Fifth Edition

LEARNING WEB DESIGN

A BEGINNER'S GUIDE TO HTML, CSS, JAVASCRIPT, AND WEB GRAPHICS

Jennifer Niederst Robbins

Beijing · Boston · Farnham · Sebastopol · Tokyo    O'REILLY®

Learning Web Design, Fifth Edition
A Beginner's Guide to HTML, CSS, JavaScript, and Web Graphics

by Jennifer Niederst Robbins

Published by O'Reilly Media, Inc., 1005 Gravenstein Highway North, Sebastopol, CA 95472.

O'Reilly Media books may be purchased for educational, business, or sales promotional use. Online editions are also available for most titles (*oreilly.com/safari*). For more information, contact our corporate/institutional sales department: 800-998-9938 or *corporate@oreilly.com*.

EDITORS: Meg Foley and Jeff Bleiel

PRODUCTION EDITOR: Kristen Brown

COVER DESIGNER: Edie Freedman

INTERIOR DESIGNER: Jennifer Robbins

PRINT HISTORY:

March 2001:	First edition.
June 2003:	Second edition.
June 2007:	Third edition.
August 2012:	Fourth edition.
May 2018:	Fifth edition.

ISBN: 978-1-491-96020-2
[TI]   [2018-04-16]

CONTENTS

PART II. HTML FOR STRUCTURE

PART IV.   JAVASCRIPT FOR BEHAVIOR

PART V.   WEB IMAGES

FOREWORD

BY JEN SIMMONS

If you travel to Silicon Valley and navigate between the global headquarters of some of the world's most famous internet companies, you can head to the Computer History Museum. Wander through the museum, past the ancient mainframes and the story of the punch card, and you'll eventually find yourself at the beginning of the Wide World Web. There's a copy of the Mosaic browser on a floppy disk tucked in a book of the same name, a copy of Netscape Navigator that was sold in a box, and something called "Internet in a Box," the #1 best-selling internet solution for Windows. Then there are the websites. Some of the earliest, most notable, and most important websites are on permanent display, including something called the "Global Network Navigator," from 1993. It was designed by none other than the author of this book, Jennifer Robbins. Long before most of us had any idea the web existed, or even before many of you were born, Jen was busy designing the first commercial website. She's been there from the very beginning, and has watched, taught, and written about every stage of evolution of the web.

Learning Web Design is now in its 5th edition, with a gazillion new pages and updates from those early days.

I am constantly asked, "What are the best resources for learning web technology?" I learned by reading books. Blog posts are great, but you also need an in-depth comprehensive look at the subject. In the beginning, all books were beginner books, teaching HTML, URLs, and how to use a browser. When CSS came along, the books assumed you'd already been using HTML, and taught you how to change to the new techniques. Then CSS3 came along, and all the books taught us how to add new CSS properties to our preexisting understanding of CSS2. Of course there were always books for beginners, but they were super basic. They never touched on professional techniques for aspiring professionals. Each new generation of books assumed that you had prior knowledge. Great for those of us in the industry. Tough for anyone new.

But how in the world are you supposed to read about two decades of techniques, discarding what is outdated, and remembering what is still correct? How are you supposed to build a career from knowledge that's so basic that you have no idea what real pros code in their everyday jobs?

You can't. That's why today when people ask me for a book recommendation, I have only one answer. This book.

This book you are reading now doesn't require any prior knowledge. You don't need to have made a web page before, or to have any idea where to get a code editor. It starts at the very beginning. And yet, unlike all the other books that start at the beginning, this one will get you to the good stuff, fast. Jen will explain every step you need, including some very advanced concepts. She's packed this book full of cutting edge, insider knowledge from top experts.

I honestly don't know how she does it. How can someone teach the basics and the advanced stuff at the same time? Usually you'll learn those things years apart, with lots of struggling in the dark in the meantime. Here, Jen will lift you up from wherever you are in your journey, and take you farther. Every one of us—myself included, and I'm on the CSS Working Group (the group of people who invent new CSS)—can learn a lot from this book. I do every time I pick it up.

Pay attention to the notes in the margins. Read the websites she recommends, watch the videos. Jen is giving you a shortcut to a professional network. Follow the people she mentions. Read the links they suggest. These might be your future colleagues. Dare to dream that you will meet them. They are, after all, only a tweet away. It is a small world, full of real people, and you can become part of it all. This book will get you started.

—Jen Simmons
Designer and Developer Advocate at Mozilla
Member of the CSS Working Group
April 2018

PREFACE

Hello and welcome to the *fifth* edition of *Learning Web Design*!

I've been documenting web design and development in books like this one for decades, and it continues to fascinate me how the web landscape changes from edition to edition. This fifth edition is no exception! Not only is this version nearly 200 pages longer than the last one, but there are also some significant updates and additions worth noting.

First, some technologies and techniques that were brand new or even experimental in the last edition have become nicely settled in. HTML5 is the new normal, and CSS is moving ahead with its modular approach, allowing new technologies to emerge and be adopted one at a time. We've largely gotten our heads around designing for a seemingly infinite range of devices. Responsive Web Design is now the de facto approach to building sites. As a result, RWD has earned its own chapter in this edition (**Chapter 17, Responsive Web Design**). Where in the last edition we pondered and argued how to handle responsive image markup, in this edition, the new responsive image elements are standardized and well supported (**Chapter 7, Adding Images**). I think we're getting the hang of this mobile thing!

I've seen a lot of seismic shifts in web design over the years, and this time, Flexbox and Grid are fundamentally changing the way we approach design. Just as we saw CSS put table-based layouts and 1-pixel spacer GIFs out of their misery, Flexbox and Grid are finally poised to kick our old float-based layout hacks to the curb. It is nothing short of a revolution, and after 25 years, it's refreshing to have an honest-to-goodness solution for layout. This edition sports a new (and hefty!) chapter on proper page layout with Flexbox and Grid (**Chapter 16, CSS Layout with Flexbox and Grid**).

Although knowledge of HTML, CSS, and JavaScript is at the heart of web development, the discipline has been evolving, and frankly, becoming more

■ ONLINE RESOURCE

The Companion Website

Be sure to visit the companion website for this book at *learningwebdesign.com*.

It features materials for the exercises, downloadable articles, lists of links from the book, contact information, and more.

complicated. I would be shirking my duty if I didn't at least introduce you to some of the new tools of the trade—CSS processors, feature detection, the command line, task runners, and Git—in a new chapter on the modern web developer toolkit (**Chapter 20, Modern Web Development Tools**). Sure, it's more stuff to learn, but the benefit is a streamlined and more efficient workflow.

The biggest surprise to me personally was how much web *image* production has changed since the fourth edition. Other than the introduction of the PNG format, my graphics chapters have remained essentially unchanged for 20 years. Not so this time around! Our old standby, GIF, is on the brink of retirement, and PNG is the default thanks to its performance advantages and new tools that let even smaller 8-bit PNGs include multiple levels of transparency. But PNG will have to keep its eye on WebP, mentioned in this edition for the first time, which may give it a run for its money in terms of file size and capabilities. The biggest web graphics story, however, is the emergence of SVG (Scalable Vector Graphics). Thanks to widespread browser support (finally!), SVG went from a small "some day" section in the previous edition to an entire "go for it!" chapter in this one (**Chapter 25, SVG**).

As in the first four editions, this book addresses the specific needs and concerns of beginners of all backgrounds, including seasoned graphic designers, programmers looking to expand their skills, and anyone else wanting to learn how to make websites. I've done my best to put the experience of sitting in my beginner web design class into a book, with exercises and tests along the way, so you get hands-on experience and can check your progress.

Whether you are reading this book on your own or using it as a companion to a web design course, I hope it gives you a good head start and that you have fun in the process.

HOW THIS BOOK IS ORGANIZED

Learning Web Design, Fifth Edition, is divided into five parts, each dealing with an important aspect of web development.

Part I: Getting Started

Part I lays a foundation for everything that follows in the book. I start off with some important general information about the web design environment, including the various roles you might play, the technologies you might learn, and tools that are available to you. You'll get your feet wet right away with HTML and CSS and learn how the web and web pages generally work. I'll also introduce you to some Big Concepts that get you thinking in the same way that modern web designers think about their craft.

Part II: HTML for Structure

The chapters in **Part II** cover the nitty-gritty of every element and attribute available to give content semantic structure. We'll cover the markup for text, links, images, tables, forms, and embedded media.

Part III: CSS for Presentation

In the course of **Part III**, you'll go from learning the basics of Cascading Style Sheets for changing the presentation of text to creating multicolumn layouts and even adding time-based animation and interactivity to the page. It provides an introduction to Responsive Web Design, as well as the tools and techniques that are part of the modern developer's workflow.

Part IV: JavaScript for Behavior

Mat Marquis starts **Part IV** out with a rundown of JavaScript syntax so that you can tell a variable from a function. You'll get to know some ways that JavaScript is used (including DOM scripting) and existing JavaScript tools such as polyfills and libraries that let you put JavaScript to use quickly, even if you aren't quite ready to write your own code from scratch.

Part V: Web Images

Part V introduces the various image file formats that are appropriate for the web, provides strategies for choosing them as part of a responsive workflow, and describes how to optimize them to make their file size as small as possible. It also includes a chapter on SVG graphics, which offer great advantages for responsive and interaction design.

Part VI: Appendices

Part VI holds reference material such as test answers, lists of HTML global attributes and CSS Selectors, and a look at HTML5 and its history.

TYPOGRAPHICAL CONVENTIONS

Italic

Used to indicate filenames and directory names, as well as for emphasis.

Colored italic

Used to indicate URLs and email addresses.

Colored roman text

Used for special terms that are being defined.

`Constant width`

Used to indicate code examples and keyboard commands.

`Colored constant width`

Used for emphasis in code examples.

`Constant width italic`

Used to indicate placeholders for attribute and style sheet property values.

→

Indicates that a line of code was broken in the text but should remain together on one line in use.

ACKNOWLEDGMENTS

Once again, many smart and lovely people had my back on this edition.

I want to say a special thanks to my two *amazing* tech reviewers. I am quite indebted to Elika J. Etemad (*fantasai*), who, as a member of the W3C CSS Working Group, helped me make this edition more accurate and up-to-date with standards than ever before. She was *tough*, but the results are worth it. Petter Dessne brought his computer science expertise as well as valuable perspective as a professor and a reader for whom English is a second language. His good humor and photos of his home in Sweden were appreciated as well!

I am also grateful for this roster of web design superstars who reviewed particular chapters and passages in their areas of expertise (in alphabetical order): Amelia Bellamy-Royds (SVG), Brent Beer (developer tools), Chris Coyier (SVG), Terence Eden (audio/video), Brad Frost (Responsive Web Design), Lyza Danger Gardner (developer tools), Jason Grigsby (images), Val Head (animation), Daniel Hengeveld (developer tools), Mat Marquis (responsive images), Eric Meyer (CSS layout), Jason Pamental (web fonts), Dan Rose (images), Arsenio Santos (embedded media), Jen Simmons (CSS layout), Adam Simpson (developer tools), and James Williamson (structured data).

Thanks also to Mat Marquis for his contribution of two lively JavaScript chapters that I could never have written myself, and to Jen Simmons for writing the Foreword and for her ongoing support of *Learning Web Design*.

I want to thank my terrific team of folks at O'Reilly Media: Meg Foley (Acquisitions Editor), Jeff Bleiel (Developmental Editor), Kristen Brown (Production Editor), Rachel Monaghan (Copyeditor), Sharon Wilkey (Proofreader), and Lucie Haskins (Indexer). Special thanks go to InDesign and book production expert Ron Bilodeau, who turned my design into a template and a set of tools that made book production an absolute joy. Special thanks also go to Edie Freedman for the beautiful cover design and half a lifetime of friendship and guidance.

Finally, no Acknowledgments would be complete without profound appreciation for the love and support of my dearest ones, Jeff and Arlo.

ABOUT THE AUTHOR

Jennifer Robbins began designing for the web in 1993 as the graphic designer for Global Network Navigator, the first commercial website. In addition to this book, she has written multiple editions of *Web Design in a Nutshell* and *HTML5 Pocket Reference*, published by O'Reilly. She is a founder and organizer of the Artifact Conference, which addresses issues related to mobile web design. Jennifer has spoken at many conferences and has taught beginning web design at Johnson and Wales University in Providence, Rhode Island. When not on the clock, Jennifer enjoys making things, indie rock, cooking, travel, and raising a cool kid.

HOW TO CONTACT US

Please address comments and questions concerning this book to the publisher:

O'Reilly Media, Inc.
1005 Gravenstein Highway North
Sebastopol, CA 95472

800-998-9938 (in the United States or Canada)
707-829-0515 (international or local)
707-829-0104 (fax)

We have a web page for this book, where we list errata, examples, and any additional information. You can access this page at *bit.ly/learningWebDesign_5e*.

To comment or ask technical questions about this book, send email to *bookquestions@oreilly.com*.

For more information about our books, courses, conferences, and news, see our website at *www.oreilly.com*.

Find us on Facebook: *facebook.com/oreilly*

Follow us on Twitter: *twitter.com/oreillymedia*

Watch us on YouTube: *www.youtube.com/oreillymedia*

GETTING STARTED

I

GETTING STARTED IN WEB DESIGN

The web has been around for more than 25 years now, experiencing euphoric early expansion, an economic-driven bust, an innovation-driven rebirth, and constant evolution along the way. One thing is certain: the web as a communication and commercial medium is here to stay. Not only that, it has found its way onto devices such as smartphones, tablets, TVs, and more. There have never been more opportunities to put web design know-how to use.

Through my experience teaching web design courses and workshops, I've had the opportunity to meet people of all backgrounds who are interested in learning how to build web pages. Allow me to introduce you to just a few:

> *"I've been a print designer for 17 years, and now I am feeling pressure to provide web design services."*

> *"I've been a programmer for years, but I want shift my skills to web development because there are good job opportunities in my area."*

> *"I tinkered with web pages in high school and I think it might be something I'd like to do for a living."*

> *"I've made a few sites using themes in WordPress, but I'd like to expand my skills and create custom sites for small businesses."*

Whatever the motivation, the first question is always the same: "Where do I start?" It may seem like there is a mountain of stuff to learn, and it's not easy to know where to jump in. But you have to start somewhere.

This chapter provides an overview of the profession before we leap into building sites. It begins with an introduction to the roles and responsibilities associated with creating websites, so you can consider which role is right for you. I will also give you a heads-up on the equipment and software you will be likely to use—in other words, the tools of the trade.

IN THIS CHAPTER

Content-related disciplines

Design specialties

Frontend development

Backend development

Recommended equipment

Web-related software

WHERE DO I START?

Maybe you are reading this book as part of a full course on web design and development. Maybe you bought it to expand your current skill set on your own. Maybe you just picked it up out of curiosity. Whatever the case, this book is a good place to start learning what makes the web tick.

There are many levels of involvement in web design, from building a small site for yourself to making it a full-blown career. You may enjoy being a "full-stack" web developer or just specializing in one skill. There are a lot of ways you can go.

If you are interested in pursuing web design or production as a career, you'll need to bring your skills up to a professional level. Employers may not require a web design degree, but they will expect to see working sample sites that demonstrate your skills and experience. These sites can be the result of class assignments, personal projects, or a site for a small business or organization. What's important is that they look professional and have well-written, clean HTML; style sheets; and scripts behind the scenes.

If your involvement is at a smaller scale—say you just have a site or two you'd like to publish—you may find using a template on an online website service is a great head start (see the sidebar **"I Just Want My Own Site"**). Most allow you to tweak the underlying code, so what you learn in this book will help you customize the template to your liking.

IT TAKES A VILLAGE (WEBSITE CREATION ROLES)

When I look at a site, I see the multitude of decisions and areas of expertise that went into building it. Sites are more than just code and pictures. They often begin with a business plan or other defined mission. Before they launch, the content must be created and organized, research is performed, design from the broadest goals to finest details must happen, code gets written, and everything must be coordinated with what's happening on the server to bring it to fruition.

Big, well-known sites are created by teams of dozens, hundreds, or even thousands of contributors. There are also sites that are created and maintained by a team with only a handful of members. It is also absolutely possible to create a respectable site with a team of only yourself. That's the beauty of the web.

In this section, I'll introduce you to the various disciplines that contribute to the creation of a site, including roles related to content, design, and code. You may end up specializing in just one area of expertise, working as part of a team of specialists. If you are designing sites on your own, you will need to wear many hats. Consider that the day-to-day upkeep of your household

---

I Just Want My Own Site

You don't necessarily need to become a web designer or developer to start publishing on the web. There are many website hosting services that provide templates and drag-and-drop interfaces that make it easy to build a site without any code know-how. They can be used for anything from full-service ecommerce solutions to small, personal sites (although some services are better suited to one more than the other).

Here are a few of the most popular site building services as of this writing:

- WordPress (*www.wordpress.com*)
- Squarespace (*squarespace.com*)
- Wix (*wix.com*)
- SiteBuilder (*sitebuilder.com*)
- Weebly (*weebly.com*)

There are many similar services available, so it's worth searching the web to find one that's right for you.

requires you to be part-time chef, housecleaner, accountant, diplomat, gardener, and construction worker—but to you it's just the stuff you do around the house. As a solo designer, you'll handle many web-related disciplines, but it will just feel like the stuff you do to make a website.

Content Wrangling

Anyone who uses the title "web designer" needs to be aware that everything we do supports the process of getting the content, message, or functionality to our users. Furthermore, good writing can help the user interfaces we create be more effective, from button labels to error messages.

Of course, someone needs to create all that content and maintain it—don't underestimate the resources required to do this successfully. Good writers and editors are an important part of the team. In addition, I want to call your attention to two content-related specialists in modern web development: the Information Architect (IA) and the Content Strategist.

Information architecture

An Information Architect (also called an Information Designer) organizes the content logically and for ease of findability. They may be responsible for search functionality, site diagrams, and how the content and data are organized on the server. Information architecture is inevitably entwined with UX and UI design (defined shortly) as well as content management. If you like organizing or are *gaga* for taxonomies, information architecture may be the job for you. The definitive text for this field as it relates to the web is *Information Architecture: For the Web and Beyond*, by Louis Rosenfeld and Peter Morville (O'Reilly).

Content strategy

When the content isn't right, the site can't be fully effective. A Content Strategist makes sure that every bit of text on a site, from long explanatory text down to the labels on buttons, supports the brand identity and marketing goals of the organization. Content strategy may also extend to data modeling and content management on a large and ongoing scale, such as planning for content reuse and update schedules. Their responsibilities may also include how the organization's voice is represented on social media. A good place to learn more is the book *Content Strategy for the Web, 2nd Edition*, by Kristina Halvorson and Melissa Rich (New Riders).

All Manner of Design

Ah, *design*! It sounds fairly straightforward, but even this simple requirement has been divided into a number of specializations when it comes to creating sites. Here are a few of the job descriptions related to designing a site, but bear in mind that the disciplines often overlap and that the person calling herself the "designer" often is responsible for more than one (if not all) of these responsibilities.

User Experience, Interaction, and User Interface design

Often, when we think of design, we think about how something looks. On the web, the first matter of business is designing how the site *works*. Before you pick colors and fonts, it is important to identify the site's goals, how it will be used, and how visitors move through it. These tasks fall under the disciplines of User Experience (UX) design, Interaction Design (IxD), and User Interface (UI) design. There is a lot of overlap between these responsibilities, and it is not uncommon for one person or team to handle all three.

The User Experience designer takes a holistic view of the design process—ensuring the entire experience with the site is favorable. UX design is based on a solid understanding of users and their needs based on observations and interviews. According to Donald Norman (who coined the term), UX design includes "all aspects of the user's interaction with the product: how it is perceived, learned, and used." For a website or application, that includes the visual design, the user interface, the quality and message of the content, and even the overall site performance. The experience must be in line with the organization's brand and business goals in order to be successful.

The goal of the Interaction Designer is to make the site as easy, efficient, and delightful to use as possible. Closely related to interaction design is User Interface design, which tends to be more narrowly focused on the functional organization of the page as well as the specific tools (buttons, links, menus, and so on) that users use to navigate content or accomplish tasks.

The following are deliverables that UX, UI, or interaction designers produce:

User research and testing reports

Understanding the needs, desires, and limitations of users is central to the success of the design of the site or web application. The approach of designing around the user's needs is referred to as User-Centered Design (UCD), and it is central to contemporary web design. Site designs often begin with user research, including interviews and observations, in order to gain a better understanding of how the site can solve problems or how it will be used. It is typical for designers to do a round of user testing at each phase of the design process to ensure the usability of their designs. If users are having a hard time figuring out where to find content or how to move to the next step in a process, then it's back to the drawing board.

Wireframe diagrams

A wireframe diagram shows the structure of a web page using only outlines for each content type and widget (FIGURE 1-1). The purpose of a wireframe diagram is to indicate how the screen real estate is divided and where functionality and content such as navigation, search boxes, form elements, and so on, are placed. Colors, fonts, and other visual identity elements are deliberately omitted so as not to distract from the structure of the page. These diagrams are usually annotated with instructions for how things should work so the development team knows what to build.

Site diagram

A site diagram indicates the structure of the site as a whole and how individual pages relate to one another. FIGURE 1-2 shows a very simple site diagram. Some site diagrams fill entire walls!

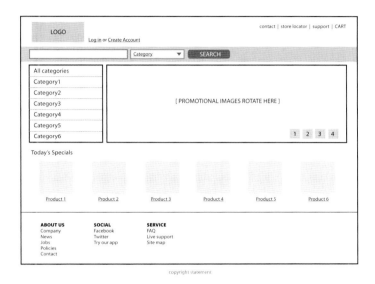

FIGURE 1-1. Wireframe diagram.

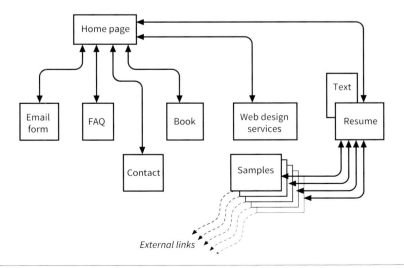

FIGURE 1-2. A simple site diagram.

Storyboards and user flow charts

A storyboard traces the path through a site or application from the point of view of a typical user (a persona in UX lingo). It usually includes a script and "scenes" consisting of screen views or the user interacting with the screen. The storyboard aims to demonstrate the steps it takes to accomplish tasks, outlines possible options, and also introduces some standard page types. FIGURE 1-3 shows a simple storyboard. A user flow chart is another method for showing how the parts of a site or application are connected, but it tends to focus on technical details rather than telling a story. For example, "when the user does *this*, it triggers *that* function on the server." It is common for designers to create a user flow chart for the steps in a process such as member registration or online payments.

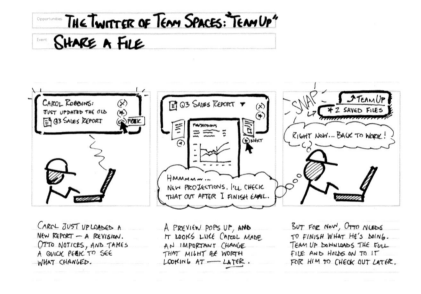

FIGURE 1-3. A typical storyboard (courtesy of Adaptive Path and Brandon Schauer).

There are many books on UX, interaction, and UI design, but these are a few of the classics to get you started:

- *The Elements of User Experience: User-Centered Design for the Web and Beyond* by Jesse James Garrett (New Riders)

- *Don't Make Me Think, Revisited: A Common Sense Approach to Web Usability* by Steve Krug (New Riders)

- *The Design of Everyday Things* by Don Norman (Basic Books)

- *About Face: The Essentials of Interaction Design, 4th Edition* by Alan Cooper, Robert Reimann, David Cronin, and Christopher Noessel (Wiley)

- *Designing Interfaces, 2nd Edition* by Jenifer Tidwell (O'Reilly)

- *100 Things Every Designer Needs to Know about People* by Susan Weinschenk (New Riders)
- *Designing User Experience: A Guide to HCI, UX and Interaction Design* by David Benyon (Pearson)

Visual (graphic) design

Because the web is a visual medium, web pages require attention to their visual presentation. First impressions are everything. A graphic designer creates the "look and feel" of the site—logos, graphics, type, colors, layout, and so on—to ensure that the site makes a good first impression and is consistent with the brand and message of the organization it represents.

There are many methods and deliverables that can be used to present a visual design to clients and stakeholders. The most traditional are sketches or mockups (created in Photoshop or a similar tool) of the way the site might look, such as the home page mockups shown in FIGURE 1-4.

Now that sites appear on screens of all sizes, many designers prefer to discuss the visual identity (colors, fonts, image style, etc.) in a way that isn't tied to a specific layout like the typical desktop view shown in FIGURE 1-4. The idea is to agree upon a visual language for the site before production begins.

One option for separating style from screen size is to use style tiles, a technique introduced by Samantha Warren (see **Note**). Style tiles include examples of color schemes, branding elements, UI treatments, text treatment, and mood (FIGURE 1-5). Once the details are decided upon, they can be implemented into working prototypes and the final site. For more on this technique, visit Samantha's excellent site, *styletil.es*, where you can download a template.

Graphic designers may also be responsible for producing the image assets for the site. They will need to know how to optimize images for the fastest delivery and how to address the requirements of varying screen sizes. It is also common for the development team to handle image optimization, but I think it is a skill every visual designer should have. We'll discuss image optimization in **Chapter 24, Image Asset Production**.

FIGURE 1-4. Look-and-feel sketches (mockups) for a simple site.

NOTE

Designer Dan Mall uses a similar approach that he calls "element collages." An element collage is a collection of design elements that give the site its unique look and feel, but like style tiles, is not tied to a particular screen layout. Read his article at v3.danielmall.com/articles/rif-element-collages/.

FIGURE 1-5. Style tile technique introduced by Samantha Warren.

Designers may also be responsible for creating a style guide that documents style choices, such as fonts, colors, and other style embellishments, in order to keep the site consistent over time. For a list of examples, articles, books, and podcasts about web style guides, visit the "Website Style Guide Resources" page at *styleguides.io*.

Do Designers Need to Learn to Code?

In short, yes. A basic familiarity with HTML and CSS is now a requirement of anybody joining a web design team. You may not be responsible for creating the final production code for the site, but as HTML and CSS are the native languages of your medium, you need to know your way around them. Some designers also learn JavaScript, but others draw the line there and let a developer handle the programming.

Code is becoming more central to the visual designer's workflow. Where once Photoshop was all you needed to mock up web page designs to send them to production, mockups fixed to a particular size fall short of describing a page that needs to flex to a wide range of screen sizes. For that reason, designers are building their own working prototypes as deliverables that communicate how the design will look and behave in users' hands.

Code Slinging

A large share of the website building process involves creating and trouble-shooting the documents, style sheets, scripts, and images that make up a site. At web design firms, the team that handles the creation of the files that make up the site (or templates for pages that get assembled dynamically) is usually called the development or production department.

Development falls under two broad categories: frontend development and backend development. Once again, these tasks may fall to specialists, but it is just as common for one person or team to handle both responsibilities.

Frontend development

Frontend refers to any aspect of the design process that appears in or relates directly to the browser. That includes HTML, CSS, and JavaScript, all of which you will need to have *intricate* knowledge of if you want a job as a web developer. Let's take a quick look at each.

Authoring/markup (HTML)

Authoring is the process of preparing content for delivery on the web, or more specifically, marking up the content with HTML tags that describe its content and function.

HTML (HyperText Markup Language) is the authoring language used to create web page documents. The current version (and the version documented

---

◼ AT A GLANCE

Frontend Development

Frontend development includes the following web technologies:

- HyperText Markup Language (HTML)
- Cascading Style Sheets (CSS)
- JavaScript and DOM scripting, including AJAX and JavaScript-based frameworks

---

in this book) is HTML 5.2. **Appendix D, From HTML+ to HTML5**, tells the history of HTML and lists what makes HTML5 unique.

HTML is not a programming language; it is a markup language, which means it is a system for identifying and describing the various components of a document such as headings, paragraphs, and lists. The markup indicates the document's underlying structure (you can think of it as a detailed, machine-readable outline). You don't need programming skills—only patience and common sense—to write HTML.

The best way to learn HTML is to write out some pages by hand, as we will be doing in the exercises in **Part II** of this book.

Styling (CSS)

While HTML is used to describe the content in a web page, Cascading Style Sheets (CSS) describe how that content should *look* (see **Note**). The way the page looks is referred to as its presentation. Fonts, colors, background images, line spacing, page layout, and so on, are all controlled with CSS. You can even add special effects and basic animation to your page.

The CSS specification also provides methods for controlling how documents will be presented in contexts other than a browser, such as in print or read aloud by a screen reader; however, we won't be covering them much here.

Although it is possible to publish web pages using HTML alone, you'll probably want to take on style sheets so you're not stuck with the browser's default styles. If you're looking into designing websites professionally, either as a designer or as a developer, proficiency at style sheets is mandatory.

JavaScript and DOM scripting

JavaScript is a scripting language that adds interactivity and behaviors to web pages, including these (to name just a few):

- Checking form entries for valid entries

- Swapping out styles for an element or an entire site

- Loading scrolling feeds with more content automatically

- Making the browser remember information about users

- Building interface widgets, such as embedded video players or special form inputs

You may also hear the term DOM scripting used in relation to JavaScript. DOM stands for Document Object Model, and it refers to the standardized list of web page elements that can be accessed and manipulated using JavaScript (or another scripting language).

Frontend developers may also be required to be familiar with JavaScript frameworks (such as React, Bootstrap, Angular, and others) that automate a lot of the production process. They'll likely also need to be handy with AJAX

The World Wide Web Consortium

The World Wide Web Consortium (called the W3C for short) is the organization that oversees the development of web technologies such as HTML, CSS, and JavaScript. The group was founded in 1994 by Tim Berners-Lee, the inventor of the web, at the Massachusetts Institute of Technology (MIT).

In the beginning, the W3C concerned itself mainly with the HTTP protocol and the development of HTML. Now, the W3C is laying a foundation for the future of the web by developing dozens of technologies and protocols that must work together in a solid infrastructure.

For the definitive answer to any web technology question, the W3C site is the place to go: *www.w3.org*.

For more information on the W3C and what it does, see this useful page: *www.w3.org/Consortium/*.

(which stands for "Asynchronous JavaScript And XML"), a technique used to load content in the background, allowing the page to update smoothly without reloading (like those automatically refreshing feeds).

Web scripting definitely requires some traditional computer programming prowess. While many web developers have degrees in computer science, it is also common for developers to be self-taught. A few developers I know started by copying and adapting existing scripts, then gradually added to their programming skills with each new project. Still, if you have no experience with programming languages, the initial learning curve may be a bit steep.

If you want to be a web developer for a living, JavaScript is a basic requirement. Designers will benefit from understanding what JavaScript can do, but may not need to learn to write it if they are working with a development team. **Chapter 21, Introduction to JavaScript**, will get you started understanding how it works, and I recommend *Learning JavaScript* by Ethan Brown (O'Reilly) to learn more.

Backend development

Backend developers focus on the server, including the applications and databases that run on it. They may be responsible for installing and configuring the server software (we'll be looking more at servers in **Chapter 2, How the Web Works**). They will certainly be required to know at least one, and probably more, server-side programming languages, such as PHP, Ruby, .NET (or ASP.NET), Python, or JSP, in order to create applications that provide the functionality required by the site. Applications handle tasks and features like forms processing, content management systems (CMSs), and online shopping, just to name a few.

Additionally, backend developers need to be familiar with configuring and maintaining databases that store all of the data for a site, such as the content that gets poured into templates, user accounts, product inventories, and more. Some common database languages include MySQL, Oracle, and SQL Server.

Backend development is well beyond the scope of this book, but it is important to know the sorts of tasks that get taken care of at the server level. You should be aware that it is possible to get functionality like shopping carts, mailing lists, and so on as prepackaged solutions from your hosting company without having to program it from scratch.

■ **AT A GLANCE**

Backend Development

The following technologies are typically in the domain of the backend developer:

- Server software (Apache, Microsoft IIS)
- Web application languages (PHP, Ruby, Python, JSP, ASP.NET)
- Database software (MySQL, Oracle, SQL Server)

Full-Stack Developers and Unicorns

When looking for a job in web development, you will frequently see posts looking for "full-stack" developers. That means a person who is fluent in both frontend (HTML, CSS, JavaScript) and backend (server applications, databases) languages.

There is a rare breed of web designer who can handle *all* of the tasks mentioned earlier—from content strategy to UX to frontend development to what happens on the server. These folks are known in the biz as "unicorns." I've met a few!

Other Roles

Not surprisingly, there are a myriad of other roles that contribute to the creation and maintenance of a site. Here are a few common roles that fall just outside the moniker "web design."

Product manager

> The product manager of a website or application guides its design and development in a way that meets business goals. This member of the team must have a thorough understanding of the target market as well as the processes involved in the creation of the site itself. Product managers develop the overall strategy for the site from a marketing perspective, including how and when it gets released.

Project manager

> The project manager coordinates the designers, developers, and everyone else who is working on the site. They manage things like timelines, development approaches, deliverables, and so on. The project manager works with the product manager and other product owners to make sure that the project gets done on time and on budget.

SEO specialist

> A website or application isn't much good if nobody knows it exists, so it is crucial that a site be easily found by search engines. Search Engine Optimization (SEO) is a discipline focused on tweaking the site structure and code in a way that increases the chances it will be highly ranked in search results. There may be an SEO specialist on the in-house team, or a company may choose to hire an outside SEO firm. SEO is sometimes perceived as a dark art, but there are many ways to improve findability that are not underhanded. In fact, the number one technique for improving SEO is simply having good content with savvy HTML markup.

Multimedia producers

> One of the cool things about the web is that you can add multimedia elements to a site, including sound, video, animation, and even interactive games. Creating multimedia elements is generally best left to artists and technicians in those fields, although they may be part of the web team if video, animation, or interactivity are core to the site's mission.

That concludes our stroll through the virtual village of workers involved in the creation of a website. The larger the site, the more likely each team member will have a narrow specialization and job titles like "UX Lead for Error Messages." More likely, everybody on the team will possess a spectrum of skills, and the lines between disciplines will blur. For example, I do Interaction and User Interface design, graphic design, HTML, and CSS, but I do not write JavaScript, work on the server, or get involved with content organization. In this book, I aim to give you a foundation in the frontend technologies that will prepare you for a number of roles.

(Soft) Skills Every Web Designer Needs

We've focused on quite a few technical skills that will be helpful in building websites. I would like to mention a few more—often overlooked—skills that are just as critical to your success.

Excellent communication skills

In your work, you will need to communicate in person, on the phone, in email, and in text messaging tools with clients, team members, and superiors. Be clear, proactive, and straightforward with what you have to say. Good communication requires not only that you express yourself clearly, but also that you be a good listener. Make sure that you understand issues being discussed, and don't be afraid to ask for clarification if you don't.

Flexibility

Be able to change direction quickly because not only does web technology change quickly, but you will no doubt be thrown curveballs in your day-to-day work as well. For example, you may arrive at work one day to find that the client has changed your priorities completely. You might find that they've cancelled your project entirely. You might be asked to learn new skills and shift positions in the team. Staying adaptable is the key to survival.

Critical thinking and good judgment

Problem-solving is central to all of the disciplines related to web design, so you need to be able to use critical thinking skills to come up with solutions and always employ basic common sense.

A good attitude

Creating sites means being part of a team, even if you work at home as a freelancer. Be mindful that the attitude with which you approach your work is contagious, so strive to be a positive and friendly team member.

GEARING UP FOR WEB DESIGN

It should come as no surprise that professional web designers require a fair amount of gear, both hardware and software. One question I'm frequently asked is, "What do I need to buy?" I can't tell you specifically what to buy, but I will provide an overview of the typical tools of the trade.

Equipment

For a comfortable web development environment, I recommend the following equipment:

A solid, up-to-date computer

Macintosh, Windows, or Linux is fine, so use whatever you have and are comfortable with. Creative departments in professional web development companies tend to be Mac-based. For backend work, Linux and Windows are popular. Although it is nice to have a super-fast machine, the files that make up web pages are very small and tend not to be too taxing on computers. Unless you're getting into sound and video editing, don't worry if your current setup is not the very latest and greatest.

A large monitor

Although not a requirement, a large monitor makes life easier. The more monitor real estate you have, the more windows and control panels you can have open at the same time. You can also see more of your page to make design decisions. If you're using a large monitor, just make sure you design for users with smaller monitors and devices in mind.

A second computer for testing

Many designers and developers find it useful to have a test computer running a different platform than the computer they use for development (i.e., if you design on a Mac, test on a PC). Because browsers work differently on Macs than on Windows machines, it's critical to test your pages in as many environments as possible, and particularly on the current Windows operating system. If you are a hobbyist web designer working at home, you could check your pages on a friend's machine. Mac users should check out the **"Run Windows on Your Mac"** sidebar.

Mobile devices for testing

The web has gone mobile! That means it is absolutely critical that you test the appearance and performance of your site on browsers on smartphones and tablet devices. Device testing is discussed in **Chapter 17, Responsive Web Design**.

A scanner and/or camera

If you anticipate making your own images and textures, you'll need some tools for creating them.

Web Production Software

There's no shortage of software available for creating web pages. In the early days, we just made do with tools originally designed for print. Today, there are wonderful tools created specifically with web design in mind that make the process more efficient. It is a delicate business listing software in a book such as this because a) there are *so many* programs, b) everyone has their personal favorite, and c) new tools come along so rapidly that there are surely newer, cooler options that you have access to that didn't exist as I wrote this.

Run Windows on Your Mac

If you have a Macintosh computer with an Intel chip running macOS (Leopard or later), you don't need a separate computer to test in a Windows environment. It is now possible to run Windows right on your Mac using the free Boot Camp application, which allows you to switch to Windows on reboot.

There are several other VM (Virtual Machine) products for macOS that allow you to toggle between Mac and Windows, including these:

- VMFusion (*www.vmware.com/fusion*) is a commercial product with a free trial you can download.
- Parallels Desktop for Mac (*www.parallels.com*) is also a commercial product with a free trial.
- Oracle VirtualBox (*virtualbox.org*) is a free program that allows you to run a number of guest operating systems, including Windows and several flavors of Unix.

All VM products require that you purchase a copy of Microsoft Windows, but it sure beats buying a whole machine.

NOTE

To do the exercises in this book, all you'll need is the text editor that came with your operating system and free image creation software. There is no need to purchase anything to follow along.

That said, here is a general overview of the types of software that comprise the tools of our trade, along with a few specific mentions of the most popular in each class.

Coding tools

Although you can get by with the simple text editors that come with your computer, a dedicated code editor makes the task of writing HTML, CSS, and JavaScript much easier. Code editors understand the syntax of the code you write, so they can do things for you like color coding, error detection, and automatically finishing simple tasks like closing HTML tags. Some provide page previews so you can view the results of your code as you work.

FIGURE 1-6 shows how an HTML document looks in the Sublime Text editor. Here are just a few of the better-known code editors for web production that are worth exploring:

- Sublime Text (*sublimetext.com*)

- Atom (free from GitHub; *atom.io*)

- Brackets (free from Adobe; *brackets.io*)

- CodeKit (*codekitapp.com*; *Mac only*)

- Adobe Dreamweaver (*www.adobe.com/products/dreamweaver.html*)

- Coda (*panic.com/coda/*)

- Microsoft Visual Studio (*visualstudio.com*)

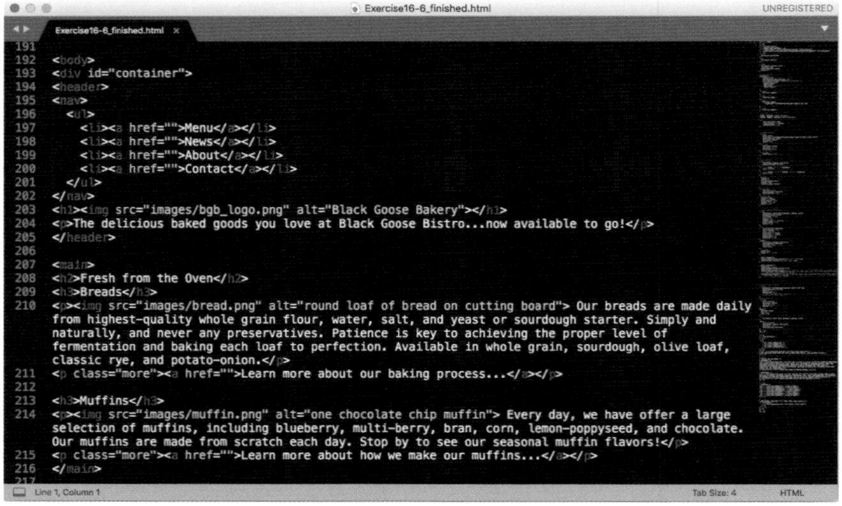

FIGURE 1-6. Sublime Text is one example of a dedicated code editor.

User interface and layout tools

There is a new breed of interface design tools made specifically for websites and other applications. Because they have been designed from scratch with interface design in mind, they seem to anticipate a web designer's every need. Interface design tools make it easy to design multiple layouts (such as layouts at various screen sizes) as well as export images and code for use in production. Some allow basic interactivity such as clicks and swipes, so your mockups can be shared online and used for basic interface testing.

Sketch (*sketchapp.com*, Mac only), shown in FIGURE 1-7, is extremely popular at the time of this writing. Other options include the following:

- Affinity Designer (*affinity.serif.com/en-us/designer/*)

- Adobe XD (*www.adobe.com/products/xd.html*)

- Figma (*figma.com*)

- UXPin (*uxpin.com*)

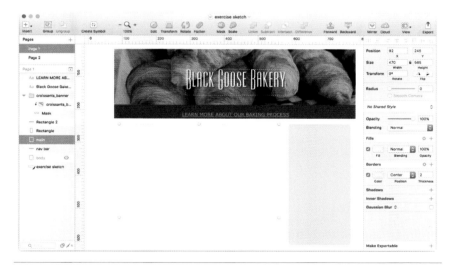

FIGURE 1-7. Sketch (Mac only) is an example of an interface design tool.

Web graphic creation tools

It is certainly possible to create all of the images you need for a site by using one of the interface design tools just listed. There are also programs that focus solely on image creation that can export files in web-appropriate formats. For professional designers, the Adobe Creative Cloud (*adobe.com*) suite of tools, which includes Photoshop (FIGURE 1-8), Illustrator, and other high-end design tools, is worth the investment.

If the Adobe monthly subscription fee is out of reach, you can try lower-cost alternatives that provide many of the same features. The number of graphics tools out there is dizzying, so I'm gathering just a few here:

- GIMP (free, open source; *gimp.org*)

- Corel PaintShop Pro (for photo editing; *paintshoppro.com*; *Windows only*)

- Corel Draw (for vector drawing; *coreldraw.com*; *Windows only*)

- Pixelmator (*pixelmator.com*; *Mac only*)

The following image editors work right in your browser, without the need to download a program, although you do need to pay for an account:

- SumoPaint (*sumopaint.com*)

- Pixlr (*pixlr.com*)

FIGURE 1-8. Adobe Photoshop is the professional standard for image editing.

A variety of browsers

One of the biggest challenges for web designers is that our sites may look and behave differently from browser to browser. For this reason, it is critical that we test our designs early and often on the widest range of browsers possible. These are the browsers designers and developers keep around for testing:

- Chrome (*google.com/chrome*)

- Firefox (*www.mozilla.org*)

- MS Edge (*www.microsoft.com/en-us/windows/microsoft-edge*; *Windows only*)

- Internet Explorer 9–11 (*www.microsoft.com*; search "Internet Explorer"; *Windows only*)

- Safari (*support.apple.com/downloads/#safari*; *Mac only*)

- Opera (*opera.com*)

You will also need to test on a variety of smartphone browsers including iOS Safari, Android browsers, and third-party mobile browsers. We will discuss mobile testing further in **Chapter 17**.

File management and transfer tools

Web design and development involves a lot of moving files around, particularly from the computer where you do your work to the server computer that hosts the site. To move files across the internet, you use an FTP (short for File Transfer Protocol) program. You will find that many hosting services offer their own FTP tools for uploading your files to their servers. Many of the code editors listed earlier also include built-in FTP functionality. Or, you can use a standalone FTP program, such as one of these:

- Filezilla (*filezilla-project.org*; *free, all platforms*)

- Cyberduck (*cyberduck.io*; *Mac and Windows*)

- WinSCP (*winscp.net/eng/index.php*; *free, Windows only*)

- Transmit (*panic.com/transmit/*; *Mac only*)

You may also find it useful to have a terminal application (command-line tool) that allows you to type Unix commands for setting file permissions, moving or copying files and directories, or managing the server software. Command-line tools, which have a number of uses in web design and development workflow, are discussed in more detail in **Chapter 20, Modern Web Development Tools**:

- Terminal (installed with macOS; shown in FIGURE 1-9)

- Cygwin (*cygwin.com*; Linux emulator for Windows that includes a command-line tool)

FIGURE 1-9. The Terminal command-line tool for macOS.

EXERCISE 1-1.
Taking stock

Now that you're taking that first step in learning web design, it might be a good time to take stock of your assets and goals. Using the lists in this chapter as a general guide, try jotting down answers to the following questions:

- What are your web design goals? To become a professional web designer? To make personal websites only?

- Which aspects of web design interest you the most?

- What current skills do you have that will be useful in creating web pages?

- Which skills will you need to brush up on?

- Which hardware and software tools do you already have for web design?

- Which tools do you need to buy? Which tools would you like to buy eventually?

WHAT YOU'VE LEARNED

I hope that this chapter has given you an overview of the many roles and responsibilities that fall under the umbrella of "web design." I also hope that you come away realizing that you don't need to learn everything. And even if you want to learn everything eventually, you don't need to learn it all at once. So relax, and don't worry. The other good news is that, while many professional tools exist, it is possible to create a basic website and get it up and running without spending much money by using freely available or inexpensive tools and your existing computer setup.

As you'll soon see, it's easy to get started making web pages—you will be able to create simple pages by the time you're done reading this book. From there, you can continue adding to your bag of tricks and find your particular niche in web design. In the meantime, try answering the questions in EXERCISE 1-1.

TEST YOURSELF

Each chapter in this book ends with a few questions that you can answer to see if you picked up the important bits of information. Answers appear in **Appendix A**.

1. Match these web professionals with the final product they might be responsible for producing:

    a. Graphic designer   _____ HTML and CSS documents

    b. Production department   _____ PHP scripts

    c. User experience designer   _____ "Look and feel" deliverables

    d. Backend programmer   _____ Storyboards

2. What does the W3C do?

3. Match the web technology with its appropriate task:

    a. HTML   _____ Checks a form field for a valid entry

    b. CSS   _____ Creates a custom server-side web application

    c. JavaScript   _____ Identifies text as a second-level heading

    d. Ruby   _____ Makes all second-level headings blue

4. What is the difference between frontend and backend web development?

5. What does an FTP tool do and how do you get one?

HOW THE WEB WORKS

I got started in web design in early 1993—pretty close to the start of the web itself. That's a quarter of a century ago (gasp!), but I still distinctly remember the first time I looked at a web page. It was difficult to tell where the information was coming from and how it all worked.

This chapter sorts out the pieces and introduces some basic terminology. We'll start with the big picture and work down to specifics.

THE INTERNET VERSUS THE WEB

No, it's not a battle to the death, just an opportunity to point out the distinction between two words that are increasingly being used interchangeably.

The internet is an international network of connected computers. No company owns the internet; it is a cooperative effort governed by a system of standards and rules. The purpose of connecting computers together, of course, is to share information. There are many ways information can be passed between computers, including email (POP3/IMAP/SMTP), file transfer (FTP), secure shell (SSH), and many more specialized modes upon which the internet is built. These standardized methods for transferring data or documents over a network are known as protocols.

The web (originally called the World Wide Web, thus the "www" in site addresses) is just one of the ways information can be shared over the internet. It is unique in that it allows documents to be linked to one another via hypertext links—thus forming a huge "web" of connected information. The web uses a protocol called HTTP (HyperText Transfer Protocol). That acronym should look familiar because it is the first four letters of nearly all website addresses, as we'll discuss in an upcoming section.

The web is a subset of the internet. It is just one of many ways information can be transferred over networked computers.

> ## A Brief History of the Web
>
> The web was born in a particle physics laboratory (CERN) in Geneva, Switzerland, in 1989. There a computer specialist named Tim Berners-Lee first proposed a system of information management that used a "hypertext" process to link related documents over a network. He and his partner, Robert Cailliau, created a prototype and released it for review. For the first several years, web pages were text-only. It's difficult to believe that in 1992, the world had only about 50 web servers, total.
>
> The real boost to the web's popularity came in 1992 when the first graphical browser (NCSA Mosaic) was introduced, and the web broke out of the realm of scientific research into mass media. The ongoing development of web technologies is overseen by the World Wide Web Consortium (W3C).
>
> If you want to dig deeper into the web's history, check out the W3C's History Archives at *www.w3.org/History.html*.
>
> **FUN FACT:** If you look at that page, you'll see a July 1993 entry for the first "WWW Wizards Workshop." Although I did not attend that meeting, I *did* design the commemorative t-shirt!

SERVING UP YOUR INFORMATION

Let's talk more about the computers that make up the internet. Because they "serve up" documents upon request, these computers are known as servers. More accurately, the server is the software (not the computer itself) that allows the computer to communicate with other computers; however, it is common to use the word "server" to refer to the computer as well. The role of server software is to wait for a request for information, and then retrieve and send that information back as quickly as possible.

There's nothing special about the computers themselves...picture anything from a high-powered Unix machine to a humble personal computer. It's the server software that makes it all happen. In order for a computer to be part of the web, it must be running special web server software that allows it to handle HyperText Transfer Protocol transactions. Web servers are also called HTTP servers.

> ■ **TERMINOLOGY**
>
> ### Open Source
>
> Open source software is developed as a collaborative effort with the intent to make its source code available to other programmers for use and modification. Open source programs are usually free to use.

There are many server software options out there, but the two most popular are Apache (open source software) and Microsoft Internet Information Services (IIS). Apache is freely available for Unix-based computers and comes installed on Macs running macOS. There is a Windows version as well. Microsoft IIS is part of Microsoft's family of server solutions.

Every computer and device (router, smartphone, car, etc.) connected to the internet is assigned a unique numeric IP address ("IP" stands for "Internet Protocol"). For example, as I write this, the computer that hosts oreilly.com has the IP address 199.27.145.64. All those numbers can be dizzying, so fortunately, the Domain Name System (DNS) was developed to allow us to refer to that server by its domain name, "oreilly.com", as well. The numeric IP address is useful for computer software, while the domain name is more accessible to humans. Matching the text domain names to their respective numeric IP addresses is the job of a separate DNS server. If you think of an IP address as a telephone number, the DNS server would be the phonebook.

It is possible to configure your web server so that more than one domain name is mapped to a single IP address, allowing several sites to share a single server.

A WORD ABOUT BROWSERS

We now know that the server does the servin', but what about the other half of the equation? The software that does the requesting is called the client. People use desktop browsers, mobile browsers, and other assistive technologies (such as screen readers) as clients to access documents on the web. The server returns the documents for the browser (also referred to as the user agent in technical circles) to display.

The requests and responses are handled via the HTTP protocol, mentioned earlier. Although we've been talking about "documents," HTTP can be used to transfer images, movies, audio files, data, scripts, and all the other web resources that commonly make up websites and applications.

It is common to think of a browser as a window on a computer monitor with a web page displayed in it. These are known as graphical browsers or desktop browsers and for a long time, they were the only web-viewing game in town. The most popular desktop browsers as of this writing include Edge and Internet Explorer for Windows, Chrome, Firefox, and Safari, with Opera and Vivaldi bringing up the rear.

These days, however, more than half of web traffic comes from mobile browsers on smartphones and tablets such as Safari on iOS, Android and Chrome browsers on Android devices, Opera Mini, and a myriad of other default and installable mobile browsers (see *en.wikipedia.org/wiki/Mobile_browser* for a complete list). Navigating the web on a touch screen is the new normal.

It is also important to keep alternative web experiences in mind. Users with impaired sight may be listening to a web page read by a screen reader (or simply make their text extremely large). Users with limited mobility may use assistive technology such as joysticks or voice commands to access links and enter content. The sites we build must be accessible and usable for all users, regardless of their browsing experiences.

The web is also finding its way onto smart TVs and gaming systems, where users access our pages with TV remotes or Xbox controllers. You never know where the web will pop up next!

■ TERMINOLOGY

Intranets and Extranets

When you think of a website, you generally assume that it is accessible to anyone surfing the web. However, many organizations take advantage of the awesome information sharing and gathering power of websites to exchange information just within their own network. These special web-based networks are called intranets. They are created and function like ordinary websites, but they use special security devices (called firewalls) that prevent the outside world from seeing them. Intranets have lots of uses, such as sharing human resource information or providing access to inventory databases.

An extranet is like an intranet, but it allows access to select users outside of the organization. For example, a manufacturing company may provide its customers with passwords that allow them to check the status of their orders in the company's orders database. Passwords determine which slice of the company's information is accessible.

■ TERMINOLOGY

Server-Side and Client-Side

Often in web design, you'll hear references to "client-side" or "server-side" applications. These terms are used to indicate which machine is doing the processing. Client-side applications run on the user's machine (also referred to as the frontend), while server-side applications and functions use the processing power of the server computer (the backend).

Browser Rendering Engines

The program that is responsible for converting HTML and CSS into what you see rendered on the screen is called a rendering engine (also browser engine or layout engine). Browsers that you use on desktop computers and mobile devices are made up of rendering engines as well as other code used for their own user interfaces and functionality. Although I talk a lot about which browsers support particular functions in this book, I'm technically referring to the browser's rendering engine. Various browsers often share a rendering engine; for example, the Blink engine powers Chrome, Opera, and a variety of Android browsers. TABLE 2-1 lists the rendering engines used by the most popular web browsers today. For more information, search Wikipedia.com for "Comparison of web browser engines" and "Comparison of web browsers."

TABLE 2-1. Current browsers and their rendering engines

Browser	Rendering engine
Chrome 28+	Blink (forked from WebKit)
Firefox (all)	Gecko (except Firefox for iOS, which uses WebKit)
Safari and Safari iOS (all)	WebKit
Internet Explorer 4–11	Trident
MS Edge (all)	EdgeHTML (forked from Trident)
Opera 15+	Blink (forked from WebKit)

The reality is that pages may look and perform differently from browser to browser. This is due to varying support for web technologies, varying device capabilities, and the users' ability to set their own browsing preferences. It is the most challenging aspect of designing and developing for our medium.

WEB PAGE ADDRESSES (URLS)

Every page and resource on the web has its own special address called a URL, which stands for Uniform Resource Locator. It's nearly impossible to get through a day without seeing a URL (pronounced "U-R-L," not "erl") plastered on the side of a bus, printed on a business card, or broadcast on a television commercial. Web addresses are fully integrated into modern vernacular.

Some URLs are short and sweet. Others may look like crazy strings of characters separated by dots (periods) and slashes, but each part has a specific purpose. Let's pick one apart.

The Parts of a URL

A complete URL is generally made up of three components: the protocol, the site name, and the absolute path to the document or resource, as shown in FIGURE 2-1.

FIGURE 2-1. The parts of a URL.

❶ `http://`

The first thing the URL does is to define the protocol that will be used for that particular transaction. The letters "HTTP" let the server know to use HyperText Transfer Protocol, or get into "web mode." You may also see a URL begin with `https://`, which I explain in the **"HTTPS, The Secure Web Protocol"** sidebar.

❷ `www.example.com`

The next portion of the URL identifies the website by its domain name. In this example, the domain name is "example.com." The "www." part at the beginning is the particular hostname at that domain. The hostname "www" has become a convention, but is not a rule. In fact, sometimes the hostname may be omitted. There can be more than one website at a domain (called subdomains). For example, there might also be "development.example.com," "clients.example.com," and so on.

❸ `/2018/samples/first.html`

This is the absolute path through directories on the server to the requested HTML document, *first.html*. The words separated by slashes are the directory names, starting with the root directory of the host (as indicated by the initial **/**). Because the internet originally comprised computers running the Unix operating system, our current way of doing things still follows Unix rules and conventions, hence the **/** separating directory names.

To sum it up, the URL in FIGURE 2-1 says it would like to use the HTTP protocol to connect to a web server on the internet called "www.example.com" and to request the document *first.html*, located in the *samples* directory, which is in the *2018* directory.

Simplified URLs

Obviously, not every URL you see is so lengthy. To get to O'Reilly's site, you'd expect to type `oreilly.com` instead of `http://www.oreilly.com/index.html`. Here's why that works.

URL Versus URI

The W3C and the development community are moving away from the term URL (Uniform Resource Locator) and toward the more generic and technically accurate URI (Uniform Resource Identifier). On the street and even on the job, however, you're still likely to hear URL.

Here's the skinny on URL versus URI: a URL is one type of a URI that identifies the resource by its location (the L in URL) on the network. The other type of URI is a URN that identifies the resource by name or namespace (the N in URN).

Because it is more familiar, I will be sticking with URL throughout this book. Just know that URLs are a subset of URIs, and the terms are often used interchangeably.

If you like to geek out on this kind of thing, I refer you to the URI Wikipedia entry: *en.wikipedia.org/wiki/Uniform_Resource_Identifier*.

HTTPS, the Secure Web Protocol

If you look at the address bar while shopping online or using a banking site, you'll notice that they use the HTTPS protocol. HTTPS, where "S" stands for "secure," is a modification of HTTP that encrypts form information when it is sent between the user's client and the server. Any web page that has form fields that accept text (such as a search bar or a login) should use HTTPS.

As of this writing, around 60% of pages (and growing!) use HTTPS, and for good reason. Not only is it a good idea to keep your user's data secure in transit, but Google is pushing along the transition to HTTPS with some serious incentives as well. If you have a site that accepts text input and you don't use HTTPS, your site won't rise as high in the Google search results. In addition, in Chrome, these sites are marked with "Not Secure" in the top bar of the browser.

HTTPS works in tandem with another protocol, SSL (for Secure Socket Layer), which needs to be enabled on the server for secure transactions to work. Hosting companies have options for enabling SSL, often for free.

Keep in mind that HTTPS protects form data as it is sent to the server, but doesn't do anything to make your site "secure" and safe from hackers.

■ **PERFORMANCE TIP**

If you want to minimize round-trips to the server, include slashes at the end of directory names in URLs in your links.

Skipping the protocol

Because nearly all web pages use the HyperText Transfer Protocol, the `http://` part is often just implied. This is the case when site names are advertised in print or on TV, as a way to keep the URL easy to remember.

Additionally, browsers are programmed to add `http://` automatically as a convenience to save you some keystrokes. It may seem like you're leaving it out, but it is being sent to the server behind the scenes.

When we begin using URLs to create hyperlinks in HTML documents in **Chapter 6, Adding Links**, you'll learn that it is necessary to include the protocol when making a link to a web page on another server.

Pointing to default files

Many addresses do not include a filename, but simply point to a directory, like these:

```
http://www.oreilly.com
http://www.jendesign.com/resume/
```

When a server receives a request for a directory name rather than a specific file, it looks in that directory for a default document, typically named *index. html*. So when someone types the previous URLs into his browser, what he'll actually see is this:

```
http://www.oreilly.com/index.html
http://www.jendesign.com/resume/index.html
```

The name of the default file (also referred to as the index file) may vary, and depends on how the server is configured. In these examples, it is named *index. html*, but some servers use the filename *default.htm*. If your site uses server-side programming to generate pages, the index file might be named *index.php* or *Default.aspx*. Just check with your server administrator or the tech support department at your hosting service to make sure you give your default file the proper name.

Another thing to notice is that in the first example, the original URL did not have a trailing slash to indicate it was a directory. If the slash is omitted, the server checks to see if the request is a file or a directory. If it is a directory, the server asks the browser to send the request again with a slash. In the end, the slash is included for directories, even if it isn't included the first time it is entered (see **Performance Tip**).

The index file is also useful for security. Some servers (depending on their configuration) display the contents of the directory if the default file is not found. FIGURE 2-2 shows how the documents in the *housepics* directory are exposed as the result of a missing default file. One way to prevent people from snooping around in your files is to be sure there is an index file in every directory. Your server administrator may also add other protections to prevent your directories from displaying in the browser.

Providing the URL for a directory (rather than a specific filename) prompts the server to look for a default file, typically called *index.html*.

Some servers are configured to return a listing of the contents of that directory if the default file is not found.

FIGURE 2-2. Some servers display the contents of the directory if an index file is not found.

THE ANATOMY OF A WEB PAGE

We're all familiar with what web pages look like in the browser window, but what's happening "under the hood"?

At the top of FIGURE 2-3, you see a minimal web page as it appears in a graphical browser. Although you see it as one coherent page, it is actually assembled from four separate files: an HTML document (*index.html*), a style sheet (*kitchen.css*), and two graphics (*foods.png* and *spoon.png*). The HTML document is running the show.

HTML Documents

You may be as surprised as I was to learn that the graphically rich and interactive pages we see on the web are generated by simple, text-only documents. The text file behind the scenes is referred to as the source document.

Take a look at *index.html*, the source document for the Jen's Kitchen web page. You can see that it contains the text content of the page plus special tags (indicated with angle brackets, < and >) that describe each element on the page.

The web page shown in this browser window consists of four separate files:

- An HTML text document
- A style sheet
- Two images

Tags in the HTML source document give the browsers instructions for how the text is structured and where the images should be placed.

index.html

```
<!DOCTYPE html>
<html>
<head>
  <meta charset="utf-8">
  <title>Jen's Kitchen</title>
  <link rel="stylesheet" href="kitchen.css" type="text/css">
</head>

<body>
<h1><img src="foods.png" alt="food illustration"> Jen's Kitchen</h1>

<p>If you love to read about <strong>cooking and eating</strong>, would like to learn about some of the best
restaurants in the world, or just want a few choice recipes to add to your collection, <em>this is the site
for you!</em></p>

<p><img src="spoon.png" alt="spoon illustration"> Your pal, Jen at Jen's Kitchen</p>

<hr>
<small>Copyright 2018, Jennifer Robbins</small>
</body>
</html>
```

kitchen.css

```
body { font: normal 1em Verdana; width: 80%; margin: 1em auto; }

h1 { font: italic 3em Georgia; color: rgb(23, 109, 109);
     margin: 1em 0 1em; }

img { margin: 0 20px 0 0; }

h1 img { margin-bottom: -20px; }

small { color: #666666; }
```

foods.png

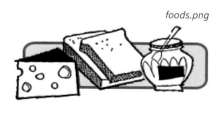

spoon.png

FIGURE 2-3. The source file, style sheet, and images that make up a simple web page.

Adding descriptive tags to a text document is known as "marking up" the document. Web pages use a markup language called HyperText Markup Language, or HTML for short, which was created especially for documents with hypertext links. HTML defines dozens of text elements that make up documents such as headings, paragraphs, emphasized text, and of course, links. There are also elements that add information about the document (such as its title), media such as images and videos, and widgets for form inputs, just to name a few.

You can view the source for any web page. EXERCISE 2-1 gives you some prompts and pointers.

The version of HTML we use today is HTML5. There have been several versions of HTML since its birth in 1989, and a few that are still in use today. There is a complete history of HTML, all its versions, and an overview of what makes HTML5 unique in **Appendix D, From HTML+ to HTML5**.

EXERCISE 2-1. View source

You can see the HTML file for any web page by viewing its source in a desktop browser. Most modern browsers keep the View Source function with the developer tools and typically open the source document in a separate window or in a developer's panel at the bottom of the current window.

Here's where to find the View Source function on the major desktop browsers:

Safari: **Develop** → **Show** → **Page Source**

Chrome: **View** → **Developer** → **View Source**

Firefox: **Tools** → **Web Developer** → **Page Source**

MS Edge: Right-click on the page and select **View Source**. If you do not see that option in the context menu, you may need to turn it on in the Developer Settings. Open a new browser window and type **about:flags** in the address bar. Under "Developer settings," check "Show View source" and "Inspect element" in the context menu. Now when you go to a web page, you can right-click on the page and access the View Source function. You may also use the Ctrl+U keyboard shortcut or F12 key.

1. With the browser of your choice, enter this URL into your browser:

    `www.learningwebdesign.com/5e/kitchen.html`

    You should see the Jen's Kitchen web page from FIGURE 2-3.

2. Follow the directions for your browser listed above to view the source HTML document for the Jen's Kitchen page. It should be the same as shown in the figure.

3. To view a page that is a little more complicated, take a look at the source for the *learningwebdesign.com* home page.

4. The source for most sites is considerably more complicated. View the source of *oreilly.com*. It's got style sheets, scripts, inline SVG graphics...the works! Don't worry if you don't understand what's going on. Much of it will look more familiar by the time you are done with this book.

WARNING

Keep in mind that while learning from others' work is fine, stealing other people's code is poor form (or even illegal). If you want to use code as you see it, ask for permission and always give credit to those who did the work.

A Quick Introduction to HTML Markup

You'll be learning the nitty-gritty of markup in **Part II**, so I don't want to bog you down with too much detail right now, but there are a few things I'd like to point out about how HTML works and how browsers interpret it.

Read through the HTML document in FIGURE 2-3 and compare it to the browser results. It's easy to see how the elements marked up with HTML tags in the source document correspond to what displays in the browser window.

First, you'll notice that the text within brackets (for example, `<body>` and `<strong>`) does not display in the final page. The browser displays only what's between the tags—the content of the element. The markup is hidden. The tag provides the name of the HTML element—usually an abbreviation such as "h1" for "heading level 1," or "em" for "emphasized text."

Second, you'll see that most of the HTML tags appear in pairs surrounding the content of the element. In our HTML document, `<h1>` indicates that the following text should be a first-level heading; `</h1>` indicates the end of the heading. Some elements, called empty elements, do not have content. In our sample, the `<hr>` tag indicates an empty element that tells the browser to "insert a horizontal rule here" as a thematic divider.

Because I was unfamiliar with computer programming when I first began writing HTML, it helped me to think of the tags and text as "beads on a string" that the browser interprets one by one, in sequence. For example, when the browser encounters an open bracket (`<`), it assumes all of the following characters are part of the markup until it finds the closing bracket (`>`). Similarly, it assumes all of the content following an opening `<h1>` tag is a heading until it encounters the closing `</h1>` tag. This is the manner in which the browser parses the HTML document. Understanding the browser's method can be helpful when troubleshooting a misbehaving HTML document.

Where Are the Pictures?

Obviously, there are no pictures in the HTML file itself, so how do they get there when you view the final page? You can see in FIGURE 2-3 that each image is a separate file. The images are placed in the flow of the text with the HTML image element (`img`), which tells the browser where to find the graphic (its URL). When the browser sees the `img` element, it makes another request to the server for the image file, and then places it in the content flow.

The browser also sends requests to the server for style sheets (like *kitchen. css*), JavaScript files (*.js*), and other embedded media like audio and videos. The browser software (or more specifically, its rendering engine) brings the separate pieces together into the final page.

The assembly of the page generally happens in an instant, so it appears as though the whole page loads all at once. Over slow connections or if the page includes huge graphics or media files, the assembly process may be more apparent as images lag behind the text. The page may even need to be redrawn as new images, fonts, and style sheets arrive (although you can construct your pages in such a way that prevents this from happening).

Adding a Little Style

I want to direct your attention to one last key ingredient of our minimal page. Near the top of the HTML document there is a `link` element that points to the style sheet document *kitchen.css*. That style sheet includes a few lines of instructions for how the page should look in the browser. These are style instructions written according to the rules of Cascading Style Sheets (CSS). CSS allows designers to add visual style instructions (known as the document's presentation) to the marked-up text (the document's structure, in web design terminology). In **Part III**, you'll get to know the power of Cascading Style Sheets.

FIGURE 2-4 shows the Jen's Kitchen page without (top) and with (bottom) the style instructions. Browsers come equipped with default styles for every HTML element they support, so if an HTML document lacks custom style instructions, the browser will use its own. That's what you see in the screenshot on the top. Even just a few style rules can make big improvements to the appearance of a page.

FIGURE 2-4. The Jen's Kitchen page without (top) and with (bottom) custom style rules.

Adding Behaviors with JavaScript

To make elements on the page *do* something, you use a scripting language called JavaScript (see **Note**). There are no scripts on the Jen's Kitchen page because I thought it best to keep things simple this early in the book, but know that JavaScript is an essential ingredient in modern websites.

Whereas HTML provides the structure and the CSS style sheet alters how things look, JavaScript adds a behavior component that controls how things work. Scripts may be standalone files on the server (with the *.js* suffix) or be written out right in the document. They may be triggered to run immediately when the page loads or be triggered by something the user does, like click or hover on an element or enter something in a form field.

You'll get a basic introduction to JavaScript in **Part IV** of this book.

NOTE

JavaScript is not required for the interactivity of links and web forms, which work using HTML alone.

PUTTING IT ALL TOGETHER

Static vs. Dynamic Sites

Static websites consist of HTML files with fixed content that display the same information to every visitor. In other words, each page you see in the browser is a view of a single HTML file on the server. This book focuses on the creation of static web pages as they are straightforward and the best starting place for beginners.

By contrast, dynamic websites are generated with backend programming such as PHP or ASP. Each page is generated by the application on the fly. Dynamic sites access content and data from a database, and the final pages may be customized for each user. For extremely large sites with hundreds or thousands of pages, setting up and maintaining a dynamic site is considerably less work than creating and storing every page as a static HTML document individually.

HTTP Status Codes

Servers issue status codes in response to browser requests. The full list of status codes is quite long (you can read about them all at *en.wikipedia.org/wiki/List_of_HTTP_status_codes*), but here are a few common responses:

200	OK
301	Moved Permanently
302	Moved Temporarily
404	Not Found
410	Gone (no longer available)
500	Internal Server Error

❶ To wrap up our introduction to how the web works, let's trace a typical stream of events that occurs with every web page that appears on your screen (FIGURE 2-5). Request a web page by either typing its URL (for example, *http://jenskitchensite.com*) directly in the browser or by clicking a link on a page. The URL contains the information needed to target a specific document on a specific web server on the internet. In this case, it points to the default file (*index.html*) in the top directory.

❷ Your browser sends an HTTP request to the server named in the URL and asks for the specific file. The request also includes information about what languages the user can read and what types of files the browser can accept. If the URL specifies a directory (not a file), it is the same as requesting the default file in that directory.

❸ The server looks for the requested file and issues an HTTP response in the form of an HTTP header. The header includes information about the file, like the last modified date, the length of the file, and its Content-Type (for example, an *.html* file has the content type "text/html").

  a. If the page cannot be found, the server returns an error message. The message typically says "404 Not Found," although more hospitable error messages may be provided. Other error types are possible as well (see the sidebar **"HTTP Status Codes"**).

  b. If the document *is* found, the server retrieves the requested file and returns it to the browser. If the site is dynamic, the server assembles the page from stored data before returning it to the browser.

❹ The browser parses the HTML document. If the page contains images (indicated by the HTML **img** element) or other external resources like scripts or style sheets, the browser contacts the server again to request each resource specified in the markup.

❺ The browser inserts each image in the document flow where indicated by the **img** element, applies styles, and runs scripts. And *voilà*! The assembled web page is displayed for your viewing pleasure.

I should note that I've depicted a traditional and simplified scenario here to tell you how web pages are put together. These days, it is common for web pages to be generated from content management systems (CMSs) that keep content in databases and use templates to assemble the data into pages on the fly. In that case, in Step 3b, there is a more complicated process of assembling the file from various parts rather than just handing off an existing file.

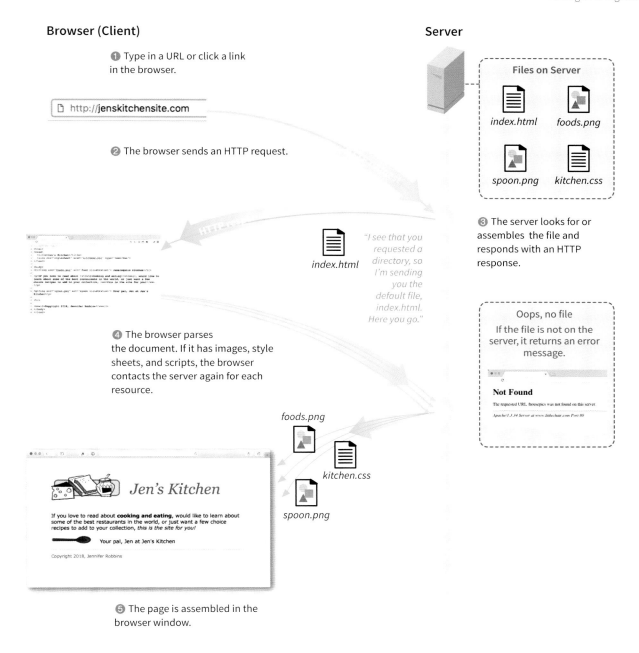

Browser (Client)

❶ Type in a URL or click a link in the browser.

http://jenskitchensite.com

❷ The browser sends an HTTP request.

❹ The browser parses the document. If it has images, style sheets, and scripts, the browser contacts the server again for each resource.

foods.png

kitchen.css

spoon.png

Jen's Kitchen

If you love to read about **cooking and eating**, would like to learn about some of the best restaurants in the world, or just want a few choice recipes to add to your collection, *this is the site for you!*

Your pal, Jen at Jen's Kitchen

Copyright 2018, Jennifer Robbins

❺ The page is assembled in the browser window.

Server

Files on Server

index.html   foods.png

spoon.png   kitchen.css

❸ The server looks for or assembles the file and responds with an HTTP response.

index.html

"I see that you requested a directory, so I'm sending you the default file, index.html. Here you go."

Oops, no file
If the file is not on the server, it returns an error message.

Not Found

The requested URL /housepics was not found on this server.

Apache/1.3.34 Server at www.littlechair.com Port 80

FIGURE 2-5. How browsers display web pages.

Getting Your Pages on the Web

If you would like more information about registering domain names and finding a server to host your site, download the article titled **"Getting Your Pages on the Web"** (PDF) at *learningwebdesign.com/articles/*.

TEST YOURSELF

Let's play a round of "Identify That Acronym!" The following are a few basic web terms mentioned in this chapter. Answers are in **Appendix A**.

1. HTML _____ a. Home of Mosaic, the first graphical browser

2. W3C _____ b. The location of a web document or resource

3. CERN _____ c. The markup language used to describe web content

4. CSS _____ d. Matches domain names with numeric IP addresses

5. HTTP _____ e. A protocol for file transfer

6. IP _____ f. Protocol for transferring web documents on the internet

7. URL _____ g. The language used to instruct how web content looks

8. NCSA _____ h. Particle physics lab where the web was born

9. DNS _____ i. Internet Protocol

10. FTP _____ j. The organization that monitors web technologies

SOME BIG CONCEPTS YOU NEED TO KNOW

As the web matures and the number of devices we access it from increases exponentially, our jobs as web designers and developers get significantly more complicated. Frankly, there's a lot more going on out there than I can fit in this book. In the chapters that follow, I will focus on the basic building blocks of web design—HTML elements, CSS styles, a taste of JavaScript, and web image production—that will give you a solid foundation for the further development of your skills.

Before we get to the nuts and bolts, I want to introduce some Big Concepts that every web designer needs to know. We'll look at ideas and concerns that inform our decisions and contribute to the contemporary web environment. I'll be referring back to the terminology introduced here frequently.

The heart of the matter is that as web designers, we never know exactly how the pages we create will be viewed. We don't know which of the dozens of browsers might be used, whether it is on a desktop computer or something more portable, how large the browser window will be, what fonts are installed, whether functionality such as JavaScript is enabled, how fast the internet connection is, whether the pages are being read by a screen reader, and so on. The Big Concepts in this chapter are primarily reactions to and methods for coping with the inescapable element of the Unknown in our medium. They include the following:

- The multitude of devices
- Web standards
- Progressive enhancement
- Responsive Web Design
- Accessibility
- Site performance

IN THIS CHAPTER

The web on mobile devices

The benefits of web standards

Progressive enhancement

Responsive Web Design

Accessibility

Site performance

Because we're just getting started, I will keep the descriptions brief and fairly non-technical. My goal is that you have a basic understanding of what I mean by terms like "progressive enhancement" when you encounter them in lessons later. Many excellent articles and books have been written on each of these topics and their related production techniques, and I'll provide pointers to resources for further reading.

A MULTITUDE OF DEVICES

Until 2007, we could be relatively certain that our users were visiting our sites while sitting at their desks, looking at a large monitor, using a speedy internet connection. We had all more or less settled on 960 pixels as a good width for a web page based on the most common monitor size. Back then, our biggest concern was dealing with the dozen or so desktop browsers and jumping through a few extra hoops to support quirky old versions of Internet Explorer. And we thought we had it rough!

Although you could access web pages and web content on mobile phones prior to 2007, the introduction of the iPhone and Android smartphones as well as faster networks heralded a huge shift in how, when, and where we do our web surfing (particularly in the United States, which lagged behind Asia and the EU in mobile technology). Since then, we've seen the introduction of phones and tablets of all different dimensions, as well as web browsers on TVs, gaming systems, and other devices. And the diversity is only going to increase. I think mobile web design expert Brad Frost sums it up nicely in his illustrations in FIGURE 3-1.

The challenge of designing for all of these devices goes beyond addressing differing screen sizes. There is a world of difference between using a site over a broadband connection and over a slow cell network. Designers need to resist making assumptions about network speed and context based on the screen size. Just because it is a small screen doesn't mean it's a slow connection or

FIGURE 3-1. Brad Frost sums up the reality of device diversity nicely (*bradfrostweb.com*).

that the person is in a hurry. It's not uncommon to leisurely browse the web on a smartphone while sitting on the couch at home with a solid WiFi connection. And iPads with larger, high-resolution displays may be accessing the internet on pokey 3G connections. In other words, it's complicated!

For a lot of sites today, more people access the web via their mobile devices than on a desktop computer. Already, a significant portion of Americans use their mobile phones as their *only* access to the internet. That means it is critical to get the design and functionality right. We've made huge strides in serving a pleasing experience to users with handheld devices, and the technology for targeting their needs continues to head in the right direction.

What I want you to learn here is that the way you see your design as you're working on it on your nice desktop machine is not how it will be experienced by everyone. Some will see it much smaller. Some will see it load painfully slowly. Some may be looking at it on a TV across the room. All web design professionals should keep this fact in mind.

> Resist making assumptions about network speed and context based on the screen size.

For Further Reading

- *Mobile First* by Luke Wroblewski (A Book Apart). Luke was way ahead of the curve in insisting that sites work well on mobile devices, and he shares his perspective in this little book, which is jam-packed with ideas.

Mobile Web?

You may hear people use the term "mobile web," but the truth is (as Stephen Hay put it in a tweet in 2011; see FIGURE 3-2), there is no Mobile Web any more than there is a Desktop Web, or a Tablet Web, or so on. There is just The Web, and it can be accessed from all manner of devices. As of this writing, "mobile web" is used as sort of a catchall term to describe our efforts to adapt our desktop design skills to accommodate a much wider variety of use cases. And, as we are finding out, there is more than one way to crack that nut.

 **Stephen Hay** @stephenhay Following

There is no Mobile Web. There is only The Web, which we view in different ways. There is also no Desktop Web. Or Tablet Web. Thank you.

 Reply Retweet Favorite

FIGURE 3-2. Stephen Hay's tweet from January 2011. Read his follow-up article at *www.the-haystack.com/2011/01/07/there-is-no-mobile-web*.

STICKING WITH THE STANDARDS

So how do we deal with this diversity? A good start is to follow the standards documented by the World Wide Web Consortium (W3C). Sticking with web standards is your primary tool for ensuring your site is consistent on all standards-compliant browsers (that's approximately 99% of browsers in current use). It also helps make your content forward-compatible as web technologies and browser capabilities evolve. Another benefit is that you can tell your clients that you create "standards-compliant" sites, and they will like you more.

The notion of standards compliance may seem like a no-brainer, but it used to be that everyone, including the browser makers, played fast and loose with HTML and scripting. The price we paid was incompatible browser implementations and the need to create sites twice to make them work for everyone. I talk more about web standards throughout this book, so I won't go into too much detail here. Suffice it to say that the web standards are your friends. Everything you learn in this book will start you off on the right foot.

> Sticking with web standards is your primary tool for ensuring your site is as consistent as possible.

For Further Reading

- The W3C site (*w3.org/standards*) is the primary resource for all web standards documents.

- The bible for standards compliance and how it makes good business sense is *Designing with Web Standards, 3rd Edition*, by Jeffrey Zeldman (New Riders). It's getting on in years, but the fundamentals are still solid.

PROGRESSIVE ENHANCEMENT

With a multitude of browsers comes a multitude of levels of support for the web standards. In fact, no browser has implemented all the standards 100%, and there are always new technologies that are slowly gaining steam. Furthermore, users can set their own browser preferences, so they may have a browser that supports JavaScript but have chosen to turn it off. The point here is that we are faced with a wide range of browser capabilities—from only basic HTML support to all the bells and whistles.

Progressive enhancement is one strategy for dealing with unknown browser capabilities (see **Note**). When designing with progressive enhancement, you start with a baseline experience that makes the content or core functionality available to even the most rudimentary browsers or assistive devices. From there, you layer on more advanced features for the browsers that can handle them. You might finish with some "nice to have" effects, like animation or wrapping text around images in interesting shapes, that enhance the experience for users with the most advanced browsers, but aren't really critical to the brand or message.

NOTE

Progressive enhancement is the flip side of an approach to browser diversity called graceful degradation, *in which you design the fully enhanced experience first, then create a series of fallbacks for non-supporting browsers. Both methods have their place in modern development. You will find many fallback techniques suggested in this book to be sure less capable browsers are accommodated.*

Progressive enhancement is an approach that informs all aspects of page design and production, including HTML, CSS, and JavaScript:

Authoring strategy

When an HTML document is written in logical order and its elements are marked up in a meaningful way, it will be usable on the widest range of browsing environments, including the oldest browsers, future browsers, and mobile and assistive devices. It may not look exactly the same, but the important thing is that your content is available. It also ensures that search engines like Google will catalog the content correctly. A clean HTML document with its elements accurately and thoroughly described is the foundation for accessibility.

Styling strategy

You can create layers of experience simply by taking advantage of the way browsers parse style sheet rules. Without going into too much technical detail, you can write a style rule that makes an element background red, but also include a style that gives it a cool gradient (a blend from one color to another) for browsers that know how to render gradients. Or you can use a cutting-edge CSS selector to deliver certain styles only to cutting-edge browsers. The knowledge that browsers simply ignore properties and rules they don't understand gives you license to innovate without bringing older browsers to their knees. You just have to be mindful of styling the baseline experience first, then adding improvements once the minimum requirements are met.

Scripting strategy

As with other web technologies, there are discrepancies in how browsers handle JavaScript (particularly on non-desktop devices), and some users opt to turn it off entirely. The first rule in progressive enhancement is to make sure basic functionality—such as linking from page to page or accomplishing essential tasks like data submission via forms—is intact even when JavaScript is off. In this way, you ensure the baseline experience, and enhance it when JavaScript is available.

> Progressive enhancement is a strategy for coping with unknown browser capabilities.

For Further Reading

- There is no better introduction to the progressive enhancement approach than the book *Adaptive Web Design: Crafting Rich Experiences with Progressive Enhancement, 2nd Edition*, by Aaron Gustafson (New Riders).

- *The Uncertain Web: Web Development in a Changing Landscape* by Rob Larson (O'Reilly).

- Once you have more chops, the book *Designing with Progressive Enhancement* by Todd Parker, Patty Toland, Scott Jehl, and Maggie Costello Wachs (New Riders) is an excellent deep-dive into techniques and best practices. Read more about it at *filamentgroup.com/dwpe/*.

RESPONSIVE WEB DESIGN

Ethan Marcotte personal site
ethanmarcotte.com

NASA
nasa.gov

FIGURE 3-3. A responsive site's layout changes based on the size of the browser window.

By default, most browsers on small devices such as smartphones and tablets shrink a web page down to fit the screen and provide mechanisms for zooming and moving around the page. Although it technically works, it is not a great experience. The text is too small to read, the links are too small to tap, and all that zooming and panning around is distracting.

Responsive Web Design (RWD) is a strategy for providing appropriate layouts to devices based on the size of the viewport (browser window). The key to Responsive Web Design is serving a single HTML document (with one URL) to all devices, but applying different style sheets based on the screen size in order to provide the most optimized layout for that device. For example, when the page is viewed on a smartphone, it appears in one column with large links for easy tapping. But when that same page is viewed on a large desktop browser, the content rearranges into multiple columns with traditional navigation elements. It's like *magic*! (Except that it's actually just CSS.)

The web design community has been abuzz about responsive design since Ethan Marcotte first wrote about it and coined the phrase in his article "Responsive Web Design" on A List Apart in 2010 (*www.alistapart.com/articles/responsive-web-design/*). It's become one of the primary tools we use to cope with unknown viewport size.

FIGURE 3-3 shows some examples of responsive sites at the typical dimensions for a desktop monitor, tablet, and smartphone. You can see many more inspirational examples at the Media Queries gallery site (*mediaqueri.es*). Try opening one of the responsive sites in your browser and then resizing the window narrow and wide. Watch as the layout changes based on window size. *Très* cool.

Responsive Web Design helps with matters of layout, but it is not a solution to all mobile web design challenges. The fact is that providing the best experiences for your users and their chosen device may require optimizations that go beyond adjusting the look and feel. You can better address some problems by using the server to detect the device and its capabilities and then making decisions on what to send back.

For some sites and services, it may be preferable to build a separate mobile site (see the **"M-dot Sites"** sidebar) with a customized interface and feature set that takes advantage of phone capabilities like geolocation. That said, although responsive design won't fix everything, it is an important part of the solution for delivering satisfactory experiences on a wide variety of browsers.

For Further Reading

I'll cover Responsive Web Design in more detail in **Chapter 17, Responsive Web Design**, once you have more code experience under your belt. There you will find plenty of resources to continue your responsive design education.

M-dot Sites

Some companies and services choose to build an entirely separate site, with a unique URL, just for mobile devices. M-dot sites (named because their URLs typically begin with "m." or "mobile.") offer a reduced set of options and may also include mobile-specific features such as geolocation. A lot of the "extra" stuff (like promotions) from the desktop site is simply stripped away. (It makes you wonder what value it adds on the desktop.) A dedicated mobile site may be the best solution if you know that your mobile users have very different usage patterns than folks seated at a desk.

FIGURE 3-4 compares CVS's primary and m-dot sites as they appeared in early 2018. You can see that phone users are offered a more streamlined set of options. Other notable sites with dedicated mobile versions are Twitter and Facebook.

The point here is that Responsive Web Design is not a universal solution. For sites that feature mainly text content, a little layout adjustment may be all that is needed to deliver a good reading experience on all devices. For complex sites and web applications, a very different experience may be preferred.

The downside of a dedicated mobile site is that it is more than twice the work. It requires additional content planning, design templates, production time, and ongoing maintenance. But if it means giving your visitors the functionality they need, it is worth the investment.

It is possible that you have a business for which mobile use is so distinct from desktop use that a separate mobile site makes sense, but in general, m-dot sites are fading away in favor of RWD. Google is helping to speed this process along by encouraging all m-dot sites to migrate to RWD before the launch of their "mobile-first index" in 2018 (*webmasters.googleblog.com/2016/11/mobile-first-indexing.html*). If search result rankings are a concern, you may get more mileage from going responsive.

> Responsive Web Design is a strategy for dealing with unknown screen size.

FIGURE 3-4. A comparison of the desktop site and the dedicated mobile site for the same business.

ONE WEB FOR ALL (ACCESSIBILITY)

We've been talking about the daunting number of browsers in use today, but so far, we've only addressed visual browsers controlled with mouse pointers or fingertips. It is critical, however, to keep in mind that people access the web in many different ways—with a keyboard, mouse, voice commands, screen readers, Braille output, magnifiers, joysticks, foot pedals, and so on. Web designers must build pages in a manner that creates as few barriers as possible to getting to information, regardless of the user's ability and the device used to access the web. In other words, you must design for accessibility.

Although intended for users with disabilities such as poor vision or limited mobility, the techniques and strategies developed for accessibility also benefit other users with less-than-optimum browsing experiences. Accessible sites are also more effectively indexed by search engines such as Google. Making your site accessible is well worth the extra effort.

There are four broad categories of disabilities that affect how people interact with their computers and the information on them:

Vision impairment

People with low or no vision may use an assistive device such as a screen reader, Braille display, or a screen magnifier to get content from the screen. They may also simply use the browser's text zoom function to make the text large enough to read.

Mobility impairment

Users with limited or no use of their hands may use special devices such as modified mice and keyboards, foot pedals, voice commands, or joysticks to navigate the web and enter information.

Auditory impairment

Users with limited or no hearing will miss out on audio aspects of multimedia, so it is necessary to provide alternatives, such as transcripts for audio tracks or captions for video.

Cognitive impairment

Users with memory, reading comprehension, problem solving, and attention limitations benefit when sites are designed simply and clearly. These qualities are helpful to anyone using your site.

The W3C started the Web Accessibility Initiative (WAI) to address the need to make the web usable for everyone. The WAI site (*www.w3.org/WAI*) is an excellent starting point for learning more about web accessibility. One of the documents produced by the WAI to help developers create accessible sites is the Web Content Accessibility Guidelines (WCAG and WCAG 2.0). You can read them all at *www.w3.org/WAI/intro/wcag.php*. The US government based its Section 508 accessibility guidelines on the Priority 1 points of the WCAG (see the sidebar **"Government Accessibility Requirements: Section 508"**). All sites benefit from these guidelines, but if you are designing a government site, adherence is a requirement.

Another W3C effort is the WAI-ARIA (Accessible Rich Internet Applications) spec, which addresses the accessibility of web applications that include dynamically generated content, scripting, and advanced interface elements that are particularly confounding to assistive devices. The ARIA Recommendation defines a number of roles for content and widgets that authors can explicitly apply using the **role** attribute. Roles include **menubar**, **progressbar**, **slider**, **timer**, and **tooltip**, to name just a few. For the complete list of roles, go to *www.w3.org/TR/wai-aria/roles#role_definitions*.

For Further Reading

The following resources are good starting points for further exploration of web accessibility:

- The Web Accessibility Initiative (WAI), *www.w3.org/WAI*

- WebAIM: Web Accessibility in Mind, *www.webaim.org*

- *Accessibility Handbook: Making 508 Compliant Websites* by Katie Cunningham (O'Reilly)

- *Universal Design for Web Applications: Web Applications That Reach Everyone* by Wendy Chisholm and Matt May (O'Reilly)

US Government Accessibility Requirements: Section 508

If you create a site receiving federal funding from the US government, you are required by law to comply with the Section 508 guidelines, which ensure that electronic information and technology are available to people with disabilities. State and other publicly funded sites may also be required to comply.

The following guidelines, excerpted from the Section 508 Standards at *www.section508.gov*, provide a good checklist for basic accessibility for all websites:

1. A text equivalent for non-text elements shall be provided (e.g., via the "alt" attribute or in element content).

2. Equivalent alternatives for any multimedia presentation shall be synchronized with the presentation.

3. Web pages shall be designed so that all information conveyed with color is also available without color—for example, from context or markup.

4. Documents shall be organized so they are readable without requiring an associated style sheet.

5. Row and column headers shall be identified for data tables.

6. Markup shall be used to associate data and header cells for tables with two or more levels of row or column headers.

7. Pages shall be designed to avoid causing the screen to flicker with a frequency greater than 2 Hz and lower than 55 Hz.

8. When pages utilize scripting languages to display content, or to create interface elements, the information provided by the script shall be identified with functional text that can be read by assistive technology.

9. When a web page requires that an applet, plug-in, or other application be present on the client system to interpret page content, the page must provide a link to a plug-in or applet that complies with §1194.21(a) through (l).

10. When electronic forms are designed to be completed online, the form shall allow people using assistive technology to access the information, field elements, and functionality required for completion and submission of the form, including all directions and cues.

11. A method shall be provided that permits users to skip repetitive navigation links.

12. When a timed response is required, the user shall be alerted and given sufficient time to indicate more time is required.

THE NEED FOR SPEED (SITE PERFORMANCE)

Although the number of users accessing the internet on slow dial-up connections is shrinking (3–5% in the US as of this writing), the percentage of folks using mobile phones to access the web is increasing dramatically; and for some sectors, such as social media and search, mobile has already exceeded desktop usage. If you have a smartphone, then you know how frustrating it is to wait for a web page to fully display over a cellular data connection.

Site performance is critical regardless of how your users access your site. A study by Google in 2009[1] showed that the addition of just 100 to 400 milliseconds to their search results page resulted in reduced searches (–0.2 to –0.6%). Amazon.com showed that reducing page load times by just 100ms resulted in a 1% increase in revenue.[2] Other studies show that users expect a site to load in under 2 seconds, and nearly a third of your audience will leave your site for another if it doesn't. Furthermore, those people aren't likely to come back. Google has added site speed to its search algorithm, so if your site is a slowpoke, it's not likely to show up in that coveted first screen of results. The takeaway here is that site performance (down to the millisecond!) matters a lot.

There are many things you can do to improve the performance of your site, and they fall under two broad categories: limiting file sizes and reducing the number of requests to the server. The following list only scratches the surface for site optimization, but it gives you a general idea of what can be done:

- Optimize images so they are the smallest file size possible without sacrificing quality. You'll learn image optimization techniques in **Chapter 24, Image Asset Production**.

- Streamline HTML markup, avoiding unnecessary levels of nested elements.

- Minimize HTML and CSS documents by removing extra character spaces and line returns.

- Keep JavaScript to a minimum.

- Add scripts in such a way that they load in parallel with other page assets and don't block rendering.

- Don't load unnecessary assets (such as images, scripts, or JavaScript libraries).

- Reduce the number of times the browser makes requests of the server (known as HTTP requests).

---

1 "Speed Matters," *googleresearch.blogspot.com/2009/06/speed-matters.html*.

2 Statistic from "Make Data Matter," PowerPoint presentation by Greg Linden of Stanford University (2006).

Every trip to the server in the form of an HTTP request takes a few milliseconds, and those milliseconds can add up. All those little Twitter widgets, Facebook Like buttons, and advertisements can make dozens of server requests each. You may be surprised to see how many server requests even a simple site makes.

If you'd like to see for yourself, you can use the Network tool available with the Developer tools in Chrome, Safari, or Firefox. The Network tool displays each request to the server and how many milliseconds it took. Here's how you use it in Chrome (but all the browsers work similarly):

1. Launch the Chrome browser and go to any web page.

2. Go to the **View** menu and select **Developer → Developer Tools**. A panel will open at the bottom of the browser.

3. Select the Network tab in the tools view and load a web page. The chart (commonly referred to as a waterfall chart) shows you all the requests made and assets downloaded. The columns on the right show the amount of time each request took in milliseconds. At the bottom of the chart, you can see a summary of the number of requests made and the total amount of data transferred.

FIGURE 3-5 shows a portion of the performance waterfall chart for *oreilly.com*. You can poke around any site on the web this way. It can be very educational.

I won't address site performance in deep technical detail in this book, but I do want you to remember the importance of keeping file sizes as small as possible and eliminating unnecessary server requests in your web design work.

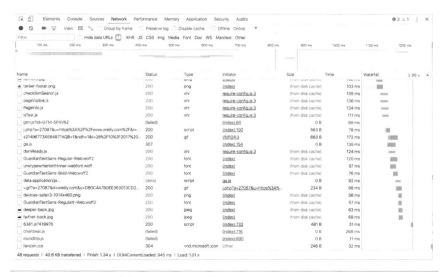

FIGURE 3-5. Waterfall charts such as this one created by the Chrome Network developer tool show the individual server requests made by a web page and the amount of time each request takes.

More Site Performance Tools

Try some of these tools for testing site performance:

- WebPageTest (*webpagetest.org*) is a tool that was originally developed for AOL, but is now available for all to use for free under an open source license. Just type in a URL, and WebPagetest returns a waterfall diagram, screenshot, and other statistics.

- Google's PageSpeed Insights (*developers.google.com/ speed/pagespeed/insights/*) is another service that analyzes the performance of any site you point it to. It also generates suggestions for making your page load faster.

- Yahoo!'s freely available YSlow tool (*yslow.org*) analyzes a site according to 23 rules of web performance, and then gives the site a grade and suggestions for improvement.

For Further Reading

There are other techniques that are too technical for this book (and frankly, for me), and I figure if you are reading this book, you are probably not quite ready to become a site performance wizard. But when you are ready to take it on, here are some resources that should help:

- Lara Hogan has assembled a list of performance-related studies, tools, and resources at *larahogan.me/design*. You can also read her book, *Designing for Performance* (O'Reilly), there for free.

- *High Performance Mobile Web: Best Practices for Optimizing Mobile Web Apps* by Maximiliano Firtman (O'Reilly) covers optimization methods and tools to check your progress.

- Google's site *Make the Web Faster* (*code.google.com/speed/*) is an excellent first stop for learning about site optimization. It compiles a number of excellent tutorials and articles as well as tools for measuring site speed.

TEST YOURSELF

Here are a few questions that check your knowledge of the Big Concepts. If you are stumped, you can find the answers in **Appendix A**.

1. List at least two unknown factors you need to consider when designing and developing a site.

2. Match the technology or practice on the left with the problem it best addresses:

   1. _____ Progressive enhancement   a. Assistive reading and input devices

   2. _____ Server-side detection   b. Slow connection speeds

   3. _____ Responsive design   c. All levels of browser capabilities

   4. _____ WAI-ARIA   d. Determining which device is being used

   5. _____ Site performance   e. A variety of screen sizes
             optimization

3. Web accessibility strategies take into account four broad categories of disabilities. Name at least three, and provide a measure you might take to ensure content is accessible for each.

4. When would you use a waterfall chart?

II

HTML FOR STRUCTURE

CREATING A SIMPLE PAGE

(HTML OVERVIEW)

Part I provided a general overview of the web design environment. Now that we've covered the big concepts, it's time to roll up our sleeves and start creating a real web page. It will be an extremely simple page, but even the most complicated pages are based on the principles described here.

In this chapter, we'll create a web page step-by-step so you can get a feel for what it's like to mark up a document with HTML tags. The exercises allow you to work along.

This is what I want you to get out of this chapter:

- Get a feel for how markup works, including an understanding of elements and attributes.

- See how browsers interpret HTML documents.

- Learn how HTML documents are structured.

- Get a first glimpse of a style sheet in action.

Don't worry about learning the specific text elements or style sheet rules at this point; we'll get to those in the following chapters. For now, just pay attention to the process, the overall structure of the document, and the new terminology.

A WEB PAGE, STEP-BY-STEP

You got a look at an HTML document in **Chapter 2, How the Web Works**, but now you'll get to create one yourself and play around with it in the browser. The demonstration in this chapter has five steps that cover the basics of page production:

Step 1: Start with content. As a starting point, we'll write up raw text content and see what browsers do with it.

Step 2: Give the document structure. You'll learn about HTML element syntax and the elements that set up areas for content and metadata.

Step 3: Identify text elements. You'll describe the content using the appropriate text elements and learn about the proper way to use HTML.

Step 4: Add an image. By adding an image to the page, you'll learn about attributes and empty elements.

Step 5: Change how the text looks with a style sheet. This exercise gives you a taste of formatting content with Cascading Style Sheets.

By the time we're finished, you'll have written the document for the page shown in FIGURE 4-1. It's not very fancy, but you have to start somewhere.

FIGURE 4-1. In this chapter, we'll write the HTML document for this page in five steps.

We'll be checking our work in a browser frequently throughout this demonstration—probably more than you would in real life. But because this is an introduction to HTML, it's helpful to see the cause and effect of each small change to the source file along the way.

LAUNCH A TEXT EDITOR

In this chapter and throughout the book, we'll be writing out HTML documents by hand, so the first thing we need to do is launch a text editor. The text editor that is provided with your operating system, such as Notepad (Windows) or TextEdit (Macintosh), will do for these purposes. Other text editors are fine as long as you can save plain-text files with the *.html* extension. If you have a visual web-authoring tool such as Dreamweaver, set it aside for now. I want you to get a feel for marking up a document manually (see the sidebar **"HTML the Hard Way"**).

HTML the Hard Way

I stand by my method of teaching HTML the old-fashioned way—by hand. There's no better way to truly understand how markup works than typing it out, one tag at a time, and then opening your page in a browser. It doesn't take long to develop a feel for marking up documents properly.

Although you may choose to use a visual or drag-and-drop web-authoring tool down the line, understanding HTML will make using your tools easier and more efficient. In addition, you will be glad that you can look at a source file and understand what you're seeing. It is also crucial for troubleshooting broken pages or fine-tuning the default formatting that web tools produce.

And for what it's worth, professional web developers tend to mark up content manually for better control over the code and the ability to make deliberate decisions about what elements to use.

This section shows how to open new documents in Notepad and TextEdit. Even if you've used these programs before, skim through for some special settings that will make the exercises go more smoothly. We'll start with Notepad; Mac users can jump ahead.

Creating a New Document in Notepad (Windows)

These are the steps to creating a new document in Notepad on Windows 10 (FIGURE 4-2):

1. Search for "Notepad" to access it quickly. Click on Notepad to open a new document window, and you're ready to start typing. ❶

2. Next, make the extensions visible. This step is not required to make HTML documents, but it will help make the file types clearer at a glance. Open the File Explorer, select the View tab, and then select the Options button on the right. In the Folder Options panel, select the View tab again. ❷

3. Find "Hide extensions for known file types" and uncheck that option. ❸

4. Click OK to save the preference ❹, and the file extensions will now be visible.

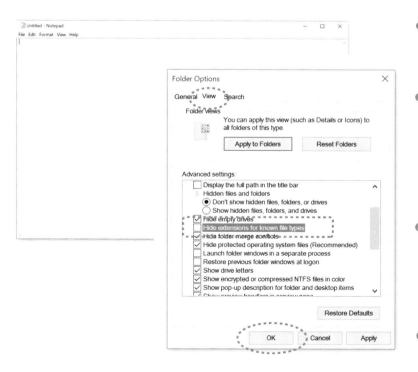

❶ Click on Notepad to open a new document.

❷ Open the File Explorer, select the View tab, and then select the Options button on the right (not shown). Select the View tab.

❸ Uncheck "Hide extensions for known file types."

❹ Click OK to save the preference, and the file extensions will now be visible.

FIGURE 4-2. Creating a new document in Notepad.

Creating a New Document in TextEdit (macOS)

By default, TextEdit creates rich-text documents—that is, documents that have hidden style-formatting instructions for making text bold, setting font size, and so on. You can tell that TextEdit is in rich-text mode when it has a formatting toolbar at the top of the window (plain-text mode does not). HTML documents need to be plain-text documents, so we'll need to change the format, as shown in this example (FIGURE 4-3):

1. Use the Finder to look in the Applications folder for TextEdit. When you've found it, double-click the name or icon to launch the application.

2. In the initial TextEdit dialog box, click the New Document button in the bottom-left corner. If you see the text formatting menu and tab ruler at the top of the Untitled document, you are in rich-text mode ❶. If you don't, you are in plain-text mode ❷. Either way, there are some preferences you need to set.

3. Close that document, and open the Preferences dialog box from the TextEdit menu.

4. Change these preferences:

   On the New Document tab, select Plain text ❸. Under Options, deselect all of the automatic formatting options ❹.

   On the Open and Save tab, select Display HTML files as HTML Code ❺ and deselect "Add '.txt' extensions to plain text files" ❻. The rest of the defaults should be fine.

5. When you are done, click the red button in the top-left corner.

6. Now create a new document by selecting File → New. The formatting menu will no longer be there, and you can save your text as an HTML document. You can always convert a document back to rich text by selecting Format → Make Rich Text when you are not using TextEdit for HTML.

❶ Formatting menu indicates rich text. ❷ Plain text documents have no menu.

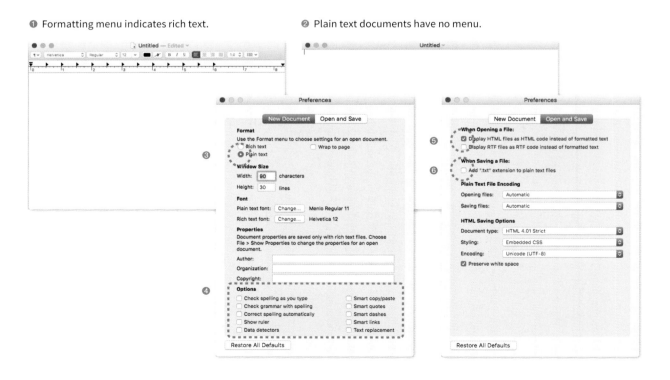

FIGURE 4-3. Launching TextEdit and choosing "Plain text" settings in the Preferences.

STEP 1: START WITH CONTENT

Now that we have our new document, it's time to get typing. A web page is all about content, so that's where we begin our demonstration. EXERCISE 4-1 walks you through entering the raw text content and saving the document in a new folder.

EXERCISE 4-1. Entering content

1. Type the home page content below into the new document in your text editor. Copy it exactly as you see it here, keeping the line breaks the same for the sake of playing along. The raw text for this exercise is also available online at *learningwebdesign.com/5e/ materials/*.

   ```
   Black Goose Bistro

   The Restaurant
   The Black Goose Bistro offers casual lunch and dinner fare in a relaxed
   atmosphere. The menu changes regularly to highlight the freshest local
   ingredients.

   Catering
   You have fun. We'll handle the cooking. Black Goose Catering can handle
   events from snacks for a meetup to elegant corporate fundraisers.

   Location and Hours
   Seekonk, Massachusetts;
   Monday through Thursday 11am to 9pm; Friday and Saturday, 11am to
   midnight
   ```

2. Select "Save" or "Save as" from the File menu to get the Save As dialog box (FIGURE 4-4). The first thing you need to do is create a new folder (click the New Folder button on both Windows and Mac) that will contain all of the files for the site. The technical name for the folder that contains everything is the local root directory.

FIGURE 4-4. Saving *index.html* in a new folder called *bistro*.

Name the new folder *bistro*, and save the text file as *index.html* in it. The filename needs to end in *.html* to be recognized by the browser as a web document. See the sidebar **"Naming Conventions"** for more tips on naming files.

3. Just for kicks, let's take a look at *index.html* in a browser.

   Windows users: Double-click the filename in the File Explorer to launch your default browser, or right-click the file for the option to open it in the browser of your choice.

   Mac users: Launch your favorite browser (I'm using Google Chrome) and choose Open or Open File from the File menu. Navigate to *index.html*, and then select the document to open it in the browser.

4. You should see something like the page shown in FIGURE 4-5. We'll talk about the results in the following section.

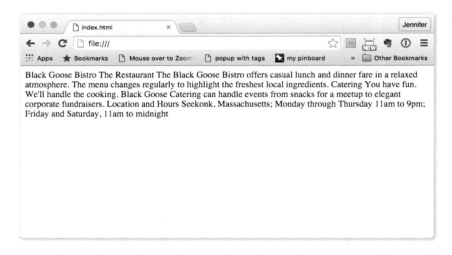

FIGURE 4-5. A first look at the content in a browser.

Naming Conventions

It is important that you follow these rules and conventions when naming your files:

Use proper suffixes for your files. HTML files must end with *.html* or *.htm*. Web graphics must be labeled according to their file format: *.gif*, *.png*, *.jpg* (*.jpeg* is also acceptable, although less common), or *.svg*.

Never use character spaces within filenames. It is common to use an underline character or hyphen to visually separate words within filenames, such as *robbins_bio.html* or *robbins-bio.html*.

Avoid special characters such as **?, %, #, /, :, ;, •,** etc. Limit filenames to letters, numbers, underscores, hyphens, and periods. It is also best to avoid international characters, such as the Swedish å.

Filenames may be case-sensitive, depending on your server configuration. Consistently using all lowercase letters in filenames, although not required, is one way to make your filenames easier to manage.

Keep filenames short. Long names are more likely to be misspelled, and short names shave a few extra bytes off the file size. If you really must give the file a long, multiword name, you can separate words with hyphens, such as *a-long-document-title.html*, to improve readability.

Self-imposed conventions. It is helpful to develop a consistent naming scheme for huge sites—for instance, always using lowercase with hyphens between words. This takes some of the guesswork out of remembering what you named a file when you go to link to it later.

Learning from Step 1

Our page isn't looking so good (FIGURE 4-5). The text is all run together into one block—that's not how it looked when we typed it into the original document. There are a couple of lessons to be learned here. The first thing that is apparent is that the browser ignores line breaks in the source document. The sidebar **"What Browsers Ignore"** lists other types of information in the source document that are not displayed in the browser window.

Second, we see that simply typing in some content and naming the document *.html* is not enough. While the browser can display the text from the file, we haven't indicated the *structure* of the content. That's where HTML comes in. We'll use markup to add structure: first to the HTML document itself (coming up in Step 2), then to the page's content (Step 3). Once the browser knows the structure of the content, it can display the page in a more meaningful way.

STEP 2: GIVE THE HTML DOCUMENT STRUCTURE

We have our content saved in an HTML document—now we're ready to start marking it up.

The Anatomy of an HTML Element

Back in **Chapter 2** you saw examples of elements with an opening tag (`<p>` for a paragraph, for example) and a closing tag (`</p>`). Before we start adding tags to our document, let's look at the anatomy of an HTML element (its syntax) and firm up some important terminology. A generic container element is labeled in FIGURE 4-6.

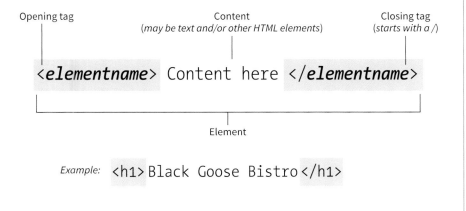

FIGURE 4-6. The parts of an HTML container element.

What Browsers Ignore

The following information in the source document will be ignored when it is viewed in a browser:

Multiple-character (white) spaces

When a browser encounters more than one consecutive blank character space, it displays a single space. So if the document contains

`long,       long          ago`

the browser displays:

`long, long ago`

Line breaks (carriage returns).

Browsers convert carriage returns to white spaces, so following the earlier "ignore multiple white spaces" rule, line breaks have no effect on formatting the page.

Tabs

Tabs are also converted to character spaces, so guess what? They're useless for indenting text on the web page (although they may make your code more readable).

Unrecognized markup

Browsers are instructed to ignore any tag they don't understand or that was specified incorrectly. Depending on the element and the browser, this can have varied results. The browser may display nothing at all, or it may display the contents of the tag as though it were normal text.

Text in comments

Browsers do not display text between the special `<!--` and `-->` tags used to denote a comment. See the upcoming **"Adding Hidden Comments"** sidebar.

Elements are identified by tags in the text source. A tag consists of the element name (usually an abbreviation of a longer descriptive name) within angle brackets (< >). The browser knows that any text within brackets is hidden and not displayed in the browser window.

The element name appears in the opening tag (also called a start tag) and again in the closing (or end) tag preceded by a slash (/). The closing tag works something like an "off" switch for the element. Be careful not to use the similar backslash character in end tags (see the tip **"Slash Versus Backslash"**).

The tags added around content are referred to as the markup. It is important to note that an element consists of both the content *and* its markup (the start and end tags). Not all elements have content, however. Some are empty by definition, such as the **img** element used to add an image to the page. We'll talk about empty elements a little later in this chapter.

One last thing: capitalization. In HTML, the capitalization of element names is not important (it is not case-sensitive). So **<img>**, **<Img>**, and **<IMG>** are all the same as far as the browser is concerned. However, most developers prefer the consistency of writing element names in all lowercase (see **Note**), as I will be doing throughout this book.

Basic Document Structure

FIGURE 4-8 shows the recommended minimal skeleton of an HTML document. I say "recommended" because the only element that is *required* in HTML is the **title**. But I feel it is better, particularly for beginners, to explicitly organize documents into metadata (**head**) and content (**body**) areas. Let's take a look at what's going on in this minimal markup example.

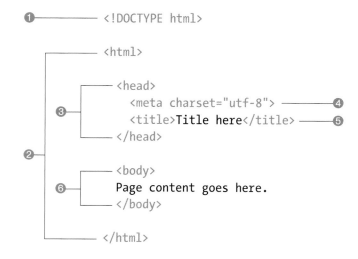

FIGURE 4-8. The minimal structure of an HTML document includes **head** and **body** contained within the **html** root element.

■ MARKUP TIP

Slash Versus Backslash

HTML tags and URLs use the slash character (/). The slash character is found under the question mark (?) on the English QWERTY keyboard (key placement on keyboards in other countries may vary).

It is easy to confuse the slash with the backslash character (\), which is found under the bar character (|); see FIGURE 4-7. The backslash key will not work in tags or URLs, so be careful not to use it.

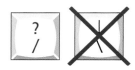

FIGURE 4-7. Slash versus backslash keys.

NOTE

There is a stricter version of HTML called XHTML that requires all element and attribute names to appear in lowercase. HTML5 has made XHTML all but obsolete except for certain use cases when it is combined with other XML languages, but the preference for all lowercase element names has persisted.

❶ I don't want to confuse things, but the first line in the example isn't an element at all. It is a document type declaration (also called DOCTYPE declaration) that lets modern browsers know which HTML specification to use to interpret the document. This DOCTYPE identifies the document as written in HTML5.

❷ The entire document is contained within an **html** element. The **html** element is called the root element because it contains all the elements in the document, and it may not be contained within any other element.

❸ Within the **html** element, the document is divided into a head and a body. The **head** element contains elements that pertain to the document that are not rendered as part of the content, such as its title, style sheets, scripts, and metadata.

❹ **meta** elements provide document metadata, information about the document. In this case, it specifies the character encoding (a standardized collection of letters, numbers, and symbols) used in the document as Unicode version UTF-8 (see the sidebar **"Introducing Unicode"**). I don't want to go into too much detail on this right now, but know that there are many good reasons for specifying the **charset** in every document, so I have included it as part of the minimal document markup. Other types of metadata provided by the **meta** element are the author, keywords, publishing status, and a description that can be used by search engines.

❺ Also in the **head** is the mandatory **title** element. According to the HTML specification, every document must contain a descriptive title.

❻ Finally, the **body** element contains everything that we want to show up in the browser window.

Are you ready to start marking up the Black Goose Bistro home page? Open the *index.html* document in your text editor and move on to EXERCISE 4-2.

Introducing Unicode

All the characters that make up languages are stored in computers as numbers. A standardized collection of characters with their reference numbers (code points) is called a coded character set, and the way in which those characters are converted to bytes for use by computers is the character encoding. In the early days of computing, computers used limited character sets such as ASCII that contained 128 characters (letters from Latin languages, numbers, and common symbols). The early web used the Latin-1 (ISO 8859-1) character encoding that included 256 Latin characters from most Western languages. But given the web was "worldwide," it was clearly not sufficient.

Enter Unicode. Unicode (also called the Universal Character Set) is a super-character set that contains over 136,000

characters (letters, numbers, symbols, ideograms, logograms, etc.) from all active modern languages. You can read all about it at *unicode.org*. Unicode has three standard encodings—UTF-8, UTF-16, and UTF-32—that differ in the number of bytes used to represent the characters (1, 2, or 3, respectively).

HTML5 uses the UTF-8 encoding by default, which allows wide-ranging languages to be mixed within a single document. It is always a good idea to declare the character encoding for a document with the **meta** element, as shown in the previous example. Your server also needs to be configured to identify HTML documents as UTF-8 in the HTTP header (information about the document that the server sends to the user agent). You can ask your server administrator to confirm the encoding of the HTML documents.

EXERCISE 4-2. Adding minimal structure

1. Open the new *index.html* document if it isn't open already and add the DOCTYPE declaration:

   ```
   <!DOCTYPE html>
   ```

2. Put the entire document in an HTML root element by adding an **<html>** start tag after the DOCTYPE and an **</html>** end tag at the very end of the text.

3. Next, create the document head that contains the title for the page. Insert **<head>** and **</head>** tags before the content. Within the **head** element, add information about the character encoding **<meta charset="utf-8">**, and the title, "Black Goose Bistro", surrounded by opening and closing **<title>** tags.

4. Finally, define the body of the document by wrapping the text content in **<body>** and **</body>** tags. When you are done, the source document should look like this (the markup is shown in color to make it stand out):

   ```
   <!DOCTYPE html>
   <html>

   <head>
     <meta charset="utf-8">
     <title>Black Goose Bistro</title>
   </head>
   ```

```
<body>
Black Goose Bistro

The Restaurant
The Black Goose Bistro offers casual lunch and
dinner fare in a relaxed atmosphere. The menu
changes regularly to highlight the freshest local
ingredients.

Catering
You have fun. We'll handle the cooking. Black
Goose Catering can handle events from snacks for a
meetup to elegant corporate fundraisers.

Location and Hours
Seekonk, Massachusetts;
Monday through Thursday 11am to 9pm; Friday and
Saturday, 11am to midnight
</body>
</html>
```

5. Save the document in the *bistro* directory, so that it overwrites the old version. Open the file in the browser or hit Refresh or Reload if it is open already. FIGURE 4-9 shows how it should look now.

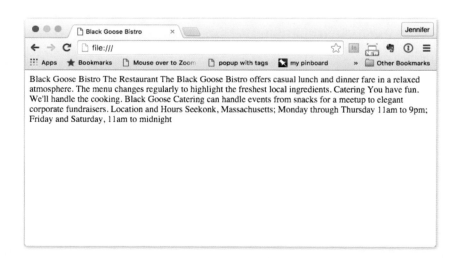

FIGURE 4-9. The page in a browser after the document structure elements have been defined.

Not much has changed in the bistro page after setting up the document, except that the browser now displays the title of the document in the top bar or tab (FIGURE 4-9). If someone were to bookmark this page, that title would be added to their Bookmarks or Favorites list as well (see the sidebar **"Don't Forget a Good Title"**). But the content still runs together because we haven't given the browser any indication of how it should be structured. We'll take care of that next.

STEP 3: IDENTIFY TEXT ELEMENTS

With a little markup experience under your belt, it should be a no-brainer to add the markup for headings and subheads (**h1** and **h2**), paragraphs (**p**), and emphasized text (**em**) to our content, as we'll do in EXERCISE 4-3. However, before we begin, I want to take a moment to talk about what we're doing and not doing when marking up content with HTML.

Mark It Up Semantically

The purpose of HTML is to add meaning and structure to the content. It is *not* intended to describe how the content should look (its presentation).

Your job when marking up content is to choose the HTML element that provides the most meaningful description of the content at hand. In the biz, we call this semantic markup. For example, the most important heading at the beginning of the document should be marked up as an **h1** because it is the most important heading on the page. Don't worry about what it looks like... you can easily change that with a style sheet. The important thing is that you choose elements based on what makes the most sense for the content.

In addition to adding meaning to content, the markup gives the document structure. The way elements follow each other or nest within one another creates relationships between them. You can think of this structure as an outline (its technical name is the DOM, for Document Object Model). The underlying document hierarchy gives browsers cues on how to handle the content. It is also the foundation upon which we add presentation instructions with style sheets and behaviors with JavaScript.

Although HTML was intended to be used strictly for meaning and structure since its creation, that mission was somewhat thwarted in the early years of the web. With no style sheet system in place, HTML was extended to give authors ways to change the appearance of fonts, colors, and alignment using markup alone. Those presentational extras are still out there, so you may run across them if you view the source of older sites or a site made with old tools. In this book, however, I'll focus on using HTML the right way, in keeping with the contemporary standards-based, semantic approach to web design.

OK, enough lecturing. It's time to get to work on that content in EXERCISE 4-3.

Don't Forget a Good Title

A **title** element is not only required for every document, but it is also quite useful. The title is what is displayed in a user's Bookmarks or Favorites list and on tabs in desktop browsers. Descriptive titles are also a key tool for improving accessibility, as they are the first things a person hears when using a screen reader (an assistive device that reads the content of a page aloud for users with impaired sight). Search engines rely heavily on document titles as well.

For these reasons, it's important to provide thoughtful and descriptive titles for all your documents and avoid vague titles, such as "Welcome" or "My Page." You may also want to keep the length of your titles in check so they are able to display in the browser's title area. Knowing that users typically have a number of tabs open or a long list of Bookmarks, put your most uniquely identifying information in the first 20 or so characters.

The purpose of HTML is to add meaning and structure to the content.

EXERCISE 4-3. Defining text elements

1. Open the document *index.html* in your text editor, if it isn't open already.

2. The first line of text, "Black Goose Bistro," is the main heading for the page, so we'll mark it up as a Heading Level 1 (**h1**) element. Put the opening tag, **<h1>**, at the beginning of the line and the closing tag, **</h1>**, after it, like this:

   ```
   <h1>Black Goose Bistro</h1>
   ```

3. Our page also has three subheads. Mark them up as Heading Level 2 (**h2**) elements in a similar manner. I'll do the first one here; you do the same for "Catering" and "Location and Hours."

   ```
   <h2>The Restaurant</h2>
   ```

4. Each **h2** element is followed by a brief paragraph of text, so let's mark those up as paragraph (**p**) elements in a similar manner. Here's the first one; you do the rest:

   ```
   <p>The Black Goose Bistro offers casual lunch and dinner fare in
   a relaxed atmosphere. The menu changes regularly to highlight the
   freshest local ingredients.</p>
   ```

5. Finally, in the Catering section, I want to emphasize that visitors should just leave the cooking to us. To make text emphasized, mark it up in an emphasis element (**em**) element, as shown here:

   ```
   <p>You have fun. <em>We'll handle the cooking.</em> Black Goose
   Catering can handle events from snacks for a meetup to elegant
   corporate fundraisers.</p>
   ```

6. Now that we've marked up the document, let's save it as we did before, and open (or reload) the page in the browser. You should see a page that looks much like the one in FIGURE 4-10. If it doesn't, check your markup to be sure that you aren't missing any angle brackets or a slash in a closing tag.

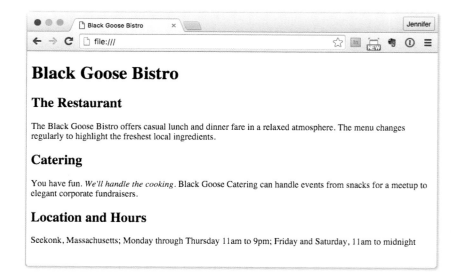

FIGURE 4-10. The home page after the content has been marked up with HTML elements.

Now we're getting somewhere. With the elements properly identified, the browser can now display the text in a more meaningful manner. There are a few significant things to note about what's happening in FIGURE 4-10.

Block and Inline Elements

Although it may seem like stating the obvious, it's worth pointing out that the heading and paragraph elements start on new lines and do not run together as they did before. That is because by default, headings and paragraphs display as block elements. Browsers treat block elements as though they are in little rectangular boxes, stacked up in the page. Each block element begins on a new line, and some space is also usually added above and below the entire element by default. In FIGURE 4-11, the edges of the block elements are outlined in red.

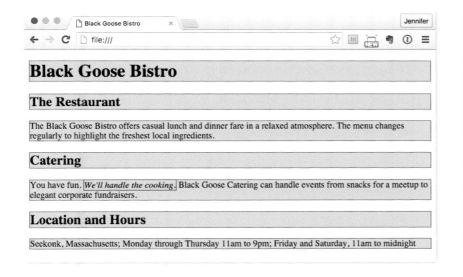

FIGURE 4-11. The outlines show the structure of the elements in the home page.

By contrast, look at the text we marked up as emphasized (**em**, outlined in blue in FIGURE 4-11). It does not start a new line, but rather stays in the flow of the paragraph. That is because the **em** element is an inline element (also called a text-level semantic element or phrasing element). Inline elements do not start new lines; they just go with the flow.

Default Styles

The other thing that you will notice about the marked-up page in FIGURES 4-10 and 4-11 is that the browser makes an attempt to give the page some

Adding Hidden Comments

You can leave notes in the source document for yourself and others by marking them up as comments. Anything you put between comment tags (`<!-- -->`) will not display in the browser and will not have any effect on the rest of the source:

```
<!-- This is a comment -->
<!-- This is a
    multiple-line comment
    that ends here. -->
```

Comments are useful for labeling and organizing long documents, particularly when they are shared by a team of developers. In this example, comments are used to point out the section of the source that contains the navigation:

```
<!-- start global nav -->
<ul>
    …
</ul>
<!-- end global nav -->
```

Bear in mind that although the browser will not display comments in the web page, readers can see them if they "view source," so be sure that the comments you leave are appropriate for everyone.

visual hierarchy by making the first-level heading the biggest and boldest thing on the page, with the second-level headings slightly smaller, and so on.

How does the browser determine what an **h1** should look like? It uses a style sheet! All browsers have their own built-in style sheets (called user agent style sheets in the spec) that describe the default rendering of elements. The default rendering is similar from browser to browser (for example, **h1**s are always big and bold), but there are some variations (the **blockquote** element for long quotes may or may not be indented).

If you think the **h1** is too big and clunky as the browser renders it, just change it with your own style sheet rule. Resist the urge to mark up the heading with another element just to get it to look better—for example, using an **h3** instead of an **h1** so it isn't as large. In the days before ubiquitous style sheet support, elements were abused in just that way. You should always choose elements based on how accurately they describe the content, and don't worry about the browser's default rendering.

We'll fix the presentation of the page with style sheets in a moment, but first, let's add an image to the page.

STEP 4: ADD AN IMAGE

What fun is a web page with no images? In EXERCISE 4-4, we'll add an image to the page with the **img** element. Images will be discussed in more detail in **Chapter 7, Adding Images**, but for now, they give us an opportunity to introduce two more basic markup concepts: empty elements and attributes.

Empty Elements

So far, nearly all of the elements we've used in the Black Goose Bistro home page have followed the syntax shown in FIGURE 4-6: a bit of text content surrounded by start and end tags.

A handful of elements, however, do not have content because they are used to provide a simple directive. These elements are said to be empty. The image element (**img**) is an example of an empty element. It tells the browser to get an image file from the server and insert it at that spot in the flow of the text. Other empty elements include the line break (**br**), thematic breaks (**hr**, a.k.a. "horizontal rules"), and elements that provide information about a document but don't affect its displayed content, such as the **meta** element that we used earlier.

FIGURE 4-12 shows the very simple syntax of an empty element (compare it to FIGURE 4-6).

$$\texttt{<element-name>}$$

Example: The **br** element inserts a line break.

```
<p>1005 Gravenstein Highway North<br>Sebastopol, CA 95472</p>
```

FIGURE 4-12. Empty element structure.

Attributes

Let's get back to adding an image with the empty **img** element. Obviously, an **<img>** tag is not very useful by itself—it doesn't indicate which image to use. That's where attributes come in. Attributes are instructions that clarify or modify an element. For the **img** element, the **src** (short for "source") attribute is required, and specifies the location (URL) of the image file.

The syntax for an attribute is as follows:

```
attributename="value"
```

Attributes go after the element name, separated by a space. In non-empty elements, attributes go in the opening tag only:

```
<element attributename="value">
```

```
<element attributename="value">Content</element>
```

You can also put more than one attribute in an element in any order. Just keep them separated with spaces:

```
<element attribute1="value" attribute2="value">
```

FIGURE 4-13 shows an **img** element with its required attributes labeled.

What Is That Extra Slash?

If you poke around in source documents for existing web pages, you may see empty elements with extra slashes at the end, like so: **<img />**, **
, **<meta />, and **<hr />**. That indicates the document was written according to the stricter rules of XHTML. In XHTML, all elements, including empty elements, must be closed (or terminated, to use the proper term). You terminate empty elements by adding a trailing slash before the closing bracket. The preceding character space is not required but was used for backward compatibility with browsers that did not have XHTML parsers, so **<img/>**, **
**, and so on are valid.

Attributes are instructions that clarify or modify an element.

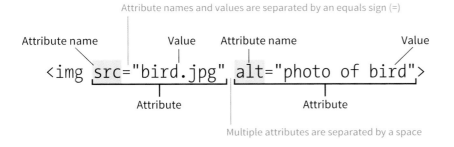

Attribute names and values are separated by an equals sign (=)

Attribute name   Value   Attribute name   Value

```
<img src="bird.jpg" alt="photo of bird">
```

Attribute   Attribute

Multiple attributes are separated by a space

FIGURE 4-13. An **img** element with two attributes.

Here's what you need to know about attributes:

- Attributes go after the element name in the opening tag only, never in the closing tag.

- There may be several attributes applied to an element, separated by spaces in the opening tag. Their order is not important.

- Most attributes take values, which follow an equals sign (=). In HTML, some attribute values are single descriptive words. For example, the **checked** attribute, which makes a form checkbox checked when the form loads, is equivalent to **checked="checked"**. You may hear this type of attribute called a Boolean attribute because it describes a feature that is either on or off.

- A value might be a number, a word, a string of text, a URL, or a measurement, depending on the purpose of the attribute. You'll see examples of all of these throughout this book.

- Wrapping attribute values in double quotation marks is a strong convention, but note that quotation marks are not required and may be omitted. In addition, either single or double quotation marks are acceptable as long as the opening and closing marks match. Note that quotation marks in HTML files need to be straight ("), not curly (").

- The attribute names and values available for each element are defined in the HTML specifications; in other words, you can't make up an attribute for an element.

- Some attributes are required, such as the **src** and **alt** attributes in the **img** element. The HTML specification also defines which attributes are required in order for the document to be valid.

Now you should be more than ready to try your hand at adding the **img** element with its attributes to the Black Goose Bistro page in EXERCISE 4-4. We'll throw a few line breaks in there as well.

EXERCISE 4-4. Adding an image

1. If you're working along, the first thing you'll need to do is get a copy of the image file on your hard drive so you can see it in place when you open the file locally. The image file is provided in the materials for this chapter (*learningwebdesign.com/5e/materials*). You can also get the image file by saving it right from the sample web page online at *learningwebdesign.com/5e/materials/ch04/bistro*. Right-click (or Control-click on a Mac) the goose image and select "Save to disk" (or similar) from the pop-up menu, as shown in FIGURE 4-14. Name the file *blackgoose.png*. Be sure to save it in the *bistro* folder with *index.html*.

2. Once you have the image, insert it at the beginning of the first-level heading by typing in the **img** element and its attributes as shown here:

```
<h1><img src="blackgoose.png" alt="logo">Black Goose Bistro</h1>
```

Windows: Right-click on the image to access the pop-up menu.

Mac: Control-click on the image to access the pop-up menu. The options may vary by browser.

FIGURE 4-14. Saving an image file from a page on the web.

The **src** attribute provides the name of the image file that should be inserted, and the **alt** attribute provides text that should be displayed if the image is not available. Both of these attributes are required in every **img** element.

3. I'd like the image to appear above the title, so add a line break (**br**) after the **img** element to start the headline text on a new line.

```
<h1><img src="blackgoose.png" alt="logo"><br>Black Goose Bistro</h1>
```

4. Let's break up the last paragraph into three lines for better clarity. Drop a **
** tag at the spots you'd like the line breaks to occur. Try to match the screenshot in FIGURE 4-15.

5. Now save *index.html* and open or refresh it in the browser window. The page should look like the one shown in FIGURE 4-15. If it doesn't, check to make sure that the image file, *blackgoose.png*, is in the same directory as *index.html*. If it is, then check to make sure that you aren't missing any characters, such as a closing quote or bracket, in the **img** element markup.

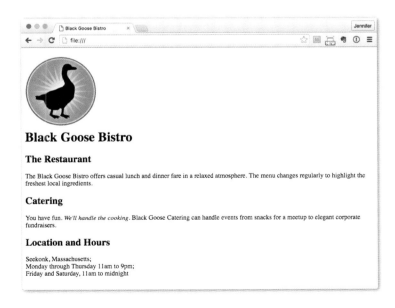

FIGURE 4-15. The Black Goose Bistro page with the logo image.

STEP 5: CHANGE THE LOOK WITH A STYLE SHEET

Depending on the content and purpose of your website, you may decide that the browser's default rendering of your document is perfectly adequate. However, I think I'd like to pretty up the Black Goose Bistro home page a bit to make a good first impression on potential patrons. "Prettying up" is just my way of saying that I'd like to change its presentation, which is the job of Cascading Style Sheets (CSS).

In EXERCISE 4-5, we'll change the appearance of the text elements and the page background by using some simple style sheet rules. Don't worry about understanding them all right now. We'll get into CSS in more detail in **Part III**. But I want to at least give you a taste of what it means to add a "layer" of presentation onto the structure we've created with our markup.

EXERCISE 4-5. Adding a style sheet

1. Open *index.html* if it isn't open already. We're going to use the **style** element to apply a very simple embedded style sheet to the page. This is just one of the ways to add a style sheet; the others are covered in **Chapter 11, Introducing Cascading Style Sheets**.

2. The **style** element is placed inside the document **head**. Start by adding the **style** element to the document as shown here:

```
<head>
    <meta charset="utf-8">
    <title>Black Goose Bistro</title>
    <style>

    </style>
</head>
```

3. Next, type the following style rules within the **style** element just as you see them here. Don't worry if you don't know exactly what's going on (although it's fairly intuitive). You'll learn all about style rules in **Part III**.

```
<style>
body {
    background-color: #faf2e4;
    margin: 0 10%;
    font-family: sans-serif;
}
h1 {
    text-align: center;
    font-family: serif;
    font-weight: normal;
    text-transform: uppercase;
    border-bottom: 1px solid #57b1dc;
    margin-top: 30px;
}
```

```
h2 {
    color: #d1633c;
    font-size: 1em;
}
</style>
```

4. Now it's time to save the file and take a look at it in the browser. It should look like the page in FIGURE 4-16. If it doesn't, go over the style sheet to make sure you didn't miss a semicolon or a curly bracket. Look at the way the page looks with our styles compared to the browser's default styles (FIGURE 4-15).

FIGURE 4-16. The Black Goose Bistro page after CSS style rules have been applied.

We're finished with the Black Goose Bistro page. Not only have you written your first web page, complete with a style sheet, but you've also learned about elements, attributes, empty elements, block and inline elements, the basic structure of an HTML document, and the correct use of markup along the way. Not bad for one chapter!

WHEN GOOD PAGES GO BAD

The previous demonstration went smoothly, but it's easy for small things to go wrong when you're typing out HTML markup by hand. Unfortunately, one missed character can break a whole page. I'm going to break my page on purpose so we can see what happens.

What if I had neglected to type the slash in the closing emphasis tag (`</em>`)? With just one character out of place (FIGURE 4-17), the remainder of the document displays in emphasized (italic) text. That's because without that slash, there's nothing telling the browser to turn "off" the emphasized formatting, so it just keeps going (see **Note**).

```
<h2>Catering</h2>
<p>You have fun. <em>We'll handle the cooking.<em> Black Goose
Catering can handle events from snacks for a meetup to elegant
corporate fundraisers.</p>
```

g. `<em>`

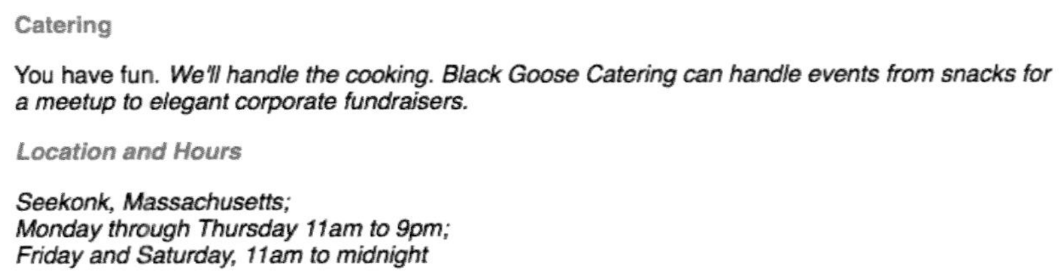

Catering

You have fun. We'll handle the cooking. Black Goose Catering can handle events from snacks for a meetup to elegant corporate fundraisers.

Location and Hours

Seekonk, Massachusetts;
Monday through Thursday 11am to 9pm;
Friday and Saturday, 11am to midnight

FIGURE 4-17. When a slash is omitted, the browser doesn't know when the element ends, as is the case in this example.

I've fixed the slash, but this time, let's see what would have happened if I had accidentally omitted a bracket from the end of the first `<h2>` tag (FIGURE 4-18).

See how the headline is missing? That's because without the closing tag bracket, the browser assumes that all the following text—all the way up to the next closing bracket (`>`) it finds—is part of the `<h2>` opening tag. Browsers don't display any text within a tag, so my heading disappeared. The browser just ignored the foreign-looking element name and moved on to the next element.

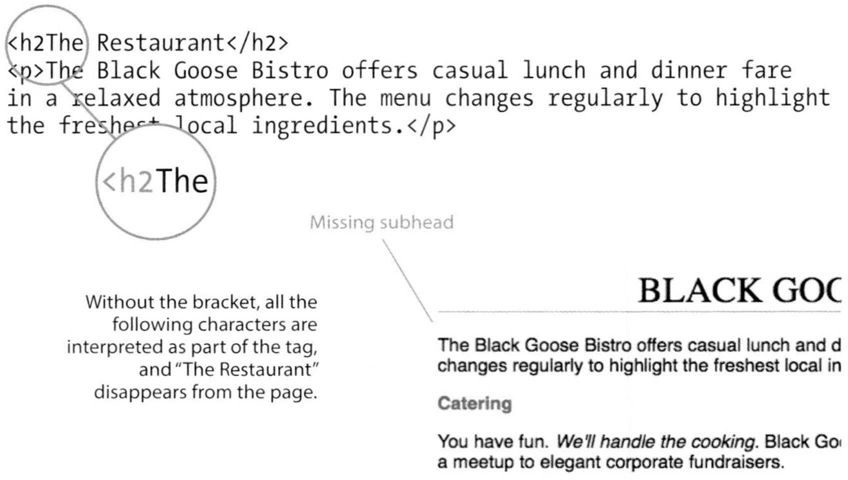

Having Problems?

The following are some typical problems that crop up when you are creating web pages and viewing them in a browser:

I've changed my document, but when I reload the page in my browser, it looks exactly the same.

It could be you didn't save your document before reloading, or you may have saved it in a different directory.

Half my page disappeared.

This could happen if you are missing a closing bracket (**>**) or a quotation mark within a tag. This is a common error when you're writing HTML by hand.

I put in a graphic by using the `img` *element, but all that shows up is a broken image icon.*

The broken graphic could mean a couple of things. First, it might mean that the browser is not finding the graphic. Make sure that the URL to the image file is correct. (We'll discuss URLs further in **Chapter 6, Adding Links**.) Make sure that the image file is actually in the directory you've specified. If the file is there, make sure it is in one of the formats that web browsers can display (PNG, JPEG, GIF, or SVG) and that it is named with the proper suffix (*.png*, *.jpeg* or *.jpg*, *.gif*, or *.svg*, respectively).

```
<h2The Restaurant</h2>
<p>The Black Goose Bistro offers casual lunch and dinner fare
in a relaxed atmosphere. The menu changes regularly to highlight
the freshest local ingredients.</p>
```

<h2The

Missing subhead

Without the bracket, all the following characters are interpreted as part of the tag, and "The Restaurant" disappears from the page.

BLACK GOC

The Black Goose Bistro offers casual lunch and d changes regularly to highlight the freshest local in

Catering

You have fun. *We'll handle the cooking.* Black Go a meetup to elegant corporate fundraisers.

FIGURE 4-18. A missing end bracket makes the browser think the following characters are part of the tag, and therefore the headline text doesn't display.

Making mistakes in your first HTML documents and fixing them is a great way to learn. If you write your first pages perfectly, I'd recommend fiddling with the code to see how the browser reacts to various changes. This can be extremely useful in troubleshooting pages later. I've listed some common problems in the sidebar **"Having Problems?"** Note that these problems are not specific to beginners. Little stuff like this goes wrong all the time, even for the pros.

VALIDATING YOUR DOCUMENTS

One way that professional web developers catch errors in their markup is to validate their documents. What does that mean? To validate a document is to check your markup to make sure that you have abided by all the rules of whatever version of HTML you are using. Documents that are error-free are said to be valid. It is strongly recommended that you validate your documents, especially for professional sites. Valid documents are more consistent on a variety of browsers, they display more quickly, and they are more accessible.

Right now, browsers don't require documents to be valid (in other words, they'll do their best to display them, errors and all), but anytime you stray from the standard, you introduce unpredictability in the way the page is handled by browsers or alternative devices.

So how do you make sure your document is valid? You could check it yourself or ask a friend, but humans make mistakes, and you aren't expected to memorize every minute rule in the specifications. Instead, use a validator, software that checks your source against the HTML version you specify. These are some of the things validators check for:

- The inclusion of a DOCTYPE declaration. Without it the validator doesn't know which version of HTML to validate against:

- An indication of the character encoding for the document.

- The inclusion of required rules and attributes.

- Non-standard elements.

- Mismatched tags.

- Nesting errors (incorrectly putting elements inside other elements).

- Typos and other minor errors.

Developers use a number of helpful tools for checking and correcting errors in HTML documents. The best web-based validator is at *html5.validator.nu*. There you can upload a file or provide a link to a page that is already online. FIGURE 4-19 shows the report the validator generates when I upload the version of the Bistro *index.html* file that doesn't have any markup. For this document, there are a number of missing elements that keep this document from being valid. It also shows the problem source code and provides an explanation of how the code should appear. Pretty darned handy!

Built-in browser developer tools for Safari and Chrome also have validators so you can check your work on the fly. Some code editors have validators built in as well.

FIGURE 4-19. The (X)HTML5 Validator (Living Validator) for checking errors in HTML documents (*html5.validator.nu*).

ELEMENT REVIEW: HTML DOCUMENT SETUP

This chapter introduced the elements that establish metadata and content portions of an HTML document. The remaining elements introduced in the exercises will be treated in more depth in the following chapters.

Element	Description
body	Identifies the body of the document that holds the content
head	Identifies the head of the document that contains information about the document itself
html	Is the root element that contains all the other elements
meta	Provides information about the document
title	Gives the page a title

TEST YOURSELF

Now is a good time to make sure you understand the basics of markup. Use what you've learned in this chapter to answer the following questions. Answers are in **Appendix A**.

1. What is the difference between a tag and an element?

2. Write out the recommended minimal markup for an HTML5 document.

3. Indicate whether each of these filenames is an acceptable name for a web document by circling "Yes" or "No." If it is not acceptable, provide the reason:

   a. *Sunflower.html*   Yes   No

   b. *index.doc*   Yes   No

   c. *cooking home page.html*   Yes   No

   d. *Song_Lyrics.html*   Yes   No

   e. *games/rubix.html*   Yes   No

   f. *%whatever.html*   Yes   No

4. All of the following markup examples are incorrect. Describe what is wrong with each one, and then write it correctly.

   a. `<img "birthday.jpg">`

   b. `<em>Congratulations!<em>`

   c. `<a href="file.html">linked text</a href="file.html">`

   d. `<p>This is a new paragraph<\p>`

5. How would you mark up this comment in an HTML document so that it doesn't display in the browser window?

   `product list begins here`

MARKING UP TEXT

Once your content is ready to go (you've proofread it, right?) and you've added the markup to structure the document (`<!DOCTYPE>`, `html`, `head`, `title`, `meta charset`, and `body`), you are ready to identify the elements in the content. This chapter introduces the elements you have to choose from for marking up text. There probably aren't as many of them as you might think, and really just a handful that you'll use with regularity. That said, this chapter is a big one and covers a lot of ground.

As we begin our tour of elements, I want to reiterate how important it is to choose elements semantically—that is, in a way that most accurately describes the content's meaning. If you don't like how it looks, change it with a style sheet. A semantically marked-up document ensures your content is available and accessible in the widest range of browsing environments, from desktop computers and mobile devices to assistive screen readers. It also allows non-human readers, such as search engine indexing programs, to correctly parse your content and make decisions about the relative importance of elements on the page.

With these principles in mind, it is time to meet the HTML text elements, starting with the most basic element of them all, the humble paragraph.

PARAGRAPHS

`<p>…</p>`
Paragraph element

Paragraphs are the most rudimentary elements of a text document. Indicate a paragraph with the **p** element by inserting an opening `<p>` tag at the beginning of the paragraph and a closing `</p>` tag after it, as shown in this example:

```
<p>Serif typefaces have small slabs at the ends of letter strokes. In
general, serif fonts can make large amounts of text easier to
read.</p>
```

IN THIS CHAPTER

Choosing the best element for your content

Paragraphs and headings

Three types of lists

Organizing content into sections

Text-level (inline) elements

Generic elements, div and span

Special characters

NOTE

I will be teaching markup according to the HTML5 standard maintained by the W3C (www.w3.org/TR/html5/). As of this writing, the latest version is the HTML 5.2 Proposed Recommendation (www. w3.org/TR/html52/).

```
<p>Sans-serif fonts do not have serif slabs; their strokes are square
on the end. Helvetica and Arial are examples of sans-serif fonts.
In general, sans-serif fonts appear sleeker and more modern.</p>
```

Visual browsers nearly always display paragraphs on new lines with a bit of space between them by default (to use a term from CSS, they are displayed as a block). Paragraphs may contain text, images, and other inline elements (called phrasing content), but they may *not* contain headings, lists, sectioning elements, or any elements that typically display as blocks by default.

Technically, it is OK to omit the closing **</p>** tag because it is not required in order for the document to be valid. A browser just assumes it is closed when it encounters the next block element. Many web developers, including myself, prefer to close paragraphs and all elements for the sake of consistency and clarity. I recommend folks who are just learning markup do the same.

No Naked Text!

You must assign an element to all the text in a document. In other words, all text must be enclosed in some sort of element. Text that is not contained within tags is called naked or anonymous text, and it will cause a document to be invalid.

HEADINGS

```
<h1>…</h1>
<h2>…</h2>
<h3>…</h3>
<h4>…</h4>
<h5>…</h5>
<h6>…</h6>
```

Heading elements

In the last chapter, we used the **h1** and **h2** elements to indicate headings for the Black Goose Bistro page. There are actually six levels of headings, from **h1** to **h6**. When you add headings to content, the browser uses them to create a document outline for the page. Assistive reading devices such as screen readers use the document outline to help users quickly scan and navigate through a page. In addition, search engines look at heading levels as part of their algorithms (information in higher heading levels may be given more weight). For these reasons, it is a best practice to start with the Level 1 heading (**h1**) and work down in numerical order, creating a logical document structure and outline.

This example shows the markup for four heading levels. Additional heading levels would be marked up in a similar manner.

```
<h1>Type Design</h1>

<h2>Serif Typefaces</h2>
<p>Serif typefaces have small slabs at the ends of letter strokes.
In general, serif fonts can make large amounts of text easier to
read.</p>

<h3>Baskerville</h3>

<h4>Description</h4>
<p>Description of the Baskerville typeface.</p>

<h4>History</h4>
<p>The history of the Baskerville typeface.</p>

<h3>Georgia</h3>
<p>Description and history of the Georgia typeface.</p>

<h2>Sans-serif Typefaces</h2>
<p>Sans-serif typefaces do not have slabs at the ends of strokes.</p>
```

The markup in this example would create the following document outline:

1. Type Design
    1. Serif Typefaces
       + text paragraph

        1. Baskerville

            1. Description
               + text paragraph

            2. History
               + text paragraph

        2. Georgia
           + text paragraph

    2. Sans-serif Typefaces
       + text paragraph

By default, the headings in our example display in bold text, starting in very large type for **h1**s, with each consecutive level in smaller text, as shown in FIGURE 5-1. You can use a style sheet to change their appearance.

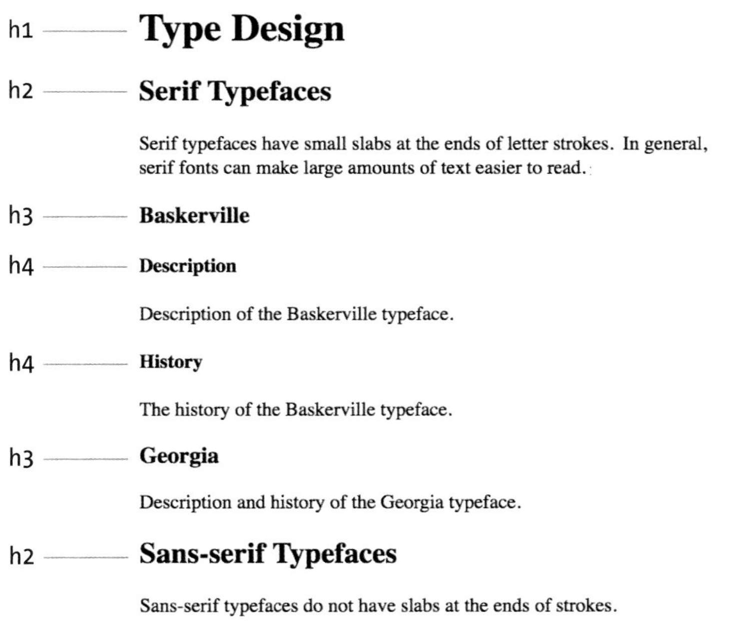

h1 ——— **Type Design**

h2 ——— **Serif Typefaces**

Serif typefaces have small slabs at the ends of letter strokes. In general, serif fonts can make large amounts of text easier to read.

h3 ——— **Baskerville**

h4 ——— **Description**

Description of the Baskerville typeface.

h4 ——— **History**

The history of the Baskerville typeface.

h3 ——— **Georgia**

Description and history of the Georgia typeface.

h2 ——— **Sans-serif Typefaces**

Sans-serif typefaces do not have slabs at the ends of strokes.

FIGURE 5-1. The default rendering of four heading levels.

THEMATIC BREAKS (HORIZONTAL RULE)

<hr>

A horizontal rule

If you want to indicate that one topic has completed and another one is beginning, you can insert what the spec calls a "paragraph-level thematic break" with the **hr** element. The **hr** element adds a logical divider between sections of a page or paragraphs without introducing a new heading level.

In older HTML versions, **hr** was defined as a "horizontal rule" because it inserts a horizontal line on the page. Browsers still render **hr** as a 3-D shaded rule and put it on a line by itself with some space above and below by default; but in the HTML5 spec, it has a new semantic name and definition. If a decorative line is all you're after, it is better to create a rule by specifying a colored border before or after an element with CSS.

hr is an empty element—you just drop it into place where you want the thematic break to occur, as shown in this example and FIGURE 5-2:

```
<h3>Times</h3>
<p>Description and history of the Times typeface.</p>
<hr>
<h3>Georgia</h3>
<p>Description and history of the Georgia typeface.</p>
```

Times

Description and history of the Times typeface.

Georgia

Description and history of the Georgia typeface.

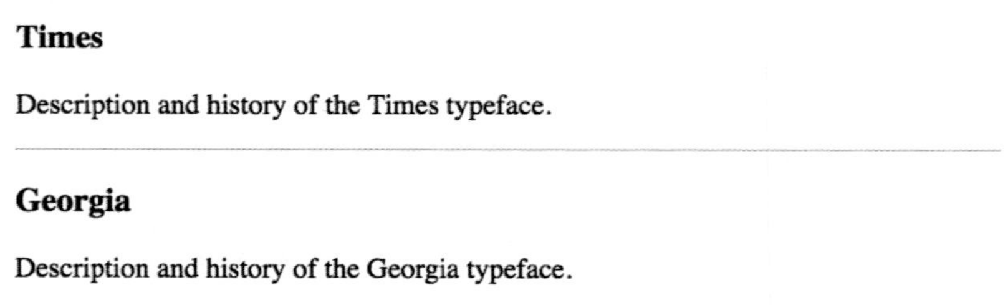

FIGURE 5-2. The default rendering of a thematic break (horizontal rule).

LISTS

Humans are natural list makers, and HTML provides elements for marking up three types of lists:

Unordered lists

Collections of items that appear in no particular order

Ordered lists

Lists in which the sequence of the items is important

Description lists

Lists that consist of name and value pairs, including but not limited to terms and definitions

All list elements—the lists themselves and the items that go in them—are displayed as block elements by default, which means that they start on a new line and have some space above and below, but that may be altered with CSS. In this section, we'll look at each list type in detail.

Unordered Lists

Just about any list of examples, names, components, thoughts, or options qualifies as an unordered list. In fact, most lists fall into this category. By default, unordered lists display with a bullet before each list item, but you can change that with a style sheet, as you'll see in a moment.

To identify an unordered list, mark it up as a **ul** element. The opening **<ul>** tag goes before the first list item, and the closing tag **</ul>** goes after the last item. Then, to mark up each item in the list as a list item (**li**), enclose it in opening and closing **li** tags, as shown in this example. Notice that there are no bullets in the source document. The browser adds them automatically (FIGURE 5-3).

The only thing that is permitted within an unordered list (that is, between the start and end **ul** tags) is one or more list items. You can't put other elements in there, and there may not be any untagged text. However, you can put any type of content element within a list item (**li**):

```
<ul>
   <li>Serif</li>
   <li>Sans-serif</li>
   <li>Script</li>
   <li>Display</li>
   <li>Dingbats</li>
</ul>
```

- Serif
- Sans-serif
- Script
- Display
- Dingbats

FIGURE 5-3. The default rendering of the sample unordered list. The browser adds the bullets automatically.

But here's the cool part. We can take that same unordered list markup and radically change its appearance by applying different style sheets, as shown in FIGURE 5-4. In the figure, I've turned off the bullets, added bullets of my own, made the items line up horizontally, and even made them look like graphical buttons. The markup stays exactly the same.

`<ul>…</ul>`
Unordered list

`<li>…</li>`
List item within an unordered list

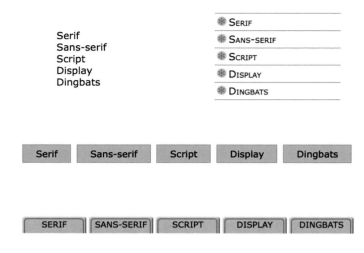

FIGURE 5-4. With style sheets, you can give the same unordered list many looks.

Ordered Lists

`<ol>...</ol>`

Ordered list

`<li>...</li>`

List item within an ordered list

NOTE

If something is logically an ordered list, but you don't want numbers to display, remember that you can always remove the numbering with style sheets. So go ahead and mark up the list semantically as an **ol** *and adjust how it displays with a style rule.*

Ordered lists are for items that occur in a particular order, such as step-by-step instructions or driving directions. They work just like the unordered lists described earlier, but they are defined with the **ol** element (for "ordered list," of course). Instead of bullets, the browser automatically inserts numbers before ordered list items (see **Note**), so you don't need to number them in the source document. This makes it easy to rearrange list items without renumbering them.

Ordered list elements must contain one or more list item elements, as shown in this example and in FIGURE 5-5:

```
<ol>
  <li>Gutenberg develops moveable type (1450s)</li>
  <li>Linotype is introduced (1890s)</li>
  <li>Photocomposition catches on (1950s)</li>
  <li>Type goes digital (1980s)</li>
</ol>
```

1. Gutenberg develops moveable type (1450s)
2. Linotype is introduced (1890s)
3. Photocomposition catches on (1950s)
4. Type goes digital (1980s)

FIGURE 5-5. The default rendering of an ordered list. The browser adds the numbers automatically.

If you want a numbered list to start at a number other than 1, you can use the **start** attribute in the **ol** element to specify another starting number, as shown here:

```
<ol start="17">
  <li>Highlight the text with the text tool.</li>
  <li>Select the Character tab.</li>
  <li>Choose a typeface from the pop-up menu.</li>
</ol>
```

The resulting list items would be numbered 17, 18, and 19, consecutively.

Description Lists

`<dl>…</dl>`

A description list

`<dt>…</dt>`

A name, such as a term or label

`<dd>…</dd>`

A value, such as a description or definition

Description lists are used for any type of name/value pairs, such as terms and their definitions, questions and answers, or other types of terms and their associated information. Their structure is a bit different from the other two lists that we just discussed. The whole description list is marked up as a **dl** element. The content of a **dl** is some number of **dt** elements indicating the names, and **dd** elements for their respective values. I find it helpful to think of them as "terms" (to remember the "t" in **dt**) and "definitions" (for the "d" in **dd**), even though that is only one use of description lists.

Here is an example of a list that associates forms of typesetting with their descriptions (FIGURE 5-6):

```
<dl>
  <dt>Linotype</dt>
  <dd>Line-casting allowed type to be selected, used, then recirculated
into the machine automatically. This advance increased the speed of
typesetting and printing dramatically.</dd>

  <dt>Photocomposition</dt>
  <dd>Typefaces are stored on film then projected onto photo-sensitive
paper. Lenses adjust the size of the type.</dd>

  <dt>Digital type</dt>
  <dd><p>Digital typefaces store the outline of the font shape in a
format such as Postscript. The outline may be scaled to any size for
output.</p>
    <p>Postscript emerged as a standard due to its support of
graphics and its early support on the Macintosh computer and Apple
laser printer.</p>
  </dd>
</dl>
```

Nesting Lists

Any list can be nested within another list; it just has to be placed within a list item. This example shows the structure of an unordered list nested in the second item of an ordered list:

```
<ol>
  <li></li>
  <li>
    <ul>
      <li></li>
      <li></li>
      <li></li>
    </ul>
  </li>
</ol>
```

When you nest an unordered list within another unordered list, the browser automatically changes the bullet style for the second-level list. Unfortunately, the numbering style is not changed by default when you nest ordered lists. You need to set the numbering styles yourself with CSS rules.

Changing Bullets and Numbering

You can use the **list-style-type** style sheet property to change the bullets and numbers for lists. For example, for unordered lists, you can change the shape from the default dot to a square or an open circle, substitute your own image, or remove the bullet altogether. For ordered lists, you can change the numbers to Roman numerals (I, II, III, or i, ii, iii), letters (A, B, C, or a, b, c), and several other numbering schemes. In fact, as long as the list is marked up semantically, it doesn't need to display with bullets or numbering at all. Changing the style of lists with CSS is covered in **Chapter 12, Formatting Text**.

Linotype
  Line-casting allowed type to be selected, used, then recirculated into the machine automatically. This advance increased the speed of typesetting and printing dramatically.
Photocomposition
  Typefaces are stored on film then projected onto photo-sensitive paper. Lenses adjust the size of the type.
Digital type

  Digital typefaces store the outline of the font shape in a format such as Postscript. The outline may may be scaled to any size for output.

  Postscript emerged as a standard due to its support of graphics and its early support on the Macintosh computer and Apple laser printer.

FIGURE 5-6. The default rendering of a definition list. Definitions are set off from the terms by an indent.

The **dl** element is allowed to contain only **dt** and **dd** elements. You cannot put headings or content-grouping elements (like paragraphs) in names (**dt**), but the value (**dd**) can contain any type of flow content. For example, the last **dd** element in the previous example contains two paragraph elements (the awkward default spacing could be cleaned up with a style sheet).

It is permitted to have multiple definitions with one term and vice versa. Here, each term-description group has one term and multiple definitions:

```
<dl>
    <dt>Serif examples</dt>
    <dd>Baskerville</dd>
    <dd>Goudy</dd>

    <dt>Sans-serif examples</dt>
    <dd>Helvetica</dd>
    <dd>Futura</dd>
    <dd>Avenir</dd>
</dl>
```

MORE CONTENT ELEMENTS

We've covered paragraphs, headings, and lists, but there are a few more special text elements to add to your HTML toolbox that don't fit into a neat category: long quotations (**blockquote**), preformatted text (**pre**), and figures (**figure** and **figcaption**). One thing these elements do have in common is that they are considered "grouping content" in the HTML5 spec (along with **p**, **hr**, the list elements, **main**, and the generic **div**, covered later in this chapter). The other thing they share is that browsers typically display them as block elements by default. The one exception is the newer **main** element, which is not recognized by any version of Internet Explorer (although it is supported in the Edge browser); see the sidebar **"HTML5 Support in Internet Explorer,"** later in this chapter, for a workaround.

Long Quotations

If you have a long quotation, a testimonial, or a section of copy from another source, mark it up as a **blockquote** element. It is recommended that content within **blockquote** elements be contained in other elements, such as paragraphs, headings, or lists, as shown in this example:

```
<p>Renowned type designer, Matthew Carter, has this to say about his
profession:</p>

<blockquote>
  <p>Our alphabet hasn't changed in eons; there isn't much latitude in
what a designer can do with the individual letters.</p>

  <p>Much like a piece of classical music, the score is written
down. It's not something that is tampered with, and yet, each
conductor interprets that score differently. There is tension in
the interpretation.</p>
</blockquote>
```

FIGURE 5-7 shows the default rendering of the **blockquote** example. This can be altered with CSS.

Renowned type designer, Matthew Carter, has this to say about his profession:

> Our alphabet hasn't changed in eons; there isn't much latitude in what a designer can do with the individual letters.
>
> Much like a piece of classical music, the score is written down. It's not something that is tampered with, and yet, each conductor interprets that score differently. There is tension in the interpretation.

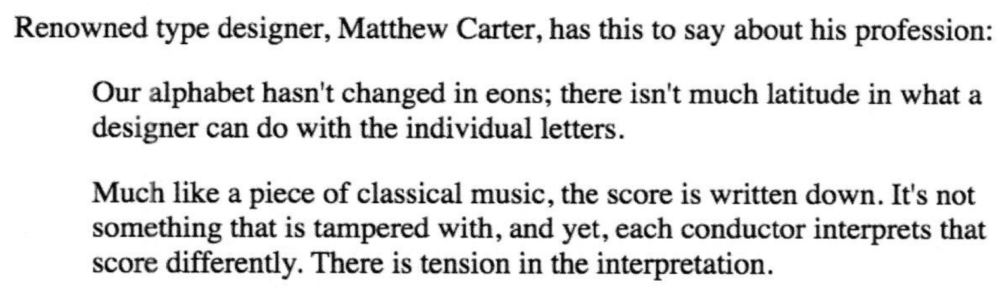

FIGURE 5-7. The default rendering of a **blockquote** element.

Preformatted Text

In the previous chapter, you learned that browsers ignore whitespace such as line returns and character spaces in the source document. But in some types of information, such as code examples or certain poems, the whitespace is important for conveying meaning. For content in which whitespace is semantically significant, use the preformatted text (**pre**) element. It is a unique element in that it is displayed exactly as it is typed—including all the carriage returns and multiple character spaces. By default, preformatted text is also displayed in a constant-width font (one in which all the characters are the same width, also called monospace), such as Courier; however, you can easily change the font with a style sheet rule.

`<blockquote>…</blockquote>`
A lengthy, block-level quotation

NOTE

*There is also the inline element **q** for short quotations in the flow of text. We'll talk about it later in this chapter.*

`<pre>…</pre>`
Preformatted text

NOTE

*The **white-space:pre** CSS property can also be used to preserve spaces and returns in the source.*

The **pre** element in this example displays as shown in FIGURE 5-8. The second part of the figure shows the same content marked up as a paragraph (**p**) element for comparison.

```
<pre>
This is                an               example of
     text with a          lot of
                          curious
                          whitespace.
</pre>

<p>
This is                an               example of
     text with a          lot of
                          curious
                          whitespace.
</p>
```

This is   an   example of
     text with a   lot of
                          curious
                          whitespace.

This is an example of text with a lot of curious whitespace.

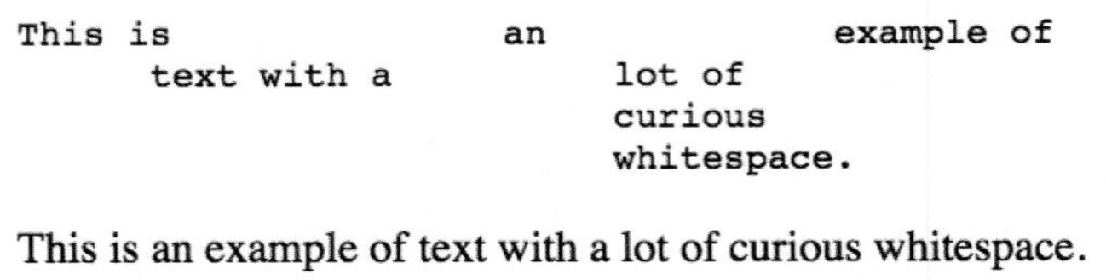

FIGURE 5-8. Preformatted text is unique in that the browser displays the whitespace exactly as it is typed into the source document. Compare it to the paragraph element, in which multiple line returns and character spaces are reduced to a single space.

Figures

`<figure>…</figure>`
Related image or resource

`<figcaption>…</figcaption>`
Text description of a figure

The **figure** element identifies content that illustrates or supports some point in the text. A figure may contain an image, a video, a code snippet, text, or even a table—pretty much anything that can go in the flow of web content. Content in a **figure** element should be treated and referenced as a self-contained unit. That means if a figure is removed from its original placement in the main flow (to a sidebar or appendix, for example), both the figure and the main flow should continue to make sense.

Although you can simply add an image to a page, wrapping it in **figure** tags makes its purpose explicitly clear semantically. It also works as a hook for applying special styles to figures but not to other images on the page:

```
<figure>
    <img src="piechart.png" alt="chart showing fonts on mobile devices">
</figure>
```

If you want to provide a text caption for the figure, use the **figcaption** element above or below the content inside the **figure** element. It is a more semantically rich way to mark up the caption than using a simple **p** element.

```
<figure>
   <pre>
     <code>
   body {
     background-color: #000;
     color: red;
   }
       </code>
   </pre>
   <figcaption>Sample CSS rule.</figcaption>
</figure>
```

In EXERCISE 5-1, you'll get a chance to mark up a document yourself and try out the basic text elements we've covered so far.

BROWSER SUPPORT NOTE

The **figure** *and* **figcaption** *elements are not supported in Internet Explorer versions 8 and earlier (see the sidebar* **"HTML5 Support in Internet Explorer,"** *later in this chapter, for a workaround).*

EXERCISE 5-1. Marking up a recipe

The owners of the Black Goose Bistro have decided to share recipes and news on their site. In the exercises in this chapter, we'll assist them with content markup.

In this exercise, you will find the raw text of a recipe. It's up to you to decide which element is the best semantic match for each chunk of content. You'll use **paragraphs**, **headings**, **lists**, and at least one **special content element**.

You can write the tags right on this page. Or, if you want to use a text editor and see the results in a browser, this text file, as well as the final version with markup, is available at *learningwebdesign.com/5e/materials*.

```
Tapenade (Olive Spread)

This is a really simple dish to prepare and it's always a big hit at
parties. My father recommends:

"Make this the night before so that the flavors have time to blend. Just
bring it up to room temperature before you serve it. In the winter, try
serving it warm."

Ingredients

1 8oz. jar sundried tomatoes
2 large garlic cloves
2/3 c. kalamata olives
1 t. capers

Instructions

Combine tomatoes and garlic in a food processor. Blend until as smooth
as possible.

Add capers and olives. Pulse the motor a few times until they are
incorporated, but still retain some
texture.

Serve on thin toast rounds with goat cheese and fresh basil garnish
(optional).
```

ORGANIZING PAGE CONTENT

So far, the elements we've covered handle very specific tidbits of content: a paragraph, a heading, a figure, and so on. Prior to HTML5, there was no way to group these bits into larger parts other than wrapping them in a generic division (**div**) element (I'll cover **div** in more detail later). HTML5 introduced new elements that give semantic meaning to sections of a typical web page or application (see **Note**), including main content (**main**), headers (**header**), footers (**footer**), sections (**section**), articles (**article**), navigation (**nav**), and tangentially related or complementary content (**aside**). Curiously, the spec lists the old **address** element as a section as well, so we'll look at that one here too.

NOTE

The new element names are based on a Google study that looked at the top 20 names that developers assigned to generic division elements (code.google.com/webstats/2005-12/classes.html).

HTML5 Support in Internet Explorer

Nearly all browsers today support the HTML5 semantic elements, and for those that don't, creating a style sheet rule that tells browsers to format each one as a block-level element is all you need to make them behave correctly:

```
section, article, nav, aside, header, footer, main {
  display: block;
}
```

Unfortunately, that fix won't work for the small fraction of users who are still using Internet Explorer versions 8 and earlier (less than 1.5% of browser traffic as of 2017). IE8 has been hanging around well past its prime because it is tied to the popular Windows Vista operating system. If you work on a large site for which 1% of users represents thousands of people, you may want to be familiar with workarounds and fallbacks for IE8. Most likely, you won't need to support it. Still, at the risk of looking outdated, I will provide notes about IE8 support throughout this book.

For example, the following is a workaround that applies only to IE8 and earlier. Not only do those browsers not recognize the HTML5 elements, but they also ignore any styles applied to them. The solution is to use JavaScript to create each element so IE knows it exists and will allow nesting and styling. Here's what a JavaScript command creating the **section** element looks like:

```
documencreateElement("section");
```

Fortunately, Remy Sharp wrote a script that creates all of the HTML5 elements for IE8 and earlier in one fell swoop. It is called "HTML5 Shiv" (or Shim) and it is available on a server that you can point to in your documents. Just copy this code in the **head** of your document and use a style sheet to style the new elements as blocks:

```
<!--[if lt IE 9]>
<script src="//cdnjs.cloudflare.com/ajax/libs/html5shiv/3.7.3/ →
html5shiv.min.js">
</script >
<![endif]-->
```

The HTML5 Shiv is also part of the Modernizr polyfill script that adds HTML5 and CSS3 functionality to older non-supporting browsers. Read more about Modernizr online at *modernizr.com*. It is also covered in **Chapter 20, Modern Web Development Tools**.

Main Content

Web pages these days are loaded with different types of content: mastheads, sidebars, ads, footers, more ads, even more ads, and so on. It is helpful to cut to the chase and explicitly point out the main content on the page. Use the **main** element to identify the primary content of a page or application. It helps screen readers and other assistive technologies know where the main content of the page begins and replaces the "Skip to main content" links that have been utilized in the past. The content of a **main** element should be unique to that page. In other words, headers, sidebars, and other elements that appear across multiple pages in a site should not be included in the **main** section:

```
<body>
<header>…</header>
<main>
  <h1>Humanist Sans Serif</h1>
  <!-- code continues -->
</main>
</body>
```

The W3C HTML5 specification states that pages should have only one **main** section and that it should not be nested within an **article**, **aside**, **header**, **footer**, or **nav**. Doing so will cause the document to be invalid.

The **main** element is the most recent addition to the roster of HTML5 grouping elements. You can use it and style it in most browsers, but for Internet Explorer (including version 11, the most current as of this writing), you'll need to create the element with JavaScript and set its display to **block** with a style sheet, as discussed in the **"HTML5 Support in Internet Explorer"** sidebar. Note that **main** is supported in MS Edge.

Headers and Footers

Because web authors have been labeling header and footer sections in their documents for years, it was kind of a no-brainer that full-fledged **header** and **footer** elements would come in handy. Let's start with headers.

Headers

The **header** element is used for introductory material that typically appears at the beginning of a web page or at the top of a section or article (we'll get to those elements next). There is no specified list of what a **header** must or should contain; anything that makes sense as the introduction to a page or section is acceptable. In the following example, the document header includes a logo image, the site title, and navigation:

```
<body>
<header>
  <img src="/images/logo.png" alt="logo">
  <h1>Nuts about Web Fonts</h1>
```

`<main>…</main>`

Primary content area of page or app

`<header>…</header>`

Introductory material for page, section, or article

`<footer>…</footer>`

Footer for page, section, or article

NOTE

The `<a href="/"></a>` code in the examples is the markup for adding links to other web pages. We'll take on links in **Chapter 6, Adding Links**. Normally the value would be the URL to the page, but I've used a simple slash as a space-saving measure.

```
<nav>
  <ul>
    <li><a href="/">Home</a></li>
    <li><a href="/">Blog</a></li>
    <li><a href="/">Shop</a></li>
  </ul>
</nav>
</header>
<!--page content-->
</body>
```

When used in an individual article, the **header** might include the article title, author, and the publication date, as shown here:

```
<article>
  <header>
    <h1>More about WOFF</h1>
    <p>by Jennifer Robbins, <time datetime="2017-11-11">November 11,
2017</time></p>
  </header>
  <!-- article content here -->
</article>
```

NOTE

Neither **header** *nor* **footer** *elements are permitted to contain nested* **header** *or* **footer** *elements.*

Footers

The **footer** element is used to indicate the type of information that typically comes at the end of a page or an article, such as its author, copyright information, related documents, or navigation. The **footer** element may apply to the entire document, or it could be associated with a particular section or article. If the footer is contained directly within the **body** element, either before or after all the other **body** content, then it applies to the entire page or application. If it is contained in a sectioning element (**section**, **article**, **nav**, or **aside**), it is parsed as the footer for just that section. Note that although it is called "footer," there is no requirement that it appear last in the document or sectioning element. It could also appear at or near the beginning if that makes sense.

In this simple example, we see the typical information listed at the bottom of an article marked up as a **footer**:

```
<article>
  <header>
    <h1>More about WOFF</h1>
    <p>by Jennifer Robbins, <time datetime="2017-11-11">November 11,
2017</time></p>
  </header>
  <!-- article content here -->
  <footer>
    <p><small>Copyright &copy;2017 Jennifer Robbins.</small></p>
```

NOTE

The **time** element will be discussed in the section **"Dates and times"** later in this chapter.

```
<nav>
  <ul>
    <li><a href="/">Previous</a></li>
    <li><a href="/">Next</a></li>
  </ul>
</nav>
  </footer>
</article>
```

Sections and Articles

Long documents are easier to use when they are divided into smaller parts. For example, books are divided into chapters, and newspapers have sections for local news, sports, comics, and so on. To divide long web documents into thematic sections, use the aptly named **section** element. Sections typically include a heading (inside the **section** element) plus content that has a meaningful reason to be grouped together.

The **section** element has a broad range of uses, from dividing a whole page into major sections or identifying thematic sections within a single article. In the following example, a document with information about typography resources has been divided into two sections based on resource type:

```
<section>
  <h2>Typography Books</h2>
  <ul>
    <li>…</li>
  </ul>
</section>

<section>
  <h2>Online Tutorials</h2>
  <p>These are the best tutorials on the web.</p>
  <ul>
    <li>…</li>
  </ul>
</section>
```

Use the **article** element for self-contained works that could stand alone or be reused in a different context (such as syndication). It is useful for magazine or newspaper articles, blog posts, comments, or other items that could be extracted for external use. You can think of it as a specialized **section** element that answers "yes" to the question "Could this appear on another site and make sense?"

A long **article** could be broken into a number of sections, as shown here:

```
<article>
  <h1>Get to Know Helvetica</h1>
  <section>
    <h2>History of Helvetica</h2>
    <p>…</p>
  </section>
```

`<section>…</section>`

Thematic group of content

`<article>…</article>`

Self-contained, reusable composition

NOTE

The HTML5 spec recommends that if the purpose for grouping the elements is simply to provide a hook for styling, use the generic **div** *element instead.*

```
    <section>
      <h2>Helvetica Today</h2>
      <p>…</p>
    </section>
  </article>
```

Conversely, a **section** in a web document might be composed of a number of articles:

```
<section id="essays">
  <article>
    <h1>A Fresh Look at Futura</h1>
    <p>…</p>
  </article>

  <article>
    <h1>Getting Personal with Humanist</h1>
    <p>…</p>
  </article>
</section>
```

The **section** and **article** elements are easily confused, particularly because it is possible to nest one in the other and vice versa. Keep in mind that if the content is self-contained and could appear outside the current context, it is best marked up as an **article**.

Aside (Sidebars)

<aside>…</aside>

Tangentially related material

The **aside** element identifies content that is separate from, but tangentially related to, the surrounding content. In print, its equivalent is a sidebar, but it couldn't be called "sidebar" because putting something on the "side" is a presentational description, not semantic. Nonetheless, a sidebar is a good mental model for using the **aside** element. **aside** can be used for pull quotes, background information, lists of links, callouts, or anything else that might be associated with (but not critical to) a document.

In this example, an **aside** element is used for a list of links related to the main article:

```
<h1>Web Typography</h1>
<p>Back in 1997, there were competing font formats and tools for
making them…</p>
<p>We now have a number of methods for using beautiful fonts on web
pages…</p>
<aside>
  <h2>Web Font Resources</h2>
  <ul>
    <li><a href="http://typekit.com/">Typekit</a></li>
    <li><a href="http://fonts.google.com">Google Fonts</a></li>
  </ul>
</aside>
```

The **aside** element has no default rendering, so you will need to make it a block element and adjust its appearance and layout with style sheet rules.

Navigation

The **nav** element gives developers a semantic way to identify navigation for a site. Earlier in this chapter, we saw an unordered list that might be used as the top-level navigation for a font catalog site. Wrapping that list in a **nav** element makes its purpose explicitly clear:

```
<nav>
  <ul>
    <li><a href="/">Serif</a></li>
    <li><a href="/">Sans-serif</a></li>
    <li><a href="/">Script</a></li>
    <li><a href="/">Display</a></li>
    <li><a href="/">Dingbats</a></li>
  </ul>
</nav>
```

Not all lists of links should be wrapped in **nav** tags, however. The spec makes it clear that **nav** should be used for links that provide primary navigation around a site or a lengthy section or article. The **nav** element may be especially helpful from an accessibility perspective.

`<nav>…</nav>`
Primary navigation links

Addresses

Last, and well, least, is the **address** element that is used to create an area for contact information for the author or maintainer of the document. It is generally placed at the end of the document or in a section or article within a document. An **address** would be right at home in a **footer** element. It is important to note that the **address** element should *not* be used for any old address on a page, such as mailing addresses. It is intended specifically for author contact information (although that could potentially be a mailing address). Following is an example of its intended use:

```
<address>
Contributed by <a href="../authors/robbins/">Jennifer Robbins</a>,
<a href="http://www.oreilly.com/">O'Reilly Media</a>
</address>
```

`<address>…</address>`
Contact information

Document Outlines

Behind the scenes, browsers look at the markup in a document and generate a hierarchical outline based on the headings in the content. A new section gets added to the outline whenever the browser encounters a new heading level.

In past versions of HTML, that was the only way the outline was created. HTML5 introduced a new outline algorithm that enables authors to explicitly add a new section to the outline by inserting a sectioning element: **article**, **section**, **aside**, and **nav**. In addition to the four sectioning elements, the spec defines some elements (**blockquote**, **fieldset**, **figure**,

dialog, **details**, and **td**) as sectioning roots, which means headings in those elements do not become part of the overall document outline.

It's a nice idea because it allows content to be repurposed and merged without breaking the outline, but unfortunately, no browsers to date have implemented it and they are unlikely to do so. The W3C has kept the sectioning elements and their intended behavior in the spec (which is why I mention this at all), but now precede it with a banner recommending sticking with the old hierarchical heading method.

THE INLINE ELEMENT ROUNDUP

Now that we've identified the larger chunks of content, we can provide semantic meaning to phrases within the chunks by using what the HTML5 specification calls text-level semantic elements. On the street, you are likely to hear them called inline elements because they display in the flow of text by default and do not cause any line breaks. That's also how they were referred to in HTML versions prior to HTML5.

Text-Level (Inline) Elements

Despite all the types of information you could add to a document, there are only a couple dozen text-level semantic elements. TABLE 5-1 lists all of them.

Although it may be handy seeing all of the text-level elements listed together in a table, they certainly deserve more detailed explanations.

Emphasized text

...

Stressed emphasis

Use the **em** element to indicate which part of a sentence should be stressed or emphasized. The placement of **em** elements affects how a sentence's meaning is interpreted. Consider the following sentences that are identical, except for which words are stressed:

```
<p><em>Arlo</em> is very smart.</p>
<p>Arlo is <em>very</em> smart.</p>
```

The first sentence indicates *who* is very smart. The second example is about *how* smart he is. Notice that the **em** element has an effect on the meaning of the sentence.

Emphasized text (**em**) elements nearly always display in italics by default (FIGURE 5-9), but of course you can make them display any way you like with a style sheet. Screen readers may use a different tone of voice to convey stressed content, which is why you should use an **em** element only when it makes sense semantically, not just to achieve italic text.

Important text

...

Strong importance

The **strong** element indicates that a word or phrase is important, serious, or urgent. In the following example, the **strong** element identifies the portion of instructions that requires extra attention. The **strong** element does not change the meaning of the sentence; it merely draws attention to the important parts:

```
<p>When returning the car, <strong>drop the keys in the red box by the front desk</strong>.</p>
```

Visual browsers typically display **strong** text elements in bold text by default. Screen readers may use a distinct tone of voice for important content, so

TABLE 5-1. Text-level semantic elements

Element	Description
a	An anchor or hypertext link (see **Chapter 6** for details)
abbr	Abbreviation
b	Added visual attention, such as keywords (bold)
bdi	Indicates text that may have directional requirements
bdo	Bidirectional override; explicitly indicates text direction (left to right, `ltr`, or right to left, `rtl`)
br	Line break
cite	Citation; a reference to the title of a work, such as a book title
code	Computer code sample
data	Machine-readable equivalent dates, time, weights, and other measurable values
del	Deleted text; indicates an edit made to a document
dfn	The defining instance or first occurrence of a term
em	Emphasized text
i	Alternative voice (italic) or alternate language
ins	Inserted text; indicates an insertion in a document
kbd	Keyboard; text entered by a user (for technical documents)
mark	Contextually relevant text
q	Short, inline quotation
ruby, rt, rp	Provides annotations or pronunciation guides under East Asian typography and ideographs
s	Incorrect text (strike-through)
samp	Sample output from programs
small	Small print, such as a copyright or legal notice (displayed in a smaller type size)
span	Generic phrase content
strong	Content of strong importance
sub	Subscript
sup	Superscript
time	Machine-readable time data
u	Indicates a formal name, misspelled word, or text that would be underlined
var	A variable or program argument (for technical documents)
wbr	Word break

The Inline Elements Backstory

Many of the inline elements that have been around since the dawn of the web were introduced to change the visual formatting of text selections because of the lack of a style sheet system. If you wanted bolded text, you marked it as **b**. Italics? Use the **i** element. In fact, there was once a **font** element used solely to change the font, color, and size of text (the horror!). Not surprisingly, HTML5 kicked the purely presentational **font** element to the curb. However, many of the old-school presentational inline elements (for example, **u** for underline and **s** for strike-through) have been kept in HTML5 and given new semantic definitions (**b** is now for "keywords," **s** for "inaccurate text").

Many inline elements have the expected style rendering (bold for the **b** element, for example). Other inline elements are purely semantic (such as **abbr** or **time**) and don't have default renderings. For any inline elements, you can use CSS rules if you want to change the way they display.

Obsolete HTML 4.01 Text Elements

Here are some old text elements that were made obsolete in HTML5: **acronym**, **applet**, **basefont**, **big**, **center**, **dir** (directory), **font**, **isindex** (search box), **menu**, **strike**, **tt** (teletype). I mention them here in case you run across them in an old document when viewing its source or if you are using an older web authoring tool. There is no reason to use them today.

mark text as **strong** only when it makes sense semantically, not just to make text bold.

The following is a brief example of our **em** and **strong** text examples. FIGURE 5-9 should hold no surprises.

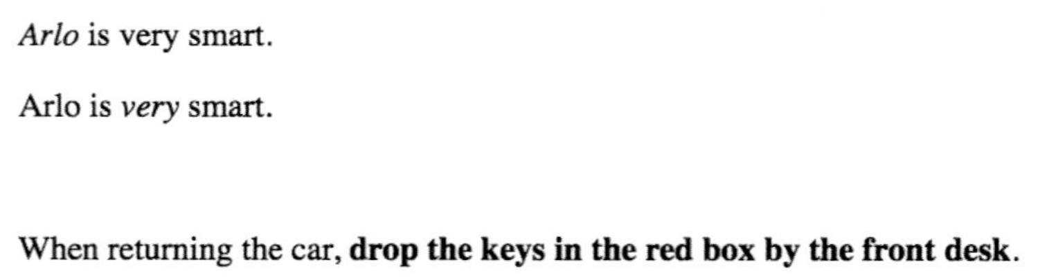

Arlo is very smart.

Arlo is *very* smart.

When returning the car, **drop the keys in the red box by the front desk**.

FIGURE 5-9. The default rendering of emphasized and strong text.

Elements originally named for their presentational properties

As long as we're talking about bold and italic text, let's see what the old **b** and **i** elements are up to now. The elements **b**, **i**, **u**, **s**, and **small** were introduced in the old days of the web as a way to provide typesetting instructions (bold, italic, underline, strike-through, and smaller text, respectively). Despite their original presentational purposes, these elements have been included in HTML5 and given updated, semantic definitions based on patterns of how they've been used. Browsers still render them by default as you'd expect (FIGURE 5-10). However, if a type style change is all you're after, using a style sheet rule is the appropriate solution. Save these for when they are semantically appropriate.

Let's look at these elements and their correct usage, as well as the style sheet alternatives.

b

Keywords, product names, and other phrases that need to stand out from the surrounding text without conveying added importance or emphasis (see **Note**). [*Old definition:* Bold]

CSS Property: For bold text, use **font-weight**. Example: **font-weight: bold;**

Example: `<p>The slabs at the ends of letter strokes are called <b>serifs</b>.</p>`

i

Indicates text that is in a different voice or mood than the surrounding text, such as a phrase from another language, a technical term, or a thought. [*Old definition:* Italic]

CSS Property: For italic text, use **font-style**. Example: **font-style: italic;**

`<b>`...`</b>`
Keywords or visually emphasized text (bold)

`<i>`...`</i>`
Alternative voice (italic)

`<s>`...`</s>`
Incorrect text (strike-through)

`<u>`...`</u>`
Annotated text (underline)

`<small>`...`</small>`
Legal text; small print (smaller type size)

NOTE

It helps me to think about how a screen reader would read the text. If I don't want the word read in a loud, emphatic tone of voice, but it really should be bold, then **b** *may be more appropriate than* **strong**.

Example: `<p>Simply change the font and <i>Voila!</i>, a new personality!</p>`

s

Indicates text that is incorrect. [*Old definition:* Strike-through text]

CSS Property: To draw a line through a selection of text, use **text-decoration**. Example: **text-decoration: line-through**

Example: `<p>Scala Sans was designed by <s>Eric Gill</s> Martin Majoor.</p>`

u

There are a few instances when underlining has semantic significance, such as underlining a formal name in Chinese or indicating a misspelled word after a spell check, such as the misspelled "Helvitica" in the following example. Note that underlined text is easily confused with a link and should generally be avoided except for a few niche cases. [*Old definition:* Underline]

CSS Property: For underlined text, use **text-decoration**. Example: **text-decoration: underline**

Example: `<p>New York subway signage is set in <u>Helviteca</u>.</p>`

small

Indicates an addendum or side note to the main text, such as the legal "small print" at the bottom of a document. [*Old definition:* Renders in font smaller than the surrounding text]

CSS Property: To make text smaller, use **font-size**. Example: **font-size: 80%**

Example: `<p><small>(This font is free for personal and commercial use.)</small></p>`

b ——— The slabs at the ends of letter strokes are called **serifs**.

i ——— Simply change the font and *Voila!*, a new personality!

s ——— Scala Sans was designed by ~~Eric Gill~~ Martin Majoor.

u ——— New York subway signage is set in <u>Helviteca</u>.

small ——— (This font is free for personal and commercial use.)

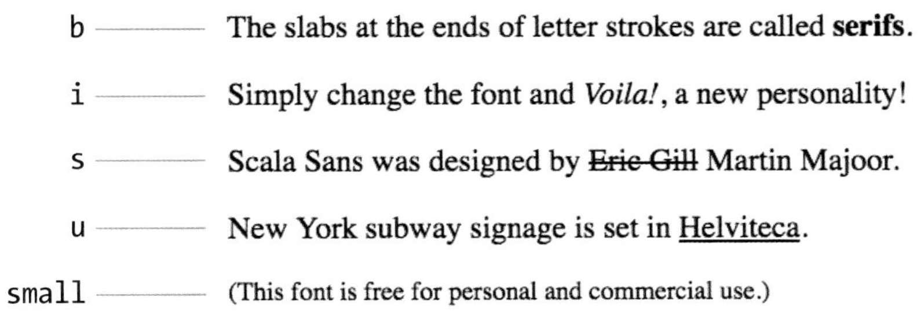

FIGURE 5-10. The default rendering of **b**, **i**, **s**, **u**, and **small** elements.

Short quotations

`<q>...</q>`

Short inline quotation

Use the quotation (**q**) element to mark up short quotations, such as "To be or not to be," in the flow of text, as shown in this example (FIGURE 5-11):

```
Matthew Carter says, <q>Our alphabet hasn't changed in eons.</q>
```

According to the HTML spec, browsers should add quotation marks around **q** elements automatically, so you don't need to include them in the source document. Some browsers, like Firefox, render curly quotes, which is preferable. Others (Safari and Chrome, which I used for my examples) render them as straight quotes as shown in the figure.

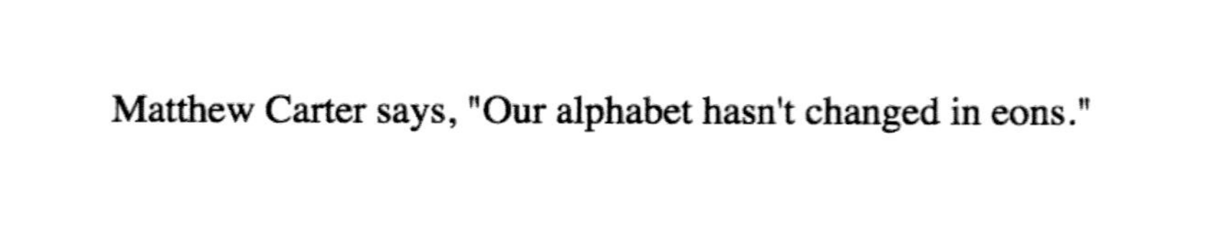

Matthew Carter says, "Our alphabet hasn't changed in eons."

FIGURE 5-11. Browsers add quotation marks automatically around **q** elements.

Abbreviations and acronyms

`<abbr>...</abbr>`

Abbreviation or acronym

Marking up acronyms and abbreviations with the **abbr** element provides useful information for search engines, screen readers, and other devices. Abbreviations are shortened versions of a word ending in a period ("Conn." for "Connecticut," for example). Acronyms are abbreviations formed by the first letters of the words in a phrase (such as NASA or USA). The **title** attribute provides the long version of the shortened term, as shown in this example:

```
<abbr title="Points">pts.</abbr>
<abbr title="American Type Founders">ATF</abbr>
```

NOTE

In HTML 4.01, there was an **acronym** *element especially for acronyms, but HTML5 has made it obsolete in favor of using the* **abbr** *for both.*

Nesting Elements

You can apply two elements to a string of text (for example, a phrase that is both a quote and in another language), but be sure they are nested properly. That means the inner element, including its closing tag, must be completely contained within the outer element, and not overlap:

```
<q><i>Je ne sais pas.</i></q>
```

Here is an example of elements that are nested incorrectly. Notice that the inner **i** element is not closed within the containing **q** element:

```
<q><i>Je ne sais pas.</q></i>
```

It is easy to spot the nesting error in an example that is this short, but when you're nesting long passages or nesting multiple levels deep, it is easy to end up with overlaps. One advantage to using an HTML code editor is that it can automatically close elements for you correctly or point out when you've made a mistake.

Citations

The **cite** element is used to identify a reference to another document, such as a book, magazine, article title, and so on. Citations are typically rendered in italic text by default. Here's an example:

```
<p>Passages of this article were inspired by <cite>The Complete Manual
of Typography</cite> by James Felici.</p>
```

`<cite>…</cite>`
Citation

Defining terms

It is common to point out the first and defining instance of a word in a document in some fashion. In this book, defining terms are set in blue text. In HTML, you can identify them with the **dfn** element and format them visually using style sheets.

```
<p><dfn>Script typefaces</dfn> are based on handwriting.</p>
```

`<dfn>…</dfn>`
Defining term

Program code elements

A number of inline elements are used for describing the parts of technical documents, such as code (**code**), variables (**var**), program samples (**samp**), and user-entered keyboard strokes (**kbd**). For me, it's a quaint reminder of HTML's origins in the scientific world (Tim Berners-Lee developed HTML to share documents at the CERN particle physics lab in 1989).

Code, sample, and keyboard elements typically render in a constant-width (also called monospace) font such as Courier by default. Variables usually render in italics.

`<code>…</code>`
Code

`<var>…</var>`
Variable

`<samp>…</samp>`
Program sample

`<kbd>…</kbd>`
User-entered keyboard strokes

Subscript and superscript

The subscript (**sub**) and superscript (**sup**) elements cause the selected text to display in a smaller size, positioned slightly below (**sub**) or above (**sup**) the baseline. These elements may be helpful for indicating chemical formulas or mathematical equations.

FIGURE 5-12 shows how these examples of subscript and superscript typically render in a browser.

```
<p>H<sub>2</sub>O</p>
```

```
<p>E=MC<sup>2</sup></p>
```

`<sub>…</sub>`
Subscript

`<sup>…</sup>`
Superscript

$$H_2O \qquad E=MC^2$$

FIGURE 5-12. Subscript and superscript

Highlighted text

<mark>...</mark>

Contextually relevant text

The **mark** element indicates a word that may be considered especially relevant to the reader. One might use it to dynamically highlight a search term in a page of results, to manually call attention to a passage of text, or to indicate the current page in a series. Some designers (and browsers) give marked text a light colored background as though it were marked with a highlighter marker, as shown in FIGURE 5-13.

```
<p> ... PART I. ADMINISTRATION OF THE GOVERNMENT. TITLE IX.
TAXATION. CHAPTER 65C. MASS. <mark>ESTATE TAX</mark>. Chapter 65C:
Sect. 2. Computation of <mark>estate tax</mark>.</p>
```

... PART I. ADMINISTRATION OF THE GOVERNMENT. TITLE IX. TAXATION. CHAPTER 65C. MASS. ESTATE TAX. Chapter 65C: Sect. 2. Computation of estate tax.

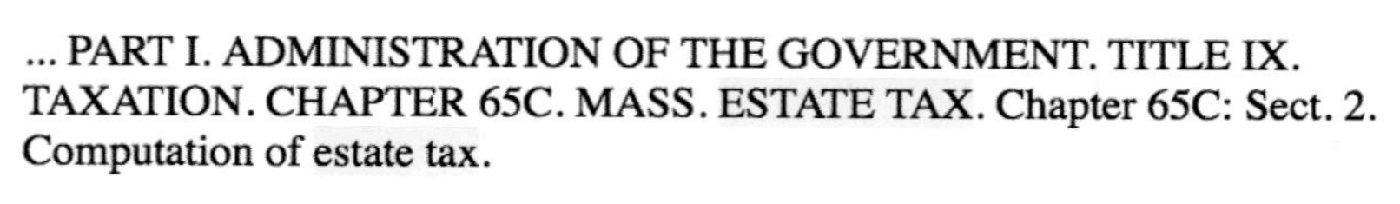

FIGURE 5-13. In this example, search terms are identified with **mark** elements and given a yellow background with a style sheet so they are easier for the reader to find.

Dates and times

<time>...</time>

Time data

When we look at the phrase "noon on November 4," we know that it is a date and a time. But the context might not be so obvious to a computer program. The **time** element allows us to mark up dates and times in a way that is comfortable for a human to read, but also encoded in a standardized way that computers can use. The content of the element presents the information to people, and the **datetime** attribute presents the same information in a machine-readable way.

The **time** element indicates dates, times, or date-time combos. It might be used to pass the date and time information to an application, such as saving an event to a personal calendar. It might be used by search engines to find the most recently published articles. Or it could be used to restyle time information into an alternate format (e.g., changing 18:00 to 6 p.m.).

The **datetime** attribute specifies the date and/or time information in a standardized time format illustrated in FIGURE 5-14. The full time format begins with the date (year–month–day). The time section begins with a letter "T" and lists hours (on the 24-hour clock), minutes, seconds (optional), and milliseconds (also optional). Finally, the time zone is indicated by the number of hours behind (-) or ahead (+) of Greenwich Mean Time (GMT). For example, "-05:00" indicates the Eastern Standard time zone, which is five hours behind GMT. When identifying dates and times alone, you can omit the other sections.

NOTE

The **time** *element is not intended for marking up times for which a precise time or date cannot be established, such as "the end of last year" or "the turn of the century."*

■ FURTHER READING

For more information on the intricate ins and outs of specifying dates and times, with examples, check out the **time** element entry in the HTML5 specification: *www.w3.org/TR/2014/REC-html5-20141028/text-level-semantics.html#the-time-element.*

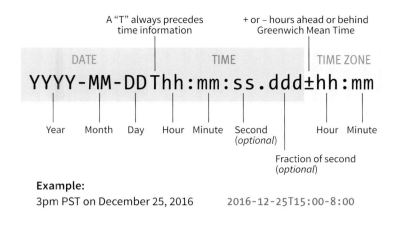

FIGURE 5-14. *Standardized date and time syntax.*

Here are a few examples of valid values for **datetime**:

- **Time only:** 9:30 p.m.

  ```
  <time datetime="21:30">9:30p.m.</time>
  ```

- **Date only:** June 19, 2016

  ```
  <time datetime="2016-06-19">June 19, 2016</time>
  ```

- **Date and time:** Sept. 5, 1970, 1:11 a.m.

  ```
  <time datetime="1970-09-05T01:11:00">Sept. 5, 1970, 1:11a.m.</time>
  ```

- **Date and time, with time zone information:** 8:00am on July 19, 2015, in Providence, RI

  ```
  <time datetime="2015-07-19T08:00:00-05:00">July 19, 2015, 8am, Providence RI</time>
  ```

Machine-readable information

The **data** element is another tool for helping computers make sense of content. It can be used for all sorts of data, including dates, times, measurements, weights, microdata, and so on. The required **value** attribute provides the machine-readable information. Here are a couple of examples:

```
<data value="12">Twelve</data>
<data value="978-1-449-39319-9">CSS: The Definitive Guide</data>
```

I'm not going to go into more detail on the **data** element, because as a beginner, you are unlikely to be dealing with machine-readable data quite yet. But it is interesting to see how markup can be used to provide usable information to computer programs and scripts as well as to your fellow humans.

> **NOTE**
>
> *You can also use the* **time** *element without the* **datetime** *attribute, but its content must be a valid date/time string:*
>
> ```
> <time>2016-06-19</time>
> ```

```
<data>…</data>
```
Machine-readable data

Inserted and deleted text

`<ins>…</ins>`
Inserted text

`<del>…</del>`
Deleted text

The **ins** and **del** elements are used to mark up edits indicating parts of a document that have been inserted or deleted (respectively). These elements rely on style rules for presentation (i.e., there is no dependable browser default). Both the **ins** and **del** elements can contain either inline or block elements, depending on what type of content they contain:

```
Chief Executive Officer: <del title="retired">Peter Pan</del><ins>Pippi
Longstocking</ins>
```

Adding Breaks

Line breaks

`<br>`
Line break

Occasionally, you may need to add a line break within the flow of text. We've seen how browsers ignore line breaks in the source document, so we need a specific directive to tell the browser to "add a line break here."

The inline line break element (**br**) does exactly that. The **br** element could be used to break up lines of addresses or poetry. It is an empty element, which means it does not have content. Just add the **br** element in the flow of text where you want a break to occur, as shown here and in FIGURE 5-15:

```
<p>So much depends <br>upon <br><br>a red wheel <br>barrow</p>
```

So much depends
upon

a red wheel
barrow

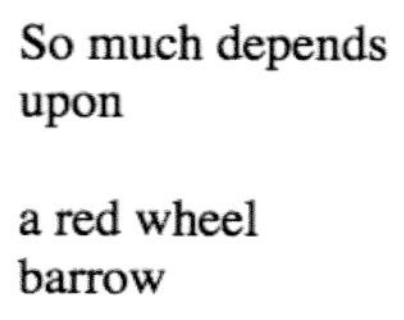

FIGURE 5-15. Line breaks are inserted at each **br** element. (Example extracted from "The Red Wheelbarrow" by William Carlos Williams.)

Unfortunately, the **br** element is easily abused. Be careful that you aren't using **br** elements to force breaks into text that really ought to be a list. For example, don't do this:

```
<p>Times<br>
Georgia<br>
Garamond
</p>
```

If it's a list, use the semantically correct unordered list element instead, and turn off the bullets with style sheets:

```
<ul>
   <li>Times</li>
   <li>Georgia</li>
   <li>Garamond</li>
</ul>
```

Word breaks

The word break (**wbr**) element lets you mark the place where a word should break (a "line break opportunity" according to the spec) should there not be enough room for the whole word (FIGURE 5-16). It takes some of the guess-work away from the browser and allows authors to control the best spot for the word to be split over two lines. If there is enough room, the word stays in one piece. Without word breaks, the word stays together, and if there is not enough room, the whole word wraps to the next line. Note that the browser does not add a hyphen when the word breaks over two lines. The **wbr** behaves as though it were a character space in the middle of the word:

```
<p>The biggest word you've ever heard and this is how it goes:
<em>supercali<wbr>fragilistic<wbr>expialidocious</em>!</p>
```

The biggest word you've ever heard and this is how it goes: *supercalifragilistic expialidocious*!

FIGURE 5-16. When there is not enough room for a word to fit on a line, it will break at the location of the **wbr** element.

You've been introduced to 32 new elements since your last exercise. I'd say it's time to give some of the inline elements a try in EXERCISE 5-2.

`<wbr>`

Word break

***

BROWSER SUPPORT NOTE

*The **wbr** element is not supported by any version of Internet Explorer as of this writing. It is supported in MS Edge.*

Accommodating Non-Western Languages

If the web is to reach a truly worldwide audience, it needs to be able to support the display of all the languages of the world, with all their unique alphabets, symbols, directionality, and specialized punctuation. The W3C's efforts for internationalization (often referred to as "i18n"—an i, then 18 letters, then an n) ensure that the formats and protocols defined in web technologies are usable worldwide.

Internationalization efforts include the following:

- Using the Unicode character encoding that contains the characters, glyph, symbols, ideographs, and the like from all active, modern languages. Unicode is discussed in **Chapter 4, Creating a Simple Page**.

- Declaring the primary language of a document by using a two-letter language code from the ISO 639-1 standard (available at *www.loc.gov/standards/iso639-2/php/code_list.php*). For example, English is "EN," Czech is "CS, "and German is "DE." Use the **lang** attribute in the **html** element to declare the language for the whole document, or in individual elements that require clarification.

- Accommodating the various writing directions of languages. In HTML, the **dir** attribute explicitly sets the direction for the document or an element to **ltr** (left-to-right) or **rtl** (right-to-left). On phrase-level elements, it also creates a bidirectional isolation, preventing text within the element from influencing the ordering of text outside it. (This can be an important consideration when you are embedding user-generated text.)

For example, to include a passage of Hebrew in an English document, use the **dir** attribute to indicate that the phrase should be displayed right-to-left:

```
<p>This is how you write Shalom:
<span dir="rtl">שלום</span></p>
```

- Providing a system that allows for ruby annotation, notes that typically appear above ideographs from East Asian languages to give pronunciation clues or translations (**ruby**, **rt**, and **rp** elements). See the spec for details if this is something you need to do.

The W3C Internationalization Activity site provides a thorough collection of HTML and CSS authoring techniques and resources to help with your internationalization efforts: *www.w3.org/International/techniques/authoring-html*.

EXERCISE 5-2. Identifying inline elements

This little post for the Black Goose Bistro News page will give you an opportunity to identify and mark up a variety of inline elements. See if you can find phrases to mark up accurately with the following elements:

b   br   cite   dfn   em

i   q   small   time

Because markup is always somewhat subjective, your resulting markup may not look exactly like my final markup, but there is an opportunity to use all of the preceding elements in the article. For extra credit, there is a phrase that could have two elements applied to it. (Hint: look for a term in another language.) Remember to nest them properly by closing the inner element before you close the outer one. Also, be sure that all text-level elements are contained *within* block elements.

You can write the tags right on this page. Or, if you want to use a text editor and see the results in a browser, this text file is available online at *learningwebdesign.com/5e/materials* along with the resulting code.

```
<article>

<header>
<p>posted by BGB, November 15, 2016</p>
</header>

<h2>Low and Slow</h2>
<p>This week I am extremely excited about a new
cooking technique called sous vide. In sous vide
cooking, you submerge the food (usually vacuum-sealed
in plastic) into a water bath that is precisely
set to the target temperature you want the food
to be cooked to. In his book, Cooking for Geeks,
Jeff Potter describes it as ultra-low-temperature
poaching.</p>
<p>Next month, we will be serving Sous Vide Salmon
with Dill Hollandaise. To reserve a seat at the chef
table, contact us before November 30.</p>

<p>blackgoose@example.com
555-336-1800</p>

<p>Warning: Sous vide cooked salmon is not
pasteurized. Avoid it if you are pregnant or have
immunity issues.</p>
</article>
```

GENERIC ELEMENTS (DIV AND SPAN)

`<div>`…`</div>`
Generic block-level element

`<span>`…`</span>`
Generic inline element

What if none of the elements we've talked about so far accurately describes your content? After all, there are endless types of information in the world, but as you've seen, not all that many semantic elements. Fortunately, HTML provides two generic elements that can be customized to describe your content perfectly. The **div** element indicates a division of content, and **span** indicates a word or phrase for which no text-level element currently exists. The generic elements are given meaning and context with the **id** and **class** attributes, which we'll discuss in a moment.

The **div** and **span** elements have no inherent presentation qualities of their own, but you can use style sheets to format them however you like. In fact, generic elements are a primary tool in standards-based web design because they enable authors to accurately describe content and offer plenty of "hooks" for adding style rules. They also allow elements on the page to be accessed and manipulated by JavaScript.

We're going to spend a little time on **div** and **span** elements, as well as the **id** and **class** attributes, to learn how authors use them to structure content.

Divide It Up with a div

Use the **div** element to create a logical grouping of content or elements on the page. It indicates that they belong together in a conceptual unit or should be treated as a unit by CSS or JavaScript. By marking related content as a **div** and giving it a unique **id** or indicating that it is part of a **class**, you give context to the elements in the grouping. Let's look at a few examples of **div** elements.

In this example, a **div** element is used as a container to group an image and two paragraphs into a product "listing":

```
<div class="listing">
   <img src="images/felici-cover.gif" alt="">
   <p><cite>The Complete Manual of Typography</cite>, James Felici</p>
   <p>A combination of type history and examples of good and bad type
design.</p>
</div>
```

By putting those elements in a **div**, I've made it clear that they are conceptually related. It also allows me to style **p** elements within listings differently than other **p** elements in the document.

Here is another common use of a **div** used to break a page into sections for layout purposes. In this example, a heading and several paragraphs are enclosed in a **div** and identified as the "news" division:

```
<div id="news">
   <h1>New This Week</h1>
   <p>We've been working on...</p>
   <p>And last but not least,... </p>
</div>
```

Now I have a custom element that I've given the name "news." You might be thinking, "Hey Jen, couldn't you use a **section** element for that?" You could! In fact, authors may turn to generic **div**s less often now that we have better semantic sectioning elements in HTML5.

Define a Phrase with span

A **span** offers the same benefits as the **div** element, except it is used for phrase elements and does not introduce line breaks. Because **span**s are inline elements, they may contain only text and other inline elements (in other words, you cannot put headings, lists, content-grouping elements, and so on, in a **span**). Let's get right to some examples.

There is no **telephone** element, but we can use a **span** to give meaning to telephone numbers. In this example, each telephone number is marked up as a **span** and classified as "tel":

```
<ul>
   <li>John: <span class="tel">999.8282</span></li>
   <li>Paul: <span class="tel">888.4889</span></li>
   <li>George: <span class="tel">888.1628</span></li>
   <li>Ringo: <span class="tel">999.3220</span></li>
</ul>
```

> ■ **MARKUP TIP**
>
> It is possible to nest **div** elements within other **div** elements, but don't go overboard. You should always strive to keep your markup as simple as possible, so add a **div** element only if it is necessary for logical structure, styling, or scripting.

You can see how the classified **span**s add meaning to what otherwise might be a random string of digits. As a bonus, the **span** element enables us to apply the same style to phone numbers throughout the site (for example, ensuring line breaks never happen within them, using a CSS `white-space: nowrap` declaration). It makes the information recognizable not only to humans but also to computer programs that know that "tel" is telephone number information. In fact, some values—including "tel"—have been standardized in a markup system known as Microformats that makes web content more useful to software (see the upcoming sidebar **"Structured Data in a Nutshell"**).

id and class Attributes

In the previous examples, we saw the **id** and **class** attributes used to provide context to generic **div** and **span** elements. **id** and **class** have different purposes, however, and it's important to know the difference.

Identification with id

The **id** attribute is used to assign a *unique* identifier to an element in the document. In other words, the value of **id** must be used only once in the document. This makes it useful for assigning a name to a particular element, as though it were a piece of data. See the sidebar **"id and class Values"** for information on providing values for the **id** attribute.

This example uses the books' ISBNs (International Standard Book Numbers) to uniquely identify each listing. No two book listings may share the same **id**.

```
<div id="ISBN0321127307">
  <img src="felici-cover.gif" alt="">
  <p><cite>The Complete Manual of Typography</cite>, James Felici</p>
  <p>A combination of type history and examples of good and bad type.
  </p>
</div>

<div id="ISBN0881792063">
  <img src="bringhurst-cover.gif" alt="">
  <p><cite>The Elements of Typographic Style</cite>, Robert Bringhurst
  </p>
  <p>This lovely, well-written book is concerned foremost with creating
beautiful typography.</p>
</div>
```

Web authors also use **id** when identifying the various sections of a page. In the following example, there may not be more than one element with the **id** of "links" or "news" in the document:

```
<section id="news">
  <!-- news items here -->
</section>

<aside id="links">
  <!-- list of links here -->
</aside>
```

id and class Values

In HTML5, the values for **id** and **class** attributes must contain one character (that is, they may not be empty) and may not contain any character spaces. You can use pretty much any character in the value.

Earlier versions of HTML had restrictions on **id** values (for example, they needed to start with a letter), but those restrictions were removed in HTML5.

Classification with class

The **class** attribute classifies elements into conceptual groups; therefore, unlike the **id** attribute, a **class** name may be shared by multiple elements. By making elements part of the same class, you can apply styles to all of the labeled elements at once with a single style rule or manipulate them all with a script. Let's start by classifying some elements in the earlier book example. In this first example, I've added **class** attributes to classify each **div** as a "listing" and to classify paragraphs as "descriptions":

```
<div id="ISBN0321127307" class="listing">
  <header>
  <img src="felici-cover.gif" alt="">
  <p><cite>The Complete Manual of Typography</cite>, James Felici</p>
  </header>
  <p class="description">A combination of type history and examples of
good and bad type.</p>
</div>

<div id="ISBN0881792063" class="listing">
  <header>
  <img src="bringhurst-cover.gif" alt="">
  <p><cite>The Elements of Typographic Style</cite>, Robert Bringhurst
</p>
  </header>
  <p class="description">This lovely, well-written book is concerned
foremost with creating beautiful typography.</p>
</div>
```

Notice how the same element may have both a **class** and an **id**. It is also possible for elements to belong to multiple classes. When there is a list of **class** values, simply separate them with character spaces. In this example, I've classified each **div** as a "book" to set them apart from possible "cd" or "dvd" listings elsewhere in the document:

```
<div id="ISBN0321127307" class="listing book">
  <img src="felici-cover.gif" alt="CMT cover">
  <p><cite>The Complete Manual of Typography</cite>, James Felici</p>
  <p class="description">A combination of type history and examples of
good and bad type.</p>
</div>

<div id="ISBN0881792063" class="listing book">
  <img src="bringhurst-cover.gif" alt="ETS cover">
  <p><cite>The Elements of Typographic Style</cite>, Robert Bringhurst
</p>
  <p class="description">This lovely, well-written book is concerned
  foremost with creating beautiful typography.</p>
</div>
```

Identify and Classify All Elements

The **id** and **class** attributes are not limited to just **div** and **span**—they are two of the global attributes (see the "**Global Attributes**" sidebar) in HTML,

---

■ **MARKUP TIP**

Use the **id** attribute to *identify*.

Use the **class** attribute to *classify*.

Global Attributes

HTML5 defines a set of attributes that can be used with every HTML element. They are called the global attributes:

> accesskey
>
> class
>
> contenteditable
>
> dir
>
> draggable
>
> hidden
>
> id
>
> lang
>
> spellcheck
>
> style
>
> tabindex
>
> title
>
> translate

Appendix B lists all of the global attributes, their values, and definitions.

which means you may use them with all HTML elements. For example, you could identify an ordered list as "directions" instead of wrapping it in a **div**:

```
<ol id="directions">
  <li>...</li>
  <li>...</li>
  <li>...</li>
</ol>
```

This should have given you a good introduction to how to use the **class** and **id** attributes to add meaning and organization to documents. We'll work with them even more in the style sheet chapters in **Part III**. The sidebar **"Structured Data in a Nutshell"** discusses more advanced ways of adding meaning and machine-readable data to documents.

IMPROVING ACCESSIBILITY WITH ARIA

As web designers, we must always consider the experience of users with assistive technologies for navigating pages and interacting with web applications. Your users may be listening to the content on the page read aloud by a screen reader and using keyboards, joysticks, voice commands, or other non-mouse input devices to navigate through the page.

Many HTML elements are plainly understood when you look at (or read) only the HTML source. Elements like the title, headings, lists, images, and tables have implicit meanings in the context of a page, but generic elements like **div** and **span** lack the semantics necessary to be interpreted by an assistive device. In rich web applications, especially those that rely heavily on JavaScript and AJAX (see **Note**), the markup alone does not provide enough clues as to how elements are being used or whether a form control is currently selected, required, or in some other state.

Fortunately, we have ARIA (Accessible Rich Internet Applications), a standardized set of attributes for making pages easier to navigate and interactive features easier to use. The specification was created and is maintained by a Working Group of the Web Accessibility Initiative (WAI), which is why you also hear it referred to as WAI-ARIA. ARIA defines roles, states, and properties that developers can add to markup and scripts to provide richer semantic information.

Roles

Roles describe an element's function or purpose in the context of the document. Some roles include **alert**, **button**, **dialog**, **slider**, and **menubar**, to name only a few. For example, as we saw earlier, you can turn an unordered list into a tabbed menu of options using style sheets, but what if you can't *see* that it is styled that way? Adding **role="toolbar"** to the list makes its purpose clear:

NOTE

AJAX (Asynchronous JavaScript and XML) is explained in a sidebar in **Chapter 22, Using JavaScript**.

Structured Data in a Nutshell

It is pretty easy for us humans to tell the difference between a recipe and a movie review. For search engines and other computer programs, however, it's not so obvious. When we use HTML alone, all browsers see is paragraphs, headings, and other semantic elements of a document. Enter structured data! Structured data allows content to be machine-readable as well, which helps search engines provide smarter, user-friendly results and can provide a better user experience—for example, by extracting event information from a page and adding it to the user's calendar app.

There are several standards for structured data, but they share a similar approach. First, they identify and name the "thing" being presented. Then they point out the properties of that thing. The "thing" might be a person, an event, a product, a movie…pretty much anything you can imagine seeing on a web page. Properties consist of name/value pairs. For example, "actor," "director," and "duration" are properties of a movie. The values of those properties appear as the content of an HTML element. A collection of the standardized terms assigned to "things," as well as their respective properties, form what is called a vocabulary.

The most popular standards for adding structured data are Microformats, Microdata, RDFa (and RDFa Lite), and JSON-LD. They differ in the syntax they use to add information about objects and their properties.

Microformats

microformats.org

This early effort to make web content more useful created standardized values for the existing **id**, **class**, and **rel** HTML attributes. It is not a documented standard, but it is a convention that is in widespread use because it is very simple to implement. There are about a dozen stable Microformat vocabularies for defining people, organizations, events, products, and more. Here is a short example of how a person might be marked up using Microformats:

```
<div class="h-card">
  <p class="p-name">Cindy Sherman</p>
  <p class="p-tel">555.999-2456</p>
</div>
```

Microdata

html.spec.whatwg.org/multipage/microdata.html

Microdata is a WHATWG (Web Hypertext Application Technology Working Group) HTML standard that uses microdata-specific attributes (**itemscope**, **itemtype**, **itemprop**, **itemid**, and **itemref**) to define objects and their properties. Here is an example of a person defined using Microdata.

```
<div itemscope itemtype="http://schema.org/Person">
  <p itemprop="name">Cindy Sherman</p>
  <p itemprop="telephone">555.999-2456</p>
</div>
```

For more information on the WHATWG, see **Appendix D, From HTML+ to HTML5**.

RDFa and RDFa Lite

www.w3.org/TR/xhtml-rdfa-primer/

The W3C dropped Microdata from the HTML5 spec in 2013, putting all of its structured data efforts behind RDFa (Resource Description Framework in Attributes) and its simplified subset, RDFa Lite. It uses specified attributes (**vocab**, **typeof**, **property**, **resource**, and **prefix**) to enhance HTML content. Here is that same person marked up with RDFa:

```
<div vocab="http://schema.org" typeof="Person">
  <p property="name">Cindy Sherman</p>
  <p property="telephone">555.999-2456</p>
</div>
```

JSON-LD

json-ld.org

JSON-LD (JavaScript Object Notation to serialize Linked Data) is a different animal in that it puts the object types and their properties in a script removed from the HTML markup. Here is the JSON-LD version of the same person:

```
<script type="application/ld+json">
{
  "@context": "http://schema.org/",
  "@type": "Person",
  "name": "Cindy Sherman"
  "telephone": "555.999-2456"
}
</script>
```

It is possible to make up your own vocabulary for use on your sites, but it is more powerful to use a standardized vocabulary. The big search engines have created Schema.org, a mega-vocabulary that includes standardized properties for hundreds of "things" like blog posts, movies, books, products, reviews, people, organizations, and so on. Schema.org vocabularies may be used with Microdata, RDFa, and JSON-LD (Microformats maintain their own separate vocabularies). You can see pointers to the Schema.org "Person" vocabulary in the preceding examples. For more information, the Schema.org "Getting Started" page provides an easy-to-read introduction: *schema.org/docs/gs.html*.

There is a lot more to say about structured data than I can fit in this book, but once you get the basic semantics of HTML down, it is definitely a topic worthy of further exploration.

```
<ul id="tabs" role="toolbar">
   <li>A-G</li>
   <li>H-O</li>
   <li>P-T</li>
   <li>U-Z</li>
</ul>
```

Here's another example that reveals that the "status" **div** is used as an alert message:

```
<div id="status" role="alert">You are no longer connected to the
server.</div>
```

Some roles describe "landmarks" that help readers find their way through the document, such as **navigation**, **banner**, **contentinfo**, **complementary**, and **main**. You may notice that some of these sound similar to the page-structuring elements that were added in HTML5, and that's no coincidence. One of the benefits of having improved semantic section elements is that they can be used as landmarks, replacing **<div id="main" role="main">** with **main**.

Most current browsers already recognize the implicit roles of the new elements, but some developers explicitly add ARIA roles until all browsers comply. The sectioning elements pair with the ARIA landmark roles in the following way:

```
<nav role="navigation">
```

```
<header role="banner">  (see Note)
```

```
<main role="main">
```

```
<aside role="complementary">
```

```
<footer role="contentinfo">
```

NOTE

The banner role is used when the **header** *applies to only the whole page, not just a section or article.*

States and Properties

ARIA also defines a long list of states and properties that apply to interactive elements such as form widgets and dynamic content. States and properties are indicated with attributes prefixed with **aria-**, such as **aria-disabled**, **aria-describedby**, and many more.

The difference between a state and property is subtle. For properties, the value of the attribute is more likely to be stable, such as **aria-labelledby**, which associates labels with their respective form controls, or **aria-haspopup**, which indicates the element has a related pop-up menu. States have values that are more likely to be changed as the user interacts with the element, such as **aria-selected**.

For Further Reading

Obviously, this is not enough ARIA coaching to allow you to start confidently using it today, but it should give you a good feel for how it works and its potential value. When you are ready to dig in and take your skills to a professional level, here is some recommended reading:

The WAI-ARIA Working Draft (*www.w3.org/TR/wai-aria-1.1/*)

This is the current Working Draft of the specification as of this writing.

ARIA in HTML (*www.w3.org/TR/html-aria/*)

This W3C Working Draft helps developers use ARIA attributes with HTML correctly. It features a great list of every HTML element, whether it has an implicit role (in which ARIA should *not* be used), and what roles, states, and properties apply.

ARIA Resources at MDN Web Docs

(*developer.mozilla.org/en-US/docs/Web/Accessibility/ARIA*)

This site features lots of links to ARIA-related and up-to-date resources. It is a good starting point for exploration.

HTML5 Accessibility (*www.html5accessibility.com*)

This site tests which new HTML5 features are accessibly supported by major browsers.

■ SPEC TIP

The W3C HTML specification now lists which ARIA roles and properties apply in the descriptions of every HTML element (*www.w3.org/TR/html52/*).

CHARACTER ESCAPES

There's just one more text-related topic before we close out this chapter. The section title makes it sound like someone left the gate open and all the characters got out. The real meaning is more mundane, albeit useful to know.

You already know that as a browser parses an HTML document, when it runs into a **<** symbol, it interprets it as the beginning of a tag. But what if you just need a less-than symbol in your text? Characters that might be misinterpreted as code need to be escaped in the source document. Escaping means that instead of typing in the character itself, you represent it by its numeric or named character entity reference. When the browser sees the character reference, it substitutes the proper character in that spot when the page is displayed.

There are two ways of referring to (escaping) a specific character:

- Using a predefined abbreviated name for the character (called a named entity; see **Note**).

- Using an assigned numeric value that corresponds to its position in a coded character set (numeric entity). Numeric values may be in decimal or hexadecimal format.

All character references begin with an **&** (ampersand) and end with a **;** (semicolon).

NOTE

HTML defines hundreds of named entities as part of the markup language, which is to say you can't make up your own entity.

An example should make this clear. I'd like to use a less-than symbol in my text, so I must use the named entity (**<**) or its numeric equivalent (**<**) where I want the symbol to appear (FIGURE 5-17):

```
<p>3 tsp. &lt; 3 Tsp.</p>
```

or:

```
<p>3 tsp. &#060; 3 Tsp.</p>
```

3 tsp. < 3 Tsp.

FIGURE 5-17. The special character is substituted for the character reference when the document is displayed in the browser.

When to Escape Characters

There are a few instances in which you may need or want to use a character reference.

HTML syntax characters

The <, >, &, ", and ' characters have special syntax meaning in HTML, and may be misinterpreted as code. Therefore, the W3C recommends that you escape <, >, and & characters in content. If attribute values contain single or double quotes, escaping the quote characters in the values is advised. Quote marks are fine in the content and do not need to be escaped. (See TABLE 5-2.)

TABLE 5-2. *Syntax characters and their character references*

Character	Description	Entity name	Decimal no.	Hexadecimal no.
<	Less-than symbol	&lt;	&#060;	&#x3C;
>	Greater-than symbol	&gt;	&#062;	&#x3E;
"	Quotation mark	&quot;	&#034;	&#x22;
'	Apostrophe	&apos;	&#039;	&#x27;
&	Ampersand	&amp;	&#038;	&#x26;

Invisible or ambiguous characters

Some characters have no graphic display and are difficult to see in the markup (TABLE 5-3). These include the non-breaking space (** **), which is used to ensure that a line doesn't break between two words. So, for instance, if I mark up my name like this:

```
Jennifer Robbins
```

I can be sure that my first and last names will always stay together on a line. Another use for non-breaking spaces is to separate digits in a long number, such as 32 000 000.

Zero-width space can be placed in languages that do not use spaces between words to indicate where the line should break. A zero-width joiner is a non-printing space that causes neighboring characters to display in their connected forms (common in Arabic and Indic languages). Zero-width non-joiners prevent neighboring characters from joining to form ligatures or other connected forms.

TABLE 5-3. *Invisible characters and their character references*

Character	Description	Entity name	Decimal no.	Hexadecimal no.
(non-printing)	Non-breaking space			
(non-printing)	En space			
(non-printing)	Em space			
(non-printing)	Zero-width space	(none)	&#8203;	&#x200B;
(non-printing)	Zero-width non-joiner	&zwnj;	&#8204;	&#x200C;
(non-printing)	Zero-width joiner	&zwj;	&#8205;	&#x200D;

Input limitations

If your keyboard or editing software does not include the character you need (or if you simply can't find it), you can use a character entity to make sure you get the character you want. The W3C doesn't endorse this practice, so use the proper character in your source if you are able. TABLE 5-4 lists some special characters that may be less straightforward to type into the source.

TABLE 5-4. *Special characters and their character references*

Character	Description	Entity name	Decimal no.	Hexadecimal no.
'	Left curly single quote	&lsquo;	&#8216;	&#x2018;
'	Right curly single quote	&rsquo;	&#8217;	&#x2019;
"	Left curly double quote	&ldquo;	&#8220;	&#x201C;
"	Right curly double quote	&rdquo;	&#8221;	&#x201D;
...	Horizontal ellipsis	&hellip;	&#8230;	&#x2026;
©	Copyright	&copy;	&#169;	&#xA9;
®	Registered trademark	&reg;	&#174;	&#xAE;
™	Trademark	&trade;	&#8482;	&#x2026;
£	Pound	&pound;	&#163;	&#xA3;
¥	Yen	&yen;	&#165;	&#xA5;
€	Euro	&euro;	&#8364;	&#x20AC;
–	En dash	&ndash;	&#8211;	&#x2013;
—	Em dash	&mdash;	&#8212;	&#x2014;

A complete list of HTML named entities and their Unicode code-points can be found as part of the HTML5 specification at *www.w3.org/TR/html5/syntax. html#named-character-references*. For a more user-friendly listing of named and numerical entities, I recommend this archived page at the Web Standards Project: *www.webstandards.org/learn/reference/charts/entities*.

PUTTING IT ALL TOGETHER

So far, you've learned how to mark up elements, and you've met all of the HTML elements for adding structure and meaning to text content. Now it's just a matter of practice. EXERCISE 5-3 gives you an opportunity to try out everything we've covered so far: document structure elements, grouping (block) elements, phrasing (inline) elements, sectioning elements, and character entities. Have fun!

EXERCISE 5-3. The Black Goose Bistro News page

Now that you've been introduced to all of the text elements, you can put them to work by marking up the News page for the Black Goose Bistro site. Get the starter text and finished markup files at *learningwebdesign.com/5e/materials*. Once you have the text, follow the instructions listed after it. The resulting page is shown in FIGURE 5-18.

```
The Black Goose Bistro News

Home
Menu
News
Contact

Summer Menu Items
posted by BGB, June 18, 2017
Our chef has been busy putting together the perfect menu for the summer
months. Stop by to try these appetizers and main courses while the days
are still long.

Appetizers
Black bean purses
Spicy black bean and a blend of Mexican cheeses wrapped in sheets of
phyllo and baked until golden. $3.95

Southwestern napoleons with lump crab -- new item!
Layers of light lump crab meat, bean and corn salsa, and our handmade
flour tortillas. $7.95

Main courses

Shrimp sate kebabs with peanut sauce
Skewers of shrimp marinated in lemongrass, garlic, and fish sauce then
grilled to perfection. Served with spicy peanut sauce and jasmine rice.
$12.95

Jerk rotisserie chicken with fried plantains -- new item!
Tender chicken slow-roasted on the rotisserie, flavored with spicy and
fragrant jerk sauce and served with fried plantains and fresh mango.
$12.95

Low and Slow
posted by BGB, November 15, 2016
<p>This week I am <em>extremely</em> excited about a new cooking
technique called <dfn><i>sous vide</i></dfn>. In <i>sous vide</i>
cooking, you submerge the food (usually vacuum-sealed in plastic) into a
water bath that is precisely set to the target temperature you want the
food to be cooked to. In his book, <cite>Cooking for Geeks</cite>, Jeff
Potter describes it as <q>ultra-low-temperature poaching.</q></p>

<p>Next month, we will be serving <b><i>Sous Vide</i> Salmon with Dill
Hollandaise</b>. To reserve a seat at the chef table, contact us before
<time datetime="20161130">November 30</time>.</p>

Location: Baker's Corner, Seekonk, MA
Hours: Tuesday to Saturday, 11am to 11pm

All content copyright 2017, Black Goose Bistro and Jennifer Robbins
```

■ MARKUP TIP

Remember that indenting each hierarchical level in your HTML source consistently makes the document easier to scan and update later.

NOTE

The "Low and Slow" paragraph is already marked up with the inline elements from EXERCISE 5-2*).*

The Black Goose Bistro News

- Home
- Menu
- News
- Contact

Summer Menu Items

posted by BGB, June 18, 2017

Our chef has been busy putting together the perfect menu for the summer months. Stop by to try these appetizers and main courses while the days are still long.

Appetizers

Black bean purses
    Spicy black bean and a blend of Mexican cheeses wrapped in sheets of phyl-lo and baked until golden. $3.95
Southwestern napoleons with lump crab — **new item!**
    Layers of light lump crab meat, bean and corn salsa, and our handmade flour tortillas. $7.95

Main courses

Shrimp sate kebabs with peanut sauce
    Skewers of shrimp marinated in lemongrass, garlic, and fish sauce then grilled to perfection. Served with spicy peanut sauce and jasmine rice. $12.95
Jerk rotisserie chicken with fried plantains — **new item!**
    Tender chicken slow-roasted on the rotisserie, flavored with spicy and fragrant jerk sauce and served with fried plantains and fresh mango. $12.95

Low and Slow

posted by BGB, November 15, 2016

This week I am *extremely* excited about a new cooking technique called *sous vide*. In *sous vide* cooking, you submerge the food (usually vacuum-sealed in plastic) into a water bath that is precisely set to the target temperature you want the food to be cooked to. In his book, *Cooking for Geeks*, Jeff Potter describes it as "ultra-low-temperature poaching."

Next month, we will be serving *Sous Vide Salmon with Dill Hollandaise*. To reserve a seat at the chef table, contact us before November 30.

Location:
Baker's Corner, Seekonk, MA

Hours:
Tuesday to Saturday, 11am to 11pm

All content copyright © 2017, Black Goose Bistro and Jennifer Robbins

---

FIGURE 5-18. The finished menu page.

1. Start by adding the DOCTYPE declaration to tell browsers this is an HTML5 document.

2. Add all the document structure elements first (**html**, **head**, **meta**, **title**, and **body**). Give the document the title "The Black Goose Bistro News."

3. The first thing we'll do is identify the top-level heading and the list of links as the header for the document by wrapping them in a **header** element (don't forget the closing tag). Within the header, the headline should be an **h1** and the list of links should be an unordered list (**ul**). Don't worry about making the list items links; we'll get to linking in the next chapter. Give the list more meaning by identifying it as the primary navigation for the site (**nav**).

4. The News page has two posts titled "Summer Menu Items" and "Low and Slow." Mark up each one as an article.

5. Now we'll get the first article into shape. Let's create a header for this article that contains the heading (**h2** this time because we've moved down in the document hierarchy) and the publication information (**p**). Identify the publication date for the article with the **time** element, just as in EXERCISE 5-2.

6. The content after the header is a simple paragraph. However, the menu has some interesting things going on. It is divided into two conceptual sections (Appetizers and Main Courses), so mark those up as section elements. Be careful that the final closing section tag (**</section>**) appears before the closing article tag (**</article>**) so the elements are nested correctly

and don't overlap. Finally, let's identify the sections with **id** attributes. Name the first one "appetizers" and the second "maincourses."

7. With our sections in place, now we can mark up the content. We're down to **h3** for the headings in each section. Choose the most appropriate list elements to describe the menu item names and their descriptions. Mark up the lists and each item within the lists.

8. Now we can add a few fine details. *Classify* each price as "price" using **span** elements.

9. Two of the dishes are new items. Change the double hyphens to an em dash character and mark up "new item!" as "strongly important." Classify the title of each new dish as "newitem" (use the existing **dt** element; there is no need to add a **span** this time). This allows us to target menu titles with the "newitem" class and style them differently than other menu items.

10. That takes care of the first article. The second article is already mostly marked up from the previous exercise, but you should mark up the header with the appropriate heading and publication date information.

11. So far, so good, right? Now make the remaining content that applies to the whole page a **footer**. Mark each line of content within the footer as a paragraph.

12. Let's give the location and hours information some context by putting them in a **div** named "about." Make the labels "Location" and "Hours" appear on a line by themselves by adding line breaks after them. Mark up the hours with the **time** element (you don't need the date or time zone portions).

13. Finally, copyright information is typically "small print" on a document, so mark it up accordingly. As the final touch, add a copyright symbol after the word "copyright" using the keyboard or the **©** character entity.

Save the as *bistro_news.html*, and check your page in a modern browser. You can also upload it to *validator.nu* and make sure it is valid (it's a great way to spot mistakes). How did you do?

▨ MARKUP TIPS

- Choose the element that best fits the meaning of the selected text.

- Don't forget to close elements with closing tags.

- Put all attribute values in quotation marks for clarity.

- "Copy and paste" is your friend when adding the same markup to multiple elements. Just be sure what you copied is correct before you paste it throughout the document.

TEST YOURSELF

Were you paying attention? Here is a rapid-fire set of questions to find out. Find the answers in **Appendix A**.

1. Add the markup to insert a thematic break between these paragraphs:

   ```
   <p>People who know me know that I love to cook.</p>

   <p>I've created this site to share some of my favorite recipes.</p>
   ```

2. What's the difference between a **blockquote** and a **q** element?

3. Which element displays whitespace exactly as it is typed into the source document?

4. What is the difference between a **ul** and an **ol** element?

5. How do you remove the bullets from an unordered list? (Be general, not specific.)

6. What element would you use to mark up "W3C" and provide its full name (World Wide Web Consortium)? Can you write out the complete markup?

7. What is the difference between **dl** and **dt**?

8. What is the difference between **id** and **class**?

9. What is the difference between an **article** and a **section**?

Want More Practice?

Try marking up your own résumé. Start with the raw text and add document structure elements, content grouping elements, and inline elements as we've done in EXERCISE 5-3. If you don't see an element that matches your information just right, try creating one using a **div** or a **span**.

ELEMENT REVIEW: TEXT ELEMENTS

The global attributes apply to all text elements. Additional attributes are listed under their respective elements.

Page sections

address	Author contact information
article	Self-contained content
aside	Tangential content (sidebar)
footer	Related content
header	Introductory content
nav	Primary navigation
section	Conceptually related group of content

Heading content

h1...h6	Headings, levels 1 through 6

Grouping content elements and attributes

blockquote	Blockquote
cite	The URL of the cited content
div	Generic division
figure	Related image or resource
figcaption	Text description of a figure
hr	Paragraph-level thematic break (horizontal rule)
main	Primary content area of page or app
p	Paragraph
pre	Preformatted text

List elements and attributes

dd	Definition
dl	Definition list
dt	Term
li	List item (for **ul** and **ol**)
value	Provides a number for an **li** in an **ol**
ol	Ordered list
reversed	Numbers the list in reverse order
start	Provides the starting number for the list
ul	Unordered list

Breaks

br	Line break
wbr	Word break

Phrasing elements and attributes

abbr	Abbreviation
b	Added visual attention (bold)
bdi	Bidirectional isolation
bdo	Bidirectional override
cite	Citation
code	Code sample
data	Machine-readable equivalent
del	Deleted text
cite	The URL of cited content.
datetime	Specifies the date and time of a change
dfn	Defining term
em	Stress emphasis
i	Alternate voice (italic)
ins	Inserted text
cite	The URL of cited content
datetime	Specifies the date and time of a change
kbd	Keyboard input
mark	Highlighted text
q	Short inline quotation
cite	The URL of the cited content
ruby	Section containing ruby text
rp	Parentheses in ruby text
rt	Ruby annotation
s	Strike-through; incorrect text
samp	Sample output
small	Annotation; "small print"
span	Generic phrase of text
strong	Strong importance
sub	Subscript
sup	Superscript
time	Machine-readable time data
datetime	Provides machine readable date/time
pubdate	Indicates the time refers to publication
u	Added attention (underline)

ADDING LINKS

If you're creating a page for the web, chances are you'll want to link to other web pages and resources, whether on your own site or someone else's. Linking, after all, is what the web is all about. In this chapter, we'll look at the markup that makes links work—links to other sites, to your own site, and within a page. There is one element that makes linking possible: the anchor (**a**).

`<a>…</a>`

Anchor element (hypertext link)

To make a selection of text a link, simply wrap it in opening and closing `<a>...</a>` tags and use the **href** attribute to provide the URL of the target page. The content of the anchor element becomes the hypertext link. Here is an example that creates a link to the O'Reilly Media site:

```
<a href="http://www.oreilly.com">Go to the O'Reilly Media site</a>
```

To make an image a link, simply put the **img** element in the anchor element:

```
<a href="http://www.oreilly.com"><img src="tarsierlogo.gif"
alt="O'Reilly Media site"></a>
```

By the way, you can put any HTML content element in an anchor to make it a link, not just images.

Nearly all graphical browsers display linked text as blue and underlined by default. Some older browsers put a blue border around linked images, but most current ones do not. Visited links generally display in purple. Users can change these colors in their browser preferences, and, of course, you can change the appearance of links for your sites using style sheets. I'll show you how in **Chapter 13, Colors and Backgrounds**.

When a user clicks or taps the linked text or image, the page you specify in the anchor element loads in the browser window. The linked image markup sample shown previously might look like FIGURE 6-1.

IN THIS CHAPTER

Linking to external pages

Linking to documents on your own server

Linking to a specific point in a page

Targeting new windows

◼ **USABILITY TIP**

One word of caution: if you choose to change your link colors, keep them consistent throughout your site so as not to confuse your users.

FIGURE 6-1. When a user clicks or taps the linked text or image, the page specified in the anchor element loads in the browser window.

THE HREF ATTRIBUTE

You'll need to tell the browser which document to link to, right? The **href** (hypertext reference) attribute provides the address of the page or resource (its URL) to the browser. The URL must always appear in quotation marks. Most of the time you'll point to other HTML documents; however, you can also point to other web resources, such as images, audio, and video files.

Because there's not much to slapping anchor tags around some content, the real trick to linking comes in getting the URL correct. There are two ways to specify the URL:

Absolute URLs

Absolute URLs provide the full URL for the document, including the protocol (**http://** or **https://**), the domain name, and the pathname as necessary. You need to use an absolute URL when pointing to a document out on the web (i.e., not on your own server):

```
href="http://www.oreilly.com/"
```

Sometimes, when the page you're linking to has a long URL pathname, the link can end up looking pretty confusing (FIGURE 6-2). Just keep in mind that the structure is still a simple container element with one attribute. Don't let the long pathname intimidate you.

Relative URLs

Relative URLs describe the pathname to a file *relative* to the current document. Relative URLs can be used when you are linking to another document on your own site (i.e., on the same server). It doesn't require the protocol or domain name—just the pathname:

```
href="recipes/index.html"
```

In this chapter, we'll add links using absolute and relative URLs to my cooking website, Jen's Kitchen (see FIGURE 6-3). Absolute URLs are easy, so let's get them out of the way first.

■ AT A GLANCE

Anchor Structure

The simplified structure of the anchor element is as follows:

```
<a href="url">linked content</a>
```

■ MARKUP TIP

URL Wrangling

If you're linking to a page with a long URL, it's helpful to copy the URL from the location toolbar in your browser and paste it into your document. That way, you avoid mistyping a single character and breaking the whole link.

Opening anchor tag

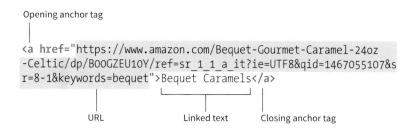

```
<a href="https://www.amazon.com/Bequet-Gourmet-Caramel-24oz
-Celtic/dp/B00GZEU10Y/ref=sr_1_1_a_it?ie=UTF8&qid=1467055107&s
r=8-1&keywords=bequet">Bequet Caramels</a>
```

URL   Linked text   Closing anchor tag

FIGURE 6-2. An example of a long URL. Although it may make the anchor tag look confusing, the structure is the same.

LINKING TO PAGES ON THE WEB

Many times, you'll want to create a link to a page that you've found on the web. This is known as an external link because it is going to a page outside of your own server or site. To make an external link, provide the absolute URL, beginning with **http://** (the protocol). This tells the browser, "Go out on the web and get the following document."

I want to add some external links to the Jen's Kitchen home page (FIGURE 6-3). First, I'll link the list item "The Food Network" to the *www.foodnetwork.com* site. I marked up the link text in an anchor element by adding opening and closing anchor tags. Notice that I've added the anchor tags *inside* the list item (**li**) element. That's because only **li** elements are permitted to be children of a **ul** element; placing an **a** element directly inside the **ul** element would be invalid HTML.

```
<li><a>The Food Network</a></li>
```

Next, I add the **href** attribute with the complete URL for the site:

```
<li><a href="http://www.foodnetwork.com">The Food Network</a></li>
```

And *voilà*! Now "The Food Network" appears as a link and takes my visitors to that site when they click or tap it. Give it a try in EXERCISE 6-1.

EXERCISE 6-1. Make an external link

Open the file *index.html* from the *jenskitchen* folder. Make the list item "Epicurious" link to its web page at *www.epicurious.com*, following my Food Network link example:

```
<ul>
  <li><a href="http://www.foodnetwork.com/">The Food Network</a></li>
  <li>Epicurious</li>
</ul>
```

When you are done, save *index.html* and open it in a browser. If you have an internet connection, you can click your new link and go to the Epicurious site. If the link doesn't take you there, go back and make sure that you didn't miss anything in the markup.

LINKING WITHIN YOUR OWN SITE

A large portion of the linking you do is between pages of your own site: from the home page to section pages, from section pages to content pages, and so on. In these cases, you can use a relative URL—one that calls for a page on your own server.

Without "http://", the browser looks on the current server for the linked document. A pathname, the notation used to point to a particular file or directory, (see **Note**) tells the browser where to find the file. Web pathnames follow the Unix convention of separating directory and filenames with forward slashes (/). A relative pathname describes how to get to the linked document starting from the location of the current document.

Relative pathnames can get a bit tricky. In my teaching experience, nothing stumps beginners like writing relative pathnames, so we'll take it one step at a time. I recommend you do EXERCISES 6-2 through 6-8 as we go along.

All of the pathname examples in this section are based on the structure of the Jen's Kitchen site shown in FIGURE 6-4. When you diagram the structure of the directories for a site, it generally ends up looking like an inverted tree with the root directory at the top of the hierarchy. For the Jen's Kitchen site, the root directory is named *jenskitchen*. For another way to look at it, there is also a view of the directory and subdirectories as they appear in the Finder on my Mac.

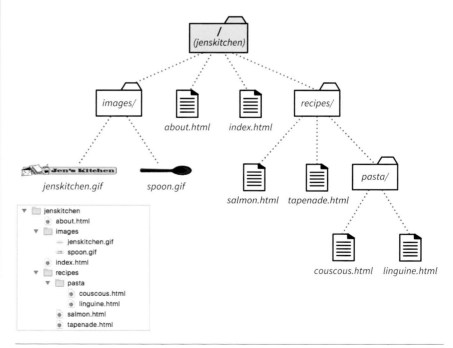

FIGURE 6-4. A diagram of the *jenskitchen* site structure.

NOTE

On PCs and Macs, files are organized into "folders," but in the web development world, it is more common to refer to the equivalent and more technical term "directory." A folder is just a directory with a cute icon.

Important Pathname Don'ts

When writing relative pathnames, follow these rules to avoid common errors:

- Don't use backslashes (\). Web URL pathnames use forward slashes (/) only.

- Don't start with the drive name (D:, C:, etc.). Although your pages will link to each other successfully while they are on your own computer, once they are uploaded to the web server, the drive name is irrelevant and will break your links.

- Don't start with file://. This also indicates that the file is local and causes the link to break when it is on the server.

Linking Within a Directory

The most straightforward relative URL points to another file within the same directory. When linking to a file in the same directory, you need to provide only the name of the file (its filename). When the URL is just a filename, the server looks in the current directory (that is, the directory that contains the document with the link) for the file.

In this example, I want to make a link from my home page (*index.html*) to a general information page (*about.html*). Both files are in the same directory (*jenskitchen*). So, from my home page, I can make a link to the information page by simply providing its filename in the URL (FIGURE 6-5):

```
<a href="about.html">About the site...</a>
```

EXERCISE 6-2 gives you a chance to mark up a simple link yourself.

A link to a filename indicates the linked file is in the same directory as the current document.

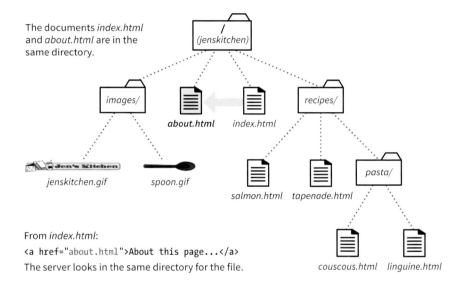

The documents *index.html* and *about.html* are in the same directory.

From *index.html*:
```
<a href="about.html">About this page...</a>
```
The server looks in the same directory for the file.

FIGURE 6-5. Writing a relative URL to another document in the same directory.

EXERCISE 6-2. Link in the same directory

Open the file *about.html* from the *jenskitchen* folder. Make the paragraph "Back to the home page" at the bottom of the page link back to *index.html*. The anchor element should be contained in the **p** element:

```
<p>Back to the home page</p>
```

When you are done, save *about.html* and open it in a browser. You don't need an internet connection to test links locally (that is, on your own computer). Clicking the link should take you back to the home page.

Linking to a Lower Directory

But what if the files aren't in the same directory? You have to give the browser directions by including the pathname in the URL. Let's see how this works.

Getting back to our example, my recipe files are stored in a subdirectory called *recipes*. I want to make a link from *index.html* to a file in the *recipes* directory called *salmon.html*. The pathname in the URL tells the browser to look in the current directory for a directory called *recipes*, and then look for the file *salmon.html* (FIGURE 6-6):

```
<li><a href="recipes/salmon.html">Garlic Salmon</a></li>
```

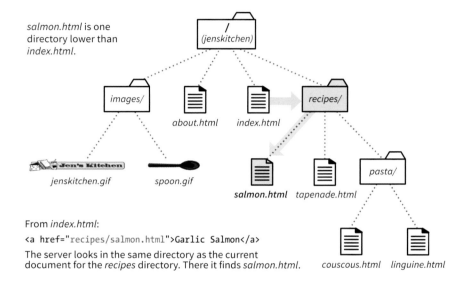

salmon.html is one directory lower than *index.html*.

From *index.html*:

```
<a href="recipes/salmon.html">Garlic Salmon</a>
```

The server looks in the same directory as the current document for the *recipes* directory. There it finds *salmon.html*.

FIGURE 6-6. Writing a relative URL to a document that is one directory level lower than the current document.

Have a try at linking to a file in a directory in EXERCISE 6-3.

EXERCISE 6-3. Link to a file in a directory

Open the file *index.html* from the *jenskitchen* folder. Make the list item "Tapenade (Olive Spread)" link to the file *tapenade.html* in the *recipes* directory. Remember to nest the elements correctly:

```
<li>Tapenade (Olive Spread)</li>
```

When you are done, save *index.html* and open it in a browser. You should be able to click your new link and see the recipe page for tapenade. If not, make sure that your markup is correct and that the directory structure for *jenskitchen* matches the examples.

Now let's link down to the file called *couscous.html*, which is located in the *pasta* subdirectory. All we need to do is provide the directions through two subdirectories (*recipes*, then *pasta*) to *couscous.html* (FIGURE 6-7):

```
<li><a href="recipes/pasta/couscous.html">Couscous...</a></li>
```

Directories are separated by forward slashes. The resulting anchor tag tells the browser, "Look in the current directory for a directory called *recipes*. There you'll find a directory called *pasta*, and in there is the file *couscous.html*."

Now that we've done two directory levels, you should get the idea of how pathnames are assembled. This same method applies for relative pathnames that drill down through any number of directories. Just start with the name of the directory that is in the same location as the current file, and follow each directory name with a slash until you get to the linked filename.

When you link to a file in a lower directory, the pathname contains the names of each subdirectory you go through to get to the file.

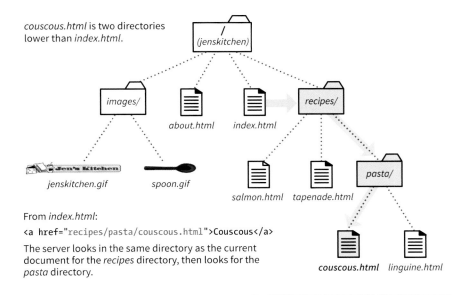

couscous.html is two directories lower than index.html.

From *index.html*:

```
<a href="recipes/pasta/couscous.html">Couscous</a>
```

The server looks in the same directory as the current document for the *recipes* directory, then looks for the *pasta* directory.

FIGURE 6-7. Writing a relative URL to a document that is two directory levels lower than the current document. You can try it yourself in EXERCISE 6-4.

EXERCISE 6-4. Link two directories down

Open the file *index.html* from the *jenskitchen* folder. Make the list item "Linguine with Clam Sauce" link to the file *linguine.html* in the *pasta* directory:

```
<li>Linguine with Clam Sauce</li>
```

When you are done, save *index.html* and open it in a browser. Click the new link to get the delicious recipe.

Linking to a Higher Directory

So far, so good, right? Now it gets more interesting. This time we're going to go in the other direction and make a link from the salmon recipe page back to the home page, which is one directory level up.

In Unix, there is a pathname convention just for this purpose, the "dot-dot-slash" (**../**). When you begin a pathname with **../**, it's the same as telling the browser "back up one directory level" and then follow the path to the specified file. If you are familiar with browsing files on your desktop, it is helpful to know that a "**../**" has the same effect as clicking the Up button in Windows Explorer or the left-arrow button in the Finder on macOS.

Let's start by making a link from *salmon.html* back to the home page (*index.html*). Because *salmon.html* is in the *recipes* subdirectory, we need to go back up to the *jenskitchen* directory to find *index.html*. This pathname tells the browser to "back up one level," then look in that directory for *index.html* (FIGURE 6-8):

```
<p><a href="../index.html">[Back to home page]</a></p>
```

Note that the **../** stands in for the name of the higher directory, and we don't need to write out *jenskitchen* in the pathname.

Each ../ at the beginning of the pathname tells the browser to go up one directory level to look for the file.

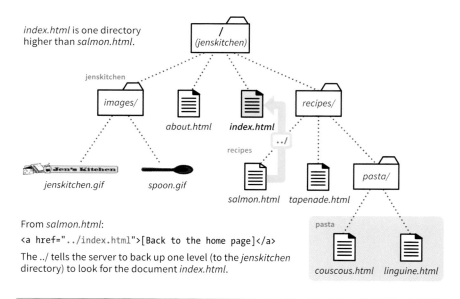

index.html is one directory higher than *salmon.html*.

From *salmon.html*:
```
<a href="../index.html">[Back to the home page]</a>
```
The ../ tells the server to back up one level (to the *jenskitchen* directory) to look for the document *index.html*.

FIGURE 6-8. Writing a relative URL to a document that is one directory level higher than the current document.

Try adding a dot-dot-slash pathname to a higher directory in EXERCISE 6-5.

But how about linking back to the home page from *couscous.html*? Can you guess how you'd back your way out of two directory levels? Simple: just use the dot-dot-slash twice (FIGURE 6-9).

A link on the *couscous.html* page back to the home page (*index.html*) would look like this:

```
<p><a href="../../index.html">[Back to home page]</a></p>
```

The first **../** backs up to the *recipes* directory; the second **../** backs up to the top-level directory (*jenskitchen*), where *index.html* can be found. Again, there is no need to write out the directory names; the **../** does it all.

Now you try (EXERCISE 6-6).

NOTE

*I confess to still sometimes silently chanting "go-up-a-level, go-up-a-level" for each **../** when trying to decipher a complicated relative URL. It helps me sort things out.*

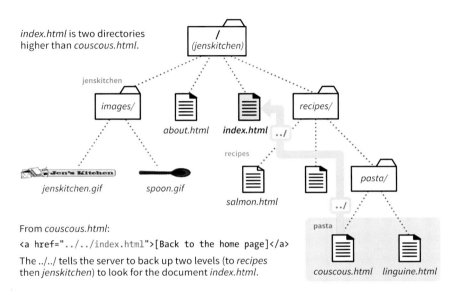

FIGURE 6-9. Writing a relative URL to a document that is two directory levels higher than the current document.

EXERCISE 6-5. Link to a higher directory

Open the file *tapenade.html* from the *recipes* directory. At the bottom of the page, you'll find this paragraph:

```
<p>[Back to the home page]</p>
```

Using the notation described in this section, make this text link back to the home page (*index.html*), located one directory level up.

EXERCISE 6-6. Link up two directory levels

OK, now it's your turn to give it a try. Open the file *linguine.html* and make the last paragraph link back to the home page by using **../../** as I have done:

```
<p>[Back to the home page]</p>
```

When you are done, save the file and open it in a browser. You should be able to link to the home page.

Linking with Site Root Relative Pathnames

All sites have a root directory, the directory that contains all the directories and files for the site. So far, all of the pathnames we've looked at are relative to the document with the link. Another way to write a relative pathname is to start at the root directory and list the subdirectory names to the file you want to link to. This type of pathname is known as site root relative.

In the Unix pathname convention, a forward slash (/) at the start of the pathname indicates that the path begins at the root directory. The site root relative pathname in the following link reads, "Go to the very top-level directory for this site, open the *recipes* directory, and then find the *salmon.html* file" (FIGURE 6-10):

```
<a href="/recipes/salmon.html">Garlic Salmon</a>
```

Site root relative links are generally preferred because of their flexibility.

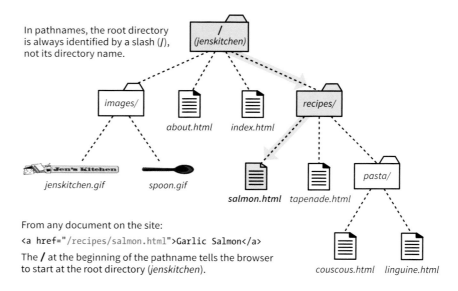

In pathnames, the root directory is always identified by a slash (/), not its directory name.

From any document on the site:
```
<a href="/recipes/salmon.html">Garlic Salmon</a>
```
The **/** at the beginning of the pathname tells the browser to start at the root directory (*jenskitchen*).

FIGURE 6-10. Writing a relative URL starting at the root directory.

WARNING

Site root relative pathnames won't work on your local computer unless it is set up as a server.

Note that you don't need to (and you shouldn't) write the name of the root directory (*jenskitchen*) in the path—the forward slash (/) at the beginning represents the top-level directory in the pathname. From there, just specify the directories the browser should look in.

Because this type of link starts at the root to describe the pathname, it works from any document on the server, regardless of which subdirectory it may be located in. Site root relative links are useful for content that might not always be in the same directory, or for dynamically generated material. They also make it easy to copy and paste links between documents.

On the downside, however, the links won't work on your local machine, because they will be relative to your hard drive. You'll have to wait until the site is on the final server to check that links are working.

Writing Pathnames to Images

The `src` attribute in the `img` element works the same as the `href` attribute in anchors. Because you'll most likely be using images from your own server, the `src` attributes within your image elements will be set to relative URLs.

Let's look at a few examples from the Jen's Kitchen site. First, to add an image to the *index.html* page, you'd use the following markup:

```
<img src="images/jenskitchen.gif" alt="">
```

The URL says, "Look in the current directory (*jenskitchen*) for the *images* directory; in there you will find *jenskitchen.gif*."

Now for the *pièce de résistance*. Let's add an image to the file *couscous.html*:

```
<img src="../../images/spoon.gif" alt="">
```

This is a little more complicated than what we've seen so far. This pathname tells the browser to go up two directory levels to the top-level directory and, once there, look in the *images* directory for an image called *spoon.gif*. Whew!

Of course, you could simplify that path by going the site root relative route, in which case the pathname to *spoon.gif* (and any other file in the *images* directory) could be accessed like this:

```
<img src="/images/spoon.gif" alt="">
```

The trade-off is that you won't see the image in place until the site is uploaded to the server, but it does make maintenance easier once it's there.

EXERCISE 6-7. Try a few more

Before we move on, you may want to try your hand at writing a few more relative URLs to make sure you've really gotten it. You can write your answers here in the book, or if you want to test your markup to see whether it works, make changes in the actual files. Note that the text shown here isn't included on the exercise pages—you'll need to add it before you can create the link (for example, type in "Go to the Tapenade recipe" for the first question). The final code is in the finished exercise files in the *materials* folder for this chapter. I also included them in **Appendix A**.

1. Create a link on *salmon.html* to *tapenade.html*:

   Go to the Tapenade recipe

2. Create a link on *couscous.html* to *salmon.html*:

   Try this with Garlic Salmon.

3. Create a link on *tapenade.html* to *linguine.html*:

   Try the Linguine with Clam Sauce

4. Create a link on *linguine.html* to *about.html*:

   About Jen's Kitchen

5. Create a link on *tapenade.html* to *www.allrecipes.com*:

   Go to Allrecipes.com

NOTE

Most of the pathnames in EXERCISE *6-7 could be site root relative, but write them relative to the listed document for the practice.*

Linking to a Specific Point in a Page

Did you know you can link to a specific point in a web page? This is useful for providing shortcuts to information at the bottom of a long, scrolling page or for getting back to the top of a page with just one click or tap. Linking to a specific point in the page is also known as linking to a document fragment.

Linking to a particular spot within a page is a two-part process. First, identify the destination, and then make a link to it. In the following example, I create an alphabetical index at the top of the page that links down to each alphabetical section of a glossary page (FIGURE 6-11). When users click the letter H, they'll jump to the "H" heading lower on the page.

Step 1: Identifying the destination

I like to think of this step as planting a flag in the document so I can get back to it easily. To create a destination, use the **id** attribute to give the target element in the document a unique name (that's "unique" as in the name may appear only once in the document, not "unique" as in funky and interesting). In web lingo, this is the fragment identifier.

You may remember the **id** attribute from **Chapter 5, Marking Up Text**, where we used it to name generic **div** and **span** elements. Here, we're going to use it to name an element so that it can serve as a fragment identifier—that is, the destination of a link.

Here is a sample of the source for the glossary page. Because I want users to be able to link directly to the "H" heading, I'll add the **id** attribute to it and give it the value "startH" (FIGURE 6-11 ❶):

```
<h2 id="startH">H</h2>
```

Step 2: Linking to the destination

With the identifier in place, now I can make a link to it.

At the top of the page, I'll create a link down to the "startH" fragment ❷. As for any link, I use the **a** element with the **href** attribute to provide the location of the link. To indicate that I'm linking to a fragment, I use the octothorpe symbol (**#**), also called a hash, pound, or number symbol, before the fragment name:

```
<p>... F | G | <a href="#startH">H</a> | I | J ...</p>
```

And that's it. Now when someone clicks the H from the listing at the top of the page, the browser will jump down and display the section starting with the "H" heading ❸.

NOTE

Linking to another spot on the same page works well for long, scrolling pages, but the effect may be lost on a short web page.

Fragment names are preceded by an octothorpe symbol (#).

① Identify the destination by using the **id** attribute.

```
<h2 id="startH">H</h2>
<dl>
<dt>hexadecimal</dt>
...
```

② Create a link to the destination. The # before the name is necessary to identify this as a fragment and not a filename.

```
<p>... | F | G | <a href="#startH">H</a> | I | J ...</p>
```

③

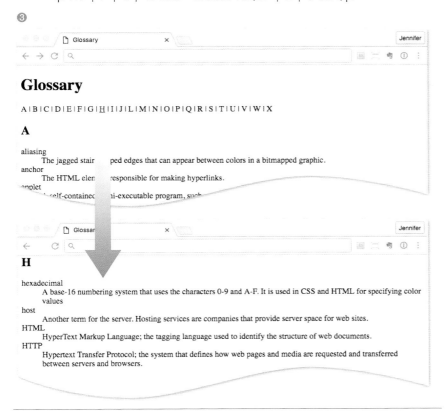

> ■ **USABILITY TIP**
>
> ## To the Top!
>
> It is common practice to add a link back up to the top of the page when linking into a long page of text. This alleviates the need for users to scroll back after every link.

FIGURE 6-11. Linking to a specific destination (a fragment) within a single web page.

Linking to a Fragment in Another Document

You can link to a fragment in another document by adding the fragment name to the end of the URL (absolute or relative). For example, to make a link to the "H" heading of the glossary page from another document in that directory, the URL would look like this:

```
<a href="glossary.html#startH">See the Glossary, letter H</a>
```

You can even link to specific destinations in pages on other sites by putting the fragment identifier at the end of an absolute URL, like so:

```
<a href="http://www.example.com/glossary.html#startH">See the Glossary,
letter H</a>
```

> **NOTE**
>
> *Some developers help their brothers and sisters out by proactively adding **id**s as anchors at the beginning of any thematic section of content (within a reasonable level, and depending on the site). That way, other people can link back to any section in their content.*

EXERCISE 6-8.
Linking to a fragment

Want some practice linking to specific destinations? Open *glossary.html* in the *materials* folder for this chapter. It looks just like the document in FIGURE 6-11.

1. Identify the **h2** "A" as a destination for a link by naming it "startA" with an **id** attribute:

   ```
   <h2 id="startA">A</h2>
   ```

2. Make the letter A at the top of the page a link to the identified fragment. Don't forget the **#**:

   ```
   <a href="#startA">A</a>
   ```

   Repeat Steps 1 and 2 for every letter across the top of the page until you really know what you're doing (or until you can't stand it anymore). You can help users get back to the top of the page, too.

3. Make the heading "Glossary" a destination named "top":

   ```
   <h1 id="top">Glossary</h1>
   ```

4. Add a paragraph element containing "TOP" at the end of each lettered section. Make "TOP" a link to the identifier that you just made at the top of the page:

   ```
   <p><a href="#top">TOP</a></p>
   ```

Copy and paste this code to the end of every letter section. Now your readers can get back to the top of the page easily throughout the document.

Of course, you don't have any control over the named fragments in other people's web pages. The destination points must be inserted by the author of those documents in order for them to be available to you. The only way to know whether they are there and where they are is to "View Source" for the page and look for them in the markup. If the fragments in external documents move or go away, the page will still load; the browser will just go to the top of the page as it does for regular links.

EXERCISE 6-8 gives you an opportunity to add links to fragments in the example glossary page.

TARGETING A NEW BROWSER WINDOW

One problem with putting links on your page is that when people click them, they may never come back to your content. The traditional solution to this dilemma has been to make the linked page open in a new browser window. That way, your visitors can check out the link and still have your content available where they left it.

Be aware that opening new browser windows can cause hiccups in the user experience of your site. Opening new windows is problematic for accessibility, and may be confusing to some users. They might not be able to tell that a new window has opened or they may never find their way back to the original page. At the very least, new windows may be perceived as an annoyance rather than a convenience. So consider carefully whether you need a new window and whether the benefits outweigh the potential drawbacks.

The method you use to open a link in a new browser window depends on whether you want to control its size. If the size of the window doesn't matter, you can use HTML markup alone. However, if you want to open the new window with particular pixel dimensions, then you need to use JavaScript (see the **"Pop-up Windows"** sidebar).

Pop-up Windows

It is possible to open a browser window to specific dimensions and with parts of the browser chrome (toolbars, scrollbars, etc.) turned on or off, but you know what…I'm not going to go into that here. First of all, it requires JavaScript. Second, in the era of mobile devices, opening a new browser window at a particular pixel size is an antiquated technique. People often turn off pop-up windows anyway.

For what it's worth, the little interstitial panels you see popping up on every web page asking you to sign up for a mailing list or showing you an ad are done with HTML elements and JavaScript, not a whole new browser window, so that is an entirely different beast.

That said, if you have a legitimate reason for opening a browser window to a specific size, I will refer you to this tutorial by Peter-Paul Koch at Quirksmode: *www.quirksmode.org/js/popup.html*.

To open a new window with markup, use the **target** attribute in the anchor (**a**) element to tell the browser the name of the window in which you want the linked document to open. Set the value of target to **_blank** or to any name of your choosing. Remember that with this method, you have no control over the size of the window, but it will generally open as a new tab or in a new window the same size as the most recently opened window in the user's browser. The new window may or may not be brought to the front depending on the browser and device used.

Setting **target="_blank"** always causes the browser to open a fresh window. For example:

```
<a href="http://www.oreilly.com" target="_blank">O'Reilly</a>
```

If you include **target="_blank"** for every link, every link will launch a new window, potentially leaving your user with a mess of open windows. There's nothing wrong with it, per se, as long as it is not overused.

Another method is to give the target window a specific name, which can then be used by subsequent links. You can give the window any name you like ("new," "sample," whatever), as long as it doesn't start with an underscore. The following link will open a new window called "display":

```
<a href="http://www.oreilly.com" target="display">O'Reilly</a>
```

If you target the "display" window from every link on the page, each linked document will open in the same second window. Unfortunately, if that second window stays hidden behind the user's current window, it may look as though the link simply didn't work.

You can decide which method (a new window for every link or reusing named windows) is most appropriate for your content and interface.

MAIL LINKS

Here's a nifty little linking trick: the **mailto** link. By using the **mailto** protocol in a link, you can link to an email address. When the user clicks a **mailto** link, the browser opens a new mail message preaddressed to that address in a designated mail program (see the **"Spam-Bots"** sidebar).

A sample **mailto** link is shown here:

```
<a href="mailto:alklecker@example.com">Contact Al Klecker</a>
```

As you can see, it's a standard anchor element with the **href** attribute. But the value is set to **mailto:**_name@address.com_.

The browser has to be configured to launch a mail program, so the effect won't work for 100% of your audience. If you use the email address itself as the linked text, nobody will be left out if the **mailto** function does not work (a nice little example of progressive enhancement).

Spam-Bots

Be aware that putting an email address in your document source makes it susceptible to receiving unsolicited junk email (known as spam). People who generate spam lists sometimes use automated search programs (called bots) to scour the web for email addresses.

If you want your email address to display on the page so that humans can figure it out but robots can't, you can deconstruct the address in a way that is still understandable to people—for example, "you [-at-] example [dot] com."

That trick won't work in a **mailto** link, because the accurate email address must be provided as an attribute value. One solution is to encrypt the email address by using JavaScript. The Enkoder Form at Hivelogic (_hivelogic.com/enkoder/_) does this for you. Simply enter the link text and the email address, and Enkoder generates code that you can copy and paste into your document.

Otherwise, if you don't want to risk getting spammed, keep your email address out of your HTML document. Using a contact form is a good alternative (web forms are coming up in **Chapter 9, Forms**).

TELEPHONE LINKS

Keep in mind that the smartphones people are using to access your site can also be used to make phone calls! Why not save your visitors a step by letting them dial a phone number on your site simply by tapping on it on the page? The syntax uses the **tel:** protocol and is very simple:

```
<a href="tel:+01-800-555-1212">Call us free at (800) 555-1212</a>
```

When mobile users tap the link, what happens depends on the device: Android launches the phone app; BlackBerry and IE11 Mobile initiate the call immediately; and iOS launches a dialog box giving the option to call, message, or add the number to Contacts. Desktop browsers may launch a dialog box to switch apps (for example, to FaceTime on Safari) or they may ignore the link.

If you don't want any interruption on desktop browsers, you could use a CSS rule that hides the link for non-mobile devices (unfortunately, that is beyond the scope of this discussion).

There are a few best practices for using telephone links:

- It is recommended that you include the full international dialing number, including the country code, for the **tel:** value because there is no way of knowing where the user will be accessing your site.

- Also include the telephone number in the content of the link so that if the link doesn't work, the telephone number is still available.

- Android and iPhone have a feature that detects phone numbers and automatically turns them into links. Unfortunately, some 10-digit numbers that are not telephone numbers might get turned into links, too. If your document has strings of numbers that might get confused as phone numbers, you can turn auto-detection off by including the following **meta** element in the **head** of your document. This will also prevent them from overriding any styles you've applied to telephone links.

```
<meta name="format-detection" content="telephone=no">
```

TEST YOURSELF

The most important lesson in this chapter is how to write URLs for links and images. Here's another chance to brush up on your pathname skills.

Using the directory hierarchy shown in FIGURE 6-12, write out the markup for the following links and graphics.

This diagram should provide you with enough information to answer the questions. If you need hands-on work to figure them out, the directory structure is available in the *test* directory in the materials for this chapter. The

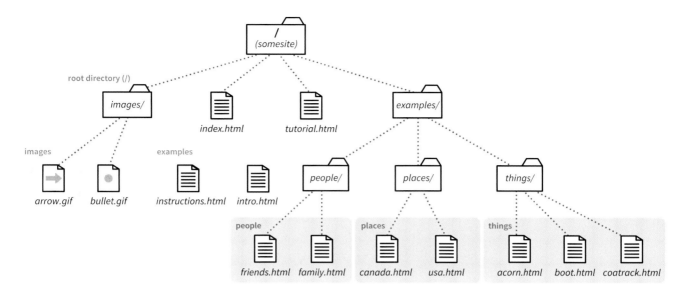

FIGURE 6-12. The directory structure for the "Test Yourself" questions.

documents are just dummy files and contain no content. I filled in the first one for you as an example. The answers are located in **Appendix A**.

1. In *index.html* (the site's home page), write the markup for a link to the *tutorial.html* page.

   ```
   <a href="tutorial.html">...</a>
   ```

2. In *index.html*, write the anchor element for a link to *instructions.html*.

3. Create a link to *family.html* from the page *tutorial.html*.

4. Create a link to *boot.html* from the *family.html* page, but this time, start with the root directory.

5. Create a link back to the home page (*index.html*) from *instructions.html*.

■ **MARKUP TIP**

The **../** (or multiples of them) always appears at the beginning of the pathname and never in the middle. If the pathnames you write have **../** in the middle, you've done something wrong.

6. Create a link to the website for this book (*learningwebdesign.com*) in the file *intro.html*.

7. Create a link to *instructions.html* from the page *usa.html*.

8. Create a link back to the home page (*index.html*) from *acorn.html*.

We haven't covered the image (**img**) element in detail yet, but you should be able to fill in the relative URLs after the **src** attribute to specify the location of the image files for these examples.

9. To place the graphic *arrow.gif* on the page *index.html*, use this URL:

```
<img src="                    " alt="">
```

10. To place the graphic *arrow.gif* on the page *intro.html*, use this URL:

```
<img src="                    " alt="">
```

11. To place the graphic *bullet.gif* on the *friends.html* page, use this URL:

```
<img src="                    " alt="">
```

ELEMENT REVIEW: LINKS

There's really only one element relevant to creating hypertext links.

Element and attributes	Description
a	Anchor (hypertext link) element
href="*URL*"	Location of the target file
target="*text string*"	Targets a browser window by name

ADDING IMAGES

The web's explosion into mass popularity was due in part to the fact that there were images on the page. Before images, the internet was a text-only tundra.

Images appear on web pages in two ways: embedded in the inline content or as background images. If the image is part of the editorial content, such as product shots, gallery images, ads, illustrations, and so on, then it should be placed in the flow of the HTML document. If the image is purely decorative, such as a stunning image in the background of the header or a patterned border around an element, then it should be added through Cascading Style Sheets. Not only does it make sense to put images that affect presentation in a style sheet, but it makes the document cleaner and more accessible and makes the design much easier to update later. I will talk about CSS background images at length in **Chapter 13, Colors and Backgrounds**.

This chapter focuses on embedding image content into the flow of the document, and it is divided into three parts. First, we'll look at the tried-and-true **img** element for adding basic images to a page the way we've been doing it since 1992. It has worked just fine for over 25 years, and as a beginner, you'll find it meets most of your needs as well.

The second part of this chapter introduces some of the methods available for embedding SVG images (Scalable Vector Graphics) in HTML documents. SVGs are a special case and demand special attention.

Finally, we'll look at the way image markup has had to adapt to the wide variety of mobile devices with an introduction to new responsive image elements (**picture** and **source**) and attributes (**srcset** and **sizes**). As the number of types of devices used to view the web began to skyrocket, we realized that a single image may not meet the needs of all viewing environments, from palm-sized screens on slow cellular networks to high-density cinema displays. We needed a way to make images "responsive"—that is, to serve images

IN THIS CHAPTER

Adding images with the img element

Image accessibility

Adding SVG images

Responsive images

appropriate for their browsing environments. After a few years of back and forth between the W3C and the development community, responsive image features were added to the HTML 5.1 specification and are beginning to see widespread browser support.

I want to point out up front that responsive image markup is not as straightforward as the examples we've seen so far in this book. It's based on more advanced web development concepts, and the syntax may be tricky for someone just getting started writing HTML (heck, it's a challenge for seasoned professionals!). I've included it in this chapter because it is relevant to adding inline images, but frankly, I wouldn't blame you if you'd like to skip the "**Responsive Image Markup**" section and come back to it after we've done more work with Responsive Web Design and you have more HTML and CSS experience under your belt.

FIRST, A WORD ON IMAGE FORMATS

We'll get to the **img** element and other markup examples in a moment, but first it's important to know that you can't put just any image on a web page; it needs to be in one of the web-supported formats.

In general, images that are made up of a grid of colored pixels (called bitmapped or raster images, as shown in FIGURE 7-1, top) must be saved in the PNG, JPEG, or GIF file formats in order to be placed inline in the content. Newer, more optimized WebP and JPEG-XR bitmapped image formats are slowly gaining in popularity, particularly now that we have markup to make them available to browsers that support them.

For vector images (FIGURE 7-1, bottom), such as the kind of icons and illustrations you create with drawing tools such as Adobe Illustrator, we have the SVG format. There is so much to say about SVGs and their features that I've given them their own chapter (**Chapter 25, SVG**), but we'll look at how to add them to HTML documents later in this chapter.

If you have a source image that is in another popular format, such as TIFF, BMP, or EPS, you'll need to convert it to a web format before you can add it to the page. If, for some reason, you must keep your graphic file in its original format (for example, a file for a CAD program), you can make it available as an external image by making a link directly to the image file, like this:

```
<a href="architecture.eps">Get the drawing</a>
```

You should name your image files with the proper suffixes—.*png*, *.jpg* (or *.jpeg*), *.gif*, *.webp*, and *.jxr*, respectively. In addition, your server must be configured to recognize and serve these various image types properly. All web server software today is configured to handle PNG, JPEG, and GIF out of the box, but if you are using SVG or one of the newer formats, you may need to deliberately add that media type to the server's official list.

Bitmapped images
are made up of a grid
of colored pixels.

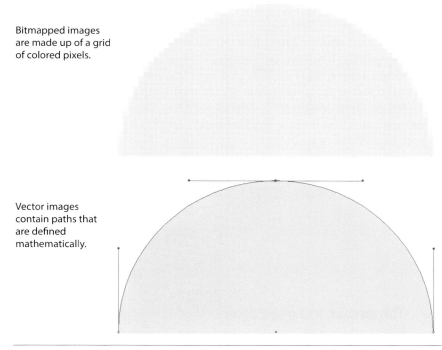

Vector images
contain paths that
are defined
mathematically.

FIGURE 7-1. A comparison of circles saved in bitmapped and vector formats.

A little background information may be useful here. Image files, and indeed any media files that may reside on a server, have an official media type (also called a MIME type) and suffixes. For example, SVG has the MIME type *image/svg+xml* and the suffixes *.svg* and *.svgz*.

Server packages have different ways of handling MIME information. The popular Apache server software uses a file in the root directory called *htaccess* that contains a list of all the file types and their acceptable suffixes. Be sure to add (or ask your server administrator to add) the MIME types of new image formats so they may be served correctly. The server looks up the suffix (*.webp*, for example) of requested files in the list and matches it with the Content-Type (*image/webp*) that it includes in its HTTP response to the browser. That tells the browser what kind of data is coming and how to parse it.

Browsers use helper applications to display media they can't handle alone. The browser matches the suffix of the file in the link to the appropriate helper application. The external image may open in a separate application window or within the browser window if the helper application is a browser plug-in. The browser may also ask the user to save the file or open an application manually. It is also possible that it won't be able to be opened at all.

Without further ado, let's take a look at the **img** element and its required and recommended attributes.

THE IMG ELEMENT

The **img** element tells the browser, "Place an image here." You've already gotten a glimpse of it used to place banner graphics in the examples in **Chapter 4, Creating a Simple Page**. You can also place an image element right in the flow of the text at the point where you want the image to appear, as in the following example. Images stay in the flow of text, aligned with the baseline of the text, and do not cause any line breaks (HTML5 calls this a phrasing element), as shown in FIGURE 7-2:

```
<p>This summer, try making pizza <img src="pizza.png" alt="">
on your grill.</p>
```

This summer, try making pizza   on your grill.

FIGURE 7-2. By default, images are aligned with the baseline of the surrounding text and do not cause a line break.

When the browser sees the **img** element, it makes a request to the server and retrieves the image file before displaying it on the page. On a fast network with a fast computer or device, even though a separate request is made for each image file, the page usually appears to arrive instantaneously. On mobile devices with slow network connections, we may be well aware of the wait for images to be fetched one at a time. The same is true for users using dial-up internet connections or other slow networks, like the expensive WiFi at luxury hotels.

The **src** and **alt** attributes shown in the sample are required. The **src** (source) attribute provides the location of the image file (its URL). The **alt** attribute provides alternative text that displays if the image is not available. We'll talk about **src** and **alt** a little more in upcoming sections.

There are a few other things of note about the **img** element:

- It is an empty element, which means it doesn't have any content. You just place it in the flow of text where the image should go.

- It is an inline element, so it behaves like any other inline element in the text flow. FIGURE 7-3 demonstrates the inline nature of image elements. When the browser window is resized, a line of images reflows to fill the new width.

The src and alt attributes are required in the img element.

FIGURE 7-3. Inline images are part of the normal document flow. They reflow when the browser window is resized.

- The **img** element is what's known as a replaced element because it is replaced by an external file when the page is displayed. This makes it different from text elements that have their content right there in the source (and thus are non-replaced).

- By default, the bottom edge of an image aligns with the baseline of text, as shown in FIGURE 7-2. Using CSS, you can float the image to the right or left margin and allow text to flow around it, crop it to a shape, control the space and borders around the image, and change its vertical alignment. We'll talk about those styles in **Part III**.

Providing the Location with src

The value of the **src** attribute is the URL of the image file. In most cases, the images you use on your pages will reside on your own server, so you will use relative URLs to point to them.

If you just read **Chapter 6, Adding Links**, you should be pretty handy with writing relative URLs. In short, if the image is in the same directory as the HTML document, you can refer to the image by name in the **src** attribute:

```
<img src="icon.gif" alt="">
```

Developers usually organize the images for a site into a directory called *images* or *img* (in fact, it helps search engines when you do it that way). There may even be separate image directories for each section of the site. If an image is not in the same directory as the document, you need to provide the pathname to the image file:

```
<img src="/images/arrow.gif" alt="">
```

Of course, you could place images from other websites by using a full URL, like this, but it is not recommended (see **Warning**):

```
<img src="http://www.example.com/images/smile.gif" alt="">
```

src="*URL*"
Source (location) of the image

WARNING

Before you use any image on your web page, be sure that you own the image, that you have explicit written permission by the copyright holder, or that it is in the public domain. Linking to an image on another server (called hotlinking*) is considered seriously uncool, so don't do it unless there is a specific use case in which you have permission. Even then, be aware that you cannot control the image and risk having it moved or renamed, which would break your link.*

■ PERFORMANCE TIP

Take Advantage of Caching

When a browser downloads an image, it stores the file in the disk cache (a space for temporarily storing files on the hard disk). That way, if it needs to redisplay the page, it can just pull up a local copy of the image without making a new server request.

If you use the same image repeatedly, be sure that the **src** attribute for each **img** element points to the same URL on the server. The image downloads once, then gets called from cache for subsequent uses. That means less traffic for the server and faster display for the user.

Providing Alternative Text with alt

alt="*text*"
Alternative text

Every **img** element must also contain an **alt** attribute that provides a text alternative to the image for those who are not able to see it. Alternative text (also called alt text) should serve as a substitute for the image content—conveying the same information and function. Alternative text is used by screen readers, search engines, and graphical browsers when the image doesn't load (FIGURE 7-4).

In this example, a PDF icon indicates that the linked text downloads a file in PDF format. In this case, the image is conveying valuable content that would be missing if the image cannot be seen. Providing the alt text "PDF file" replicates the purpose of the image:

```
<a href="application.pdf">High school application</a> <img src="images/→
pdflogo.png alt="PDF file">
```

A screen reader might indicate the image by reading its **alt** value this way:

"High school application. Image: PDF file"

Sometimes images function as links, in which case providing alternative text is critical because the screen reader needs something to read for the link. In the next example, an image of a book cover is used as a link to the book's website. Its alt text does not describe the cover itself, but rather performs the same function as the cover image on the page (indicating a link to the site):

```
<a href="http://learningwebdesign.com"><img src="/images/LWD_cover.png"
alt="Learning Web Design site"></a>
```

If an image does not add anything meaningful to the text content of the page, it is recommended that you leave the value of the **alt** attribute empty (null). In the following example, a decorative floral accent is not contributing to the content of the page, so its **alt** value is null. (You may also consider whether it is more appropriately handled as a background image in CSS, but I digress.) Note that there is no character space between the quotation marks:

```
<img src="/images/floralembellishment.png" alt="">
```

```
<p>If you're <img src="happy.gif" alt="happy">
and you know it clap your hands.</p>
```

With image displayed

If you're   and you know it clap your hands.

Firefox

If you're happy and you know it clap your hands.

Chrome (Mac & Windows)

If you're ⊡happy and you know it clap your hands.

MS Edge (Windows)

If you're ⊠ happy and you know it clap your hands.

Safari (iOS)

If you're happy and you know it clap your hands.

Safari (Mac)

If you're   ▪   and you know it clap your hands.

FIGURE 7-4. Most browsers display alternative text in place of the image if the image is not available. Safari for macOS is a notable exception. Firefox's substitution is the most seamless.

For each inline image on your page, consider what the alternative text would sound like when read aloud and whether that enhances the experience or might be obtrusive to a user with assistive technology.

Alternative text may benefit users with graphical browsers as well. If the user has opted to turn images off in the browser preferences or if the image simply fails to load, the browser may display the alternative text to give the user an idea of what is missing. The handling of alternative text is inconsistent among modern browsers, however, as shown in FIGURE 7-4.

Providing the Dimensions with width and height

The **width** and **height** attributes indicate the dimensions of the image in number of pixels. Browsers use the specified dimensions to hold the right amount of space in the layout while the images are loading rather than reconstructing the page each time a new image arrives, resulting in faster page display. If only one dimension is set, the image will scale proportionally.

These attributes have become less useful in the age of modern web development. They should never be used to resize an image (use your image-editing program or CSS for that), and they should be omitted entirely when you're using one of the responsive image techniques introduced later in this chapter. They may be used with images that will appear at the same fixed size across all devices, such as a logo or an icon, to give the browser a layout hint.

Be sure that the pixel dimensions you specify are the actual dimensions of the image. If the pixel values differ from the actual dimensions of your image, the browser resizes the image to match the specified values (FIGURE 7-5). If you are using **width** and **height** attributes and your image looks distorted or even slightly blurry, check to make sure that the values are in sync.

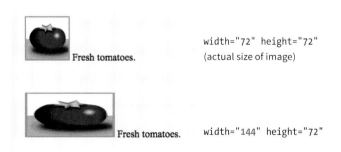

width="72" height="72"
(actual size of image)

width="144" height="72"

FIGURE 7-5. Browsers resize images to match the provided **width** and **height** values, but you should not resize images this way.

Now that you know the basics of the **img** element, you should be ready to add a few photos to the Black Goose Bistro Gallery site in EXERCISE 7-1.

■ **ACCESSIBILITY TIP**

Avoid using "image of" or "graphic of" in alt text values. It will be clear that it is an image. If the medium of the image, for example painting, photograph, or illustration, is relevant to the content, then it is fine to include the descriptive term.

width="*number*"
Image width in pixels

height="*number*"
Image height in pixels

■ **FURTHER READING**

Image Accessibility

Some types of images, such as data charts and diagrams, require long descriptions that aren't practical as **alt** values. These cases require alternate accessibility strategies, which you will find in these resources:

- "Accessible Images" at WebAIM (*webaim.org/techniques/ images/*)
- "Alternative Text" at WebAIM (*webaim.org/techniques/alttext/*)
- The Web Content Accessibility Guidelines (WCAG 2.0) at the W3C (*www.w3.org/TR/WCAG20-TECHS/*) include techniques for improving accessibility across all web content. Warning: this one is pretty dense.

FIGURE 7-6. Photo gallery pages.

EXERCISE 7-1. Adding and linking images

In this exercise, you'll add images to pages and use them as links. All of the full-size photos and thumbnails (small versions of the images) you need have been created for you, and I've given you a head start on the HTML files with basic styles as well. The starter files and the resulting code are available at *learningwebdesign.com/5e/materials*. Put a copy of the *gallery* folder on your hard drive, making sure to keep it organized as you find it.

This little site is made up of a main page (*index.html*) and three separate HTML documents containing each of the larger image views (FIGURE 7-6). First, we'll add the thumbnails, and then we'll add the full-size versions to their respective pages. Finally, we'll make the thumbnails link to those pages. Let's get started.

Open the file *index.html*, and add the small thumbnail images to this page to accompany the text. I've done the first one for you:

```
<p><img src="thumbnails/bread-200.jpg" alt="close-up of sliced rustic
bread" width="200" height="200"><br>We start our day at the…
```

I've put the image at the beginning of the paragraph, just after the opening **<p>** tag. Because all of the thumbnail images are located in the *thumbnails* directory, I provided the pathname in the URL. I added a description of the image with the **alt** attribute, and because I know these thumbnails will appear at exactly 200 pixels wide and high on all devices, I've included the **width** and **height** attributes as well to tell the browser how much space to leave in the layout. Now it's your turn.

1. Add the thumbnail images *burgers-200.jpg* and *fish-200.jpg* at the beginning of the paragraphs in their respective sections, following my example. Be sure to include the pathnames and thoughtful alternative text descriptions. Finally, add a line break (**
) after the **img element.

   When you are done, save the file and open it in the browser to be sure that the images are visible and appear at the right size.

2. Next, add the images to the individual HTML documents. I've done *bread.html* for you:

```
<h1>Gallery: Baked Goods</h1>
<p><img src="photos/bread-800.jpg" alt="close-up of sliced rustic
bread" width="800" height="600"></p>
```

   Notice that the full-size images are in a directory called *photos*, so that needs to be reflected in the pathnames. Notice also that because this page is not designed to be responsive, and the images will be a fixed size across devices, I went ahead and included the **width** and **height** attributes here as well.

   Add images to *burgers.html* and *fish.html*, following my example. Hint: all of the images are 800 pixels wide and 600 pixels high.

   Save each file, and check your work by opening them in the browser window.

3. Back in *index.html*, link the thumbnails to their respective files. I've done the first one:

```
<p><a href="bread.html"><img src="thumbnails/bread-200.jpg" alt="close-
up of sliced rustic bread" width="200" height="200"></a><br>We start
our day at the crack of dawn…
```

   Notice that the URL is relative to the current document (*index.html*), not to the location of the image (the *thumbnails* directory).

   Make the remaining thumbnail images link to each of the documents. If all the images are visible and you are able to link to each page and back to the home page again, then congratulations, you're done!

That takes care of the basics of adding images to a page. Next we'll take on adding SVG images, which are a special case, both in terms of the underlying format and the ways they can be added to HTML.

ADDING SVG IMAGES

No lesson on adding images to web pages would be complete without an introduction to adding SVGs (Scalable Vector Graphics). After all, the popularity of SVG images has been gaining momentum thanks to nearly ubiquitous browser support and the need for images that can resize without loss of quality. For illustration-style images, they are a responsive dream come true. I'm saving my deep-dive into all things SVG for **Chapter 25**, but for now I'll give you a quick peek at what they're made of so that the embedding markup makes sense.

As I mentioned at the beginning of this chapter, SVGs are an appropriate format for storing vector images (FIGURE 7-1). Instead of a grid of pixels, vectors are made up of shapes and paths that are defined mathematically. And even more interesting, in SVGs those shapes and paths are specified by instructions written out in a text file. Let that sink in: they are *images* that are written out in *text*! All of the shapes and paths as well as their properties are written out in the standardized SVG markup language (see **Note**). As HTML has elements for paragraphs (**p**) and tables (**table**), SVG has elements that define shapes like rectangle (**rect**), circle (**circle**), and paths (**path**).

A simple example will give you the general idea. Here is the SVG code that describes a rectangle (**rect**) with rounded corners (**rx** and **ry**, for x-radius and y-radius) and the word "hello" set as **text** with attributes for the font and color (FIGURE 7-7). Browsers that support SVG read the instructions and draw the image exactly as I designed it:

```
<svg xmlns="http://www.w3.org/2000/svg" viewBox="0 0 300 180">
  <rect width="300" height="180" fill="purple" rx="20" ry="20"/>
  <text x="40" y="114" fill="yellow" font-family="'Verdana-Bold'"
font-size="72">
    hello!
  </text>
</svg>
```

NOTE

SVG is an example, or application, of XML (Extensible Markup Language), which provides the rules and standards for how markup languages should be written and work together. As a result, SVG plays well alongside HTML content.

FIGURE 7-7. A simple SVG made up of a rectangle and text.

SVGs offer some significant advantages over their bitmapped counterparts for certain image types:

- Because they save only instructions for what to draw, they generally require less data than an image saved in a bitmapped format. That means faster downloads and better performance.

- Because they are vectors, they can resize as needed in a responsive layout without loss of quality. An SVG is always nice and crisp. No fuzzy edges.

- Because they are text, they integrate well with HTML/XML and can be compressed with tools like Gzip and Brotli, just like HTML files.

- They can be animated.

- You can change how they look with Cascading Style Sheets.

- You can add interactivity with JavaScript so things happen when users hover their mouse over or click the image.

Again, all of the ins and outs of creating SVGs, as well as their many features, are discussed in detail in **Chapter 25**. For now, I'd like to focus on the HTML required to place them in the flow of a web page. You have a few options: embedded with the **img** element, written out in code as an inline **svg** element, embedded with **object**, and used as a background image with CSS.

Embedded with the img Element

SVG text files saved with the *.svg* suffix (sometimes referred to as a stand-alone SVG) can be treated as any other image, including placing it in the document by using the **img** element. You're an expert on the **img** element by now, so the following example should be clear:

```
<img src="/images/circle.svg" alt="">
```

Pros and cons

The advantage to embedding an SVG with **img** is that it is universally supported in browsers that support SVG.

This approach works fine when you are using a standalone SVG as a simple substitute for a GIF or a PNG, but there are a few disadvantages to embedding SVGs with **img**:

- You cannot apply styles to the items within the SVG by using an external style sheet, such as a *.css* file applied to the whole page. The *.svg* file may include its own internal style sheet using the **style** element, however, for styling the elements within it. You can also apply styles to the **img** element itself.

- You cannot manipulate the elements within the SVG with JavaScript, so you lose the option for interactivity. Scripts in your web document can't see the content of the SVG, and scripts in the SVG file do not run at all. Other interactive effects, like links or :hover styles, are never triggered inside an SVG embedded with img as well.

- You can't use *any* external files, such as embedded images or web fonts, within the SVG.

In other words, standalone SVGs behave as though they are in their own little, self-contained bubble. But for static illustrations, that is just fine.

Browser support for SVG with img

The good news is that all modern browsers support SVGs embedded with the img element. The two notable exceptions are Internet Explorer versions 8 and earlier, and the Android browser prior to version 3. As of this writing, users with those browsers may still show up in small but significant numbers in your user logs. If you see a reason for your site to support these older browsers, there are workarounds, which I address briefly in the upcoming "**SVG Fallbacks**" section.

> ### SVG Server Configuration
>
> If you are using SVGs and they are not showing up correctly when your site is uploaded, you may need to configure the server to recognize the SVG image type, as discussed at the beginning of this chapter. Here's how to do it on the Apache server, but similar configurations can be done in other server languages:
>
> AddType image/svg+xml .svg

Inline in the HTML Source

Another option for putting an SVG on a web page is to copy the content of the SVG file and paste it directly into the HTML document. This is called using the SVG inline. Here is an example that looks a lot like the inline **img** example that we saw way back in FIGURE 7-2, only this time our pizza is a vector image drawn with circles and inserted with the **svg** element (FIGURE 7-8). Each **circle** element has attributes that describe the fill color, the position of its center point (**cx** and **cy**), and the length of its radius (**r**):

```
<p>This summer, try making pizza

<svg xmlns="http://www.w3.org/2000/svg" viewBox="0 0 72 72" width="100"
height="100">
   <circle fill="#D4AB00" cx="36" cy="36" r="36"/>
   <circle opacity=".7" fill="#FFF" stroke="#8A291C" cx="36.1" cy="35.9"
r="31.2"/>
   <circle fill="#A52C1B" cx="38.8" cy="13.5" r="4.8"/>
   <circle fill="#A52C1B" cx="22.4" cy="20.9" r="4.8"/>
   <circle fill="#A52C1B" cx="32" cy="37.2" r="4.8"/>
   <circle fill="#A52C1B" cx="16.6" cy="39.9" r="4.8"/>
   <circle fill="#A52C1B" cx="26.2" cy="53.3" r="4.8"/>
   <circle fill="#A52C1B" cx="42.5" cy="27.3" r="4.8"/>
   <circle fill="#A52C1B" cx="44.3" cy="55.2" r="4.8"/>
   <circle fill="#A52C1B" cx="54.7" cy="42.9" r="4.8"/>
   <circle fill="#A52C1B" cx="56" cy="28.3" r="4.8"/>
</svg>

  on your grill.</p>
```

```
<svg>
```

An inline SVG image

This summer, try making pizza   on your grill.

FIGURE 7-8. This pizza image is an SVG made up of 11 **circle** elements. Instead of an **img** element, the SVG source code is placed right in the HTML document with an **svg** element.

This code was generated by Adobe Illustrator, where I created the illustration and saved it in SVG format. I also optimized it to strip out a lot of cruft that Illustrator adds in there. We'll discuss SVG optimization in **Chapter 25**.

Pros and cons

Inline SVGs allow developers to take full advantage of SVG features. When the SVG markup is alongside the HTML markup, all of its elements are part of the main DOM tree. That means you can access and manipulate SVG objects with JavaScript, making them respond to user interaction or input. There are similar benefits for style sheets because the elements in the SVG can inherit styles from HTML elements. That makes it easy to apply the same styles to elements on the page and within the SVG graphic.

On the downside, the code for SVG illustrations can get extremely long and unwieldy, resulting in bloated HTML documents that are difficult to read. Even that little pepperoni pizza requires a serious block of code. It also makes the images for a site more difficult to maintain, since they are tucked away in the HTML documents. Another disadvantage is that inline SVGs are not cached by the browser separate from the HTML file, so avoid this method for large images that are reused across many HTML pages.

Browser support

The good news is that all modern browsers support SVG images placed inline with the **svg** element. The following older browser versions lack support: Internet Explorer versions 8 and earlier, Safari versions 5 and earlier, Android mobile browser prior to version 3, and iOS prior to version 5.

Embedded with the object Element

HTML has an all-purpose media embedding element called **object**. We'll talk about it more in **Chapter 10, Embedded Media**, but for now, know that **object** is another option for embedding an SVG in a web page. It is a good compromise between **img** and inline SVG, allowing a fully functional SVG that is still encapsulated in a separate, cacheable file.

The opening **object** tag specifies the media type (an **svg+xml** image) and points to the file to be used with the **data** attribute. The **object** element comes with its own fallback mechanism—any content within the **object** gets rendered if the media specified with **data** can't be displayed. In this case, a PNG version of the image will be placed with an **img** if the *.svg* is not supported or fails to load:

```
<object type="image/svg+xml" data="pizza.svg">
  <img src="pizza.png" alt="pizza">
</object>
```

There is one catch, however. Some browsers download the fallback image even if they support SVG and don't need it. Useless downloads are not ideal. The workaround is to make the fallback image a CSS background image in an empty **div** container. Unfortunately, it is not as flexible for scaling and sizing, but it does solve the extra download issue.

```
<object type="image/svg+xml" data="pizza.svg">
  <div style="background-image: url(pizza.png); width 100px; height:
100px;" role="img" aria-label="pizza">
</object>
```

Pros and cons

The main advantage to embedding SVGs with the **object** element is that they can be scripted and load external files. They can also use scripts to access the parent HTML document (with some security restrictions). However, because they are separate files and not part of the DOM for the page, you can't use a style sheet in the HTML document to style elements within the SVG. Embedded SVGs may also have some buggy behaviors in browsers, so be sure to test thoroughly.

Used as a Background Image with CSS

I know that this is an HTML chapter, but I'd be remiss if I didn't at least mention that SVGs can be used as background images with CSS. This style rule example puts a decorative image in the background of a **header**:

```
header {
  background-image: url(/images/decorative.svg);
}
```

SVG Fallbacks

As mentioned earlier, all modern browsers support SVGs either embedded as an **img**, embedded as an **object**, or included inline, which is very good news. However, if your server logs show significant traffic from Internet Explorer 8 and earlier, Android version 3 and earlier, or Safari 5 and earlier, or if your

Other Embedding Options

Older techniques for adding SVGs involve using two other HTML elements for embedding media: **embed** and **iframe** (we'll talk about them in **Chapter 10**). You may still see these in use with SVGs out there, and they work fine for browsers that support SVG, but most developers consider them to be outdated methods. Stick with **img**, inline **svg**, **object**, and CSS **background-image**.

client just requires support for those browsers, you may need to use a fallback technique. One option is to use the **object** element to embed the SVG on the page and take advantage of its fallback content feature shown earlier.

If you are using SVG as an image with the **img** element, another option is to use the **picture** element (it's discussed as part of the **"Responsive Image Markup"** section later in this chapter). The **picture** element can be used to provide several versions of an image in different formats. Each version is suggested with the **source** element, which in the following example points to the *pizza.svg* image and defines its media type. The **picture** element also has a built-in fallback mechanism. If the browser doesn't support the suggested **source** files, or if it does not support the **picture** element, users will see the PNG image provided with the good old **img** element instead:

```
<picture>
  <source type="image/svg+xml" srcset="pizza.svg">
  <img srcset="pizza.png" alt="No SVG support">
</picture>
```

If you Google for "SVG fallbacks," you'll likely get quite a few hits, many of which use JavaScript to detect support. For more detailed information on SVG fallbacks, I recommend reading Amelia Bellamy-Royd's article, "A Complete Guide to SVG Fallbacks" (*css-tricks.com/a-complete-guide-to-svg-fallbacks/*) or Chris Coyier's book, *Practical SVG* (A Book Apart) when you are ready. Ideally, you will be reading this in a world where old Internet Explorer and Android versions are no longer an issue.

Are you ready to give SVGs a spin? Try out some of the embedding techniques we discussed in EXERCISE 7-2.

EXERCISE 7-2. Adding an SVG to a page

In this exercise, we'll add some SVG images to the Black Goose Bistro page that we worked on in **Chapter 4**. The materials for this exercise are available online at *learningwebdesign.com/5e/materials*. You will find everything in a directory called *svg*. The resulting code is provided with the materials.

This exercise has two parts: first, we'll replace the logo with an SVG version, and second, we'll add a row of social media icons at the bottom of the page (FIGURE 7-9).

Part I: Replacing the logo

1. Open *blackgoosebistro.html* in a text editor. It should look just like we left it in **Chapter 4**.

2. Just for fun, let's see what happens when you make the current PNG logo really large. Add **width="500" height="500"** to the **img** tag. Save the file and open it in the browser to see how blurry bitmapped images get when you size them larger. Yuck.

3. Let's replace it with an SVG version of the same logo by using the inline SVG method. In the *svg* folder, you will find a file called *blackgoose-logo.svg*. Open it in your text editor and copy all of the text (from **<svg>** to **</svg>**).

BLACK GOOSE BISTRO

The Restaurant

The Black Goose Bistro offers casual lunch and dinner fare in a relaxed atmosphere. The menu changes regularly to highlight the freshest local ingredients.

Catering

You have fun. *We'll handle the cooking.* Black Goose Catering can handle events from snacks for a meetup to elegant corporate fundraisers.

Location and Hours

Seekonk, Massachusetts;
Monday through Thursday 11am to 9pm;
Friday and Saturday, 11am to midnight

Please visit our social media pages

FIGURE 7-9. The Black Goose Bistro page with SVG images.

4. Go back to the *blackgoosebistro.html* file and delete the entire **img** element (be careful not to delete the surrounding markup). Paste the SVG text in its place. If you look closely, you will see that the SVG contains two circles, a gradient definition, and two paths (one for the starburst shape and one for the goose).

5. Next, set the size the SVG should appear on the page. In the opening **svg** tag, add **width** and **height** attributes set to 200px each.

```
<h1><svg width="200px" height="200px" …
```

Save the file and open the page in the browser. You should see the SVG logo in place, looking a lot like the old one.

6. Try seeing what happens when you make the SVG logo really big! Change the width and height to 500 pixels, save the file, and reload the page in the browser. It should be big and *sharp*! No blurry edges like the PNG. OK, now put the size back to 200 × 200 or whatever looks good to you.

Part II: Adding icons

7. Next we're going to create a footer at the bottom of the page for social media icons. Below the Location & Hours section, add the following (the empty paragraph is where we'll add the logos):

```
<footer>
  <p>Please visit our social media pages</p>
  <p> </p>
</footer>
```

8. Use the **img** element to place three SVG icons: *twitter.svg*, *facebook.svg*, and *instagram.svg*. Note that they are located in the *icons* directory. There are also icons for Tumblr and GitHub if you'd like extra practice. Here's a head start on the first one:

```
<p><img src="icons/twitter.svg" alt="twitter"></p>
```

9. Save the file and open it in the browser. The icons should be there, but they are *huge*. Let's write a couple of style rules to make the footer look nice. We haven't done much with style rules yet, so just copy exactly what you see here inside the **style** element in the **head** of the document:

```
footer {
  border-top: 1px solid #57b1dc;
  text-align: center;
  padding-top: 1em;
}
footer img {
  width: 40px;
  height: 40px;
  margin-left: .5em;
  margin-right: .5em;
}
```

10. Save the file again and open it in the browser (you should see a page that looks like FIGURE 7-9). Go ahead and play around with the style settings, or even the code in the inline SVG, if you'd like to get a feel for how they affect the appearance of the images. It's kinda fun.

RESPONSIVE IMAGE MARKUP

Pretty quickly after smartphones, tablets, "phablets," and other devices hit the scene, it became clear that large images that look great on a large screen were overkill on smaller screens. All that image data...downloaded and wasted. Forcing huge images onto small devices slows down page display and may cost real money too, depending on the user's data plan (and your server costs). Conversely, small images that download quickly may be blurry on large, high-resolution screens. Just as we need a way to make whole web pages respond and adapt to various screen sizes, we need a way to make images on those page "responsive" as well. Our trusty `img` element with its single `src` attribute just doesn't cut it in most cases.

It took a couple of years of proposals, experimentation, and discussion between browser makers and the web development community, but we now have a way to suggest alternate images by using HTML markup alone. No complicated JavaScript or server-side hacks. The resulting responsive image features (`srcset` and `sizes` attributes as well as the `picture` element) have been incorporated into the HTML 5.1 specification, and browser support is growing steadily, led by the Chrome browser in September 2014.

Thanks to a foolproof fallback and scripts that add support to older browsers, you can start using these techniques right away. That said, none of this is set in stone. Responsive image solutions are likely to be tweaked and improved, or perhaps one day even made obsolete. If you are going to include them in your sites, a good starting place for getting up-to-speed is the Responsive Images Community Group (*responsiveimages.org*). RICG is a group of developers who worked together to hammer out the current spec with the browser creators. They are on top of this stuff. You should also look for recent articles and perhaps even crack open the spec.

How It Works

When we say "responsive images," we are talking about providing images that are tailored to the user's viewing environment. First and foremost, responsive image techniques prevent browsers on small screens from downloading more image data than they need. They also include a mechanism to give high-resolution displays on fast networks images large enough to look extra-gorgeous. In addition, they provide a way for developers to take advantage of new, more efficient image formats.

In short, responsive images work this way: you provide multiple images, sized or cropped for different screen sizes, and the browser picks the most appropriate one based on what it knows about the current viewing environment. Screen dimensions are one factor, but resolution, network speed, what's already in its cache, user preferences, and other considerations may also be involved.

You provide multiple images, sized or cropped for different screen sizes, and the browser picks the most appropriate one based on what it knows about the current viewing environment.

The responsive image attributes and elements address the following four basic scenarios:

- Providing extra-large images that look crisp on **high-resolution screens**

- Providing a set of images of various dimensions for use on **different screen sizes**

- Providing versions of the image with varying amount of detail based on the device size and orientation (known as the **art direction** use case)

- Providing **alternative image formats** that store the same image at much smaller file sizes

Let's take a look at each of these common use cases.

High-Density Displays (x-descriptor)

Everything that you see on a screen display is made up of little squares of colored light called pixels. We call the pixels that make up the screen itself device pixels (you'll also sometimes see them referred to as hardware pixels or physical pixels). Until recently, screens commonly fit 72 or 96 device pixels in an inch (now 109 to 160 is the norm). The number of pixels per inch (ppi) is the resolution of the screen.

Bitmapped images, like JPEG, PNG, and GIF, are made up of a grid of pixels too. It used to be that the pixels in images as well as pixel dimensions specified in our style sheets mapped one-to-one with the device pixels. An image or box element that was 100 pixels wide would be laid out across 100 device pixels. Nice and straightforward.

Device-pixel-ratios

It should come as no surprise that it's not so straightforward today. Manufacturers have been pushing screen resolutions higher and higher in an effort to improve image quality. The result is that device pixels have been getting smaller and smaller, so small that our images and text would be illegibly tiny if they were mapped one-to-one.

To compensate, devices use a measurement called a reference pixel for layout purposes. Reference pixels are also known as points (PT) in iOS, Device Independent Pixels (DP or DiP) in Android, or CSS pixels because they are the unit of measurement we use in style sheets. The iPhone 8 has a screen that is made up of 750 × 1334 device pixels, but it uses a layout grid of 375 × 667 points or CSS pixels (a ratio of 2 device pixels to 1 layout pixel—2:1 or 2x). A box sized to 100 pixels wide in CSS would be laid out across 200 device pixels on the iPhone8. The iPhone X has a screen that is made up of 1125 × 2436 pixels, but it uses a layout grid of 375 × 812 points (a ratio of 3 device pixels to one point—or 3x). A box sized to 100 pixels is laid out across 300 device pixels on the iPhone X.

> Devices use a measurement called a reference pixel for layout purposes.

The ratio of the number of device pixels to CSS pixels is called the device-pixel-ratio (FIGURE 7-10). Common device-pixel-ratios on handheld devices are 1.325x, 1.5x, 1.7x, 2x, 2.4x, 3x, and even 4x (the "x" is the convention for indicating a device-pixel-ratio). Even large desktop displays are featuring ratios of 2x, 3x, and 4x.

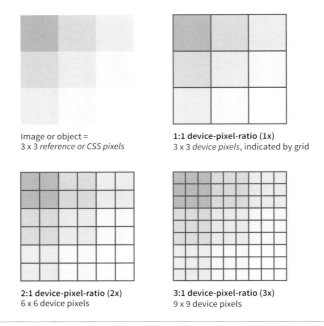

Image or object =
3 x 3 *reference or CSS pixels*

1:1 device-pixel-ratio (1x)
3 x 3 *device pixels*, indicated by grid

2:1 device-pixel-ratio (2x)
6 x 6 device pixels

3:1 device-pixel-ratio (3x)
9 x 9 device pixels

FIGURE 7-10. Device pixels compared to CSS/reference pixels.

Let's say you have an image that you want to appear 200 pixels wide on all displays. You can make the image exactly 200px wide (px is short for pixels), and it will look fine on standard-resolution displays, but it might be a little blurry on high-resolution displays. To get that image to look sharp on a display with a device-pixel-ratio of 2x, you'd need to make that same image 400 pixels wide. It would need to be 600 pixels wide to look sharp on a 3x display. Unfortunately, the larger images may have file sizes that are four or more times the size of the original. Who wants to send all that extra data to a 1x device that really only needs the smaller image?

Introducing srcset

We now have a way to serve larger images just to the browsers on displays that benefit from them. We do it using the new **srcset** attribute with our old friend the **img** element. **srcset** allows developers to specify a list of image source options for the browser to choose from.

The value of **srcset** is a comma-separated list of options. Each item in that list has two parts: the URL of an image and an x-descriptor that specifies the target device-pixel-ratio. Note that the whole list is the value of **srcset** and goes inside a single set of quotation marks. This sample shows the structure of a **srcset** value:

```
srcset="image-URL #x, image-URL #x"
```

The **src** attribute is still required, and is generally used to specify the default 1x image for browsers that don't support **srcset**. Make sure there is an **alt** attribute as well:

```
<img src="image-URL" alt="" srcset="image-URL #x, image-URL #x">
```

Let's look at an example. I have an image of a turkey that I'd like to appear 200 pixels wide. For standard resolution, I created the image at 200 pixels wide and named it *turkey-200px.jpg*. I'd also like it to look crisp in high-resolution displays, so I have two more versions: *turkey-400px.jpg* (for 2x) and *turkey-600px.jpg* (for 3x). Here is the markup for adding the image and indicating its high-density equivalents with x-descriptors:

```
<img src="/images/turkey-200px.jpg" alt=""
srcset="/images/turkey-400px.jpg 2x, /images/turkey-600px.jpg 3x" >
```

Because browsers ignore line returns and spaces in the source document, I can also write that same element stacked in this way to make it a little easier to read, as I will be doing throughout this chapter:

```
<img
   src="/images/turkey-200px.jpg" alt=""
   srcset="/images/turkey-400px.jpg 2x,
          /images/turkey-600px.jpg 3x" >
```

That makes the options and structure more clear at a glance, don't you think?

Browsers that recognize the **srcset** attribute check the screen resolution and download what they believe to be the most appropriate image. If the browser is on a Mac with a 2x Retina display, it may download *image-400px.jpg*. If the device-pixel-ratio is 1.5x, 2.4x, or something else, it checks the overall viewing environment and makes the best selection. It is important to know that when we use **srcset** with the **img** element, we are handing the keys to the browser to make the final image selection.

When to use x-descriptors

X-descriptors tell the browser to make a selection based on screen resolution only, with no regard for the dimensions of the screen or viewport. For this reason, x-selectors are best used for images that stay the same pixel dimensions regardless of the screen size, such as logos, social media badges, or other fixed-width images.

It is much more likely that you'll want images to resize based on the size of the screen and to be able to serve small images to small handheld devices, and large images to desktops (that's kind of the crux of this responsive image thing, after all). Now that you are familiar with using the **srcset** attribute, let's see how it can be used to deliver images targeted to various screen sizes. Here's where **srcset** really shines.

> The srcset attribute specifies a list of image options for the browser to choose from.

> When we use srcset with the img element, we are allowing the browser to make the best image selection.

Variable-Width Images (w-descriptor)

When you're designing a responsive web page, chances are you'll want image sizes to change based on the size of the browser viewport (see **Note**). This is known as a viewport-based selection. And because you are the type of web developer who cares about how fast pages display, you'll want to limit unnecessary data downloads by providing appropriately sized images.

To achieve this goal, use the **srcset** and **sizes** attributes with the **img** element. As we saw in previous examples, the **srcset** gives the browser a set of image file options, but this time, it uses a w-descriptor (width descriptor) that provides the *actual pixel width* of each image. Using **srcset** with a w-descriptor is appropriate when the images are identical except for their dimensions (in other words, they differ only in scale). Here's an example of a **srcset** attribute that provides four image options and specifies their respective pixel widths via w-descriptors. Note again that the whole list is in a single set of quotation marks:

```
srcset="strawberries-480.jpg 480w,
        strawberries-960.jpg 960w,
        strawberries-1280.jpg 1280w,
        strawberries-2400.jpg 2400w"
```

Using the sizes attribute

The sizes attribute is required when you use width descriptors.

That's a good start, but whenever you use w-descriptors, you also need to use the **sizes** attribute to tell the browser the approximate size that the image will appear in the page's layout. There is a very good reason (in addition to being required in the spec), and it is worth understanding.

When a browser downloads the HTML document for a web page, the first thing it does is look through the whole document and establish its outline structure (its Document Object Model, or DOM). Then, almost immediately, a preloader goes out to get all the images from the server so they are ready to go. Finally, the CSS and the JavaScript are downloaded. It is likely that the style sheet has instructions for layout and image sizes, but by the time the browser sees the styles, the images are already downloaded. For that reason, we have to give the browser a good hint with the **sizes** attribute whether the image will fill the whole viewport width or only a portion of it. That allows the preloader to pick the correct image file from the **srcset** list.

We'll start with the simplest scenario in which the image is a banner and always appears at 100% of the viewport width, regardless of the device (FIGURE 7-11). Here's the complete **img** element:

```
<img src="strawberries-640.jpg"
     alt="baskets of ripe strawberries"
     srcset="strawberries-480.jpg 480w,
             strawberries-960.jpg 960w,
             strawberries-1280.jpg 1280w,
             strawberries-2400.jpg 2400w"
     sizes="100vw">
```

NOTE

On a mobile device, the viewport fills the whole screen. On a desktop browser, the viewport is the area where the page displays, not including the scrollbars and other browser "chrome."

FIGURE 7-11. The image fills 100% of the viewport width, regardless of its size.

In this example, the **sizes** attribute tells the browser that the image fills the full viewport by using viewport width units (**vw**), the most common unit for the **sizes** attribute, so the browser can pick the best image for the job. For example, **100vw** translates to 100% of the viewport width, **50vw** would be 50%, and so on. You can also use **em**, **px**, and a few other CSS units, but you cannot use percentages. Browsers that do not support **srcset** and **sizes** simply use the image specified in the **src** attribute.

Sizing an image to fill the whole width of the browser is a pretty specific case. More likely, your images will be one component in a responsive page layout that resizes and rearranges to make best use of the available screen width. FIGURE 7-12 shows a sidebar of food photos that take up the full width of the screen on small devices, take up a portion of the width on larger devices, and appear three across in a layout for large browser windows.

Browsers that do not support srcset and sizes use the image specified in the src attribute.

FIGURE 7-12. The width of the images changes based on the width of the viewport.

For cases like these, use the **sizes** attribute to tell the browser something about how the image will be sized for each layout. The **sizes** value is a comma-separated list in which each item has two parts. The first part in parentheses is a media condition that describes a parameter such as the width of the viewport. The second part is a length that indicates the width that image will occupy in the layout if the media condition is met. Here's how that syntax looks:

```
sizes="(media-feature: condition) length,
       (media-feature: condition) length,
       (media-feature: condition) length"
```

I've added some media conditions to the previous example, and now we have a complete valid **img** element for one of the photo images in FIGURE 7-12:

```
<img src="strawberries-640.jpg" alt="baskets of ripe strawberries"
    srcset="strawberries-240.jpg 240w,
            strawberries-480.jpg 480w,
            strawberries-672.jpg 672w"
    sizes="(max-width: 480px) 100vw,
           (max-width: 960px) 70vw,
           240px">
```

The **sizes** attribute tells the browser the following:

- If the viewport is 480 pixels wide or smaller (maximum width is 480 pixels), the image fills 100% of the viewport width.

- If the viewport is wider than 480 pixels but no larger than 960 pixels (**max-width: 960px**), then the image will appear at 70% of the viewport. (This layout has 15% margins on the left and the right of the images, or 30% total.)

- If the viewport is larger than 960 pixels and doesn't meet any of the prior media conditions, the image gets sized to exactly 240 pixels.

Now that the browser knows the width of the viewport and how big the image will appear within it, it can select the most appropriate image from the **srcset** list to download.

There's a bit more to using **sizes** than shown here—other media conditions, additional length units, even the ability to ask the browser to calculate widths for you. If you plan on using viewport-width-based images in your designs, I recommend reading the spec to take full advantage of the possibilities.

WARNING

*The **sizes** attribute will resize an image even if there is no CSS applied to it. If there is a CSS rule specifying image size that conflicts with the value of the **sizes** attribute, the style rule wins (i.e., it overrides the **sizes** value).*

NOTE

Strategies and tools for producing the image sets for responsive layouts are introduced in **Chapter 24, Image Asset Production**.

Art Direction (picture Element)

So far, we've looked at image selection based on the resolution of the screen and the size of the viewport. In both of these scenarios, the content of the image does not change but merely resizes.

But sometimes, resizing isn't enough. You might want to crop into important details of an image when it is displayed on a small screen. You may want to change or remove text from the image if it gets too small to be legible. Or you might want to provide both landscape (wide) and portrait (tall) versions of the same image for different layouts.

For example, in FIGURE 7-13, the whole image of the table as well as the dish reads fine on larger screens, but at smartphone size, it gets difficult to see the delicious detail. It would be nice to provide alternate versions of the image that make sense for the browsing conditions.

![That dinner looks delicious on desktop browsers. (1280px wide)](image)

That dinner looks delicious on desktop browsers.
(1280px wide)

Detail is lost when the full image is shrunk down on small devices.
(300px wide)

Cropping to the most important detail may make better sense.
(300px wide)

FIGURE 7-13.   Some images are illegible when resized smaller for mobile devices.

This scenario is known as an art-direction-based selection and it is accomplished with the **picture** element. The **picture** element has no attributes; it is just a wrapper for some number of **source** elements and an **img** element. The **img** element is required and must be the last element in the list. If the **img** is left out, no image will display at all because it is the piece that is actually

---

`<picture>…</picture>`
Specifies a number of image options

`<source>…</source>`
Specifies alternate image sources

Use the picture element when simply resizing the image is not enough.

---

placing the image on the page. Let's look at a sample **picture** element and then pick it apart:

```
<picture>
  <source media="(min-width: 1024px)" srcset="icecream-large.jpg">
  <source media="(min-width: 760px)" srcset="icecream-medium.jpg">
  <img src="icecream-small.jpg" alt="hand holding ice cream cone and
text that reads Savor the Summer">
</picture>
```

This example tells the browser that if the viewport is 1024 pixels wide or larger, use the large version of the ice cream cone image. If it is wider than 760 pixels (but smaller than 1024, such as on a tablet), use the medium version. Finally, for viewports that are smaller than 760 pixels and therefore don't match any of the media queries in the previous **source** elements, the small version should be used (FIGURE 7-14). The small version, as specified in the **img** element, will be used for browsers that do not recognize **picture** and **source**.

Each **source** element includes a **media** attribute and a **srcset** attribute. It can also use the **sizes** attribute, although that is not shown in the previous example. The **media** attribute supplies a media query for checking the current browsing conditions. It is similar to the media conditions we saw in the earlier **srcset** example, but the **media** attribute specifies a full-featured CSS media query (we'll talk more about media queries in **Chapter 17, Responsive Web Design**). The **srcset** attribute supplies the URL for the image to use if the media query is a match. In the previous example, there is just one image specified, but it could also be a comma-separated list if you wanted to provide several options using x- or w-descriptors.

Browsers download the image from the first **source** that matches the current conditions, so the order of the **source** elements is important. The URL provided in the **srcset** attribute gets passed to the **src** attribute in the **img**

iPhone   iPad

Chrome browser on desktop

FIGURE 7-14. The **picture** element provides different image versions to be sourced at various screen sizes.

element. Again, it's the `img` that places the image on the page, so don't omit it. The `alt` attribute for the `img` element is required, but `alt` is not permitted in the `source` element.

Art direction is the primary use of the `picture` element, but let's look at one more thing it can do to round out our discussion on responsive images.

Alternative Image Formats (type Attribute)

Once upon a time, in the early 1990s, the only image type you could put on a web page was a GIF. JPEGs came along not long after, and we waited nearly a *decade* for reliable browser support for the more feature-rich PNG format. It takes a notoriously long time for new image formats to become universally supported. In the past, that meant simply avoiding newer formats.

In an effort to reduce image file sizes, more efficient image formats have been developed—such as WebP, JPEG 2000, and JPEG XR—that can compress images significantly smaller than their JPEG and PNG counterparts (see **Note**). And once again, some browsers support them and some don't. The difference is that today we can use the `picture` element to serve the newer image formats to browsers that can handle them, and a standard image format to browsers that can't. We no longer have to wait for universal browser support.

In the following example, the `picture` element specifies two image alternatives before the fallback JPEG listed in the `img` element:

```
<picture>
  <source type="image/webp" srcset="pizza.webp">
  <source type="image/jxr" srcset="pizza.jxr">
  <img src="pizza.jpg" alt="">
</picture>
```

For image-format-based selections, each `source` element has two attributes: the `srcset` attribute that we've seen before, and the `type` attribute for specifying the type of file (also known as its MIME type, see the **"File (MIME) Types"** sidebar). In this example, the first `source` points to an image that is in the WebP format, and the second specifies a JPEG XR. Again, the browser uses the image from the first source that matches the browser's image support, so it makes sense to put them in order from smallest to largest file size.

Browser Support

As I write this section, it seems like a new browser is adding support for `picture`, `srcset`, and `sizes` every day, but of course, old browser versions have a bad habit of sticking around for years. This is not a reason to avoid using responsive images, however. First of all, all of these features are designed to include the `img` element as a built-in fallback for browsers that don't recognize the newer markup. In the worst case, the browser grabs the image specified in the `img` element.

NOTE

The bitmapped image formats, including WebP, JPEG 2000, and JPEG XR, are discussed in more detail in **Chapter 23, Web Image Basics**.

File (MIME) Types

The web uses a standardized system to communicate the type of media files being transferred between the server and browser. It is based on MIME (Multipurpose Internet Mail Extension), which was originally developed for sending attachments via email. Every file format has a standardized type (such as **image**, **application**, **audio**, or **video**), subtype that identifies the specific format, and one or more file extensions. In our example, the **type** attribute specifies the WebP option with its type/subtype (**image/webp**) and uses the proper file extension (*.webp*). Other examples of media MIME types are **image/jpeg** (extensions *.jpg*, *.jpeg*), **video/mpeg** (extensions *.mpg*, *.mpe*, *.mpeg*, *.m1v*, *.mp2*, *.mp3*, and *.mpa*), and **application/pdf** (*.pdf*). The complete listing of registered MIME types is published by the IANA (Internet Assigned Numbers Authority) at *www.iana.org/assignments/media-types*.

If that isn't good enough, try including Picturefill with your web pages. Picturefill is an example of a polyfill, a script that makes older browsers behave as though they support a new technology—in this case, responsive images. It was created by Scott Jehl of Filament Group, creators of many fine responsive design and frontend development tools. Go to *scottjehl.github.io/picturefill/* to download the script and read the very thorough tutorial on how it works and how to use it.

Responsive Images Summary

This has been a long discussion about responsive images, and we've really only scratched the surface. We've looked at how to use the **img** element with **srcset** and **sizes** to make *pixel-ratio-based* and *viewport-size-based* selections (you can try them yourself in EXERCISE 7-3). We also saw how the **picture** element can be used for *art-direction-based* and *image-type-based* selections.

I've kept my examples short and sweet, but know that it is possible to combine techniques in different ways, often resulting in a tower of code for each image. To see some examples of how these responsive image techniques might be combined to target more than one condition, I recommend Andreas Bovens's article "Responsive Images: Use Cases and Documented Code Snippets to Get You Started" on the Dev.Opera site (*dev.opera.com/articles/responsive-images/*).

I also recommend the 10-part "Responsive Images 101" tutorial by Jason Grigsby at Cloud Four. He goes into a bit more detail than I was able to here and provides links to other good resources. Start with "Part 1: Definitions" (*cloudfour.com/thinks/responsive-images-101-definitions/*).

| BROWSER SUPPORT
TIP

The site *CanIUse.com* is a great tool for checking on the browser support for HTML, CSS, and other frontend web technologies. Type in **picture**, **srcset**, or **sizes** to see where browser support stands.

EXERCISE 7-3. Adding responsive images

Ready to try out some of this responsive image stuff? I recommend downloading the latest version of Google Chrome (*google.com/chrome/*) or Firefox (*firefox.com*) so you are certain it supports the responsive image HTML features. The materials for this exercise are provided at *learningwebdesign.com/5e/materials*. Use the *responsivegallery* directory that contains a starter HTML file and *images* directory.

We're going to give the Black Goose Bistro Gallery page a makeover using responsive images. Now, instead of the user clicking a thumbnail and going to a separate page, the large images appear right on the page and resize to fill the available space. Small devices and browsers that don't support **picture** get a 400-pixel-square version of each image (FIGURE 7-15).

1. Open the file *index.html* located in the *responsivegallery* directory in a text or HTML editor. I've added a **meta** element that sets the viewport to the same size as the device width, which is required to make this page responsive. I also added a style for **img** elements that sets their maximum width to 100% of the available space. That is the bit that makes the images scale down for smaller screen widths. We'll talk a lot more about

Small devices like the iPhone show the cropped 400-pixel-square image.

BLACK GOOSE BISTRO GALLERY

On viewports larger than 480 pixels, like the iPad shown here, the full version of the image is used. It resizes to fill the available width of the page between the margins.

On very large desktop displays, the full version of the image resizes to fill the available width.

Browsers that do not support **picture** display the 400-pixel-square image specified by the **img** element.

FIGURE 7-15. The Black Goose Bistro Gallery with responsive images in place. Smaller devices see a square cropped version of the image. Larger browsers get the full image that resizes to fill the content width.

responsive design in **Chapter 17**, so don't worry about it too much now. I just wanted to point out changes from our previous exercise.

2. Because we want to change between horizontal and square versions of the image on this page, we'll need to use the **picture** element. Start by adding the bare bones of a **picture** element in the first paragraph after "Our Baked Goods," including the **picture** wrapper and its required **img** element. The **img** element points to the default square version of the image (*bread-400.jpg*). Add a line break element after the **picture** element to start the text on the next line:

EXERCISE 7-3. Continued

```
<p>
<picture>
   <img src="images/bread-400.jpg" alt="close-up of sliced rustic
bread">
</picture>
<br>We start our day…
```

3. That takes care of small devices and the fallback for non-supporting devices. Now add a **source** element that tells browser to use a 1200-pixel-wide landscape version of the image when the viewport is larger than 480 pixels:

```
<p>
<picture>
   <source media="(min-width: 480px)"
           srcset="images/bread-1200.jpg">
   <img src="images/bread-400.jpg" alt="close-up of sliced rustic
bread">
</picture>
<br>We start our day…
```

Note that because there is only one image specified in the **source**, we could have used a simple **src** attribute here, but we have more work to do, so the **srcset** gets us ready for the next step.

4. Because we don't want to force such a large image on everyone, let's give the browser an 800-pixel-wide version as well. (Even more versions would be useful, but for the sake of keeping this exercise manageable, we'll stop at two.) Remember that the **srcset** attribute specifies a comma-separated list of images and their respective pixel widths with w-descriptors. I've added the **1200w** descriptor to the original image and added the 800-pixel option to the **srcset**. Finally, use the **sizes** attribute to let the browser know that the image will occupy 80% of the viewport width (the style sheet adds a 10% margin on the left and right sides, leaving 80% for the content). Now the browser can choose the most appropriate size.

```
<p>
<picture>
   <source media="(min-width: 480px)"
           srcset="images/bread-1200.jpg 1200w,
                   images/bread-800.jpg 800w"
           sizes="80vw">
   <img src="images/bread-400.jpg" alt="close-up of sliced rustic
bread">
</picture>
<br>We start our day…
```

5. Save the file. Launch the Chrome or Firefox desktop browser and resize the window to as narrow as it will go. Open *index.html* and you should see the square cropped version of the bread photo. Slowly drag the corner of the browser window to make the window wider. When it gets wider than 480 pixels, it should switch to the full version of the photo. If you see a little "800" in the corner of the image, that means the browser has downloaded *bread-800.jpg* for this task. Keep expanding the window, and the image should keep getting larger. If you see "1200," it means it is using *bread-1200.jpg*. Once the larger image is in the browser's cache, you won't see the 800-pixel version again. Try making the window narrow and wide again and watch what changes. Congratulations! You are now an official responsive web designer! Making windows narrow and wide is how we spend a good portion of our workday.

6. Add the remaining two images to the page, following my example. Try experimenting with different min- and max-widths in the **media** attribute.

NOTE

If you don't see the images at all, it could be that your pathnames are incorrect or the *images* directory hasn't copied to your computer.

WHEW! WE'RE FINISHED

That wraps up our exploration of images. We've seen how to place images with the `img` element and its required `src` and `alt` attributes. We've talked about the importance of good alternative text for accessibility. We also looked at a few ways to embed SVG images into a web page. Finally, we took on the newly minted responsive image features, including `srcset` and `sizes` for the `img` element to target high-density displays or to provide a variety of image sizes for the browser to choose from, and the `picture` and `source` elements for art direction and alternative image formats. Now try answering a few questions to test your knowledge.

TEST YOURSELF

Images are a big part of the web experience. Answer these questions to see how well you've absorbed the key concepts of this chapter. The correct answers can be found in **Appendix A**.

1. Which attributes must be included in every `img` element?

2. Write the markup for adding an image called *furry.jpg* that is in the same directory as the current document.

3. Name two reasons to include alternative text for an `img` element.

4. What might be going wrong if your images don't appear when you view the page in a browser? There are three possible explanations.

5. What is the difference between an x-descriptor and a w-descriptor?

6. What is the difference between a device pixel and a CSS (reference) pixel?

Alternatives to Responsive Images

Although it is terrific to have an HTML solution for getting the right images to the right browsers, the current system is cumbersome with stacks of code and the need to produce multiple images. If you work on an image-heavy site, it could prove to be unmanageable. Image processing is a task that begs to be automated. The solution: let the *server* do it!

Fortunately, there are many tools and services, both open source and for pay, that let the server do the work of creating appropriate image versions on the fly. You upload the largest available size of the image and let the server handle the rest—no need to create and store multiple versions of every image. In general, image-generation services address only resizing, and not art direction or alternative image types; however, at least one service (*Cloudinary.com*) uses face detection as a basis for image cropping.

Some content management systems (CMSs) have image resizing features built in. Another option is to install software on your own server. Bear in mind, however, that requiring JavaScript to be running is less than ideal. There are also many third-party solutions that provide image-resizing services (like Cloudinary.com and Kraken.io), usually for a fee. For large, image-heavy sites, they are worth looking into.

Jason Grigsby of Cloud Four has compiled a spreadsheet of image-resizing software and services that serves as a good jumping-off point. You can get to it from his article, "Image Resizing Services" (*cloudfour. com/thinks/image-resizing-services/*) or at *tinyurl.com/pmpbyzj*.

7. Match the responsive image scenarios with the HTML solutions:

   a. `<img src="" alt="" srcset="URL x-descriptor">`

   b. `<img src="" alt=" srcset="URL w-descriptor" sizes="#">`

   c.
   ```
   <picture>
      <source type="…" srcset="">
      <img src="" alt="">
   </picture>
   ```

   d.
   ```
   <picture>
      <source media="()" srcset="">
      <img src="" alt="">
   </picture>
   ```

   _____ You want the image to always fill the width of the browser window.

   _____ You want to take advantage of the file savings of the WebP image format.

   _____ You want to remove the text from an image when it is on small screens.

   _____ You want your product images to look as sharp as possible on high-resolution screens.

   _____ You want to show a close-up of the action in a news image on small screens.

   _____ You want the image to resize smaller when it is part of the layout on a large screen.

8. Challenge question: Describe what this example tells the browser to do:

```
<picture>
  <source sizes="(min-width: 480px) 80vw,
                 100vw"
          srcset="photo-200.webp 200w
                  photo-400.webp 400w,
                  photo-800.webp 800w,
                  photo-1200.webp 1200w"
        type="image/webp">
  <img src=" photo-400.jpg" alt=""
      sizes="(min-width: 480px) 80vw,
             100vw"
      srcset="photo-200.jpg 200w,
              photo-400.jpg 400w,
              photo-800.jpg 800w,
              photo-1200.jpg 1200w">
</picture>
```

9. What is cache and how does it affect web page performance?

10. Name one advantage and one disadvantage of adding an SVG to a page with the **img** element.

■ **PHOTO CREDITS**

Many of the images in this chapter are from the fabulous royalty-free photo site, *Unsplash.com*: ravioli by Davide Ragusa, burgers by Niklas Rhöse, ice cream cone by Alex Jones, dinner table by Jay Wennington, strawberries by Priscilla Fong. From Flickr's "No Rights Restrictions" collection: fish dish by Renata Maia, muffins by Hasma Kanouni. All others are uncredited public domain images.

11. Name one advantage and one disadvantage of inline SVG.

12. When would it be appropriate to add an SVG to a page as a background image with CSS?

13. What is this bit of code describing, and when might you need to use it?

```
image/svg+xml
```

14. What is this bit of code describing, and where would you find it?

```
http://www.w3.org/2000/svg
```

ELEMENT REVIEW: IMAGES

Following are the elements you learned in your exploration of image markup.

Element and attributes	Description
`img`	Inserts an inline image
`alt="text"`	Alternative text
`src="url"`	The location of the image file
`srcset="list of urls with descriptors"`	Images to use in different situations
`sizes="list media conditions and layout sizes"`	Image sizes for different layouts
`width="number"`	Width of the graphic
`height="number"`	Height of the graphic
`usemap="usemap"`	Indicates the client-side image map to use
`picture`	Container that provides multiple sources to its contained **img** element
`source`	Provides alternate sources for the **img** element
`src="URL"`	Address of the image resource
`srcset="URL"`	Images to use in different situations
`sizes="source size list"`	Image sizes for different page layouts
`media="media query"`	Query to determine applicable media
`type="media type"`	Media (MIME) type of embedded image file
`svg`	Adds an inline SVG image

TABLE MARKUP

Before we launch into the markup for tables, let's check in with our progress so far. We've covered a lot of territory: how to establish the basic structure of an HTML document, how to mark up text to give it meaning and structure, how to make links, and how to embed simple images on the page.

This chapter and the next two chapters, **Chapter 9, Forms**, and **Chapter 10, Embedded Media**, describe the markup for specialized content that you might not have a need for right away. If you're getting antsy to make your pages look good, skip right to **Part III** and start playing with Cascading Style Sheets. The tables, forms, and media chapters will be here when you're ready for them.

Are you still with me? Great. Let's talk tables. We'll start out by reviewing how tables should be used, then learn the elements used to create them. Remember, this is an HTML chapter, so we're going to focus on the markup that structures the content into tables, and we won't be concerned with how the tables look (that will be tackled in various CSS chapters in **Part III**).

HOW TO USE TABLES

HTML tables were created for instances when you need to add tabular material (data arranged into rows and columns) to a web page. Tables may be used to organize schedules, product comparisons, statistics, or other types of information, as shown in FIGURE 8-1. Note that "data" doesn't necessarily mean numbers. A table cell may contain any sort of information, including numbers, text elements, and even images and multimedia objects.

In visual browsers, the arrangement of data in rows and columns gives readers an instant understanding of the relationships between data cells and their respective header labels. Bear in mind when you are creating tables, however,

Element	Description	Categories	Parents†	List of elements Children	Attributes	Interface
a	Hyperlink	flow; phrasing*; interactive	phrasing	transparent*	globals; href; target; rel; media; hreflang; type	HTMLAnchorElement
abbr	Abbreviation	flow; phrasing	phrasing	phrasing	globals	HTMLElement
address	Contact information for a page or section	flow; formatBlock candidate	flow	flow*	globals	HTMLElement
area	Hyperlink or dead area on an image map	flow; phrasing	phrasing*	empty	globals; alt; coords; shape; href; target; rel; media; hreflang; type	HTMLAreaElement
article	Self-contained syndicatable or reusable composition	flow; sectioning; formatBlock candidate	flow	flow	globals	HTMLElement
aside	Sidebar for tangentially related content	flow; sectioning; formatBlock candidate	flow	flow	globals	HTMLElement
audio	Audio player	flow; phrasing; embedded; interactive	phrasing	source*; transparent*	globals; src; preload; autoplay; mediagroup; loop; controls	HTMLAudioElement
b	Keywords	flow; phrasing	phrasing	phrasing	globals	HTMLElement
base	Base URL and default target browsing context for hyperlinks and forms	metadata	head	empty	globals; href; target	HTMLBaseElement
bdi	Text directionality isolation	flow; phrasing	phrasing	phrasing	globals	HTMLElement
bdo	Text directionality formatting	flow; phrasing	phrasing	phrasing	globals	HTMLElement
blockquote	A section quoted from another source	flow; sectioning root; formatBlock candidate	flow	flow	globals; cite	HTMLQuoteElement

w3c.org

PM	7:30	8:00	8:30	9:00	9:30	10:00	10:30
ABC	The Adventures of Ozzie and Harriet	The Patty Duke Show	Gidget	The Big Valley		Amos Burke — Secret Agent*	
CBS	Lost in Space		The Beverly Hillbillies #8 25.9 rating	Green Acres #11 24.6 rating	The Dick Van Dyke Show #16 23.6 rating	The Danny Kaye Show	
NBC	The Virginian #25 22.0 rating			Bob Hope Presents the Chrysler Theatre / Chrysler Presents a Bob Hope Special		I Spy	

wikipedia.org

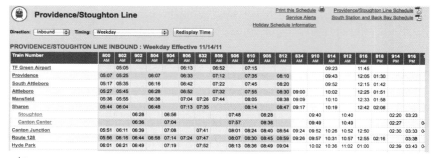

mbta.org

FIGURE 8-1. Examples of tables used for tabular information, such as charts, calendars, and schedules.

that some readers will be hearing your data read aloud with a screen reader or reading Braille output. Later in this chapter, we'll discuss measures you can take to make table content accessible to users who don't have the benefit of visual presentation.

In the days before style sheets, tables were the only option for creating multicolumn layouts or controlling alignment and whitespace. Layout tables, particularly the complex nested table arrangements that were once standard web design fare, have gone the way of the dodo. If you need rows and columns for presentation purposes, there are alternatives that use CSS to achieve the desired effect. In one approach known as CSS Tables, nested **div**s provide the markup, and CSS Table properties make them behave like rows and cells in the browser. You can also achieve many of the effects that previously required table markup using Flexbox and Grid Layout techniques (see **Chapter 16, CSS Layout with Flexbox and Grid**).

That said, this chapter focuses on HTML table elements used to semantically mark up rows and columns of data as described in the HTML specification.

MINIMAL TABLE STRUCTURE

Let's take a look at a simple table to see what it's made of. Here is a small table with three rows and three columns that lists nutritional information.

Menu item	Calories	Fat (g)
Chicken noodle soup	120	2
Caesar salad	400	26

FIGURE 8-2 reveals the structure of this table according to the HTML table model. All of the table's content goes into cells that are arranged into rows. Cells contain either header information (titles for the columns, such as "Calories") or data, which may be any sort of content.

```
table
  row    Menu item   header cell    Calories   header cell    Fat        header cell
  row    Chicken noodle soup  data cell   120   data cell    2          data cell
  row    Caesar salad  data cell   400   data cell    26         data cell
```

FIGURE 8-2. Tables are made up of rows that contain cells. Cells are the containers for content.

Simple enough, right? Now let's look at how those parts translate into elements (FIGURE 8-3).

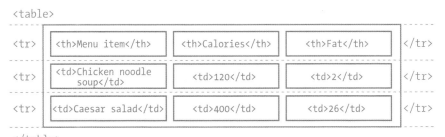

```
<table>
  <tr>   <th>Menu item</th>        <th>Calories</th>    <th>Fat</th>    </tr>
  <tr>   <td>Chicken noodle soup</td>   <td>120</td>    <td>2</td>     </tr>
  <tr>   <td>Caesar salad</td>      <td>400</td>    <td>26</td>    </tr>
</table>
```

FIGURE 8-3. The elements that make up the basic structure of a table.

Stylin' Tables

Once you build the structure of the table in the markup, it's no problem to add a layer of style to customize its appearance.

Style sheets can and should be used to control these aspects of a table's visual presentation. We'll get to all the formatting tools you'll need in the following chapters:

Chapter 12, Formatting Text:

- Font settings for cell contents
- Text color in cells

Chapter 13, Colors and Backgrounds:

- Background colors
- Tiling background images

Chapter 14, Thinking Inside the Box:

- Table dimensions (width and height)
- Borders
- Cell padding (space around cell contents)
- Margins around the table

Chapter 19, More CSS Techniques:

- Special properties for controlling borders and spacing between cells

■ FUN WITH THE SPEC

According to the HTML5 spec, a **table** element may contain "in this order: optionally a **caption** element, followed by zero or more **colgroup** elements, followed optionally by a **thead** element, followed by either zero or more **tbody** elements or one or more **tr** elements, followed optionally by a **tfoot** element (but there can only be one **tfoot** element child in total)."

Well, I'm glad we cleared that up!

FIGURE 8-3 shows the elements that identify the table (**table**), rows (**tr**, for "table row"), and cells (**th**, for "table headers," and **td**, for "table data"). Cells are the heart of the table, because that's where the actual content goes. The other elements just hold things together.

What we don't see are column elements. The number of columns in a table is implied by the number of cells in each row. This is one of the things that make HTML tables potentially tricky. Rows are easy—if you want the table to have three rows, just use three **tr** elements. Columns are different. For a table with four columns, you need to make sure that every row has four **td** or **th** elements. (There's more to the column story, which I cover in the section **"Row and Column Groups"** later in this chapter.)

Written out in a source document, the markup for the table in FIGURE 8-3 looks like the following sample. It is common to stack the **th** and **td** elements in order to make them easier to find in the source. This does not affect how the browser renders them.

```
<table>
    <tr>
        <th>Menu item</th>
        <th>Calories</th>
        <th>Fat (g)</th>
    </tr>
    <tr>
        <td>Chicken noodle soup</td>
        <td>120</td>
        <td>2</td>
    </tr>
    <tr>
        <td>Caesar salad</td>
        <td>400</td>
        <td>26</td>
    </tr>
</table>
```

Remember, all the content must go in cells—that is, within **td** or **th** elements. You can put any content in a cell: text, a graphic, or even another table.

Start and end **table** tags identify the beginning and end of the tabular material. The **table** element may directly contain only some number of **tr** (row) elements, a caption and, optionally, the row and column group elements listed in the **"Row and Column Groups"** section. The only thing that can go in the **tr** element is some number of **td** or **th** elements. In other words, there may be no text content within the **table** and **tr** elements that isn't contained within a **td** or **th**.

Finally, FIGURE 8-4 shows how the table would look in a simple web page, as displayed by default in a browser. I know it's not exciting. Excitement happens in the CSS. What is worth noting is that tables always start on new lines by default in browsers.

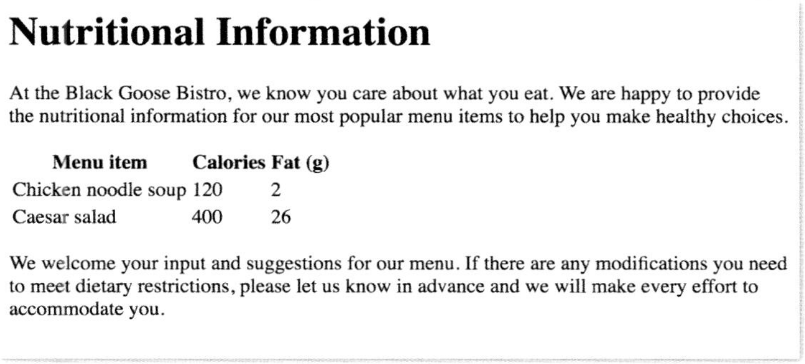

Nutritional Information

At the Black Goose Bistro, we know you care about what you eat. We are happy to provide the nutritional information for our most popular menu items to help you make healthy choices.

Menu item	Calories	Fat (g)
Chicken noodle soup	120	2
Caesar salad	400	26

We welcome your input and suggestions for our menu. If there are any modifications you need to meet dietary restrictions, please let us know in advance and we will make every effort to accommodate you.

FIGURE 8-4. The default rendering of our sample table in a browser.

Here is the source for another table. Can you tell how many rows and columns it will have when it is displayed in a browser?

```
<table>
    <tr>
        <th>Burgers</th>
        <td>Organic Grass-fed Beef</td>
        <td>Black Bean Veggie</td>
    </tr>
    <tr>
        <th>Fries</th>
        <td>Hand-cut Idaho potato</td>
        <td>Seasoned sweet potato</td>
    </tr>
</table>
```

If you guessed that it's a table with two rows and three columns, you are correct! Two **tr** elements create two rows; one **th** and two **td** elements in each row create three columns.

TABLE HEADERS

As you can see in FIGURE 8-4, the text marked up as headers (**th** elements) is displayed differently from the other cells in the table (**td** elements). The difference, however, is not purely cosmetic. Table headers are important because they provide information or context about the cells in the row or column they precede. The **th** element may be handled differently than **td**s by alternative browsing devices. For example, screen readers may read the header aloud before each data cell ("Menu item: Caesar salad, Calories: 400, Fat-g: 26").

In this way, headers are a key tool for making table content accessible. Don't try to fake them by formatting a row of **td** elements differently than the rest of the table. Conversely, don't avoid using **th** elements because of their default rendering (bold and centered). Instead, mark up the headers semantically and change the presentation later with a style rule.

That covers the basics. Before we get fancier, try your hand at EXERCISE 8-1.

EXERCISE 8-1.
Making a simple table

Try writing the markup for the table shown in FIGURE 8-5. You can open a text editor or just write it down on paper. The finished markup is provided in the *materials* folder (*www. learningwebdesign.com/5e/materials*).

Note that I've added a 1-pixel border around cells with a style rule just to make the structure clear. If you would like borders on your tables, copy this **style** element into the **head** of the document(s) you create for the exercises in this chapter:

```
<style>
td, th {
   border: 1px solid gray;
}
</style>
```

Be sure to close all table elements. Technically, you are not *required* to close **tr**, **th**, and **td** elements, but I want you to get in the habit of writing tidy source code for maximum predictability across all browsing devices.

Album	Year
Rubber Soul	1965
Revolver	1966
Sgt. Pepper's	1967
The White Album	1968
Abbey Road	1969

FIGURE 8-5. Write the markup for this table.

EXERCISE 8-2.
Column spans

Try writing the markup for the table shown in FIGURE 8-7. You can open a text editor or just write it down on paper. I've added borders to reveal the cell structure in the figure, but your table won't have them unless you add the style sheet shown in EXERCISE 8-1. Again, the final markup is provided in the *materials* folder.

Some hints:

- The first and third rows show that the table has a total of three columns.
- When a cell is spanned over, its **td** element does not appear in the table.

7:00pm	7:30pm	8:00pm
The Sunday Night Movie		
Perry Mason	Candid Camera	What's My Line?
Bonanza	The Wackiest Ship in the Army	

FIGURE 8-7. Practice column spans by writing the markup for this table.

WARNING

*Be careful with **colspan** values. If you specify a number that exceeds the number of columns in the table, browsers add columns to the existing table, which typically screws things up.*

SPANNING CELLS

One fundamental feature of table structure is cell spanning, which is the stretching of a cell to cover several rows or columns. Spanning cells allows you to create complex table structures, but it has the side effect of making the markup a little more difficult to keep track of. It can also make it potentially more difficult for users with screen readers to follow.

You make a header or data cell span by adding the **colspan** or **rowspan** attributes, as we'll discuss next.

Column Spans

Column spans, created with the **colspan** attribute in the **td** or **th** element, stretch a cell to the right to span over the subsequent columns (FIGURE 8-6). Here a column span is used to make a header apply to two columns (I've added a border around the cells to reveal the structure of the table in the screenshot).

```
<table>
    <tr>
        <th colspan="2">Fat</th>
    </tr>
    <tr>
        <td>Saturated Fat (g)</td>
        <td>Unsaturated Fat (g)</td>
    </tr>
</table>
```

Fat	
Saturated Fat (g)	Unsaturated Fat (g)

FIGURE 8-6. The **colspan** attribute stretches a cell to the right to span the specified number of columns.

Notice in the first row (**tr**) that there is only one **th** element, while the second row has two **td** elements. The **th** for the column that was spanned over is no longer in the source; the cell with the **colspan** stands in for it. Every row should have the same number of cells or equivalent **colspan** values. For example, there are two **td** elements and the **colspan** value is 2, so the implied number of columns in each row is equal.

Try your hand at column spanning in EXERCISE 8-2.

Row Spans

Row spans, created with the **rowspan** attribute, work just like column spans, but they cause the cell to span downward over several rows. In this example, the first cell in the table spans down three rows (FIGURE 8-8).

```
<table>
    <tr>
        <th rowspan="3">Serving Size</th>
        <td>Small (8oz.)</td>
    </tr>
    <tr>
        <td>Medium (16oz.)</td>
    </tr>
    <tr>
        <td>Large (24oz.)</td>
    </tr>
</table>
```

Again, notice that the **td** elements for the cells that were spanned over (the first cells in the remaining rows) do not appear in the source. The **rowspan="3"** implies cells for the subsequent two rows, so no **td** elements are needed.

If you loved spanning columns, you'll love spanning rows in EXERCISE 8-3.

	Small (8oz.)
Serving Size	Medium (16oz.)
	Large (24oz.)

FIGURE 8-8. The **rowspan** attribute stretches a cell downward to span the specified number of rows.

Space in and Between Cells

By default, tables expand just enough to fit the content of the cells, which can look a little cramped. Old versions of HTML included **cellpadding** and **cellspacing** attributes for adding space within and between cells, but they have been kicked out of HTML5 as they are obsolete, presentational markup. The proper way to adjust table cell spacing is with style sheets, of course. The **"Styling Tables"** section in **Chapter 19, More CSS Techniques** addresses cell spacing.

TABLE ACCESSIBILITY

As a web designer, it is important that you always keep in mind how your site's content is going to be used by visitors with impaired sight. It is especially challenging to make sense of tabular material by using a screen reader, but the HTML specification provides measures to improve the experience and make your content more understandable.

Row spans

Try writing the markup for the table shown in FIGURE 8-9. Remember that cells that are spanned over do not appear in the table code.

Some hints:

- Rows always span downward, so the "oranges" cell is part of the first row even though its content is vertically centered.

- Cells that are spanned over do not appear in the code.

apples		pears
bananas	oranges	
lychees		pineapple

FIGURE 8-9. Practice row spans by writing the markup for this table.

`<caption>...</caption>`

Title or description to be displayed
with the table

Describing Table Content

The most effective way to give sight-impaired users an overview of your table is to give it a title or description with the **caption** element. Captions display next to the table (generally, above it) and can be used to describe the table's contents or provide hints on how it is structured.

When used, the **caption** element must be the first thing within the **table** element, as shown in this example, which adds a caption to the nutritional chart from earlier in the chapter:

```
<table>
    <caption>Nutritional Information</caption>
    <tr>
        <th>Menu item</th>
        <th>Calories</th>
        <th>Fat (g)</th>
    </tr>
    <!-- table continues -->
</table>
```

The caption is displayed above the table by default, as shown in FIGURE 8-10, although you can use a style sheet property to move it below the table (**caption-side: bottom**).

Nutritional Information

Menu item	Calories	Fat (g)
Chicken noodle soup	120	2
Caesar salad	400	26

FIGURE 8-10. The table caption is displayed above the table by default.

For longer descriptions, you could consider putting the table in a **figure** element and using the **figcaption** element for the description. The HTML5 specification has a number of suggestions for providing table descriptions (*www.w3.org/TR/html5/tabular-data.html#table-descriptions-techniques*).

Connecting Cells and Headers

We discussed headers briefly as a straightforward method for improving the accessibility of table content, but sometimes it may be difficult to know which header applies to which cells. For example, headers may be at the left or right edge of a row rather than at the top of a column. And although it may be easy for sighted users to understand a table structure at a glance, for users hearing the data as text, the overall organization is not as clear. The **scope** and **headers** attributes allow authors to explicitly associate headers and their respective content.

scope

The **scope** attribute associates a table header with the row, column, group of rows (such as **tbody**), or column group in which it appears by using the values **row**, **col**, **rowgroup**, or **colgroup**, respectively. This example uses the **scope** attribute to declare that a header cell applies to the current row:

```
<tr>
    <th scope="row">Mars</th>
    <td>.95</td>
    <td>.62</td>
    <td>0</td>
</tr>
```

Accessibility experts recommend that every **th** element contain a **scope** attribute to make its associated data explicitly clear.

headers

For really complicated tables in which **scope** is not sufficient to associate a table data cell with its respective header (such as when the table contains multiple spanned cells), the **headers** attribute is used in the **td** element to explicitly tie it to a header's **id** value. In this example, the cell content ".38" is tied to the header "Diameter measured in earths":

```
<th id="diameter">Diameter measured in earths</th>
<!-- many other cells -->
<td headers="diameter">.38</td>
<!-- many other cells -->
```

Unfortunately, support of the **id**/**headers** feature is unreliable. The recommended best practice is to create tables in a way that a simple **scope** attribute will do the job.

This section is obviously only the tip of the iceberg of table accessibility. In-depth instruction on authoring accessible tables is beyond the scope of this beginner book. If you'd like to learn more, I recommend "Creating Accessible Tables" at WebAIM (*webaim.org/techniques/tables/data*) as an excellent starting point.

There is one more important set of elements for helping make the semantic structure of a table clear: row and column grouping elements.

ROW AND COLUMN GROUPS

The sample tables we've been looking at so far in this chapter have been stripped down to their bare essentials to make the structure clear while you're learning how tables work. But tables in the real world are not always so simple. Check out the beauty in FIGURE 8-11 from the CSS Writing Modes Level 3 spec. You can identify three groups of columns (one with headers, two with two columns each), and three groupings of rows (headers, data, and a footnote).

Conceptual table groupings like these are marked up with row group and column group elements that provide additional semantic structure and more "hooks" for styling or scripting. For example, the row and column groups in FIGURE 8-11 were styled with thicker borders to make them stand out visually.

> **VIEW SOURCE**
>
> View the source of the table in FIGURE 8-11 at *www.w3.org/TR/css-writing-modes-3/#unicode-bidi* (you need to scroll down a little). The source is too long to print here, but it is clearly marked up and easy to follow. Note that it uses all the row group elements, column groups, and the **scope** attribute we saw in the last section to associate headers with rows. There are several interesting tables on this page for your source-viewing pleasure.

Bidi control codes injected by 'unicode-bidi' at the start/end of 'display: inline' boxes

'unicode-bidi' **value**	'direction' **value**			
	'ltr'		'rtl'	
	start	**end**	**start**	**end**
'normal'	—	—	—	—
'embed'	LRE (U+202A)	PDF (U+202C)	RLE (U+202B)	PDF (U+202C)
'isolate'	LRI (U+2066)	PDI (U+2069)	RLI (U+2067)	PDI (U+2069)
'bidi-override'*	LRO (U+202D)	PDF (U+202C)	RLO (U+202E)	PDF (U+202C)
'isolate-override'*	FSI,LRO (U+2068,U+202D)	PDF,PDI (U+202C,U+2069)	FSI,RLO (U+2068,U+202E)	PDF,PDI (U+202C,U+2069)
'plaintext'	FSI (U+2068)	PDI (U+2069)	FSI (U+2068)	PDI (U+2069)

* The LRO/RLO+PDF pairs are also applied to the root inline box of a block container if these values of 'unicode-bidi' were specified on the block container.

FIGURE 8-11. An example of a table with row and column groups (from the CSS Writing Modes Level 3 specification).

Row Group Elements

<thead>…</thead>
Table header row group

<tbody>…</tbody>
Table body row group

<tfoot>…</tfoot>
Table footer row group

You can describe rows or groups of rows as belonging to a header, footer, or the body of a table by using the **thead**, **tfoot**, and **tbody** elements, respectively. Some user agents (another word for a browser) may repeat the header and footer rows on tables that span multiple pages. For example, the head and foot rows may print on every page of a multipage table. Authors may also use these elements to apply styles to various regions of a table.

Row group elements may only contain one or more **tr** elements. They contain no direct text content. The **thead** element should appear first, followed by any number of **tbody** elements, followed by an optional **tfoot**.

This is the row group markup for the table in FIGURE 8-11 (**td** and **th** elements are hidden to save space):

```
<table>
…
<thead>
  <!-- headers in these rows-->
  <tr></tr>
  <tr></tr>
  <tr></tr>
<thead>
<tbody>
  <!-- data -->
  <tr></tr>
  <tr></tr>
  <tr></tr>
  <tr></tr>
  <tr></tr>
  <tr></tr>
</tbody>
```

```
<tfoot>
  <!-- footnote -->
  <tr></tr>
</tfoot>
</table>
```

Column Group Elements

As you've learned, columns are implied by the number of cells (**td** or **th**) in each row. You can semantically group columns (and assign **id** and **class** values) using the **colgroup** element.

Column groups are identified at the start of the table, just after the **caption** if there is one, and they give the browser a little heads-up as to the column arrangement in the table. The number of columns a **colgroup** represents is specified with the **span** attribute. Here is the column group section at the beginning of the table in FIGURE 8-11:

```
<table>
  <caption>…</caption>
  <colgroup></colgroup>
  <colgroup span="2"></colgroup>
  <colgroup span="2"></colgroup>
  <!-- rest of table... -->
```

That's all there is to it. If you need to access individual columns within a **colgroup** for scripting or styling, identify them with **col** elements. The previous column group section could also have been written like this:

```
<colgroup></colgroup>
<colgroup>
  <col class="start">
  <col class="end">
</colgroup>
<colgroup>
  <col class="start">
  <col class="end">
</colgroup>
```

Note that the **colgroup** elements contain no content—they only provide an indication of semantically relevant column structure. The empty **col** elements are used as handles for scripts or styles, but are not required.

WRAPPING UP TABLES

This chapter gave you a good overview of the components of HTML tables. EXERCISE 8-4 combines most of what we've covered to give you a little more practice at authoring tables.

`<colgroup>…</colgroup>`

A semantically related group of columns

`<col>…</col>`

One column in a column group

NOTE

When **colgroup** *elements contain* **col** *elements, they must not have a* **span** *attribute.*

EXERCISE 8-4. The table challenge

Now it's time to put together the table writing skills you've acquired in this chapter. Your challenge is to write out the source document for the table shown in FIGURE 8-12.

	A common header for two subheads		Header 3
	Header 1	Header 2	
Thing A	data A1	data A2	data A3
Thing B	data B1	data B2	data B3
Thing C	data C1	data C2	data C3

Your Content Here

FIGURE 8-12. The table challenge.

I'll walk you through it one step at a time.

1. First, open a new document in your text editor and set up its overall structure (**DOCTYPE**, **html**, **head**, **title**, and **body** elements). Save the document as *table.html* in the directory of your choice.

2. Next, in order to make the boundaries of the cells and table clear when you check your work, I'm going to have you add some simple style sheet rules to the document. Don't worry about understanding exactly what's happening here (although it's fairly intuitive); just insert this **style** element in the **head** of the document exactly as you see it here:

```
<head>
  <title>Table Challenge</title>
  <style>
    td, th { border: 1px solid #CCC; }
    table { border: 1px solid black; }
  </style>
</head>
```

3. Now it's time to start building the table. I usually start by setting up the table and adding as many empty row elements as I'll need for the final table as placeholders, as shown here. You can tell from the figure that there are five rows in this table:

```
<body>
  <table>
    <tr></tr>
    <tr></tr>
    <tr></tr>
    <tr></tr>
    <tr></tr>
  </table>
</body>
```

4. Start with the top row, and fill in the **th** and **td** elements from left to right, including any row or column spans as necessary. I'll help with the first row.

The first cell (the one in the top-left corner) spans down the height of two rows, so it gets a **rowspan** attribute. I'll use a **th** here to keep it consistent with the rest of the row. This cell has no content:

```
<table>
  <tr>
    <th rowspan="2"></th>
  </tr>
```

The cell in the second column of the first row spans over the width of two columns, so it gets a **colspan** attribute:

```
<table>
  <tr>
    <th rowspan="2"></th>
    <th colspan="2">A common header for two subheads</th>
  </tr>
```

The cell in the third column has been spanned over by the **colspan** we just added, so we don't need to include it in the markup. The cell in the fourth column also spans down two rows:

```
<table>
  <tr>
    <th rowspan="2"></th>
    <th colspan="2">A common header for two subheads</th>
    <th rowspan="2">Header 3</th>
  </tr>
```

5. Now it's your turn. Continue filling in the **th** and **td** elements for the remaining four rows of the table. Here's a hint: the first and last cells in the second row have been spanned over. Also, if it's bold in the example, make it a header.

6. To complete the content, add the title over the table by using the **caption** element.

7. Use the **scope** attribute to make sure that the Thing A, Thing B, and Thing C headers are associated with their respective rows.

8. Finally, give the table row and column groups for greater sematic clarity. There is no **tfoot** in this table. There are two column groups: one column for headers, the rest for data. Use the **span** attribute (no need for individual column identification).

9. Save your work and open the file in a browser. The table should look just like the one on this page. If not, go back and adjust your markup. If you're stumped, the final markup for this exercise is provided in the *materials* folder.

TEST YOURSELF

The answers to these questions appear in **Appendix A**.

1. What are the parts (elements) of a basic HTML table?

2. What elements can a **table** contain directly (i.e., first-level children)?

3. What elements can a **tr** contain?

4. When would you use the **col** (column) element?

5. Find five errors in this table markup:

```
<caption>Primetime Television 1965</caption>
<table>
  Thursday Night
  <tr></tr>
    <th>7:30</th>
    <th>8:00</th>
    <th>8:30</th>
  <tr>
    <td>Shindig</td>
    <td>Donna Reed Show</td>
    <td>Bewitched</td>
  <tr>
    <colspan="2">Laredo</colspan>
    <td>Daniel Boone</td>
  </tr>
</table>
```

ELEMENT REVIEW: TABLES

The following is a summary of the elements we covered in this chapter.

Element and attributes	Description
table	Establishes a table element
tr	Establishes a row within a table
td	Establishes a cell within a table row
colspan="*number*"	Number of columns the cell should span
rowspan="*number*"	Number of rows the cell should span
headers="*header name*"	Associates the data cell with a header
th	Table header associated with a row or column
abbr="*text*"	Alternative label for when the header cell is referenced in other contexts
colspan="*number*"	Number of columns the cell should span
rowspan="*number*"	Number of rows the cell should span
headers="*header name*"	Associates a header with another header
scope="row|col|rowgroup|colgroup"	Associates the header with a row, row group, column, or column group
caption	Gives the table a title that displays in the browser
colgroup	Declares a group of columns
span="*number*"	Number of columns the column group spans; may not be used when the **colgroup** contains **col** elements
col	Declares a column
span="*number*"	Number of columns the column spans
tbody	Identifies a table body row group
thead	Identifies a table header row group
tfoot	Identifies a table footer row group

FORMS

It didn't take long for the web to shift from a network of pages to read to a place where you go to get things *done*—making purchases, booking plane tickets, signing petitions, searching a site, posting a tweet...the list goes on! Web forms handle all of these interactions.

In fact, in response to this shift from page to application, HTML5 introduced a bonanza of new form controls and attributes that make it easier for users to fill out forms and for developers to create them. Tasks that have traditionally relied on JavaScript may be handled by markup and native browser behavior alone. HTML5 introduces a number of new form-related elements, 12 new input types, and many new attributes (they are listed in TABLE 9-1 at the end of this chapter). Some of these features are waiting for browser implementation to catch up, so I will be sure to note which controls may not be universally supported.

This chapter introduces web forms, how they work, and the markup used to create them. I'll also briefly discuss the importance of web form design.

HOW FORMS WORK

There are two parts to a working form. The first part is the form that you see on the page itself that is created using HTML markup. Forms are made up of buttons, input fields, and drop-down menus (collectively known as form controls) used to collect information from the user. Forms may also contain text and other elements.

The other component of a web form is an application or script on the server that processes the information collected by the form and returns an appropriate response. It's what makes the form *work*. In other words, posting an

HTML document with form elements isn't enough. Web applications and scripts require programming know-how that is beyond the scope of this book, but the **"Getting Your Forms to Work"** sidebar, later in this chapter, provides some options for getting the scripts you need.

From Data Entry to Response

If you are going to be creating web forms, it is beneficial to understand what is happening behind the scenes. This example traces the steps of a transaction using a simple form that gathers names and email addresses for a mailing list; however, it is typical of the process for many forms.

1. Your visitor—let's call her Sally—opens the page with a web form in the browser window. The browser sees the form control elements in the markup and renders them with the appropriate form controls on the page, including two text-entry fields and a Submit button (shown in FIGURE 9-1).

2. Sally would like to sign up for this mailing list, so she enters her name and email address into the fields and submits the form by hitting the Submit button.

3. The browser collects the information she entered, encodes it (see the sidebar **"A Word About Encoding"**), and sends it to the web application on the server.

4. The web application accepts the information and processes it (that is, does whatever it is programmed to do with it). In this example, the name and email address are added to a mailing list database.

5. The web application also returns a response. The kind of response sent back depends on the content and purpose of the form. Here, the response is a simple web page saying thank you for signing up for the mailing list. Other applications might respond by reloading the form page with updated information, by moving the user on to another related form page, or by issuing an error message if the form is not filled out correctly, to name only a few examples.

6. The server sends the web application's response back to the browser, where it is displayed. Sally can see that the form worked and that she has been added to the mailing list.

A Word About Encoding

Form data is encoded via the same method used for URLs. Spaces and other characters that are not permitted get translated into their hexadecimal equivalents. For example, each space character in the collected form data is represented by the character **+** or **%20** and a slash (**/**) character is replaced with **%2F**. You don't need to worry about this; the browser handles it automatically.

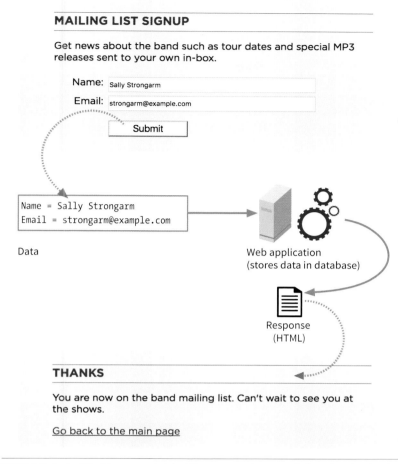

FIGURE 9-1. What happens behind the scenes when a web form is submitted.

THE FORM ELEMENT

Forms are added to web pages with (no surprise here) the **form** element. The **form** element is a container for all the content of the form, including some number of form controls, such as text-entry fields and buttons. It may also contain block elements (**h1**, **p**, and lists, for example). However, it may *not* contain another **form** element.

This sample source document contains a form similar to the one shown in FIGURE 9-1:

```
<!DOCTYPE html>
<html>
<head>
  <title>Mailing List Signup</title>
  <meta charset="utf-8">
</head>
```

`<form>...</form>`

Interactive form

■ **MARKUP TIP**

Be careful not to nest **form** elements or allow them to overlap. A **form** element must be closed before the next one begins.

NOTE

*It is current best practice to wrap form controls in semantic HTML elements such as lists or **div**s. Ordered lists, as shown in this example, are a popular solution, but know that there are often default styles that you'll need to clear out before styling them, particularly on mobile browsers. The **fieldset**, **legend**, and **label** elements used in the example improve accessibility. They are explained later in this chapter.*

```
<body>
  <h1>Mailing List Signup</h1>

  <form action="/mailinglist.php" method="POST">
    <fieldset>
      <legend>Join our email list</legend>
      <p>Get news about the band such as tour dates and special MP3
releases sent to your own in-box.</p>
      <ol>
        <li><label for="firstlast">Name:</label>
          <input type="text" name="fullname" id="firstlast"></li>
        <li><label for="email">Email:</label>
          <input type="text" name="email" id="email"></li>
      </ol>
      <input type="submit" value="Submit">
    </fieldset>
  </form>

</body>
</html>
```

In addition to being a container for form control elements, the **form** element has some attributes that are necessary for interacting with the form processing program on the server. Let's take a look at each.

The action Attribute

The **action** attribute provides the location (URL) of the application or script that will be used to process the form. The **action** attribute in this example sends the data to a script called *mailinglist.php*:

```
<form action="/mailinglist.php" method="POST">...</form>
```

The *.php* suffix indicates that this form is processed by a script written in the PHP scripting language, but web forms may be processed by any of the following technologies:

- PHP (*.php*) is an open source scripting language most commonly used with the Apache web server. It is the most popular and widely supported forms processing option.

- Microsoft ASP (Active Server Pages; *.asp*) is a programming environment for the Microsoft Internet Information Server (IIS).

- Microsoft's ASP.NET (Active Server Page; *.aspx*) is a newer Microsoft language that was designed to compete with PHP.

- Ruby on Rails. Ruby is the programming language that is used with the Rails platform. Many popular web applications are built with it.

- JavaServer Pages (*.jsp*) is a Java-based technology similar to ASP.

- Python is a popular scripting language for web and server applications.

There are other form-processing options that may have their own suffixes or none at all (as is the case for the Ruby on Rails platform). Check with your programmer, server administrator, or script documentation for the proper name and location of the program to be provided by the **action** attribute (see **Web Hosting Tip**).

Sometimes there is form processing code such as PHP embedded right in the HTML file. In that case, leave the action empty, and the form will post to the page itself.

The method Attribute

The **method** attribute specifies how the information should be sent to the server. Let's use this data gathered from the sample form in FIGURE 9-1 as an example.

```
fullname = Sally Strongarm
email = strongarm@example.com
```

When the browser encodes that information for its trip to the server, it looks like this (see the earlier sidebar if you need a refresher on encoding):

```
fullname=Sally+Strongarm&email=strongarm%40example.com
```

There are only two methods for sending this encoded data to the server: POST or GET, indicated by the **method** attribute in the **form** element. The method is optional and will default to GET if omitted. We'll look at the difference between the two methods in the following sections. Our example uses the POST method, as shown here:

```
<form action="/mailinglist.php" method="POST">...</form>
```

The GET method

With the GET method, the encoded form data gets tacked right onto the URL sent to the server. A question mark character separates the URL from the following data, as shown here:

```
get http://www.bandname.com/mailinglist.php?name=Sally+Strongarm&email=→
strongarm%40example.com
```

GET is inappropriate if the form submission performs an action, such as deleting something or adding data to a database, because if the user goes back, it gets submitted again.

The POST method

When the form's method is set to POST, the browser sends a separate server request containing some special headers followed by the data. In theory, only the server sees the content of this request, and thus it is the best method for sending secure information such as a home address or other personal information. In practice, make sure HTTPS is enabled on your server so the user's data is encrypted and inaccessible in transit. (HTTPS is discussed in **Chapter 2, How the Web Works**.)

Getting Your Forms to Work

If you aren't a programmer, don't fret. You have a few options for getting your forms operational:

Use hosting plan goodies

Many site hosting plans include access to scripts for simple functions such as mailing lists. More advanced plans may even provide everything you need to add a full shopping cart system to your site as part of your monthly hosting fee. Documentation or a technical support person should be available to help you use them.

Hire a programmer

If you need a custom solution, you may need to hire a programmer who has server-side programming skills. Tell your programmer what you are looking to accomplish with your form, and she will suggest a solution. Again, you need to make sure you have permission to install scripts on your server under your current hosting plan, and that the server supports the language you choose.

NOTE

POST and GET are not case-sensitive and are commonly listed in all uppercase by convention. In XHTML documents, however, the value of the **method** *attribute (post or get) must be provided in all lowercase letters.*

All form controls (except submit and reset buttons) must include a name attribute.

The POST method is also preferable for sending a lot of data, such as a lengthy text entry, because there is no character limit as there is for GET.

The GET method is appropriate if you want users to be able to bookmark the results of a form submission (such as a list of search results). Because the content of the form is in plain sight, GET is not appropriate for forms with private personal or financial information. In addition, GET may not be used when the form is used to upload a file.

In this chapter, we'll stick with the more prevalent POST method. Now that we've gotten through the technical aspects of the **form** element, let's turn our attention to form controls.

VARIABLES AND CONTENT

Web forms use a variety of controls that allow users to enter information or choose between options. Control types include various text-entry fields, buttons, menus, and a few controls with special functions. They are added to the document with a collection of form control elements that we'll be examining one by one in the upcoming **"The Great Form Control Roundup"** section.

As a web designer, you need to be familiar with control options to make your forms easy and intuitive to use. It is also useful to have an idea of what form controls are doing behind the scenes.

The name Attribute

The job of each form control is to collect one bit of information from a user. In the previous form example, text-entry fields collect the visitor's name and email address. To use the technical term, "fullname" and "email" are two variables collected by the form. The data entered by the user ("Sally Strongarm" and "strongarm@example.com") is the value or content of the variables.

The **name** attribute provides the variable name for the control. In this example, the text gathered by a **textarea** element is defined as the "comment" variable:

```
<textarea name="comment" rows="4" cols="45" placeholder="Leave us a comment."></textarea>
```

When a user enters a comment in the field ("This is the best band ever!"), it would be passed to the server as a name/value (variable/content) pair like this:

```
comment=This+is+the+best+band+ever%21
```

All form control elements must include a **name** attribute so the form processing application can sort the information. You may include a **name** attribute for **submit** and **reset** button elements, but they are not required, because they have special functions (submitting or resetting the form) not related to data collection.

Naming Your Variables

You can't just name controls willy-nilly. The web application that processes the data is programmed to look for specific variable names. If you are designing a form to work with a preexisting application or script, you need to find out the specific variable names to use in the form so they are speaking the same language. You can get the variable names from the instructions provided with a ready-to-use script on your server, your system administrator, or the programmer you are working with.

If the script or application will be created later, be sure to name your variables simply and descriptively and to document them well. In addition, to avoid confusion, you are advised to name each variable uniquely—that is, don't use the same name for two variables (however, there may be exceptions for which it is desirable). You should also avoid putting character spaces in variable names. Use an underscore or hyphen instead.

We've covered the basics of the **form** element and how variables are named. Now we can get to the real meat of form markup: the controls.

THE GREAT FORM CONTROL ROUNDUP

This is the fun part—playing with form controls to the page. This section introduces the following:

- Text-entry controls
- Specialized text-entry
- Submit and reset but
- Radio and checkbox
- Pull-down and scro
- File selection and u
- Hidden controls
- Dates and times
- Numerical contr
- Color picker co

We'll pause along the way out by constructing the pizza ordering form shown in FIGURE 9-2.

As you will see, the majority of controls are added to a form via the **input** element. The functionality and appearance of the **input** element changes based on the value of the **type** attribute in the tag. In HTML5.2, there are *twenty-two* types of input controls. We'll take a look at them all.

NOTE

The attributes associated with each input type are listed in TABLE 9-1 *at the end of this chapter.*

Black Goose Bistro | Pizza-on-Demand

Our 12" wood-fired pizzas are available for delivery. Build your custom pizza and we'll deliver it within an hour.

Your Information
Name:
Address:
Telephone Number:
Email:
Delivery instructions:
No more than 400 characters long.

Design Your Dream Pizza:

Pizza specs
Crust *(Choose one)*:
- Classic white
- Multigrain
- Cheese-stuffed crust
- Gluten-free

Toppings *(Choose as many as you want)*:
- ☑ Red sauce
- ☐ White sauce
- ☐ Mozzarella Cheese
- ☐ Pepperoni
- ☐ Mushrooms
- ☐ Peppers
- ☐ Anchovies

Number
How many pizzas: 1

Bring me a pizza! | Reset

FIGURE 9-2. The pizza ordering form we'll build in the exercises in this chapter.

Text-Entry Controls

One of the most common web form tasks is entering text information. Which element you use to collect text input depends on whether users are asked to enter a single line of text (**input**) or multiple lines (**textarea**).

Be aware that if your form has text-entry fields, it needs to use the secure HTTPS protocol to protect the user-entered content while their data is in transit to the server (see the **"HTTPS, the Secure Web Protocol"** sidebar in   for more information).

Single-line text field

One of the most straightforward form input types is the text-entry field for entering a single word or line of text. In fact, it is the default input type, which means it is what you'll get if you forget to include the **type** attribute or include an unrecognized value. Add a text input field to a form by inserting an **input** element with its **type** attribute set to **text**, as shown here and in FIGURE 9-3:

```
<li><label>Favorite color: <input type="text" name="favcolor"
value="Red" maxlength="50"></label></li>
```

NOTE

The markup examples throughout this section include the **label** *element, which is used to improve accessibility. We will discuss* **label** *in the upcoming* **"Form Accessibility Features"** *section, but in the meantime, I want you to get used to seeing proper form markup.*

`<input type="text">`

Single-line text-entry control

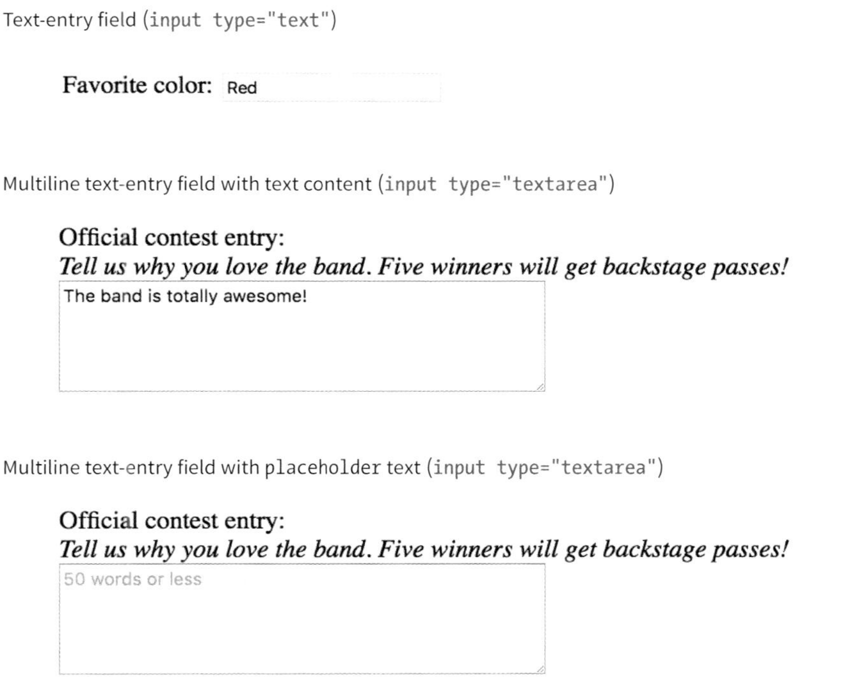

Text-entry field (`input type="text"`)

Favorite color: Red

Multiline text-entry field with text content (`input type="textarea"`)

Official contest entry:
Tell us why you love the band. Five winners will get backstage passes!

The band is totally awesome!

Multiline text-entry field with placeholder text (`input type="textarea"`)

Official contest entry:
Tell us why you love the band. Five winners will get backstage passes!

50 words or less

FIGURE 9-3. Examples of the text-entry control options for web forms.

NOTE

The specific rendering style of form controls varies by operating system and browser version.

There are a few attributes in there that I'd like to point out:

`name`

    The **name** attribute is required for indicating the variable name.

`value`

    The **value** attribute specifies default text that appears in the field when the form is loaded. When you reset a form, it returns to this value. The value of the **value** attribute gets submitted to the server, so in this example, the value "Red" will be sent with the form unless the user changes it. As an alternative, you could use the **placeholder** attribute to provide a hint of what to type in the field, such as "My favorite color". The value of **placeholder** is not submitted with the form, and is purely a user interface enhancement. You'll see it in action in the upcoming section.

BROWSER SUPPORT NOTE

Versions of Internet Explorer prior to version 11 and older versions of Android do not support **placeholder**.

`maxlength, minlength`

    By default, users can type an unlimited number of characters in a text field regardless of its size (the display scrolls to the right if the text exceeds the character width of the box). You can set a maximum character limit using the **maxlength** attribute if the form-processing program you are using requires it. The **minlength** attribute specifies the minimum number of characters.

size

The **size** attribute specifies the length of the input field in number of visible characters. It is more common, however, to use style sheets to set the size of the input area. By default, a text input widget displays at a size that accommodates 20 characters.

Multiline text-entry field

<textarea>…</textarea>
Multiline text-entry control

At times, you'll want your users to be able to enter more than just one line of text. For these instances, use the **textarea** element, which is replaced by a multiline, scrollable text entry box when displayed by the browser (FIGURE 9-3).

Unlike the empty **input** element, you can put content between the opening and closing tags in the **textarea** element. The content of the **textarea** element shows up in the text box when the form is displayed in the browser. It also gets sent to the server when the form is submitted, so carefully consider what goes there.

```
<p><label>Official contest entry: <br>
<em>Tell us why you love the band. Five winners will get backstage
passes!</em><br>
<textarea name="contest_entry" rows="5" cols="50">The band is totally
awesome!</textarea></label></p>
```

The **rows** and **cols** attributes provide a way to specify the size of the **textarea** with markup. **rows** specifies the number of lines the text area should display, and **cols** specifies the width in number of characters (although it is more common to use CSS to specify the width of the field). Scrollbars will be provided if the user types more text than fits in the allotted space.

There are also a few attributes not shown in the example. The **wrap** attribute specifies whether the soft line breaks (where the text naturally wraps at the edge of the box) are preserved when the form is submitted. A value of **soft** (the default) does not preserve line breaks. The **hard** value preserves line breaks when the **cols** attribute is used to set the character width of the box. The **maxlength** and **minlength** attributes set the maximum and minimum number of characters that can be typed into the field.

It is not uncommon for developers to put nothing between the opening and closing tags, and provide a hint of what should go there with a **placeholder** attribute instead. Placeholder text, unlike **textarea** content, is not sent to the server when the form is submitted. Examples of **textarea** content and placeholder text are shown in FIGURE 9-3.

```
<p>Official contest entry:<br>
<em>Tell us why you love the band. Five winners will get backstage
passes!</em><br>
<textarea name="contest_entry" placeholder="50 words or less" rows="5"
cols="50"></textarea>
</p>
```

disabled and readonly

The **disabled** and **readonly** attributes both prevent users from interacting with a form control, but they work slightly differently.

When a form element is disabled, it cannot be selected. Visual browsers may render the control as grayed-out by default (which you can change with CSS, of course). The disabled state can only be changed with a script. This is a useful attribute for restricting access to some form fields based on data entered earlier in the form and can be applied to any form control or **fieldset**.

The **readonly** attribute prevents the user from changing the value of the form control (although it can be selected). This enables developers to use scripts to set values for controls contingent on other data entered earlier in the form. Inputs that are **readonly** should have strong visual cues that they are somehow different from other inputs, or they could be confusing to users who are trying to change their values. The **readonly** attribute can be used with **textarea** and text-based input controls (see TABLE 9-1 at the very end of this chapter).

The most important difference is that **readonly** fields are submitted when the form is submitted, but **disabled** ones are not.

Specialized Text-Entry Fields

In addition to the generic single-line text entry, there are a number of input types for entering specific types of information such as passwords, search terms, email addresses, telephone numbers, and URLs.

Password entry field

A password field works just like a text-entry field, except the characters are obscured from view by asterisk (*) or bullet (•) characters, or another character determined by the browser.

```
<input type="password">
```
Password text control

It's important to note that although the characters entered in the password field are not visible to casual onlookers, the form does not encrypt the information, so it should not be considered a real security measure.

Here is an example of the markup for a password field. FIGURE 9-4 shows how it might look after the user enters a password in the field.

```
<li><label for="form-pswd">Password:</label><br>
  <input type="password" name="pswd" maxlength="12" id="form-pswd"></li>
```

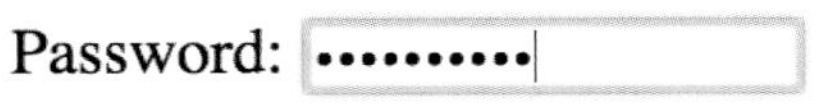

Password: ●●●●●●●●●

FIGURE 9-4. Passwords are converted to bullets in the browser display.

Search, email, telephone numbers, and URLs

`<input type="search">`

Search field

`<input type="email">`

Email address

`<input type="tel">`

Telephone number

`<input type="url">`

Location (URL)

Until HTML5, the only way to collect email addresses, telephone numbers, URLs, or search terms was to insert a generic text input field. In HTML5, the `email`, `tel`, `url`, and `search` input types give the browser a heads-up as to what type of information to expect in the field. These input types use the same attributes as the generic text input type described earlier (`name`, `maxlength`, `minlength`, `size`, and `value`), as well as a number of other attributes (see TABLE 9-1 at the end of the chapter).

All of these input types are typically displayed as single-line text inputs. But browsers that support them can do some interesting things with the extra semantic information. For example, Safari on iOS uses the input type to provide a keyboard well suited to the entry task, such as the keyboard featuring a Search button for the `search` input type or a ".com" button when the input type is set to `url` (FIGURE 9-5). Browsers usually add a one-click "clear field" icon (usually a little X) in search fields. A supporting browser could check the user's input to see that it is valid—for example, by making sure text entered in an `email` input follows the standard email address structure (in the past, you needed JavaScript for validation). For example, the Opera (FIGURE 9-6) and Chrome browsers display a warning if the input does not match the expected format.

Although email, search, telephone, and URL inputs are well supported by up-to-date browsers, there may be inconsistencies in the way they are handled. Older browsers, such as Opera Mini and any version of Internet Explorer prior to 11, do not recognize them at all, but will display the default generic text input instead, which works perfectly fine.

FIGURE 9-5. Safari on iOS provides custom keyboards based on the input type.

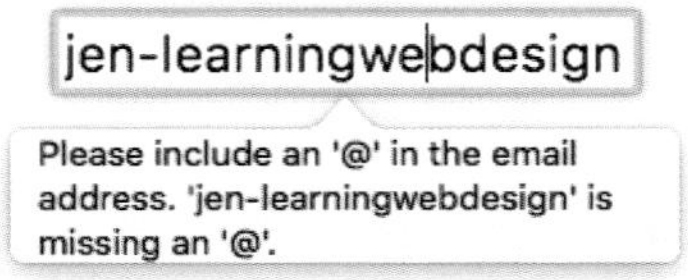

FIGURE 9-6. Opera displays a warning when input does not match the expected **email** format as part of its client-side validation support.

Drop-Down Suggestions

```
<datalist>…</datalist>
```
Drop-down menu input

The **datalist** element allows the author to provide a drop-down menu of suggested values for any type of text input. It gives the user some shortcuts to select from, but if none are selected, the user can still type in their own text. Within the **datalist** element, suggested values are marked up as **option** elements. Use the **list** attribute in the **input** element to associate it with the **id** of its respective **datalist**.

In the following example (FIGURE 9-7), a **datalist** suggests several education level options for a text input:

```
<p>Education completed: <input type="text" list="edulevel"
name="education">

<datalist id="edulevel">
  <option value="High School">
  <option value="Bachelors Degree">
  <option value="Masters Degree">
  <option value="PhD">
</datalist>
```

As of this writing, browser support for datalists remains spotty. Chrome and Opera support it, but there is a bug that makes datalists unscrollable (i.e., unusable) if the list is too long, so it is best used for short lists of options. IE11 and Edge have buggy implementations, and Safari and iOS don't support it at all. The good news is if it is unsupported, browsers present a simple text input, which is a perfectly acceptable fallback. You could also use a JavaScript polyfill to create **datalist** functionality.

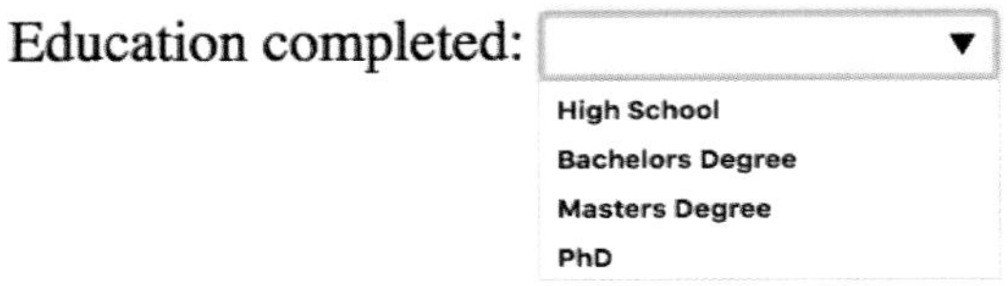

FIGURE 9-7. A **datalist** creates a pop-up menu of suggested values for a text-entry field.

WARNING

The values from form controls should be checked by the server code (PHP, ASP.NET, etc.), as they can be hacked or manipulated. So, although they make controlling and validating user input easier, it is still vital to perform server-side checks before updating the data-base on the server.

A Few More Buttons

A Few More Buttons

There are a handful of custom button elements that are a little off the beaten path for beginners, but in the interest of thoroughness, here they are tucked off in a sidebar.

Image buttons

`<input type="image">`

This type of **input** control allows you to replace the submit button with an image of your choice. The image will appear flat, not like a 3-D button. Unfortunately, this type of button has accessibility issues, so be sure to include a carefully chosen **alt** value.

Custom input button

`<input type="button">`

Setting the type of the **input** element to "button" creates a button that can be customized with JavaScript. It has no predefined function on its own, unlike submit and reset buttons.

The button element

`<button>...</button>`

The **button** element is a flexible element for creating custom buttons similar to those created with the **input** element. The content of the **button** element (text and/or images) is what gets displayed on the button.

For more information on what you can do with the **button** element, read "Push My Button" by Aaron Gustafson at *digital-web.com/articles/push_my_button*. "When to Use the Button Element," by Chris Coyier is another helpful read (*css-tricks.com/use-button-element/*).

Submit and Reset Buttons

`<input type="submit">`
Submits the form data to the server

`<input type="reset">`
Resets the form controls to their default settings

There are several kinds of buttons that can be added to web forms. The most fundamental is the submit button. When clicked or tapped, the submit button immediately sends the collected form data to the server for processing. A reset button returns the form controls to the state they were in when the form initially loaded. In other words, resetting the form doesn't simply clear all the fields.

Both submit and reset buttons are added via the **input** element. As mentioned earlier, because these buttons have specific functions that do not include the entry of data, they are the only form control elements that do not require the **name** attribute, although it is OK to add one if you need it.

Submit and reset buttons are straightforward to use. Just place them in the appropriate place in the form, which in most cases is at the very end. By default, the submit button displays with the label "Submit" or "Submit Query," and the reset button is labeled "Reset." You can change the text on the button by using the **value** attribute, as shown in the reset button in this example (FIGURE 9-8).

```
<p><input type="submit"> <input type="reset" value="Start over"></p>
```

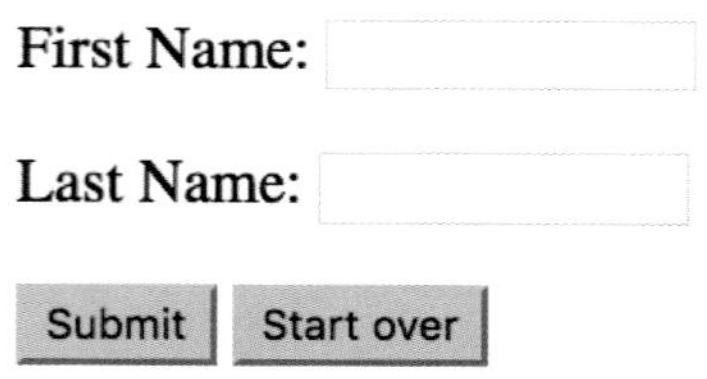

First Name: [   ]

Last Name: [   ]

[Submit] [Start over]

FIGURE 9-8. Submit and reset buttons.

The reset button is not used in forms as commonly as it used to be. That is because in contemporary form development, we use JavaScript to check the validity of form inputs along the way, so users get feedback as they go along. With thoughtful design and assistance, fewer users should get to the end of the form and need to reset the whole thing. Still, it is a good function to be aware of.

At this point, you know enough about form markup to start building the questionnaire shown in FIGURE 9-2.

EXERCISE 9-1 walks you through the first steps.

EXERCISE 9-1. Starting the pizza order form

Here's the scenario. You are the web designer in charge of creating an online pizza ordering form for Black Goose Bistro. The owner has handed you a sketch (FIGURE 9-9) of the form's content. There are sticky notes from the programmer with information about the script and variable names you need to use.

Your challenge is to turn the sketch into a functional form. I've given you a head start by creating a bare-bones document with text content and minimal markup and styles. This document, *pizza.html*, is available online at *learningwebdesign.com/5e/ materials*. The finished form is also provided.

Black Goose Bistro | Pizza-on-Demand

Our 12" wood-fired pizzas are available for delivery. Build your custom pizza and we'll deliver it within an hour.

Your Information

Name: [   ]

Address: [   ]

Telephone Number: [   ]

Email: [   ]

Delivery instructions:

This form should be sent to **http://blackgoosebistro.com/pizza.php** *via the POST method.*

Name the text fields **customername, address, telephone, email,** *and* **instructions,** *respectively.*

[*Limit characters and add placeholder text "No more than 400 characters long"*]

Design Your Dream Pizza:
Pizza specs

Name the controls in this section **crust, toppings[],** *and* **number,** *respectively.*

Note that the brackets ([]) after "toppings" are required in order for the script to process it correctly.

Crust (Choose one):
   ( ) Classic white
   ( ) Multigrain
   ( ) Cheese-stuffed crust
   ( ) Gluten-free

Toppings (Choose as many as you want):
   [X] Red sauce
   [   ] White sauce
   [   ] Mozzarella Cheese
   [   ] Pepperoni
   [   ] Mushrooms
   [   ] Peppers
   [   ] Anchovies

Make sure "red sauce" is selected when the page loads.

Number
How many pizzas: [**1**]

Pull down menu for ordering up to 6 pizzas.

[Bring me a pizza!]   [Reset]

Change the Submit button text.

FIGURE 9-9. A sketch of the Black Goose Bistro pizza ordering form.

EXERCISE 9-1. Continued

1. Open the file *pizza.html* in a text editor.

2. The first thing we'll do is put everything after the intro paragraph into a **form** element. The programmer has left a note specifying the **action** and the **method** to use for this form. The resulting **form** element should look like this (keep it on one line):

```
<form action="http://www.blackgoosebistro.com/
pizza.php" method="POST">
…
</form>
```

3. In this exercise, we'll work on the "Your Information" section of the form. Start with the first four short text-entry form controls that are marked up appropriately as an unordered list. Here's the first one; you insert the other three:

```
<li>Name: <input type="text" name="customername">
</li>
```

HINTS: Choose the most appropriate input type for each entry field. Be sure to name the input elements as specified in the programmer's note.

4. After "Delivery instructions:" add a line break and a multiline text area. Because we aren't writing a style sheet for this form, use markup to make it four rows long and 60 characters wide (in the real world, CSS is preferable because it gives you more fine-tuned control):

```
<li>Delivery instructions:<br>
<textarea name="instructions" rows="4" cols="60"
maxlength="400" placeholder="No more than 400
characters long"></textarea></li>
```

5. We'll skip the rest of the form for now until we get a few more controls under our belt, but we can add the submit and reset buttons at the end, just before the **</form>** tag. Note that they've asked us to change the text on the submit button.

```
<p><input type="submit" value="Bring me a
pizza!"><input type="reset"></p>
```

6. Now, save the document and open it in a browser. The parts that are finished should generally match FIGURE 9-2. If they don't, then you have some more work to do.

Once the document looks right, take it for a spin by entering some information and submitting the form. You should get a response like the one shown in FIGURE 9-10. Yes, *pizza.php* actually works, but sorry, no pizzas will be delivered.

FIGURE 9-10. You should see a response page like this if your form is working. The pizza description fields will be added in later exercises, so they will return "empty" for now.

NOTE

I have omitted the **fieldset** *and* **label** *elements from the code examples for radio buttons, checkboxes, and menus in order to keep the markup structure as simple and clear as possible. In the upcoming section* **"Form Accessibility Features,"** *you will learn why it is important to include them in your markup for all form elements.*

Radio and Checkbox Buttons

Both checkbox and radio buttons make it simple for your visitors to choose from a number of provided options. They are similar in that they function like little on/off switches that can be toggled by the user and are added with the **input** element. They serve distinct functions, however.

A form control made up of a collection of radio buttons is appropriate when only one option from the group is permitted—in other words, when the selections are mutually exclusive (such as "Yes or No," or "Pick-up or Delivery"). When one radio button is "on," all of the others must be "off," sort of the way buttons used to work on old radios: press one button in, and the rest pop out.

When checkboxes are grouped together, however, it is possible to select as many or as few from the group as desired. This makes them the right choice for lists in which more than one selection is OK.

Radio buttons

Radio buttons are added to a form via the **input** element with the **type** attribute set to "radio." Here is the syntax for a minimal radio button:

```
<input type="radio" name="variable" value="value">
```

The **name** attribute is required and plays an important role in binding multiple radio inputs into a set. When you give a number of radio button inputs the same **name** value ("age" in the following example), they create a group of mutually exclusive options.

In this example, radio buttons are used as an interface for users to enter their age group. A person can't belong to more than one age group, so radio buttons are the right choice. FIGURE 9-11 shows how radio buttons are rendered in the browser.

```
<p>How old are you?</p>
<ol>
  <li><input type="radio" name="age" value="under24" checked> under
24</li>
  <li><input type="radio" name="age" value="25-34"> 25 to 34</li>
  <li><input type="radio" name="age" value="35-44"> 35 to 44</li>
  <li><input type="radio" name="age" value="over45"> 45+</li>
</ol>
```

Notice that all of the **input** elements have the same variable name ("age"), but their values are different. Because these are radio buttons, only one button can be checked at a time, and therefore, only one value will be sent to the server for processing when the form is submitted.

You can decide which button is checked when the form loads by adding the **checked** attribute to the **input** element (see **Note**). In this example, the button next to "under 24" will be checked when the page loads.

```
<input type="radio">
```
Radio button

NOTE

It may look like the **checked** *attribute has no value, but it is one of the attributes in HTML that can be minimized to one word. Behind the scenes, the minimized* **checked** *attribute stands for the rather redundant:*

```
checked="checked"
```

One of the rules of the stricter XHTML syntax is that attributes cannot be minimized in this way.

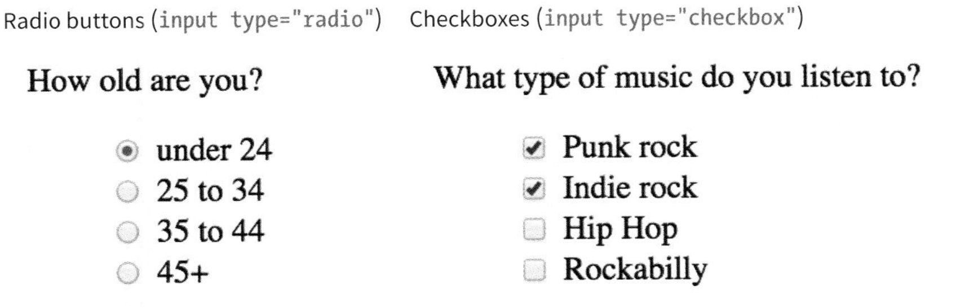

Radio buttons (`input type="radio"`)   Checkboxes (`input type="checkbox"`)

How old are you?

- ◉ under 24
- ○ 25 to 34
- ○ 35 to 44
- ○ 45+

What type of music do you listen to?

- ☑ Punk rock
- ☑ Indie rock
- ☐ Hip Hop
- ☐ Rockabilly

FIGURE 9-11. Radio buttons (left) are appropriate when only one selection is permitted. Checkboxes (right) are best when users may choose any number of choices, from none to all of them.

Checkbox buttons

`<input type="checkbox">`

Checkbox button

Checkboxes are added via the **input** element with its type set to **checkbox**. As with radio buttons, you create groups of checkboxes by assigning them the same **name** value. The difference, as we've already noted, is that more than one checkbox may be checked at a time. The value of every checked button will be sent to the server when the form is submitted. Here's an example of a group of checkbox buttons used to indicate musical interests; FIGURE 9-11 shows how they look in the browser:

```
<p>What type of music do you listen to?</p>
<ul>
  <li><input type="checkbox" name="genre" value="punk" checked> Punk
rock</li>
  <li><input type="checkbox" name="genre" value="indie" checked> Indie
rock</li>
  <li><input type="checkbox" name="genre" value="hiphop"> Hip Hop</li>
  <li><input type="checkbox" name="genre" value="rockabilly">
Rockabilly</li>
</ul>
```

Checkboxes don't necessarily need to be used in groups, of course. In this example, a single checkbox is used to allow visitors to opt in to special promotions. The value of the control will be passed along to the server only if the user checks the box.

```
<p><input type="checkbox" name="OptIn" value="yes"> Yes, send me news
and special promotions by email.</p>
```

Checkbox buttons also use the **checked** attribute to make them preselected when the form loads.

In EXERCISE 9-2, you'll get a chance to add both radio and checkbox buttons to the pizza ordering form.

EXERCISE 9-2. Adding radio buttons and checkboxes

The next section of the Black Goose Bistro pizza ordering form uses radio buttons and checkboxes for selecting pizza options. Open the *pizza.html* document and follow these steps:

1. In the "Design Your Dream Pizza" section, there are lists of Crust and Toppings options. The Crust options should be radio buttons because pizzas have only one crust. Insert a radio button before each option. Follow this example for the remaining crust options:

   ```
   <li><input type="radio" name="crust" value="white"> Classic white</li>
   ```

2. Mark up the Toppings options as you did the Crust options, but this time, the **type** should be **checkbox**. Be sure the variable name for each is **toppings[ ]**, and that the "Red sauce" option is preselected (**checked**), as noted on the sketch.

3. Save the document and check your work by opening it in a browser to make sure it looks right; then submit the form to make sure it's functioning properly.

Menus

Another way to provide a list of choices is to put them in a drop-down or scrolling menu. Menus tend to be more compact than groups of buttons and checkboxes.

You add both drop-down and scrolling menus to a form with the **select** element. Whether the menu pulls down or scrolls is the result of how you specify its size and whether you allow more than one option to be selected. Let's take a look at both menu types.

Drop-down menus

The **select** element displays as a drop-down menu (also called a pull-down menu) by default when no size is specified or if the **size** attribute is set to 1. In pull-down menus, only one item may be selected. Here's an example (shown in FIGURE 9-12):

```
<p>What is your favorite 80s band?
<select name="EightiesFave">
    <option>The Cure</option>
    <option>Cocteau Twins</option>
    <option>Tears for Fears</option>
    <option>Thompson Twins</option>
    <option value="EBTG">Everything But the Girl</option>
    <option>Depeche Mode</option>
    <option>The Smiths</option>
    <option>New Order</option>
</select>
</p>
```

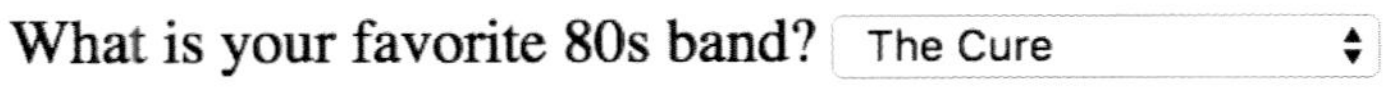

What is your favorite 80s band? | The Cure ⏏ |

FIGURE 9-12. Pull-down menus pop open when the user clicks the arrow or bar.

You can see that the **select** element is just a container for a number of **option** elements. The content of the chosen **option** element is what gets passed to the web application when the form is submitted. If, for some reason, you want to send a different value than what appears in the menu, use the **value** attribute to provide an overriding value. For example, if someone selects "Everything But the Girl" from the sample menu, the form submits the value "EBTG" for the "EightiesFave" variable. For the others, the content between the **option** tags will be sent as the value.

Scrolling menus

To make the menu display as a scrolling list, simply specify the number of lines you'd like to be visible using the **size** attribute. This example menu has

`<select>…</select>`
Menu control

`<option>…</option>`
An option within a menu

`<optgroup>…</optgroup>`
A logical grouping of options within a menu

the same options as the previous one, except it has been set to display as a scrolling list that is six lines tall (FIGURE 9-13):

```
<p>What 80s bands did you listen to?
<select name="EightiesBands" size="6" multiple>
    <option>The Cure</option>
    <option>Cocteau Twins</option>
    <option selected>Tears for Fears</option>
    <option selected>Thompson Twins</option>
    <option value="EBTG">Everything But the Girl</option>
    <option>Depeche Mode</option>
    <option>The Smiths</option>
    <option>New Order</option>
</select>
</p>
```

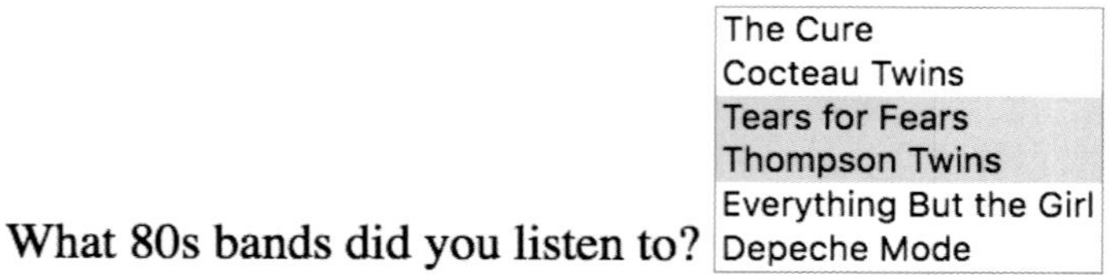

> The Cure
> Cocteau Twins
> Tears for Fears
> Thompson Twins
> Everything But the Girl
> Depeche Mode

What 80s bands did you listen to?

FIGURE 9-13. A scrolling menu with multiple options selected.

You may notice a few minimized attributes tucked in there. The **multiple** attribute allows users to make more than one selection from the scrolling list. Note that pull-down menus do not allow multiple selections; when the browser detects the **multiple** attribute, it displays a small scrolling menu automatically by default.

Use the **selected** attribute in an **option** element to make it the default value for the menu control. Selected options are highlighted when the form loads. The **selected** attribute can be used with pull-down menus as well.

Grouping menu options

You can use the **optgroup** element to create conceptual groups of options. The required **label** attribute provides the heading for the group (see **Note**). FIGURE 9-14 shows how option groups are rendered in modern browsers.

NOTE

*The **label** attribute in the **optgroup** element is not the same as the **label** element used to improve accessibility (discussed later in this chapter).*

```
<select name="icecream" size="7" multiple>
  <optgroup label="traditional">
    <option>vanilla</option>
    <option>chocolate</option>
  </optgroup>
  <optgroup label="fancy">
    <option>Super praline</option>
    <option>Nut surprise</option>
    <option>Candy corn</option>
  </optgroup>
</select>
```

traditional
vanilla
chocolate
fancy
Super praline
Nut surprise
Candy corn

FIGURE 9-14. Option groups.

In EXERCISE 9-3, you will use the **select** element to let Black Goose Bistro customers choose a number of pizzas for their order.

File Selection Control

`<input type="file">`

File selection field

Web forms can collect more than just data. They can also be used to transmit external documents from a user's hard drive. For example, a printing company could use a web form to upload artwork for a business card order. A magazine could use a form to collect digital photos for a photo contest.

The file selection control makes it possible for users to select a document from the hard drive to be submitted with the form data. We add it to the form by using our old friend, the **input** element, with its **type** set to **file**.

The markup sample here (FIGURE 9-15) shows a file selection control used for photo submissions:

```
<form action="/client.php" method="POST" enctype="multipart/form-data">
  <label>Send a photo to be used as your online icon <em>(optional)
</em><br>
  <input type="file" name="photo"></label>
</form>
```

The file upload widget varies slightly by browser and operating system, but it is generally a button that allows you to access the file organization system on your computer (FIGURE 9-15).

File input (on Chrome browser)

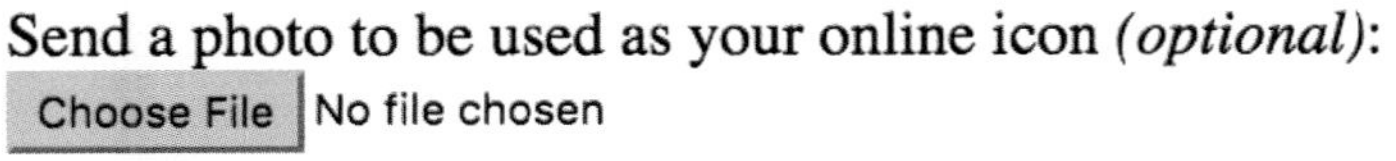

Send a photo to be used as your online icon *(optional)*:

Choose File | No file chosen

FIGURE 9-15. A file selection form field.

Adding a menu

The only other control that needs to be added to the order form is a pull-down menu for selecting the number of pizzas to have delivered.

1. Insert a **select** menu element with the option to order between 1 and 6 pizzas:

```
<p>How many pizzas:
<select name="pizzas"
size="1">
    <option>1</option>
<-- more options here -->
  </select>
</p>
```

2. Save the document and check it in a browser. You can submit the form, too, to be sure that it's working. You should get the "Thank You" response page listing all of the information you entered in the form.

Congratulations! You've built your first working web form. In EXERCISE 9-4, we'll add markup that makes it more accessible to assistive devices.

It is important to note that when a form contains a file selection input element, you must specify the encoding type (`enctype`) as `multipart/form-data` in the `form` element and use the POST method.

The file input type has a few attributes. The `accept` attribute gives the browser a heads-up on what file types may be accepted (audio, video, image, or some other format identified by its media type). Adding the `multiple` attributes allows multiple files to be selected for upload. The `required` attribute, as it says, requires a file to be selected.

Hidden Controls

<div markdown="1" style="float:left">

`<input type="hidden">`

Hidden control field

</div>

There may be times when you need to send information to the form processing application that does not come from the user. In these instances, you can use a hidden form control that sends data when the form is submitted, but is not visible when the form is displayed in a browser.

Hidden controls are added via the `input` element with the `type` set to `hidden`. Its sole purpose is to pass a name/value pair to the server when the form is submitted. In this example, a hidden form element is used to provide the location of the appropriate thank-you document to display when the transaction is complete:

WARNING

It is possible for users to access and manipulate hidden form controls. If you should become a professional web developer, you will learn to program defensively for this sort of thing.

```
<input type="hidden" name="success-link" value="http://www.example.com/
thankyou.html">
```

I've worked with forms that have had dozens of hidden controls in the `form` element before getting to the parts that the user actually fills out. This is the kind of information you get from the application programmer, system administrator, or whoever is helping you get your forms processed. If you are using an existing script, be sure to check the accompanying instructions to see if any hidden form variables are required.

Date and Time Controls

`<input type="date">`

Date input control

`<input type="time">`

Time input control

`<input type="datetime-local">`

Date/time control

`<input type="month">`

Specifies a month in a year

`<input type="week">`

Specifies a particular week in a year

If you've ever booked a hotel or a flight online, you've no doubt used a little calendar widget for choosing the date. Chances are, that little calendar was created with JavaScript. HTML5 introduced six new input types that make date and time selection widgets part of a browser's standard built-in display capabilities, just as they can display checkboxes, pop-up menus, and other widgets today. As of this writing, the date and time pickers are implemented on only a few browsers (Chrome, Microsoft Edge, Opera, Vivaldi, and Android), but on non-supporting browsers, the date and time input types display as a perfectly usable text-entry field instead. FIGURE 9-16 shows date and time widgets as rendered in Chrome on macOS.

input type="time"

12:06 --

input type="date"

input type="datetime-local"

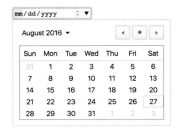

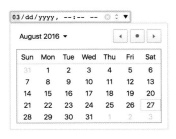

input type="month"

input type="week"

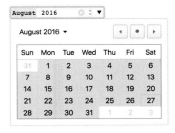

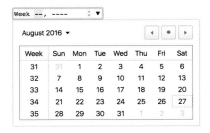

FIGURE 9-16. Date and time picker inputs (shown in Chrome on macOS).

The new date- and time-related input types are as follows:

`<input type="date" name="name" value="2017-01-14">`

Creates a date input control, such as a pop-up calendar, for specifying a date (year, month, day). The initial value must be provided in ISO date format (YYYY-MM-DD).

`<input type="time" name="name" value="03:13:00">`

Creates a time input control for specifying a time (hour, minute, seconds, fractional sections) with no time zone indicated. The value is provided as hh:mm:ss.

`<input type="datetime-local" name="name" value="2017-01-14T03:13:00">`

Creates a combined date/time input control with no time zone information (YYYY-MM-DDThh:mm:ss).

NOTE

The value attribute is optional but may be included to provide a starting date or time in the widget. It is included here to demonstrate date and time formats.

```
<input type="month" name="name" value="2017-01">
```

Creates a date input control that specifies a particular month in a year (YYYY-MM).

```
<input type="week" name="name" value="2017-W2">
```

Creates a date input control for specifying a particular week in a year using an ISO week numbering format (YYYY-W#).

Numerical Inputs

`<input type="number">`
Number input

`<input type="range">`
Slider input

The **number** and **range** input types collect numerical data. For the **number** input, the browser may supply a spinner widget with up and down arrows for selecting a specific numerical value (a text input may display in user agents that don't support the input type). The **range** input is typically displayed as a slider (FIGURE 9-17) that allows the user to select a value within a specified range:

```
<label>Number of guests <input type="number" name="guests" min="1"
max="6"></label>

<label>Satisfaction (0 to 10) <input type="range" name="satisfaction"
min="0" max="10" step="1"></label>
```

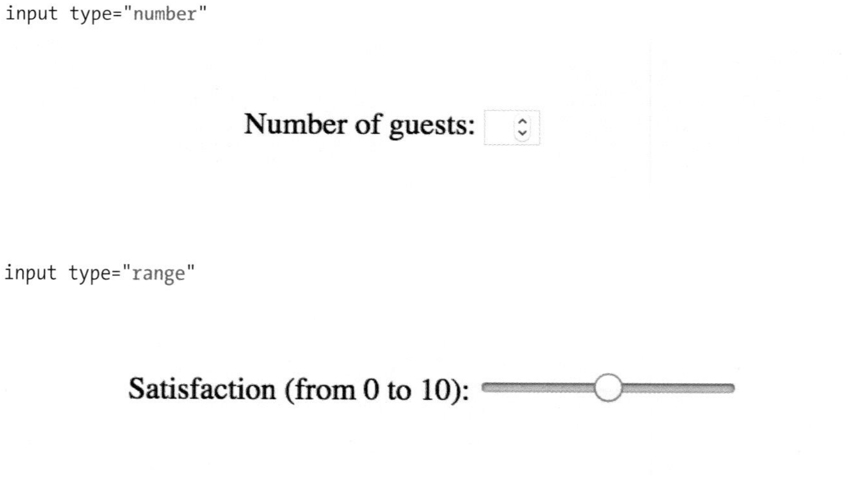

input type="number"

Number of guests: ⟨⟩

input type="range"

Satisfaction (from 0 to 10): ══════◯══════

FIGURE 9-17. The **number** and **range** input types (shown in Chrome on macOS).

Both the **number** and **range** input types accept the **min** and **max** attributes for specifying the minimum and maximum values allowed for the input (again, the browser could check that the user input complies with the constraint). Both **min** and **max** are optional, and you can also set one without the other. Negative values are allowed. When the element is selected, the value can be increased or decreased with the number keys on a computer keyboard, in addition to being moved with the mouse or a finger.

The **step** attribute allows developers to specify the acceptable increments for numerical input. The default is 1. A value of ".5" would permit values 1, 1.5, 2, 2.5, and so on; a value of 100 would permit 100, 200, 300, and so on. You can also set the **step** attribute to **any** to explicitly accept any value increment.

These two elements allow for only the calculated step values, not for a specified list of allowed values (such as 1, 2, 3, 5, 8, 13, 21). If you need customized values, you need to use JavaScript to program that behavior.

Because these are newer elements, browser support is inconsistent. Some UI widgets include up and down arrows for increasing or decreasing the amount, but many don't. Mobile browsers (iOS Safari, Android, Chrome for Android) currently do not support **min**, **max**, and **step**. Internet Explorer 9 and earlier do not support number and range inputs at all. Again, browsers that don't support these new input types display a standard text input field instead, which is a fine fallback.

Color Selector

The intent of the color control type is to create a pop-up color picker for visually selecting a color value similar to those used in operating systems or image-editing programs. Values are provided in hexadecimal RGB values (#RRGGBB). FIGURE 9-18 shows the color picker in Chrome on macOS (it is the same as the macOS color picker). Non-supporting browsers—currently all versions of IE, iOS Safari, and older versions of Android—display the default text input instead.

```
<label>Your favorite color: <input type="color" name="favorite">
</label>
```

`<input type="color">`

Color picker

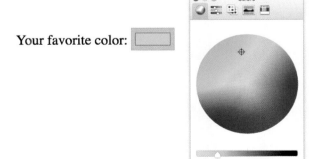

FIGURE 9-18. The **color** input type (shown in Chrome on macOS).

That wraps up the form control roundup. Learning how to insert form controls is one part of the forms production process, but any web developer worth her salt will take the time to make sure the form is as accessible as possible. Fortunately, there are a few things we can do in markup to describe the form's structure.

A Few More Form Elements

For the sake of completeness, let's look at the remaining form elements. These were added in HTML5 and, as of this writing, they still have spotty browser support. They are somewhat esoteric anyway, so you may wait a while to add these to your HTML toolbox. We've already covered the **datalist** element for providing suggested values for text inputs. HTML5 also introduced the following elements:

progress

`<progress>…</progress>`

Indicates the state of an ongoing process

The **progress** element gives users feedback on the state of an ongoing process, such as a file download. It may indicate a specific percentage of completion (determinate), like a progress bar, or just indicate a "waiting" state (indeterminate), like a spinner. The **progress** element requires scripting to function.

```
Percent downloaded: <progress max="100" id="fave">0</progress>
```

meter

`<meter>…</meter>`

Represents a measurement within a range

meter represents a measurement within a known range of values (also known as a gauge). It has a number of attributes: **min** and **max** indicate the highest and lowest values for the range (they default to 0 and 100); **low** and **high** could be used to trigger warnings at undesirable levels; and **optimum** specifies a preferred value.

```
<meter min="0" max="100" name="volume">60%</meter>
```

output

`<output>…</output>`

Calculated output value

Simply put, the **output** element indicates the result of a calculation by a script or program. This example, taken from the HTML5.2 specification, uses the **output** element and JavaScript to display the sum of numbers entered into inputs a and b.

```
<form onsubmit="return false" oninput="o.value = a.valueAsNumber +
b.valueAsNumber">
<input name=a type=number step=any>
+ <input name=b type=number step=any> =
<output name=o for="a b"></output>
</form>
```

FORM ACCESSIBILITY FEATURES

It is essential to consider how users without the benefit of visual browsers will be able to understand and navigate through your web forms. The `label`, `fieldset`, and `legend` form elements improve accessibility by making the semantic connections between the components of a form clear. Not only is the resulting markup more semantically rich, but there are also more elements available to act as "hooks" for style sheet rules. Everybody wins!

Labels

Although we may see the label "Address" right next to a text field for entering an address in a visual browser, in the source, the label and field input may be separated. The `label` element associates descriptive text with its respective form field. This provides important context for users with speech-based browsers. Another advantage to using labels is that users can click or tap anywhere on them to select or focus the form control. Users with touch devices will appreciate the larger tap target.

Each `label` element is associated with exactly one form control. There are two ways to use it. One method, called implicit association, nests the control and its description within a `label` element. In the following example, `label`s are assigned to individual checkboxes and their related text descriptions. (By the way, this is the way to label radio buttons and checkboxes. You can't assign a label to the entire group.)

`<label>...</label>`

Attaches information to form controls

```
<ul>
  <li><label><input type="checkbox" name="genre" value="punk"> Punk
rock</label></li>
  <li><label><input type="checkbox" name="genre" value="indie"> Indie
rock</label></li>
  <li><label><input type="checkbox" name="genre" value="hiphop"> Hip
Hop</label></li>
  <li><label><input type="checkbox" name="genre" value="rockabilly">
Rockabilly</label></li>
</ul>
```

The other method, called explicit association, matches the label with the control's `id` reference. The `for` attribute says which control the label is for. This approach is useful when the control is not directly next to its descriptive text in the source. It also offers the potential advantage of keeping the label and the control as two distinct elements, which you may find handy when aligning them with style sheets.

```
<label for="form-login-username">Login account</label>
<input type="text" name="login" id="form-login-username">

<label for="form-login-password">Password</label>
<input type="password" name="password" id="form-login-password">
```

> ### ▣ MARKUP TIP
>
> To keep form-related **id**s distinct from other **id**s on the page, consider prefacing them with "form-" as shown in the examples.
>
> Another technique for keeping forms organized is to give the **form** element an ID name and include it as a prefix in the IDs for the controls it contains as follows:
>
> ```
> <form id="form-login">
> <input id="form-login-user">
> <input id="form-login-passwd">
> ```

fieldset and legend

<fieldset>…</fieldset
Groups related controls and labels

<legend>…</legend>
Assigns a caption to a fieldset

The **fieldset** element indicates a logical group of form controls. A **fieldset** may also include a **legend** element that provides a caption for the enclosed fields.

FIGURE 9-19 shows the default rendering of the following example, but you could use style sheets to change the way the **fieldset** and **legend** appear (see **Warning**):

```
<fieldset>
  <legend>Mailing List Sign-up</legend>
  <ul>
    <li><label>Add me to your mailing list <input type="radio"
    name="list" value="yes" checked></label></li>
    <li><label>No thanks <input type="radio" name="list" value="no">
  </label></li>
  </ul>
</fieldset>

<fieldset>
  <legend>Customer Information</legend>
  <ul>
    <li><label>Full name: <input type="text" name="fullname"></label>
</li>
    <li><label>Email: <input type="text" name="email"></label></li>
    <li><label>State: <input type="text" name="state"></label></li>
  </ul>
</fieldset>
```

WARNING

Fieldsets and legends tend to throw some curveballs when it comes to styling. For example, background colors in fieldsets are handled differently from browser to browser. Legends are unique in that their text doesn't wrap. The solution is to put a **span** *or* **b** *element in them and control presentation of the contained element without sacrificing accessibility. Be sure to do lots of testing if you style these form elements.*

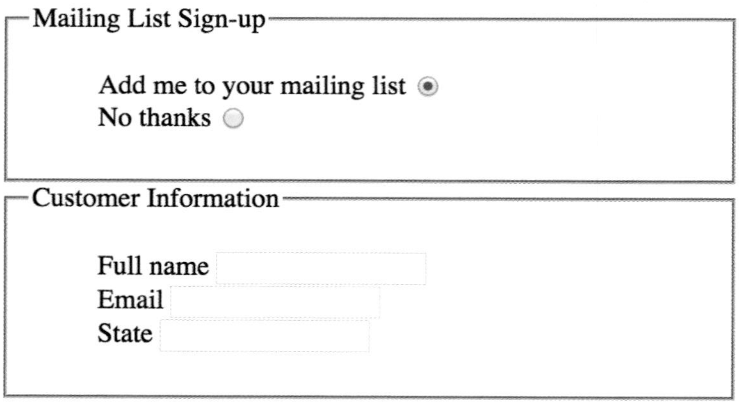

FIGURE 9-19. The default rendering of fieldsets and legends.

In EXERCISE 9-4, we'll wrap up the pizza order form by making it more accessible with labels and fieldsets.

EXERCISE 9-4. Labels and fieldsets

Our pizza ordering form is working, but we need to label it appropriately and create some **fieldsets** to make it more usable on assistive devices. Once again, open the *pizza.html* document and follow these steps.

I like to start with the broad strokes and fill in details later, so we'll begin this exercise by organizing the form controls into fieldsets, and then we'll do all the labeling. You could do it the other way around, and ideally, you'd just mark up the labels and fieldsets as you go along instead of adding them all later.

1. The "Your Information" section at the top of the form is definitely conceptually related, so let's wrap it all in a **fieldset** element. Change the markup of the section title from a paragraph (**p**) to a **legend** for the fieldset:

```
<fieldset>
  <legend>Your Information</legend>
  <ul>
    <li>Name: <input type="text" name="fullname">
    </li>
      …
  </ul>
</fieldset>
```

2. Next, group the Crust, Toppings, and Number questions in a big fieldset with the legend "Pizza specs" (the text is there; you just need to change it from a **p** to a **legend**):

```
<h2>Design Your Dream Pizza:</h2>
<fieldset>
<legend>Pizza specs</legend>
  Crust…
  Toppings…
  Number…
</fieldset>
```

3. Create another fieldset just for the Crust options, again changing the description in a paragraph to a **legend**. Do the same for the Toppings and Number sections. In the end, you will have three fieldsets contained within the larger "Pizza specs" fieldset. When you are done, save your document and open it in a browser. Now it should look very close to the final form shown back in FIGURE 9-2, given the expected browser differences:

```
<fieldset>
<legend>Crust <em>(Choose one)</em>:</legend>
  <ul>…</ul>
</fieldset>
```

4. OK, now let's get some labels in there. In the "Your Information" fieldset, explicitly tie the label to the text input by using the **for/id** label method. Wrap the description in **label** tags and add the **id** to the input. The **for/id** values should be descriptive and they must match. I've done the first one for you; you do the other four:

```
<li><label for="form-name">Name:</label> <input
type="text" name="fullname" id="form-name"></li>
```

5. For the radio and checkbox buttons, wrap the **label** element around the **input** and its value label. In this way, the button will be selected when the user clicks or taps anywhere inside the **label** element. Here's the first one; you do the rest:

```
<li><label><input type="radio" name="crust"
value="white"> Classic White</label></li>
```

Save your document, and you're done! Labels don't have any effect on how the form looks by default, but you can feel good about the added semantic value you've added and maybe even use them to apply styles at another time.

DIY Form Widgets

Despite having dozens of form widgets straight out of HTML to choose from, it is common for developers to "roll their own" form widgets using markup, CSS, and JavaScript. This might be preferable if you want to provide custom functionality or to make the styling of the form extra-fancy. For example, you could create a drop-down menu using an unordered list inside a **div** instead of the standard **select** element:

```
<div class="select" role="listbox">
  <ul class="optionlist">
    <li class="option" role="option">Red</li>
    <li class="option" role="option">Yellow</li>
  </ul>
</div>
```

To help assistive technologies like screen readers recognize this as a form element, use the ARIA **role** attribute to describe the intended function of the **div** (a listbox) and each **li** (an option in that listbox). There are also many ARIA states and properties that make forms, both standard and custom, usable with assistive devices. For a complete list, see *www.w3.org/TR/wai-aria/states_and_properties*.

Custom form widgets require scripting and CSS well beyond the scope of this book, but I wanted you to be aware of the technique. It's also extremely easy to mess up, making a user's interaction with the form awkward and frustrating (even for sighted users), so "roll your own" with caution.

The article "How to Build Custom Form Widgets" on MDN Web Docs provides a nice overview (*developer.mozilla.org/en-US/docs/Web/Guide/HTML/Forms/How_to_build_custom_form_widgets*). You might also choose to use a premade custom widget from one of the available JavaScript Libraries like jQuery UI (*jqueryui.com*).

FORM LAYOUT AND DESIGN

I can't close this chapter without saying a few words about form design, even though this chapter is about markup, not presentation.

Usable Forms

A poorly designed form can ruin a user's experience on your site and negatively impact your business goals. Badly designed forms mean lost customers, so it is critical to get it right—both on the desktop and for small-screen devices with their special requirements. You want the path to a purchase or other action to be as frictionless as possible.

The topic of good web form design is a rich one that could fill a book in itself. In fact, there is such a book: *Web Form Design* (Rosenfeld Media) by web form expert Luke Wroblewski, and I recommend it highly. Luke's subsequent book, *Mobile First* (A Book Apart), includes tips for how to format forms in a mobile context. You can browse over a hundred articles about forms on his site at *www.lukew.com/ff?tag=forms*.

Here I'll offer just a very small sampling of tips from *Web Form Design* to get you started, but the whole book is worth a read:

Avoid unnecessary questions.

Help your users get through your form as easily as possible by not including questions that are not absolutely necessary to the task at hand. Extra questions, in addition to slowing things down, may make a user wary of your motivations for asking. If you have another way of getting the information (for example, the type of credit card can be determined from the first four numbers of the account), then use alternative means and don't put the burden on the user. If there is information that might be nice to have but is not required, consider asking at a later time, after the form has been submitted and you have built a relationship with the user.

Consider the impact of label placement.

The position of the label relative to the input affects the time it takes to fill out the form. The less the user's eye needs to bounce around the page, the quicker the form completion. Putting the labels above their respective fields creates a single alignment for faster scans and completion, particularly when you're asking for familiar information (name, address, etc.). Top-positioned labels can also accommodate labels of varying lengths and work best on narrow, small-screen devices. They do result in a longer form, however, so if vertical space is a concern, you can position the labels to the left of the inputs. Left alignment of labels results in the slowest form completion, but it may be appropriate if you want the user to slow down or be able to scan and consider the types of required information.

Choose input types carefully.

As you've seen in this chapter, there are quite a few input types to choose from, and sometimes it's not easy to decide which one to use. For example, a list of options could be presented as a pull-down menu or a number of choices with checkboxes. Weigh the pros and cons of each control type carefully, and follow up with user testing.

Group related inputs.

It is easier to parse the many fields, menus, and buttons in a form if they are visually grouped by related topic. For example, a user's contact information could be presented in a compact group so that five or six inputs are perceived as one unit. Usually, all you need is a very subtle indication, such as a fine horizontal rule and some extra space. Don't overdo it.

Clarify primary and secondary actions.

The primary action at the end of the form is usually some form of submit button ("Buy," "Register," etc.) that signals the completion of the form and the readiness to move forward. You want that button to be visually dominant and easy to find (aligning it along the main axis of the form is helpful as well). Using JavaScript, you can gray out the submit button as non-functioning until all necessary data has been filled in.

Secondary actions tend to take you a step back, such as clearing or reset-ting the form. If you must include a secondary action, make sure that it is styled to look different and less important than the primary action. It is also a good idea to provide an opportunity to undo the action.

Styling Forms

As we've seen in this chapter, the default rendering of form markup is not up to par with the quality we see on most professional web forms today. As for other elements, you can use style sheets to create a clean form layout as well as change the appearance of most form controls. Something as simple as nice alignment and a look that is consistent with the rest of your site can go a long way toward improving the impression you make on a user.

Keep in mind that form widgets are drawn by the browser and are informed by operating system conventions. However, you can still apply dimensions, margins, fonts, colors, borders, and background effects to form elements such as text inputs, select menus, textareas, fieldsets, labels, and legends. Be sure to test in a variety of browsers to check for unpleasant surprises. **Chapter 19, More CSS Techniques**, in **Part III**, lists some specific techniques once you have more experience with CSS. For more help, a web search for "CSS for forms" will turn up a number of tutorials.

TEST YOURSELF

Ready to put your web form know-how to the test? Here are a few questions to make sure you've gotten the basics. You'll find the answers in **Appendix A**.

1. Decide whether each of these forms should be sent via the GET or POST method:

   a. A form for accessing your bank account online   _____

   b. A form for sending t-shirt artwork to the printer   _____

   c. A form for searching archived articles   _____

   d. A form for collecting long essay entries   _____

2. Which form control element is best suited for the following tasks? When the answer is "input," be sure to also include the type. Some tasks may have more than one correct answer.

   a. Choose your astrological sign from 12 signs.

   b. Indicate whether you have a history of heart disease (yes or no).

   c. Write up a book review.

   d. Select your favorite ice cream flavors from a list of eight flavors.

   e. Select your favorite ice cream flavors from a list of 25 flavors.

3. Each of these markup examples contains an error. Can you spot it?

   a. `<input name="country" value="Your country here.">`

   b. `<checkbox name="color" value="teal">`

   c.
   ```
   <select name="popsicle">
       <option value="orange">
       <option value="grape">
       <option value="cherry">
   </select>
   ```

   d. `<input type="password">`

   e.
   ```
   <textarea name="essay" width="100" height="6">Your story.
   </textarea>
   ```

ELEMENT REVIEW: FORMS

The following table lists all of the form-related elements and attributes included in HTML 5.2 (some attributes were not covered in this chapter). The attributes for each input type are listed in TABLE 9-1.

Element and attributes	Description
button	Generic input button
autofocus	Automatically focuses the form control when the page is loaded
name="*text*"	Supplies a unique variable name for the control
disabled	Disables the input so it cannot be selected
type="submit|reset|button"	The type of custom button
value="*text*"	Specifies the value to be sent to the server
menu="*idvalue*"	Specifies a designated pop-up menu
form,formaction, formenctype, formmethod, formnovalidate, formtarget	Form submission-related attributes used for submit and reset type buttons
datalist	Provides a list of options for text inputs
fieldset	Groups related controls and labels
disabled	Disables all the inputs in the fieldset so they cannot be selected, edited, or submitted
form="*idvalue*"	Associates the element with a specific form
name="*text*"	Supplies a unique variable name for the control
form	Form element
action="*url*"	Location of forms processing program (*required*)
method="get|post"	The method used to submit the form data
enctype="*content type*"	The encoding method, generally either **application/x-www-form-urlencoded** (default) or **multipart/form-data**
accept-charset="*characterset*"	Character encodings to use
autocomplete	Default setting for autofill feature for controls in the form
name="*text*"	Name of the form to use in the **document.forms** API
novalidate	Bypasses form control validation for this form
target="text|_blank|_self|_parent|_top"	Sets the browsing context

Element and attributes	Description
input	Creates a variety of controls, based on the **type** value
autofocus	Indicates the control should be ready for input when the document loads
type="submit|reset|button| text|password|checkbox|radio| image|file|hidden|email|tel| search|url|date|time| datetime-local|month|week| number|range|color"	The type of input
See TABLE 9-1 *for a full list of attributes associated with each input type.*	
disabled	Disables the input so it cannot be selected, edited, or submitted
form="*form id value*"	Associates the control with a specified form
label	Attaches information to controls
for="*text*"	Identifies the associated control by its **id** reference
legend	Assigns a caption to a **fieldset**
meter	Represents a fractional value within a known range
high="*number*"	Indicates the range that is considered "high" for the gauge
low="*number*"	Indicates the range that is considered "low" for the gauge
max="*number*"	Specifies the highest value for the range
min="*number*"	Specifies the lowest value for the range
optimum="*number*"	Indicates the number considered to be "optimum"
value="*number*"	Specifies the actual or measured value
optgroup	Defines a group of options
disabled	Disables the **optgroup** so it cannot be selected
label="*text*"	Supplies a label for a group of options
option	An option within a select menu control
disabled	Disables the **option** so it cannot be selected
label="*text*"	Supplies an alternate label for the option
selected	Preselects the option
value="*text*"	Supplies an alternate value for the option
output	Represents the results of a calculation
for="*text*"	Creates a relationship between output and another element
form="*form id value*"	Associates the control with a specified form
name="*text*"	Supplies a unique variable name for the control

Element and attributes	Description
progress	Represents the completion progress of a task (can be used even if the maximum value of the task is not known)
max="*number*"	Specifies the total value or final size of the task
value="*number*"	Specifies how much of the task has been completed
select	Pull-down menu or scrolling list
autofocus	Indicates the control should be highlighted and ready for input when the document loads
disabled	Indicates the control is nonfunctional; can be activated with a script
form="*form id value*"	Associates the control with a specified form
multiple	Allows multiple selections in a scrolling list
name="*text*"	Supplies a unique variable name for the control
required	Indicates the user input is required for this control
size="*number*"	The height of the scrolling list in text lines
textarea	Multiline text-entry field
autocomplete	Hint for form autofill feature
autofocus	Indicates the control should be highlighted and ready for input when the document loads
cols="*number*"	The width of the text area in characters
dirname="*text*"	Allows text directionality to be submitted
disabled	Disables the control so it cannot be selected
form="*form id value*"	Associates the control with a specified form
inputmode	Hint for selecting an input modality
maxlength="*text*"	Specifies the maximum number of characters the user can enter
minlength="*text*"	Specifies the minimum number of characters the user can enter
name="*text*"	Supplies a unique variable name for the control
placeholder="*text*"	Provides a short hint to help the user enter the correct data
readonly	Makes the control unalterable by the user
required	Indicates user input is required for this control
rows="*number*"	The height of the text area in text lines
wrap="hard|soft"	Controls whether line breaks in the text input are returned in the data; **hard** preserves line breaks, while **soft** does not

TABLE 9-1. *Available attributes for each input type*

Attribute	submit	reset	button	text	password	checkbox	radio	image	file	hidden
accept									•	
alt								•		
autocomplete				•	•					
autofocus	•	•	•	•	•	•	•	•	•	
checked						•	•			
disabled	•	•	•	•	•	•	•	•	•	•
form	•	•	•	•	•	•	•	•	•	•
formaction	•							•		
formenctype	•							•		
formmethod	•							•		
formnovalidate	•							•		
formtarget	•							•		
height								•		
list				•						
max										
min										
maxlength				•	•				•	
minlength				•	•				•	
multiple									•	
name	•	•	•	•	•	•	•	•	•	•
pattern				•	•					
placeholder				•	•					
readonly				•	•					
required				•	•	•	•		•	
size				•	•				•	
src								•		
step										
value	•	•	•	•	•	•	•		•	•
width								•		

Attribute	email	telephone, search, url	number	range	date, time, datetime-local, month, week	color
accept						
alt						
autocomplete	•	•	•	•	•	•
autofocus	•	•	•	•	•	•
checked						
disabled	•	•	•	•	•	•
form	•	•	•	•	•	•
formaction						
formenctype						
formmethod						
formnovalidate						
formtarget						
height						
list	•	•	•	•	•	•
max			•	•	•	
min			•	•	•	
maxlength	•	•				
minlength	•	•				
multiple	•				•	
name	•	•	•	•	•	•
pattern	•	•				
placeholder	•	•				
readonly	•	•	•			
required	•	•	•		•	
size	•	•				
src						
step			•	•	•	
value	•	•	•	•	•	•
width						

EMBEDDED MEDIA

The HTML specification defines embedded content as follows:

> content that imports another resource into the document, or content from another vocabulary that is inserted into the document

In **Chapter 7, Adding Images**, you saw examples of both parts of that definition because images are one type of embedded content. The `img` and `picture` elements point to an external image resource using the `src` or `srcset` attributes, and the `svg` element embeds an image file written in the SVG vocabulary right in the page.

But images certainly aren't the only things you can stick in a web page. In this chapter, we'll look at other types of embedded content and their respective markup, including the following:

- A window for viewing an external HTML source (`iframe`)

- Multipurpose embedding elements (`object` and `embed`)

- Video and audio players (`video` and `audio`)

- A scriptable drawing area that can be used for animations or game-like interactivity (`canvas`)

WINDOW-IN-A-WINDOW (IFRAME)

The `iframe` (short for inline frame) element lets you embed a separate HTML document or other web resource in a document. It has been around for many years, but it has recently become one of the most popular ways to share content between sites.

`<iframe>…</iframe>`
A nested browsing window

For example, when you request the code to embed a video from YouTube or a map from Google Maps, they provide iframe-based code to copy and paste into your page. Many other media sites are following suit because it allows them to control aspects of the content you are putting on your page. Inline frames have also become a standard tool for embedding ad content that might have been handled with Flash back in the day. Web tutorial sites may use inline frames to embed code samples on pages.

Adding an **iframe** to the page creates a little window-in-a-window (or a nested browsing context, as it is known in the spec) that displays the external resource. You place an inline frame on a page similarly to an image, specifying the source (**src**) of its content. The **width** and **height** attributes specify the dimensions of the frame. The content in the **iframe** element itself is fallback content for browsers that don't support the element, although virtually all browsers support iframes at this point.

In this very crude example, the parent document displays the web page *glossary.html* in an inline frame (FIGURE 10-1). This iframe has its own set of scrollbars because the embedded HTML document is too long to fit. To be honest, you don't often see iframes used this way in the wild (except for code examples, perhaps), but it is a good way to understand how they work.

```
<h1>An Inline Frame</h1>

<iframe src="glossary.html" width="400" height="250" >
  Read the <a href="glossary.html">glossary</a>.
</iframe>
```

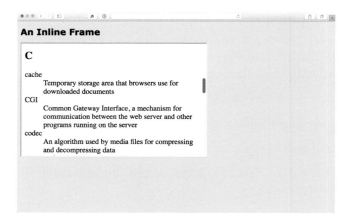

FIGURE 10-1. Inline frames (added with the **iframe** element) are like a browser window within the browser that displays external HTML documents and resources.

In modern uses of **iframe**, the window is not so obvious. In fact, there is usually no indication that there is an embedded frame there at all, as shown by the Google Maps example in FIGURE 10-2.

FIGURE 10-2. The edges of an **iframe** are usually not detectable, as shown in this embedded Google Map.

There are some security concerns with using iframes because they may act like open windows through which hackers can sneak. The **sandbox** attribute puts restrictions on what the framed content can do, such as not allowing forms, pop ups, scripts, and the like.

Iframe security is beyond the scope of this chapter, but you'll need to brush up if you are going to make use of iframes on your site. I recommend the MDN Web Docs article "From object to iframe: Other Embedding Technologies" (*developer.mozilla.org/en-US/docs/Learn/HTML/Multimedia_and_embedding/ Other_embedding_technologies*), which provides a good overview of iframe security issues.

To get a feel for how iframes work, use one to embed your favorite video on a page in EXERCISE 10-1.

EXERCISE 10-1. Embedding a video with iframe

If you'd like to poke around with an **iframe**, it's easy to grab one from YouTube to embed your favorite video on a page.

Start by creating a new HTML document, including the basic structural elements that we covered in **Chapter 4, Creating a Simple Page**.

Go to YouTube and once you are on the page for your chosen video, look for the Share button; then choose the Embed option. The **iframe** code is there for you to copy and paste. If you click "Show more," there will be further configuration options. Just copy the **iframe** code and paste it into the new HTML document. Open it in a browser, and you're done!

MULTIPURPOSE EMBEDDER (OBJECT)

`<object>...</object>`
Represents external resource

`<param>`
Parameters of an object

A plug-in is software that gives a browser functionality that it doesn't have natively.

In the early days, web browsers were extremely limited in what they were able to render, so they relied on plug-ins to help them display media that they couldn't handle natively. Java applets, Flash movies, RealMedia (an old web video and audio format), and other media required third-party plug-ins in order to be played in the browser. Heck, even JPEG images once required a plug-in to display.

To embed those media resources on the page, we used the **object** and **embed** elements. They have slightly different uses. The **object** element is a multipurpose object placer. It can be used to place an image, create a nested browsing context (like an iframe), or embed a resource that must be handled by a plug-in. The **embed** element was for use with plug-ins only.

To put it frankly, although still in use, **object** is going out of style, and **embed** is all but extinct (I've tucked it away in a brief sidebar). Media like Java applets and Flash movies are disappearing fast, and modern browsers use APIs to display many types of media natively. In addition, mobile browsers as well as the desktop Microsoft Edge browser don't support plug-ins.

That said, let's take a look at the **object** element. At its most minimal, the **object** element uses the **data** attribute to point to the resource and the **type** attribute to provide its MIME type. Any content within the **object** element tags will be used as a fallback for browsers that don't support the embedded resource type. Here is a simple **object** element that places an SVG image on the page and provides a PNG fallback:

```
<object data="picture.svg" type="image/svg+xml">
  <img src="picture.png" alt="">
</object>
```

Additional attributes for the **object** element are available and vary according to the type of media it is placing. The media format may also require that the **object** contain a number of **param** elements that set parameters specific to that type of media.

The embed Element

The **embed** element was created by Netscape for use with plug-in technologies. It has always been well supported, but it wasn't adopted into a formal specification until HTML5. With so many other options for embedding media, the **embed** element is not as useful as it once was. It is often used as a fallback when there is a good reason to support extremely old browser versions.

embed is an empty element that points to an external resource with the **src** attribute:

```
<embed type="video/quicktime"
src="movies/hekboy.mov"
width="320" height="256">
```

There are additional media-specific attributes that set parameters similar to the **param** element, but I'm not going to cover them all here. In fact, I think that's all there is to say about **embed**.

Farewell Flash

Apple's announcement that it would not support Flash on its iOS devices, *ever*, gave HTML5 an enormous push forward and eventually led to Adobe stopping development on its mobile Flash products. Not long after, Microsoft announced that it was discontinuing its Silverlight media player in lieu of HTML5 alternatives. As of this writing, HTML5 is a long way from being able to reproduce the vast features and functionality of Flash, but it's getting there gradually. We are likely to occasionally see Flash players on the desktop, but the trajectory away from plug-ins and toward standard web technologies seems clear.

In this example, **param** elements specify whether the movie starts automatically (no) or has visible controls (yes):

```
<object type="video/quicktime" data="movies/hekboy.mov" width="320"
height="256">
  <param name="autostart" value="false">
  <param name="controller" value="true">
</object>
```

VIDEO AND AUDIO

Until recently, browsers did not have built-in capabilities for handling video or sound, so they used plug-ins to fill in the gap. With the development of the web as an open standards platform, and with broadband connections allowing for heftier downloads than previously, it seemed to be time to make multimedia support part of browsers' out-of-the-box capabilities. Enter the new **video** and **audio** elements and their respective APIs (see the **"API"** sidebar).

The Good News and the Bad News

The good news is that the **video** and **audio** elements are well supported in modern browsers, including IE 9+, Safari, Chrome, Opera, and Firefox for the desktop and iOS Safari 4+, Android 2.3+, and Opera Mobile (however, not Opera Mini).

But if you're envisioning a perfect world where all browsers are supporting video and audio in perfect harmony, I'm afraid it's not that simple. Although they have all lined up on the markup and JavaScript for embedding media players, unfortunately they have not agreed on which formats to support. Let's take a brief journey through the land of media file formats. If you want to add video or audio to your page, this stuff is important to understand.

How Media Formats Work

When you prepare audio or video content for web delivery, there are two format decisions to make. The first is how the media is encoded (the algorithms used to convert the source to 1s and 0s and how they are compressed). The method used for encoding is called the codec, which is short for "code/decode" or "compress/decompress." There are a bazillion codecs out there (that's an estimate). Some probably sound familiar, like MP3; others might sound new, such as H.264, Vorbis, Theora, VP8, and AAC.

Second, you need to choose the container format for the media. You can think of it as a ZIP file that holds the compressed media and its metadata together in a package. Usually a container format is compatible with more than one codec type, and the full story is complicated. Because space is limited in this chapter, I'm going to cut to the chase and introduce the most common container/codec combinations for the web. If you are going to add video or audio to your site, I encourage you to get more familiar with all of these formats.

■ TERMINOLOGY

API

An API (Application Programming Interface) is a standardized set of commands, data names, properties, actions, and so on, that lets one software application communicate with another. HTML5 introduced a number of APIs that give browsers programmable features that previously could only be achieved with third-party plug-ins.

Some APIs have a markup component, such as embedding multimedia with the new HTML5 **video** and **audio** elements (Media Player API). Others happen entirely behind the scenes with JavaScript or server-side components, such as creating web applications that work even without an internet connection (Offline Web Application API).

The W3C is working on lots and lots of APIs for use with web applications, all in varying stages of completion and implementation. Most have their own specifications, separate from the HTML5 spec itself, but they are generally included under the wide HTML5 umbrella that covers web-based applications.

A list of all HTML5 APIs and specs in development is available at *html5-overview.net*, maintained by Erik Wilde. You will also find introductions to better-known APIs in **Appendix D**.

Meet the video formats

For video, the most common options are as follows:

MPEG-4 container + H.264 video codec + AAC audio codec. This combination is generally referred to as "MPEG-4," and it takes the *.mp4* or *.m4v* file suffix. H.264 is a high-quality and flexible video codec, but it is patented and must be licensed for a fee. All current browsers that support HTML5 video can play MPEG-4 files with the H.264 codec. The newer H.265 codec (also known as HEVC, High Efficiency Video Coding) is in development and reduces the bitrate by half, but is not well supported as of this writing.

WebM container + VP8 video codec + Vorbis audio codec. "WebM" is a container format that has the advantage of being open source and royalty-free. It uses the *.webm* file extension. It was originally designed to work with VP8 and Vorbis codecs.

WebM container + VP9 video codec + Opus audio codec. The VP9 video codec from the WebM project offers the same video quality as VP8 and H.264 at half the bitrate. Because it is newer, it is not as well supported, but it is a great option for browsers that can play it.

Ogg container + Theora video codec + Vorbis audio codec. This is typically called "Ogg Theora," and the file should have an *.ogv* suffix. All of the codecs and the container in this option are open source and unencumbered by patents or royalty restrictions, but some say the quality is inferior to other options. In addition to new browsers, it is supported on some older versions of Chrome, Firefox, and Android that don't support WebM or MP4, so including it ensures playback for more users.

Of course, the problem that I referred to earlier is that browser makers have not agreed on a single format to support. Some go with open source, royalty-free options like Ogg Theora or WebM. Others are sticking with H.264 despite the royalty requirements. What that means is that we web developers need to make multiple versions of videos to ensure support across all browsers. TABLE 10-1 lists which browsers support the various video options (see the **"Server Setup"** sidebar).

Server Setup

In TABLES 10-1 and 10-2, the Type column identifies the MIME type of each media format. If your site is running on the Apache server, to make sure that video and audio files are served correctly, you may need to add their respective types to the server's *.htaccess* file. The following example adds the MP4 type/subtype and extensions:

```
AddType video/mp4 mp4 m4v
```

Meet the audio formats

The landscape looks similar for audio formats: several to choose from, but no format that is supported by all browsers (TABLE 10-2).

MP3. The MP3 (short for MPEG-1 Audio Layer 3) format is a codec and container in one, with the file extension.*mp3*. It has become ubiquitous as a music download format.

WAV. The WAV format (.*wav*) is also a codec and container in one. This format is uncompressed so it is only good for very short clips, like sound effects.

Ogg container + Vorbis audio codec. This is usually referred to as "Ogg Vorbis" and is served with the .*ogg* or .*oga* file extension.

MPEG 4 container + AAC audio codec. "MPEG4 audio" (.*m4a*) is less common than MP3.

WebM container + Vorbis audio codec. The WebM (.*webm*) format can also contain audio only.

WebM container + Opus audio codec. Opus is a newer, more efficient audio codec that can be used with WebM.

▌ FOR FURTHER EXPLORATION

HLS (HTTP Streaming Video)

If you are serious about web video, you should become familiar with HLS (HTTP Streaming Video), a streaming format that can adapt its bitrate on the fly. The HLS Wikipedia entry is as good a place as any to get started: *en.wikipedia.org/wiki/ HTTP_Live_Streaming*.

TABLE 10-1. *Video support in desktop and mobile browsers (as of 2017)*

Format	Type	IE	MS Edge	Chrome	Firefox	Safari	Opera	Android	iOS Safari
MP4 (H.264)	video/mp4 mp4 m4v	9.0+	12+	4+	Yes*	3.2+	25+	4.4+	3.2+
WebM (VP8)	video/webm webm webmv	–	–	6+	4.0+	–	15+	2.3+	–
WebM (VP9)	video/webm webm webmv	–	14+	29+	28+	–	16+	4.4+	–
Ogg Theora	video/ogg ogv	–	–	3.0+	3.5+	–	13+	2.3+	–

* *Firefox version varies by operating system.*

TABLE 10-2. *Audio support in current browsers (as of 2017)*

Format	Type	IE	MS Edge	Chrome	Firefox	Opera	Safari	iOS Safari	Android
MP3	audio/mpeg mp3	9.0+	12+	3.0+	22+	15+	4+	4.1	2.3+
WAV	audio/wav or audio/wave	–	12+	8.0+	3.5+	11.5+	4+	3.2+	2.3+
Ogg Vorbis	audio/ogg ogg oga	–	–	4.0+	3.5+	11.5+	–	–	2.3+
MPEG-4/AAC	audio/mp4 m4a	11.0+	12+	12.0+	–	15+	4+	4.1+	3.0+
WebM/Vorbis	audio/webm webm	–	–	6.0+	4.0+	11.5+	–	–	2.3.3+
WebM/Opus	audio/webm webm	–	14+	33+	15+	20+	–	–	–

Adding a Video to a Page

<video>…</video>

Adds a video player to the page

I guess it's about time we got to the markup for adding a video to a web page (this is an HTML chapter, after all). Let's start with an example that assumes you are designing for an environment where you know exactly what browser your user will be using. When this is the case, you can provide only one video format using the **src** attribute in the **video** tag (just as you do for an **img**). FIGURE 10-3 shows a movie with the default player in the Chrome browser.

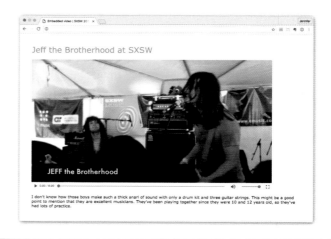

FIGURE 10-3. An embedded movie using the **video** element (shown in Chrome on a Mac).

Video and Audio Encoding Tools

There are scores of options for editing and encoding video and audio files, so I can't cover them all here, but the following tools are free and get the job done.

Video conversion

- **Handbrake** (*handbrake.fr*) is a popular open source tool for converting to MPEG4 with H.264, H.265, VP8, and Theora. It is available for Windows, macOS, and Linux.

- **Firefogg** (*firefogg.org*) is an extension to Firefox for converting video to the WebM (VP8 and VP9) and Ogg Theora formats. Simply install the Firefogg extension to Firefox (cross-platform); then visit the Firefogg site and convert video by using its online interface.

- **FFmpeg** (*ffmpeg.org*)is an open source, command-line tool for converting just about any video format. If you are not comfortable with the command line, there are a number of software packages (some for pay, some free) that offer a user interface to FFmpeg to make it more user-friendly.

- **Freemake** (*freemake.com*) is a free video and audio conversion tool for Windows that supports over 500 media formats.

Audio conversion

- **Audio Converter** (*online-audio-converter.com*) is one of the free audio and video tools from *123Apps.com* that converts files to MP3, WAV, OGG, and more.

- **Media.io** (*media.io*) is a free web service that converts audio to MP3, WAV, and OGG.

- **MediaHuman Audio Converter** (*www.mediahuman.com/audio-converter/*) is free for Mac and Windows and can convert to all of the audio formats listed in this chapter and more. It has an easy drag-and-drop interface, but is pretty much no-frills.

- **Max** (*sbooth.org/Max/*) is an open source audio converter (Mac only).

- **Audacity** (*www.audacityteam.org*) is free, open source, cross-platform audio software for multitrack recording and editing. It can import and export files in many of the formats listed in this chapter.

Here is a simple video element that embeds a movie and player on a web page:

```
<video src="highlight_reel.mp4" width="640" height="480"
poster="highlight_still.jpg" controls autoplay>
   Your browser does not support HTML5 video. Get the <a
href="highlight_reel.mp4">MP4 video</a>
</video>
```

Browsers that do not support **video** display whatever content is provided within the **video** element. In this example, it provides a link to the movie that your visitor could download and play in another player.

There are also some attributes in that example worth looking at in detail:

width="*pixel measurement*"
height="*pixel measurement*"

Specifies the size of the box the embedded media player takes up on the screen. Generally, it is best to set the dimensions to exactly match the pixel dimensions of the movie. The movie will resize to match the dimensions set here.

poster="*url of image*"

Provides the location of an image that is shown in place of the video before it plays.

controls

Adding the **controls** attribute prompts the browser to display its built-in media controls, generally a play/pause button, a "seeker" that lets you move to a position within the video, and volume controls. It is possible to create your own custom player interface using CSS and JavaScript if you want more consistency across browsers.

autoplay

Makes the video start playing automatically after it has downloaded enough of the media file to play through without stopping. In general, use of **autoplay** should be avoided in favor of letting the user decide when the video should start. **autoplay** does not work on iOS Safari and some other mobile browsers in order to protect users from unnecessary data downloads.

In addition, the **video** element can use the **loop** attribute to make the video play again after it has finished (ad infinitum), **muted** for playing the video track without the audio, and **preload** for suggesting to the browser whether the video data should be fetched as soon as the page loads (**preload="auto"**) or wait until the user clicks the play button (**preload="none"**). Setting **preload="metadata"** loads information about the media file, but not the media itself. A device can decide how to best handle the **auto** setting; for example, a browser in a smartphone may protect a user's data usage by not preloading media, even when it is set to **auto**.

Providing video format options

Do you remember back in **Chapter 7** when we supplied multiple image formats with the **picture** element using a number of **source** elements? Well, **picture** got that idea from **video**!

As you've seen, it is not easy to find one video format to please all browsers (although MPEG4/H.264 gets close). In addition, new efficient video formats like VP9 and H.265 are available but not supported in older browsers. Using **source** elements, we can let the browsers use what they can.

In the markup, a series of **source** elements inside the **video** element point to each video file. Browsers look down the list until they find one they support and download only that version. The following example provides a video clip in the souped-up WebM/VP9 format for supporing browsers, as well as an MP4 and Ogg Theora for other browsers. This will cover pretty much all browsers that support HTML5 video (see the sidebar **"Flash Video Fallback"**).

```
<video id="video" controls poster="img/poster.jpg">
  <source src="clip.webm" type="video/webm">
  <source src="clip.mp4" type="video/mp4">
  <source src="clip.ogg" type="video/ogg">
  <a href="clip.mp4">Download the MP4 of the clip.</a>
</video>;
```

Custom video players

One of the powerful things about the **video** element and the Media Player API is that the system allows for a lot of customization. You can change the appearance of the control buttons with CSS and manipulate the functionality with JavaScript. That is all beyond the scope of this chapter, but I recommend the article "Creating a Cross-Browser Video Player" by Eric Shepherd, Chris Mills, and Ian Devlin (*developer.mozilla.org/en-US/Apps/Fundamentals/Audio_and_video_delivery/cross_browser_video_player*) for a good overview.

You may also be interested in trying out a prefab video player that provides good looks and advanced performance such as support for streaming video formats. You can implement many of them by adding a line or two of JavaScript to your document and then by using the **video** element, so it's not hard to get started. There's a nice roundup of plug-and-play video player options listed at VideoSWS (*videosws.praegnanz.de/*).

Flash Video Fallback

Older browsers—most notably Internet Explorer versions 8 and earlier—do not support **video**. If f IE8 is making a significant blip in your site statistics, you may choose to provide a Flash movie fallback. The "Creating a Cross-Browser Video Player" article mentioned previously has thorough explanation of the technique. Another article worth a read is Kroc Camen's "Video for Everybody" (*camendesign.com/code/video_for_everybody*). It is a bit dated, but I'm sure would be helpful, balanced with your up-to-date browser support knowledge.

Adding Audio to a Page

If you've wrapped your head around the **video** markup example, you already know how to add audio to a page. The **audio** element uses the same attributes as the **video** element, with the exception of **width**, **height**, and **poster** (because there is nothing to display). Just like the **video** element, you can provide a stack of audio format options using the **source** element, as shown in the example here. FIGURE 10-4 shows how the audio player might look when it's rendered in the browser.

`<audio>…</audio>`
Adds an audio file to the page

```
<p>Play "Percussion Gun" by White Rabbits</p>

<audio id="whiterabbits" controls preload="auto">
  <source src="percussiongun.mp3" type="audio/mp3">
  <source src="percussiongun.ogg" type="audio/ogg">
  <source src="percussiongun.webm" type="audio/webm">
  <p>Download "Percussion Gun":</p>
  <ul>
    <li><a href="percussiongun.mp3">MP3</a></li>
    <li><a href="percussiongun.ogg">Ogg Vorbis</a></li>
  </ul>
</audio>
```

Play "Percussion Gun" by White Rabbits

FIGURE 10-4. Audio player as rendered in Firefox.

If you have only one audio file, you can simply use the **src** attribute instead. If you want to be evil, you could embed audio in a page, set it to play automatically and then loop, and not provide any controls to stop it like this:

```
<audio src="jetfighter.mp3" autoplay loop></audio>
```

But you would never, *ever* do something like that, right? *Right?!* Of course you wouldn't.

Adding Text Tracks

The **track** element provides a way to add text that is synchronized with the timeline of a video or audio track. Some uses include the following:

`<track>…</track>`
Adds synchronized text to embedded media

- **Subtitles** in alternative languages

- **Captions** for the hearing impaired

- **Descriptions** of what is happening in a video for the sight impaired

- **Chapter titles** to allow for navigation through the media

- **Metadata** that is not displayed but can be used by scripts

Clearly, adding text tracks makes the media more accessible, but it has the added bonus of improving SEO (Search Engine Optimization). It can also allow for deep linking, linking to a particular spot within the media's timeline.

FIGURE 10-5 shows how captions might be rendered in a browser that supports the **track** element.

FIGURE 10-5. A video with captions.

Use the **track** element inside the **video** or **audio** element you wish to annotate. The **track** element must appear after all the **source** elements, if any, and may include these attributes:

src

Points to the text file.

kind

Specifies the type of text annotation you are providing (**subtitles**, **captions**, **descriptions**, **chapters**, or **metadata**). If **kind** is set to **subtitle**, you must also specify the language (**srclang** attribute) by using a standardized IANA two-letter language tag (see **Note**).

label

Provides a name for the track that can be used in the interface for selecting a particular track.

default

Marks a particular track as the default and it may be used on only one track within a media element.

NOTE

The full list of two-letter language codes is published at www.iana.org/assignments/language-subtag-registry/language-subtag-registry.

The following code provides English and French subtitle options for a movie:

```
<video width="640" height="320" controls>
  <source src="japanese_movie.mp4" type="video/mp4">
  <source src="japanese_movie.webm" type="video/webm">
  <track src="english_subtitles.vtt"
         kind="subtitles"
         srclang="en"
         label="English subtitles"
         default>
  <track src="french.vtt"
         kind="subtitles"
         srclang="fr"
         label="Sous-titres en français">
</video>
```

WebVTT

You'll notice in the previous example that the track points to a file with a *.vtt* suffix. That is a text file in the WebVTT (Web Video Text Tracks) format that contains a list of cues. It looks like this:

```
WEBVTT

00:00:01.345 --> 00:00:03.456
Welcome to Artifact [applause]

00:00:06.289 --> 00:00:09.066
There is a lot of new mobile technology to discuss.

00:00:06.289 --> 00:00:13.049
We're glad you could all join us at the Alamo Drafthouse.
```

Cues are separated by empty line spaces. Each cue has a start and end time in *hours:minutes:seconds:milliseconds* format, separated by an "arrow" (**-->**). The cue text (subtitle, caption, description, chapter, or metadata) is on a line below. Optionally, an ID can be provided for each cue on the line above the time sequence.

You can probably guess that there's a lot more to mastering text tracks for video and audio. Take a look at the following resources:

- "Adding Captions and Subtitles to HTML5 Video" at MDN Web Docs (*developer.mozilla.org/en-US/Apps/Fundamentals/Audio_and_video_delivery/Adding_captions_and_subtitles_to_HTML5_video*)

- Subtitle tutorial on Miracle Tutorials (*www.miracletutorials.com/how-to-create-captionssubtitles-for-video-and-audio-in-webtvv-srt-dfxp-format/*)

- The WebVTT specification at the W3C is available at *www.w3.org/TR/webvtt1/*

If you'd like to play around with the **video** element, spend some time with EXERCISE 10-2.

NOTE

Other timed text formats include SRT captioning (replaced by WebVTT) and TML/DFXP, which is maintained by the W3C and supported by Internet Explorer but it is not recommended in the HTML5 specification for **track***.*

EXERCISE 10-2. Embedding a video player

In this exercise, you'll add a video to a page with the **video** element. In the materials for **Chapter 10**, you will find the small movie about wind tunnel testing in MPEG-4, OGG/Theora, and WebM formats.

1. Create a new document with the proper HTML5 setup, or you can use the same document you used in EXERCISE 10-1.

2. Start by adding the **video** element with the **src** attribute pointed to *windtunnel.mp4* because MP4 video has the best browser support. Be sure to include the width (320 pixels) and height (262 pixels), as well as the **controls** attribute so you'll have a way to play and pause it. Include some fallback copy within the **video** element—either a message or a link to the video:

```
<video src="windtunnel.mp4" width="320"
height="262" controls>
  Sorry, your browser doesn't support HTML5 video.
</video>
```

3. Save and view the document in your browser. If you see the fallback message, your browser is old and doesn't support the **video** element. If you see the controls but no video, it doesn't support MP4, so try it again with one of the other formats.

4. The **video** element is pretty straightforward so you may feel done at this point, but I encourage you to play around with it a little to see what happens. Here are some things to try:

   • Resize the video player with the **width** and **height** attributes.

   • Add the **autoplay** attribute.

   • Remove the **controls** attribute and see what that's like as a user.

   • Rewrite the **video** element using **source** elements for each of the three provided video formats.

CANVAS

Another cool, "Look Ma, no plug-ins!" addition in HTML5 is the **canvas** element and the associated Canvas API. The **canvas** element creates an area on a web page for drawing with a set of JavaScript functions for creating lines, shapes, fills, text, animations, and so on. You could use it to display an illustration, but what gives the **canvas** element so much potential (and has the web development world so delighted) is that it's all generated with scripting. That means it is dynamic and can draw things on the fly and respond to user input. This makes it a nifty platform for creating animations, games, and even whole applications—all using the native browser behavior and without proprietary plug-ins like Flash.

It is worth noting that the canvas drawing area is raster-based, meaning that it is made up of a grid of pixels. This sets it apart from the other drawing standard, SVG, which uses vector shapes and paths that are defined with points and mathematics.

NOTE

If you have a good reason to support IE8, the FlashCanvas JavaScript library (flashcanvas.net) adds canvas support using the Flash drawing API.

The good news is that every current browser supports the **canvas** element as of this writing, with the exception of Internet Explorer 8 and earlier (see **Note**). It has become so well established that Adobe's Animate software (the replacement for Flash Pro) now exports to canvas format.

FIGURE 10-6 shows a few examples of the **canvas** element used to create games, drawing programs, an interactive molecule structure tool, and an asteroid animation. You can find more examples at EnvatoTuts+ (*code. tutsplus.com/articles/21-ridiculously-impressive-html5-canvas-experiments- -net-14210*), on David Walsh's blog (*davidwalsh.name/canvas-demos*), as well as the results of your own web search.

mahjong.frvr.com/

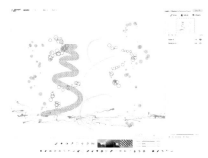

muro.deviantart.com/

www.effectgames.com/demos/canvascycle/

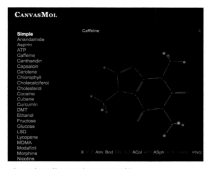

alteredqualia.com/canvasmol/

FIGURE 10-6. A few examples of the **canvas** element used for games, animations, and applications.

Mastering the **canvas** element is more than we can take on here, particularly without any JavaScript experience under our belts, but I will give you a taste of what it is like to draw with JavaScript. That should give you a good idea of how it works, and also a new appreciation for the complexity of some of those examples.

The canvas Element

You add a canvas space to the page with the **canvas** element and specify the dimensions with the **width** and **height** attributes. And that's really all there is to the markup. For browsers that don't support the **canvas** element, you can provide some fallback content (a message, image, or whatever seems appropriate) inside the tags:

`<canvas>`...`</canvas>`

Adds a 2-D dynamic drawing area

```
<canvas width="600" height="400" id="my_first_canvas">
Your browser does not support HTML5 canvas. Try using Chrome, Firefox,
Safari or MS Edge.
</canvas>
```

The markup just clears a space upon which the drawing will happen. You can affect the drawing space itself with CSS (add a border or a background color, for example), but all of the contents of the canvas are generated by scripting and cannot be selected for styling with CSS.

Drawing with JavaScript

The Canvas API includes functions for creating shapes, such as **strokeRect()** for drawing a rectangular outline and **beginPath()** for starting a line drawing. Some functions move things around, such as **rotate()** and **scale()**. It also includes attributes for applying styles (for example, **lineWidth**, **font**, **stroke-Style**, and **fillStyle**).

Sanders Kleinfeld created the following code example for his book *HTML5 for Publishers* (O'Reilly). He was kind enough to allow me to use it in this book. FIGURE 10-7 shows the simple smiley face we'll be creating with the Canvas API.

FIGURE 10-7. The finished product of our "Hello Canvas" example. See the original at *examples.oreilly.com/0636920022473/my_first_canvas/my_first_canvas.html*.

And here is the script that created it. Don't worry that you don't know any JavaScript yet. Just skim through the script and pay attention to the inline comments. I'll also describe some of the functions in use at the end. I bet you'll get the gist of it just fine.

```
<script type="text/javascript">
window.addEventListener('load', eventWindowLoaded, false);
function eventWindowLoaded() {
    canvasApp();
}

function canvasApp(){
var theCanvas = document.getElementById('my_first_canvas');
var my_canvas = theCanvas.getContext('2d');
my_canvas.strokeRect(0,0,200,225)
    // to start, draw a border around the canvas
```

```
        //draw face
my_canvas.beginPath();
my_canvas.arc(100, 100, 75, (Math.PI/180)*0, (Math.PI/180)*360, false);
        // circle dimensions
my_canvas.strokeStyle = "black"; // circle outline is black
my_canvas.lineWidth = 3; // outline is three pixels wide
my_canvas.fillStyle = "yellow"; // fill circle with yellow
my_canvas.stroke(); // draw circle
my_canvas.fill(); // fill in circle
my_canvas.closePath();

        // now, draw left eye
my_canvas.fillStyle = "black"; // switch to black for the fill
my_canvas.beginPath();
my_canvas.arc(65, 70, 10, (Math.PI/180)*0, (Math.PI/180)*360, false);
        // circle dimensions
my_canvas.stroke(); // draw circle
my_canvas.fill(); // fill in circle
my_canvas.closePath();

        // now, draw right eye
my_canvas.beginPath();
my_canvas.arc(135, 70, 10, (Math.PI/180)*0, (Math.PI/180)*360, false);
        // circle dimensions
my_canvas.stroke(); // draw circle
my_canvas.fill(); // fill in circle
my_canvas.closePath();

        // draw smile
my_canvas.lineWidth = 6; // switch to six pixels wide for outline
my_canvas.beginPath();
my_canvas.arc(99, 120, 35, (Math.PI/180)*0, (Math.PI/180)*-180, false);
        // semicircle dimensions
my_canvas.stroke();
my_canvas.closePath();

        // Smiley Speaks!
my_canvas.fillStyle = "black"; // switch to black for text fill
my_canvas.font        = '20px _sans'; // use 20 pixel sans serif font
my_canvas.fillText  ("Hello Canvas!", 45, 200); // write text
}
</script>
```

Finally, here is a little more information on the Canvas API functions used in the example:

strokeRect(*x1, y1, x2, y2*)

Draws a rectangular outline from the point (x1, y1) to (x2, y2). By default, the origin of the canvas (0, 0) is the top-left corner, and *x* and *y* coordinates are measured to the right and down.

beginPath()

Starts a line drawing.

closePath()

Ends a line drawing that was started with **beginPath()**.

`arc(x, y, arc_radius, angle_radians_beg, angle_radians_end)`

> Draws an arc where (x,y) is the center of the circle, **arc_radius** is the length of the radius of the circle, and **angle_radians_beg** and **_end** indicate the beginning and end of the arc angle.

`stroke()`

> Draws the line defined by the path. If you don't include this, the path won't appear on the canvas.

`fill()`

> Fills in the path specified with **beginPath()** and **endPath()**.

`fillText(your_text, x1, y1)`

> Adds text to the canvas starting at the (x,y) coordinate specified.

In addition, the following attributes were used to specify colors and styles:

`lineWidth`

> Width of the border of the path.

`strokeStyle`

> Color of the border.

`fillStyle`

> Color of the fill (interior) of the shape created with the path.

`font`

> The font and size of the text.

Of course, the Canvas API includes many more functions and attributes than we've used here. For a complete list, see the W3C's HTML5 Canvas 2D Context specification at *www.w3.org/TR/2dcontext*. A web search will turn up lots of Canvas tutorials should you be ready to learn more. In addition, I can recommend these resources:

- The book *HTML5 Canvas, Second Edition*, by Steve Fulton and Jeff Fulton (O'Reilly).

- If video is more your speed, try this tutorial by David Geary: *HTML5 Canvas for Developers* (*shop.oreilly.com/product/0636920030751.do*).

TEST YOURSELF

We've looked at all sorts of ways to stick things in web pages in this chapter. We've seen how to use **iframe** to create a "window-in-a-window" for displaying external web resources; **object** for resources that require plug-ins, video and audio players; and the **canvas** 2-D scriptable drawing space. Now see if you were paying attention. As always, answers are in **Appendix A**.

1. What is a "nested browsing context," and how would you create one?

2. Why would you use the **sandbox** attribute with an **iframe**?

3. Name some instances when you might need to know the MIME type for your media file.

4. Identify each of the following as a container format, video codec, or audio codec:

   a. Ogg   _____

   b. H.264   _____

   c. VP8   _____

   d. Vorbis   _____

   e. WebM   _____

   f. Theora   _____

   g. Opus   _____

   h. MPEG-4   _____

5. What does the **poster** attribute do?

6. What is a _.vtt_ file?

7. List at least two differences between SVG and Canvas.

8. List the two Canvas API functions you would use to draw a rectangle and fill it with red. You don't need to write the whole script.

ELEMENT REVIEW: EMBEDDED MEDIA

The following elements are used to embed media files of many types into web pages.

Element and Attributes	Description
audio	Embeds an audio player on the page
src="*URL*"	Address of the resource
crossorigin="anonymous| use-credentials"	How the element handles requests from other origins (servers)
preload="auto|none|metadata"	Indicates how much the media resource should be buffered on page load
autoplay	Indicates the media can play as soon as the page is loaded
loop	Indicates the media file should start playing again automatically once it reaches the end
muted	Disables the audio output
controls	Indicates the browser should display a set of playback controls for the media file
canvas	Represents a two-dimensional area that can be used for rendering dynamic bitmap graphics
height	The height of the canvas area
width	The width of the canvas area
embed	Embeds a multimedia object that requires a plug-in for playback on the page. Certain media types require custom attributes not listed below.
src="*URL*"	Address of the media resource
type="*media type*"	The media (MIME) type of the media
width="*number*"	The horizontal dimension of the video player in pixels
height="*number*"	The vertical dimension of the video player in pixels
iframe	Creates a nested browsing context to display HTML resources in a page
src="*URL*"	Address of the HTML resource
srcdoc="*HTML source code*"	The HTML source of a document to display in the inline frame
name="*text*"	Assigns a name to the inline frame to be referenced by targeted links

sandbox=
    "allow-forms|
    allow-pointer-lock|
    allow-popups|
    allow-same-origin|
    allow-scripts|
    allow-top-navigation"
	Security rules for nested content

allowfullscreen	Indicates the objects in the inline frame are allowed to use **requestFullScreen()**
width="*number*"	The horizontal dimension of the video player in pixels
height="*number*"	The vertical dimension of the video player in pixels

Element and Attributes	Description
object	A generic element for embedding an external resource
data="*URI*"	Address of the resource
type="*media type*"	The media (MIME) type of the resource
typemustmatch	Indicates the resource is to be used only if the value of the **type** attribute and the content type of the resource match
name="*text*"	The name of the object to be referenced by scripts
form="*form ID*"	Associates the **object** with a **form** element
width="*number*"	The horizontal dimension of the video player in pixels
height="*number*"	The vertical dimension of the video player in pixels
param	Supplies a parameter within an **object** element
name="*text*"	Defines the name of the parameter
value="*text*"	Defines the value of the parameter
source	Allows authors to specify multiple versions of a media file (used with **video** and **audio**)
src="*text*"	The address of the resource
type="*media type*"	The media (MIME) type of the resource
track	Specifies an external resource (text or audio) that is timed with a media file that improves accessibility, navigation, or SEO
kind="subtitles|captions|descriptions|chapters|metadata"	Type of text track
src="*text*"	Address of external resource
srclang="*valid language tag*"	Language of the text track
label="*text*"	A title for the track that may be displayed by the browser
default	Indicates the track should be used by default if it does not override user preferences
video	Embeds a video player on the page
src="*URL*"	Address of the resource
crossorigin="anonymous|use-credentials"	How the element handles requests from other origins (servers)
poster="*URL*"	The location of an image file that displays as a placeholder before the video begins to play
preload="auto|none|metadata"	Hints how much buffering the media resource will need
autoplay	Indicates the media can play as soon as the page is loaded
loop	Indicates the media file should start playing again automatically once it reaches the end
muted	Disables the audio output
controls	Indicates the browser should display a set of playback controls for the media file
width="*number*"	Specifies the horizontal dimension of the video player in pixels
height="*number*"	Specifies the vertical dimension of the video player in pixels

III

CSS FOR PRESENTATION

INTRODUCING CASCADING STYLE SHEETS

You've heard style sheets mentioned quite a bit already, and now we'll finally put them to work and start giving our pages some much-needed style. Cascading Style Sheets (CSS) is the W3C standard for defining the presentation of documents written in HTML, and in fact, any XML language. Presentation, again, refers to the way the document is delivered to the user, whether shown on a computer screen, displayed on a cell phone, printed on paper, or read aloud by a screen reader. With style sheets handling the presentation, HTML can handle the business of defining document structure and meaning, as intended.

CSS is a separate language with its own syntax. This chapter covers CSS terminology and fundamental concepts that will help you get your bearings for the upcoming chapters, where you'll learn how to change text and font styles, add colors and backgrounds, and even do basic page layout. By the end of **Part III**, I aim to give you a solid foundation for further reading on your own and lots of practice.

THE BENEFITS OF CSS

Not that you need further convincing that style sheets are the way to go, but here is a quick rundown of the benefits of using style sheets.

- **Precise type and layout controls.** You can achieve print-like precision using CSS. There is even a set of properties aimed specifically at the printed page (but we won't be covering them in this book).

- **Less work.** You can change the appearance of an entire site by editing one style sheet. This also ensures consistency of formatting throughout the site.

- **More accessible sites.** When all matters of presentation are handled by CSS, you can mark up your content meaningfully, making it more accessible for non-visual or mobile devices.

Come to think of it, there really aren't any disadvantages to using style sheets. There are some lingering hassles from browser inconsistencies, but they can either be avoided or worked around if you know where to look for them.

The Power of CSS

We're not talking about minor visual tweaks here, like changing the color of headlines or adding text indents. When used to its full potential, CSS is a robust and powerful design tool. My eyes were first opened to the possibilities of using CSS for design by the variety and richness of the designs at CSS Zen Garden (*www.csszengarden.com*).

In the misty days of yore (2003), when developers were still hesitant to give up their table-based layouts for CSS, David Shea's CSS Zen Garden site demonstrated exactly what could be accomplished using CSS alone. David posted an HTML document and invited designers to contribute their own style sheets that gave the document a visual design. FIGURE 11-1 shows just a few of my favorites. All of these designs use the *exact same* HTML source document.

Not only that, they don't include a single **img** element (all of the images are in the background of elements). But look at how different each page looks—and how sophisticated. That's all done with style sheets. It is proof of the power in keeping CSS separate from HTML, and presentation separate from structure.

The CSS Zen Garden is no longer being updated and now is considered a historical document of a turning point in the adoption of web standards. Despite its age, I still find it to be a nice one-stop lesson for demonstrating exactly what CSS can do.

Granted, it takes a lot of practice to be able to create CSS layouts like those shown in FIGURE 11-1. Killer graphic design skills help too (unfortunately, you won't get those in this book). I'm showing this to you up front because I want you to be aware of the potential of CSS-based design, particularly because the examples in this beginners' book tend to be simple and straightforward. Take your time learning, but keep your eye on the prize.

HOW STYLE SHEETS WORK

It's as easy as 1-2-3!

1. Start with a document that has been marked up in HTML.

2. Write style rules for how you ' d like certain elements to look.

CSS Zen Dragen
by Matthew Buchanan

By the Pier
by Peter Ong Kelmscott

Organica Creativa
by Eduardo Cesario

Shaolin Yokobue
by Javier Cabrera

FIGURE 11-1. These pages from the CSS Zen Garden use the same HTML source document, but the design is changed with CSS alone (used with permission of CSS Zen Garden and the individual designers).

3. Attach the style rules to the document. When the browser displays the document, it follows your rules for rendering elements (unless the user has applied some mandatory styles, but we'll get to that later).

OK, so there's a bit more to it than that, of course. Let's give each of these steps a little more consideration.

1. Marking Up the Document

You know a lot about marking up content from the previous chapters. For example, you know that it is important to choose elements that accurately describe the meaning of the content. You also heard me say that the markup

EXERCISE 11-1.
A first look

In this chapter, we'll add a few simple styles to a short article. The document, *cooking.html*, and its associated image, *salads.jpg*, are available at *learningwebdesign.com/5e/materials/*.

For now, just open the document in a browser to see how it looks by default (it should look something like FIGURE 11-2). You can also open the document in a text editor to get ready to follow along in the next two exercises.

FIGURE 11-2. This is what the article looks like without any style sheet instructions. Although we won't be making it beautiful, you will get a feel for how style sheets work.

creates the structure of the document, sometimes called the structural layer, upon which the presentation layer can be applied.

In this and the upcoming chapters, you'll see that having an understanding of your document's structure and the relationships between elements is central to your work as a style sheet author.

In the exercises throughout this chapter you will get a feel for how simple it is to change the look of a document with style sheets. The good news is that I've whipped up a little HTML document for you to play with. You can get acquainted with the page we'll be working with in EXERCISE 11-1.

2. Writing the Rules

A style sheet is made up of one or more style instructions (called style rules) that describe how an element or group of elements should be displayed. The first step in learning CSS is to get familiar with the parts of a rule. As you'll see, they're fairly intuitive to follow. Each rule *selects* an element and *declares* how it should look.

The following example contains two rules. The first makes all the **h1** elements in the document green; the second specifies that the paragraphs should be in a large, sans-serif font. Sans-serif fonts do not have a little slab (a serif) at the ends of strokes and tend to look more sleek and modern.

```
h1 { color: green; }
p  { font-size: large; font-family: sans-serif; }
```

In CSS terminology, the two main sections of a rule are the selector that identifies the element or elements to be affected, and the declaration that provides the rendering instructions. The declaration, in turn, is made up of a property (such as **color**) and its value (**green**), separated by a colon and a space. One or more declarations are placed inside curly brackets, as shown in FIGURE 11-3.

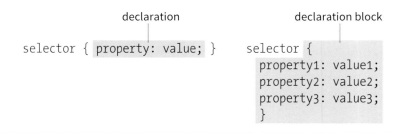

FIGURE 11-3. The parts of a style rule.

Selectors

In the previous small style sheet example, the **h1** and **p** elements are used as selectors. This is called an element type selector, and it is the most basic type of selector. The properties defined for each rule will apply to every **h1** and **p** element in the document, respectively.

Another type of selector is an ID selector, which selects an element based on the value of an element's **id** attribute. It is indicated with the **#** symbol. For example, the selector **#recipe** targets an element with **id="recipe"**.

In upcoming chapters, I'll introduce you to more sophisticated selectors that you can use to target elements, including ways to select groups of elements, and elements that appear in a particular context. See the **"Selectors in this Book"** sidebar for details.

Mastering selectors—that is, choosing the best type of selector and using it strategically—is an important step in mastering CSS.

Declarations

The declaration is made up of a property/value pair. There can be more than one declaration in a single rule; for example, the rule for the **p** element shown earlier in the code example has both the **font-size** and **font-family** properties. Each declaration must end with a semicolon to keep it separate from the following declaration (see **Note**). If you omit the semicolon, the declaration and the one following it will be ignored. The curly brackets and the declarations they contain are often referred to as the declaration block (FIGURE 11-3).

Because CSS ignores whitespace and line returns within the declaration block, authors typically write each declaration in the block on its own line, as shown in the following example. This makes it easier to find the properties applied to the selector and to tell when the style rule ends.

```
p {
  font-size: large;
  font-family: sans-serif;
}
```

Note that nothing has really changed here—there is still one set of curly brackets, semicolons after each declaration, and so on. The only difference is the insertion of line returns and some character spaces for alignment.

Properties

The heart of style sheets lies in the collection of standard properties that can be applied to selected elements. The complete CSS specification defines dozens of properties for everything from text indents to how table headers should be read aloud. This book covers the most common and best-supported properties that you can begin using right away.

Selectors in This Book

Instead of throwing the selectors at you all at once, I've spread them out so you can master a few at a time. Here is where you will find them:

Chapter 11:

Chapter 12:

Chapter 13:

NOTE

Technically, the semicolon is not required after the last declaration in the block, but it is recommended that you get into the habit of always ending declarations with a semicolon. It will make adding declarations to the rule later that much easier.

Values

Values are dependent on the property. Some properties take length measurements, some take color values, and others have a predefined list of keywords. When you use a property, it is important to know which values it accepts; however, in many cases, simple common sense will serve you well. Authoring tools such as Dreamweaver or Visual Studio provide hints of suitable values to choose from. Before we move on, why not get a little practice writing style rules yourself in EXERCISE 11-2?

EXERCISE 11-2. Your first style sheet

Open *cooking.html* in a text editor. In the **head** of the document you will find that I have set up a **style** element for you to type the rules into. The **style** element is used to embed a style sheet in an HTML document. To begin, we'll simply add the small style sheet that we just looked at in this section. Type the following rules into the document, just as you see them here:

```
<style>
h1 {
  color: green;
}
p {
  font-size: large;
  font-family: sans-serif;
}
</style>
```

Save the file, and take a look at it in the browser. You should notice some changes (if your browser already uses a sans-serif font, you may see only a size change). If not, go back and check that you included both the opening and closing curly bracket and semicolons. It's easy to accidentally omit these characters, causing the style sheet not to work.

Now we'll edit the style sheet to see how easy it is to write rules and see the effects of the changes. Here are a few things to try.

IMPORTANT: Remember that you need to save the document after each change in order for the changes to be visible when you reload it in the browser.

- Make the **h1** element "gray" and take a look at it in the browser. Then make it "blue". Finally, make it "orange". (We'll run through the complete list of available color names in **Chapter 13, Colors and Backgrounds**.)

- Add a new rule that makes the **h2** elements orange as well.

- Add a 100-pixel left margin to paragraph (**p**) elements by using this declaration:

```
margin-left: 100px;
```

Remember that you can add this new declaration to the existing rule for **p** elements.

- Add a 100-pixel left margin to the **h2** headings as well.

- Add an orange, 1-pixel border to the bottom of the **h1** element by using this declaration:

```
border-bottom: 1px solid orange;
```

- Move the image to the right margin, and allow text to flow around it with the **float** property. The shorthand **margin** property shown in this rule adds zero pixels of space on the top and bottom of the image and 12 pixels of space on the left and right of the image (the values are mirrored in a manner explained in **Chapter 14, Thinking Inside the Box**):

```
img {
  float: right;
  margin: 0 12px;
}
```

When you are done, the document should look something like the one shown in FIGURE 11-4.

FIGURE 11-4. The article after we add a small style sheet. Not beautiful—just different.

3. Attaching the Styles to the Document

In the previous exercise, we embedded the style sheet right in the document by using the **style** element. That is just one of three ways that style information can be applied to an HTML document. You'll get to try out each of these soon, but it is helpful to have an overview of the methods and terminology up front.

External style sheets

An external style sheet is a separate, text-only document that contains a number of style rules. It must be named with the *.css* suffix. The *.css* document is then linked to (via the **link** element) or imported (via an **@import** rule in a style sheet) into one or more HTML documents. In this way, all the files in a website may share the same style sheet. This is the most powerful and preferred method for attaching style sheets to content. We'll discuss external style sheets more and start using them in the exercises in **Chapter 13**.

Embedded style sheets

This is the type of style sheet we worked with in the exercise. It is placed in a document via the **style** element, and its rules apply only to that document. The **style** element must be placed in the **head** of the document. This example also includes a comment (see the **"Comments in Style Sheets"** sidebar).

```
<head>
    <title>Required document title here</title>
    <style>
      /* style rules go here */
    </style>
</head>
```

Inline styles

You can apply properties and values to a single element by using the **style** *attribute* in the element itself, as shown here:

```
<h1 style="color: red">Introduction</h1>
```

To add multiple properties, just separate them with semicolons, like this:

```
<h1 style="color: red; margin-top: 2em">Introduction</h1>
```

Inline styles apply only to the particular element in which they appear. Inline styles should be avoided, unless it is absolutely necessary to override styles from an embedded or external style sheet. Inline styles are problematic in that they intersperse presentation information into the structural markup. They also make it more difficult to make changes because every **style** attribute must be hunted down in the source.

EXERCISE 11-3 gives you an opportunity to write an inline style and see how it works. We won't be working with inline styles after this point for the reasons listed earlier, so here's your chance.

Comments in Style Sheets

Sometimes it is helpful to leave yourself or your collaborators comments in a style sheet. CSS has its own comment syntax, shown here:

```
/* comment goes here */
```

Content between the **/*** and ***/** will be ignored when the style sheet is parsed, which means you can leave comments anywhere in a style sheet, even within a rule:

```
body {
   font-size: small;
  /* change this later */
}
```

One use for comments is to label sections of the style sheet to make things easier to find later; for example:

```
/* FOOTER STYLES */
```

CSS comments are also useful for temporarily hiding style declarations in the design process. When I am trying out a number of styles, I can quickly switch styles off by enclosing them in **/*** and ***/**, check the design in a browser, then remove the comment characters to make the style appear again. It's much faster than retyping the entire thing.

Applying an inline style

Open the article *cooking.html* in whatever state you last left it in EXERCISE 11-2. If you worked to the end of the exercise, you will have a rule that makes the **h2** elements orange.

Write an inline style that makes the second **h2** gray. We'll do that right in the opening **h2** tag by using the **style** attribute, as shown here:

```
<h2 style="color: gray">The
Main Course</h2>
```

Note that it must be gray-with-an-a (not grey-with-an-e) because that is the way the color is defined in the spec.

Save the file and open it in a browser. Now the second heading is gray, overriding the orange color set in the embedded style sheet. The other **h2** heading is unaffected.

THE BIG CONCEPTS

There are a few big ideas that you need to get your head around to be comfortable with how Cascading Style Sheets behave. I'm going to introduce you to these concepts now so we don't have to slow down for a lecture once we're rolling through the style properties. Each of these ideas will be revisited and illustrated in more detail in the upcoming chapters.

Inheritance

Are your eyes the same color as your parents'? Did you inherit their hair color? Well, just as parents pass down traits to their children, styled HTML elements pass down certain style properties to the elements they contain. Notice in EXERCISE 11-1, when we styled the **p** elements in a large, sans-serif font, the **em** element in the second paragraph became large and sans-serif as well, even though we didn't write a rule for it specifically (FIGURE 11-5). That is because the **em** element inherited the styles from the paragraph it is in. Inheritance provides a mechanism for styling elements that don't have any explicit styles rules of their own.

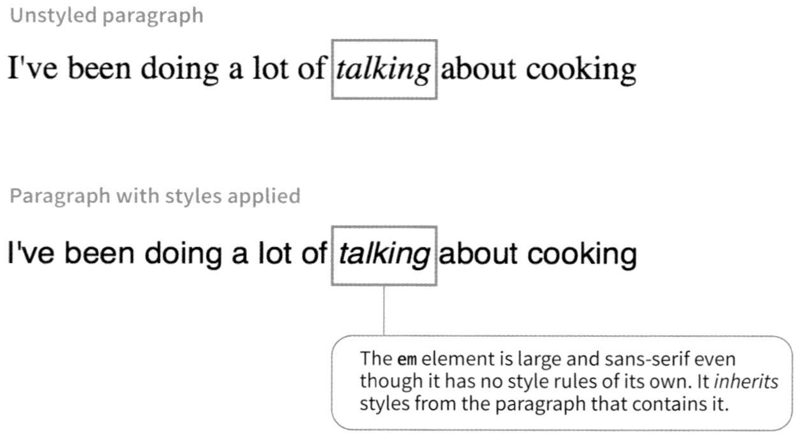

Unstyled paragraph

I've been doing a lot of *talking* about cooking

Paragraph with styles applied

I've been doing a lot of *talking* about cooking

> The **em** element is large and sans-serif even though it has no style rules of its own. It *inherits* styles from the paragraph that contains it.

FIGURE 11-5. The **em** element inherits styles that were applied to the paragraph.

Document structure

This is where an understanding of your document's structure becomes important. As I've noted before, HTML documents have an implicit structure, or hierarchy. For example, the sample article we've been playing with has an **html** root element that contains a **head** and a **body**, and the **body** contains heading and paragraph elements. A few of the paragraphs, in turn, contain inline elements such as images (**img**) and emphasized text (**em**). You can visualize the structure as an upside-down tree, branching out from the root, as shown in FIGURE 11-6.

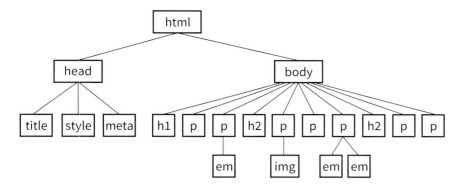

FIGURE 11-6. The document tree structure of the sample document, *cooking.html*.

Parents and children

The document tree becomes a family tree when it comes to referring to the relationship between elements. All the elements contained within a given element are said to be its descendants. For example, the **h1**, **h2**, **p**, **em**, and **img** elements in the document in FIGURE 11-6 are all descendants of the **body** element.

An element that is directly contained within another element (with no intervening hierarchical levels) is said to be the child of that element. Conversely, the containing element is the parent. For example, the **em** element is the child of the **p** element, and the **p** element is its parent.

All of the elements higher than a particular element in the hierarchy are its ancestors. Two elements with the same parent are siblings. We don't refer to "aunts" or "cousins," so the analogy stops there. This may all seem academic, but it will come in handy when you're writing CSS selectors.

Pass it on

When you write a font-related style rule using the **p** element as a selector, the rule applies to all of the paragraphs in the document as well as the inline text elements they contain. We've seen the evidence of the **em** element inheriting the style properties applied to its parent (**p**) back in FIGURE 11-5. FIGURE 11-7 demonstrates what's happening in terms of the document structure diagram. Note that the **img** element is excluded because font-related properties do not apply to images.

Notice that I've been saying "certain" properties are inherited. It's important to note that some style sheet properties inherit and others do not. In general, properties related to the styling of text—font size, color, style, and the like— are passed down. Properties such as borders, margins, backgrounds, and so on that affect the boxed area around the element tend not to be passed down. This makes sense when you think about it. For example, if you put a border

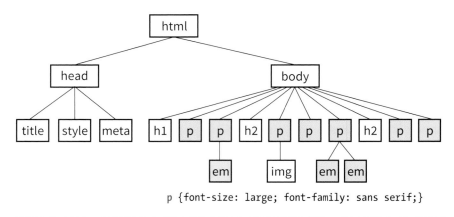

p {font-size: large; font-family: sans serif;}

FIGURE 11-7. Certain properties applied to the **p** element are inherited by their children.

around a paragraph, you wouldn't want a border around every inline element (such as **em**, **strong**, or **a**) it contains as well.

You can use inheritance to your advantage when writing style sheets. For example, if you want all text elements to be blue, you could write separate style rules for every element in the document and set the **color** to "blue". A *better* way would be to write a single style rule that applies the **color** property to the **body** element, and let all the elements contained in the **body** inherit that style (FIGURE 11-8).

Any property applied to a specific element overrides the inherited values for that property. Going back to the article example, if we specify that the **em** element should be orange, that would override the inherited blue setting.

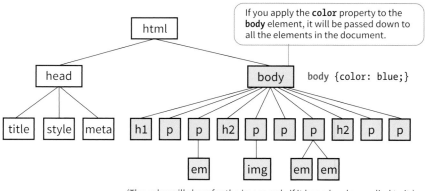

If you apply the **color** property to the **body** element, it will be passed down to all the elements in the document.

body {color: blue;}

(The color will show for the image only if it has a border applied to it.)

FIGURE 11-8. All the elements in the document inherit certain properties applied to the **body** element.

Conflicting Styles: The Cascade

Ever wonder why they are called "cascading" style sheets? CSS allows you to apply several style sheets to the same document, which means there are bound to be conflicts. For example, what should the browser do if a document's imported style sheet says that **h1** elements should be red, but its embedded style sheet has a rule that makes **h1**s purple? The two style rules with **h1** selectors have equal weight, right?

The folks who wrote the style sheet specification anticipated this problem and devised a hierarchical system that assigns different weights to the various sources of style information. The cascade refers to what happens when several sources of style information vie for control of the elements on a page: style information is passed down ("cascades" down) until it is overridden by a style rule with more weight. Weight is considered based on the *priority* of the style rule source, the *specificity* of the selector, and *rule order*.

Priority

If you don't apply any style information to a web page, it renders according to the browser's internal style sheet. We've been calling this the default rendering; the W3C calls it the user agent style sheet. Individual users can apply their own styles as well (the user style sheet, also called the reader style sheet), which override the default styles in their browser. However, if the author of the web page has attached a style sheet (the author style sheet), that overrides both the user and the user agent styles. The sidebar **"Style Rule Hierarchy"** provides an overview of the cascading order from highest to lowest priority.

The only exception is if the user has identified a style as "important," in which case that style will override all competing styles (see the **"Assigning Importance"** sidebar). This permits users to keep settings accommodating a disability such as extra large type for sight impairment.

Specificity

It is possible for conflicts to arise in which an element is getting style instructions from more than one rule. For example, there may be a rule that applies to paragraphs and another rule for a paragraph that has the ID "intro." Which rule should the intro paragraph use?

When two rules in a style sheet conflict, the type of selector is used to determine the winner. The more specific the selector, the more weight it is given to override conflicting declarations. In our example, the selector that includes the ID name (**#intro**) is more specific than a general element selector (like **p**), so that rule would apply to the "intro" paragraph, overriding the rules set for all paragraphs.

It's a little soon to be discussing specificity because we've looked at only two types of selectors. For now, put the term specificity and the concept that some

---

The "cascade" refers to what happens when several sources of style information vie for control of the elements on a page.

Style Rule Hierarchy

Style information can come from various origins, listed here from highest priority to lowest. In other words, items higher in the list override items below.

- Any style rule marked **!important** by the reader (user)
- Any style rule marked **!important** by the author
- Style sheets written by the author
- Style sheets created by the reader (user)
- Browser's default style rules ("user agent style sheet")

When two rules in a single style sheet conflict, the type of selector is used to determine the winner.

Assigning Importance

If you want a rule not to be overridden by a subsequent conflicting rule, include the **!important** indicator just after the property value and before the semicolon for that rule. For example, to guarantee paragraph text will be blue, use the following rule:

```
p {color: blue !important;}
```

Even if the browser encounters an inline style later in the document (which should override a document-wide style sheet), like this one:

```
<p style="color: red">
```

that paragraph will still be blue because the rule with the **!important** indicator cannot be overridden by other styles in the author's style sheet.

The only way an **!important** rule may be overridden is by a conflicting rule in a reader (user) style sheet that has also been marked **!important**. This is to ensure that special reader requirements, such as large type or high-contrast text for the visually impaired, are never overridden.

Based on the previous examples, if the reader's style sheet includes this rule

```
p {color: black;}
```

the text would still be blue because all author styles (even those not marked **!important**) take precedence over the reader's styles. However, if the conflicting reader's style is marked **!important**, like this

```
p {color: black !important;}
```

the paragraphs will be black and cannot be overridden by any author-provided style.

Beware that the **!important** indicator is not a get-out-of-jail-free card. Best practices dictate that it should be used sparingly, if at all, and certainly never just to get yourself out of a sticky situation with inheritance and the cascade.

---

selectors have more "weight," and therefore override others, on your radar. We will revisit specificity in much more detail in **Chapter 12, Formatting Text** when you have more selector types under your belt.

Rule order

After all the style sheet sources have been sorted by priority, and after all the linked and imported style sheets have been shuffled into place, there are likely to be conflicts in rules with equal weights. When that is the case, the order in which the rules appear is important. The cascade follows a "last one wins" rule. Whichever rule appears last has the last word.

Within a style sheet, if there are conflicts within style rules of identical weight, whichever one comes last in the list "wins." Take these three rules, for example:

```
<style>
  p { color: red; }
  p { color: blue; }
  p { color: green; }
</style>
```

In this scenario, paragraph text will be green because the last rule in the style sheet—that is, the one closest to the content in the document—overrides the earlier ones. Procedurally, the paragraph is assigned a color, then assigned a new one, and finally a third one (green) that gets used. The same thing happens when conflicting styles occur within a single declaration stack:

> The cascade follows a "last one wins" rule. Whichever rule appears last has the last word.

```
<style>
  p { color: red;
      color: blue;
      color: green; }
</style>
```

The resulting color will be green because the last declaration overrides the previous two. It is easy to accidentally override previous declarations within a rule when you get into compound properties, so this is an important behavior to keep in mind. That is a very simple example. What happens when style sheet rules from different sources come into play?

Let's consider an HTML document that has an embedded style sheet (added with the **style** element) that starts with an **@import** rule for importing an external *.css* file. That same HTML document also has a few inline **style** attributes applied to particular **h1** elements.

STYLE DOCUMENT (*external.css***):**

```
…
h1 { color: red }
…
```

HTML DOCUMENT:

```
<!DOCTYPE html>
<html>
<head>
  <title>…</title>
  <style>
    @import url(external.css);   /* set to red first */
    h1 { color: purple;}   /* overridden by purple */
  </style>
</head>
<body>
  <h1 style="color: blue">Heading</h1>   /* blue comes last and wins */
    …
</body>
</html>
```

When the browser parses the file, it gets to the imported style sheet first, which sets **h1**s to red. Then it finds a rule with equal weight in the embedded style sheet that overrides the imported rule, so **h1**s are set to purple. As it continues, it encounters a style rule right in an **h1** that sets its color to blue. Because that rule came last, it's the winner, and that **h1** will be blue. That's the effect we witnessed in EXERCISE 11-3. Note that other **h1**s in this document without inline style rules would be purple, because that was the last **h1** color applied to the whole document.

The Box Model

As long as we're talking about Big CSS Concepts, it is only appropriate to introduce the cornerstone of the CSS visual formatting system: the box model. The easiest way to think of the box model is that browsers see every element on the page (both block and inline) as being contained in a little

---

Using Rule Order for Fallbacks

Many CSS properties are tried and true and are supported by all browsers; however, there are always useful, new properties emerging that take a while to be implemented by browsers. It is common for just one or two browsers to support a new feature and for others to lag behind or never support it at all. It also takes a long time for some old browsers to completely fade from existence.

Fortunately, there are a number of ways to provide fallbacks (alternative styles using better-supported properties) to non-supporting browsers. The most straightforward method takes advantage of browsers' built-in behavior of ignoring any declaration they don't understand and then using rule order strategically.

In this example, I have added a decorative border image to an element by using the **border-image** property and provided a fallback solid border with the tried-and-true **border** property. Supporting browsers use the image because it is the last rule in the stack. Non-supporting browsers set a solid border but stop there when they get to the **border-image** property they don't understand. They won't crash or throw an error. They just ignore it. The border displays as the fallback solid red line on those browsers, which is fine, but users with supporting browsers will see the decorative border as intended.

```
h1 {
  /* fallback first */
  border: 25px solid #eee;
  /* newer technique */
  border-image: url(fancyframe.
  png) 55 fill / 55px / 25px;
}
```

You'll see this method of providing fallbacks by putting newer properties last throughout this book.

A Quick History of CSS

The first official version of CSS (the **CSS Level 1 Recommendation**, a.k.a **CSS1**) was released in 1996, and included properties for adding font, color, and spacing instructions to page elements. Unfortunately, lack of browser support prevented the widespread adoption of CSS for several years.

CSS Level 2 (CSS2), released in 1998, most notably added properties for positioning that allowed CSS to be used for page layout. It also introduced styles for other media types (such as print and handheld) and more sophisticated methods for selecting elements. **CSS Level 2, Revision 1 (CSS2.1)** made some minor adjustments to CSS2 and became a Recommendation in 2011.

CSS Level 3 (CSS3) is different from prior versions in that it is divided into individual modules, each addressing a feature such as animation, multiple column layouts, or borders. While some modules are being standardized, others remain experimental. In that way, browser developers can begin implementing (and we can begin using!) one feature at a time instead of waiting for an entire specification to be "ready."

Now that each CSS module is on its own track, modules have their own Level numbers. No more big, all-encompassing CSS versions. Newly introduced modules, such as the Grid Layout Module, start out at Level 1. Modules that have been around a while may have already reached Level 4.

You won't believe how many individual specifications are in the works! For an overview of the specifications in their various states of "doneness," see the W3C's CSS current work page at *www.w3.org/Style/CSS/current-work*.

rectangular box. You can apply properties such as borders, margins, padding, and backgrounds to these boxes, and even reposition them on the page.

We're going to go into a lot more detail about the box model in **Chapter 14**, but having a general feel for it will benefit you even as we discuss text and backgrounds in the following two chapters.

To see the elements roughly the way the browser sees them, I've written style rules that add borders around every content element in our sample article:

```
h1 { border: 1px solid blue; }
h2 { border: 1px solid blue; }
p { border: 1px solid blue; }
em { border: 1px solid blue; }
img { border: 1px solid blue; }
```

FIGURE 11-9 shows the results. The borders reveal the shape of each block element box. There are boxes around the inline elements (**em** and **img**) as well. If you look at the headings, you will see that block element boxes expand to fill the available width of the browser window, which is the nature of block elements in the normal document flow. Inline boxes encompass just the characters or image they contain.

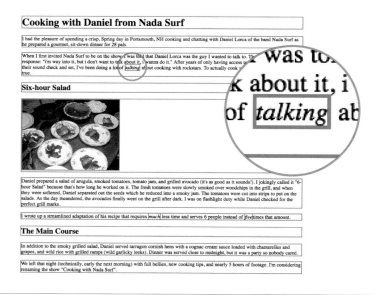

FIGURE 11-9. Rules around all the elements reveal their element boxes.

Grouped Selectors

Hey! This is a good opportunity to show you a handy style rule shortcut. If you ever need to apply the same style property to a number of elements, you can group the selectors into one rule by separating them with commas. This one rule has the same effect as the five rules listed previously. Grouping them makes future edits more efficient and results in a smaller file size:

```
h1, h2, p, em, img { border: 1px solid blue; }
```

Now you have two selector types in your toolbox: a simple element selector and grouped selectors.

CSS UNITS OF MEASUREMENT

This chapter lays the groundwork for upcoming lessons, so it's a good time to get familiar with the units of measurement used in CSS. You'll be using them to set font size, the width and height of elements, margins, indents, and so on. The complete list is provided in the sidebar **"CSS Units."**

Some will look familiar (like inches and millimeters), but there are some units that bear more explanation: absolute units, rem, em, and vw/vh. Knowing how to use CSS units effectively is another one of those core CSS skills.

Pop Quiz

Can you guess why I didn't just add the **border** property to the **body** element and let it inherit to all the elements in the grouped selector?

Answer:

Because **border** is one of the properties that are not inherited.

CSS Units

CSS3 provides a variety of units of measurement. They fall into two broad categories: absolute and relative.

Absolute units

Absolute units have predefined meanings or real-world equivalents. With the exception of pixels, they are not appropriate for web pages that appear on screens.

px	pixel, defined as equal to 1/96 of an inch in CSS3.
in	inches.
mm	millimeters.
cm	centimeters.
q	¼ millimeter.
pt	points (1/72 inch). Points are a unit commonly used in print design.
pc	picas (1 pica = 12 points or 1/6 inch). Points are a unit commonly used in print design.

Relative units

Relative units are based on the size of something else, such as the default text size or the size of the parent element.

em	a unit of measurement equal to the current font size.
ex	x-height, approximately the height of a lowercase "x" in the font.
rem	root em, equal to the em size of the root element (`html`).
ch	zero width, equal to the width of a zero (0) in the current font and size.
vw	viewport width unit, equal to 1/100 of the current viewport (browser window) width.
vh	viewport height unit, equal to 1/100 of the current viewport height.
vmin	viewport minimum unit, equal to the value of **vw** or **vh**, whichever is smaller.
vmax	viewport maximum unit, equal to the value of **vw** or **vh**, whichever is larger.

NOTES

- Although not a "unit," percentages are another common measurement value for web page elements. Percentages are calculated relative to another value, such as the value of a property applied to the current element or its parent or ancestor. The spec always says what a percentage value for a property is calculated on.

  When used for page layouts, percentage values ensure that page elements stay proportional.

- Child elements do not inherit the relative values of their parent, but rather the resulting *calculated* value.

- IE9 supports **vm** instead of **vmin**. IE and Edge (all versions as of 2017) do not support **vmax**.

Absolute Units

Absolute units have predefined meanings or real-world equivalents. They are always the same size, regardless of the context in which they appear.

The most popular absolute unit for web design is the pixel, which CSS3 defines as 1/96 inch. Pixels are right at home on a pixel-based screen and offer precise control over the size of the text and elements on the page. For a while there, pixels were all we used. Then we realized they are too rigid for pages that need to adapt to a wide variety of screen sizes and user preferences. Relative measurements like rem, em, and % are more appropriate to the fluid nature of the medium.

As long as we are kicking **px** to the curb, all of the absolute units—such as **pt**, **pc**, **in**, **mm**, and **cm**—are out because they are irrelevant on screens, although they may be useful for print style sheets. That narrows down your unit choices a bit.

That said, pixels do still have their place in web design for elements that truly should stay the same size regardless of context. Border widths are appropriate in pixels, as are images that have inherent pixel dimensions.

Relative Units

As I just established, relative units are the way to go for most web measurements, and there are a few options: rem, em, and **vw/vh**.

The rem unit

CSS3 introduced a relative measurement called a rem (for root em) that is based on the font size of the root (**html**) element, whatever that happens to be. In modern browsers, the default root font size is 16 pixels; therefore, a rem is equivalent to a 16-pixel unit (unless you set it explicitly to another value). An element sized to 10rem would measure 160 pixels.

For the most part, you can use rem units like an absolute measurement in style rules; however, because it is relative, if the base font size changes, so does the size of a rem. If a user changes the base font size to 24 pixels for easier reading from a distance, or if the page is displayed on a device that has a default font size of 24 pixels, that 10rem element becomes 240 pixels. That seems dodgy, but rest assured that it is a feature, not a bug. There are many instances in which you want a layout element to expand should the text size increase. It keeps the page proportional with the font size, which can help maintain optimum line lengths.

The em unit

An em is a relative unit of measurement that, in traditional typography, is based on the width of the capital letter M (thus the name "em"). In the CSS

Rem Fallbacks for Old IE Browsers

The drawback to rems is that IE8 and earlier do not support them at all, and you need to provide a fallback declaration with the equivalent measurement in pixels. There are production tools that can convert all your rem units to pixels automatically, which are discussed in **Chapter 20, Modern Development Tools**.

specification, an em is calculated as the distance between baselines when the font is set without any extra space between the lines (also known as leading). For text with a font size of 16 pixels, an em measures 16 pixels; for 12-pixel text, an em equals 12 pixels; and so on, as shown in FIGURE 11-10.

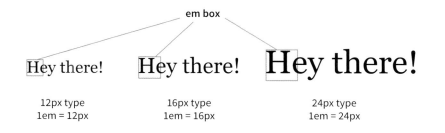

em box

Hey there!

12px type
1em = 12px

Hey there!

16px type
1em = 16px

Hey there!

24px type
1em = 24px

FIGURE 11-10. An em is based on the size of the text.

NOTE

Don't confuse the em unit of measurement with the **em** *HTML element used to indicate emphasized text. They are totally different things.*

Once the dimension of an em for a text element is calculated by the browser, it can be used for all sorts of other measurements, such as indents, margins, the width of the element on the page, and so on. Basing measurements on text size helps keep everything in proportion should the text be resized.

The trick to working with ems is to remember they are always relevant to the current font size of the element. To borrow an example from Eric Meyer and Estelle Weyl's *CSS: The Definitive Guide* (O'Reilly), if you set a 2em left margin on an **h1**, **h2**, and **p**, those elements will not line up nicely because the em units are based on their respective element's sizes (FIGURE 11-11).

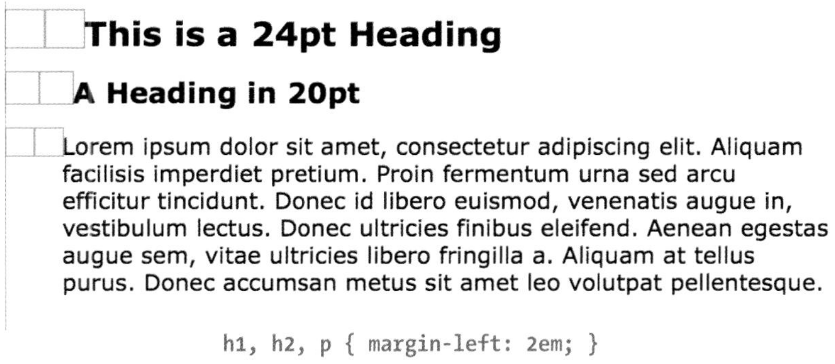

This is a 24pt Heading

A Heading in 20pt

Lorem ipsum dolor sit amet, consectetur adipiscing elit. Aliquam facilisis imperdiet pretium. Proin fermentum urna sed arcu efficitur tincidunt. Donec id libero euismod, venenatis augue in, vestibulum lectus. Donec ultricies finibus eleifend. Aenean egestas augue sem, vitae ultricies libero fringilla a. Aliquam at tellus purus. Donec accumsan metus sit amet leo volutpat pellentesque.

```
h1, h2, p { margin-left: 2em; }
```

FIGURE 11-11. Em measurements are always relevant to the element's font size. An em for one element may not be the same for another.

Viewport percentage lengths (vw/vh)

The viewport width (**vw**) and viewport height (**vh**) units are relative to the size of the viewport (browser window). A **vw** is equal to 1/100 the width of the viewport. Similarly, a **vh** is equal to 1/100 the height of the viewport. Viewport-based units are useful for making images and text elements stay the full width or height of the viewport:

```
header {
   width: 100vw;
   height: 100vh; }
```

It's also easy to specify a unit to be a specific percentage of the window size, such as 50%:

```
img {
   width: 50vw;
   height: 50vh; }
```

BROWSER SUPPORT NOTE

IE9 supports **vm** *instead of* **vmin***. IE and Edge (all versions as of 2017) do not support* **vmax***.*

Related are the **vmin** unit (equal to the value of **vw** or **vh**, whichever is smaller) and **vmax** (equal to the value of **vw** or **vh**, whichever is larger).

That should give you a good introduction to the units you'll be using in your style sheets. I recommend reading the full CSS Values and Units Module (*www.w3.org/TR/css3-values/*) to deepen your knowledge and make the values listed for properties in this book easier to understand. In addition to length units, it includes text-based values (such as keywords, text strings, and URLs), numbers and percentage values, colors, and more.

DEVELOPER TOOLS RIGHT IN YOUR BROWSER

Because of the cascade, a single page element may have styles applied from a number of sources. This can make it tricky to debug a page when styles aren't displaying the way you think they should. Fortunately, every major browser comes with developer tools that can help you sort things out.

I've opened the simple *cooking.html* document that we've been working on in the Chrome browser, then selected View → Developer → Developer Tools from the menu. The Developer Tools panel opens at the bottom of the document, as you can see in FIGURE 11-12. You can also make it its own separate window by clicking the windows icon in the top left.

In the Elements tab on the left, I can see the HTML source for the document. The content is initially hidden so you can see the structure of the document more clearly, but clicking the arrows opens each section. When I click the element in the source (like the second **p** element shown in the figure), that element is also highlighted in the browser window view.

In the Styles tab on the right, I can see all of the styles that are being applied to the selected element. In the example, I see the `font-size`, `font-family`, and `margin-left` properties from the **style** element in the document. If there were external CSS documents, they'd be listed too. I can also see the "User Agent Style Sheet," which is the browser's default styles. In this case, the browser style sheet adds the margin space around the paragraph. Chrome also provides a box model diagram for the selected element that shows the content dimensions, padding, border, and margins that are applied. This is a great tool for troubleshooting unexpected spacing in layouts.

Elements selected in code are highlighted in the browser view.

HTML source for the page.

All styles that are applied to the selected element.

Margins, borders, and paddings applied to the element.

FIGURE 11-12. The Chrome browser with the Developer Tools panel open.

The *cool* thing is that when you edit the style rules in the panel, the changes are reflected in the browser view of the page in real time! If I select the **h1** element and change the color from orange to green, it turns green in the window. It's a great way to experiment with or troubleshoot a design; however, the changes are not being made to the document itself. It's just a preview, so you'll have to duplicate the changes in your source.

You can inspect *any* page on the web in this way, play around with turning styles off and on, and even add some of your own. Nothing you do has any effect on the actual site, so it is just for your education and amusement.

The element and style inspectors are just the tip of the iceberg of what browser developer tools can do. You can also tweak and debug JavaScript, check performance, view the document in various device simulations, and much more. The good news is that all major browsers now have built-in tools with similar features. As a web developer, you'll find they are your best friend.

- Chrome DevTools (View → Developer → Developer Tools)
  developer.chrome.com/devtools

- Firefox (Tools → Web Developer)
  developer.mozilla.org/en-US/docs/Tools

- Microsoft Edge (open with F12 key)
  developer.microsoft.com/en-us/microsoft-edge/platform/documentation/ f12-devtools-guide/

- Safari (Develop → Show Web Inspector)
  developer.apple.com/library/content/documentation/AppleApplications/ Conceptual/Safari_Developer_Guide/Introduction/Introduction.html)

- Opera (View → Developer Tools → Opera Dragonfly)
  www.opera.com/dragonfly/

- Internet Explorer 9+ (open with F12 key)
  msdn.microsoft.com/en-us/library/gg589512(v=vs.85).aspx

MOVING FORWARD WITH CSS

This chapter covered all the fundamentals of Cascading Style Sheets, including rule syntax, ways to apply styles to a document, and the central concepts of inheritance, the cascade (including priority, specificity, and rule order), and the box model. Style sheets should no longer be a mystery, and from this point on, we'll merely be building on this foundation by adding properties and selectors to your arsenal and expanding on the concepts introduced here.

CSS is a vast topic, well beyond the scope of this book. Bookstores and the web are loaded with information about style sheets for all skill levels. I've compiled a list of the resources I've found the most useful during my learning process. I've also provided a list of popular tools that assist in writing style sheets.

Books

There is no shortage of good books on CSS out there, but these are the ones that taught me, and I feel good recommending them.

- *CSS: The Definitive Guide, 4th Edition* by Eric A. Meyer and Estelle Weyl (O'Reilly)

- *CSS Cookbook* by Christopher Schmitt (O'Reilly)

Online Resources

The sites listed here are good starting points for online exploration of style sheets.

CSS-Tricks (*css-tricks.com*)

   The is the blog of CSS guru Chris Coyier. Chris *loves* CSS and enthusiastically shares his research and tinkering on his site.

World Wide Web Consortium (*www.w3.org/TR/CSS/*)

   The World Wide Web Consortium oversees the development of web technologies, including CSS. This page is a "snapshot" of the CSS specifications. See also *www.w3.org/Style/CSS/current-work*.

MDN Web Docs (*developer.mozilla.org*)

The CSS pages at MDN include detailed reference pages, step-by-step tutorials, and demos. It's a great hub for researching any web technology.

A List Apart (*www.alistapart.com/topics/code/css/*)

This online magazine features some of the best thinking and writing on cutting-edge, standards-based web design. It was founded in 1998 by Jeffrey Zeldman and Brian Platz.

TEST YOURSELF

Here are a few questions to test your knowledge of the CSS basics. Answers are provided in **Appendix A**.

1. Identify the various parts of this style rule:

   ```
   blockquote { line-height: 1.5; }
   ```

   selector: _____   value: _____

   property: _____   declaration: _____

2. What color will paragraphs be when this embedded style sheet is applied to a document? Why?

   ```
   <style type="text/css">
       p { color: purple; }
       p { color: green; }
       p { color: gray; }
   </style>
   ```

3. Rewrite each of these CSS examples. Some of them are completely incorrect, and some could just be written more efficiently.

   a.
   ```
   p {font-family: sans-serif;}
   p {font-size: 1em;}
   p {line-height: 1.2em;}
   ```

   b.
   ```
   blockquote {
       font-size: 1em
       line-height: 150%
       color: gray }
   ```

   c.
   ```
   body
   {background-color: black;}
   {color: #666;}
   {margin-left: 12em;}
   {margin-right: 12em;}
   ```

d. `p {color: white;}`
   `blockquote {color: white;}`
   `li {color: white;}`

e. `<strong style="red">Act now!</strong>`

4. Circle all the elements that you would expect to appear in red when the following style rule is applied to a document with the structure diagrammed in FIGURE 11-13.

   `div#intro { color: red;}`

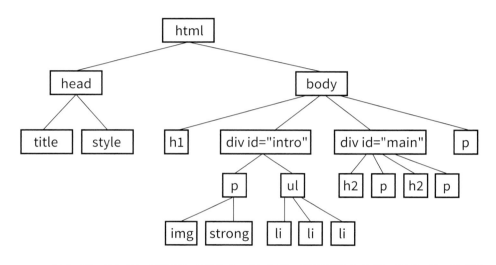

FIGURE 11-13. The document structure of a sample document.

FORMATTING TEXT

Now that you've gotten your feet wet formatting text, are you ready to jump into the deep end? By the end of this chapter, you'll pick up over 40 additional CSS properties used to manipulate the appearance of text. Along the way, you'll also learn how to use more powerful selectors for targeting elements in a particular context and with a specific `id` or `class` name.

The nature of the web makes specifying type tricky, if not downright frustrating, particularly if you have experience designing for print or even formatting text in a word processing program. There is no way to know for sure whether the font you specify will be available or how large or small the type will appear when it hits your users' browsers. We'll address the best practices for dealing with these challenges as we go along.

Throughout this chapter, we'll be sprucing up a Black Goose Bistro online menu similar to the one we marked up back in **Chapter 5, Marking Up Text.** I encourage you to work along with the exercises to get a feel for how the properties work. FIGURE 12-1 shows how the menu looks before and after we're done. It's not a masterpiece, because we're just scratching the surface of CSS here, but at least the text has more personality.

BASIC FONT PROPERTIES

When I design a text document (for print or the web), one of the first things I do is specify a font. In CSS, fonts are specified using a set of font-related properties for typeface, size, weight, font style, and special characters. There are also shortcut properties that let you specify multiple font attributes in a single rule.

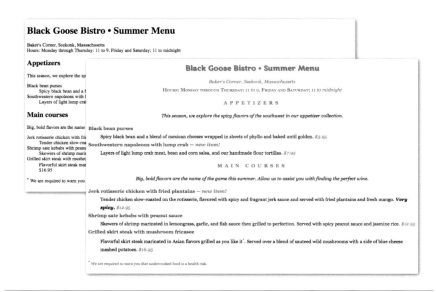

FIGURE 12-1. Before and after views of the Black Goose Bistro menu that we'll be working on in this chapter.

A Word About Property Listings

Each CSS property listing in this book is accompanied by information on how it behaves and how to use it. Property listings include:

Values:

These are the accepted values for the property. Predefined keyword values appear in code font (for example, **small**, **italic**, or **small-caps**) and must be typed in exactly as shown.

Default:

This is the value that will be used for the property by default (its initial value)— that is, if no other value is specified. Note that the default browser style sheet values may vary from the defaults defined in CSS.

Applies to:

Some properties apply only to certain types of elements.

Inherits:

This indicates whether the property is passed down to the element's descendants.

CSS-wide keywords

All CSS properties accept the three CSS-wide keywords: **initial**, **inherit**, and **unset**. Because they are shared by all properties, they are not listed with the values for individual property listings.

- The **initial** keyword explicitly sets the property to its default (initial) value.

- The **inherit** keyword allows you to explicitly force an element to inherit a style property from its parent. This may come in handy to override other styles applied to that element and to guarantee that the element always matches its parent.

- Finally, **unset** erases declared values occurring earlier in the cascade, setting the property to either **inherit** or **initial**, depending on whether it inherits or not.

Specifying the Font Name

Choosing a typeface, or font family as it is called in CSS, for your text is a good place to start. Let's begin with the **font-family** property and its values.

font-family

Values: *one or more font or generic font family names, separated by commas*

Default: depends on the browser

Applies to: all elements

Inherits: yes

Use the **font-family** property to specify a font or list of fonts (known as a font stack) by name, as shown in these examples:

```
body { font-family: Arial; }
var { font-family: Courier, monospace; }
p { font-family: "Duru Sans", Verdana, sans-serif; }
```

Here are some important syntax requirements:

- All font names, with the exception of generic font families, must be capitalized. For example, use **Arial** instead of **arial**.

- Use commas to separate multiple font names, as shown in the second and third examples.

- Notice that font names that contain a character space (such as Duru Sans in the third example) must appear within quotation marks.

You might be asking, "Why specify more than one font?" That's a good question, and it brings us to one of the challenges of specifying fonts for the web.

Font limitations

Browsers are limited to displaying fonts they have access to. Traditionally, that meant the fonts that were already installed on the user's hard drive. In 2010, however, there was a boom in browser support for embedded web fonts using the CSS **@font-face** rule, so it became possible for designers to provide their own fonts. See the sidebar **"Say Hello to Web Fonts"** for more information.

But back to our **font-family** rule. Even when you specify that the font should be Futura in a style rule, if the browser can't find it (for example, if that font is not installed on the user's computer or the provided web font fails to load), the browser uses its default font instead.

Fortunately, CSS allows us to provide a list of back-up fonts (that font stack we saw earlier) should our first choice not be available. If the first specified font is not found, the browser tries the next one, and down through the list until it finds one that works. In the third **font-family** rule shown in the previous code example, if the browser does not find Duru Sans, it will use Verdana, and if Verdana is not available, it will substitute some other sans-serif font.

■ **AT A GLANCE**

Font Properties

The CSS2.1 font-related properties are universally supported:

```
font-family
font-size
font-weight
font-style
font-variant
font
```

The CSS Font Module Level 3 adds these properties for more sophisticated font handling, although browser support is inconsistent as of this writing:

```
font-stretch
font-variant-ligatures
font-variant-position
font-variant-caps
font-variant-numeric
font-variant-alternates
font-variant-east-asian
font-size-adjust
font-kerning
font-feature-settings
font-language-override
```

Say Hello to Web Fonts

The ability to provide your own font for use on a web page has been around since 1998, but it was never feasible because of browser inconsistencies. Fortunately, that story has changed, and now web fonts are a perfectly viable option. The web has never looked better!

There is a lot to say about web fonts, so this sidebar is merely an introduction, starting with the challenges.

Web font formats

There have been two main hurdles to including fonts with web pages. First, there is the problem that different browsers support different font formats. Most fonts come in OpenType (OTF) or TrueType (TTF) format, but older versions of Internet Explorer accept only its proprietary Embedded Open Type (EOT).

The good news is that there is a new standard for packaging fonts for delivery to web pages that all browser vendors, even IE, are implementing. The new format, WOFF/WOFF2 (for Web Open Font Format versions 1 and 2), is a container that packages font files for web delivery. Now that IE9 supports WOFF, one day it may be all we need. As of this writing, however, it is still a best practice to provide the same font in a number of different formats (more on that in just a moment).

The other issue with providing fonts on web pages is that the font companies, or foundries, are concerned (a polite way to say "freaked out") that their fonts will be sitting vulnerably on servers and available for download. Fonts cost a lot to create and are very valuable. Most come with licenses that cover very specific uses by a limited number of machines, and "free to download for whatever" is usually not included.

So, to link to a web font, you need to use the font legally and provide it in a way that all browsers support. There are two general approaches to providing fonts: host them yourself or use a web font service. Let's look at both options.

Host your own

In the "host your own" option, you find the font you want, put it on your server in all the required formats, and link it to your web page by using the CSS3 **@font-face** rule. It is worth noting that each font file corresponds to a single weight or variant of a typeface. So if you want to use regular, bold, and italic versions, you have to host three different font files and reference each in your CSS.

Step 1: Find a font. This can be a bit of a challenge because the End User License Agreement (EULA) for virtually all commercial fonts does not cover web usage. Be sure to purchase the additional web license if it is available. However, thanks to demand, some foundries are opening fonts up for web use, and there are a growing number of open source fonts that you can use for free. The service Fontspring (*fontspring.com*), by Ethan Dunham, is a great place to purchase fonts that have a web license that you can use on your site or your own computer. The site Font Squirrel (*fontsquirrel.com*), also by Ethan Dunham, is a great source for open source fonts that can be used for commercial purposes for free.

Step 2: Save it in multiple formats. As of this writing, providing multiple formats (EOT, WOFF, TTF, SVG) is a reality. The recommended source for the various formats is the font vendor where you purchased the font, as they will be the best quality and approved under the EULA. If you have an open source font (one that is free from licensing restrictions) and you need alternative formats, there is a service that will take your font and make everything you need for you—the "@font-face Generator" from Font Squirrel (*www.fontsquirrel.com/fontface/generator*). Go to that page and upload your font, and it gives back the font in TTF, EOT, WOFF, WOFF2, and SVG, as well as the CSS code you need to make it work.

Step 3: Upload to the server. Developers typically keep their font files in the same directory as the CSS files, but that's just a matter of preference. If you download a package from Font Squirrel, be sure to keep the pieces together as you found them.

Step 4: Write the code. Link the font to your site by using the **@font-face** rule in your *.css* document. The "at-rule" gives the font a **font-family** name that you can then reference later in your style sheet. It also lists the locations of the font files in their various formats. This cross-browser code example was developed by Ethan Dunham (yep, him again!) to address a bug in IE. I recommend reading the full article at *blog.fontspring. com/2011/02/further-hardening-of-the-bulletproof-syntax/*. See also Paul Irish's updated version at *paulirish.com/2009/ bulletproof-font-face-implementation-syntax/*.

```
@font-face {
    font-family: 'MyWebFont';
    src: url('webfont.eot'); /* IE9 Compat Modes */
    src: url('webfont.eot?#iefix') format('embedded-
opentype'), /* IE6-IE8 */
    url('webfont.woff') format('woff'),
        /* Modern Browsers */
    url('webfont.ttf')  format('truetype'),
        /* Safari, Android, iOS */
    url('webfont.svg#svgFontName') format('svg');
        /* Legacy iOS */
}
```

Then you just refer to the established font name in your font rules, like so:

```
p {font-family: MyWebFont; }
```

Use a font embedding service

If that seems like a lot of work, you may want to sign up with one of the font embedding services that do all the heavy lifting for you. For a fee, you get access to high-quality fonts, and the service handles font licensing and font protection for the foundries. They also generally provide an interface and tools that make embedding a font as easy as copy and paste.

The services have a variety of fee structures. Some charge monthly fees; some charge by the font. Some have a surcharge for bandwidth as well. There are generally tiered plans that range from free to hundreds of dollars per month.

Here are some font embedding services that are popular as of this writing, but it's worth doing a web search to see what's currently offered.

Google Web Fonts (www.google.com/webfonts)

Google Web Fonts is a free service that provides access to hundreds of open source fonts that are free for commercial use. All you have to do is choose a font, and then copy and paste the code they generate for you. If you don't have a font budget and you aren't too particular about fonts, this is a wonderful way to go. We'll use it in the first exercise in this chapter.

Typekit, from Adobe (www.typekit.com)

Typekit was the first web font service and is now part of Adobe. Their service uses JavaScript to link the fonts to your site in a way that improves performance and quality in all browsers. I also recommend their blog for excellent articles on how type works (see *blog.typekit.com/ category/type-rendering/*).

Fonts.com (fonts.com)

Fonts.com boasts the largest font collection from the biggest font foundries. If you need a particular font, they are likely to have it.

Other services include Cloud Typography by Hoefler & Co. (*www.typography.com/cloud/welcome/*), Typotheque (*www. typotheque.com/webfonts*), and Fonts Live (*www.fontslive. com*). They differ in the number of fonts they offer and their fee structures, so you may want to shop around. Fontstand (*fontstand.com/*) allows you to rent fonts on a monthly basis, which, depending on your use, could work out to be a fraction of the cost of buying the font outright.

Summing up web fonts

Which method you use to add fonts to your site is up to your discretion. If you like total control, hosting your own font (legally, of course) may be a good way to go. If you need a very particular, well-known font because your client's brand depends on it, you will probably find it on one of the web font services for a price. If you want to experiment with web fonts and are happy to choose from what's freely available, then Google Web Fonts is for you.

You now have a good foundation in including web fonts on your web pages. The landscape is likely to change quickly over the next few years, so be sure to do your own research when you are ready to get started.

Generic font families

That last option, "some other sans-serif font," bears more discussion. "Sans-serif" is just one of five generic font families that you can specify with the `font-family` property. When you specify a generic font family, the browser chooses an available font from that stylistic category. FIGURE 12-2 shows examples from each family.

FIGURE 12-2. Examples of the five generic font families.

`serif`

> *Examples: Times, Times New Roman, Georgia*
>
> Serif typefaces have decorative slab-like appendages (serifs) on the ends of certain letter strokes.

`sans-serif`

> *Examples: Arial, Arial Black, Verdana, Trebuchet MS, Helvetica, Geneva*
>
> Sans-serif typefaces have straight letter strokes that do not end in serifs.

`monospace`

> *Examples: Courier, Courier New, and Andale Mono*
>
> In monospace (also called constant width) typefaces, all characters take up the same amount of space on a line. For example, a capital W will be no wider than a lowercase i. Compare this to proportional typefaces (such as the one you're reading now) that allot different widths to different characters.

`cursive`

> *Examples: Apple Chancery, Zapf-Chancery, and Comic Sans*
>
> Cursive fonts emulate a script or handwritten appearance.

`fantasy`

> *Examples: Impact, Western, or other decorative font*
>
> Fantasy fonts are purely decorative and would be appropriate for headlines and other display type.

Font stack strategies

The best practice for specifying fonts for web pages is to start with your first choice, provide some similar alternatives, and then end with a generic font family that at least gets users in the right stylistic ballpark. For example, if you want an upright, sans-serif font, you might start with a web font if you are providing one (Oswald), list a few that are more common (Univers, Tahoma, Geneva), and finish with the generic sans-serif. There is no limit to the number of fonts you can include, but many designers strive to keep it under 10.

```
font-family: Oswald, Univers, Tahoma, Geneva, sans-serif;
```

A good font stack should include stylistically related fonts that are known to be installed on most computers. Sticking with fonts that come with the Windows, macOS, and Linux operating systems, as well as fonts that get installed with popular software packages such as Microsoft Office and Adobe Creative Suite, gives you a solid list of "web-safe" fonts to choose from. A good place to look for stylistically related web-safe fonts is CSS Font Stack (*www.cssfontstack.com*). There are many articles on font stack strategies that are just a Google search away. I recommend Michael Tuck's "8 Definitive Font Stacks" (*www.sitepoint.com/eight-definitive-font-stacks*), which is an oldie but goodie.

So, as you see, specifying fonts for the web is more like merely suggesting them. You don't have absolute control over which font your users will see. You might get your first choice; you might get the generic fallback. It's one of those web design quirks you learn to live with.

Now seems like a good time to get started formatting the Black Goose Bistro menu. We'll add new style rules one at a time as we learn new properties, staring with EXERCISE 12-1.

EXERCISE 12-1. Formatting a menu

In this exercise, we'll change the fonts for the body and main heading of the Black Goose Bistro menu document, *menu.html*, which is available at *learningwebdesign.com/5e/materials*. Open the document in a text editor. You can also open it in a browser to see its "before" state. It should look something like FIGURE 12-1. Hang on to this document, because this exercise will continue as we pick up additional font properties.

I've included an embedded font in this exercise to show you how easy it is to do with a service like Google Web Fonts.

1. Use an embedded style sheet for this exercise. Start by adding a **style** element in the **head** of the document, like this:

```
<head>
    <title>Black Goose Bistro</title>
    <style>

    </style>
</head>
```

2. I would like the main text to appear in Verdana or some other sans-serif font. Instead of writing a rule for every element in the document, we will write one rule for the **body** element that will be inherited by all the elements it contains. Add this rule to the embedded style sheet:

```
<style>
    body {font-family: Verdana, sans-serif;}
</style>
```

3. I want a fancy font for the "Black Goose Bistro, Summer Menu" headline, so I chose a free display font called Marko One from Google Web Fonts (*www.google.com/webfonts*). Google gave me the code for linking the font file on their server to my HTML file (it's actually a link to an external style sheet). It must be placed in the **head** of the document, so copy it exactly as it appears, but keep it on one line. Put it after the **title** and before the **style** element.

```
<head>
<title>Black Goose Bistro</title>
<link href="http://fonts.googleapis.com/→
css?family=Marko+One" rel="stylesheet">
<style>
…
```

4. Now write a rule that applies it to the **h1** element. Notice I've specified Georgia or another serif font as fallbacks:

```
<style>
    body {font-family: Verdana, sans-serif;}
    h1 {font-family: "Marko One", Georgia, serif;}
</style>
```

5. Save the document and reload the page in the browser. It should look like FIGURE 12-3. Note that you'll need to have an internet connection and a current browser to view the Marko One headline font. We'll work on the text size in the next exercise.

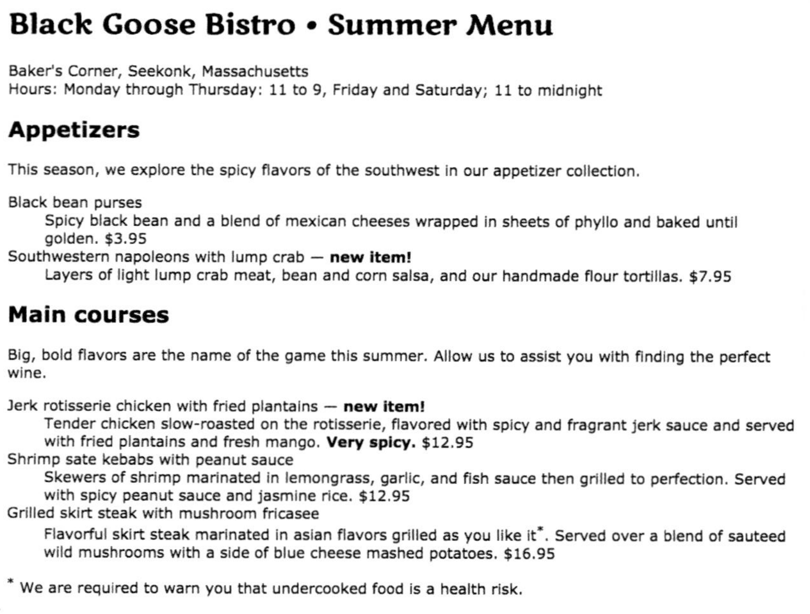

Black Goose Bistro • Summer Menu

Baker's Corner, Seekonk, Massachusetts
Hours: Monday through Thursday: 11 to 9, Friday and Saturday; 11 to midnight

Appetizers

This season, we explore the spicy flavors of the southwest in our appetizer collection.

Black bean purses
    Spicy black bean and a blend of mexican cheeses wrapped in sheets of phyllo and baked until golden. $3.95
Southwestern napoleons with lump crab — **new item!**
    Layers of light lump crab meat, bean and corn salsa, and our handmade flour tortillas. $7.95

Main courses

Big, bold flavors are the name of the game this summer. Allow us to assist you with finding the perfect wine.

Jerk rotisserie chicken with fried plantains — **new item!**
    Tender chicken slow-roasted on the rotisserie, flavored with spicy and fragrant jerk sauce and served with fried plantains and fresh mango. **Very spicy.** $12.95
Shrimp sate kebabs with peanut sauce
    Skewers of shrimp marinated in lemongrass, garlic, and fish sauce then grilled to perfection. Served with spicy peanut sauce and jasmine rice. $12.95
Grilled skirt steak with mushroom fricasee
    Flavorful skirt steak marinated in asian flavors grilled as you like it*. Served over a blend of sauteed wild mushrooms with a side of blue cheese mashed potatoes. $16.95

* We are required to warn you that undercooked food is a health risk.

FIGURE 12-3. The menu after we change only the font family.

Specifying Font Size

Use the aptly named **font-size** property to specify the size of the text.

font-size

Values: *length unit* | *percentage* | xx-small | x-small | small | medium | large | x-large | xx-large | smaller | larger

Default: medium

Applies to: all elements

Inherits: yes

You can specify text size in several ways:

- Using one of the CSS length units, as shown here:

  h1 { font-size: 1.5em; }

  When specifying a number of units, be sure the unit abbreviation immediately follows the number, with no extra character space in between (see the sidebar "**Providing Measurement Values**").

  CSS length units are discussed in **Chapter 11, Introducing Cascading Style Sheets**. See also the "**CSS Units Cheat Sheet**" sidebar.

- As a percentage value, sized up or down from the element's inherited font size:

  h1 { font-size: 150%; }

- Using one of the absolute keywords (**xx-small**, **x-small**, **small**, **medium**, **large**, **x-large**, **xx-large**). On most current browsers, **medium** corresponds to the default font size.

  h1 { font-size: x-large; }

- Using a relative keyword (**larger** or **smaller**) to nudge the text larger or smaller than the surrounding text:

  strong { font-size: larger; }

I'm going to cut to the chase and tell you that, despite all these options, the preferred values for **font-size** in contemporary web design are the relative length units **em** and **rem**, as well as percentage values. You can specify font size in pixels (**px**), but in general, they do not provide the flexibility required in web page design. All of the other absolute units (**pt**, **pc**, **in**, etc.) are out too, unless you are creating a style sheet specifically for print.

I'll explain the keyword-based **font-size** values in a moment, but let's start our discussion with the best practice using relative values.

Providing Measurement Values

When you're providing measurement values, the unit must immediately follow the number, like this:

    margin: 2em;

Adding a space before the unit will cause the property not to work:

    INCORRECT: margin: 2 em;

It is acceptable to omit the unit of measurement for zero values:

    margin: 0;

■ AT A GLANCE

CSS Units Cheat Sheet

As a quick reference, here are the CSS length units again:

Relative units

em	ex	rem	ch
vw	vh	vmin	vmax

Absolute units

px	in	mm	cm
q	pt	pc	

The preferred font-size values are em, rem, and %.

Sizing text with relative values

The best practice for setting the font size of web page elements is to do it in a way that respects the user's preference. Relative sizing values %, rem, and em allow you to use the default font size as the basis for proportional sizing of other text elements. It's usually not important that the headlines are exactly 24 pixels; it is important that they are 1.5 times larger than the main text so they stand out. If the user changes their preferences to make their default font size larger, the headlines appear larger, too.

To maintain the browser's default size, set the **font-size** of the root element to 100% (see **Note**):

```
html {
    font-size: 100%;
}
```

That sets the basis for relative sizing. Because the default font size for all modern browsers is 16 pixels, we'll assume our base size is 16 pixels going forward (we'll also keep in mind that it could be different).

Rem values

The rem unit, which stands for "root em," is always relative to the size of the root (**html**) element. If the root size is 16 pixels, then a rem equals 16 pixels. What's nice about rem units is, because they are always relative to the same element, they are the same size wherever you use them throughout the document. In that way, they work like an absolute unit. However, should the root size be something other than 16 pixels, elements specified in rem values will resize accordingly and proportionally. It's the best of both worlds.

Here is that same heading sized with rem values:

```
h1 { font-size: 1.5rem; }   /* 1.5 x 16 = 24 */
```

Em measurements

Em units are based on the font size of the current element. When you specify **font-size** in ems, it will be relative to the inherited size for that element. Once the em is calculated for an element, it can be used for other measurements as well, such as margins, padding, element widths, and any other setting you want to always be relative to the size of the font.

Here I've used em units to specify the size of an **h1** that has inherited the default 16-pixel font size from the root:

```
h1 { font-size: 1.5em; }   /* 1.5 x 16 = 24 */
```

There are a few snags to working with ems. One is that because of rounding errors, there is some inconsistency in how browsers and platforms render text set in ems.

NOTE

*It is also common practice to set the **body** to 100%, but setting it on the **html** element is a more flexible approach.*

BROWSER SUPPORT NOTE

*Note that rem units are not supported in Internet Explorer 8 and earlier. If for some reason you need to support old browsers, you'll need to provide a fallback declaration set in pixels. There are also tools that change all your rem units to pixels automatically, as discussed in **Chapter 20, Modern Web Development Tools**.*

The other tricky aspect to using ems is that they are based on the *inherited* size of the element, which means that their size is based on the context in which they are applied.

The **h1** in the previous example was based on an inherited size of 16 pixels. But if this **h1** had appeared in an **article** element that had its font size set to 14 pixels, it would inherit the 14-pixel size, and its resulting size would be just 21 pixels (1.5 × 14 = 21). FIGURE 12-4 shows the results.

THE MARKUP

```
<h1>Headline in Body</h1>
<p>Pellentesque ligula leo,…</p>
<article>
  <h1>Headline in Article</h1>
  <p>Vivamus …</p>
</article>
```

THE STYLES

```
h1 {
  font-size: 1.5em;    /* sets all h1s to 1.5em */
}
article {
  font-size: .875em    /* 14 pixels based on 16px default */
}
```

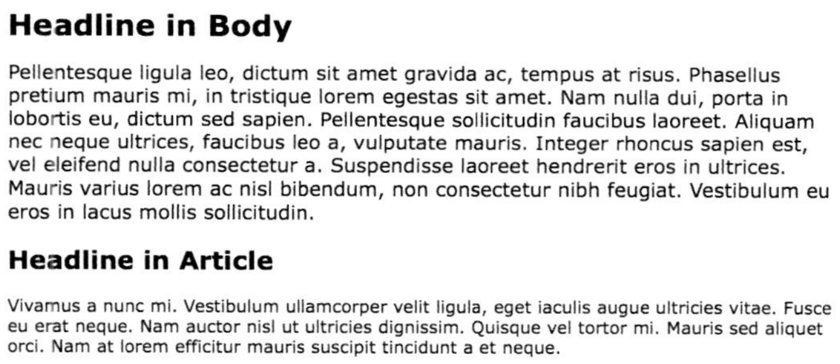

Headline in Body

Pellentesque ligula leo, dictum sit amet gravida ac, tempus at risus. Phasellus pretium mauris mi, in tristique lorem egestas sit amet. Nam nulla dui, porta in lobortis eu, dictum sed sapien. Pellentesque sollicitudin faucibus laoreet. Aliquam nec neque ultrices, faucibus leo a, vulputate mauris. Integer rhoncus sapien est, vel eleifend nulla consectetur a. Suspendisse laoreet hendrerit eros in ultrices. Mauris varius lorem ac nisl bibendum, non consectetur nibh feugiat. Vestibulum eu eros in lacus mollis sollicitudin.

Headline in Article

Vivamus a nunc mi. Vestibulum ullamcorper velit ligula, eget iaculis augue ultricies vitae. Fusce eu erat neque. Nam auctor nisl ut ultricies dignissim. Quisque vel tortor mi. Mauris sed aliquet orci. Nam at lorem efficitur mauris suscipit tincidunt a et neque.

FIGURE 12-4. All **h1** elements are sized at 1.5em, but they are different sizes because of the context in which they appear.

From this example, you can see that an element set in ems might appear at different sizes in different parts of the document. If you wanted the **h1** in the article to be 24 pixels as well, you could calculate the em value by dividing the target size by its context: 24 / 14 = 1.71428571 em. (No need to round that figure down…the browser knows what to do with it.)

If you have elements nested several layers deep, the size increase or decrease compounds, which can create problems. With many layers of nesting, text may end up being way too small. When working with ems, pay close attention and write style rules in a way that takes the context into account.

This compounding nature of the em is what has driven the popularity of the predictable rem unit.

NOTE

Ethan Marcotte introduced the **target ÷ context = result** *formula in his book* **Responsive Web Design** *(A Book Apart). It is useful for converting pixel values into percentages and ems.*

To calculate % and em values, use this formula: target size ÷ size of context = result.

Percentage values

We saw a percentage value (100%) used to preserve the default font size, but you can use percentage values for any element. They are pretty straightforward.

In this example, the **h1** inherits the default 16px size from the **html** element, and applying the 150% value multiplies that *inherited* value, resulting in an **h1** that is 24 pixels:

```
h1 { font-size: 150%; }  /* 150% of 16 = 24 */
```

Working with keywords

An alternative way to specify **font-size** is by using one of the predefined absolute keywords: **xx-small**, **x-small**, **small**, **medium**, **large**, **x-large**, and **xx-large**. The keywords do not correspond to particular measurements, but rather are scaled consistently in relation to one another. The default size is **medium** in current browsers. FIGURE 12-5 shows how each of the absolute keywords renders in a browser when the default text is set at 16 pixels. I've included samples in Verdana and Times to show that, even with the same base size, there is a big difference in legibility at sizes **small** and below. Verdana was designed to be legible on screens at small font sizes; Times was designed for print so is less legible in that context.

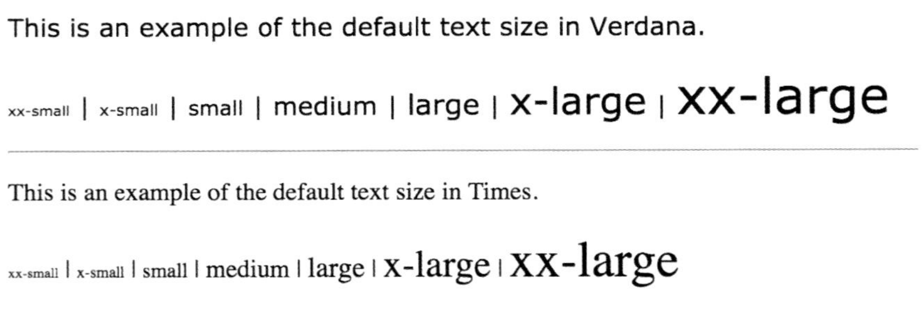

This is an example of the default text size in Verdana.

xx-small | x-small | small | medium | large | x-large | xx-large

This is an example of the default text size in Times.

xx-small | x-small | small | medium | large | x-large | xx-large

FIGURE 12-5. Text sized with absolute keywords.

The relative keywords, **larger** and **smaller**, are used to shift the size of text relative to the size of the parent element text. The exact amount of the size change is determined by each browser and is out of your control. Despite that limitation, it is an easy way to nudge type a bit larger or smaller if the exact proportions are not critical.

You can apply your new CSS font knowledge in EXERCISE 12-2.

EXERCISE 12-2. Setting font size

Let's refine the size of some of the text elements to give the online menu a more sophisticated appearance. Open *menu.html* in a text editor and follow the steps. You can save the document at any point and take a peek in the browser to see the results of your work. You should also feel free to try out other size values along the way.

1. There are many approaches to sizing text on web pages. In this example, start by putting a stake in the ground and setting the **font-size** of the **body** element to 100%, thus clearing the way for em measurements thereafter:

```
body {
    font-family: Verdana, sans-serif;
    font-size: 100%;
}
```

2. The browser default of 16 pixels is a fine size for the main page text, but I would like to improve the appearance of the heading levels. I'd like the main heading to be 24 pixels, or one and a half times larger than the body text [target (24) ÷ context (16) = 1.5]. I'll add a new rule that sets the size of the **h1** to 1.5em. I could have used 150% to achieve the same thing.

```
h1 {
    font-size: 1.5em;
}
```

3. Now make the **h2**s the same size as the body text so they blend in with the page better:

```
h2 {
    font-size: 1em;
}
```

FIGURE 12-6 shows the result of our font-sizing efforts.

Black Goose Bistro • Summer Menu

Baker's Corner, Seekonk, Massachusetts
Hours: Monday through Thursday: 11 to 9, Friday and Saturday; 11 to midnight

Appetizers

This season, we explore the spicy flavors of the southwest in our appetizer collection.

Black bean purses
    Spicy black bean and a blend of mexican cheeses wrapped in sheets of phyllo and baked until golden. $3.95
Southwestern napoleons with lump crab — **new item!**
    Layers of light lump crab meat, bean and corn salsa, and our handmade flour tortillas. $7.95

Main courses

Big, bold flavors are the name of the game this summer. Allow us to assist you with finding the perfect wine.

FIGURE 12-6. The online menu after a few minor font-size changes to the headings.

Font Weight (Boldness)

After font families and size, the remaining font properties are straightforward. For example, if you want a text element to appear in bold, use the **font-weight** property to adjust the boldness of type.

font-weight

Values:	normal | bold | bolder | lighter | 100 | 200 | 300 | 400 | 500 | 600 | 700 | 800 | 900
Default:	normal
Applies to:	all elements
Inherits:	yes

As you can see, the **font-weight** property has many predefined values, including descriptive terms (**normal**, **bold**, **bolder**, and **lighter**) and nine numeric values (**100** to **900**) for targeting various weights of a font if they are available.

Because most fonts commonly used on the web have only two weights, normal (or Roman) and bold, the only font weight value you will use in most cases is **bold**. You may also use **normal** to make text that would otherwise appear in bold (such as strong text or headlines) appear at a normal weight.

The numeric chart may come in handy when using web fonts with a large range of weights (I've seen a few Google web fonts that require numeric size values). If multiple weights are not available, numeric settings of 600 and higher generally result in bold text, as shown in FIGURE 12-7 (although even that can vary by browser).

If a separate bold face is not available, the browser may "synthesize" a bold font by beefing up the available normal face (see **Note**).

NOTE

The CSS Fonts Module Level 3 introduced the **font-synthesis** *property, which allows authors to turn off (with a value of* **none***) or allow synthesized bold fonts (value of* **weight***); however, it is still considered experimental at this time.*

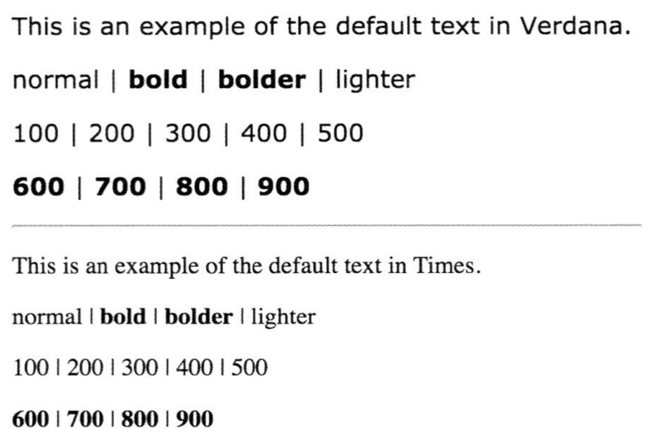

This is an example of the default text in Verdana.

normal | **bold** | **bolder** | lighter

100 | 200 | 300 | 400 | 500

600 | 700 | 800 | 900

This is an example of the default text in Times.

normal | **bold** | **bolder** | lighter

100 | 200 | 300 | 400 | 500

600 | 700 | 800 | 900

FIGURE 12-7. The effect (and lack thereof!) of **font-weight** values.

Font Style (Italics)

The **font-style** property affects the posture of the text—that is, whether the letter shapes are vertical (**normal**) or slanted (**italic** and **oblique**).

font-style

Values: normal | italic | oblique
Default: normal
Applies to: all elements
Inherits: yes

Use the **font-style** property to make text **italic**. Another common use is to make text that is italicized in the browser's default styles (such as emphasized text) display as **normal**. There is an **oblique** value that specifies a slanted version of the font; however, browsers generally display **oblique** exactly the same as **italic**.

Try out weight and style in EXERCISE 12-3.

EXERCISE 12-3. Making text bold and italic

Back to the menu. I've decided that I'd like all of the menu item names to be in bold text. What I'm not going to do is wrap each one in **<b>** tags…that would be so 1996! I'm also not going to mark them up as **strong** elements…that is not semantically accurate. Instead, the right thing to do is simply apply a style to the semantically correct **dt** (definition term) elements to make them all bold at once. Add this rule to the end of the style sheet, save the file, and try it out in the browser:

```
dt { font-weight: bold; }
```

Now that all the menu item names are bold, some of the text I've marked as **strong** isn't standing out very well, so I think I'll make them italic for further emphasis. To do this, simply apply the **font-style** property to the **strong** element:

```
strong { font-style: italic;}
```

Once again, save and reload. It should look like the detail shown in FIGURE 12-8.

Black Goose Bistro • Summer Menu

Baker's Corner, Seekonk, Massachusetts
Hours: Monday through Thursday: 11 to 9, Friday and Saturday; 11 to midnight

Appetizers

This season, we explore the spicy flavors of the southwest in our appetizer collection.

Black bean purses
Spicy black bean and a blend of mexican cheeses wrapped in sheets of phyllo and baked until golden. $3.95
Southwestern napoleons with lump crab — *new item!*
Layers of light lump crab meat, bean and corn salsa, and our handmade flour tortillas. $7.95

Main courses

Big, bold flavors are the name of the game this summer. Allow us to assist you with finding the perfect wine.

Jerk rotisserie chicken with fried plantains — *new item!*
Tender chicken slow-roasted on the rotisserie, flavored with spicy and fragrant jerk sauce and served with fried plantains and fresh mango. ***Very spicy.*** $12.95
Shrimp sate kebabs with peanut sauce
Skewers of shrimp marinated in lemongrass, garlic, and fish sauce then grilled to perfection. Served with spicy peanut sauce and jasmine rice. $12.95

FIGURE 12-8. Applying the **font-weight** and **font-style** properties.

Font Variant in CSS2.1 (Small Caps)

font-variant

Values:	normal | small-caps
Default:	normal
Applies to:	all elements
Inherits:	yes

Some typefaces come in a "small caps" variant. This is a separate font design that uses small uppercase-style letters in place of lowercase letters. Small caps characters are designed to match the size and density of lowercase text so they blend in.

Small caps should be used for strings of three or more capital letters appearing in the flow of text, such as acronyms and abbreviations, that may look jarring as full-sized capitals. Compare NASA and USA in the standard font to NASA and USA in small caps. Small caps are also recommended for times, like 1AM or 2017AD.

When the **font-variant** property was introduced in CSS2.1, it was a one-trick pony that allowed designers to specify a small-caps font for text elements. CSS3 has greatly expanded the role of **font-variant**, as I will cover in the upcoming section **"Advanced Typography with CSS3."** For now, we'll look at only the CSS2.1 version of **font-variant**.

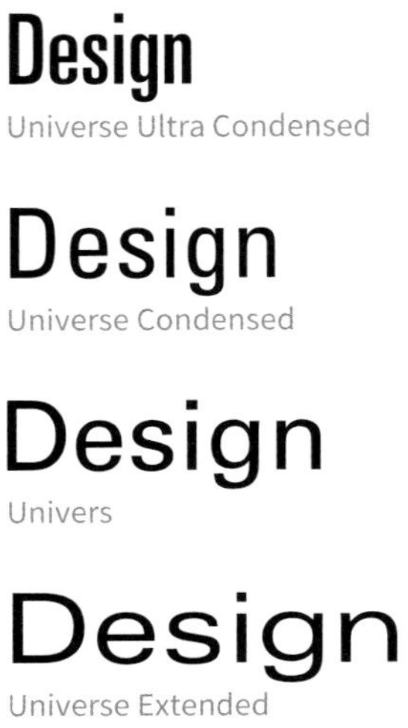

Design

Universe Ultra Condensed

Design

Universe Condensed

Design

Univers

Design

Universe Extended

FIGURE 12-9. Examples of condensed, normal, and extended versions of the Universe typeface.

WARNING

Be careful when using shorthand properties like **font**. **Any omitted property resets to its default value.** *On the flip side, the shorthands are a good way to get a blank slate if you need one.*

■ **CROSS-BROWSER SUPPORT TIP**

If you include values for the newer **font-stretch** property in the **font** shorthand, first list a version that omits stretch for browsers that don't support it. You will end up with two declarations like this:

```
h3 {
   font: bold 1.25em Helvetica;
   font: bold extended 1.25em
Helvetica;
}
```

In most cases, browsers simulate small caps by scaling down uppercase letters in the current font. To typography sticklers, this is less than ideal and results in inconsistent stroke weights, but you may find it an acceptable option for adding variety to small amounts of text. You will see an example of small caps when we use the **font-variant** property in EXERCISE 12-5.

Font Stretch (Condensed and Extended)

font-stretch

Values:	normal | ultra-condensed | extra-condensed | condensed | semi-condensed | semi-expanded | expanded | extra-expanded | ultra-expanded
Default:	normal
Applies to:	all elements
Inherits:	yes

The CSS3 **font-stretch** property tells the browser to select a normal, condensed, or extended font in the font family (FIGURE 12-9). If the browser cannot find a matching font, it will *not* try to synthesize the width by stretching or squeezing text; it may just substitute a font of a different width. Browser support is just beginning to kick in for this property. As of this writing, it works on IE11+, Edge, Firefox, Chrome 48+, Opera, and Android 52+, but it is not yet supported on Safari or iOS Safari; however, that may change.

The Shortcut font Property

Specifying multiple font properties for each text element can get repetitive and lengthy, so the creators of CSS provided the shorthand **font** property, which compiles all the font-related properties into one rule.

font

Values:	*font-style font-weight font-variant font-stretch font-size/line-height font-family* | caption | icon | menu | message-box | small-caption | status-bar
Default:	depends on default value for each property listed
Applies to:	all elements
Inherits:	yes

The value of the **font** property is a list of values for all the font properties we just looked at, separated by character spaces. It is important to note that only the CSS2.1 version of **font-variant** (**small-caps**) can be used in the **font** shortcut (which is one reason I kept it separate). In this property, the order of the values is important:

```
{ font: style weight stretch variant size/line-height font-family; }
```

At minimum, the **font** property *must* include a **font-size** value and a **font-family** value, in that order. Omitting one or putting them in the wrong order causes the entire rule to be invalid. This is an example of a minimal font property value:

```
p { font: 1em sans-serif; }
```

Once you've met the size and family requirements, the other values are optional and may appear in any order *prior* to the **font-size**. When style, weight, stretch, or variant is omitted, its value is set to **normal**. That makes it easy to accidentally override a previous setting with the shorthand property, so be careful when you use it.

There is one value in there, **line-height**, that we have not seen yet. As it sounds, it adjusts the height of the text line and is used to add space between lines of text. It appears just after **font-size**, separated by a slash, as shown in these examples. The **line-height** property is covered in more detail later in this chapter.

```
h3 { font: oblique bold small-caps 1.5em/1.8em Verdana, sans-serif; }
h2 { font: bold 1.75em/2 sans-serif; }
```

In EXERCISE 12-4, we'll use the shorthand **font** property to make some changes to the **h1** headings in the bistro menu.

System font keywords

The **font** property also has a number of keyword values (**caption**, **icon**, **menu**, **message-box**, **small-caption**, and **status-bar**) that represent system fonts, the fonts used by operating systems for things like labels for icons and menu items. These may be useful when you're designing a web application so that it matches the environment the user is working on. These are considered shorthand values because they encapsulate the font, size, style, and weight of the font used for each purpose with only one keyword.

Like the shorthand **font** property, EXERCISE 12-4 is short and sweet.

ADVANCED TYPOGRAPHY WITH CSS3

Now you have a good basic toolkit for formatting fonts with CSS. If you want to get fancy, you should read up on all the properties in the *CSS Fonts Module Level 3*, which give you far more control over character selection and position. I'm going to keep my descriptions brief because of space restraints and the fact that many of these features are still experimental or have very limited browser support. But if nice typography is your thing, I urge you to do more research, starting with the specification at *www.w3.org/TR/css-fonts-3*.

EXERCISE 12-4.
Using the shorthand font property

One last tweak to the menu, and then we'll take a brief break. To save space, we can replace all the font properties we've specified for the **h1** element with one declaration with the shorthand **font** property:

```
h1 {
    font: bold 1.5em "Marko One",
  Georgia, serif;
}
```

You might find it redundant that I included the bold font weight value in this rule. After all, the **h1** element was already bold by default, right? The thing about shorthand properties is that if you omit a value, it is reset to the default value for that *property*, not the browser's default value.

In this case, the default **font-weight** value within a **font** declaration is **normal**. Because our style sheet overrides the browser's default bold heading style, the **h1** would appear in normal-weight text if we don't explicitly make it bold in the **font** property. Shorthand properties can be tricky that way…pay attention so you don't leave something out and override a default or inherited value you were counting on.

You can save this and look at it in the browser. If you've done your job right, it should look exactly the same as in the previous step.

Font Variant in CSS3

The collection of **font-variant-** prefixed properties in CSS3 aims to give designers and developers access to special characters (glyphs) in fonts that can make the typography on a page more sophisticated.

As I mentioned earlier, the CSS3 Font Module greatly expanded the definition of **font-variant**. Now it can serve as a shorthand property for a number of **font-variant-** prefixed properties. These properties are still considered experimental, although browser support is starting to pick up. Still, it's interesting to see how font control in web design is evolving, so let's take a look.

NOTE

With the exception of **font-variant-position***, which has a specific purpose, the other* **font-variant** *properties are great opportunities to practice progressive enhancement. They are nice to have but OK to lose.*

font-variant-ligatures

NOTE

The **font-variant-ligatures** *property has a long list of values, which you can find at www.w3.org/TR/css-fonts-3/#propdef-font-variant-ligatures.*

A ligature is a glyph that combines two or more characters into one symbol. One common example is the combination of a lowercase f and i, where the dot on the i becomes part of the f (fi). Ligatures can smooth out the appearance of known awkward letter pairings, and ligature glyphs are included in many fonts. The **font-variant-ligatures** property provides a way to control the use of ligatures on web pages. This one is better supported than the others, and already works in IE10+, Chrome 34+, as well as Safari and Opera (with the **-webkit-** prefix). I would expect browser support to steadily improve.

font-variant-caps

Allows the selection of small-cap glyphs (**small-caps**) from the font's character set rather than simulating them in the browser. The **all-small-caps** value uses small caps for upper- and lowercase letters. **unicase** uses small caps for uppercase only, and lowercase letters in the word stay the same. **titling-caps** is used for all-caps titles but is designed to be less strong. Other options are **petite-caps** and **all-petite-caps**.

font-variant-position

Selects superscript (**super**) or subscript (**sub**) glyphs from the font's character set when they are available. Otherwise, the browser creates superscript or subscript text for the **sup** and **sub** elements by shrinking the character and moving it above or below the baseline.

font-variant-numeric

Allows the selection of various number character styles if they are available. For example, you can pick numerals that are proportional or line up in columns as for a spreadsheet (**proportional-numbers**/**tabular-numbers**) opt for old-style numerals (**old-style-nums**) where some characters dip below the baseline, and specify whether fractions should be on a diagonal or stacked (**diagonal-fractions**/**stacked-fractions**). It also allows you to make ordinal numbers look like 2nd instead of 2nd (**ordinal**) and gives you a way to use zeros with slashes through them as is preferred in some contexts (**slashed-zero**).

font-variant-alternates

Fonts sometimes offer more than one glyph for a particular character—for example, a few swash designs for the letter S, or an old-fashioned s that looks more like an f. **font-variant-alternates** provides a way to specify swashes and other alternative characters. Many of its values are font-specific and must be defined first with the **@font-features-values** at-rule. I'll leave a deeper explanation to the spec.

font-variant-east-asian

Allows selection of particular Asian glyphs.

Finally, the old **font-variant** property that has been around since the beginning of CSS has been upgraded to be a shorthand property for all of the properties listed here. You can use it today with the original **small-caps** value, and it will be perfectly valid. Once these properties gain traction, it will be able to do a whole lot more.

Other CSS3 Properties

It's time to finish up our review of the font properties in the Fonts Module Level 3. I'll give you a general idea of what is available (or will be, after browser support catches up) and you can dig deeper in the spec on your own:

font-size-adjust

The size text *looks* on the page often has more to do with the height of the lowercase x (its x-height) than the specified size of the text. For example, 10-point type with relatively large x-height is likely easier to read than 10-point type with dainty little lowercase letters. The **font-size-adjust** property allows the browser to adjust the size of a fallback font until its x-height matches the x-height of the first-choice font. This can ensure better legibility even when a fallback font needs to be used.

font-kerning

Kerning is the space between character glyphs. Fonts typically contain metadata about which letter pairs need to be cozied up together to make the spacing in a word look consistent. The **font-kerning** property allows the font's kerning information to be applied (**normal**), turned off (**none**), or left to the browser's discretion (**auto**).

font-feature-settings

This property gives authors the ability to control advanced typographic features in OpenType fonts that are not widely used, such as swashes, small caps, ligatures, automatic fractions, and more. Those features should look familiar, as many of them can be controlled with various **font-variant** properties. In fact, the spec recommends you use **font-variant** whenever possible and reserve **font-feature-settings** for edge cases. As of this writing, however, the **font-feature-settings** property has better browser support, so for the time being it may be a better option. Just be aware that it cascades poorly, meaning it is easy to undo a setting when you use it later to set something else. CSS-Tricks provides a good overview by Robin Rendle (*css-tricks.com/almanac/properties/f/font-feature-settings*).

font-language-override

This experimental property controls the use of language-specific glyphs.

We've finally made our way through the various ways to control fonts in CSS (it took a while!), but that is just one aspect of text presentation. Changing the color of text is another common design choice.

> ■ **FURTHER READING**
>
> For a nice overview of OpenType features and why they are worthwhile, read "Caring about OpenType Features" by Tim Brown at Adobe Typekit (*practice.typekit.com/lesson/caring-about-opentype-features/*).

CHANGING TEXT COLOR

You got a glimpse of how to change text color in **Chapter 11, Introducing Cascading Style Sheets**, and to be honest, there's not a lot more to say about it here. You change the color of text with the **color** property.

color

Values:	*color value (name or numeric)*
Default:	depends on the browser and user's preferences
Applies to:	all elements
Inherits:	yes

Using the **color** property is very straightforward. The value of the **color** property can be a predefined color name (see the "**Color Names**" sidebar) or a numeric value describing a specific RGB color. Here are a few examples, all of which make the **h1** elements in a document gray:

```
h1 { color: gray; }
h1 { color: #666666; }
h1 { color: #666; }
h1 { color: rgb(102,102,102); }
```

Don't worry about the numeric values for now; I just wanted you to see what they look like. RGB color is discussed in detail in **Chapter 13, Colors and Backgrounds,** so in this chapter, we'll just stick with color names for demonstration purposes.

Color is inherited, so you can change the color of all the text in a document by applying the **color** property to the **body** element, as shown here:

```
body { color: fuchsia; }
```

OK, so you probably wouldn't want all your text to be fuchsia, but you get the idea.

For the sake of accuracy, I want to point out that the **color** property is not strictly a text-related property. In fact, according to the CSS specification, it is used to change the foreground (as opposed to the background) color of an element. The foreground of an element consists of both the text it contains as well as its border. So, when you apply a color to an element (including image elements), know that color will be used for the border as well, unless there is a specific **border-color** property that overrides it. We'll talk more about borders and border color in **Chapter 14, Thinking Inside the Box.**

Before we add color to the online menu, I want to take a little side trip and introduce you to a few more types of selectors that will give us more flexibility in targeting elements in the document for styling.

A FEW MORE SELECTOR TYPES

So far, we've been using element names as selectors. In the last chapter, you saw how to group selectors together in a comma-separated list so you can apply properties to several elements at once. Here are examples of the selectors you already know:

Element selector   `p { color: navy; }`

Grouped selectors   `p, ul, td, th { color: navy; }`

The disadvantage of selecting elements this way, of course, is that the property (in this case, navy blue text) is applied to every paragraph and other listed elements in the document. Sometimes you want to apply a rule to a particular paragraph or paragraphs. In this section, we'll look at three selector types that allow us to do just that: descendant selectors, ID selectors, and class selectors.

Descendant Selectors

A descendant selector targets elements that are contained within (and therefore are descendants of) another element. It is an example of a contextual selector because it selects the element based on its context or relation to another element. The sidebar **"Other Contextual Selectors"** lists some more.

AT A GLANCE

Color Names

CSS2.1 defines 17 standard color names:

black	white	purple
lime	navy	aqua
silver	maroon	fuchsia
olive	blue	orange
gray	red	green
yellow	teal	

The updated CSS Color Module Level 3 allows names from a larger set of 140 color names to be specified in style sheets. You can see samples of each in FIGURE 13-2 and at *learningwebdesign.com/colornames.html*.

A character space between element names means that the second element must be contained within the first.

Descendant selectors are indicated in a list separated by a character space. This example targets emphasized text (**em**) elements, but *only* when they appear in list items (**li**). Emphasized text in paragraphs and other elements would be unaffected (FIGURE 12-10).

```
li em { color: olive; }
```

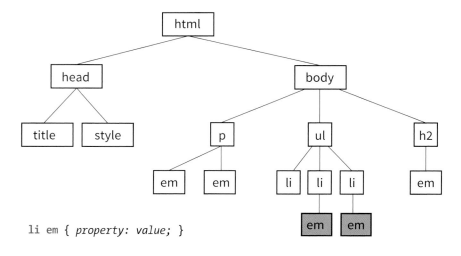

```
li em { property: value; }
```

FIGURE 12-10. Only **em** elements within **li** elements are selected. The other **em** elements are unaffected.

Here's another example that shows how contextual selectors can be grouped in a comma-separated list, just as we saw earlier. This rule targets **em** elements, but only when they appear in **h1**, **h2**, and **h3** headings:

```
h1 em, h2 em, h3 em { color: red; }
```

It is also possible to nest descendant selectors several layers deep. This example targets **em** elements that appear in anchors (**a**) in ordered lists (**ol**):

```
ol a em { font-variant: small-caps; }
```

ID Selectors

The # symbol identifies an ID selector.

Back in **Chapter 5, Marking Up Text**, we learned about the **id** attribute, which gives an element a unique identifying name (its id reference). The **id** attribute can be used with any element, and it is commonly used to give meaning to the generic **div** and **span** elements. ID selectors allow you to target elements by their **id** values. The symbol that identifies ID selectors is the octothorpe (**#**), also known as a hash or pound symbol.

Here is an example of a list item with an **id** reference:

```
<li id="sleestak">Sleestak T-shirt</li>
```

Now you can write a style rule just for that list item using an ID selector, like so (notice the **#** preceding the **id** reference):

```
li#sleestak { color: olive; }
```

Because **id** values must be unique in the document, it is acceptable to omit the element name. The following rule is equivalent to the last one:

```
#sleestak { color: olive; }
```

You can also use an ID selector as part of a contextual selector. In this example, a style is applied only to **a** elements that appear within the element identified as "resources." In this way, you can treat links in the element named "resources" differently than all the other links on the page without any additional markup.

```
#resources a { text-decoration: none; }
```

You should be beginning to see the power of selectors and how they can be used strategically along with well-planned semantic markup.

Other Contextual Selectors

Descendant selectors are one of four types of contextual selectors (called combinators in the Selectors specifications Level 3 and Level 4). The other three are child selectors, next-sibling selectors, and subsequent-sibling selectors.

Child selector

A child selector is similar to a descendant selector, but it targets only the direct children of a given element. There may be no other hierarchical levels in between. They are indicated with the greater-than symbol (**>**). The following rule affects emphasized text, but only when it is directly contained in a **p** element. An **em** element inside a link (**a**) within the paragraph would not be affected.

```
p > em {font-weight: bold;}
```

Next-sibling selector

A next-sibling selector targets an element that comes directly after another element with the same parent. It is indicated with a plus (**+**) sign. This rule gives special treatment to paragraphs that follow an **h1**. Other paragraphs are unaffected.

```
h1 + p {font-style: italic;}
```

Subsequent-sibling selectors

A subsequent-sibling selector selects an element that shares a parent with the specified element and occurs after it in the source order. They do not need to follow one another directly. This type of selector is new in CSS3 and is not supported by Internet Explorer 8 and earlier. The following rule selects any **h2** that both shares a parent element (such as a **section** or **article**) with an **h1** and appears after it in the document.

```
h1 ~ h2 {font-weight: normal;}
```

The period (.) symbol indicates a class selector.

Class Selectors

One last selector type, and then we can get back to text style properties. The other element identifier you learned about in **Chapter 5** is the **class** identifier, used to classify elements into a conceptual group. Unlike the **id** attribute, multiple elements may share a **class** name. Not only that, but an element may belong to more than one class.

You can target elements belonging to the same class with—you guessed it—a class selector. Class names are indicated with a period (**.**) at the beginning of the selector. For example, to select all paragraphs with **class="special"**, use this selector (the period indicates the following word is a class selector):

```
p.special { color: orange; }
```

To apply a property to *all* elements of the same class, omit the element name in the selector (be sure to leave the period; it's the character that indicates a class). This example targets all paragraphs and any other element that has been marked up with **class="special"**:

```
.special { color: orange; }
```

Specificity 101

In **Chapter 11**, I introduced you to the term specificity, which refers to the fact that more specific selectors have more weight when it comes to handling style rule conflicts. Now that you know a few more selectors, it is a good time to revisit this very important concept.

This list of selector types from most to least specific should serve you well in most scenarios:

- **Inline styles** with the **style** attribute are more specific than (and will override…)

- **ID selectors**, which are more specific than (and will override…)

- **Class selectors**, which are more specific than (and will override…)

- **Individual element selectors**

The full story is a little more complicated, but here it is in a nutshell. To calculate specificity, start by drawing three boxes:

Now count up the number of IDs in the selector, and put that number in the first box. Next count up the number of classes and pseudo-classes in the selector, and put that number in the second box. Third, count up the element names, and put that number in the third box.

Specificity is compared box by box. The first box that is not a tie determines which selector wins. Here is a simple example of two conflicting rules for the **h1** element:

```
h1 { color: red;}              [0] [0] [1]
h1.special { color: lime; }    [0] [1] [1]
```

The second one has a class selector and the first one doesn't; therefore, the second one is more specific and has more weight.

How about something more complicated?

```
article#main aside.sidebar:hover > h1:first-of-type  [1] [3] [3]

.x.x.x.x.x.x.x.x  a:link       [0] [8] [1]
```

The second selector targets a link in an element with a string of class names (represented by ".x"). But the first selector has an ID (**#main**) and is therefore more specific.

You may need to do this full specificity calculation, but in most cases you'll have a feel for which selector is more specific by following previously listed general guidelines.

You can use specificity strategically to keep your style sheets simple and your markup minimal. For example, it is possible to set a style for an element (**p**, in this example), and then override when necessary by using more specific selectors.

```
p { line-height: 1.2em; }          [0] [0] [1]
blockquote p { line-height: 1em; } [0] [0] [2]
p.intro { line-height: 2em; }      [0] [1] [1]
```

In these examples, **p** elements that appear within a **blockquote** have a smaller line height than ordinary paragraphs. However, all paragraphs with a **class** of "intro" will have a 2em line height, even if it appears within a **blockquote**, because class selectors are more specific.

Understanding the concepts of inheritance and specificity is critical to mastering CSS, and there is a lot more to be said about specificity. The **"More About Specificity"** sidebar provides useful references.

Now, back to the menu. Fortunately, our Black Goose Bistro page has been marked up thoroughly and semantically, so we have a lot of options for selecting specific elements. Give these new selectors a try in EXERCISE 12-5.

More About Specificity

The specificity overview in this chapter is enough to get you started, but when you get more experienced and your style sheets become more complicated, you may find that you need a more thorough understanding of the inner workings.

For the technical explanation of exactly how specificity is calculated, see the CSS Selectors Module Level 4 specification at *www.w3.org/TR/selectors4/#specificity*.

Eric Meyer provides a thorough, yet more digestible, description of this system in his book *Selectors, Specificity, and the Cascade: Applying CSS to Documents* (O'Reilly). This material is also included in his book co-authored with Estelle Weyl, *CSS: The Definitive Guide, 4e* (O'Reilly).

If you are looking for help online, I recommend the *Smashing Magazine* article "CSS Specificity: Things You Should Know" (*coding.smashingmagazine.com/2007/07/27/css-specificity-things-you-should-know/*) by Vitaly Friedman. It's over a decade old, but the concepts hold true.

As for most web design topics, the MDN Web Docs site provides a comprehensive explanation: *developer.mozilla.org/en-US/docs/Web/CSS/Specificity*.

The Universal Selector

The universal element selector (*****) matches any element , like a wildcard in programming languages. The style rule

```
* { border: 1px solid gray; }
```

puts a 1-pixel gray border around every element in the document. It is also useful as a contextual selector, as shown in this example that selects all elements in an "intro" section:

```
#intro * { color: gray; }
```

Be aware that every element will be selected with the universal selector, including some that you might not be expecting to style. For example, some styles might mess up your form controls, so if your page contains form inputs, the safest bet is to avoid the universal selector.

EXERCISE 12-5. Using selectors

This time, we'll add a few more style rules using descendant, ID, and class selectors combined with the **font** and **color** properties we've learned about so far.

1. I'd like to add some attention-getting color to the "new item!" elements next to certain menu item names. They are marked up as **strong**, so we can apply the **color** property to the **strong** element. Add this rule to the embedded style sheet, save the file, and reload it in the browser:

```
strong {
  font-style: italic;
  color: tomato;
}
```

That worked, but now the **strong** element "Very spicy" in the description is "tomato" red too, and that's not what I want. The solution is to use a contextual selector that targets only the **strong** elements that appear in **dt** elements. Remove the **color** declaration you just wrote from the **strong** rule, and create a new rule that targets only the **strong** elements within definition list terms:

```
dt strong { color: tomato; }
```

2. Look at the document source, and you will see that the content has been divided into three unique **div**s: **info**, **appetizers**, and **entrees**. We can use these to our advantage when it comes to styling. For now, let's do something simple and apply a teal color to the text in the **div** with the ID "info". Because color inherits, we need to apply the property only to the **div** and it will be passed down to the **h1** and **p**:

```
#info { color: teal; }
```

3. Now let's get a little fancier and make the paragraph inside the "info" section italic in a way that doesn't affect the other paragraphs on the page. Again, a contextual selector is the answer. This rule selects only paragraphs contained within the **info** section of the document:

```
#info p { font-style: italic; }
```

4. I want to give special treatment to all of the prices on the menu. Fortunately, they have all been marked up with **span** elements:

```
<span class="price">$3.95</span>
```

So now all we have to do is write a rule using a class selector to change the font to Georgia or some serif font, make the prices italic, and gray them back:

```
.price {
  font-family: Georgia, serif;
  font-style: italic;
  color: gray;
}
```

5. Similarly, in the "info" **div**, I can change the appearance of the spans that have been marked up as belonging to the "label" class to make the labels stand out:

```
.label {
  font-weight: bold;
  font-variant: small-caps;
  font-style: normal;
}
```

6. Finally, there is a warning at the bottom of the page that I want to make small and red. It has been given the class "warning," so I can use that as a selector to target just that paragraph for styling. While I'm at it, I'm going to apply the same style to the **sup** element (the footnote asterisk) earlier on the page so they match. Note that I've used a grouped selector, so I don't need to write a separate rule.

```
p.warning, sup {
  font-size: small;
  color: red;
}
```

FIGURE 12-11 shows the results of all these changes. We now have some touches of color and special typography treatments.

Black Goose Bistro • Summer Menu

Baker's Corner, Seekonk, Massachusetts
Hours: Monday through Thursday: *11 to 9,* **Friday and Saturday:** *11 to midnight*

Appetizers

This season, we explore the spicy flavors of the southwest in our appetizer collection.

Black bean purses
   Spicy black bean and a blend of mexican cheeses wrapped in sheets of phyllo and baked until golden. *$3.95*
Southwestern napoleons with lump crab — *new item!*
   Layers of light lump crab meat, bean and corn salsa, and our handmade flour tortillas. *$7.95*

Main courses

Big, bold flavors are the name of the game this summer. Allow us to assist you with finding the perfect wine.

Jerk rotisserie chicken with fried plantains — *new item!*
   Tender chicken slow-roasted on the rotisserie, flavored with spicy and fragrant jerk sauce and served with fried plantains and fresh mango. ***Very spicy.*** *$12.95*
Shrimp sate kebabs with peanut sauce
   Skewers of shrimp marinated in lemongrass, garlic, and fish sauce then grilled to perfection. Served with spicy peanut sauce and jasmine rice. *$12.95*
Grilled skirt steak with mushroom fricasee
   Flavorful skirt steak marinated in asian flavors grilled as you like it*. Served over a blend of sauteed wild mushrooms with a side of blue cheese mashed potatoes. *$16.95*

* We are required to warn you that undercooked food is a health risk.

FIGURE 12-11. The current state of the bistro menu.

TEXT LINE ADJUSTMENTS

The next batch of text properties has to do with the treatment of whole lines of text rather than the shapes of characters. They allow web authors to format web text with indents, extra space between lines (leading), and different horizontal alignments, similar to print.

Line Height

line-height

Values: *number | length measurement | percentage |* normal

Default: normal

Applies to: all elements

Inherits: yes

The **line-height** property defines the minimum distance from baseline to baseline in text. We saw it earlier as part of the shorthand **font** property. The **line-height** property is said to specify a "minimum" distance because if you put a tall image or large characters on a line, the height of that line expands to accommodate it.

A baseline is the imaginary line upon which the bottoms of characters sit. Setting a line height in CSS is similar to adding leading in traditional typesetting; however, instead of space being added between lines, the extra space is split above and below the text. The result is that **line-height** defines the height of a line-box in which the text line is vertically centered (FIGURE 12-12).

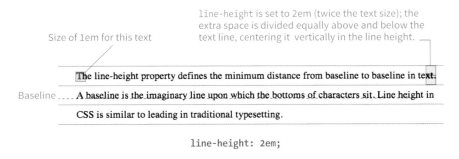

FIGURE 12-12. Text lines are centered vertically in the line height.

These examples show three different ways to make the line height twice the height of the font size:

```
p { line-height: 2; }
p { line-height: 2em; }
p { line-height: 200%; }
```

When a number is specified alone, as shown in the first example, it acts as a scaling factor that is multiplied by the current font size to calculate the **line-height** value.

Line heights can also be specified in one of the CSS length units. Ems and percentage values are based on the current font size of the element. In the three examples, if the font size is 16 pixels, the calculated line height would be 32 pixels (see FIGURE 12-12).

The difference between using a scaling factor (number value) and a relative value (em or %) is how they inherit. If you set the line height with a scaling factor for a whole document on the **body** element, its descendants inherit the multiplier. If the scaling factor is set to 2 for the **body**, a 24-pixel headline will end up with a line height of 48 pixels.

If you set the **line-height** on the **body** element using ems or percentages, its descendants inherit the *calculated* size based on the body's font size. For example, if the line height is set to **1em** for the **body** element (calculated at 16 pixels), a 24-pixel headline inherits the calculated 16-pixel line height, not the 1em value. This is likely not the effect you are after, making number values a more intuitive option.

Indents

The **text-indent** property indents the first line of text by a specified amount.

text-indent

Values:	*length measurement* | *percentage*
Default:	0
Applies to:	block containers
Inherits:	yes

You can specify a length measurement or a percentage value for **text-indent**. The results are shown in FIGURE 12-13. Here are a few examples:

```
p#1 { text-indent: 2em; }
p#2 { text-indent: 25%; }
p#3 { text-indent: -35px; }
```

Percentage values are calculated based on the width of the *parent* element, and they are passed down to their descendant elements as percentage values (not calculated values). So if a **div** has a **text-indent** of 10%, so will all of its descendants.

In the third example, notice that a negative value was specified, and that's just fine. It will cause the first line of text to hang out to the left of the left text edge (also called a hanging indent).

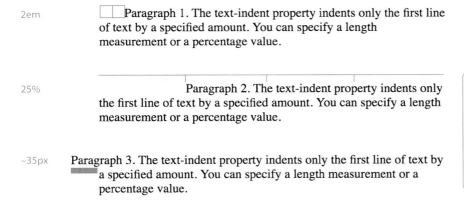

2em

Paragraph 1. The text-indent property indents only the first line of text by a specified amount. You can specify a length measurement or a percentage value.

25%

Paragraph 2. The text-indent property indents only the first line of text by a specified amount. You can specify a length measurement or a percentage value.

−35px

Paragraph 3. The text-indent property indents only the first line of text by a specified amount. You can specify a length measurement or a percentage value.

FIGURE 12-13. Examples of the **text-indent** property.

Horizontal Text Alignment

You can align text for web pages just as you would in a word processing or desktop publishing program with the **text-align** property.

text-align

Values:	left | right | center | justify | start | end
Default:	start
Applies to:	block containers
Inherits:	yes

This is a fairly straightforward property to use. The results of the various CSS2.1 **text-align** values are shown in FIGURE 12-14.

text-align: **left**	Aligns text on the left margin
text-align: **right**	Aligns text on the right margin
text-align: **center**	Centers the text in the text block
text-align: **justify**	Aligns text on both right and left margins

The CSS Text Module Level 3 added the **start** and **end** values, which specify the side of the line box the text should align to (see **Note**). This accommodates languages that are written vertically and right to left. For left-to-right reading languages, **start** corresponds to **left**.

Good news—only five more text properties to go! Then we'll be ready to try a few of them in the Black Goose Bistro menu.

NOTE

*The CSS Text Module Level 3 also defines two new properties related to text alignment—***text-align-last*** (for aligning the last line of text) and ***text-justify*** (for more fine-tuned control over how space is inserted in justified text).*

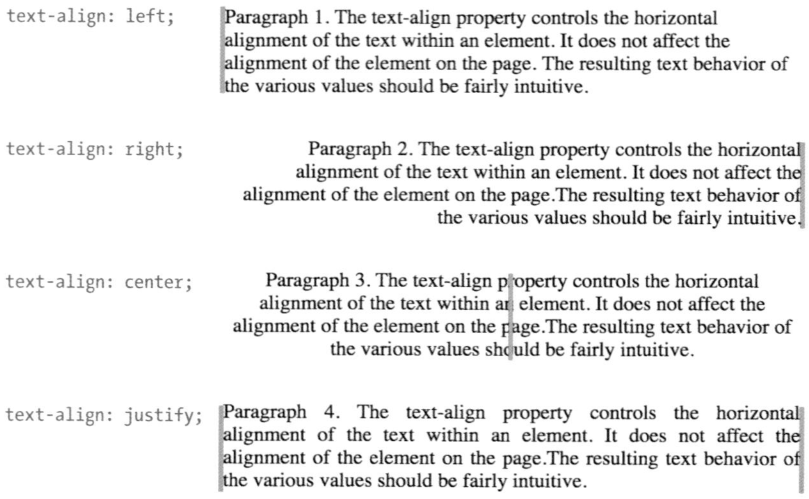

text-align: left;	Paragraph 1. The text-align property controls the horizontal alignment of the text within an element. It does not affect the alignment of the element on the page. The resulting text behavior of the various values should be fairly intuitive.
text-align: right;	Paragraph 2. The text-align property controls the horizontal alignment of the text within an element. It does not affect the alignment of the element on the page. The resulting text behavior of the various values should be fairly intuitive.
text-align: center;	Paragraph 3. The text-align property controls the horizontal alignment of the text within an element. It does not affect the alignment of the element on the page. The resulting text behavior of the various values should be fairly intuitive.
text-align: justify;	Paragraph 4. The text-align property controls the horizontal alignment of the text within an element. It does not affect the alignment of the element on the page. The resulting text behavior of the various values should be fairly intuitive.

FIGURE 12-14. Examples of CSS2.1 **text-align** values.

NOTE

The CSS3 Text Module includes enhancements to **text-decoration***, including* **text-decoration-line***,* **text-decoration-color***,* **text-decoration-style***,* **text-decoration-skip***, and* **text-underline-position***. No version of IE or Edge supports these properties, but with the exception of* **-skip***, they are supported in other modern browsers. See CanIUse.com for specifics.*

UNDERLINES AND OTHER "DECORATIONS"

If you want to put a line under, over, or through text, or if you'd like to turn of the underline under links, then **text-decoration** is the property for you.

text-decoration

Values:	none | underline | overline | line-through | blink
Default:	none
Applies to:	all elements
Inherits:	no, but since lines are drawn across child elements, they may look like they are "decorated" too

The values for **text-decoration** are intuitive and are shown in FIGURE 12-15.

underline	Underlines the element
overline	Draws a line over the text
line-through	Draws a line through the text

The most popular use of the **text-decoration** property is turning off the underlines that appear automatically under linked text, as shown here:

```
a { text-decoration: none; }
```

There are a few cautionary words to be said regarding **text-decoration**:

- First, if you get rid of the underlines under links, be sure there are other cues to compensate, such as color and weight.

I've got laser eyes.

text-decoration: underline;

I've got laser eyes.

text-decoration: overline;

I've got laser eyes.

text-decoration: line-through;

FIGURE 12-15. Examples of **text-decoration** values.

- On the flip side, because underlines are such a strong visual cue to "click here," underlining text that is *not* a link may be misleading and frustrating. Consider whether italics may be an acceptable alternative.

- Finally, there is no reason to make your text blink. Browser makers agree and therefore have dropped support for blinking text. IE never supported it in the first place.

CHANGING CAPITALIZATION

I remember when desktop publishing programs introduced a feature that let me change the capitalization of text on the fly (OK, I'm dating myself here). This made it easy to see how my headlines might look in all capital letters without needing to retype them. CSS includes this feature as well with the **text-transform** property.

text-transform

Values:	none | capitalize | lowercase | uppercase | full-width
Default:	none
Applies to:	all elements
Inherits:	yes

When you apply the **text-transform** property to a text element, it changes its capitalization when it renders without changing the way it is typed in the source. The values are as follows (FIGURE 12-16):

none	As it is typed in the source
capitalize	Capitalizes the first letter of each word
lowercase	Makes all letters lowercase
uppercase	Makes all letters uppercase
full-width	Chooses a "full-width" version of a character if one exists (not well supported)

text-transform: none; *(as it was typed in the source)*	And I know what you're thinking.
text-transform: capitalize;	And I Know What You're Thinking.
text-transform: lowercase;	and i know what you're thinking.
text-transform: uppercase;	AND I KNOW WHAT YOU'RE THINKING.

FIGURE 12-16. The **text-transform** property changes the capitalization of characters when they are displayed, regardless of how they are typed in the source.

SPACED OUT

The next two text properties are used to insert space between letters (**letter-spacing**) or words (**word-spacing**) when the text is displayed.

letter-spacing

Values:	*length measurement* | normal
Default:	normal
Applies to:	all elements
Inherits:	yes

word-spacing

Values:	*length measurement* | normal
Default:	normal
Applies to:	all elements
Inherits:	yes

The **letter-spacing** and **word-spacing** properties do what they say: add space between the letters of the text or words in a line, respectively.

FIGURE 12-17 shows the results of letter spacing and word spacing applied to the simple paragraph shown here:

```
<p>Black Goose Bistro Summer Menu</p>
```

B l a c k   G o o s e   B i s t r o   S u m m e r   M e n u

```
p { letter-spacing: 8px; }
```

Black   Goose   Bistro   Summer   Menu

```
p { word-spacing: 1.5em; }
```

FIGURE 12-17. **letter-spacing** (top) and **word-spacing** (bottom).

It is worth noting that when you specify em measurements, the calculated size is passed down to child elements, even if they have a smaller font size than the parent.

In EXERCISE 12-6 later in this chapter, we'll make one last trip back to the Black Goose Bistro menu and use the **letter-spacing** property on **h2**s.

TEXT SHADOW

The **text-shadow** property adds a "shadow" below your text that makes it seem to hover or pop out above the page. Since flat-color design has become the fashion, drop shadows have gone out of style, but they can still be a useful visual tool, particularly when your text is in front of a patterned or photographic background.

Text shadows are drawn behind the text but in front of the background and border if there is one. Text shadows are supported by all current browsers. Internet Explorer versions 9 and earlier lack support.

text-shadow

Values:	*'horizontal offset' 'vertical offset' 'blur radius' 'color'* | none
Default:	none
Applies to:	all elements
Inherits:	yes

The value for the **text-shadow** property is two or three measurements (a horizontal offset, vertical offset, and an optional blur radius) and a color. FIGURE 12-18 shows an example of a minimal text shadow declaration.

```
h1 {
   color: darkgreen;
   text-shadow: .2em .2em silver;
}
```

```
h1 {
   color: darkgreen;
   text-shadow: -.3em -.3em silver;
}
```

The first value is a horizontal offset that positions the shadow to the right of the text (a negative value pulls the shadow to the *left* of the text). The second measurement is a vertical offset that moves the shadow down by the specified amount (a negative value moves the shadow *up*). The declaration ends with the color specification (silver). If the color is omitted, the text color will be used.

That should give you an idea for how the first two measurements work, but that sharp shadow doesn't look very...well...shadowy. What it needs is a blur radius measurement. Zero (0) is no blur, and the blur gets softer with higher values (FIGURE 12-19). Usually, you just have to fiddle with values until you get the effect you want.

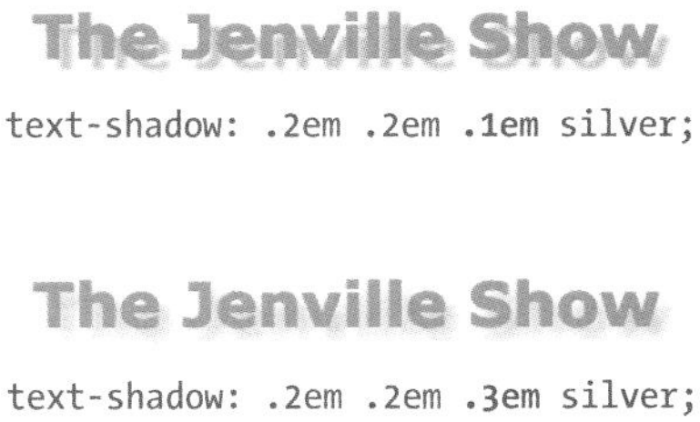

It is possible to apply several text shadows to the same element. If you vary the position and blur amounts, you can give the text the appearance of multiple light sources.

The Jenville Show

text-shadow: .2em .2em silver;

The Jenville Show

text-shadow: -.3em -.3em silver;

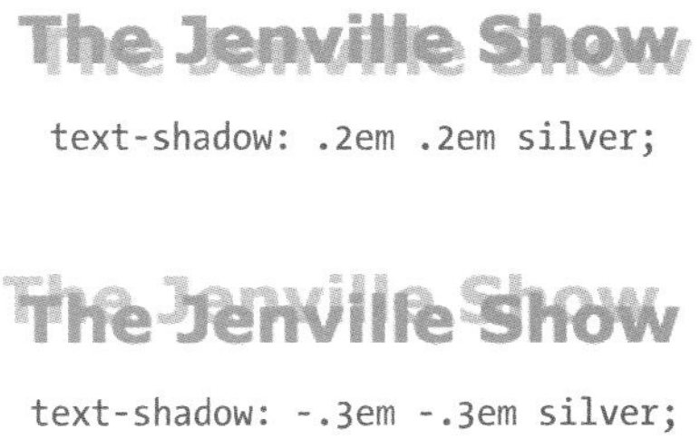

FIGURE 12-18. A minimal text drop shadow.

The Jenville Show

text-shadow: .2em .2em .1em silver;

The Jenville Show

text-shadow: .2em .2em .3em silver;

FIGURE 12-19. Adding a blur radius to a text drop shadow.

So go have some fun with text shadows, but be careful not to overdo it. Not only can drop shadows make text difficult to read, but adding a shadow to everything can slow down page performance (scrolling, mouse interactions, etc.) as well, which is particularly problematic for mobile browsers without much processing power. In addition, be careful that your text doesn't require a shadow in order to be visible. Folks with non-supporting browsers won't see a thing. My advice is to use drop shadows as an enhancement in a way that isn't critical if they don't appear.

EXERCISE 12-6 gives you a chance to try out more text formatting properties to put a little polish on the Black Goose Bistro menu.

The Other Text Properties

In the interest of saving space and keeping this an introductory-level book, I haven't given these properties the full treatment, but they are worth mentioning. Each is labeled with the CSS Level in which it was introduced.

For even more text-related properties in development, see the following CSS Text Modules:

- CSS Text Module Level 3:
  www.w3.org/TR/css-text-3

- CSS Text Decoration Module Level 3:
  www.w3.org/TR/css-text-decor-3

- CSS Text Module Level 4 (still in Working Draft and considered experimental):
  www.w3.org/TR/css-text-4

white-space (*CSS2*) Specifies how whitespace in the element source is handled in layout. For example, the **pre** value preserves the character spaces and returns found in the source, similar to the **pre** HTML element.

vertical-align (*CSS2*) Specifies the vertical alignment of an inline element's baseline relative to the baseline of the surrounding text. It is also used to set the vertical alignment of content in a table cell (**td**).

word-break *and* **line-break** (*CSS3*) Affects how text wrapping is calculated within words and lines, respectively, in various languages, including East Asian (Chinese, Japanese, Korean).

text-justify (*CSS3*) Specifies the manner in which space is to be added within and between words when the **text-align** property on the element is set to **justify**.

text-align-last (*CSS3*) Specifies how the last line of a block of text should be justified when the **text-align** property on the element is set to **justify**. For example, it is often preferable to have the last line left-justified for justified text to avoid awkwardly spaced words.

tab-size (*CSS3*) Specifies the length of the tab character (Unicode point 0009) in number of characters or a length measurement.

hyphens (*CSS3*) Provides control over how text is hyphenated. **manual** means hyphenation happens only when there is a hyphen added in the source. **auto** gives control to the browser, and **none** turns off hyphenation completely.

overflow-wrap (*CSS3*) Specifies whether browsers are allowed to break words to fit text in its bounding box.

hanging-punctuation (*CSS3*) Determines whether the punctuation mark may be outside the element's line box at the start or end of a line. Hanging punctuation can make margins appear more tidy.

The following properties are in the spec, but should not be used. Use the **dir** HTML attribute instead.

direction (*CSS3*) Specifies the direction in which the text reads: left to right (**ltr**) or right to left (**rtl**).

unicode-bidi (*CSS2*) Related to bidirectional features of Unicode. The Recommendation states that it allows the author to generate levels of embedding within the Unicode embedding algorithm. If you have no idea what this means, don't worry. Neither do I.

EXERCISE 12-6. Finishing touches

Let's add a few finishing touches to the online menu, *menu.html*. It might be useful to save the file and look at it in the browser after each step to see the effect of your edits and to make sure you're on track. The finished style sheet is provided in the *materials* folder for this chapter.

1. First, I have a few global changes to the **body** element in mind. I've had a change of heart about the **font-family**. I think that a serif font such as Georgia would be more sophisticated and appropriate for a bistro menu. Let's also use the **line-height** property to open up the text lines and make them easier to read. Make these updates to the **body** style rule, as shown:

```
body {
    font-family: Georgia, serif;
    font-size: small;
    line-height: 1.75em;
}
```

2. I also want to redesign the "info" section of the document. Remove the teal color setting by deleting that whole rule. Once that is done, make the **h1** olive green and the paragraph in the header gray. Add color declarations to the existing rules:

```
#info { color: teal; }  /* delete */
h1 {
    font: bold 1.5em "Marko One", Georgia, serif;
    color: olive;}
#info p {
    font-style: italic;
    color: gray;}
```

3. Next, to imitate a fancy restaurant menu, I'm going to center a few key elements on the page with the **text-align** property. Write a rule with a grouped selector to center the headings and the "info" section:

```
h1, h2, #info {
    text-align: center;}
```

4. I want to make the "Appetizer" and "Main Courses" **h2** headings more eye-catching. Instead of large, bold type, I'm going to use all uppercase letters, extra letter spacing, and color to call attention to the headings. Here's the new rule for **h2** elements that includes all of these changes:

```
h2 {
    font-size: 1em;
    text-transform: uppercase;
    letter-spacing: .5em;
    color: olive;}
```

5. We're really close now; just a few more tweaks to those paragraphs right after the **h2** headings. Let's center those too and make them italic:

```
h2 + p {
    text-align: center;
    font-style: italic;}
```

Note that I've used a next-sibling selector (**h2 + p**) to select any paragraph that follows an **h2**.

6. Next, add a softer color to the menu item names (in **dt** elements). I've chosen "sienna," one of the names from the CSS3 color module. Note that the **strong** elements in those **dt** elements stay "tomato" red because the color applied to the **strong** elements overrides the color inherited by their parents.

```
dt {
    font-weight: bold;
    color: sienna;}
```

7. Finally, for kicks, add a drop shadow under the **h1** heading. You can play around with the values a little to see how it works. I find it to look a little clunky against a white background, but when you have a patterned background image, sometimes a drop shadow provides the little punch you need to make the text stand out. Notice how small the shadow values are—a little goes a long way!

```
h1 {
    font: bold 1.5em "Marko One", Georgia, serif;
    color: olive;
    text-shadow: .05em .05em .1em lightslategray;}
```

And we're done! FIGURE 12-20 shows how the menu looks now—an improvement over the unstyled version, and we used only text and color properties to do it. Notice that we didn't touch a single character of the document markup in the process. That's the beauty of keeping style separate from structure.

FIGURE 12-20. The formatted Black Goose Bistro menu.

CHANGING LIST BULLETS AND NUMBERS

Before we close out this chapter on text properties, I want to show you a few tweaks you can make to bulleted and numbered lists. As you know, browsers automatically insert bullets before unordered list items, and numbers before items in ordered lists (the list markers). For the most part, the rendering of these markers is determined by the browser. However, CSS provides a few properties that allow authors to choose the type and position of the marker, or turn them off entirely.

Choosing a Marker

Apply the **list-style-type** property to the **ul**, **ol**, or **li** element select the type of marker that appears before each list item (see **Note**).

list-style-type

Values:	none | disc | circle | square | decimal | decimal-leading-zero | lower-alpha | upper-alpha | lower-latin | upper-latin | lower-roman | upper-roman | lower-greek
Default:	disc
Applies to:	ul, ol, and li (or elements whose display value is list-item)
Inherits:	yes

More often than not, developers use the **list-style-type** property with its value set to **none** to remove bullets or numbers altogether. This is handy when you're using list markup as the foundation for a horizontal navigation menu or the entries in a web form. You can keep the semantics but get rid of the pesky markers.

The **disc**, **circle**, and **square** values generate bullet shapes just as browsers have been doing since the beginning of the web itself (FIGURE 12-21). Unfortunately, there is no way to change the appearance (size, color, etc.) of generated bullets, so you're stuck with the browser's default rendering.

NOTE

This section documents the CSS2.1 **list-style** *types that are well supported on current browsers. CSS3 extends the marker functionality shown here, including a method for authors to define their own list styles, allowing for numbering in many languages (www.w3.org/TR/css3-lists/).*

NOTE

CSS3 introduces the **@counter-style** *rule, which provides* **box**, **check**, **diamond**, *and* **dash** *marker types as well as the ability to specify your own markers when a predefined one won't do. See the spec for details.*

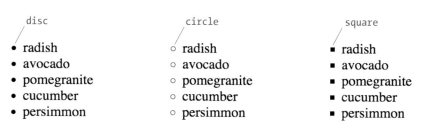

FIGURE 12-21. The **list-style-type** values **disc**, **circle**, and **square**.

The remaining keywords (TABLE 12-1) specify various numbering and lettering styles for use with ordered lists.

TABLE 12-1. Lettering and numbering system (CSS2.1)

Keyword	System
decimal	1, 2, 3, 4, 5...
decimal-leading-zero	01, 02, 03, 04, 05...
lower-alpha	a, b, c, d, e...
upper-alpha	A, B, C, D, E...
lower-latin	a, b, c, d, e... (same as lower-alpha)
upper-latin	A, B, C, D, E... (same as upper-alpha)
lower-roman	i, ii, iii, iv, v...
upper-roman	I, II, III, IV, V...
lower-greek	α, β, γ, δ, ε...

Marker Position

By default, the marker hangs outside the content area for the list item, displaying as a hanging indent. The **list-style-position** property allows you to pull the bullet inside the content area so it runs into the list content.

list-style-position

Values:	inside │ outside │ hanging
Default:	outside
Applies to:	ul, ol, and li (or elements whose display value is list-item)
Inherits:	yes

I've applied a light green background color to the list items in FIGURE 12-22 to reveal the boundaries of their content area boxes.

You can see that when the position is set to **out-side** (top), the markers fall outside the content area. When it is set to **inside** (bottom), the markers are tucked into the content area.

```
li {background-color: #F99;}
ul#outside {list-style-position: outside;}
ul#inside {list-style-position: inside;}
```

CSS3 adds the **hanging** value for **list-style-position**. it is similar to **inside**, but the markers appear outside and abutting the left edge of the shaded area.

List Item Display Role

You may have noticed that the list style properties apply to "elements whose display value is **list-item**." The CSS2.1 specification allows any element to perform like a list item by setting its **display** property to **list-item**. This property can be applied to any HTML element or elements in other XML languages. For example, you could automatically bullet or number a series of paragraphs by setting the **display** property of paragraph (**p**) elements to **list-item**, as shown in this example:

```
p.lettered {
  display: list-item;
  list-style-type: upper-alpha;
}
```

outside

- **Radish.** Praesent in lacinia risus. Morbi urna ipsum, efficitur id erat pellentesque, tincidunt commodo sem. Phasellus est velit, porttitor vel dignissim vitae, commodo ut urna.
- **Avocado.** Class aptent taciti sociosqu ad litora torquent per conubia nostra, per inceptos himenaeos. Curabitur lacinia accumsan est, ut malesuada lorem consectetur eu.
- **Pomegranite.** Nam euismod a ligula ac bibendum. Aenean ac justo eget lorem dapibus aliquet. Vestibulum vitae luctus orci, id tincidunt nunc. In a mauris odio. Duis convallis enim nunc.

inside

- **Radish.** Praesent in lacinia risus. Morbi urna ipsum, efficitur id erat pellentesque, tincidunt commodo sem. Phasellus est velit, porttitor vel dignissim vitae, commodo ut urna.
- **Avocado.** Class aptent taciti sociosqu ad litora torquent per conubia nostra, per inceptos himenaeos. Curabitur lacinia accumsan est, ut malesuada lorem consectetur eu.
- **Pomegranite.** Nam euismod a ligula ac bibendum. Aenean ac justo eget lorem dapibus aliquet. Vestibulum vitae luctus orci, id tincidunt nunc. In a mauris odio. Duis convallis enim nunc.

FIGURE 12-22. The **list-style-position** property.

Make Your Own Bullets

You can also use your own image as a bullet by using the **list-style-image** property.

list-style-image

Values: url(*location*) | none

Default: none

Applies to: **ul**, **ol**, and **li** (or elements whose display value is **list-item**)

Inherits: yes

The value of the **list-style-image** property is the URL of the image you want to use as a marker. The **list-style-type** is set to **disc** as a backup in case the image does not display or the property isn't supported by the browser or other user agent. The result is shown in FIGURE 12-23.

```
ul {
   list-style-type: disc;
   list-style-image: url(/images/rainbow.gif);
   list-style-position: outside;
}
```

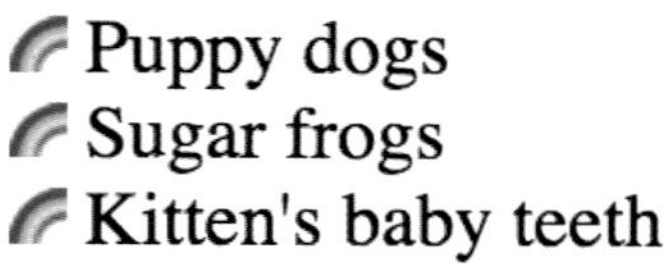

 Puppy dogs
 Sugar frogs
 Kitten's baby teeth

FIGURE 12-23. Using an image as a marker.

> **■ CSS TIP**
>
> There is a **list-style** shorthand property that combines the values for type, position, and image, in any order. For example:
>
> ```
> ul {
>    list-style: url(/images/rainbow.gif) disc outside;
> }
> ```
>
> As for all shorthands, be careful not to override list style properties set earlier in the style sheet.

Wow! Whatta chapter! We started by looking at properties for specifying fonts and character shapes followed by a review of all the text-level settings and effects. You also got to use descendent, ID, and class selectors and looked a little more closely at specificity. We topped it off with the properties available for adding some style to lists. I don't expect you to have all of these properties committed to memory (although many will become second nature the more you practice), but let's see how you do on the following questions.

TEST YOURSELF

It's time to see how well you understand the font properties and selectors introduced in this chapter. Check **Appendix A** for the answers if you get stuck.

1. Match the style property with the text samples in FIGURE 12-24.

    a. _____ {font-size: 1.5em;}

    b. _____ {text-transform: capitalize;}

    c. _____ {text-align: right;}

    d. _____ {font-family: Verdana; font-size: 1.5em;}

    e. _____ {letter-spacing: 3px;}

    f. _____ {font: bold italic 1.2em Verdana;}

    g. _____ {text-transform: uppercase;}

    h. _____ {text-indent: 2em;}

    i. _____ {font-variant: small-caps;}

Look for the good in others and they'll see the good in you.

default font and size

❶ Look For The Good In Others And They'll See The Good In You.

❷ Look for the good in others and they'll see the good in you.

❸ Look for the good in others and they'll see the good in you.

❹ Look for the good in others and they'll see the good in you.

❺ 　　　Look for the good in others and they'll see the good in you.

❻ Look for the good in others and they'll see the good in you.

❼ 　　　　　　　　　　Look for the good in others and they'll see the good in you.

❽ LOOK FOR THE GOOD IN OTHERS AND THEY'LL SEE THE GOOD IN YOU.

❾ *Look for the good in others and they'll see the good in you.*

FIGURE 12-24. Styled text samples.

2. Here is a chance to get a little practice writing selectors. Using the diagram shown in FIGURE 12-25, write style rules that make each of the elements described here red (**color: red;**). Write the selector as efficiently as possible.

   a. All text elements in the document

   b. **h2** elements

   c. **h1** elements and all paragraphs

   d. Elements belonging to the class **special**

   e. All elements in the "intro" section

   f. **strong** elements in the "main" section

   g. Extra credit: just the paragraph that appears after an **h2**

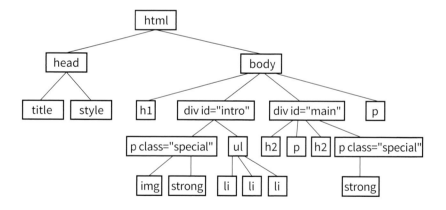

FIGURE 12-25. Sample document structure.

CSS REVIEW: FONT AND TEXT PROPERTIES

In this chapter, we covered the properties used to format text elements. Here is a summary in alphabetical order.

Property	Description
color	Specifies the foreground color (text and borders) for an element
direction	Indicates whether the text reads left-to-right or right-to-left
font	A shorthand property that combines font properties
font-family	Specifies a typeface or generic font family
font-feature-settings	Allows access to lesser-used OpenType features
font-kerning	Controls how browsers implement kerning data (space between characters)
font-language-override	Controls use of language-specific glyphs
font-size	Specifies the size of the font
font-size-adjust	Matches the x-height of a fallback font with the specified font
font-stretch	Selects a condensed, normal, or extended font
font-style	Specifies italic or oblique fonts
font-synthesis	Controls whether a browser may simulate bold or italic fonts
font-variant	Specifies a small-caps font
font-variant-alternates	Selects alternate versions of character glyphs
font-variant-caps	Selects small caps and similar alternates when available
font-variant-east-asian	Selects alternate glyphs in Chinese, Japanese, and Korean
font-variant-ligatures	Selects ligatures for certain letter pairs when available
font-variant-numeric	Selects alternate number glyphs
font-variant-position	Selects subscript or superscript character glyphs
font-weight	Specifies the boldness of the font
hanging-punctuation	Indicates whether the punctuation may hang outside the content box
hyphens	Controls how text is hyphenated
letter-spacing	Inserts space between letters
line-break	Describes rules for breaking lines
line-height	Indicates the distance between baselines of neighboring text lines

Property	Description
list-style-image	Specifies an image to be used as a list marker
list-style-position	Puts a list marker inside or outside the content area
list-style-type	Selects the marker type for list items
overflow-wrap	Specifies whether the browser can break lines within words to prevent overflow
tab-size	Specifies the length of a tab character
text-align	Indicates the horizontal alignment of text
text-align-last	Specifies how the last line in justified text is aligned
text-decoration	Specifies underlines, overlines, and lines through
text-indent	Specifies the amount of indentation of the first line in a block
text-justify	Denotes how space is distributed in justified text
text-shadow	Adds a drop shadow under the text
text-transform	Changes the capitalization of text when it displays
unicode-bidi	Works with Unicode bidirectional algorithms
vertical-align	Adjusts the vertical position of inline elements relative to the baseline
white-space	Specifies how whitespace in the source is displayed
word-break	Specifies whether to break lines within words
word-spacing	Inserts space between words
word-wrap	Indicates whether the browser can break lines within words to prevent overflow (same as **overflow-wrap**)

COLORS AND BACKGROUNDS

PLUS MORE SELECTORS AND EXTERNAL STYLE SHEETS

If you had seen the web back in 1993, you would have found it to be a dreary affair by today's standards—every background was gray, and all the text was black. Then came Netscape Navigator and, with it, a handful of HTML attributes that allowed rudimentary (but welcome) control over font colors and backgrounds. For years, we made do. But thankfully, we now have style sheet properties that have laid those unmentionable presentational attributes to rest.

We're going to cover a *lot* of ground in this chapter. Of course, I'll introduce you to all of the properties for specifying colors and backgrounds. This chapter also rounds out your collection of selector types and shows you how to create an external style sheet. Our first order of business, however, is to explore the options for specifying color in CSS, including a primer on the nature of color on computer monitors.

SPECIFYING COLOR VALUES

There are two main ways to specify colors in style sheets—with a predefined color name, as we have been doing so far:

```
color: red;          color: olive;          color: blue;
```

Or, more commonly, with a numeric value that describes a particular RGB color (the color model on computer monitors). You may have seen color values that look like these:

```
color: #FF0000;     color: #808000;        color: #00F;
```

We'll get to all the ins and outs of RGB color in a moment, but first, a short and sweet section on the standard color names.

Color Names

The most intuitive way to specify a color is to call it by name. Unfortunately, you can't make up just any color name and expect it to work. It has to be one of the color keywords predefined in the CSS Recommendation. CSS1 and CSS2 adopted the 16 standard color names originally introduced in HTML 4.01. CSS2.1 tossed in **orange** for a total of 17 (FIGURE 13-1).

CSS3 adds support for the extended set of 140 (rather fanciful) color names. Now we can specify names like **burlywood**, **peachpuff**, **oldlace**, and my long-time favorite, **papayawhip**! The extended colors are shown in FIGURE 13-2, but if you want a more accurate view, point your browser at *learningwebdesign.com/colornames.html*. CSS3 also added the **transparent** keyword, which can be used with any property that has a color value.

Color names are easy to use—just drop one into place as the value for any color-related property:

```
color: silver;
background-color: gray;
border-bottom-color: teal;
```

■ **FUN FACT**

The extended color names, also known as the X11 color names, were originally provided with the X Window System for Unix.

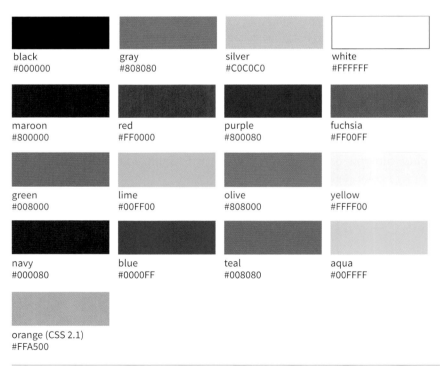

black #000000	gray #808080	silver #C0C0C0	white #FFFFFF
maroon #800000	red #FF0000	purple #800080	fuchsia #FF00FF
green #008000	lime #00FF00	olive #808000	yellow #FFFF00
navy #000080	blue #0000FF	teal #008080	aqua #00FFFF
orange (CSS 2.1) #FFA500			

FIGURE 13-1. The 17 standard color names in CSS2.1. (Note that "gray" must be spelled with an "a.")

aliceblue 240,248,255 F0F8FF	**cornsilk** 255,248,220 FFF8DC	**darkturquoise** 0,206,209 00CED1	**hotpink** 255,105,180 FF69B4	**lightskyblue** 135,206,250 87CEFA	**midnightblue** 25,25,112 191970	**peru** 205,133,63 CD853F	**snow** 255,250,250 FFFAFA
antiquewhite 250,235,215 FAEBD7	**crimson** 220,20,60 DC143C	**darkviolet** 148,0,211 9400D3	**indianred** 205,92,92 CD5C5C	**lightslategray** 119,136,153 778899	**mintcream** 245,255,250 F5FFFA	**pink** 255,192,203 FFC0CB	**springgreen** 0,255,127 00FF7F
aqua 0,255,255 00FFFF	**cyan** 0,255,255 00FFFF	**deeppink** 255,20,147 FF1493	**indigo** 75,0,130 4B0082	**lightsteelblue** 176,196,222 B0C4DE	**mistyrose** 255,228,225 FFE4E1	**plum** 221,160,221 DDA0DD	**steelblue** 70,130,180 46,82,B4
aquamarine 127,255,212 7FFFD4	**darkblue** 0,0,139 00008B	**deepskyblue** 0,191,255 00BFFF	**ivory** 255,240,240 FFFFF0	**lightyellow** 255,255,224 FFFFE0	**moccasin** 255,228,181 FFE4B5	**powderblue** 176,224,230 B0E0E6	**tan** 210,180,140 D2B48C
azure 240,255,255 F0FFFF	**darkcyan** 0,139,139 008B8B	**dimgray** 105,105,105 69,69,69	**khaki** 240,230,140 F0D58C	**lime** 0,255,0 00FF00	**navajowhite** 255,222,173 FFDEAD	**purple** 128,0,128 800080	**teal** 0,128,128 008080
beige 245,245,220 F5F5DC	**darkgoldenrod** 184,134,11 B8860B	**dodgerblue** 30,144,255 1E90FF	**lavender** 230,230,250 E6E6FA	**limegreen** 50,205,50 32CD32	**navy** 0,0,128 000080	**red** 225,0,0 FF0000	**thistle** 216,191,216 D8BFD8
bisque 255,228,196 FFE4C4	**darkgray** 169,169,169 A9A9A9	**firebrick** 178,34,34 B22222	**lavenderblush** 255,240,245 FFF0F5	**linen** 250,240,230 FAF0E6	**oldlace** 253,245,230 FDF5E6	**rosybrown** 188,143,143 BC8F8F	**tomato** 253,99,71 FF6347
black 0,0,0 000000	**darkgreen** 0,100,0 006400	**floralwhite** 255,250,240 FFFAF0	**lawngreen** 124,252,0 7CFC00	**magenta** 255,0,255 FF00FF	**olive** 128,128,0 808000	**royalblue** 65,105,225 4169E1	**turquoise** 64,224,208 40E0D0
blanchedalmond 255,255,205 FFFFCD	**darkkhaki** 189,183,107 BDB76B	**forestgreen** 34,139,34 228B22	**lemonchiffon** 255,250,205 FFFACD		**olivedrab** 107,142,35 6B8E23	**saddlebrown** 139,69,19 8B4513	**violet** 238,130,238 EE82EE
blue 0,0,255 0000FF	**darkmagenta** 139,0,139 8B008B	**fuchsia** 255,0,255 FF00FF	**lightblue** 173,216,230 ADD8E6	**mediumaquamarine** 102,205,170 66CDAA	**orange** 255,165,0 FFA500	**salmon** 250,128,114 FA8072	**white** 255,255,255 FFFFFF
blueviolet 138,43,226 8A2BE2	**darkolivegreen** 85,107,47 556B2F	**gainsboro** 220,220,220 DCDCDC	**lightcoral** 240,128,128 F08080	**mediumblue** 0,0,205 0000CD	**orchid** 218,112,214 DA70D6	**sandybrown** 244,164,96 F4A460	**wheat** 245,222,179 F5DEB3
brown 165,42,42 A52A2A	**darkorange** 255,140,0 FF8C00	**ghostwhite** 248,248,255 F8F8FF	**lightgoldenrodyellow** 250,250,210 FAFAD2	**mediumorchid** 186,85,211 BA55D3	**orangered** 255,69,0 FF4500	**seagreen** 46,139,87 2E8B57	**whitesmoke** 245,245,245 F5F5F5
burlywood 222,184,135 DEB887	**darkred** 139,0,0 8B0000	**gold** 255,215,0 FFD700	**lightcyan** 224,255,255 E0FFFF	**mediumpurple** 147,112,219 9370DB	**palegoldenrod** 238,232,170 EEE8AA	**seashell** 255,245,238 FFF5EE	**yellow** 255,255,0 FFFF00
cadetblue 95,158,160 5F9EA0	**darkorchid** 153,50,204 9932CC	**goldenrod** 218,165,32 DAA520	**lightgreen** 144,238,144 90EE90	**mediumseagreen** 60,179,113 3CB371	**palegreen** 152,251,152 98FB98	**sienna** 160,82,45 A0522D	**yellowgreen** 154,205,50 9ACD32
chartreuse 127,255,0 7FFF00	**darksalmon** 233,150,122 E9967A	**gray** 128,128,128 808080	**lightgrey** 211,211,211 D3D3D3	**mediumslateblue** 123,104,238 7B68EE	**paleturquoise** 175,238,238 AFEEEE	**silver** 192,192,192 C0C0C0	
chocolate 210,105,30 D2691E	**darkseagreen** 143,188,143 8FBC8F	**green** 0,128,0 008000	**lightpink** 255,182,193 FFB6C1	**mediumspringgreen** 0,250,154 00FA9A	**palevioletred** 219,112,147 DB7093	**skyblue** 135,206,235 87CEEB	
coral 255,127,80 FF7F50	**darkslateblue** 72,61,139 483D8B	**greenyellow** 173,255,47 ADFF2F	**lightsalmon** 255,160,122 FFA07A	**mediumturquoise** 72,209,204 48D1CC	**papayawhip** 255,239,213 FFEFD5	**slateblue** 106,90,205 6A5ACD	
cornflowerblue 100,149,237 6495ED	**darkslategray** 47,79,79 2F4F4F	**honeydew** 240,255,240 F0FFF0	**lightseagreen** 32,178,170 20B2AA	**mediumvioletred** 199,21,133 C71585	**peachpuff** 255,239,213 FFEFD5	**slategray** 112,128,144 708090	

FIGURE 13-2. The 140 extended color names in CSS3. Bear in mind that these look quite different on a screen.

RGB Color Values

Names are easy, but as you can see, they are limited. By far, the most common way to specify a color is by its RGB value. It also gives you millions of colors to choose from.

For those who are not familiar with how computers deal with color, I'll start with the basics before jumping into the CSS syntax.

A word about RGB color

Computers create the colors you see on a monitor by combining three colors of light: red, green, and blue. This is known as the RGB color model. You can provide recipes (of sorts) for colors by telling the computer how much of each color to mix in. The amount of light in each color "channel" is typically described on a scale from 0 (none) to 255 (full blast), although it can also be provided as a percent. The closer the three values get to 255 (100%), the closer the resulting color gets to white (FIGURE 13-3). Wondering why the scale is from 0 to 255? See the **"Why 255?"** sidebar.

Any color you see on your monitor can be described by a series of three numbers: a red value, a green value, and a blue value. This is one of the ways that image editors such as Adobe Photoshop keep track of the colors for every pixel in an image. With the RGB color system, a pleasant lavender can be described as R:200, G:178, B:230.

Taken together, 255 colors in each channel can define around 16.7 million color combinations. This color space of millions of colors is known as Truecolor. There are different ways to encode those colors (that is, convert them to bytes for computers), and the web uses an encoding called sRGB. So, if you see an option for saving images as sRGB in a graphics program, click Yes.

> ### Why 255?
>
> In true RGB color, 8 bits of information are devoted to each color channel. Because 8 bits can describe 256 shades ($2^8 = 256$), colors are measured on a scale from 0 to 255.

The RGB Color Model

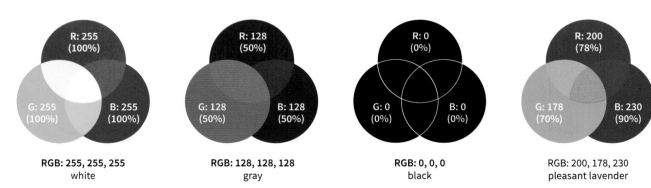

FIGURE 13-3. Computers create colors on a monitor by mixing different amounts of red, green, and blue light (thus, RGB). The color in the middle of each diagram shows what happens when the three color channels are combined. The more light there is in each channel (i.e., the higher the number value), the closer the combination is to white.

Picking a color

There are a number of ways to pick a color and find its RGB color values. One quick and easy option is to go to Google.com and search "color picker," and *voilà*—a full-featured color picker (FIGURE 13-4, left)! If you tend to keep an image-editing program such as Adobe Photoshop open and handy, you can use its built-in color picker (FIGURE 13-4, right).

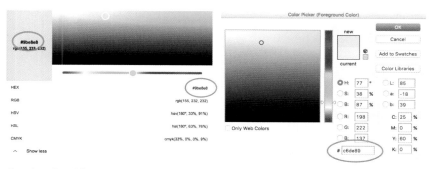

Google color picker   Photoshop color picker

FIGURE 13-4. Color pickers such as the one at Google.com (search "color picker") and in Photoshop.

Both the Google and image editor color pickers show how the selected color would be expressed in a variety of color models (to reveal the values in Google, click "Show color values" below the picker). RGB is the most common for web design, so we're focusing our attention on that one. HSL (Hue Saturation Lightness or Luminosity) is another option for specifying color in style sheets, and we'll take a look at it in a moment (see **Note**). CMYK (Cyan Magenta Yellow blacK) is used primarily for print media, so you won't use it except perhaps to translate print colors to their screen equivalents.

When you select a color from the spectrum in the color picker, the red, green, and blue values are listed, as pointed out in FIGURE 13-4. And look next to the # symbol—those are the same three values, converted to hexadecimal equivalents so they are ready to go in a style sheet. I'll explain the six-digit hex values in a moment.

Writing RGB values in style sheets

CSS allows RGB color values to be specified in a number of formats. Going back to that pleasant lavender, we could add it to a style sheet by listing each value on a scale from 0 to 255:

```
color: rgb(200, 178, 230);
```

You can also list them as percentage values, although that is less common:

```
color: rgb(78%, 70%, 90%);
```

The Web Palette

You may come across the terms web palette or web-safe colors in web production tools like Dreamweaver or Photoshop. The web got its start in the days when computer monitors typically could display only 256 colors at a time. The web palette was a collection of 216 colors that could be displayed on both Windows and Macintosh operating systems without dithering, and thus they were "safe" for the web. That era is long behind us, as is the need to restrict our color choices to the web palette.

NOTE

HSL is not the same as HSB (Hue Saturation Brightness), another color model provided in Photoshop and other image editors.

Specifying RGB Values

There are four formats for providing RGB values in CSS:

    rgb(255, 255, 255)

    rgb(100%, 100%, 100%)

    #FFFFFF

    #FFF

All of these examples specify white.

Or, you can provide the six-digit hexadecimal version that we saw in the color pickers. These six digits represent the same three RGB values, except they have been converted into hexadecimal (or hex for short) equivalents. Note that hex RGB values are preceded by the # symbol and do not require the `rgb()` notation shown in the previous examples. They may be upper- or lowercase, but it is recommended that you be consistent:

    color: #C8B2E6;

There is one last shorthand way to specify hex color values. If your value happens to be made up of three pairs of double digits or letters, such as

    color: #FFCC00; or color: #993366;

you can condense each pair down to one digit or letter. It's easier to type and to read, and it slightly reduces the size of your file. These examples are equivalent to the ones just listed:

    color: #FC0; or color: #936;

About hexadecimal values

It's time to clarify what's going on with that six-digit string of characters. What you're looking at is actually a series of three two-digit numbers, one each for red, green, and blue. But instead of decimal (base-10, the system we're used to), these values are written in hexadecimal, or base-16. FIGURE 13-5 shows the structure of the hex RGB value.

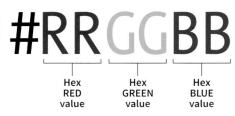

FIGURE 13-5. Hexadecimal RGB values are made up of three two-digit numbers, one for red, one for green, and one for blue.

Handy Hex Values

White = #FFFFFF or #FFF
(the equivalent of 255,255,255)

Black = #000000 or #000
(the equivalent of 0,0,0)

The hexadecimal numbering system uses 16 digits: 0–9 and A–F (for representing the quantities 10–15). FIGURE 13-6 shows how this works. The hex system is used widely in computing because it reduces the space it takes to store certain information. For example, the RGB values are reduced from three to two digits once they're converted to hexadecimal.

Now that most graphics and web development software provides easy access to hexadecimal color values (as we saw in FIGURE 13-4), there isn't much need to translate RGB values to hex yourself, as we needed to do back in the old days. Should you need to, there are plenty of decimal-to-hexadecimal converters online.

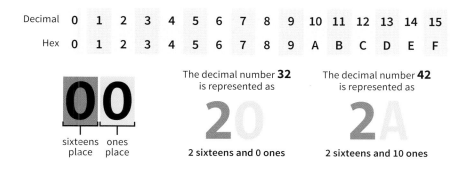

FIGURE 13-6. The hexadecimal numbering system is base-16.

RGBa Color

RGBa color allows you to specify a color and make it as transparent or as opaque as you like. The "a" in "RGBa" stands for alpha, which is an additional channel that controls the level of transparency on a scale from 0 (fully transparent) to 1 (fully opaque). Here's how it looks written in a style rule:

```
color: rgba(0, 0, 0, .5);
```

The first three values in the parentheses are regular old RGB values, in this case creating the color black. The fourth value, .5, is the transparency level. So this color is black with 50% transparency. That allows other colors or background patterns to show through slightly (FIGURE 13-7).

BROWSER SUPPORT NOTE

Internet Explorer versions 8 and earlier do not support RGBa color, so if a significant percentage of your users have those browsers, you may want to provide a fallback. Pick an RGB color that approximates the look you're going for and list it first in the style rule. IE ignores the RGBa value, and supporting browsers will override the opaque color when they get to the second declaration.

```
h1 {
   color: rgb(120, 120, 120);
   color: rgba(0, 0, 0, .5);
}
```

Playing with RGBa — color: rgba(0, 0, 0, .1);

Playing with RGBa — color: rgba(0, 0, 0, .5);

Playing with RGBa — color: rgba(0, 0, 0, 1);

FIGURE 13-7. Headings with various levels of transparency using RGBa values.

HSL Color

CSS3 introduced the ability to specify colors by their HSL values: Hue (color), Saturation, and Lightness (or Luminosity). In this system, the colors are spread out around a circle in the order of the rainbow, with red at the top (12 o'clock) position. Hue values are then measured in degrees around the circle: red at 0°/360°, green at 120°, and blue at 240°, with other colors in between. Saturation is a percentage value from 0% (gray) to 100% (color at full blast). Lightness (or brightness) is also a percentage value from 0% (darkest) to 100% (lightest).

BROWSER SUPPORT NOTE

HSL and HSLa color are not supported in Internet Explorer versions 8 and earlier, so use a fallback if you must support those browsers.

FIGURE 13-8 shows one hue, cyan (located at 180° on the wheel) with its associated saturation and lightness levels. You can see why some people find this system more intuitive to use, because once you lock into a hue, it is easy to make it stronger, darker, or lighter by increasing or decreasing the percentage values. RGB values are not intuitive at all, although some practiced designers develop a feel for them.

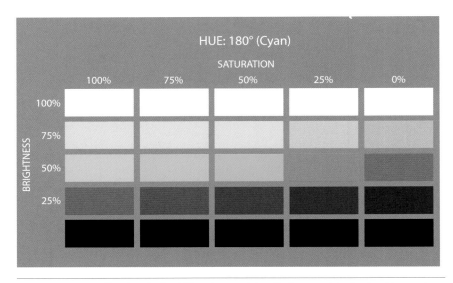

FIGURE 13-8. One hue in the HSL color model, with its associated saturation and lightness values.

In CSS, HSL values are provided as the hue value and two percentages. They are never converted to hexadecimal values, as may be done for RGB. Here is that lavender from FIGURE 13-3 as it would be specified using HSL:

```
color: hsl(265, 51%, 80%);
```

Picking HSL color

There are a number of HSL color pickers online. In the Google color picker, click "Show color values" below the panel to reveal the HSL values for your selected color. Here are some other cool tools worth checking out:

- A Most Excellent HSL Color Picker by Brandon Mathis (*hslpicker.com/*)
- HSL Color Picker (*www.workwithcolor.com/hsl-color-picker-01.htm*)
- HSLa Explorer by Chris Coyier at CSS-Tricks (*css-tricks.com/examples/HSLaExplorer/*)

WARNING

Be aware that the HSB color model listed in Photoshop's color picker is not the same as HSL and cannot be used for CSS.

HSLa color

As with RGB, you can add an alpha channel to set the transparency of HSL colors, resulting in the HSLa color model. As for RGBa, the fourth value is the degree of transparency on a scale from 0 (fully transparent) to 1 (fully opaque). This example specifies a spring green color that is 65% opaque:

```
color: hsla(70, 60%, 58%, .65);
```

Summing Up Color Values

It took us a few pages to get here, but the process for picking and specifying colors in style sheets is actually easy:

- Pick one of the predefined color names,

or

- Use a color picker to select a color and copy down the RGB values (preferably the six-digit hex values). Put those values in the style rule using one of the four RGB value formats, and you're done. Or you could use HSL, if that feels easier to you.

There is one more colorful way to fill an element, and that's gradients (colors that fade from one hue to another), but I'm going to save them for the end of this chapter.

FOREGROUND COLOR

Now that we know how to write color values, let's get to the color-related properties. You can specify the foreground and background colors for any HTML element. There are also **border-color** properties that take color values, but we'll get to those in **Chapter 14, Thinking Inside the Box.**

The foreground of an element consists of its text and border (if one is specified). You specify a foreground color with the **color** property, as we saw in the last chapter when we rolled it out to give text a little pizzazz. Here are the details for the **color** property one more time.

> The foreground of an element consists of its text and border (if one is specified).

color

Values:	*color value (name or numeric)*
Default:	depends on the browser and user's preferences
Applies to:	all elements
Inherits:	yes

In the following example, the foreground of a **blockquote** element is set to green with a color name. You can see that applying the **color** property to the **blockquote** element means the color is inherited by the **p** and **em** elements it contains (FIGURE 13-9). The thick dashed border around the whole block-quote is green as well; however, if we were to apply a **border-color** property to this same element, that color would override the green foreground setting.

THE STYLE RULE

```
blockquote {
   border: 4px dashed;
   color: green;
}
```

THE MARKUP

```
<blockquote>
In the latitude of central New England, cabbages are not secure ...
</blockquote>
```

In the latitude of central New England, cabbages are not secure from injury from frost with less than a foot of earth thrown over the heads. In mild winters a covering of half that depth will be sufficient; but as we have no prophets to foretell our mild winters, a foot of earth is safer than six inches.

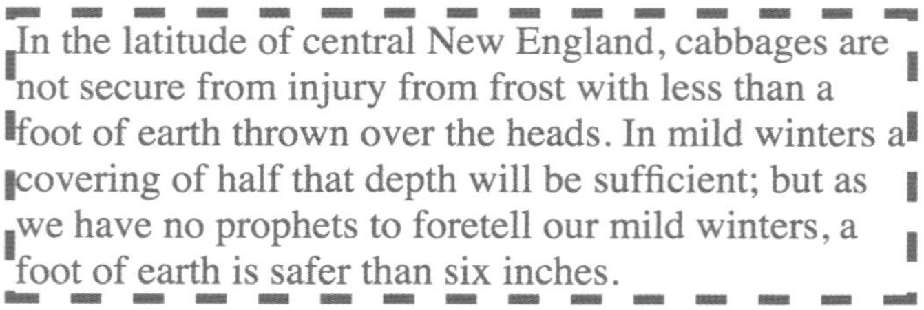

FIGURE 13-9. Applying a color to the foreground of an element.

BACKGROUND COLOR

Use **background-color** to apply a background color to any element.

background-color

Values:	*color value (name or numeric)* | transparent
Default:	transparent
Applies to:	all elements
Inherits:	no

A background color fills the canvas behind the element that includes the content area, and any padding (extra space) added around the content, extending behind the border out to its outer edge. Let's see what happens when we use the **background-color** property to make the background of the same sample **blockquote** light green (FIGURE 13-10):

```
blockquote {
   border: 4px dashed;
   color: green;
   background-color: #c6de89;
}
```

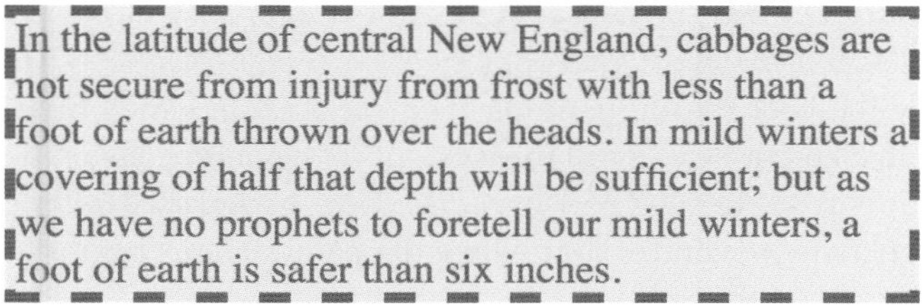

FIGURE 13-10. Adding a light green background color to the sample blockquote.

As expected, the background color fills the area behind the text, all the way to the border. Look closely at the gaps in the border, and you'll see that the background color goes to its outer edge. But that's where the background stops; if we apply a margin around this element, the background will not extend into the margin. We'll revisit all these components of an element when we talk about the CSS box model. For now, just know that, by default, if your border has gaps, the background will show through.

It's worth noting that background colors do not inherit, but because the default background setting for all elements is **transparent**, the parent's background color shows through its descendant elements. For example, you can change the background color of a whole page by applying the **background-color** property to the **body** element and the color will show through all the elements on the page (see **"An Important Exception"**).

In addition to setting the color of the whole page, you can change the background color of any element, both block-level (like the **blockquote** shown in the previous example) as well as inline. In this example, I've used the **color** and **background-color** properties to highlight a word marked up as a "glossary" term. You can see in FIGURE 13-11 that the background color fills the little box created by the inline **dfn** element.

> **AN IMPORTANT EXCEPTION**
>
> When you apply a background to the **body** (or more generically, on the root **html**) element, it is treated specially. It doesn't get clipped to the box, but instead extends to cover the entire viewport.

> To color the background of the whole page, apply the background-color property to the body element.

THE STYLE RULE

```
.glossary {
  color: #0378a9;   /* blue */
  background-color: yellow;
}
```

THE MARKUP

```
<p>Every variety of cabbage had their origin in the wild cabbage of
Europe (<dfn class="glossary"><i>Brassica oleracea</i></dfn>)</p>
```

Every variety of cabbage had their origin in the wild cabbage of Europe (*Brassica oleracea*)

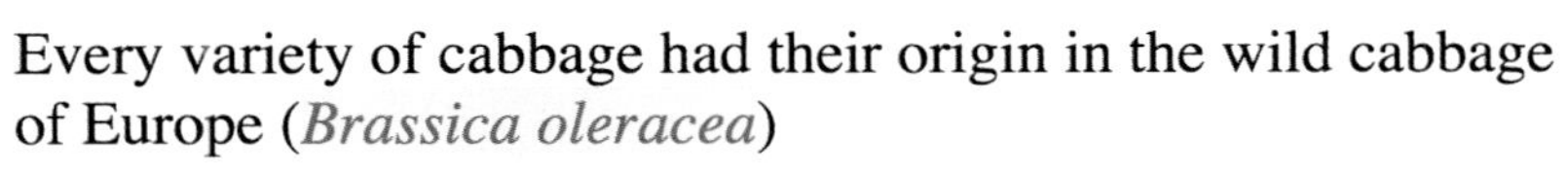

FIGURE 13-11. Applying the background-color property to an inline element.

CLIPPING THE BACKGROUND

Traditionally, the background painting area (the area on which fill colors are applied) of an element extends all the way out to the outer edge of the border, as we saw in FIGURE 13-10. CSS3 introduced the **background-clip** property to give designers more control over where the painting area begins and ends.

background-clip

Values:	border-box | padding-box | content-box
Default:	border-box
Applies to:	all elements
Inherits:	no

The default **border-box** value draws the painting area to the outside edge of the border, as we've seen. FIGURE 13-12 shows that **padding-box** starts the painting area on the outside edge of the padding area for the element (and to the inside edge of the border). Finally, **content-box** allows the background to fill only the content area for the element.

I can't help but feel like I'm spoiling the surprise of the element box model and its properties here a little, since I was saving that for the next chapter. I've added some padding (space between the content and the border) so the effects of the clip settings will be more apparent.

```
blockquote {
    padding: 1em; border: 4px dashed; color: green; background-color: #C6DE89;}
}
```

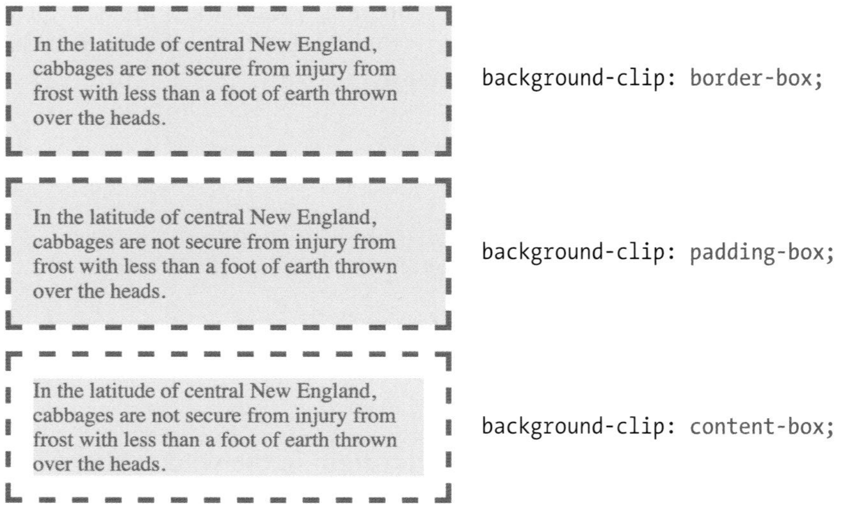

background-clip: border-box;

background-clip: padding-box;

background-clip: content-box;

FIGURE 13-12. The **background-clip** property.

PLAYING WITH OPACITY

Earlier, we talked about the RGBa color format, which adds a level of transparency when it is applied to a color or background. There is another way to make an element slightly see-through, however—the CSS3 **opacity** property.

opacity

Values: *number* (0 to 1)

Default: 1

Applies to: all elements

Inherits: no

The value for **opacity** is a number between 0 (completely transparent) and 1 (completely opaque). A value of .5 gives the element an opacity of 50%. The **opacity** setting applies to the entire element—both the foreground and the background (if one has been set). If you want to affect just one or the other, use an RGBa color value instead.

In the following code example (and FIGURE 13-13), a heading has been given a color of gold and a background color of white. When the **opacity** property is set, it allows the blue background of the page to show through both the text and the element box.

```
h1 {color: gold; background: white; opacity: .25;}
h1 {color: gold; background: white; opacity: .5;}
h1 {color: gold; background: white; opacity: 1;}
```

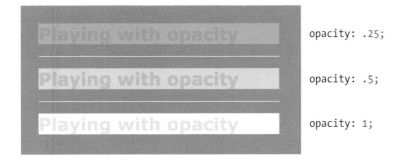

opacity: .25;

opacity: .5;

opacity: 1;

FIGURE 13-13. Setting the opacity on an element affects both the foreground and background colors.

You may be itching to take these color and background properties out for a spin, and we will in a moment, but first, I want to introduce you to some of the fancier CSS selectors and round out your collection. The **"At a Glance"** sidebar lists the selectors you should feel comfortable with so far.

The opacity setting applies to the entire element—both the foreground and the background.

BROWSER SUPPORT NOTE

The **opacity** *property is not supported in Internet Explorer versions 8 and earlier. If you need to support IE8, use a style rule with Microsoft's proprietary* **filter** *property, then override it with the standard opacity style rule.*

```
h1 {
    filter:alpha(opacity=50);
    opacity: .5;
}
```

PSEUDO-CLASS SELECTORS

Have you ever noticed that a link is often one color when you click it and another color when you go back to that page? That's because, behind the scenes, your browser is keeping track of which links have been clicked (or "visited," to use the lingo). The browser keeps track of other states too, such as whether the user's cursor is over an element (hover state), whether an element is the first of its type, whether it's the first or last child of its parent, and whether a form element has been checked or disabled, just to name a few.

In CSS, you can apply styles to elements in these states by using a special kind of selector called a pseudo-class selector. It's an odd name, but you can think of it as though elements in a certain state belong to the same class. However, the class name isn't in the markup—it's something the browser just keeps track of. So it's *kinda* like a class...it's a *pseudo-class*.

Pseudo-class selectors are indicated by the colon (:) character. They typically go immediately after an element name—for example, `li:first-child`.

There are quite a few pseudo-classes in CSS3, and the W3C has been going a little crazy in the CSS Selector Module Level 4 slinging around new pseudo-classes, the majority of which have no browser support as of this writing. In this section, I'll introduce you to the most commonly used and the best supported as a solid starter kit. You can explore the cutting-edge selectors as you gain more experience. The full list of CSS selectors (including Level 4), with descriptions, can be found in **Appendix C**.

Link Pseudo-Classes

The most basic pseudo-class selectors target links (**a** elements) based on whether they have been clicked. Link pseudo-classes are a type of dynamic pseudo-class because they are applied as the result of the user interacting with the page rather than something in the markup.

`:link`	Applies a style to unclicked (unvisited) links
`:visited`	Applies a style to links that have already been clicked

By default, browsers typically display linked text as blue and links that have been clicked as purple, but you can change that with a few style rules. There are limitations on what properties may be applied to `:visited` links, as explained in the **"Visited Links and Security"** sidebar.

In these examples, I've changed the color of unclicked links to maroon and visited links to gray. It is common for visited links to be a more muted color than unclicked links:

```
a:link {
   color: maroon;
}
a:visited {
   color: gray;
}
```

User Action Pseudo-Classes

Another type of dynamic pseudo-class targets states that result from direct user actions.

`:focus`	Applies when the element is selected and ready for input
`:hover`	Applies when the mouse pointer is over the element
`:active`	Applies when the element (such as a link or button) is in the process of being clicked or tapped

Focus state

If you've ever used a web form, then you should be familiar with how a browser visually emphasizes a form element when you select it. When an element is highlighted and ready for input, it is said to have "focus." The `:focus` selector lets you apply custom styles to elements when they are in the focused state.

In this example, when a user selects a text input, it gets a yellow background color to make it stand out from the other form inputs:

```
input:focus { background-color: yellow; }
```

Hover state

The `:hover` selector is an interesting one. It targets elements while the user's mouse pointer is directly over them. You can use the hover state with any element, although it is most commonly used with links to give the user visual feedback that an action is possible. Hover states are also used to trigger pop-up menus for navigation or for revealing more information about an object on the page.

This rule gives links a light pink background color while the mouse hovers over them:

```
a:hover {
  color: maroon;
  background-color: #ffd9d9;
}
```

In the previous chapter, we saw the **text-decoration** property used to turn off underlines under links. You could use the `:hover` selector to make the underlines appear only "on hover":

```
a:hover {
  text-decoration: underline;
}
```

It is important to note that there is no true hover state on touch-screen devices such as smartphones and tablets, so hover effects must be used with care and alternative solutions (see the sidebar **"Hover on Touch Devices"**).

Visited Links and Security

Browsers keep track of what links have been visited, but for some users, a record of their visited links (which could be stolen by a malicious site) may be undesirable. For people in regions with severe restrictions on viewing online content, that record in the wrong hands could even be life threatening. When it was determined that visual styles applied to visited links, as well as the methods browsers use to keep track of them, could be used to track users' viewing histories, some changes were made to how visited links are handled.

The first change was to limit the visual presentation properties that can be applied to visited links. Style rules with `:visited` pseudo-class selectors may use only the following properties: **color**, **background-color**, **border-color** (and individual side border properties), and **outline-color**. Any other property will be ignored. Furthermore, you cannot use any value that makes the link transparent, including the **transparent** keyword and RGBa and HSLa color values.

Under the hood, the DOM mechanism that keeps track of what links have been visited will always return a "not visited" state, even when visited styles are displayed on the screen. This keeps browsing history hidden at the DOM level as well.

The fate of the `:visited` pseudo-class is uncertain, so do not apply styles that are critical to the usability of your site.

Active state

Finally, the `:active` selector applies styles to an element while it is in the process of being activated. In the case of a link, it is the style that is applied while it is being clicked or while a fingertip is in contact with it on a touch screen. This style may be displayed only for an instant, but it can give a subtle indication that something has happened. In this example, I've brightened up the color for the active state (from maroon to red):

```css
a:active {
    color: red;
    background-color: #ffd9d9;
}
```

Putting It All Together

Web designers commonly provide styles for all of these link states because it is an easy way to give a nice bit of feedback at every stage of clicking a link (and it usually improves on the browser defaults). In fact, users have come to expect this feedback: seeing at a glance which links have been followed, having links do something when they point at them, and receiving confirmation when the links are successfully clicked.

When you apply styles to **a** elements with all five pseudo-classes, the order in which they appear is important for them to function properly. For example, if you put `:link` or `:visited` last, they override the other states, preventing them from appearing. The required order for link pseudo-classes is `:link`, `:visited`, `:focus`, `:hover`, `:active` (LVFHA, which you can remember with LoVe For Hairy Animals, or the mnemonic device of your choice).

The required order for pseudo-classes is:

:link

:visited

:focus

:hover

:active

Hover on Touch Devices

On the desktop, the mouse pointer can hover over elements on the screen, but touch devices respond only when the screen is actually touched. This can make hover effects problematic on smartphones and tablets.

When hover effects are applied to a link (an **a** element), mobile operating systems may display the hover state styles after a single tap. To follow the link, the user must tap again. Other hover-triggered elements, such as pop-up menus, may get stuck open, requiring the user to tap elsewhere or reload the page to clear it (not a good user experience, and a deal-breaker for some designs).

There is no single CSS-based solution to this issue. Always including `:focus` and `:active` state styles along with the `:hover` styles may help in some situations. Otherwise, your options are to use JavaScript to program the desired effect

for mobile devices or to avoid the `:hover` state and stick with outright clicks. It is possible to serve the hover-free styles in a style sheet targeted specifically to touch devices.

JavaScript solutions are beyond the scope of this chapter, so I recommend these resources to get started. Some knowledge of JavaScript is required.

- "4 novel ways to deal with sticky `:hover` effects on mobile devices" (*www.javascriptkit.com/dhtmltutors/sticky-hover-issue-solutions.shtml*).

- Search for "hover states on touch devices" on StackOverflow.com and see questions and answers related to this issue. Stack Overflow is a forum where programmers can ask questions and get help from fellow programmers. You'll find a lot of solutions, but also some dead ends.

It is recommended that you provide a `:focus` style for users who use the keyboard to tab through links on a page rather than clicking with a mouse. Applying the same style used for `:hover` is common, although not required.

To sum things up, the link styles I've shown should look like this in the style sheet. FIGURE 13-14 shows the results.

```
a { text-decoration: none; }  /* turns underlines off for all links */
a:link { color: maroon; }
a:visited { color: gray; }
a:focus { color: maroon; background-color: #ffd9d9; }
a:hover { color: maroon; background-color: #ffd9d9; }
a:active { color: red; background-color: #ffd9d9; }
```

Samples of my work:

- Pen and Ink Illustrations
- Paintings
- Collage

`a:link`

Links are maroon and not underlined.

Samples of my work:

- Pen and Ink Illustrations
- Paintings
- Collage

`a:focus`
`a:hover`

While the mouse is over the link or when the link has focus, the pink background color appears.

Samples of my work:

- Pen and Ink Illustrations
- Paintings
- Collage

`a:active`

As the mouse button is being pressed, the link turns bright red.

Samples of my work:

- Pen and Ink Illustrations
- Paintings
- Collage

`a:visited`

After that link has been visited, the link is gray.

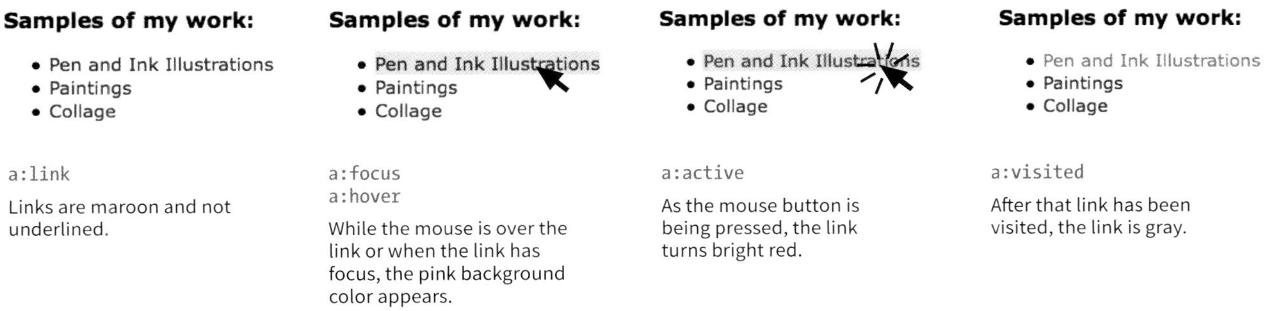

FIGURE 13-14. Changing the colors and backgrounds of links with pseudo-class selectors.

Other Pseudo-Class Selectors

OK…five CSS3 pseudo-classes down, only 40 more to go! Well, I don't know about you, but that sounds like it would take a while, and we have other selector types to explore. However, I do want you to know what is possible today and what is in the works, so I've tucked the CSS3 pseudo-class selectors into the **"More CSS Pseudo-Classes"** sidebar. In addition, you can find the complete list of Level 3 and 4 selectors in **Appendix C, CSS Selectors, Level 3 and 4** with brief descriptions.

I also highly recommend reading "An Ultimate Guide to CSS Pseudo-Classes and Pseudo-Elements" by Ricardo Zea of *Smashing Magazine* (*www.smashingmagazine.com/2016/05/an-ultimate-guide-to-css-pseudo-classes-and-pseudo-elements/*). He's done the hard work of providing explanations and examples of all of the CSS3 pseudo-class selectors in one big roundup.

More CSS3 Pseudo-Classes

The W3C has been creating all sorts of interesting ways to select content for styling based on states the browser keeps track of on the fly.

CSS3 introduced a whole slew of pseudo-classes, most of which are supported by browsers today. Of course, Internet Explorer 8 and earlier lack support, but you could use the Selectivizr polyfill (*selectivizr.com*) to emulate support in the rare event you need to support IE 6–8.

An excellent resource for learning more about these CSS Level 3 and 4 selectors, including browser support information, is *CSS4-selectors.com* by Nelly Brekardin.

Structural pseudo-classes

These allow selection based on where the element is in the structure of the document (the document tree):

    :root
    :empty
    :first-child
    :last-child
    :only-child
    :first-of-type
    :last-of-type
    :only-of-type
    :nth-child()
    :nth-last-child()
    :nth-of-type()
    :nth-last-of-type()

Input pseudo-classes

These selectors apply to states that are typical for form inputs:

    :enabled
    :disabled
    :checked

Location pseudo-classes (in addition to :link and :visited)

    :target (fragment identifier)

Linguistic pseudo-class

    :lang()

Logical pseudo-class

    :not()

PSEUDO-ELEMENT SELECTORS

Pseudo-classes aren't the only kind of pseudo-selectors. There are also four pseudo-elements that act as though they are inserting fictional elements into the document structure for styling. In CSS3, pseudo-elements are indicated by a double colon (::) symbol to differentiate them from pseudo-classes. However, all browsers support the single-colon syntax (:) as they were defined in CSS2, so many developers stick with that to ensure backward compatibility with older browsers.

First Letter and Line

NOTE

*There are a few properties in this list that you haven't seen yet. We'll cover the box-related properties (*margin*, padding*, *border*) in* **Chapter 14, Thinking Inside the Box.** *The* float *property is introduced in* **Chapter 15, Floating and Positioning.**

The following pseudo-elements are used to select the first line or the first letter of text in an element as displayed in the browser.

`::first-line`

This selector applies a style rule to the first line of the specified element. The only properties you can apply, however, are as follows:

color	text-decoration
font properties	vertical-align
background properties	text-transform
word-spacing	line-height
letter-spacing	

`::first-letter`

This applies a style rule to the first letter of the specified element. The properties you can apply are limited to the following:

color	vertical-align (if float is none)
font properties	padding properties
background properties	margin properties
letter-spacing	border properties
word-spacing	line-height
text-decoration	float
text-transform	

FIGURE 13-15 shows examples of the `::first-line` and `::first-letter` pseudo-element selectors.

```
p::first-line { letter-spacing: 9px; }

p::first-letter { font-size: 300%; color: orange; }
```

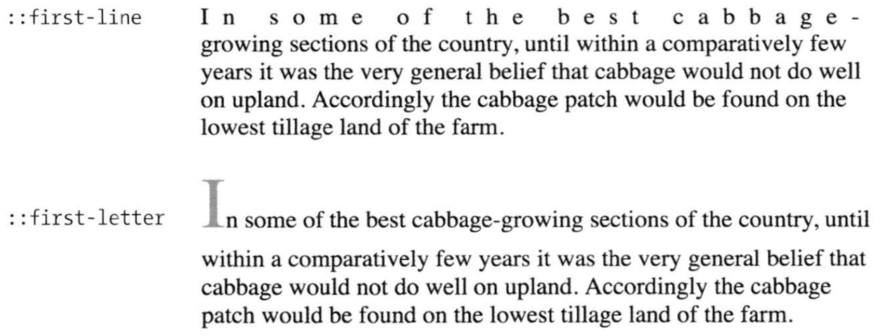

::first-line   In   some   of   the   best   cabbage-growing sections of the country, until within a comparatively few years it was the very general belief that cabbage would not do well on upland. Accordingly the cabbage patch would be found on the lowest tillage land of the farm.

::first-letter   In some of the best cabbage-growing sections of the country, until within a comparatively few years it was the very general belief that cabbage would not do well on upland. Accordingly the cabbage patch would be found on the lowest tillage land of the farm.

FIGURE 13-15. Examples of `::first-line` and `::first-letter` pseudo-element selectors.

Generated Content with ::before and ::after

You've seen how browsers add bullets and numbers to lists automatically, even though they are not actually in the HTML source. That is an example of generated content, content that browsers insert on the fly. It is possible to tell browsers to generate content before or after any element you like by using the `::before` and `::after` pseudo-elements (see **Note**).

Generated content could be used to add icons before list items, to display URLs next to links when web documents get printed out, to add language-appropriate quotation marks around a quote, and much more. Here's a simple example that inserts an image by using the `url()` function before the paragraph and "Thank you." at the end of the paragraph. Compare the markup to what you see rendered in the browser (FIGURE 13-16).

NOTE

Although double colons are specified in CSS3, you can use single colons for backward compatibility. Browsers are also required to support single colons going forward.

THE STYLES:

```
p.warning::before {
  content: url(exclamation.png);
  margin-right: 6px;
}

p.warning::after {
  content: " Thank you.";
  color: red;
}
```

THE MARKUP:

```
<p class="warning">We are required to warn you that undercooked food is
a health risk.</p>
```

 We are required to warn you that undercooked food is a health risk. Thank you.

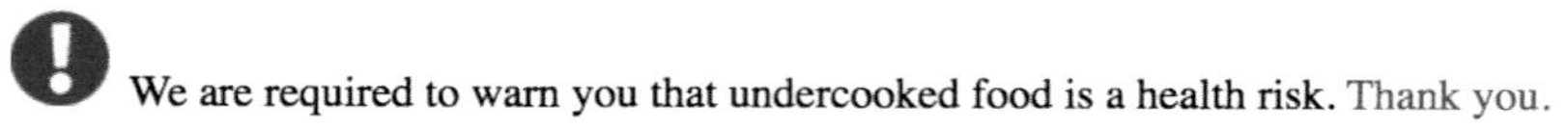

FIGURE 13-16. Generated content added with the `::before` and `::after` pseudo-selectors.

There are a few things of note in this example:

- The pseudo-element selector goes immediately after the target element without any space.

- The pseudo-element rule both inserts the content and specifies how it should be styled in one declaration block.

- The **content** property, which provides the content you want inserted, is required. The selector won't do anything without it.

- If you want spaces between the generated content and the content from the source document, you must include the character spaces inside the value's quotation marks or apply a margin.

If you want to insert an image, such as an icon or other mark, specify the URL without quotations marks:

```
li:before { content: url(images/star.png) }
```

When using generated content, keep in mind that whatever you insert does not become part of the document's DOM. It exists in the browser's display only and is not accessible to assistive devices like screen readers. It is best to use generated content for decorations and other "extras" that are not critical to your meaning and message.

> ■ **FURTHER READING**
>
> "Learning to Use the :before and :after Pseudo-Elements in CSS" by Louis Lazaris (*www.smashingmagazine.com/2011/07/learning-to-use-the-before-and-after-pseudo-elements-in-css/*).

ATTRIBUTE SELECTORS

We're finally in the home stretch with selectors. Attribute selectors target elements based on attribute names or values, which provides a lot of flexibility for selecting elements without needing to add a lot of **class** or **id** markup. The CSS3 attribute selectors are listed here:

element[*attribute*]

The simple attribute selector targets elements with a particular attribute regardless of its value. The following example selects any image that has a **title** attribute.

```
img[title] {border: 3px solid;}
```

element[*attribute*="*exact value*"]

The exact attribute value selector selects elements with a specific value for the attribute. This selector matches images with exactly the **title** value "first grade".

```
img[title="first grade"] {border: 3px solid;}
```

element[*attribute*~="*value*"]

The partial attribute value selector (indicated with a tilde, ~) allows you to specify one part of an attribute value. The following example looks for the word "grade" in the title, so images with the **title** value "first grade" and "second grade" would be selected.

```
img[title~="grade"] {border: 3px solid;}
```

element[*attribute*|="*value*"]

The hyphen-separated attribute value selector (indicated with a bar, |) targets hyphen-separated values. This selector matches any link that points to a document written in a variation on the English language (**en**), whether the attribute value is **en-us** (American English), **en-in** (Indian English), **en-au-tas** (Australian English), and so on.

```
[hreflang|="en"] {border: 3px solid;}
```

element[*attribute*^="*first part of the value*"]

The beginning substring attribute value selector (indicated with a carat, ^) matches elements whose specified attribute values *start* in the string of characters in the selector. This example applies the style only to images that are found in the */images/icons* directory.

```
img[src^="/images/icons"] {border: 3px solid;}
```

element[*attribute*$="*last part of the value*"]

The ending substring attribute value selector (indicated with a dollar sign, **$**) matches elements whose specified attribute values *end* in the string of characters in the selector. In this example, you can apply a style to just the **a** elements that link to PDF files.

```
a[href$=".pdf"] {border-bottom: 3px solid;}
```

```
element[attribute*="any part of the value"]
```

> The arbitrary substring attribute value selector (indicated with an aster-isk, *) looks for the provided text string in any part of the attribute value specified. This rule selects any image that contains the word "February" somewhere in its **title**.
>
> ```
> img[title*="February"] {border: 3px solid;}
> ```

OK, we're done with selectors! You've been a real trouper. I think it's definitely time to try out foreground and background colors as well as a few of these new selector types in EXERCISE 13-1 before moving on to background images.

BACKGROUND IMAGES

We've seen how to add images to the content of the document by using the **img** element, but most decorative images are added to pages and elements as backgrounds with CSS. After all, decorations such as tiling background patterns are firmly part of presentation, not structure. We've come a long way from the days when sites were giant graphics cut up and held together with tables (*shudder*).

In this section, we'll look at the collection of properties used to place and push around background images, starting with the basic **background-image** property.

Adding a Background Image

The **background-image** property adds a background image to any element. Its primary job is to provide the location of the image file.

background-image

Values:	url(*location of image*) | none
Default:	none
Applies to:	all elements
Inherits:	no

The value of **background-image** is a sort of URL holder that contains the location of the image (see **Note**).

The URL is relative to wherever the CSS rule is at the time. If the rule is in an embedded style sheet (a **style** element in the HTML document), then the pathname in the URL should be relative to the location of the HTML file. If the CSS rule is in an external style sheet, then the pathname to the image should be relative to the location of the *.css* file.

As an alternative, providing site root relative URLs for images ensures that the background image can be found regardless of the location of the style rules.

NOTE

The proper term for that "URL holder" is a functional notation. It is the same syntax used to list decimal and percentage RGB values.

EXERCISE 13-1. Adding color to a document

In this exercise, we'll start with a simple black-and-white menu and give it some personality with foreground and background colors (FIGURE 13-17). You should have enough experience writing style rules by this point that I'm not going to hold your hand as much as I have in previous exercises. This time, you write the rules. You can check your work against the finished style sheet provided with the materials for this chapter.

Open the file *summer-menu.html* (get it at *learningwebdesign. com/5e/materials*) in a text editor. You will find that there is already an embedded style sheet that provides basic text formatting. You'll just need to work on the colors. Feel free to save the document at any step along the way and view your progress in a browser.

1. Make the **h1** heading purple (R:153, G:51, B:153, or **#993399**) by adding a new declaration to the existing **h1** rule. Note that because this value has all double digits, you can use the condensed version (**#939**).

2. Make the **h2** headings light brown (R:204, G:102, B:0, **#cc6600** or **#c60**).

3. Make the background of the entire page a light green (R:210, G:220, B:157, or **#d2dc9d**). Now might be a nice time to save, have a look in a browser, and troubleshoot if the background and headings do not appear in color.

4. Make the background of the **header** white with 50% transparency (R:255, G:255, B:255, .5) so a hint of the background color shows through.

5. I've already added a rule that turns underlines off under links (**text-decoration:none**), so we'll be relying on color to make the links pop. Write a rule that makes links the same purple as the **h1** (**#939**).

6. Make visited links a muted purple (**#937393**).

7. When the mouse is placed over links, make the text a brighter purple (**#c700f2**) and add a white background color (**#fff**). This will look a little like the links are lighting up when the mouse is pointing at it. Use these same style rules for when the links are in focus.

8. As the mouse is being clicked (or tapped on a touch device), add a white background color and make the text turn a vibrant purple (**#ff00ff**). Make sure that all of your link pseudo-classes are in the correct order.

When you are done, your page should look like FIGURE 13-17. We'll be adding background images to this page later, so if you'd like to continue experimenting with different colors on different elements, make a copy of this document and give it a new name. Remember that the Google color picker is an easy destination for colors and their RGB equivalents.

WARNING

Don't forget the # character before hex values. The rule won't work without it.

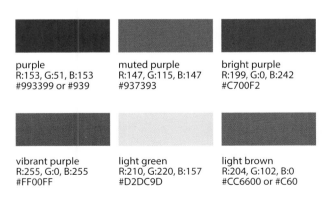

purple
R:153, G:51, B:153
#993399 or #939

muted purple
R:147, G:115, B:147
#937393

bright purple
R:199, G:0, B:242
#C700F2

vibrant purple
R:255, G:0, B:255
#FF00FF

light green
R:210, G:220, B:157
#D2DC9D

light brown
R:204, G:102, B:0
#CC6600 or #C60

FIGURE 13-17. The Black Goose Bistro menu page with colors applied.

■ AT A GLANCE

Background Properties

The properties related to the background are:

background-color
background-image
background-repeat
background-position
background-attachment
background-clip
background-size
background

■ DESIGN TIP

Tiling Background Images

When working with background images, keep these guidelines and tips in mind:

- Use a simple image that won't interfere with the legibility of the text over it.

- Always provide a background-color value that matches the primary color of the background image. If the background image fails to display, at least the overall design of the page will be similar. This is particularly important if the text color would be illegible against the browser's default white background.

- As usual for the web, keep the file size of background images as small as possible.

The root directory is indicated by a slash at the beginning of the URL. For example:

```
background-image: url(/images/background.jpg);
```

The downside, as for all site root relative URLs, is that you won't be able to test it locally (from your own computer) unless you have it set up as a server.

These examples and FIGURE 13-18 show background images applied behind a whole page (**body**) and a single **blockquote** element with padding and a border applied.

```
body {
    background-image: url(star.png);
}

blockquote {
    background-image: url(dot.png);
    padding: 2em;
    border: 4px dashed;
}
```

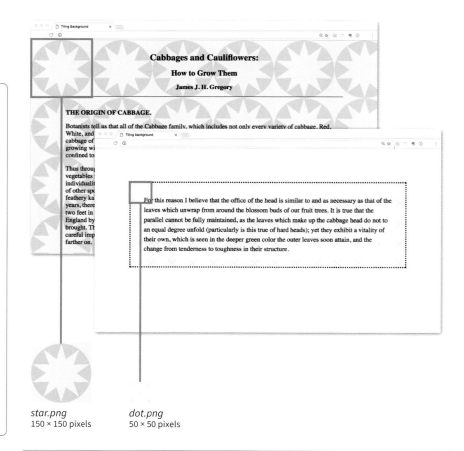

star.png
150 × 150 pixels

dot.png
50 × 50 pixels

FIGURE 13-18. Tiling background images added with the **background-image** property.

Here you can see the default behavior of **background-image**. The image starts in the top-left corner and tiles horizontally and vertically until the entire element is filled (although you'll learn how to change that in a moment). Like background colors, tiling background images fill the area behind the content area, fill the extra padding space around the content, and extend to the outer edge of the border (if there is one). You can change the background painting area with the **background-clip** property.

If you provide both a **background-color** and a **background-image** to an element, the image is placed on top of the color. In fact, it is recommended that you *do* provide a backup color that is similar in hue, in the event that the image fails to download.

Now you can try your hand at adding a tiling background image to a page in EXERCISE 13-2.

Always specify a similar background color should your background image fail to load.

EXERCISE 13-2. Adding a tiling background image

In this exercise, we're going to add a simple tiling background image to the menu. The images provided for this exercise should be in the *images* directory.

Add a declaration to the **body** style rule that makes the image *bullseye.png* tile in the background of the page. Be sure to include the pathname relative to the style sheet (in this case, the current HTML document).

```
background-image: url(images/bullseye.png);
```

Easy, isn't it? When you save and view the page in the browser, it should look like FIGURE 13-19.

I want to point out that *bullseye.png* is a slightly transparent PNG graphic, so it blends into any background color. Try temporarily changing the **background-color** for the **body** element by adding a second **background-color** declaration lower in the stack so it overrides the previous one. Play around with different colors and notice how the circles blend in. When you are done experimenting, delete the second declaration so the background is green again and you're ready to go for upcoming exercises.

FIGURE 13-19. The menu with a simple tiling background image.

Background Repeating

As we saw in FIGURE 13-18, images tile left and right, up and down, when left to their own devices. You can change this behavior with the **background-repeat** property.

background-repeat

Values:	repeat | no-repeat | repeat-x | repeat-y | space | round
Default:	repeat
Applies to:	all elements
Inherits:	no

If you want a background image to appear just once, use the **no-repeat** keyword value:

```
body {
   background-image: url(star.png);
   background-repeat: no-repeat;
}
```

You can also restrict the image to tiling only horizontally (**repeat-x**) or vertically (**repeat-y**), as shown in these examples:

```
body {
   background-image: url(star.png);
   background-repeat: repeat-x;
}
body {
   background-image: url(star.png);
   background-repeat: repeat-y;
}
```

FIGURE 13-20 shows examples of each of these keyword values. Notice that in all the examples, the tiling begins in the top-left corner of the element (or browser window when an image is applied to the **body** element). In the next section, I'll show you how to change that.

The remaining keyword values, **space** and **round**, attempt to fill the available background painting area an even number of times.

When **background-repeat** is set to **space**, the browser calculates how many background images can fit across the width and height of the background area, then adds equal amounts of space between each image. The result is even rows and columns and no clipped images (FIGURE 13-21).

The **round** keyword makes the browser squish the background image horizontally and vertically (not necessarily proportionally) to fit in the background area an even number of times (FIGURE 13-21).

Let's try out some background repeating patterns in EXERCISE 13-3.

BROWSER SUPPORT NOTE

Internet Explorer 8 and earlier do not support the **space** *and* **round** *keywords for* **background-repeat***.*

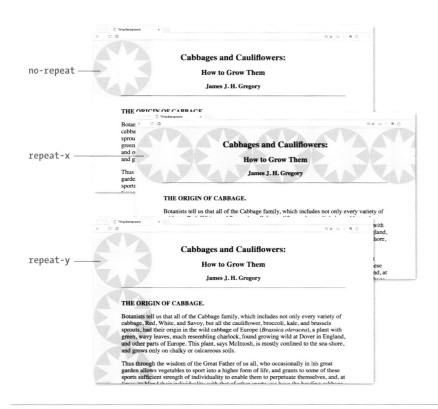

FIGURE 13-20. Turning off automatic tiling with **no-repeat** (top), applying horizontal-axis tiling with **repeat-x** (middle), and applying vertical-axis tiling with **repeat-y** (bottom).

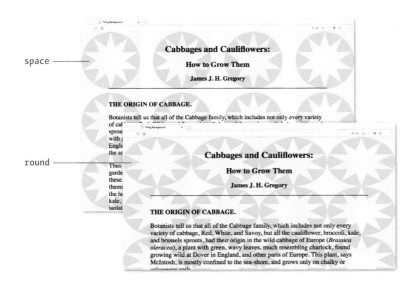

FIGURE 13-21. Examples of **space** and **round** keywords for **background-repeat**. The "space" example would be less clunky if the background color matched the image, but I've left it white to better demonstrate how the **space** value works.

EXERCISE 13-3. Controlling tile direction

Now let's try some slightly more sophisticated tiling on the Summer Menu page. This time we'll add a tiling background just along the top edge of the **header** element.

1. In the **header** rule, add the image *purpledot.png* and set it to repeat horizontally only:

```
header {
  margin-top: 0;
  padding: 3em 1em 2em 1em;
  text-align: center;
  background-color: rgba(255,255,255,.5);
  background-image: url(images/purpledot.png);
  background-repeat: repeat-x;
}
```

2. Save the file and look at it in the browser. It should look something like FIGURE 13-22. I recommend resizing your browser window wider and narrower and paying attention to the position of the background pattern. See how it's always anchored on the left? You're going to learn how to adjust position next. Try changing the style rule to make the dot repeat vertically only; then make it not repeat at all (set it back to **repeat-x** and save when you're done).

FIGURE 13-22. Adding a horizontal tiling image to the **header**.

3. Finally, try out the **space** and **round** repeat values on the **body** background image and see if you like the effect. Note that the tiles are evenly spaced within the body of the document, not just the viewport, so you may see some cut-off circles at the bottom edge of your browser. Delete the **background-repeat** declaration so it goes back to the default **repeat** for upcoming exercises:

```
body {
  …
  background-repeat: space;
}
```

Background Position

The **background-position** property specifies the position of the origin image in the background. You can think of the origin image as the first image that is placed in the background from which tiling images extend. Here is the property and its various values.

background-position

Values: *length measurement* | *percentage* | left | center | right | top | bottom

Default: 0% 0% (same as left top)

Applies to: all elements

Inherits: no

To position the origin image, provide horizontal and vertical values that describe where to place it. There are a variety of ways to do it.

Keyword positioning

The keyword values (**left**, **right**, **top**, **bottom**, and **center**) position the origin image relative to the outer edges of the element's padding. For example, **left** positions the image all the way to the left edge of the background area. The default origin position corresponds to **left top**.

Keywords are typically used in pairs, as in these examples:

```
background-position: left bottom;
background-position: right center;
```

The keywords may appear in any order. If you provide only one keyword, the missing keyword is assumed to be **center**. Thus, **background-position: right** has the same effect as **background-position: right center**.

Length measurements

Specifying position using length measurements such as pixels or ems indicates an amount of offset from the top-left corner of the element to the top-left corner of the background origin image. When you are providing length values, the horizontal measurement always goes first. Specifying negative values is allowed and causes the image to hang outside the visible background area.

This example positions the top-left corner of the image 200 pixels from the left edge and 50 pixels down from the top edge of the element (or more specifically, the padding edge by default):

```
background-position: 200px 50px;
```

Percentages

Percentage values are provided in horizontal/vertical pairs, with **0% 0%** corresponding to the top-left corner and **100% 100%** corresponding to the bottom-right corner. As with length values, the horizontal measurement always goes first.

When you are providing length or percentage values, the horizontal measurement always goes first.

It is important to note that the percentage value applies to both the canvas area *and* the image itself. A horizontal value of 25% positions the point 25% from the left edge of the image at a point that is 25% from the left edge of the background positioning area. A vertical value of 100% positions the bottom edge of the image at the bottom edge of the positioning area.

```
background-position: 25% 100%;
```

As with keywords, if you provide only one percentage, the other is assumed to be 50% (centered).

FIGURE 13-23 shows the results of each of the aforementioned **background-position** examples with the **background-repeat** set to **no-repeat** for clarity. It is

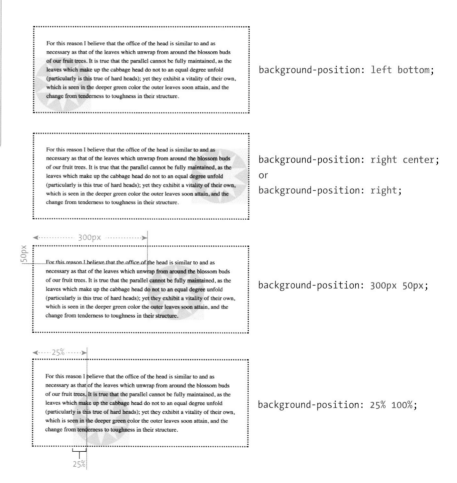

FIGURE 13-23. Positioning a non-repeating background image. If these background images were allowed to repeat, they would extend left and right and/or up and down from the initial positions.

Background Edge Offsets

The CSS3 specification also includes a four-part syntax for **background-position** that allows you to specify an offset (in length or percentage from a particular edge). This is the syntax:

```
background-position:
    edge-keyword offset
    edge-keyword offset;
```

In this example, an origin image is positioned 50 pixels from the right edge and 50 pixels from the bottom of the element's positioning area:

```
background-position:
    right 50px bottom 50px;
```

This four-part syntax is not supported by IE 8 and earlier, Safari and iOS Safari 6 and earlier, and Android 4.3 and earlier.

possible to position the origin image and let it tile from there, in both directions or just horizontally or vertically. When the image tiles, the position of the initial image might not be obvious, but you can use **background-position** to make a tile pattern start at a point other than the left edge of the image. This might be used to keep a background pattern centered and symmetrical.

Background Position Origin

Notice in FIGURE 13-23 that when the origin image was placed in the corner of an element, it was placed inside the border (only repeated images extend under the border to its outer edge). This is the default position, but you can change it with the **background-origin** property.

background-origin

Values:	border-box | padding-box | content-box
Default:	padding-box
Applies to:	all elements
Inherits:	no

This property defines the boundaries of the background positioning area in the same way **background-clip** defined the background painting area. You can set the boundaries to the **border-box** (so the origin image is placed under the outer edge of the border, **padding-box** (outer edge of the padding, just inside the border), or **content-box** (the actual content area of the element). These terms will become more meaningful once you get more familiar with the box model in the next chapter. In the meantime, FIGURE 13-24 shows the results of each of the keyword options.

BROWSER SUPPORT NOTE

background-origin *is not supported by Internet Explorer 8 and earlier.*

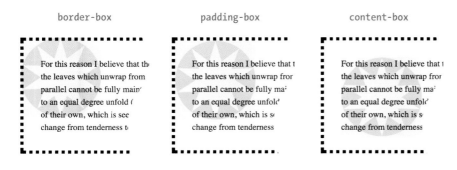

FIGURE 13-24. Examples of **background-origin** keywords.

Before we move on to the remaining background properties, check out EXERCISE 13-4 to get a feel for background positioning.

EXERCISE 13-4. Positioning background images

Let's have some fun with the position of the background image in the menu. First we're going to make some subtle adjustments to the background images that are already there, and then we'll swap them out for a whole different background and play around some more. We are still working with the *summer-menu.html* document, which should have repeating tile patterns in the **body** and **header** elements.

1. I'm thinking that because the main elements of the menu are centered, it would be nice if the background patterns stayed centered, too. Add this declaration to both the **body** and **header** rules; then save and look at it in the browser.

   ```
   background-position: center top;
   ```

   You may not notice the difference until you resize the browser wide and narrow again. Now the pattern is anchored in the center and reveals more or less on both edges, not just the right edge as before.

2. For kicks, alter the **background-position** values so that the purple dots are along the bottom edge of the **header** (**center bottom**). (That doesn't look so good; I'm putting mine back to **top**.) Then try moving *bullseye.png* down 200 pixels (**center 200px**). Notice that the pattern still fills the entire screen—we moved the origin image down, but the background is still set to tile in all directions. FIGURE 13-25 shows the result of these changes.

3. That looks good, but let's get rid of the background on the **body** for now. I want to show you a little trick. During the design process, I prefer to hide styles in comments instead of deleting them entirely. That way, I don't need to remember them or type them in again; I only have to remove the comment indicators, and they're back. When the design is done and it's time to publish, I strip unused styles out to keep the file size down.

Here's how to hide declarations as CSS comments:

```
body {
    …
    background-color: #d2dc9d;
    /*  background-image: url(images/bullseye.png);
    background-position: center 200px; */
}
```

4. Now, add the *blackgoose.png* image (also a semi-transparent PNG) to the background of the page. Set it to not repeat, and center it at the top of the page:

   ```
   background-image: url(images/blackgoose.png);
   background-repeat: no-repeat;
   background-position: center top;
   ```

   Take a look in the browser window and watch the background scroll up with the content when you scroll the page.

5. I want you to get a feel for the various position keywords and numeric values. Try each of these out and look at it in the browser. Be sure to scroll the page and watch what happens. Note that when you provide a percentage or keyword to the vertical position, it is based on the height of the entire document, not just the browser window. You can try your own variations as well.

   ```
   background-position: right top;
   ```

   ```
   background-position: right bottom;
   ```

   ```
   background-position: left 50%;
   ```

   ```
   background-position: center 100px;
   ```

6. Leave the image positioned at **center 100px** so you are ready to go for the next exercise. Your page should look like the one shown on the right in FIGURE 13-25.

Centered background pattern

Positioned non-repeating image

FIGURE 13-25. The results of positioning the origin image in the tiling background patterns (left) and positioning a single background logo (right).

Background Attachment

In the previous exercise, I asked you to scroll the page and watch what happens to the background image. As expected, it scrolls along with the document and off the top of the browser window, which is its default behavior. However, you can use the **background-attachment** property to free the background from the content and allow it to stay fixed in one position while the rest of the content scrolls.

background-attachment

Values:	scroll | fixed | local
Default:	scroll
Applies to:	all elements
Inherits:	no

With the **background-attachment** property, you have the choice of whether the background image scrolls with the content or stays in a fixed position. When an image is **fixed**, it stays in the same position relative to the viewport of the browser (as opposed to being relative to the element it fills). You'll see what I mean in a minute (and you can try it yourself in EXERCISE 13-5).

In the following example, a large, non-tiling image is placed in the background of the whole document (the **body** element). By default, when the document scrolls, the image scrolls too, moving up and off the page, as shown in FIGURE 13-26. However, if you set the value of **background-attachment** to **fixed**, it stays where it is initially placed, and the text scrolls up over it.

```
body {
    background-image: url(images/bigstar.gif);
    background-repeat: no-repeat;
    background-position: center 300px;
    background-attachment: fixed;
}
```

The **local** value, which was added in CSS3, is useful when an element has its own scrolling mechanism. Instead of scrolling with the viewport's scroller, **local** makes the background image fixed to the content of the scrolling element. This keyword is not supported in IE8 and earlier and may also be problematic on mobile browsers.

A large non-repeating background image in the **body** of the document.

background-attachment: `scroll`;

By default, the background image is attached to the **body** element and scrolls off the page when the content scrolls.

background-attachment: `fixed`;

When **background-attachment** is set to **fixed**, the image stays in its position relative to the browser viewing area and does not scroll with the content.

FIGURE 13-26. Preventing the background image from scrolling with the **background-attachment** property.

EXERCISE 13-5.
Fixed position

When we last left the bistro menu, we had applied a large, non-repeating logo image to the background of the page. We'll leave it just like that, but we'll use the **background-attachment** property to keep it in the same place even when the page scrolls:

```
body {
    background-image: url(images/
blackgoose.png);
    background-repeat: no-repeat;
    background-position: center
100px;
    background-attachment: fixed;
}
```

Save the document, open it in the browser, and try scrolling. The background image stays put in the viewing area of the browser. Cool, huh?

For extra credit, see what happens when you fix the attachment of the dot pattern in the **header**. (Spoiler: it stays in the same place, but only within the **header** itself. When the **header** slides out of view, so does its background.)

Background Size

OK, we have just one more background image property to cover before we wrap it all up with the **background** shorthand property. So far, the background images we've seen are displayed at the actual size of the image itself. You can change the size of the image by using the **background-size** property.

background-size

Values:	*length*	*percentage*	auto	cover	contain
Default:	auto
Applies to:	all elements
Inherits:	no

There are several ways to specify the size of the background image. Perhaps the most straightforward is to specify the dimensions in length units such as pixels or ems. As usual, when two values are provided, the first one is used as the horizontal measurement. If you provide just one value, it is used as the horizontal measurement, and the vertical value is set to **auto**.

This example resizes the *target.png* background image, which has an intrinsic size of 300 pixels by 300 pixels (FIGURE 13-27):

```
header {
    background-image: url(images/target.png);
    background-size: 600px 150px;
}
```

Percentage values are calculated based on the background positioning area, which by default runs to the inside edge of the border, but may have been altered with **background-origin**—something to keep in mind. So a horizontal value of 50% does not make the image half its width; rather, it sizes it to 50% of the width of the positioning area (FIGURE 13-27). Again, the horizontal value goes first. It is OK to mix percentage and length values, as shown in this example:

```
header {
    background-image: url(images/target.png);
    background-size: 50% 10em;
}
```

The **auto** keyword resizes the image in whatever direction is necessary to maintain its proportions. Bitmapped images such as GIF, JPEG, and PNG have intrinsic proportions, so they will always stay proportional when one sizing value is set to **auto**. Some images, such as SVG and CSS gradients, don't have intrinsic proportions. In that case, **auto** sets the width or height to 100% of the width or height of the background positioning area.

The **cover** and **contain** keywords are interesting additions in CSS3. When you set the background size to **cover**, the browser resizes a background image large enough to reach all the sides of the background positioning area. There will be only one image because it fills the whole element, and it is likely that

target.png
300 × 300 pixels

`background-size: 600px 300px;`

`background-size: 50% 10em;`

FIGURE 13-27. Resizing a background image with specific length units and percentages.

portions of the image will fall outside the positioning area if the proportions of the image and the positioning area do not match (FIGURE 13-28).

By contrast, **contain** sizes the image just large enough to fill either the width or the height of the positioning area (depending on the proportions of the image). The whole image will be visible and "contained" within the background area (FIGURE 13-28). If there is leftover space, the background image repeats unless **background-repeat** is set to **no-repeat**.

```
div#A {
    background-image: url(target.png);
    background-size: cover; }

div#B {
    background-image: url(target.png);
    background-size: contain; }
```

`background-size: cover;`

The entire background area of the element is covered, and the image maintains its proportions even if it is clipped.

`background-size: contain;`

The image is sized proportionally so it fits entirely in the element. There may be room left over for tiling (as shown).

FIGURE 13-28. Examples of the **cover** and **contain** background size keywords.

THE SHORTHAND BACKGROUND PROPERTY

You can use the handy **background** property to specify *all* of your background styles in one declaration.

background

Values:	*background-color background-image background-repeat background-attachment background-position background-clip background-origin background-size*
Default:	see individual properties
Applies to:	all elements
Inherits:	no

The value of the **background** property is a list of values that would be provided for the individual background properties previously listed. For example, this one background rule

```
body { background: white url(star.png) no-repeat right top fixed; }
```

replaces this rule with five separate declarations:

```
body {
    background-color: white;
    background-image: url(star.png);
    background-repeat: no-repeat;
    background-position: right top;
    background-attachment: fixed;
}
```

All of the property values for **background** are optional and may appear in any order. The only restriction is that when you are providing the coordinates for the **background-position** property, the horizontal value must appear first, immediately followed by the vertical value. As with any shorthand property, be aware that if any value is omitted, it will be reset to its default value. See the **"Watch Out for Overrides"** sidebar.

In EXERCISE 13-6, you can convert your long-winded background properties to a single declaration with **background**.

Watch Out for Overrides

The **background** property is efficient, but use it carefully. We've addressed this before, but it bears repeating. Because **background** is a shorthand property, when you omit a value, that property will be reset to its default. Be careful that you do not accidentally override style rules earlier in the style sheet with a later shorthand rule that reverts your settings to their defaults.

In this example, the background image *dots.gif* will *not* be applied to **h3** elements because by omitting the value for **background-image**, you essentially set that value to **none**:

```
h1, h2, h3 {
background: red url(dots.gif)
repeat-x;
}
h3 {
background: green;
}
```

To override particular properties, use the specific background property you intend to change. For example, if the intent in the preceding example were to change just the background color of **h3** elements, the **background-color** property would be the correct choice.

EXERCISE 13-6. Convert to shorthand property

This one is easy. Replace all of the background-related declarations in the **body** of the bistro menu with a single **background** property declaration:

```
body {
    font-family: Georgia, serif;
    font-size: 100%;
```

```
    line-height: 175%;
    margin: 0 15%;
    background: #d2dc9d url(images/blackgoose.png)
no-repeat center 100px fixed;
}
```

Do the same for the **header** element, and you're done.

Multiple Backgrounds

CSS3 introduced the ability to apply multiple background images to a single element. To apply multiple values for **background-image**, put them in a list separated by commas. Additional background-related property values also go in comma-separated lists; the first value listed applies to the first image, the second value to the second, and so on.

Although CSS declarations usually work on a "last one wins" rule, for multiple background images, whichever is listed last goes on the bottom, and each image prior in the list layers on top of it. You can think of them like Photoshop layers in that they get stacked in the order in which they appear in the list. Put another way, the image defined by the first value will go in front, and others line up behind it, in the order in which they are listed.

```
body {
    background-image: url(image1.png), url(image2.png), url(image3.png);
    background-position: left top, center center, right bottom;
    background-repeat: no-repeat, no-repeat, no-repeat;
    …
}
```

Alternatively, you can take advantage of the **background** shorthand property to make the rule simpler. Now the **background** property has three value series, separated by commas:

```
body {
    background:
      url(image1.png) left top no-repeat,
      url(image2.png) center center no-repeat,
      url(image3.png) right bottom no-repeat;
}
```

FIGURE 13-29 shows the result. The big, orange 1 is positioned in the top-left corner, the 2 is centered vertically and horizontally, and the 3 is in the bottom-right corner. All three background images share the background positioning area of one **body** element. Try it out for yourself in EXERCISE 13-7.

BROWSER SUPPORT NOTE

Internet Explorer 8 and earlier do not support multiple background images and will entirely ignore any background declaration with more than one value. The fix is to choose one **background-image** *for the element as a fallback for IE and other non-supporting browsers, and then specify the multiple* **background** *rules that override it:*

```
body {
/* for non-supporting browsers */
  background: url(image_fallback.
png) top left no-repeat;
/* multiple backgrounds */
background:
  url(image1.png) left top
no-repeat,
  url(image2.png) center center
no-repeat,
  url(image3.png) right bottom
no-repeat;
/* background color */
background-color: papayawhip;
}
```

Cabbage Recipes

From *The Whitehouse Cookbook* (1887)

FIGURE 13-29. Three separate background images added to the **body** element.

EXERCISE 13-7. Multiple background images

In this exercise, we'll give multiple background images a try (be sure you aren't using an old version of IE, or this won't work).

I'd like the dot pattern in the **header** to run along the left and right sides. I also have a little goose silhouette (*gooseshadow.png*) that might look cute walking along the bottom of the header. I'm making this example friendly for non-supporting browsers (IE8 and earlier) by providing a fallback declaration with just one image and separating out the **background-color** declaration so it doesn't get overridden. If IE8 is not a concern, you don't need the fallback.

You can see in the example that we are placing three images in a single header: dots on the left side, dots on the right, and a goose at the bottom.

```
header {
  …
  background: url(images/purpledot.png) center top
repeat-x;
  background:
    url(images/purpledot.png) left top repeat-y,
    url(images/purpledot.png) right top repeat-y,
    url(images/gooseshadow.png) 90% bottom no-repeat;
  background-color: rgba(255,255,255,.5);
}
```

FIGURE 13-30 shows the final result. Meh, I liked it better before, but you get the idea.

FIGURE 13-30. The bistro menu header with two rows of dots and a small goose graphic in the **header** element.

LIKE A RAINBOW (GRADIENTS)

A gradient is a transition from one color to another, sometimes through multiple colors. In the past, the only way to put a gradient on a web page was to create one in an image-editing program and add the resulting image with CSS.

Now we can specify color gradients by using CSS notation alone, leaving the task of rendering color blends to the browser. Although they are specified with code, gradients are *images*. They just happen to be generated on the fly. A gradient image has no intrinsic size or proportions; the size matches the element it gets applied to. Gradients can be applied anywhere an image may be applied: **background-image**, **border-image**, and **list-style-image**. We'll stick with **background-image** examples in this chapter.

There are two types of gradients:

- Linear gradients change colors along a line, from one edge of the element to the other.

- Radial gradients start at a point and spread outward in a circular or elliptical shape.

Gradients are images that browsers generate on the fly. Use them as you would use a background image.

Linear Gradients

The **linear-gradient()** notation provides the angle of the gradient line and one or more points along that line where the pure color is positioned (color stops). You can use color names or any of the numerical color values discussed earlier in the chapter, including transparency. The angle of the gradient line is specified in degrees (*n***deg**) or with keywords. With degrees, **0deg** points upward, and positive angles go around clockwise so that **90deg** points to the right. Therefore, if you want to go from aqua on the top edge to green on the bottom edge, set the rotation to **180deg**:

```
background-image: linear-gradient(180deg, aqua, green);
```

The keywords describe direction in increments of 90° (**to top**, **to right**, **to bottom**, **to left**). Our **180deg** gradient could also be specified with the **to bottom** keyword. The result is shown in FIGURE 13-31 (top):

```
background-image: linear-gradient(to bottom, aqua, green);
```

You can use the "to" syntax to point to corners as well. The following gradient would be drawn from the bottom-left corner to the top-right corner. The resulting angle of a gradient drawn between corners is determined by the aspect ratio of the box.

```
background-image: linear-gradient(to top right, aqua, green);
```

In the following example, the gradient now goes from left to right (**90deg**) and includes a third color, orange, which appears 25% of the way across the gradient line (FIGURE 13-31, middle). You can see that the placement of the color stop is indicated after the color value. You can use percentages or any length measurement. The first and last color stops don't require positions because they are set to 0% and 100%, respectively, by default.

```
background-image: linear-gradient(90deg, yellow, orange 25%, purple);
```

You certainly aren't limited to right angles. Specify any degree you like to make the linear gradient head in that direction. You can also specify as many colors as you like. If no positions are specified, the colors are spaced evenly across the length of the gradient line. If you position the last color stop short of the end of the gradient line (such as the blue at 50% in this example), the last color continues to the end of the gradient line (FIGURE 13-31, bottom):

```
background-image: linear-gradient(54deg, red, orange, yellow, green,
  blue 50%);
```

■ **PERFORMANCE TIP**

Gradients offer both advantages and disadvantages when it comes to performance. On the plus side, they do not require an extra call to the server and require fewer bytes to download than images. On the other hand, all that rendering on the fly requires time and processing power that can hurt performance. Radial gradients are the worst culprits. They can be particularly problematic on mobile devices, where processing power may be limited. Consider serving a separate style sheet without gradients to mobile devices.

```
linear-gradient(180deg, aqua, green);
or
linear-gradient(to bottom, aqua, green);
```

```
linear-gradient(90deg, yellow, orange 25%, purple);
```

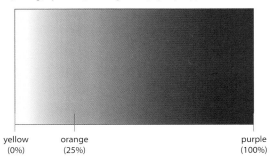

```
linear-gradient(54deg, red, orange, yellow, green, blue 50%);
```

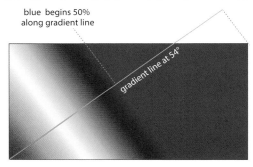

FIGURE 13-31. Examples of linear gradients.

These examples are pretty garish, but if you choose your colors and stops right, gradients are a nice way to give elements subtle shading and a 3-D appearance. The button in FIGURE 13-32 uses a background gradient to achieve a 3-D look without graphics.

FIGURE 13-32. A 3-D button made with only CSS.

```css
a.button-like {
  background: linear-gradient(to bottom, #e2e2e2 0%, #dbdbdb 50%,
  #d1d1d1 51%, #fefefe 100%);
}
```

That concludes our quick-and-dirty tour of linear gradients. You should know that I really only scratched the surface of linear gradient behavior and possibilities, so you may want to check out the resources in the **"Further Reading"** sidebar. It's time to move on to radial gradients.

Radial Gradients

Radial gradients, like the name says, radiate out from a point in a circle along a gradient ray (like a gradient line, but it always points outward from the center). At minimum, a radial gradient requires two color stops, as shown in this example:

```
background-image: radial-gradient(yellow, green);
```

By default, the gradient fills the available background area, and its center is positioned in the center of the element (FIGURE 13-33). The result is an ellipse if the containing element is a rectangle and a circle if the element is square.

FIGURE 13-33. A minimal radial gradient with default size and position.

That looks pretty spiffy already, but you don't have to settle for the default. The **radial-gradient()** notation allows you to specify the shape, size, and center position of the gradient:

Shape

In most cases, the shape of the radial gradient will result from the shape of the element or an explicit size you apply to it, but you can also specify the shape by using the **circle** or **ellipse** keywords. When you make a gradient a **circle** (without conflicting size specifications), it stays circular even when it is in a rectangular element (FIGURE 13-34, top).

```
background-image: radial-gradient(circle, yellow, green);
```

Size

The size of the radial gradient can be specified in length units or percentages, which apply to the gradient ray, or with keywords. If you supply just one length, it is used for both width and height, resulting in a circle. When you provide two lengths, the first one is the horizontal measurement and the second is vertical (FIGURE 13-34, middle). For ellipses, you can provide percentage values as well, or mix percentages with length values.

```
background-image: radial-gradient(200px 80px, aqua, green);
```

■ FURTHER READING

The most in-depth coverage of CSS gradient syntax that I've read is in Eric Meyer's book, *Colors, Backgrounds, and Gradients* (O'Reilly). The same content is available in *CSS: The Definitive Guide*, by Eric Meyer and Estelle Weyl (also from O'Reilly).

Online, I recommend these overviews and tutorials:

- "CSS Gradients" by Chris Coyier (*css-tricks.com/css3-gradients/*)
- "Using CSS Gradients" at MDN Web Docs (*developer.mozilla. org/en-US/docs/Web/CSS/CSS_ Images/Using_CSS_gradients*)
- "CSS3 Gradients," part of the *CSS Mine* e-book by Martin Michalek (*www.cssmine.com/ebook/css3-gradients*)

```
radial-gradient(circle, yellow, green);
```

```
radial-gradient(200px 80px, aqua, green);
```

```
radial-gradient(farthest-side at right bottom, yellow, orange 50%, purple);
```

FIGURE 13-34. Examples of sizing and positioning radial gradients.

There are also four keywords—**closest-side**, **closest-corner**, **farthest-side**, and **farthest-corner**—that set the length of the gradient ray relative to points on the containing element.

Position

By default, the center of the gradient is positioned at **center center**, but you can change that by using the positioning syntax we covered for the **background-position** property. The syntax is the same, but it should be preceded by the **at** keyword, as in this example (FIGURE 13-34, bottom). Notice that in this example, I have included an additional color stop of orange at the 50% mark.

```
background-image: radial-gradient(farthest-side at right bottom,
yellow, orange 50%, purple);
```

Repeating Gradients

If you'd like your gradient pattern to repeat, use the **repeating-linear-gra-dient()** or **repeating-radial-gradient()** notation. The syntax is the same as for single gradients, but adding "repeating-" causes the pattern to repeat the color stops infinitely in both directions. This is commonly used to create interesting striped patterns. In this simple example, a gradient from white to silver (light gray) repeats every 30 pixels because the silver color stop is set to 30px (FIGURE 13-35, top):

```
background: repeating-linear-gradient(to bottom, white, silver 30px);
```

This example makes a diagonal pattern of orange and white stripes (FIGURE 13-35, bottom). The edges are sharp because the white stripe starts at exactly the point where the orange one ends (at 12px) with no fading:

```
background: repeating-linear-gradient(45deg, orange, orange 12px, white 12px, white 24px);
```

`repeating-linear-gradient(to bottom, white, silver 30px);`

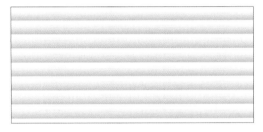

`repeating-linear-gradient(45deg, orange, orange 12px, white 12px, white 24px);`

FIGURE 13-35. Repeating gradient pattern.

Browser Support and Vendor Prefixes

All of the major browsers started adding support for the standard gradient syntax between 2012 and 2013 (see **Browser Support Note**), so they've been reliable for a good number of years. However, if you need to support older browsers, you can do so using each browser's proprietary gradient syntax with a vendor prefix (see the **"Vendor Prefixes"** sidebar). For Internet Explorer 9 and earlier, you can use its proprietary **filter** function. Or, go the progressive enhancement route and use a solid color as a fallback.

BROWSER SUPPORT NOTE

Standard gradient syntax is supported in Internet Explorer 10+, Edge, Firefox 16+, Chrome 26+, Safari 6.1+, iOS 7.1+, and Android 4.4+.

Vendor Prefixes

Browser makers usually start tinkering with proprietary solutions for cutting-edge web technologies before the specs are fully settled. For many years, they kept their experimentation separate from the final implementation by adding a vendor prefix (or browser prefix) to the property or function name. The prefix indicates that the implementation is proprietary and still a work in progress. For example, while Safari was implementing text-wrap shapes, it used its own **-webkit-** prefixed version of the standard **shape-outside** property:

```
-webkit-shape-outside: url(cube.png);
```

TABLE 13-1 lists the prefixes used by the major browsers.

TABLE 13-1. Browser vendor prefixes

Prefix	Organization	Most popular browsers
-ms-	Microsoft	Internet Explorer
-moz-	Mozilla Foundation	Firefox, Camino, SeaMonkey
-o-	Opera Software	Opera, Opera Mini, Opera Mobile
-webkit-	Originally Apple; now open source	Safari, Chrome, Android, Silk, BlackBerry, WebOS, many others

Vendor prefixes allowed developers to start using cool new CSS features on the browsers that supported them, which was a plus for moving web design and the specification forward. On the downside, the whole system turned out to be complicated and often misused. In the end, the browser makers agreed to put the prefix system to rest and not release any more proprietary properties.

These days, browsers hide experimental features behind "flags" (options you can turn on or off) or in separate technology preview releases that developers can access for testing purposes only. When a feature seems stable, it is made public in the formal browser release. We'll look at methods for testing for individual CSS features in **Chapter 19, More CSS Techniques**.

However, there are a few CSS properties and features that came into vogue during the prefix era that still require prefixes in order to work in older browsers, should you choose to support them. Gradient syntax is one of those features.

Prefixing Tools

Writing all those redundant prefixed properties is a big pain, but fortunately, there are some tools that will generate them for you automatically.

If you use one of the CSS preprocessor syntaxes (like Sass, LESS, or Stylus), you can take advantage of their prefixing "mixins." We'll talk more about preprocessors in **Chapter 19**.

If you write your CSS in the standard syntax, you can run it through a postprocessor like AutoPrefixer when you are done. Autoprefixer parses your styles, then automatically adds prefixes just for the properties and notations that need them. The prefixing happens as part of a "build step" via a build tool like Grunt. For a good overview, see "Autoprefixer: A Postprocessor Dealing with Vendor Prefixes in the Best Possible Way" at CSS-Tricks (*css-tricks.com/autoprefixer/*). I'll talk more about build tools in **Chapter 20, Modern Web Development Tools**.

A gradient for all browsers

The following example shows the yellow-to-green linear gradient written to address every browser, past and present, with the Internet Explorer **filter** equivalent thrown in for good measure. Notice that there are differences in syntax. Where the CSS3 spec uses the **to bottom** keyword, most of the others use **top**. A very old version used by WebKit browsers used **-webkit-gradient** for both linear and radial gradients, but it was quickly replaced with separate functions. Another difference not evident in this example is that in the old syntax, **0deg** pointed to the right edge, not to the top edge as was standardized in CSS3, and the angles increased counterclockwise.

This is a serious chunk of code for a single gradient, and thankfully, we are very close to this no longer being necessary:

```
background: #ffff00; /* Old browsers */
background: -moz-linear-gradient(top, #ffff00 0%, #00ff00 100%);
/* FF3.6+ */
background: -webkit-gradient(linear, left top, left bottom, color-
stop(0%,#ffff00), color-stop(100%,#00ff00));
/* Chrome,Safari4+ */
background: -webkit-linear-gradient(top, #ffff00 0%,#00ff00 100%);
/* Chrome10+,Safari5.1+ */
background: -o-linear-gradient(top, #ffff00 0%,#00ff00 100%);
/* Opera 11.10+ */
background: -ms-linear-gradient(top, #ffff00 0%,#00ff00 100%);
/* IE10+ */
background: linear-gradient(to bottom, #ffff00 0%,#00ff00 100%);
/* W3C Standard */
filter: progid:DXImageTransform.Microsoft.gradient(
startColorstr='#ffff00', endColorstr='#00ff00',GradientType=0 );
/* IE6-9 */
```

In upcoming chapters, whenever a property requires vendor prefixes, I will be sure to note it. Otherwise, you can assume that the standard CSS is all you need.

Designing Gradients

That last code example was a doozy! Vendor prefixes aside, just the task of describing gradients can be daunting. Although it is not impossible to write the code by hand, I recommend you do what I do—use an online gradient tool. One option is the Ultimate CSS Gradient Generator from Colorzilla (*www.colorzilla.com/gradient-editor/*), shown in FIGURE 13-36. Simply enter as many color stops as you'd like, slide the sliders around until you get the look you want, and then copy the code. That's exactly what I did to get the example we just looked at. The CSS Gradient Generator by Virtuosoft is another fine option that also includes support for repeating gradients (*www.virtuosoft.eu/tools/css-gradient-generator/*).

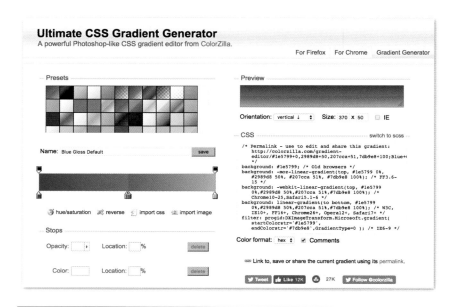

FIGURE 13-36. The Ultimate CSS Gradient Generator (*www.colorzilla.com/gradient-editor*) makes creating CSS gradients a breeze.

CSS3 Patterns Gallery

FIGURE 13-37. CSS3 Patterns Gallery assembled by Lea Verou (*lea.verou.me/css3patterns*). You may also enjoy Lea's book, *CSS Secrets: Better Solutions to Everyday Web Design Problems* (O'Reilly).

If you want your mind blown, take a look at the wild background patterns made with gradients assembled by Lea Verou in her CSS3 Patterns Gallery (*lea.verou.me/css3patterns*) (FIGURE 13-37). It's inspirational, and you can take a peek at the code used to create them.

FINALLY, EXTERNAL STYLE SHEETS

Back in **Chapter 11, Introducing Cascading Style Sheets,** I told you that there are three ways to connect style sheets to an HTML document: inline with the **style** attribute, embedded with the **style** element, and as an external *.css* document linked to or imported into the document. In this section, we finally get to that third option.

External style sheets are by far the most powerful way to use CSS because you can make style changes across an entire site simply by editing a single style sheet document. That is the advantage to having all the style information in one place, and not mixed in with the document source.

Furthermore, because a single style document is downloaded and cached by the browser for the whole site, there is less code to download with every document, resulting in better performance.

First, a little bit about the style sheet document itself. An external style sheet is a plain-text document with at least one style sheet rule. It may *not* include any HTML tags (there's no reason to include them, anyway). It may contain comments, but they must use the CSS comment syntax that you've seen already:

```
/* This is the end of the section */
```

The style sheet should be named with the *.css* suffix (there are some exceptions to this rule, but you're unlikely to encounter them as a beginner). It may also begin with the **@charset** at-rule to declare the character encoding, although you really need to do that only if you are using an encoding other than UTF-8. If you use **@charset**, it must be the first element in the style sheet, with no characters, including comments or style rules, preceding it.

FIGURE 13-38 shows how a short style sheet document looks in my text editor.

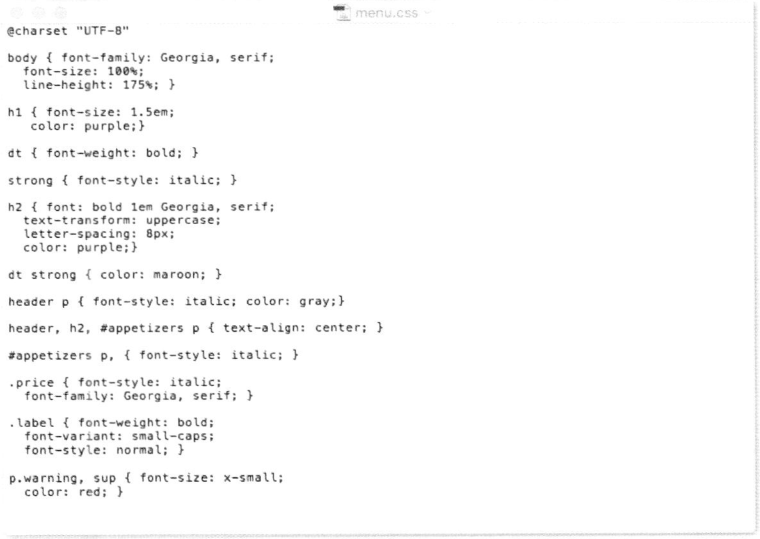

```
                                    menu.css
@charset "UTF-8"

body { font-family: Georgia, serif;
   font-size: 100%;
   line-height: 175%; }

h1 { font-size: 1.5em;
    color: purple;}

dt { font-weight: bold; }

strong { font-style: italic; }

h2 { font: bold 1em Georgia, serif;
   text-transform: uppercase;
   letter-spacing: 8px;
   color: purple;}

dt strong { color: maroon; }

header p { font-style: italic; color: gray;}

header, h2, #appetizers p { text-align: center; }

#appetizers p, { font-style: italic; }

.price { font-style: italic;
   font-family: Georgia, serif; }

.label { font-weight: bold;
   font-variant: small-caps;
   font-style: normal; }

p.warning, sup { font-size: x-small;
   color: red; }
```

FIGURE 13-38. External style sheets contain only CSS rules and comments in a plain-text document.

There are two ways to apply an external style sheet: the **link** element and an **@import** rule. Let's look at both of these attachment methods.

Using the link Element

The **link** element defines a relationship between the current document and an external resource. By far, its most popular use is to link to style sheets. The **link** element goes in the **head** of the document, as shown here:

```
<head>
  <title>Titles are required.</title>
  <link rel="stylesheet" href="/path/stylesheet.css">
</head>
```

You need to include two attributes in the **link** element:

EXERCISE 13-8.
Making an external style sheet

It is OK to use an embedded style sheet while designing a page, but it is probably best moved to an external style sheet once the design is finished so it can be reused by multiple documents in the site. We'll do just that for the summer menu style sheet.

1. Open the latest version of *summer-menu.html*. Select and cut all of the rules within the **style** element, but leave the **<style>...</style>** tags because we'll be using them in a moment.

2. Create a new plain ASCII text document and paste all of the style rules. Make sure that no markup got in there by accident.

3. Save this document as *menustyles.css* in the same directory as the *summer-menu.html* document.

4. Now, back in *summer-menu.html*, add an **@import** rule to attach the external style sheet:

   ```
   <style>
   @import url(menustyles.css);
   </style>
   ```

   Save the file and reload it in the browser. It should look exactly the same as it did when the style sheet was embedded. If not, go back and make sure that everything matches the examples.

5. Delete the whole **style** element, and this time we'll add the style sheet with a **link** element in the **head** of the document.

   ```
   <link rel="stylesheet"
   href="menustyles.css">
   ```

   Again, test your work by saving the document and taking a look at it in the browser.

`rel="stylesheet"`

Defines the linked document's relation to the current document. The value of the **rel** attribute is always **stylesheet** when you are linking to a style sheet.

`href="`*`url`*`"`

Provides the location of the *.css* file.

You can include multiple **link** elements to different style sheets, and they'll all apply. If there are conflicts, whichever one is listed last will override previous settings, because of the rule order and the cascade.

Importing with @import

The other method for attaching an external style sheet to a document is to import it with an **@import** rule. The **@import** at-rule is another type of rule you can add to a style sheet, either in an external *.css* style sheet document, or right in the **style** element, as shown in the following example:

```
<head>
  <style>
    @import url("/path/stylesheet.css");
    p { font-face: Verdana;}
  </style>
  <title>Titles are required.</title>
</head>
```

In this example, a relative URL is shown, but it could also be an absolute URL (beginning with **http://**). The **@import** rule must go at the beginning of the style sheet *before any selectors*. You can import more than one style sheet, and they all will apply, but rules from the last style sheet listed take precedence over earlier ones.

You can also limit a style sheet's import to specific media types (such as screen, print, or projection, to name a few) or viewing environments (orientation, screen size, etc.) using media queries. Media queries are a method for applying styles based on the medium used to display the document. They appear after the **@import** rule in a comma-separated list. For example, if you have created a style sheet that should be imported and used only when the document is printed, use this rule:

```
@import url(print_styles.css) print;
```

Or to serve a special style sheet just for small devices, you could also query the viewport:

```
@import url(small_device.css) screen and (max-width: 320px;);
```

We'll talk a lot more about media queries in **Chapter 17, Responsive Web Design**, but I mention them here as they are relevant to importing style sheets.

You can try both the **link** and **@import** methods in EXERCISE 13-8.

Using Modular Style Sheets

Because you can compile information from multiple external style sheets, modular style sheets have become a popular technique for style management. Many developers keep styles they frequently reuse—such as typography treatments, layout rules, or form-related styles—in separate style sheets, then combine them in mix-and-match fashion using **@import** rules. Again, the **@import** rules need to go before rules that use selectors.

Here's an example of a style sheet that imports multiple external style sheets:

```
/* basic typography */
@import url("type.css");

/* form inputs */
@import url("forms.css");

/* navigation */
@import url("list-nav.css");

/* site-specific styles */
body { background: orange; }

/* more style rules */
```

This is a good technique to keep in mind as you build experience in creating sites. You'll find that there are some solutions that work well for you, and it is nice not to have to reinvent the wheel for every new site. Modular style sheets are a good time-saving and organizational device; however, they can be a problem for performance and caching.

If you use this method, it is recommended that you compile all of the styles into a single document before delivering them to a browser. Not to worry, you don't need to do it manually; there are tools out there that will do it for you. The LESS and Sass CSS preprocessors (which will be formally introduced in **Chapter 20**) are just two tools that offer compiling functionality.

NOTE

You can also supply the URL without the **url()** *notation:*

> @import "/path/style.css";

Again, absolute pathnames, beginning at the root, will ensure that the .css document will always be found.

WRAPPING IT UP

We've covered a lot of ground (or *background*, to be more accurate) in this chapter. We looked at ways to set the foreground and background colors for an element by using various numeric systems and color names. We looked at options for adjusting the level of transparency with the **opacity** property and RGBa, and HSLa color spaces. We spent a long time exploring the various ways to add a background image and adjust how it repeats, where the origin image is placed, and how it is sized. We saw how linear and radial gradients can be used as background images as well. Along the way, you picked up pseudo-class, pseudo-element, and attribute selectors and looked at ways to attach external style sheets. I think that's enough for one chapter! See how much you remember with this little quiz.

TEST YOURSELF

This time I'll test your background prowess entirely with matching and multiple-choice questions. Answers appear in **Appendix A**.

1. Which of these areas gets filled with a background color by default?

    a. The area behind the content

    b. Any padding added around the content

    c. The area under the border

    d. The margin space around the element

    e. All of the above

    f. a and b

    g. a, b, and c

2. Which of these is *not* a way to specify the color white in CSS?

    a. `#FFFFFF`

    b. `#FFF`

    c. `rgb(255, 255, 255)`

    d. `rgb(FF, FF, FF)`

    e. `white`

    f. `rgb(100%, 100%, 100%)`

3. Match the pseudo-class with the elements it targets.

    a. `a:link`   1. Links that have already been clicked

    b. `a:visited`   2. An element that is highlighted and ready for input

    c. `a:hover`   3. An element that is the first child element of its parent

    d. `a:active`   4. A link with the mouse pointer over it

    e. `:focus`   5. Links that have not yet been visited

    f. `:first-child`   6. A link that is in the process of being clicked

4. Match the following rules with their respective samples as shown in FIGURE 13-39. All of the samples in the figure use the same source document, consisting of one paragraph element to which some padding and a border have been applied.

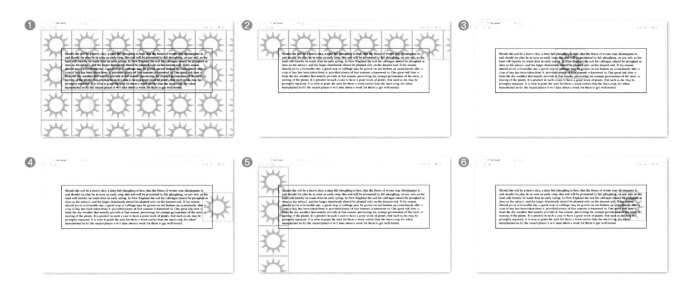

FIGURE 13-39. Samples for Question 4.

a. ```
body {
    background-image: url(graphic.gif);
}
```

b. ```
p {
    background-image: url(graphic.gif);
    background-repeat: no-repeat;
    background-position: 50% 0%;
}
```

c. ```
body {
    background-image: url(graphic.gif);
    background-repeat: repeat-x;
}
```

d. ```
p {
    background: url(graphic.gif) no-repeat right center;
}
```

e. ```
body {
    background-image: url(graphic.gif);
    background-repeat: repeat-y;
}
```

f. ```
body {
    background: url(graphic.gif) no-repeat right center;
}
```

CSS REVIEW: COLOR AND BACKGROUND PROPERTIES

Here is a summary of the properties covered in this chapter, in alphabetical order.

Property	Description
background	Shorthand property that combines background properties
background-attachment	Specifies whether the background image scrolls or is fixed
background-clip	Specifies how far the background image should extend
background-color	Specifies the background color for an element
background-image	Provides the location of an image to use as a background
background-origin	Determines how the **background-position** is calculated (from edge of border, padding, or content box)
background-position	Specifies the location of the origin background image
background-repeat	Specifies whether and how a background image repeats (tiles)
background-size	Specifies the size of the background image
color	Specifies the foreground (text and border) color
opacity	Specifies the transparency level of the foreground and background

THINKING INSIDE THE BOX

In **Chapter 11, Introducing Cascading Style Sheets,** I described the box model as one of the fundamental concepts of CSS. According to the box model, every element in a document generates a box to which properties such as width, height, padding, borders, and margins can be applied. You probably already have a feel for how element boxes work from adding backgrounds to elements. This chapter covers all the box-related properties, beginning with an overview of the components of an element box, and then taking on the box properties from the inside out: content dimensions, padding, borders, and margins.

THE ELEMENT BOX

As we've seen, every element in a document, both block-level and inline, generates a rectangular element box. The components of an element box are diagrammed in FIGURE 14-1. Pay attention to the new terminology—it will be helpful in keeping things straight later in the chapter.

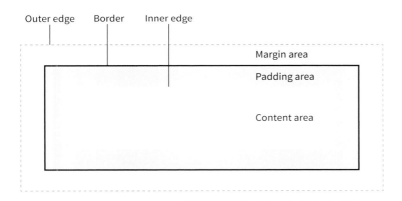

FIGURE 14-1. The parts of an element box according to the CSS box model.

Content area

At the core of the element box is the content itself. In FIGURE 14-1, the content area is indicated by a white box.

Inner edges

The edges of the content area are referred to as the inner edges of the element box. Although the inner edges are made distinct by a color change in FIGURE 14-1, in real pages, the edge of the content area is invisible.

Padding

The padding is the area between the content area and an optional border. In the diagram, the padding area is indicated by a yellow-orange color. Padding is optional.

Border

The border is a line (or stylized line) that surrounds the element and its padding. Borders are also optional.

Margin

The margin is an optional amount of space added on the *outside* of the border. In the diagram, the margin is indicated with light-blue shading, but in reality, margins are always transparent, allowing the background of the parent element to show through.

Outer edge

The outside edges of the margin area make up the outer edges of the element box. This is the total area the element takes up on the page, and it includes the width of the content area plus the total amount of padding, border, and margins applied to the element. The outer edge in the diagram is indicated with a dotted line, but in real web pages, the edge of the margin is invisible.

All elements have these box components; however, as you will see, some properties behave differently based on whether the element is block or inline. In fact, we'll see some of those differences right away as we look at box dimensions.

SPECIFYING BOX DIMENSIONS

`width`

Values:	*length* | *percentage* | auto
Default:	auto
Applies to:	block-level elements and replaced inline elements (such as images)
Inherits:	no

> The amount of space taken up by an element on the page includes the content plus the total amount of padding, borders, and margins applied to the element.

`height`

Values:	*length*	*percentage*	auto
Default:	auto
Applies to:	block-level elements and replaced inline elements (such as images)
Inherits:	no

`box-sizing`

Values:	content-box	border-box
Default:	content-box
Applies to:	all elements
Inherits:	no

By default, the width and height of a block element are calculated automatically by the browser (thus the default **auto** value). The box will be as wide as the browser window or other containing block element, and as tall as necessary to fit the content. However, you can use the **width** and **height** properties to make the content area of an element a specific width or height.

Unfortunately, setting box dimensions is not as simple as just dropping those properties in your style sheet. You have to know exactly which part of the element box you are sizing.

There are two ways to specify the size of an element. The default method—introduced way back in CSS1—applies the width and height values to the *content box*. That means that the resulting size of the element will be the dimensions you specify *plus* the amount of padding and borders that have been added to the element. The other method—introduced as part of the **box-sizing** property in CSS3—applies the width and height values to the *border box*, which includes the content, padding, and border. With this method, the resulting visible element box, including padding and borders, will be exactly the dimensions you specify. We're going to get familiar with both methods in this section.

Regardless of the method you choose, you can specify the width and height only for block-level elements and non-text inline elements such as images. The **width** and **height** properties do not apply to inline text (non-replaced) elements and are ignored by the browser. In other words, you cannot specify the width and height of an anchor (**a**) or **strong** element (see **Note**).

Sizing the Content Box

By default (that is, if you do not include a **box-sizing** rule in your styles), the **width** and **height** properties are applied to the content box. That is the way all current browsers interpret width and height values, but you can explicitly specify this behavior by setting **box-sizing: content-box**.

BROWSER SUPPORT TIP

The major browsers began supporting the **box-sizing** *property in 2011 and 2012. For browsers released prior to that (Chrome <10, Safari <5.1, Safari iOS <5.1, or Android <4.3), there is the prefixed version* **-webkit-box-sizing***, but at this point, the prefix is considered no longer necessary. Internet Explorer 6 and 7 do not support* **box-sizing** *at all, but they are fairly extinct.*

NOTE

Actually, there is a way to apply **width** *and* **height** *properties to inline elements such as anchors (***a***): by forcing them to behave as block elements with the* **display** *property, covered at the end of this chapter.*

In the following example and in FIGURE 14-2, a simple box is given a width of 500 pixels and a height of 150 pixels, with 20 pixels of padding, a 5-pixel border, and a 20-pixel margin all around. In the default content box model, the **width** and **height** values are applied to the *content area only*.

```
p {
    background: #f2f5d5;
    width: 500px;
    height: 150px;
    padding: 20px;
    border: 5px solid gray;
    margin: 20px;
}
```

The resulting width of the *visible* element box ends up being 550 pixels: the content plus 40px padding (20px left and right) and 10px of border (5px left and right).

Visible element box =

5px + 20px + 500px width **+ 20px + 5px = 550 pixels**

When you throw in 40 pixels of margin, the width of the *entire* element box is 590 pixels. Knowing the resulting size of your elements is critical to getting layouts to behave predictably.

Element box =

20px + 5px + 20px + 500px width **+ 20px + 5px + 20px = 590 pixels**

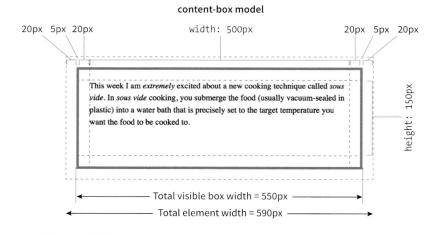

FIGURE 14-2. Specifying the **width** and **height** with the **content-box** model.

Using the border-box Model

The other way to specify the size of an element is to apply width and height dimensions to the entire visible box, including the padding and border. Because this is not the default browser behavior, you need to explicitly set **box-sizing: border-box** in the style sheet.

Let's look at the same paragraph example from the previous section and see what happens when we make it 500 pixels using the **border-box** method (FIGURE 14-3). All other style declarations for the box stay the same.

```
p {
  …
  box-sizing: border-box;
  width: 500px;
  height: 150px;
}
```

Now the width of the visible box is 500 pixels (compare to 550 pixels in the content-box model), and the total element widh is 540px. Many developers find the **border-box** model to be a more intuitive way to size elements. It is particularly helpful for specifying widths in percentages, which is a cornerstone of responsive design. For example, you can make two columns 50% wide and know that they will fit next to each other without having to mess around with adding calculated padding and border widths to the mix (although you still need to account for margins).

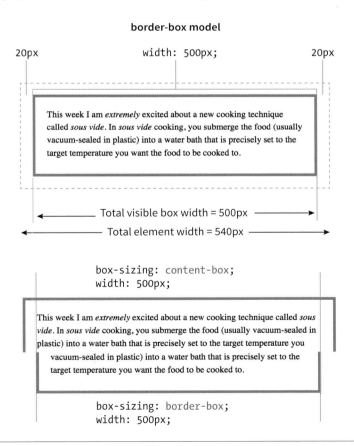

FIGURE 14-3. Sizing an element with the **border-box** method. The bottom diagram compares the resulting boxes from each sizing method.

In fact, many developers simply set *everything* in the document to use the **border-box** model by setting it on the root (**html**) element, then setting all other elements to inherit, like this:

```
html {box-sizing: border-box;}

*, *:before, *:after {box-sizing: inherit;}
```

For more information on this technique, read Chris Coyier's article "Inheriting box-sizing Probably Slightly Better Best-Practice" (*css-tricks.com/inheriting-box-sizing-probably-slightly-better-best-practice*).

Specifying Height

The **height** property works just the same as **width**. In general practice, it is less common to specify the height of elements. It is more in keeping with the nature of the medium to allow the height to be calculated automatically, allowing the element box to change based on the font size, user settings, or other factors. If you do specify a height for an element containing text, be sure to also consider what happens should the content not fit. Fortunately, CSS gives you some options, as we'll see in the next section.

Handling Overflow

When an element is sized too small for its contents, you can specify what to do with the content that doesn't fit by using the **overflow** property.

overflow

Values:	visible | hidden | scroll | auto
Default:	visible
Applies to:	block-level elements and replaced inline elements (such as images)
Inherits:	no

FIGURE 14-4 demonstrates the predefined values for **overflow**. In the figure, the various values are applied to an element that is 150 pixels square. The background color makes the edges of the content area apparent.

visible

> The default value is **visible**, which allows the content to hang out over the element box so that it all can be seen.

hidden

> When **overflow** is set to **hidden**, the content that does not fit gets clipped off and does not appear beyond the edges of the element's content area.

scroll

> When **scroll** is specified, scrollbars are added to the element box to let users scroll through the content. Be aware that they may become

---

Maximum and Minimum Dimensions

If you want to set a limit on the size of a block element, use the **max-** and **min-** width and height properties.

max-height, max-width, min-height, min-width

Values: *length* | *percentage* | none

These properties work with block-level and replaced elements (like images) only. When the **content-box** model is used, the value applies to the content area only, so if you apply padding, borders, or margins, it will make the overall element box larger, even if a **max-width** or **max-height** property has been specified. Note also that IE8 does not support **box-sizing** on elements with **max-/min-** sizes.

WARNING

*Avoid using **max-** and **min-** widths and heights with the **border-box** model. They are known to cause browser problems.*

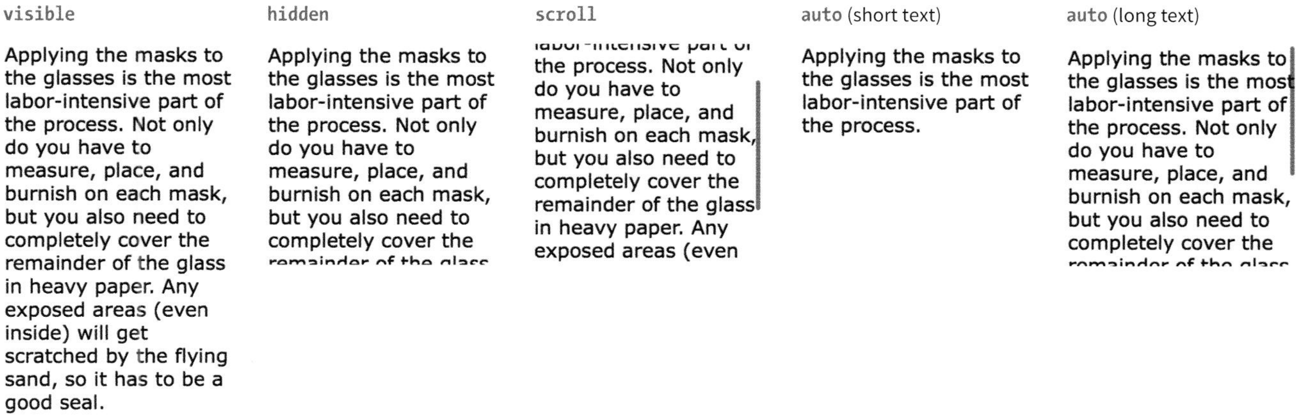

visible	hidden	scroll	auto (short text)	auto (long text)
Applying the masks to the glasses is the most labor-intensive part of the process. Not only do you have to measure, place, and burnish on each mask, but you also need to completely cover the remainder of the glass in heavy paper. Any exposed areas (even inside) will get scratched by the flying sand, so it has to be a good seal.	Applying the masks to the glasses is the most labor-intensive part of the process. Not only do you have to measure, place, and burnish on each mask, but you also need to completely cover the remainder of the glass	labor-intensive part of the process. Not only do you have to measure, place, and burnish on each mask, but you also need to completely cover the remainder of the glass in heavy paper. Any exposed areas (even	Applying the masks to the glasses is the most labor-intensive part of the process.	Applying the masks to the glasses is the most labor-intensive part of the process. Not only do you have to measure, place, and burnish on each mask, but you also need to completely cover the remainder of the glass

FIGURE 14-4. Options for handling content overflow. The scroll and auto options have narrow gray scrollbars to the right of the text (as rendered on macOS).

visible only when you click the element to scroll it. There is an issue with this value on old iOS (<4), Android (<2.3), and a few other older mobile browsers, so it may be worthwhile to use a simpler alternative to `overflow:scroll` for mobile.

auto

The **auto** value allows the browser to decide how to handle overflow. In most cases, scrollbars are added only when the content doesn't fit and they are needed.

PADDING

Padding is the space between the content area and the border (or the place the border would be if one isn't specified). I find it helpful to add padding to elements when using a background color or a border. It gives the content a little breathing room, and prevents the border or edge of the background from bumping right up against the text.

You can add padding to the individual sides of any element (block-level or inline). There is also a shorthand **padding** property that lets you add padding on all sides at once.

Padding is the space between the content and the border.

`padding-top`, `padding-right`, `padding-bottom`, `padding-left`

Values:	*length* | *percentage*
Default:	0
Applies to:	all elements
Inherits:	no

```
padding
```

Values: *length | percentage*

Default: 0

Applies to: all elements

Inherits: no

The **padding-top**, **padding-right**, **padding-bottom**, and **padding-left** proper-ties specify an amount of padding for each side of an element, as shown in this example and FIGURE 14-5 (note that I've also added a background color to make the outer edges of the padding area apparent).

```
blockquote {
   padding-top: 2em;
   padding-right: 4em;
   padding-bottom: 2em;
   padding-left: 4em;
   background-color: #D098D4; /* light green */
}
```

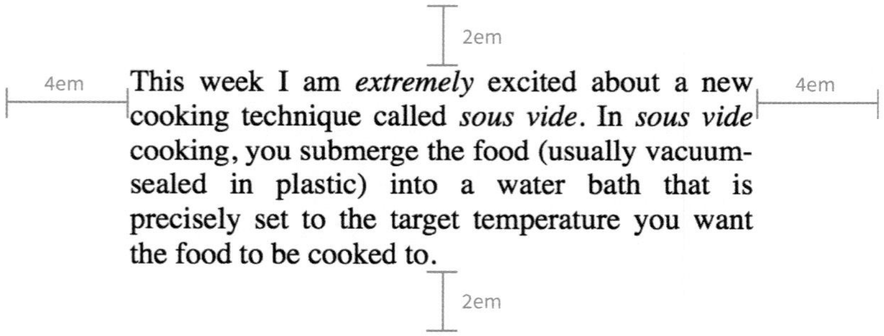

FIGURE 14-5. Adding padding around the content of an element.

Specify padding in any of the CSS length units (**em** and **px** are the most com-mon) or as a percentage of the *width* of the parent element. Yes, the parent's width is used as the basis, even for top and bottom padding. If the width of the parent element changes, so will the padding values on all sides of the child element, which makes percentage values somewhat tricky to manage.

The Shorthand padding Property

As an alternative to setting padding one side at a time, you can use the short-hand **padding** property to add padding all around the element. The syntax is interesting; you can specify four, three, two, or one value for a single **padding** property. Let's see how that works, starting with four values.

When you supply four **padding** values, they are applied to each side in *clockwise* order, starting at the top. Some people use the mnemonic device "TRouBLe" for the order *Top Right Bottom Left*. This is a common syntax for applying shorthand values in CSS, so take a careful look:

```
padding: top right bottom left;
```

Using the **padding** property, we could reproduce the padding specified with the four individual properties in the previous example like this:

```
blockquote {
  padding: 2em 4em 2em 4em;
  background-color: #D098D4;
}
```

If the left and right padding are the same, you can shorten it by supplying only three values. The value for "right" (the second value in the string) will be mirrored and used for "left" as well. It is as though the browser assumes the "left" value is missing, so it just uses the "right" value on both sides. The syntax for three values is as follows:

```
padding: top right/left bottom;
```

This rule would be equivalent to the previous example because the padding on both the left and right edges of the element is set to 4em:

```
blockquote {
  padding: 2em 4em 2em;
  background-color: #D098D4;
}
```

Continuing with this pattern, if you provide only two values, the first one is used for the top and the bottom edges, and the second one is used for the left and right edges:

```
padding: top/bottom right/left;
```

Again, the same effect achieved by the previous two examples could be accomplished with this rule:

```
blockquote {
  padding: 2em 4em;
  background-color: #D098D4;
}
```

Note that all of the previous examples have the same visual effect as shown in FIGURE 14-5.

Finally, if you provide just one value, it will be applied to all four sides of the element. This declaration applies 15 pixels of padding on all sides of a **div** element:

```
div#announcement {
  padding: 15px;
  border: 1px solid;
}
```

Get a feel for adding padding to elements in EXERCISE 14-1.

■ **AT A GLANCE**

Shorthand Values

1 value

`padding: 10px;`

Applied to all sides.

2 values

`padding: 10px 6px;`

First is top and bottom; second is left and right.

3 values

`padding: 10px 6px 4px;`

First is top; second is left and right; third is bottom.

4 values

`padding: 10px 6px 4px 10px;`

Applied clockwise to top, right, bottom, and left edges consecutively (TRBL).

EXERCISE 14-1. Adding a little padding

In this exercise, we'll begin adding box properties to improve the appearance of a site for the fictional Black Goose Bakery. I've given you a head start by marking up the source (*bakery.html*). Unlike pages in previous exercises, the bakery page uses an external style sheet, *bakery-styles.css*. Everything we will be doing to format this site over the next few chapters happens in the CSS file, so you should never need edit the HTML document; however, that is the file you will open in the browser to see the results of your style changes. All the files are available at *learningwebdesign.com/5e/materials*.

FIGURE 14-6 shows before and after shots of the site. It's going to take several exercises over three chapters to get there, and padding is just the beginning. In **Chapter 16, CSS Layout with Flexbox and Grid**, we'll turn that ugly navigation list into a nice navigation menu bar (in the meantime, please avert your eyes) and give the page a two-column layout suitable for larger screens.

NOTE

This design uses a Google web font called Stint. You will need to have an internet connection in order to see it. If you are working offline, you will see Georgia or some serif font instead, which is just fine for these purposes, but your page won't look exactly like the ones in the figures.

Start by getting familiar with the source document. Open *bakery.html* in a browser and a text editor to see what you've got to work with. The style sheet has been added with an **@import** rule in the **style** element. The document has been marked up with **header** (including a **nav** section), **main**, **aside**, and **footer** sections.

Now take a look at *bakery-styles.css* in your text editor. I used comments in the style sheet to organize the styles related to each section (bonus points for you if you keep the styles organized as you go along!). You will find styles for text formatting, colors, and backgrounds—all properties that we've covered so far in this book, so they should look familiar. Now let's add some rules to *bakery-styles.css* to add padding to the elements.

FIGURE 14-6. Before and after shots of the Black Goose Bakery site.

1. The first thing we'll do is to set the **box-sizing** model to **border-box** for all the elements in the document. Add these new rules to the existing **style** element. This will make measurements simpler going forward.

```
html {
    box-sizing: border-box;
}
* {
    box-sizing: inherit;
}
```

2. Now find the styles for the **header** and give it a height. It will fill 100% of the width of the page by default, so the width is taken care of. I picked 15em for the height because it seemed tall enough to accommodate the content and show a nice amount of the croissant background image, but you can play around with it.

```
header {
    …
    height: 15em;
}
```

3. The **main** section is going to need a little padding, so add 1em of padding on all sides. You can add this declaration after the existing **main** styles.

```
main {
    …
    padding: 1em;
}
```

4. Next, we'll get a little fancier with the **aside** element ("Hours"). We'll need extra padding on the left side for the tiling scallop background image to be visible. There are several approaches to applying different padding amounts to each side, but I'm going to do it in a way that gives you experience deliberately overriding earlier declarations.

Use the **padding** shorthand property to add 1em of padding on all sides of the **aside** element. Then write a second declaration that adds 45 pixels of padding on just the left side. Because the **padding-left** declaration comes second, it will override the 1em setting applied with the shorthand.

```
aside {
    …
    padding: 1em;
    padding-left: 45px;
}
```

5. Finally, that footer is looking skinny and cramped. Let's add padding, which will increase the height of the footer and give the content some space.

```
footer {
    …
    padding: 1em;
}
```

6. Save the *bakery-styles.css* document, and then open (or reload) *bakery.html* in the browser to see the result of your work. The changes at this point are pretty subtle. FIGURE 14-7 highlights the padding additions.

FIGURE 14-7. The shaded areas indicate the padding added to **main** (blue), **aside** (pink), and **footer** (yellow). Colors added for demo purposes but wouldn't render in the browser.

BORDERS

A border is simply a line drawn around the content area and its (optional) padding. You can choose from eight border styles and make them any width and color you like. Borders can be applied all around the element or just on a particular side or sides. CSS3 introduced properties for rounding the corners or applying images to borders. We'll start our border exploration with the various border styles.

Border Style

The style is the most important of the border properties because, according to the CSS specification, if there is no border style specified, the border does not exist (the default is **none**). In other words, you must always declare the style of the border, or the other border properties will be ignored.

Border styles can be applied one side at a time or with the shorthand **border-style** property.

`border-top-style`, `border-right-style`,
`border-bottom-style`, `border-left-style`

Values:	none | solid | hidden | dotted | dashed | double | groove | ridge | inset | outset
Default:	none
Applies to:	all elements
Inherits:	no

`border-style`

Values:	none | solid | hidden | dotted | dashed | double | groove | ridge | inset | outset
Default:	none
Applies to:	all elements
Inherits:	no

The value of the **border-style** property is one of 10 keywords describing the available border styles, as shown in FIGURE 14-8. The value **hidden** is equivalent to **none**.

Use the side-specific border style properties (**border-top-style**, **border-right-style**, **border-bottom-style**, and **border-left-style**) to apply a style to one side of the element. If you do not specify a width, the default medium width will be used. If there is no color specified, the border uses the foreground color of the element (same as the text).

In the following example, I've applied a different style to each side of an element to show the single-side border properties in action (FIGURE 14-9).

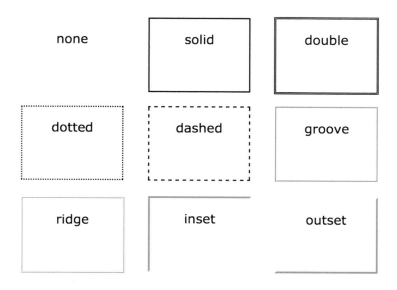

FIGURE 14-8. The available border styles (shown at the default medium width).

```
div#silly {
  border-top-style: solid;
  border-right-style: dashed;
  border-bottom-style: double;
  border-left-style: dotted;
  width: 300px;
  height: 100px;
}
```

The **border-style** shorthand property works on the clockwise (TRouBLe) system described for **padding** earlier. You can supply four values for all four sides or fewer values when the left/right and top/bottom borders are the same. The silly border effect in the previous example could also be specified with the **border-style** property as shown here, and the result would be the same as shown in FIGURE 14-9:

```
border-style: solid dashed double dotted;
```

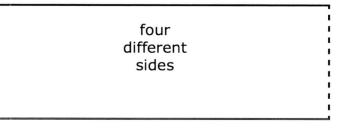

FIGURE 14-9. Border styles applied to individual sides of an element.

Border Width (Thickness)

Use one of the **border-width** properties to specify the thickness of the border. Once again, you can target each side of the element with a single-side property, or specify several sides at once in clockwise order with the shorthand **border-width** property.

border-top-width, border-right-width,
border-bottom-width, border-left-width

Values:	*length* | thin | medium | thick
Default:	medium
Applies to:	all elements
Inherits:	no

border-width

Values:	*length* | thin | medium | thick
Default:	medium
Applies to:	all elements
Inherits:	no

The most common way to specify the width of borders is using a pixel or em measurement; however, you can also specify one of the keywords (**thin**, **medium**, or **thick**) and leave the rendering up to the browser.

I've included a mix of values in this example (FIGURE 14-10). Notice that I've also included the **border-style** property because if I didn't, the border would not render at all:

```
div#help {
  border-top-width: thin;
  border-right-width: medium;
  border-bottom-width: thick;
  border-left-width: 12px;
  border-style: solid;
  width: 300px;
  height: 100px;
}
```

or:

```
div#help {
  border-width: thin medium thick 12px;
  border-style: solid;
  width: 300px;
  height: 100px;
}
```

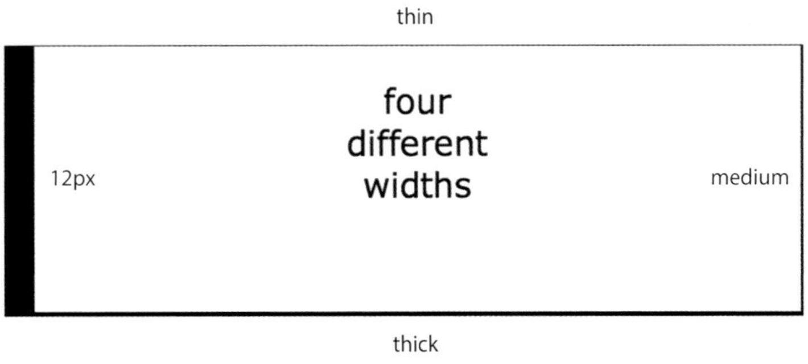

FIGURE 14-10. Specifying the width of borders.

Border Color

Border colors are specified in the same way: via the side-specific properties or the **border-color** shorthand property. When you specify a border color, it overrides the foreground color as set by the **color** property for the element.

`border-top-color, border-right-color,`
`border-bottom-color, border-left-color`

Values:	*color name* or *RGB/HSL value* | transparent
Default:	the value of the color property for the element
Applies to:	all elements
Inherits:	no

`border-color`

Values:	*color name* or *RGB/HSL value* | transparent
Default:	the value of the color property for the element
Applies to:	all elements
Inherits:	no

You know all about specifying color values, and you should be getting used to the shorthand properties as well, so I'll keep this example short and sweet (FIGURE 14-11). Here, I've provided two values for the shorthand **border-color** property to make the top and bottom of a **div** maroon and the left and right sides aqua:

```
div#special {
   border-color: maroon aqua;
   border-style: solid;
   border-width: 6px;
   width: 300px;
   height: 100px;
}
```

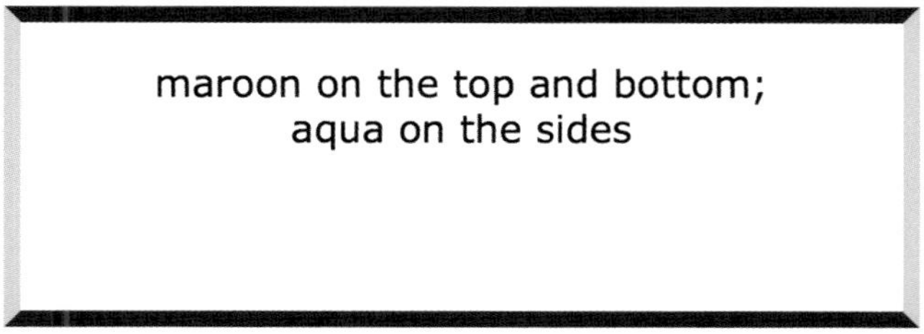

> **■ DESIGN TIP**
>
> Setting **border-color** to **transparent** allows the background to show through the border, yet holds the width of the border as specified. This may be useful when you're creating rollover (**:hover**) effects with borders, because the space where the border will appear is maintained even when the mouse is not over the element.

> maroon on the top and bottom;
> aqua on the sides

FIGURE 14-11. Specifying the color of borders.

Outlines are a good tool for checking your page layout as you work.

CSS Outlines

Another type of rule you can draw around an element is an outline. Outlines look like borders, and the syntax is the same, but there is an important difference. Outlines, unlike borders, are not calculated in the width of the element box. They just lay on top, not interfering with anything. Outlines are drawn on the outside edge of the border (if one is specified) and overlap the margin.

Because outlines do not affect layout, they're a great tool for checking your design. You can turn them on and off without affecting width measurements to see where and how element boxes are positioned.

The outline properties are similar to border properties with one important difference: It is not possible to specify outlines for particular sides of the element box—it's all or nothing.

outline-style

Values:	auto | solid | none | dotted | dashed | double | groove | ridge | inset | outset
Default:	none

These are the same as the **border-style** values, with the addition of **auto**, which lets the browser choose the style. Also, you cannot set the **outline-style** to **hidden**.

outline-width

Values:	*length* | thin | medium | thick
Default:	medium

Same as **border-width** values.

outline-color

Values:	*color name* or *RGB/HSL value* | invert
Default:	invert

The default **invert** value applies the inverse of the background color to the outline, but it has very little browser support.

outline-offset

Values:	*length*
Default:	0

By default, the outline is drawn just outside the border edge. **outline-offset** moves the outline beyond the border by a specified length.

outline

Values:	*outline-style outline-width outline-color*
Default:	Defaults of individual properties

The shorthand **outline** property combines values for **outline-style**, **outline-width**, and **outline-color**. Remember that you can specify them only for all sides of the element at once.

```
div#story { outline: 2px dashed red; }
```

Combining Style, Width, and Color

The authors of CSS didn't skimp when it came to border shortcuts. They also created properties for providing style, width, and color values in one declaration, one side at a time. You can specify the appearance of specific sides, or use the **border** property to change all four sides at once.

border-top, border-right, border-bottom, border-left

Values:	*border-style border-width border-color*
Default:	defaults for each property
Applies to:	all elements
Inherits:	no

border

Values:	*border-style border-width border-color*
Default:	defaults for each property
Applies to:	all elements
Inherits:	no

The values for **border** and the side-specific border properties may include style, width, and color values in any order. You do not need to declare all three, but if the border style value is omitted, no border will render.

The **border** shorthand property works a bit differently than the other shorthand properties that we've covered in that it takes one set of values and always applies them to all four sides of the element. In other words, it does not use the clockwise TRBL system that we've seen with other shorthand properties.

Here is a smattering of valid border shortcut examples to give you an idea of how they work:

```
h1 { border-left: red .5em solid; }     /* left border only */
h2 { border-bottom: 1px solid; }         /* bottom border only */
p.example { border: 2px dotted #663; }   /* all four sides */
```

Rounded Corners with border-radius

Perhaps you'd like your element boxes to look a little softer and rounder. Well, then, the **border-radius** property is for you! There are individual corner properties as well as a **border-radius** shorthand.

border-top-left-radius, border-top-right-radius, border-bottom-right-radius, border-bottom-left-radius

Values:	*length*	*percentage*
Default:	0
Applies to:	all elements
Inherits:	no

```
p {
  width: 200px;
  height: 100px;
  background: darkorange;
}
```

border-radius: 1em;

border-radius: 50px;

border-top-right-radius: 50px;

border-top-left-radius: 1em;
border-top-right-radius: 2em;
border-bottom-right-radius: 1em;
border-bottom-left: 2em;

FIGURE 14-12. Make the corners of element boxes rounded with the **border-radius** properties.

border-radius

Values:	*1, 2, 3, or 4 length or percentage values*
Default:	0
Applies to:	all elements
Inherits:	no

To round off the corner of an element, simply apply one of the **border-radius** properties, but keep in mind that you will see the result only if the element has a border or background color. Values are typically provided in ems or pixels. Percentages are allowed and are nice for keeping the curve proportional to the box should it resize, but you may run into some browser inconsistencies.

You can target the corners individually or use the shorthand **border-radius** property. If you provide one value for **border-radius**, it is applied to all four corners. Four values are applied clockwise, starting in the top-left corner (top-left, top-right, bottom-right, bottom-left). When you supply two values, the first one is used for top-left and bottom-right, and the second is for the other two corners.

Compare the **border-radius** values to the resulting boxes in FIGURE 14-12. You can achieve many different effects, from slightly softened corners to a long capsule shape, depending on how you set the values.

BROWSER SUPPORT NOTE

*All browsers have been supporting **border-radius** properties using the standard syntax (that is, without prefixes) since about 2010. There are prefixed properties for Firefox <3.6 and Safari <5.0, but they're so old it's probably not worth worrying about. Internet Explorer 8 and earlier, however, do not support **border-radius** at all. But in this case, chances are the usability of your site doesn't depend on rounded corners, so this is a good opportunity to practice progressive enhancement: non-supporting browsers get perfectly acceptable square corners, and all modern browsers get a little something extra.*

Elliptical corners

So far, the corners we've made are sections of perfect circles, but you can also make a corner elliptical by specifying two values: the first for the horizontal radius and the second for the vertical radius (see FIGURE 14-13, Ⓐ and Ⓑ).

Ⓐ border-top-right-radius: 100px 50px;

Ⓑ border-top-right-radius: 50px 20px;
    border-top-left-radius: 50px 20px;

If you want to use the shorthand property, the horizontal and vertical radii get separated by a slash (otherwise, they'd be confused for different corner values). The following example sets the horizontal radius on all corners to 60px and the vertical radius to 40px (FIGURE 14-13, Ⓒ):

Ⓒ border-radius: 60px / 40px;

If you want to see something really nutty, take a look at a **border-radius** shorthand property that specifies a different ellipse for each of the four corners. All of the horizontal values are lined up on the left of the slash in clockwise order (top-left, top-right, bottom-right, bottom-left), and all of the corresponding vertical values are lined up on the right (FIGURE 14-13, **D**):

D border-radius: 36px 40px 60px 20px / 12px 10px 30px 36px;

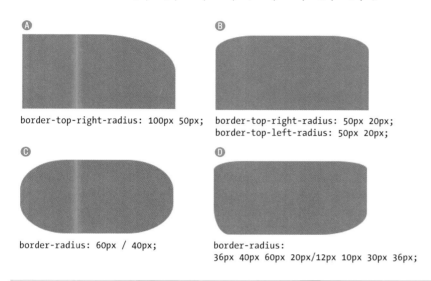

border-top-right-radius: 100px 50px;

border-top-right-radius: 50px 20px;
border-top-left-radius: 50px 20px;

border-radius: 60px / 40px;

border-radius:
36px 40px 60px 20px/12px 10px 30px 36px;

FIGURE 14-13. Applying elliptical corners to boxes.

Now it's time to try your hand at borders. EXERCISE 14-2 will not only give you some practice, but it should also give you some ideas on the ways borders can be used to add visual interest to designs.

EXERCISE 14-2. Border tricks

In this exercise, we'll have some fun with borders on the Black Goose Bakery page. In addition to putting borders around content sections of the page, we'll use borders to beef up the headlines and as an alternative to underlines under links.

1. Open *bakery-styles.css* in a text editor if it isn't already. We'll start with the basics by using the shorthand **border** property to add a tan double rule around the **main** element. Add the new declaration to the existing rule for **main**:

```
main {
    …
    padding: 1em;
    border: double 4px #EADDC4;
}
```

2. Now try out some **border-radius** properties to add generous rounded corners to the **main** and **aside** sections. A 25-pixel radius should do. Pixels are my choice over ems here because I don't want the radius to scale with the text. Start by adding this declaration to the styles for **main**:

```
border-radius: 25px;
```

And give just the top-right corner of the **aside** a matching rounded corner:

```
aside {
    …
    border-top-right-radius: 25px;
}
```

3. Just for fun (and practice), we'll add a decorative border on two sides of the baked goods headings (**h3**). Find the existing rule for **h3** elements and add a declaration that adds a 1-pixel solid rule on the top of the headline. Add another that adds a thicker 3-pixel solid rule on the left. I want the borders to be the same color as the text, so we don't need to specify the **border-color**. Finally, to prevent the text from bumping into the left border, add a little bit of padding (1em) to the left of the headline content:

```
h3 {
  ...
  border-top: 1px solid;
  border-left: 3px solid;
  padding-left: 1em;
}
```

4. The last thing we'll do is to replace the standard underline with a decorative bottom border under links. Start by turning off the underline for all links. Add this rule in the "link styles" section of the style sheet:

```
a {
  text-decoration: none;
}
```

Then add a 1-pixel dotted border to the bottom edge of links:

```
a {
  text-decoration: none;
  border-bottom: 1px dotted;
}
```

As is often the case when you add a border to an element, it is a good idea to also add a little padding to keep things from bumping together:

```
a {
  text-decoration: none;
  border-bottom: 1px dotted;
  padding-bottom: .2em;
}
```

Now you can save the style sheet and reload *bakery.html* in the browser. FIGURE 14-14 shows a detail of how your page should be looking so far.

MUFFINS

Every day, we offer a large selection of muffins, including blueberry, multi-berry, bran, corn, lemon-poppyseed, and chocolate. Our muffins are made from scratch each day. Stop by to see our seasonal muffin flavors!

LEARN MORE ABOUT HOW WE MAKE OUR MUFFINS...

Hours

FIGURE 14-14. The results of our border additions.

Picture-Perfect Borders

CSS3 introduced the **border-image-*** properties, which let you fill in the sides and corners of a border box with an image of your choice, as shown in FIGURE 14-15.

Border images are applied with a collection of five properties:

- **border-image-source** indicates the location of the image
- **border-image-slice** divides the image into nine sections using offset measurements
- **border-image-width** specifies the width of the border area
- **border-image-repeat** specifies whether the image should stretch or repeat along the sides
- **border-image-outset** pushes the border away from the content by the specified amount

There is also a shorthand **border-image** property that combines the individual properties in the following syntax:

```
border-image: source slice / width / outset
repeat;
```

The style rules for the image border in FIGURE 14-15 are as follows:

```
border: 5px solid #d1214a; /* red */
border-image: url(fancyframe.png) 55 fill / 55px /
25px stretch;
```

The **border** shorthand provides a fallback style for the border should the image not load or if the **border-image** isn't supported by the browser.

The **border-image** rule tells the browser to apply the image *fancyframe.png* to the border, slice it **55** pixels from the edges, and use the center of the image to **fill** the center of the box. The width of the border area is **55px**, and the image should be pushed toward the margins by **25px**. Finally, the image areas that make up the sides should **stretch** to fill the width and height of the box.

That's not much of an explanation, I know, but I've written an article, **"Border Images,"** which goes into more detail. You can download it at *learningwebdesign.com/articles/*. For even more information on border images, check out these resources:

- The CSS Background and Borders Module Level 3 (*www.w3.org/TR/css3-background/#the-border-image-source*)
- The **border-image** listing on CSS-Tricks (*css-tricks.com/almanac/properties/b/border-image/*), for a less dense explanation

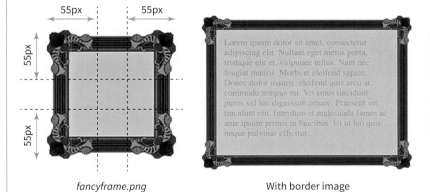

fancyframe.png	With border image	Without border image

FIGURE 14-15. Examples of a border image applied to a box.

■ CSS TIP

Browser Default Margins

You may have noticed that space is added automatically around headings, paragraphs, and other block elements. That's the browser's default style sheet at work, applying margin amounts above and below those elements.

It's good to keep in mind that the browser is applying its own values for margins and padding behind the scenes. These values will be used unless you specifically override them with your own style rules.

If you are working on a design and coming across mysterious amounts of space that you didn't add, the browser's default styles may be the culprit. To troubleshoot, I recommend using your browser's Web Inspector tool, which will show you the source of all the styles applied to the element. Or if you just don't want to worry about browser styles at all, one solution is to reset the padding and margins for all elements to zero, which is discussed in the "CSS Reset" section in **Chapter 19, More CSS Techniques**.

■ POWER TOOL

Centering with auto Margins

Setting the margin to **auto** on the left and right sides of a sized element has the effect of centering the element in its container.

MARGINS

A margin is an optional amount of space that you can add on the outside of the border. Margins keep elements from bumping into one another or the edge of the browser window or viewport.

The side-specific and shorthand **margin** properties work much like the **padding** properties we've looked at already; however, margins have some special behaviors to be aware of.

`margin-top`, `margin-right`, `margin-bottom`, `margin-left`

Values:	*length* | *percentage* | auto
Default:	auto
Applies to:	all elements
Inherits:	no

`margin`

Values:	*length* | *percentage* | auto
Default:	auto
Applies to:	all elements
Inherits:	no

The margin properties are very straightforward to use. You can either specify an amount of margin to appear on each side of the element or use the **margin** property to specify all sides at once.

The shorthand **margin** property works the same as the **padding** shorthand. When you supply four values, they are applied in clockwise order (top, right, bottom, left) to the sides of the element. If you supply three values, the middle value applies to both the left and right sides. When two values are provided, the first is used for the top and bottom, and the second applies to the left and right edges. Finally, one value will be applied to all four sides of the element.

As with most web measurements, ems, pixels, and percentages are the most common ways to specify margins. Be aware, however, that if you specify a percentage value, it is calculated based on the *width* of the parent element. If the parent's width changes, so will the margins on all four sides of the child element (padding has this behavior as well). The **auto** keyword allows the browser to fill in the amount of margin necessary to fit or fill the available space (see **Power Tool** sidebar).

FIGURE 14-16 shows the results of the following margin examples. I've added a red border to the elements in the examples to make their boundaries more clear. The dotted rules were added in the figure illustration to indicate the outer edges of the margins for clarity purposes only, but they are not something you'd see in the browser.

```
Ⓐ  p#A {
       margin: 4em;
       border: 2px solid red;
       background: #e2f3f5;
    }
Ⓑ  p#B {
       margin-top: 2em;
       margin-right: 250px;
       margin-bottom: 1em;
       margin-left: 4em;
       border: 2px solid red;
       background: #e2f3f5;
    }
Ⓒ  body {
       margin: 0 20%;
       border: 3px solid red;
       background-color: #e2f3f5;
    }
```

Adding a margin to the body element adds space between the page content and the edges of the viewport.

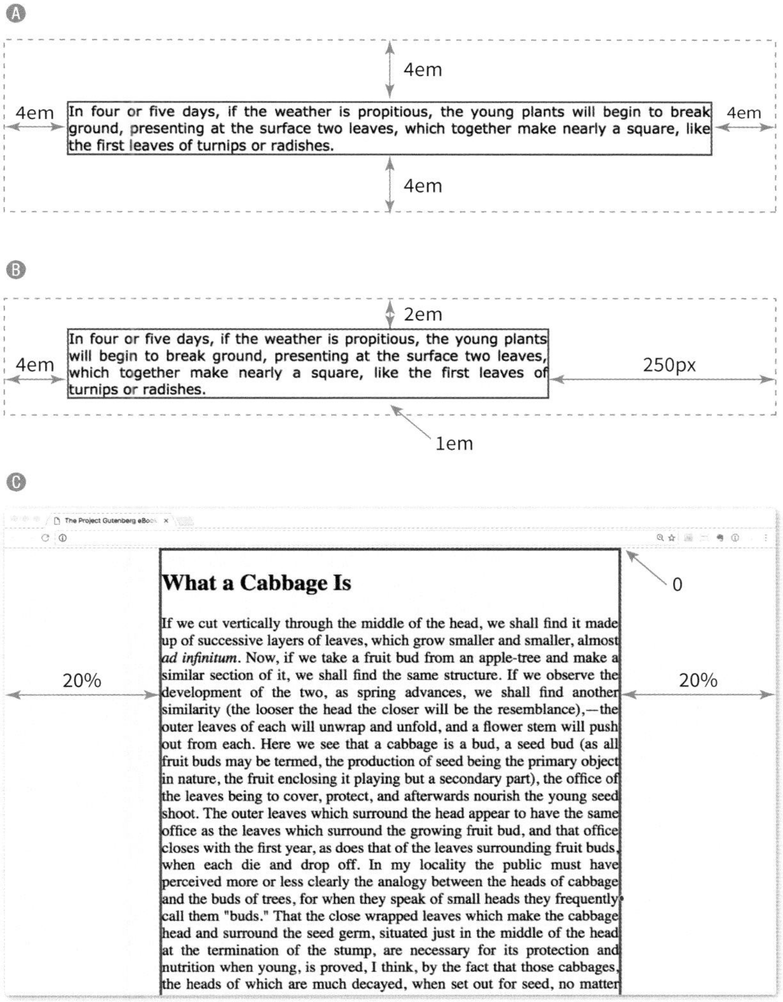

Ⓐ

```
                              4em
    ┌───────────────────────────────────────────────────────┐
4em │ In four or five days, if the weather is propitious, the young plants will begin to break │ 4em
    │ ground, presenting at the surface two leaves, which together make nearly a square, like │
    │ the first leaves of turnips or radishes.                │
    └───────────────────────────────────────────────────────┘
                              4em
```

Ⓑ

```
                            2em
    ┌──────────────────────────────────┐
    │ In four or five days, if the weather is propitious, the young plants │
    │ will begin to break ground, presenting at the surface two leaves, │
4em │ which together make nearly a square, like the first leaves of │   250px
    │ turnips or radishes.             │
    └──────────────────────────────────┘
                            1em
```

Ⓒ

What a Cabbage Is

If we cut vertically through the middle of the head, we shall find it made up of successive layers of leaves, which grow smaller and smaller, almost *ad infinitum*. Now, if we take a fruit bud from an apple-tree and make a similar section of it, we shall find the same structure. If we observe the development of the two, as spring advances, we shall find another similarity (the looser the head the closer will be the resemblance),—the outer leaves of each will unwrap and unfold, and a flower stem will push out from each. Here we see that a cabbage is a bud, a seed bud (as all fruit buds may be termed, the production of seed being the primary object in nature, the fruit enclosing it playing but a secondary part), the office of the leaves being to cover, protect, and afterwards nourish the young seed shoot. The outer leaves which surround the head appear to have the same office as the leaves which surround the growing fruit bud, and that office closes with the first year, as does that of the leaves surrounding fruit buds, when each die and drop off. In my locality the public must have perceived more or less clearly the analogy between the heads of cabbage and the buds of trees, for when they speak of small heads they frequently call them "buds." That the close wrapped leaves which make the cabbage head and surround the seed germ, situated just in the middle of the head at the termination of the stump, are necessary for its protection and nutrition when young, is proved, I think, by the fact that those cabbages, the heads of which are much decayed, when set out for seed, no matter

20%   0   20%

FIGURE 14-16. Applying margins to the **body** and to individual elements.

Take a look at Example ❸ in FIGURE 14-16. Here I've applied the `margin` property to the **body** element of the document. For this particular design, I set the top margin to zero (0) so the **body** starts flush against the top edge of the browser window. Adding equal amounts of margin to the left and right sides of the **body** keeps the content of the page centered and gives it a little breathing room.

Margin Behavior

Although it is easy to write rules that apply margin amounts around HTML elements, it is important to be familiar with some of the quirks of margin behavior.

Collapsing margins

The most significant margin behavior to be aware of is that the top and bottom margins of neighboring elements collapse. This means that instead of accumulating, adjacent margins overlap, and only the largest value is used.

Using the two paragraphs from the previous figure as an example, if the top element has a bottom margin of 4em, and the following element has a top margin of 2em, the resulting margin space between elements does not add up to 6ems Rather, the margins collapse and the resulting margin between the paragraphs will be 4em, the largest specified value. This is demonstrated in FIGURE 14-17.

The only time top and bottom margins *don't* collapse is for floated or absolutely positioned elements (we'll get to that in **Chapter 15, Floating and Positioning**). Margins on the left and right sides never collapse, so they're nice and predictable.

> Adjacent margins overlap, and only the largest value will be used.

■ **FURTHER READING**

Collapsing Margins

When spacing between and around elements behaves unpredictably, collapsing margins are often to blame. Here are a few articles that dig deep into collapsing margin behavior. Although they were written long ago, the information is still solid and may help you understand what is happening behind the scenes in your layouts.

- "No Margin for Error" by Andy Budd (*www.andybudd.com/ archives/2003/11/no_margin_for_ error*)
- "Uncollapsing Margins" by Eric Meyer (*www.complexspiral. com/publications/uncollapsing- margins*)

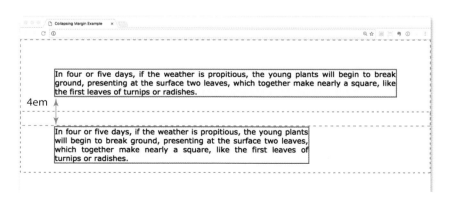

FIGURE 14-17. Vertical margins of neighboring elements collapse so that only the larger value is used.

Margins on inline elements

You can apply top and bottom margins to inline text elements (or "non-replaced inline elements," to use the proper CSS terminology), but it won't add vertical space above and below the element, and the height of the line will not change. However, when you apply left and right margins to inline text elements, margin space *will* be held clear before and after the text in the flow of the element, even if that element breaks over several lines.

Just to keep things interesting, margins on replaced inline elements, such as images, *do* render on all sides, and therefore do affect the height of the line. See FIGURE 14-18 for examples of each.

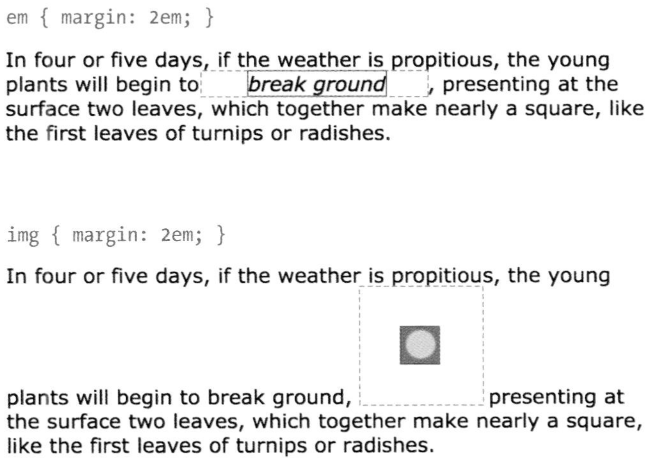

```
em { margin: 2em; }
```

In four or five days, if the weather is propitious, the young plants will begin to   *break ground*   , presenting at the surface two leaves, which together make nearly a square, like the first leaves of turnips or radishes.

```
img { margin: 2em; }
```

In four or five days, if the weather is propitious, the young

plants will begin to break ground,   presenting at the surface two leaves, which together make nearly a square, like the first leaves of turnips or radishes.

FIGURE 14-18. Examples of margins on inline elements. Only horizontal margins are rendered on non-replaced elements (top). Margins are rendered on all sides of replaced elements such as images.

Negative margins

It is worth noting that it is possible to specify negative values for margins. When you apply a negative margin, the content, padding, and border are moved in the opposite direction that would have resulted from a positive margin value.

I'll make this clear with an example. FIGURE 14-19 shows two neighboring paragraphs with different-colored borders applied to show their boundaries. In the left view, I've added a 3em bottom margin to the top paragraph, which has the effect of pushing the following paragraph *down* by that amount. If I specify a negative value (−3em), the following element moves *up* by that amount and overlaps the element with the negative margin.

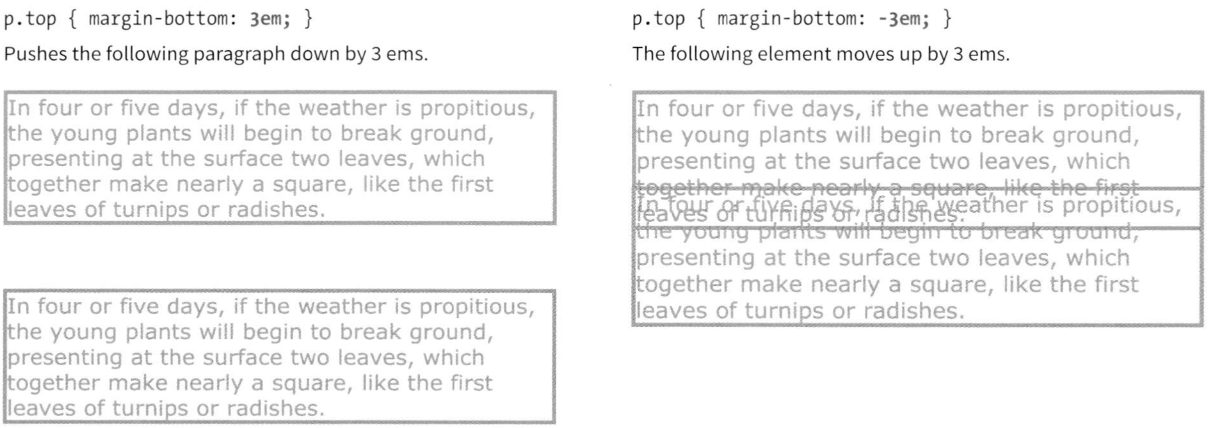

p.top { margin-bottom: 3em; }

Pushes the following paragraph down by 3 ems.

> In four or five days, if the weather is propitious, the young plants will begin to break ground, presenting at the surface two leaves, which together make nearly a square, like the first leaves of turnips or radishes.

> In four or five days, if the weather is propitious, the young plants will begin to break ground, presenting at the surface two leaves, which together make nearly a square, like the first leaves of turnips or radishes.

p.top { margin-bottom: -3em; }

The following element moves up by 3 ems.

> In four or five days, if the weather is propitious, the young plants will begin to break ground, presenting at the surface two leaves, which together make nearly a square, like the first leaves of turnips or radishes.
> In four or five days, if the weather is propitious, the young plants will begin to break ground, presenting at the surface two leaves, which together make nearly a square, like the first leaves of turnips or radishes.

FIGURE 14-19. Using negative margins.

This may seem like a strange thing to do, and in fact, you probably wouldn't make blocks of text overlap as shown. The point here is that you can use margins with both positive and negative values to move elements around on the page. This is the basis of some older CSS layout techniques.

Now let's use margins to add some space between parts of the Black Goose Bakery home page in EXERCISE 14-3.

ASSIGNING DISPLAY TYPES

As long as we're talking about boxes and the CSS layout model, this is a good time to introduce the **display** property. You should already be familiar with the display behavior of block and inline elements. Although HTML assigns display behaviors (or display types, to use the latest CSS term) to the elements it defines, there are other XML-based languages that can use CSS that don't do the same. For this reason, the **display** property was created to allow authors to specify how elements should behave in layouts.

display

Values:	inline | block | run-in | flex | grid | flow | flow-root | list-item | table | table-row-group | table-header-group | table-footer-group | table-row | table-cell | table-column-group | table-column | table-caption | ruby | ruby-base | ruby-text | ruby-base-container | ruby-text-container | inline-block | inline-table | inline-flex | inline-grid | contents | none
Default:	inline
Applies to:	all elements
Inherits:	yes

EXERCISE 14-3. Adding margin space around elements

It's time to adjust the margins around the elements on the bakery page. We'll start by adjusting margins on the whole document, and then make tweaks to each section from top to bottom. You should have *bakery-styles.css* open in a text editor.

1. It is a common practice to set the margin for the **body** element to zero, thus clearing out the browser's default margin setting. Add this margin declaration to the **body** styles, and then save the file and open it in a browser. You'll see that the elements now go to the very edge of the window with no space between.

```
body {
    …
    margin: 0;
}
```

NOTE

When the value is 0, you don't need to provide a specific unit.

2. If you are a careful observer, you may have noticed that there is still a bit of whitespace above the colored navigation bar. That happens to be the top margin of the **ul** list pushing the whole **nav** element down from the top edge of the browser. Let's take care of that. Add a new style rule in the "nav styles" section of the style sheet:

```
nav ul {
    margin: 0;
}
```

3. Margins are good for nudging elements around in the layout. For example, I think I'd like to move the **h1** with the logotype down a bit, so I'll add a margin to its top edge. I played around with a few values before deciding on 1.5em for this new style rule:

```
header h1 {
    margin-top: 1.5em;
}
```

I'd like the intro paragraph in the header to be a little closer to the logotype, so let's get wacky and use a *negative* top margin to pull it *up*. Add this declaration to the existing style rule:

```
header p {
    …
    margin-top: -12px;
}
```

4. Give the **main** section a 2.5% margin on all sides:

```
main {
    …
    margin: 2.5%;
}
```

5. Add a little extra space above the **h3** headings in the main area. I've chosen 2.5em, but you can play around with different values to see what you like best:

```
h3 {
    …
    margin-top: 2.5em;
}
```

6. Finally, add some space around the **aside**. This time, we'll do different amounts on each side for kicks. Put 1em on the top, 2.5% on the right side, 0 on the bottom, and 10% margin on the left. I'm going to let you do this one yourself. Can you make all those changes with one declaration? If you want to check your work, my finished version of the Black Goose Bakery page so far is available with the exercise materials for this chapter.

7. Save the style sheet again, and reload the page in the browser. It should look like the one in FIGURE 14-20. This isn't the most beautiful design, particularly if your browser window is set wide. However, if you resize your browser window narrow, you'll find that it wouldn't be too bad as the small-screen version in a responsive design. (Bet you can't wait for the Responsive Web Design chapter to learn how to fix this!)

FIGURE 14-20. The Black Goose Bakery home page after padding, borders, and margins are added.

The **display** property defines the type of element box an element generates in the layout. In addition to the familiar **inline** and **block** display types, you can also make elements display as list items or the various parts of a table. There are also a number of values for ruby annotation for East Asian languages. As you can see from the list of values, there are a lot of display types, but there are only a few that are used in everyday practice.

Display type assignment is useful for achieving layout effects while keeping the semantics of the HTML source intact. For example, it is common practice to make **li** elements (which usually display with the characteristics of block elements) display as inline elements to turn a list into a horizontal navigation bar. You may also make an otherwise inline **a** (anchor) element display as a block in order to give it a specific width and height:

```
ul.navigation li { display: inline; }

ul.navigation li a { display: block; }
```

Another useful value for the **display** property is **none**, which removes the content from the normal flow entirely. Unlike **visibility: hidden**, which just makes the element invisible but keeps the space it would have occupied blank, **display: none** removes the content, and the space it would have occupied is closed up.

One popular use of **display: none** is to prevent certain content in the source document from displaying in specific media, such as when the page is printed or displayed on devices with small screens. For example, you could display URLs for links in a document when it is printed, but not when it is displayed on a computer screen where the links are interactive.

Be aware that content that has its **display** set to **none** still downloads with the document. Setting some content to **display:none** for devices with small screens may keep the page shorter, but it is not doing anything to reduce data usage or download times.

BOX DROP SHADOWS

We've arrived at the last stop on the element box tour. In **Chapter 12, Formatting Text,** you learned about the **text-shadow** property, which adds a drop shadow to text. The **box-shadow** property applies a drop shadow around the entire visible element box (excluding the margin).

box-shadow

Values:	*'horizontal offset' 'vertical offset' 'blur distance' 'spread distance' color* inset | none
Default:	none
Applies to:	all elements
Inherits:	no

The value of the **box-shadow** property should seem familiar to you after working with **text-shadow**: specify the horizontal and vertical offset distances, the amount the shadow should blur, and a color. For box shadows, you can also specify a spread amount, which increases (or decreases with negative values) the size of the shadow. By default, the shadow color is the same as the foreground color of the element, but specifying a color overrides it.

FIGURE 14-21 shows the results of the following code examples.  adds a simple box shadow 6 pixels to the right and 6 pixels down, without blur or spread. **B** adds a blur value of 5 pixels, and **C** shows the effect of a 10-pixel spread value. Box shadows are always applied to the area *outside* the border of the element (or the place it would be if a border isn't specified). If the element has a transparent or translucent background, you will not see the box shadow in the area behind the element.

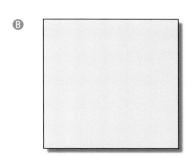

A `box-shadow: 6px 6px gray;`

B `box-shadow: 6px 6px 5px gray; /* 5 pixel blur */`

C `box-shadow: 6px 6px 5px 10px gray; /* 5px blur, 10px spread */`

You can make the shadow render inside the edges of the visible element box by adding the **inset** keyword to the rule. This makes it look like the element is pressed into the screen (FIGURE 14-22).

```
box-shadow: inset 6px 6px 5px gray;
```

FIGURE 14-21. Adding drop shadows around an element with the **box-shadow** property.

FIGURE 14-22. An inset box shadow renders on the inside of the element box.

As for **text-shadow**, you can specify multiple box shadows on an element by providing the values in a comma-separated list. The values that come first get placed on top, and subsequent shadows are placed behind it in the order in which they appear in the list.

WARNING

Box shadows, text shadows, and gradients take a lot of processor power because you are shifting the burden of interpreting and rendering them onto the browser. The more you use, the slower performance will be, and as we all know, performance is everything on the web. So go easy on them.

TEST YOURSELF

At this point, you should have a good feel for element boxes and how to manipulate the space within and around them. In the next chapter, we'll start moving the boxes around on the page, but first, why not get some practice at writing rules for padding, borders, and margins in the following test?

In this test, your task is to write the declarations that create the effects shown in each example in FIGURE 14-23 (see **Useful Hints**). All the paragraphs shown here share a rule that sets the dimensions and the background color for each paragraph. You just need to provide the box-related property declarations. Answers, as always, appear in **Appendix A**.

Ⓐ

Ⓑ

Ⓒ

Ⓓ

Ⓔ

Ⓕ

CSS REVIEW: BOX PROPERTIES

Property	Description
border	A shorthand property that combines border properties
border-top border-right border-bottom border-left	Combines border properties for each side of the element
border-color	Shorthand property for specifying the color of borders
border-top-color border-right-color border-bottom-color border-left-color	Specifies the border color for each side of the element
border-image	Adds an image inside the border area
border-image-outset	How far the border image should be positioned away from the border area.
border-image-repeat	The manner in which the image fills the sides of the border
border-image-slice	The points at which the border image should be divided into corners and sides
border-image-source	The location of the image file to be used for the border image

Table continues...

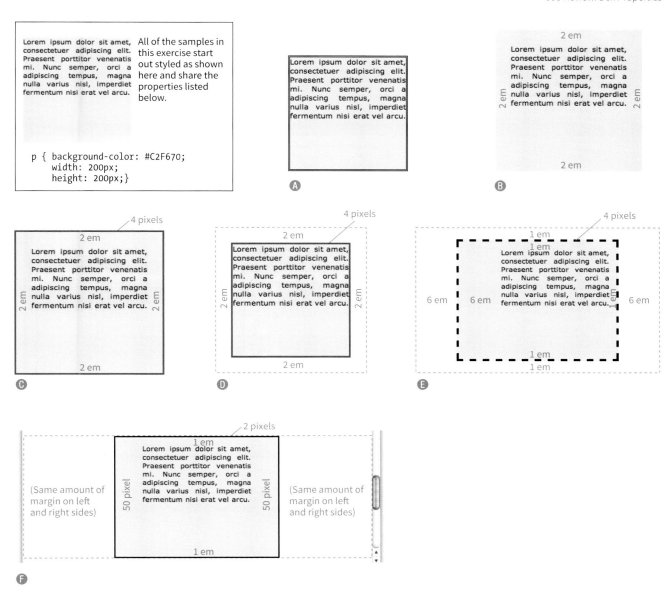

All of the samples in this exercise start out styled as shown here and share the properties listed below.

```
p { background-color: #C2F670;
    width: 200px;
    height: 200px;}
```

FIGURE 14-23. Write the declarations for these examples.

Property	Description
border-image-width	The width of the space the border image should occupy
border-radius	Shorthand property for rounding the corners of the visible element box
border-top-left-radius border-top-right-radius border-bottom-right-radius border-bottom-left-radius	Specifies the radius curve for each individual corner
border-style	Shorthand property for specifying the style of borders
border-top-style border-right-style border-bottom-style border-left-style	Specifies the border style for each side of the element
border-width	Shorthand property for specifying the width of borders
border-top-width border-right-width border-bottom-width border-left-width	Specifies the border width for each side of the element
box-sizing	Specifies whether width and height dimensions apply to the content box or the border box
box-shadow	Adds a drop shadow around the visible element box
display	Defines the type of element box an element generates
height	Specifies the height of the element's content box or border box
margin	Shorthand property for specifying margin space around an element
margin-top margin-right margin-bottom margin-left	Specifies the margin amount for each side of the element
max-height	Specifies the maximum height of an element
max-width	Specifies the maximum width of an element
min-height	Specifies the minimum height of an element
min-width	Specifies the minimum width of an element
outline	Shorthand property for adding an outline around an element
outline-color	Sets the color of the outline
outline-offset	Sets space between an outline and the outer edge of the border
outline-style	Sets the style of the outline
outline-width	Sets the width of the outline
overflow	Specifies how to handle content that doesn't fit in the content area
padding	Shorthand property for specifying space between the content area and the border
padding-top padding-right padding-bottom padding-left	Specifies the padding amount for each side of the element
width	Specifies the width of an element's content box or border box

FLOATING AND POSITIONING

At this point, you've learned dozens of CSS properties that let you change the appearance of text elements and the boxes they generate. But so far, we've merely been formatting elements as they appear in the flow of the document.

In this chapter, we'll look at floating and positioning, the CSS methods for breaking out of the normal flow and arranging elements on the page. Floating an element moves it to the left or right and allows the following text to wrap around it. Positioning is a way to specify the location of an element anywhere on the page with pixel precision.

Before we start moving elements around, let's be sure we are well acquainted with how they behave in the normal flow.

NORMAL FLOW

We've covered the normal flow in previous chapters, but it's worth a refresher. In the CSS layout model, text elements are laid out from top to bottom in the order in which they appear in the source, and from left to right in left-to-right reading languages (see **Note**). Block elements stack up on top of one another and fill the available width of the browser window or other containing element. Inline elements and text characters line up next to one another to fill the block elements.

When the window or containing element resizes, the block elements expand or contract to the new width, and the inline content reflows to fit as shown in FIGURE 15-1.

Objects in the normal flow affect the layout of the objects around them. This is the behavior you've come to expect in web pages—elements don't overlap or bunch up. They make room for one another.

NOTE

For right-to-left reading languages such as Arabic and Hebrew, the normal flow is top to bottom and right to left.

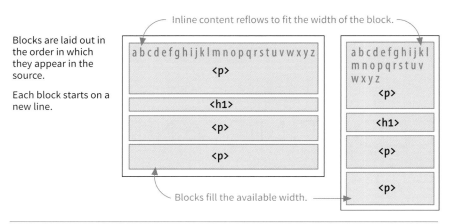

Blocks are laid out in the order in which they appear in the source.

Each block starts on a new line.

Inline content reflows to fit the width of the block.

Blocks fill the available width.

FIGURE 15-1. One more example of the normal flow behavior.

We've seen all of this before, but in this chapter we'll be paying attention to whether elements are in the flow or removed from the flow. Floating and positioning change the relationship of elements to the normal flow in different ways. Let's first look at the special behavior of floated elements (or "floats" for short).

FLOATING

Simply stated, the **float** property moves an element as far as possible to the left or right, allowing the following content to wrap around it. It is a unique feature built into CSS with some interesting behaviors.

float

Values:	left | right | none
Default:	none
Applies to:	all elements
Inherits:	no

The best way to explain floating is to demonstrate it. In this example, the **float** property is applied to an **img** element to float it to the right. FIGURE 15-2 shows how the paragraph and the contained image are rendered by default (top) and how it looks when the **float** property is applied (bottom).

THE MARKUP

```
<p><img src="icecreambowl.png" alt=""> After the cream is frozen rather
stiff,…
```

THE STYLES

```
img {
  float: right;
}
```

Floating an element moves it to the left or right and allows the following text to wrap around it.

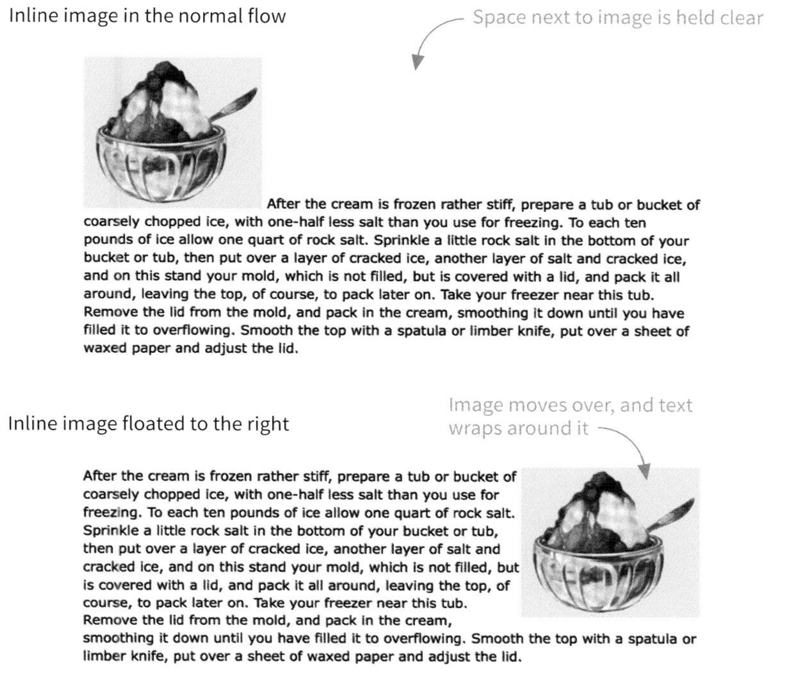

Inline image in the normal flow

Space next to image is held clear

After the cream is frozen rather stiff, prepare a tub or bucket of coarsely chopped ice, with one-half less salt than you use for freezing. To each ten pounds of ice allow one quart of rock salt. Sprinkle a little rock salt in the bottom of your bucket or tub, then put over a layer of cracked ice, another layer of salt and cracked ice, and on this stand your mold, which is not filled, but is covered with a lid, and pack it all around, leaving the top, of course, to pack later on. Take your freezer near this tub. Remove the lid from the mold, and pack in the cream, smoothing it down until you have filled it to overflowing. Smooth the top with a spatula or limber knife, put over a sheet of waxed paper and adjust the lid.

Inline image floated to the right

Image moves over, and text wraps around it

After the cream is frozen rather stiff, prepare a tub or bucket of coarsely chopped ice, with one-half less salt than you use for freezing. To each ten pounds of ice allow one quart of rock salt. Sprinkle a little rock salt in the bottom of your bucket or tub, then put over a layer of cracked ice, another layer of salt and cracked ice, and on this stand your mold, which is not filled, but is covered with a lid, and pack it all around, leaving the top, of course, to pack later on. Take your freezer near this tub. Remove the lid from the mold, and pack in the cream, smoothing it down until you have filled it to overflowing. Smooth the top with a spatula or limber knife, put over a sheet of waxed paper and adjust the lid.

FIGURE 15-2. The layout of an image in the normal flow (top), and with the **float** property applied (bottom).

That's a nice effect. We've gotten rid of a lot of wasted space on the page, but now the text is bumping right up against the image. How do you think you would add some space between the image element and the surrounding text? If you guessed "add a margin," you're absolutely right. I'll add 1em of space on all sides of the image with the **margin** property (FIGURE 15-3). You can begin to see how the box properties work together to improve page layout.

```
img {
    float: right;
    margin: 1em;
}
```

Indicates outer margin edge
(dotted line does not appear in the browser)

After the cream is frozen rather stiff, prepare a tub or bucket of coarsely chopped ice, with one-half less salt than you use for freezing. To each ten pounds of ice allow one quart of rock salt. Sprinkle a little rock salt in the bottom of your bucket or tub, then put over a layer of cracked ice, another layer of salt and cracked ice, and on this stand your mold, which is not filled, but is covered with a lid, and pack it all around, leaving the top, of course, to pack later on. Take your freezer near this tub. Remove the lid from the mold, and pack in the cream, smoothing it down until you have filled it to overflowing. Smooth the top with a spatula or limber knife, put over a sheet of waxed paper and adjust the lid.

FIGURE 15-3. Adding a 1em margin around the floated image.

The previous two figures demonstrate some key behaviors of floated elements:

A floated element is like an island in a stream.

First and foremost, you can see that the image is removed from its position in the normal flow yet continues to influence the surrounding content. The subsequent paragraph text reflows to make room for the floated **img** element. One popular analogy compares floats to islands in a stream—they are not in the flow, but the stream has to flow around them. This behavior is unique to floated elements.

Floats stay in the content area of the containing element.

It is also important to note that the floated image is placed within the *content area* (the inner edges) of the paragraph that contains it. It does not extend into the padding area of the paragraph.

Margins are maintained.

In addition, margins are held on all sides of the floated image, as indicated in FIGURE 15-3 by the dotted line. In other words, the entire element box, from outer edge to outer edge, is floated.

Floating Inline and Block elements

Those are the basics, so now let's look at more examples and explore additional floating behaviors. It is possible to float any HTML element, both inline and block-level, as we'll see in the following examples.

Floating an inline text element

In the previous example, we floated an inline image element. This time, let's look at what happens when you float an inline text (non-replaced) element—in this case, a span of text (FIGURE 15-4).

THE MARKUP

```
<p><span class="tip">TIP: Make sure that your packing tub or bucket
has a hole below the top of the mold so  the  water will drain
off.</span>After the cream is frozen rather stiff, prepare a tub or
bucket of…</p>
```

THE STYLES

```
span.tip {
  float: right;
  margin: 1em;
  width: 200px;
  color: #fff;
  background-color: lightseagreen;
  padding: 1em;
}
```

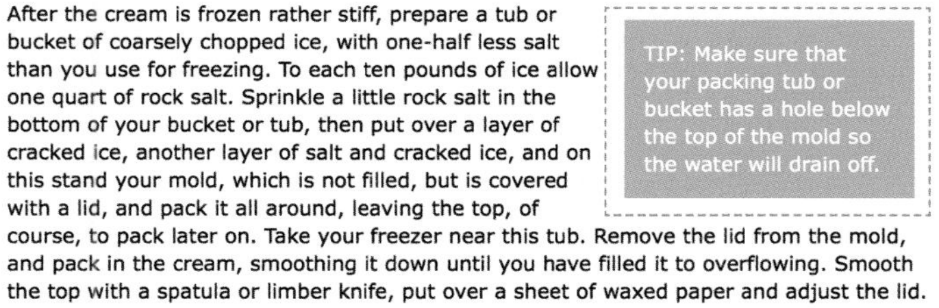

After the cream is frozen rather stiff, prepare a tub or bucket of coarsely chopped ice, with one-half less salt than you use for freezing. To each ten pounds of ice allow one quart of rock salt. Sprinkle a little rock salt in the bottom of your bucket or tub, then put over a layer of cracked ice, another layer of salt and cracked ice, and on this stand your mold, which is not filled, but is covered with a lid, and pack it all around, leaving the top, of course, to pack later on. Take your freezer near this tub. Remove the lid from the mold, and pack in the cream, smoothing it down until you have filled it to overflowing. Smooth the top with a spatula or limber knife, put over a sheet of waxed paper and adjust the lid.

> TIP: Make sure that your packing tub or bucket has a hole below the top of the mold so the water will drain off.

FIGURE 15-4. Floating an inline text (non-replaced) element.

At a glance, it is behaving the same as the floated image, which is what we'd expect. But there are some subtle things at work here that bear pointing out:

Always provide a width for floated text elements.

First, you'll notice that the style rule that floats the **span** includes the **width** property. It is necessary to specify a width for a floated text element because without one, its box is sized wide enough to fit its content (**auto**). For short phrases that are narrower than the container, that might not be an issue. However, for longer, wrapped text, the box expands to the width of the container, making it so wide that there wouldn't be room to wrap anything around it. Images have an inherent width, so we didn't need to specify a width in the previous example (although we certainly could have).

> It is necessary to specify the width for floated text elements.

Floated inline elements behave as block elements.

Notice that the margin is held on all four sides of the floated **span** text, even though top and bottom margins are usually not rendered on inline elements (see FIGURE 14-20 in the previous chapter). That is because all floated elements behave like block elements. Once you float an inline element, it follows the display rules for block-level elements, and margins are rendered on all four sides.

Margins on floated elements do not collapse.

In the normal flow, abutting top and bottom margins collapse (overlap), but margins for floated elements are maintained on all sides as specified.

Floating block elements

Let's look at what happens when you float a block within the normal flow. In this example, the whole second paragraph element is floated to the left (FIGURE 15-5).

THE MARKUP

```
<p>If you wish to pack ice cream...</p>
<p id="float">After the ice cream is rather stiff,...</p>
<p>Make sure that your packing tub or bucket...</p>
<p>As cold water is warmer than the ordinary...</p>
```

THE STYLES

```
p {
  border: 2px red solid;
}

#float {
  float: left;
  width: 300px;
  margin: 1em;
  background: white;
}
```

FIGURE 15-5. Floating a block-level element.

I've added a red border around all **p** elements to reveal their boundaries. In addition, I've made the background of the floated paragraph white so it stands out and added a 1em margin on all sides (indicated with a blue dotted line). The bottom view in FIGURE 15-5 shows how it looks with all the extra stuff turned off, as it would more likely appear on a real page.

Just as we saw with the image, the paragraph moves off to the side (left this time), and the following content wraps around it, even though blocks normally stack on top of one another. There are a few things I want to point out in this example:

You must provide a width for floated block elements.

If you do not provide a `width` value, the width of the floated block will be set to `auto`, which fills the available width of the browser window or other containing element. There's not much sense in having a full-width floated box, because the idea is to wrap text next to the float, not start below it.

Elements do not float higher than their reference in the source.

A floated block will float to the left or right relative to where it occurs in the source, allowing the following elements in the flow to wrap around it. It stays below any block elements that precede it in the flow (in effect, it is "blocked" by them). That means you can't float an element up to the top corner of a page, even if its nearest ancestor is the **body** element. If you want a floated element to start at the top of the page, it must appear first in the document source (see **Note**).

Non-floated elements maintain the normal flow.

The red borders in the top image reveal that the element boxes for the surrounding paragraphs still extend the full width of the normal flow. Only the content of those elements wraps around the float. This is a good model to keep in mind.

For example, adding a left margin to the surrounding paragraphs would add space on the left edge of the page, not between the text and the floated element. If you want space between the float and the wrapped text, you need to apply the margin to the float itself.

Clearing Floated Elements

If you're going to be floating elements around, it's important to know how to turn the text wrapping *off* and get back to normal flow as usual. You do this by clearing the element that you want to start below the float. Applying the **clear** property to an element prevents it from appearing next to a floated element and forces it to start against the next available "clear" space below the float.

`clear`

Values:	left | right | both | none
Default:	none
Applies to:	block-level elements only
Inherits:	no

Keep in mind that you apply the **clear** property to the element you want to start below the floated element, not the floated element itself. The **left** value starts the element below any elements that have been floated to the left. Similarly, the **right** value makes the element clear all floats on the right edge of the containing block. If there are multiple floated elements, and you

NOTE

Absolute positioning is the CSS method for placing elements on a page regardless of how they appear in the source. We'll get to absolute positioning later in this chapter. You can also change the order in which elements display by using Flexbox and Grid as discussed in **Chapter 16, CSS Layout with Flexbox and Grid**.

want to be sure an element starts below all of them, use the **both** value to clear floats on both sides.

In this example, the **clear** property has been used to make **h2** elements start below left-floated elements. FIGURE 15-6 shows how the **h2** heading starts at the next available clear edge below the float.

```
img {
  float: left;
  margin-right: .5em;
}
h2 {
  clear: left;
  margin-top: 2em;
}
```

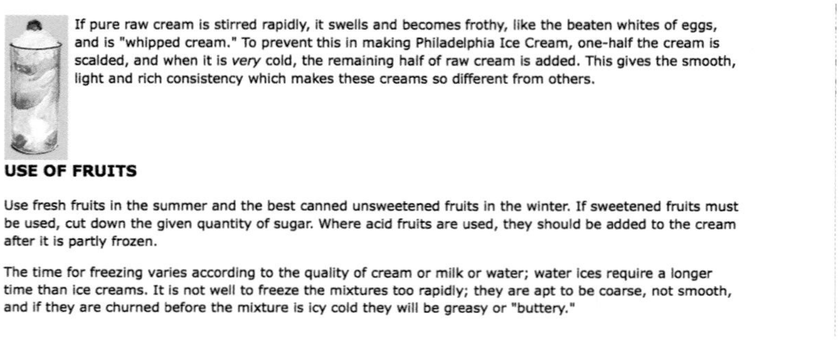

If pure raw cream is stirred rapidly, it swells and becomes frothy, like the beaten whites of eggs, and is "whipped cream." To prevent this in making Philadelphia Ice Cream, one-half the cream is scalded, and when it is very cold, the remaining half of raw cream is added. This gives the smooth, light and rich consistency which makes these creams so different from others.
USE OF FRUITS
Use fresh fruits in the summer and the best canned unsweetened fruits in the winter. If sweetened fruits must be used, cut down the given quantity of sugar. Where acid fruits are used, they should be added to the cream after it is partly frozen.
The time for freezing varies according to the quality of cream or milk or water; water ices require a longer time than ice creams. It is not well to freeze the mixtures too rapidly; they are apt to be coarse, not smooth, and if they are churned before the mixture is icy cold they will be greasy or "buttery."

FIGURE 15-6. Clearing a left-floated element.

Notice in FIGURE 15-6 that although there is a 2em top margin applied to the **h2** element, it is not rendered between the heading and the floated image. That's the result of collapsing vertical margins in the flow. If you want to make sure space is held between a float and the following text, apply a bottom margin to the floated element itself.

By now you have enough float know-how to give it a try in EXERCISE 15-1.

Float-Based Layouts

Curiously, there were no tools for true page layout in CSS1 or CSS2. Some clever designers realized we could use the CSS float behavior to line up elements horizontally, and floats started being used to turn lists into navigation bars and even turn whole sections of a document into columned layouts.

Float-based layouts are still prevalent on the web as I write this, but now that better CSS layout tools like Flexbox and Grid are gaining browser support, we are recognizing our float-based layouts for the hacks they are. Float-based layouts will eventually vanish like the table-based layouts of the 1990s.

That said, we are in a time of transition. Not all browsers in use today support newer standards like Flexbox and Grid, so depending on the browsers you need to support, you may still need to provide a fallback design that is universally supported. Floats will get the job done.

If you need to support older browsers that do not support Flexbox and Grid, you can download my article **"Page Layout with Floats and Positioning"** (PDF), which is available at *learningwebdesign.com/articles/*. It contains lessons on how to create navigation bars with floats and a number of templates for creating multicolumn layouts with floats and positioning. You may never need to know these techniques, but the information is there if you do.

Floating Multiple Elements

It's perfectly fine to float multiple elements on a page or even within a single element. In fact, for years, floats have been the primary method for lining up elements like navigation menus and even for creating whole page layouts (please take time to read the sidebar **"Float-Based Layouts"**).

When you float multiple elements, there is a complex system of behind-the-scenes rendering rules that ensures floated elements do not overlap. You can consult the CSS specification for details, but the upshot of it is that floated elements will be placed as far left or right (as specified) and as high up as space allows.

EXERCISE 15-1. Floating images

In the exercises in this chapter, we'll make further improvements to the Black Goose Bakery home page that we worked on in **Chapter 14, Thinking Inside the Box**. If you did not follow along in the last chapter, or if you would just like a fresh start, there is a copy of the document in its most recent state (*bakery_ch15.html*) in the **Chapter 15** materials (*learningwebdesign.com/5e/materials*).

1. Open the CSS file in a text editor and the HTML document in the browser. We'll start by removing wasted vertical space next to the baked good images by floating those images to the left. We'll create a new style rule with a contextual selector to target only the images in the **main** section:

   ```
   main img {
     float: left;
   }
   ```

   Save the CSS file and refresh the page in the browser, and you'll see that we have some post-float tidying up to do.

2. I want the "Learn more" links to always appear below the images so they are clearly visible and consistently on the left side of the page. Fortunately, the paragraphs with those links are marked up with the class "more" and there is already a style rule for them using a class selector. Make those paragraphs clear any floats on the left edge.

   ```
   p.more {
     …
     clear: left;
   }
   ```

3. Lastly, we'll adjust the spacing around the floated images. Give both images a 1em margin on the right and bottom sides by using the shorthand **margin** property:

   ```
   main img {
     float: left;
     margin: 0 1em 1em 0;
   }
   ```

   I feel like the muffin image could use extra space on the left side so it lines up better with the bread. Use this nifty attribute selector to grab any image whose **src** attribute contains the word *muffin* (there's only one):

   ```
   img[src*="muffin"] {
     margin-left: 50px;
   }
   ```

FIGURE 15-7 shows the new and improved "Fresh from the Oven" section.

Fresh from the Oven

BREADS

Our breads are made daily from highest-quality whole grain flour, water, salt, and yeast or sourdough starter. Simply and naturally, and never any preservatives. Patience is key to achieving the proper level of fermentation and baking each loaf to perfection. Available in whole grain, sourdough, olive loaf, classic rye, and potato-onion.

LEARN MORE ABOUT OUR BAKING PROCESS...

MUFFINS

Every day, we offer a large selection of muffins, including blueberry, multi-berry, bran, corn, lemon-poppyseed, and chocolate. Our muffins are made from scratch each day. Stop by to see our seasonal muffin flavors!

LEARN MORE ABOUT HOW WE MAKE OUR MUFFINS...

FIGURE 15-7. The product section with floated images and wrapped text has less wasted space.

FIGURE 15-8 shows what happens when a series of sequential paragraphs is floated to the same side. The first three floats start stacking up from the left edge, but when there isn't enough room for the fourth, it moves down and to the left until it bumps into something—in this case, the edge of the browser window. However, if one of the floats, such as P2, had been very long, it would have bumped up against the edge of the long float instead. Notice that the next paragraph in the normal flow (P6) starts wrapping at the highest point it can find, just below P1.

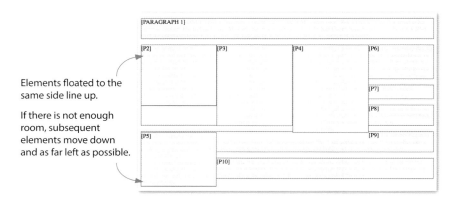

Elements floated to the same side line up.

If there is not enough room, subsequent elements move down and as far left as possible.

FIGURE 15-8. Multiple floated elements line up and do not overlap.

THE MARKUP

```
<p>[PARAGRAPH 1] ONCE upon a time…</p>
<p class="float">[P2]…</p>
<p class="float">[P3]…</p>
<p class="float">[P4]…</p>
<p class="float">[P5]…</p>
<p>[P6]…</p>
<p>[P7]…</p>
<p>[P8]…</p>
<p>[P9]…</p>
<p>[P10]…</p>
```

THE STYLES

```
p.float {
   float: left;
   width: 200px;
   margin: 0px;
   background: #F2F5d5;
   color: #DAEAB1;
}
```

Containing Floats

This is a good time to address a quirky float behavior: float containment. By default, floats are designed to hang out of the element they are contained in. That's just fine for allowing text to flow around a floated image, but sometimes it can cause some unwanted behaviors.

Take a look at the example in FIGURE 15-9. It would be nicer if the border expanded around all the content, but the floated image hangs out the bottom.

SUNDAE BUFFET
Topping list

FIGURE 15-9. The containing element does not expand to accommodate the floated image as indicated by its blue border.

If you float *all* the elements in a container element, there will be no elements remaining in the flow to hold the containing element open. This phenomenon is illustrated in FIGURE 15-10. The **#container div** contains two paragraphs. The view of the normal flow (top) shows that the **#container** has a background color and border that wraps around the content.

```
<div id="container">
  <p>…</p>
  <p>…</p>
</div>

#container {
  background: #f2f5d5;
  border: 2px dashed green;
}
```

However, when both paragraphs (that is, all of the content within the **div**) are floated, as shown in the figure on the bottom), the element box for the **#container** closes up to a height of zero, leaving the floats hanging down below (you can still see the empty border at the top). There's no content left in the normal flow to give the containing **div** height. This clearly is not the effect we are after.

```
p {
  float: left;
  width: 44%;
  padding: 2%;
}
```

In the normal flow, the container div encloses the paragraphs.

Etiam convallis, nulla ut ullamcorper mollis, ipsum purus imperdiet tellus, ut ultrices massa tortor vitae nulla. Fusce non arcu quam. Nullam lacinia facilisis lacus, et varius ligula imperdiet ut. Morbi molestie auctor magna, quis venenatis felis adipiscing sed. Aliquam ipsum nibh, dapibus sit amet tristique at, tincidunt in leo. Quisque accumsan lobortis lacus, id gravida tortor luctus et. Donec quis diam et odio volutpat blandit nec nec enim. Nam vitae vestibulum risus. Cras in adipiscing odio. Nam vel dolor id purus pretium suscipit quis in quam. Proin varius tincidunt facilisis. Maecenas eget felis ut nisi ullamcorper ornare. Suspendisse vestibulum leo sed lectus posuere eget convallis nisi placerat. Vestibulum porttitor egestas ornare.

Cras id ipsum dui. Donec semper congue lectus quis vulputate. Ut felis leo, bibendum at blandit non, luctus ac lorem. Nunc vitae ligula ut neque convallis sagittis. Quisque consequat orci sed arcu tincidunt et volutpat tellus tempor. Nulla vulputate ante nec felis elementum auctor. Duis magna neque, posuere eu hendrerit sit amet, dapibus quis quam. Pellentesque habitant morbi tristique senectus et netus et malesuada fames ac turpis egestas. Class aptent taciti sociosqu ad litora torquent per conubia nostra, per inceptos himenaeos. Nunc dapibus dui dignissim nibh sagittis. Morbi non dolor diam, nec iaculis neque. Aenean at eros sit amet velit iaculis porttitor. Nam lobortis sodales augue, sit amet tincidunt erat sagittis eu. Class aptent taciti sociosqu ad litora torquent per conubia nostra, per inceptos himenaeos. Donec ut ultricies velit. Quisque tempor fermentum ante, quis tempus est fringilla eu.

When both paragraphs are floated, the container does not stretch around them.

Etiam convallis, nulla ut ullamcorper mollis, ipsum purus imperdiet tellus, ut ultrices massa tortor vitae nulla. Fusce non arcu quam. Nullam lacinia facilisis lacus, et varius ligula imperdiet ut. Morbi molestie auctor magna, quis venenatis felis adipiscing sed. Aliquam ipsum nibh, dapibus sit amet tristique at, tincidunt in leo. Quisque accumsan lobortis lacus, id gravida tortor luctus et. Donec quis diam et odio volutpat blandit nec nec enim. Nam vitae vestibulum risus. Cras in adipiscing odio. Nam vel dolor id purus pretium suscipit quis in quam. Proin varius tincidunt facilisis. Maecenas eget felis ut nisi ullamcorper ornare. Suspendisse vestibulum leo sed lectus posuere eget convallis nisi placerat. Vestibulum porttitor egestas ornare.

Cras id ipsum dui. Donec semper congue lectus quis vulputate. Ut felis leo, bibendum at blandit non, luctus ac lorem. Nunc vitae ligula ut neque convallis sagittis. Quisque consequat orci sed arcu tincidunt et volutpat tellus tempor. Nulla vulputate ante nec felis elementum auctor. Duis magna neque, posuere eu hendrerit sit amet, dapibus quis quam. Pellentesque habitant morbi tristique senectus et netus et malesuada fames ac turpis egestas. Class aptent taciti sociosqu ad litora torquent per conubia nostra, per inceptos himenaeos. Nunc dapibus dui dignissim dolor rutrum vel consequat nibh sagittis. Morbi non dolor diam, nec iaculis neque. Aenean at eros sit amet velit iaculis porttitor. Nam lobortis sodales augue, sit amet tincidunt erat sagittis eu. Class aptent taciti sociosqu ad litora torquent per conubia nostra, per inceptos himenaeos. Donec ut ultricies velit. Quisque tempor fermentum ante, quis tempus est fringilla eu.

FIGURE 15-10. The container box disappears entirely when all its contents are floated.

Fortunately, there are a few fixes to this problem, and they are pretty straightforward. The most popular and foolproof solution is the "clearfix" technique. It uses the `:after` pseudo-element to insert a character space after the container, set its display to "block," and clear it on both sides. For more information on this version of clearfix, see Thierry Koblentz's article "The very latest clearfix reloaded" (*cssmojo.com/the-very-latest-clearfix-reloaded*). Here it is applied to the `#container div` in FIGURE 15-10:

```
#container:after {
  content: " ";
  display: block;
  clear: both;
  background-color: #f2f5d5; /*light green*/
  border: 2px dashed green;
  padding: 1em;
}
```

Another option is to float the containing element as well and give it a width of 100%:

```
#container {
  float: left;
  width: 100%;
  …
}
```

FIGURE 15-11 shows the result of applying a containment technique to the previous examples. Either will do the trick.

SUNDAE BUFFET
Topping list

Etiam convallis, nulla ut ullamcorper mollis, ipsum purus imperdiet tellus, ut ultrices massa tortor vitae nulla. Fusce non arcu quam. Nullam lacinia facilisis lacus, et varius ligula imperdiet ut. Morbi molestie auctor magna, quis venenatis felis adipiscing sed. Aliquam ipsum nibh, dapibus sit amet tristique at, tincidunt in leo. Quisque accumsan lobortis lacus, id gravida tortor luctus et. Donec quis diam et odio volutpat blandit nec nec enim. Nam vitae vestibulum risus. Cras in adipiscing odio. Nam vel dolor id purus pretium suscipit quis in quam. Proin varius tincidunt facilisis. Maecenas eget felis ut nisi ullamcorper pretium non at nulla. Etiam suscipit aliquet velit ac facilisis. Etiam egestas ante eu velit ullamcorper ornare. Suspendisse vestibulum leo sed lectus posuere eget convallis nisi placerat. Vestibulum porttitor egestas ornare.

Cras id ipsum dui. Donec semper congue lectus quis vulputate. Ut felis leo, bibendum at blandit non, luctus ac lorem. Nunc vitae ligula ut neque convallis sagittis. Quisque consequat orci sed arcu tincidunt et volutpat tellus tempor. Nulla vulputate ante nec felis elementum auctor. Duis magna neque, posuere eu hendrerit sit amet, dapibus quis quam. Pellentesque habitant morbi tristique senectus et netus et malesuada fames ac turpis egestas. Class aptent taciti sociosqu ad litora torquent per conubia nostra, per inceptos himenaeos. Nunc dapibus dui dignissim dolor rutrum vel consequat nibh sagittis. Morbi non dolor diam, nec iaculis neque. Aenean at eros sit amet velit iaculis porttitor. Nam lobortis sodales augue, sit amet tincidunt erat sagittis eu. Class aptent taciti sociosqu ad litora torquent per conubia nostra, per inceptos himenaeos. Donec ut ultricies velit. Quisque tempor fermentum ante, quis tempus est fringilla eu.

FIGURE 15-11. Our hanging floats are now contained.

That covers the fundamentals of floating. If you are thinking that rectangular text wraps are a little *ho-hum*, you could add some pizzazz (or just eliminate extra whitespace) by using CSS Shapes.

FANCY TEXT WRAP WITH CSS SHAPES

Look at the previous float examples, and you will see that the text always wraps in a rectangular shape around a floated image or element box. However, you can change the shape of the wrapped text to a circle, ellipse, polygon, or any image shape by using the **shape-outside** property. This is an up-and-coming CSS feature, so be sure to check the **Browser Support Note**. Following is a quick introduction to CSS Shapes, which should inspire and prepare you for more exploration on your own.

shape-outside

Values:	none	circle()	ellipse()	polygon()	url()	 [margin-box	padding-box	content-box]
Default:	none
Applies to:	floats
Inherits:	no

FIGURE 15-12 shows the default text wrap around a floated image (left) and the same wrap with **shape-outside** applied (right). This is the kind of thing you'd expect to see in a print magazine, but now we can do it on the web!

It is worth noting that you can change the text wrap shape around any floated element (see **Note**), but I will focus on images in this discussion, as text elements are generally boxes that fit nicely in the default rectangular wrap.

There are two approaches to making text wrap around a shape. One way is to provide the path coordinates of the wrap shape with **circle()**, **ellipse()**, or **polygon()**. Another way is to use **url()** to specify an image that has transparent areas (such as a GIF or a PNG). With the image method, text flows into the transparent areas of the image and stops at the opaque areas. This is the shape method shown in FIGURE 15-12 and the method I'll introduce first.

BROWSER SUPPORT NOTE

As of this writing in 2018, text wrap shapes are supported only by Chrome 37+, Opera 24+, Safari 7.1+ (with prefix; without starting in 10.1), iOS Safari 8+ (with prefix; without in 10.3+), and Android 56+. The feature is under consideration at Microsoft Edge and in development at Firefox, so the support situation may be better by the time you are reading this. Check CanIUse.com for the current state of support.

For the time being, feel free to use it as a progressive enhancement for designs in which a rectangular text wrap would be perfectly acceptable. Another alternative is to use a feature query (@supports) to serve a fallback set of styles to non-supporting browsers. Feature queries are introduced in **Chapter 19, More CSS Techniques**.

NOTE

shape-outside *works only on floated elements for now, but it is believed that this will change in the future.*

Ordinary fruit creams may be made with condensed milk at a cost of about fifteen cents a quart, which, of course, is cheaper than ordinary milk and cream.

In places where neither cream nor condensed milk can be purchased, a fair ice cream is made by adding two tablespoonfuls of olive oil to each quart of milk. The cream for Philadelphia Ice Cream should be rather rich, but not double cream.

If pure raw cream is stirred rapidly, it swells and becomes frothy, like the beaten whites of eggs, and is "whipped cream." To prevent this in making Philadelphia Ice Cream, one-half the cream is scalded, and when it is *very* cold, the remaining half of raw cream is added. This gives the smooth, light and rich consistency which makes these creams so different from others.

The time for freezing varies according to the quality of cream or milk or water; water ices require a longer time than ice creams. It is not well to freeze the mixtures too rapidly; they are apt to be coarse, not smooth, and if they are churned before the mixture is icy cold they will be greasy or "buttery."

Default text wrap

Ordinary fruit creams may be made with condensed milk at a cost of about fifteen cents a quart, which, of course, is cheaper than ordinary milk and cream.

In places where neither cream nor condensed milk can be purchased, a fair ice cream is made by adding two tablespoonfuls of olive oil to each quart of milk. The cream for Philadelphia Ice Cream should be rather rich, but not double cream.

If pure raw cream is stirred rapidly, it swells and becomes frothy, like the beaten whites of eggs, and is "whipped cream." To prevent this in making Philadelphia Ice Cream, one-half the cream is scalded, and when it is *very* cold, the remaining half of raw cream is added. This gives the smooth, light and rich consistency which makes these creams so different from others.

The time for freezing varies according to the quality of cream or milk or water; water ices require a longer time than ice creams. It is not well to freeze the mixtures too rapidly; they are apt to be coarse, not smooth, and if they are churned before the mixture is icy cold they will be greasy or "buttery."

Text wrap with **shape-outside** using the transparent areas of the image as a guide

FIGURE 15-12. Example of text wrapping around an image with **shape-outside**.

Using a Transparent Image

In the example in FIGURE 15-12, I placed the *sundae.png* image in the HTML document to display on the page, and I've specified the same image in the style rule using **url()** so that its transparent areas define the wrap shape (see important Warning). It makes sense to use the same image in the document and for the CSS shape, but it is not required. You could apply a wrap shape derived from one image to another image on the page.

WARNING

There is a security setting in Chrome and Opera that makes image-based text wraps a little tricky to use. Without getting into too much sys-admin detail, the browser restricts the use of the image used to create the CSS shape if it isn't on the same domain as the file requesting it. This is not a bug; they are following the rules set out in the specification.

The rule also means that compliant browsers won't allow images to be used for shapes when the files are served locally (i.e., on your computer). They need to be uploaded to a server to work, which makes the design process a little more cumbersome, especially for beginners.

If you use image-based text wraps, you know your CSS is written correctly, but you aren't seeing wrapping in the browser, this security setting (related to Cross-Origin Resource Sharing, or CORS, if you're curious) is probably the culprit.

THE MARKUP

```
<p><img src="sundae.png" class="wrap" alt=""> In places…</p>
```

THE STYLES

```
img.wrap {
  float: left;
  width: 300px;
  height: 300px;
  -webkit-shape-outside: url(sundae.png); /* prefix required in 2018 */
  shape-outside: url(sundae.png);
```

Notice that the wrapped text is now bumping right into the image. How about we give it a little extra space with **shape-margin**?

shape-margin

Values: *length* | *percentage*

Default: 0

Applies to: floats

Inherits: no

The **shape-margin** property specifies an amount of space to hold between the shape and the wrapped text. In FIGURE 15-13, you can see the effect of adding 1em of space between the opaque image areas and the wrapped text lines. It gives it a little breathing room the way any good margin should.

```
-webkit-shape-margin: 1em;
shape-margin: 1em;
```

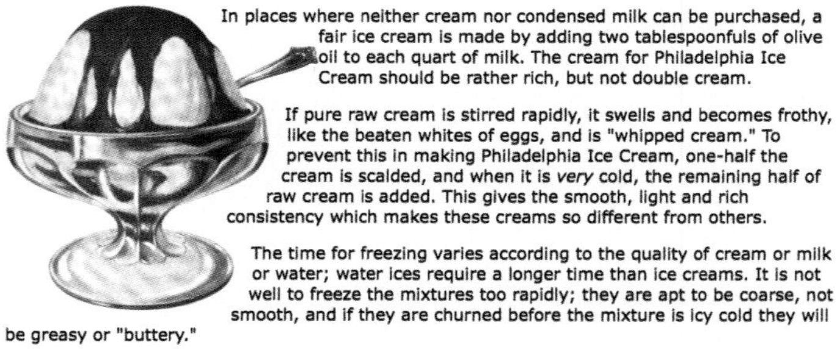
In places where neither cream nor condensed milk can be purchased, a fair ice cream is made by adding two tablespoonfuls of olive oil to each quart of milk. The cream for Philadelphia Ice Cream should be rather rich, but not double cream.
If pure raw cream is stirred rapidly, it swells and becomes frothy, like the beaten whites of eggs, and is "whipped cream." To prevent this in making Philadelphia Ice Cream, one-half the cream is scalded, and when it is very cold, the remaining half of raw cream is added. This gives the smooth, light and rich consistency which makes these creams so different from others.
The time for freezing varies according to the quality of cream or milk or water; water ices require a longer time than ice creams. It is not well to freeze the mixtures too rapidly; they are apt to be coarse, not smooth, and if they are churned before the mixture is icy cold they will be greasy or "buttery."

FIGURE 15-13. Adding a margin between the shape and the wrapped text.

Opacity Threshold

If you have a source image with multiple levels of transparency, such as the gradient shadow, the **shape-image-threshold** property allows text to creep into the image but stop when it encounters a specific transparency level. The value of this property is a number between 0 and 1, representing a percentage of transparency. For example, if you set the threshold to .2, text will wrap into areas that are up to 20% transparent, but stop when it gets to more opaque levels.

Using a Path

The other method for creating a text wrap shape is to define it using one of the path keywords: **circle()**, **ellipse()**, and **polygon()**.

The **circle()** notation creates a circle shape for the text to wrap around. The value provided within the parentheses represents the length of the radius of the circle:

```
circle(radius)
```

In this example, the radius is 150px, half of the image width of 300 pixels. By default, the circle is centered vertically and horizontally on the float:

```
img.round {
    float: left;
    -webkit-shape-outside: circle(150px);
    shape-outside: circle(150px);
}
```

FIGURE 15-14 shows this style rule applied to different images. Notice that the transparency of the image is not at play here. It's just a path overlaid on the image that sets the boundaries for text wrap. Any path can be applied to any image or other floated element.

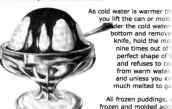

FIGURE 15-14. The same **circle()** shape applied to different images in the source.

This is a good point to demonstrate a critical behavior of wrap shapes. They allow text to flow *into* the floated image or element, but they cannot hold space free beyond it.

In the example in FIGURE 15-15, I've increased the diameter of the circle path from 150px to 200px. Notice that the text lines up along the right edge of the image, even though the circle is set 50 pixels beyond the edge. The path does not push text away from the float. If you need to keep wrapped text away from the outside edge of the floated image or element, apply a margin to the element itself (it will be the standard rectangular shape, of course).

```
img.round {
  float: left;
  -webkit-shape-outside: circle(200px);
  shape-outside: circle(200px);
}
```

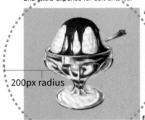

A CSS shape allows text to wrap into floated elements, but does not push text away from them.

FIGURE 15-15. CSS shapes allow text to wrap into the floated element but do not hold space beyond it.

Elliptical shapes are created with the **ellipse()** notation, which provides the horizontal and vertical radius lengths followed by the word **at** and then the x,y coordinates for the center of the shape. Here is the syntax:

```
ellipse(rx ry at x y);
```

The position coordinates can be listed as a specific measurement or a percentage. Here I've created an ellipse with a 100-pixel horizontal radius and a 150-pixel vertical radius, centered in the floated element it is applied to (FIGURE 15-16):

```
img.round {
  float: left;
  -webkit-shape-outside: ellipse(200px 100px at 50% 50%);
  shape-outside: ellipse(200px 100px at 50% 50%);
}
```

The edges of the image (blue) and ellipse path (dotted orange) revealed

FIGURE 15-16. An elliptical text wrap created with **ellipse()**.

Finally, we come to **polygon()**, which lets you create a custom path using a series of comma-separated x,y coordinates along the path. This style rule creates the wrap effect shown in FIGURE 15-17:

```
img.wrap {
   float: left;
   width: 300px;
   height: 300px;
   shape-outside: polygon(0px 0px, 186px 0px, 225px 34px, 300px 34px,
300px 66px, 255px 88px, 267px 127px, 246px 178px, 192px 211px, 226px
236px, 226px 273px, 209px 300px, 0px 300px);
}
```

The edges of the image (blue) and
polygon path (dotted orange) revealed

FIGURE 15-17. A custom path created with **polygon()**.

Holy coordinates! That's a lot of numbers, and my path was fairly simple. I'd like to be able to point you to a great tool for drawing and exporting polygon paths, but sadly, as of this writing I have none to recommend (see **Note**). I got the coordinates for my polygon examples by opening the image in Photoshop and gathering them manually, which, although possible, is not ideal.

CSS Shapes Resources

There are some finer points regarding CSS Shapes that I must leave to you to research further. Here are a few resources to get you started:

- CSS Shapes Module, Level 1 (*www.w3.org/TR/css-shapes-1/*)

- "Getting Started with CSS Shapes" by Razvan Caliman (*www.html5rocks. com/en/tutorials/shapes/getting-started*)

- CSS Shapes at the Experimental Layout Lab of Jen Simmons (*labs.jensimmons.com/#shapes*)

- "A Redesign with CSS Shapes" by Eric Meyer (*alistapart.com/article/redesign-with-css-shapes*)

Why don't we make the text wrap around the images in the Black Goose Bakery page in a more interesting way for users with browsers that support it (EXERCISE 15-2)?

NOTE

A CSS Shapes Editor will be included in a future version of Firefox that will likely be available by the time you are reading this (developer.mozilla.org/en-US/docs/Tools/Page_Inspector/How_to/Edit_CSS_shapes).

◼ **WEB SEARCH TIP**

If you search for "CSS Shapes" you will certainly come across that term used for a technique that uses CSS to draw geometric shapes such as triangles, arrows, circles, and so on. It's a little confusing, although those other "CSS shapes" are pretty nifty and something you might want to tinker with. I introduce them briefly in **Chapter 23, Web Image Basics**.

EXERCISE 15-2. Adding shapes around floats

The bread and muffin images on the Black Goose Bakery page provide a nice opportunity to try out CSS Shapes. You will need to use a supporting browser such as a recent version of Chrome, Safari, or Opera to see the wrapping effect.

Open the latest version of the bakery style sheet and look for the section labeled **/* main "products" styles */**. We'll put the image wrap styles there to keep our style sheet organized.

Target each image individually using an attribute selector (there is one set up for "muffin" already). Start out simply and make the text wrap around a circle. Set the radius of the circle to 125px for the bread image and 110px for the muffin.

```
img[src*="bread"] {
  -webkit-shape-outside: circle(125px);
  shape-outside: circle(125px);
}
img[src*="muffin"] {
  margin-left: 50px;
  -webkit-shape-outside: circle(110px);
  shape-outside: circle(110px);
}
```

Save the styles and take a look at the page in a supporting browser. The circles look pretty good, but I think I could improve the wrap around the bread by making it an ellipse. Add these

after the circle declarations, and the ellipse wrap will override the previous styles (or delete and replace):

```
img[src*="bread"] {
  -webkit-shape-outside: ellipse(130px 95px at 50% 50%);
  shape-outside: ellipse(130px 95px at 50% 50%);
}
```

If you're feeling ambitious, you could add a polygon wrap shape around the muffin image instead of the circle. You'll need to copy these coordinates or just copy and paste from the finished exercise provided in the materials for this chapter. Or just stick with the circle, and nobody will judge you.

```
img[src*="muffin"] {
  …
  shape-outside: polygon(0px 0px, 197px 0px, 241px
  31px, 241px 68px, 226px 82px, 219px 131px, 250px
  142px, 250px 158px, 0px 158px);
}
```

The final result is shown in FIGURE 15-18. It is most apparent when the browser window is sufficiently narrow that enough lines wrap to reveal the shape. For browsers that don't support shapes, the rectangular whitespace is just fine.

Fresh from the Oven

BREADS

Our breads are made daily from highest-quality whole grain flour, water, salt, and yeast or sourdough starter. Simply and naturally, and never any preservatives. Patience is key to achieving the proper level of fermentation and baking each loaf to perfection. Available in whole grain, sourdough, olive loaf, classic rye, and potato-onion.

LEARN MORE ABOUT OUR BAKING PROCESS…

MUFFINS

Every day, we offer a large selection of muffins, including blueberry, multi-berry, bran, corn, lemon- poppyseed, and chocolate. Our muffins are made from scratch each day. Stop by to see our seasonal muffin flavors!

LEARN MORE ABOUT HOW WE MAKE OUR MUFFINS…

FIGURE 15-18. The bakery page with text wrapping around images in an ellipse (bread) and polygon (muffin) using CSS Shapes.

Well, that covers floating! You've learned how to float elements left and right, clear the following elements so they start below the floats, and even make fancy text wrapping shapes. Now let's move on to the other approach to moving elements around on the page—positioning.

POSITIONING BASICS

CSS provides several methods for positioning elements on the page. They can be positioned relative to where they would normally appear in the flow, or removed from the flow altogether and placed at a particular spot on the page. You can also position an element relative to the viewport, and it will stay put while the rest of the page scrolls.

Types of Positioning

position

Values:	static | relative | absolute | fixed
Default:	static
Applies to:	all elements
Inherits:	no

The **position** property indicates that an element is to be positioned and specifies which positioning method to use. I'll introduce each keyword value briefly here, and then we'll take a more detailed look at each method in the remainder of this chapter.

static

> This is the normal positioning scheme in which elements are positioned as they occur in the normal document flow.

relative

> Relative positioning moves the element box relative to its original position in the flow. The distinctive behavior of relative positioning is that the space the element would have occupied in the normal flow is preserved as empty space.

absolute

> Absolutely positioned elements are removed from the document flow entirely and positioned with respect to the viewport or a containing element (we'll talk more about this later). Unlike relatively positioned elements, the space they would have occupied is closed up. In fact, they have no influence at all on the layout of surrounding elements.

> **■ TERMINOLOGY**
>
> ## Viewport
>
> I'll be sticking with the more formal term *viewport* throughout the positioning discussions, but keep in mind it could be a browser window on a desktop computer, the full screen of a mobile device, or the frame of an **iframe** element from the perspective of the web page loaded in that frame. It is any space that visually displays a web page.

`fixed`

> The distinguishing characteristic of fixed positioning is that the element stays in one position in the viewport even when the document scrolls. Fixed elements are removed from the document flow and positioned relative to the viewport rather than another element in the document.

`sticky`

> Sticky positioning is a combination of relative and fixed in that it behaves as though it is relatively positioned, until it is scrolled into a specified position relative to the viewport, at which point it remains fixed.
>
> The MDN Web Docs site has this description for a potential use case:
>
> > *Sticky positioning is commonly used for the headings in an alphabetized listing. The B heading will appear just below the items that begin with A until they are scrolled offscreen. Rather than sliding offscreen with the rest of the content, the B heading will then remain fixed to the top of the viewport until all the B items have scrolled offscreen, at which point it will be covered up by the C heading.*
>
> The **sticky** position value is supported by current versions of Chrome, Firefox, Opera, MS Edge, Android, as well as Safari and iOS Safari with the **-webkit-** prefix. No version of IE supports it. Happily, **sticky** positioning degrades gracefully, as the element simply stays inline and scrolls with the document if it is not supported.

Each positioning method has its purpose, but absolute positioning is the most versatile. With absolute positioning, you can place an object anywhere in the viewport or within another element. Absolute positioning has been used to create multicolumn layouts, but it is more commonly used for small tasks, like positioning a search box in the top corner of a header. It's a handy tool when used carefully and sparingly.

Specifying Position

Once you've established the positioning method, the actual position is specified with some combination of up to four offset properties.

`top`, `right`, `bottom`, `left`

Values:	*length*	*percentage*	auto
Default:	auto
Applies to:	positioned elements (where `position` value is relative, absolute, or fixed)
Inherits:	no

The value provided for each offset property defines the distance the element should be moved *away* from that respective edge. For example, the value of **top** defines the distance the top outer edge of the positioned element should be offset from the top edge of the browser or other containing element. A positive value for **top** results in the element box moving *down* by that amount (see **Note**). Similarly, a positive value for **left** would move the positioned element to the right (toward the center of the containing block) by that amount.

Further explanations and examples of the offset properties will be provided in the discussions of each positioning method. We'll start our exploration of positioning with the fairly straightforward **relative** method.

RELATIVE POSITIONING

As mentioned previously, relative positioning moves an element relative to its original spot in the flow. The space it would have occupied is preserved and continues to influence the layout of surrounding content. This is easier to understand with a simple example.

Here I've positioned an inline **em** element. A bright background color on the **em** and a border on the containing paragraph make their boundaries apparent. First, I used the **position** property to set the method to **relative**, and then I used the **top** offset property to move the element 2em down from its initial position, and the **left** property to move it 3em to the right. Remember, offset property values move the element *away* from the specified edge, so if you want something to move to the right, as I did here, you use the **left** offset property. The results are shown in FIGURE 15-19.

```
em {
    position: relative;
    top: 2em; /* moves element down */
    left: 3em; /* moves element right */
    background-color: fuchsia;
}
```

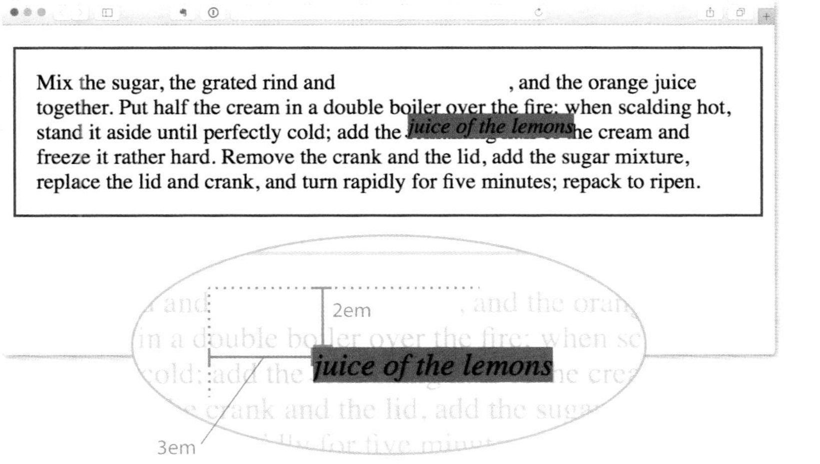

NOTE

*Negative values are acceptable and move the element in the opposite direction of positive values. For example, a negative value for **top** would have the effect of moving the element up.*

When an element is relatively positioned, the space it once occupied is preserved.

FIGURE 15-19. When an element is positioned with the relative method, the space it would have occupied is preserved.

I want to point out a few things that are happening here:

The original space in the document flow is preserved.

You can see that there is a blank space where the emphasized text would have been if the element had not been positioned. The surrounding content is laid out as though the element were still there, and therefore we say that the element still "influences" the surrounding content.

Overlap happens.

Because this is a positioned element, it can potentially overlap other elements, as happens in FIGURE 15-19.

The empty space left behind by relatively positioned objects can be a little awkward, so this method is not used as often as absolute positioning. However, relative positioning is commonly used to create a "positioning context" for an absolutely positioned element. Remember that term *positioning context*—I'll explain it in the next section.

ABSOLUTE POSITIONING

Absolute positioning works a bit differently and is a more flexible method for accurately placing items on the page than relative positioning.

Now that you've seen how relative positioning works, let's take the same example as shown in FIGURE 15-19, only this time we'll change the value of the **position** property to **absolute** (FIGURE 15-20):

```
em {
    position: absolute;
    top: 2em;
    left: 3em;
    background-color: fuchsia;
}
```

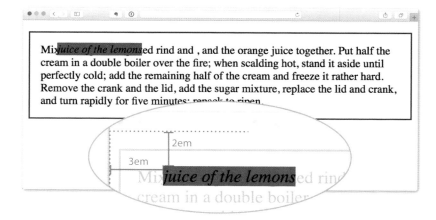

FIGURE 15-20. When an element is absolutely positioned, it is removed from the flow and the space is closed up.

As you can see in FIGURE 15-20, the space once occupied by the **em** element is now closed up, as is the case for all absolutely positioned elements. In its new position, the element box overlaps the surrounding content. In the end, absolutely positioned elements have no influence whatsoever on the layout of surrounding elements.

The most significant difference here, however, is the location of the positioned element. This time, the offset values position the **em** element 2em down and 3em to the right of the top-left corner of the *viewport* (browser window).

But wait—before you start thinking that absolutely positioned elements are always placed relative to the viewport, I'm afraid that there's more to it than that.

What actually happens in absolute positioning is that the element is positioned relative to its nearest *containing block*. It just so happens that the nearest containing block in FIGURE 15-20 is the root (**html**) element, also known as the initial containing block, so the offset values position the **em** element relative to the whole document.

Getting a handle on the containing block concept is the first step to tackling absolute positioning.

Containing Blocks

The CSS Positioned Layout Module, Level 3, states, "The position and size of an element's box(es) are sometimes computed relative to a certain rectangle, called the containing block of the element." It is critical to be aware of the containing block of the element you want to position. We sometimes refer to this as the positioning context.

The spec lays out a number of intricate rules for determining the containing block of an element, but it basically boils down to this:

- If the positioned element is *not* contained within another positioned element, then it will be placed relative to the initial containing block (created by the **html** element).

- But if the element has an ancestor (i.e., is contained within an element) that has its position set to **relative**, **absolute**, or **fixed**, the element will be positioned relative to the edges of *that* element instead.

FIGURE 15-20 is an example of the first case: the **p** element that contains the absolutely positioned **em** element is *not* positioned itself, and there are no other positioned elements higher in the hierarchy. Therefore, the **em** element is positioned relative to the initial containing block, which is equivalent to the viewport area.

Let's deliberately turn the **p** element into a containing block and see what happens. All we have to do is apply the **position** property to it; we don't have to actually move it. The most common way to make an element into a containing block is to set its **position** to **relative**, but not move it with any

> When an element is absolutely positioned, the space it once occupied is closed up.

offset values. This is what I was talking about earlier when I said that relative positioning is used to create a *positioning context* for an absolutely positioned element.

In this example, we'll keep the style rule for the **em** element the same, but we'll add a **position** property to the **p** element, thus making it the containing block for the positioned **em** element. FIGURE 15-21 shows the results.

```
p {
    position: relative;
    padding: 15px;
    background-color: #F2F5D5;
    border: 2px solid purple;
}
```

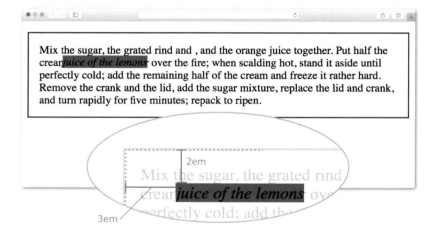

FIGURE 15-21. The relatively positioned **p** element acts as a containing block for the **em** element.

You can see that the **em** element is now positioned 2em down and 3em from the top-left corner of the paragraph box, not the browser window. Notice also that it is positioned relative to the *padding edge* of the paragraph (just inside the border), not the content area edge. This is the normal behavior when block elements are used as containing blocks (see **Note**).

I'm going to poke around at this some more to reveal additional aspects of absolutely positioned objects. This time, I've added **width** and **margin** properties to the positioned **em** element (FIGURE 15-22):

```
em {
    width: 200px;
    margin: 25px;
    position: absolute;
    top: 2em;
    left: 3em;
    background-color: fuchsia;
}
```

NOTE

When inline elements are used as containing blocks (and they can be), the positioned element is placed relative to the content area edge, not the padding edge.

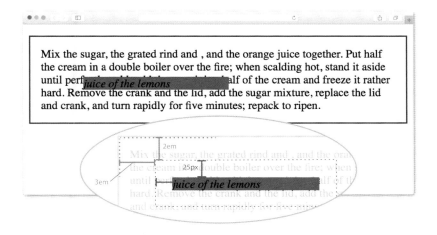

FIGURE 15-22. Adding a width and margins to the positioned element.

Here we can see that:

- The offset values apply to the outer edges of the element box (the outer margin edge) for absolutely positioned elements (see **Note**).

- Absolutely positioned elements always behave as block-level elements. For example, the margins on all sides are maintained, even though this is an inline element. It also permits a width to be set for the element.

It is important to keep in mind that once you've positioned an element, it becomes the new containing block for all the elements it contains. Say you position a narrow **div** at the top-left corner of a page, creating a column. If you were to absolutely position an image within that **div** with offset values that place it in the top-right corner, it appears in the top-right corner of that **div**, not the entire page. Once the parent element is positioned, it acts as the containing block for the **img** and any other contained elements.

Specifying Position

Now that you have a better feel for the containing block concept, let's take some time to get better acquainted with the offset properties. So far, we've only seen an element moved a few ems down and to the right, but that's not all you can do, of course.

Pixel measurements

As mentioned previously, positive offset values push the positioned element box *away* from the specified edge and toward the center of the containing block. If there is no value provided for a side, it is set to **auto**, and the browser adds enough space to make the layout work. In this example, **div#B** is contained within **div#A**, which has been given the dimensions 600 pixels wide by 300 pixels high. I've used pixel lengths for all four offset properties to place

NOTE

For relatively positioned elements, the offset is measured to the box itself (not the outer margin edge).

the positioned element (#B) at a particular spot in its containing element (#A) (FIGURE 15-23).

THE MARKUP

```
<div id="A">
  <div id="B"> </div>
</div>
```

THE STYLES

```
div#A {
  position: relative;    /* creates the containing block */
  width: 600px;
  height: 300px;
  background-color: #C6DE89; /* green */
}

div#B {
  position: absolute;
  top: 25px;
  right: 50px;
  bottom: 75px;
  left: 100px;
  background-color: steelblue;
}
```

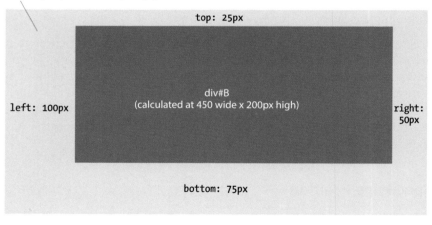

FIGURE 15-23. Setting offset values for all four sides of a positioned element.

Notice that by setting offsets on all four sides, I have indirectly set the dimensions of the positioned **div#B.** It fills the 450 × 200 pixel space that is left over within the containing block after the offset values are applied. If I had also specified a width and other box properties for **div#B**, there is the potential for conflicts if the total of the values for the positioned box and its offsets does not match the available space within the containing block.

The CSS specification provides a daunting set of rules for handling conflicts, but the upshot is that you should just be careful not to over-specify box properties and offsets. In general, a width (factoring in margins as well as padding and border if you are using the **content-box** box-sizing model) and one or two offset properties are all that are necessary to achieve the layout you're looking for. Let the browser take care of the remaining calculations.

Percentage values

You can also specify positions with percentage values. In the first example in FIGURE 15-24, the image is positioned halfway (50%) down the left edge of the containing block. In the second example on the right, the **img** element is positioned so that it always appears in the bottom-right corner of the containing block.

```
img#A {
   position: absolute;
   top: 50%;
   left: 0%;
}
img#B {
   position: absolute;
   bottom: 0%;
   right: 0%;
}
```

Although the examples here specify both a vertical and horizontal offset, it is common to provide just one offset for a positioned element—for example, to move it left or right into a margin using either **left** or **right** properties.

In EXERCISE 15-3, we'll make further changes to the Black Goose Bakery home page, this time using absolute positioning.

WARNING

*Be careful when positioning elements at the bottom of the initial containing block (the **html** element). Although you may expect it to be positioned at the bottom of the whole page, browsers actually place the element at the bottom of the browser window. Results may be unpredictable. If you want something positioned at the bottom of your page, put it in a containing block element at the end of the document source, and go from there.*

NOTE

The % symbol could be omitted for a 0 value, which essentially turns it into a 0 length but achieves an equivalent result.

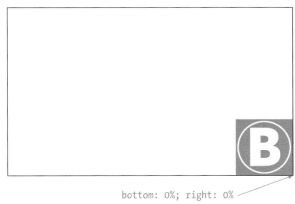

FIGURE 15-24. Using percentage values to position an element in a containing block.

EXERCISE 15-3. Absolute positioning

In this exercise, we'll use absolute positioning to add an award graphic to the home page. Open the version of the site you saved in EXERCISE 15-2.

1. Good news! Black Goose Bakery won the Farmers' Market Award, and we have the privilege of displaying an award medal on the home page. Because this is new content, we'll need to add it to the markup in *bakery.html*. Because it is nonessential information, add the image in a new **div** in the **footer** of the document:

   ```
   <footer>
     <p>All content copyright &copy; 2017, Black
   Goose Bistro.</p>
     <div id="award"><img src="images/award.png"
   alt="Farmers' Market Award"></div>
   </footer>
   ```

2. Just because the award is at the end of the source document doesn't mean it needs to display there. We can use absolute positioning to place the award in the top-left corner of the viewport by adding a new rule to the style sheet that positions the **div**, like so (I put mine in the **/* misc styles */** section):

   ```
   #award {
     position: absolute;
     top: 30px;
     left: 50px;
   }
   ```

Save the document and take a look (FIGURE 15-25). Resize the browser window very narrow, and you will see that the positioned award image overlaps the header content. Notice also that when you scroll the document, the image scrolls with the rest of the page. Try playing around with other offset properties to get a feel for positioning in the viewport (or the "initial containing block" to be precise).

P.S. I know that the navigation list still looks bad, but we'll fix it up in **Chapter 16**.

Fresh from the Oven

FIGURE 15-25. An absolutely positioned award graphic.

Stacking Order

Before we close the book on absolute positioning, there is one last related concept that I want to introduce. As we've seen, absolutely positioned elements overlap other elements, so it follows that multiple positioned elements have the potential to stack up on one another.

By default, elements stack up in the order in which they appear in the document, but you can change the stacking order with the **z-index** property (see **Note**). Picture the z-axis as a line that runs perpendicular to the page, as though from the tip of your nose, through this page, and out the other side.

NOTE

*The **z-index** property is also useful for items in a grid, which also have the potential to overlap, as discussed in **Chapter 16**.*

`z-index`

Values:	*number* | auto
Default:	auto
Applies to:	positioned elements
Inherits:	no

The value of the **z-index** property is a number (positive or negative). The higher the number, the higher the element will appear in the stack (that is, closer to your nose). Lower numbers and negative values move the element lower in the stack. Let's look at an example to make this clear (FIGURE 15-26).

Here are three paragraph elements, each containing a letter image (A, B, and C, respectively) that have been absolutely positioned in such a way that they overlap on the page. By default, paragraph C would appear on top because it appears last in the source. However, by assigning higher **z-index** values to paragraphs A and B, we can force them to stack in our preferred order.

Note that the values of **z-index** do not need to be sequential, and they do not relate to anything in particular. All that matters is that higher number values position the element higher in the stack.

THE MARKUP

```
<p id="A"><img src="A.gif" alt="A"></p>
<p id="B"><img src="B.gif" alt="B"></p>
<p id="C"><img src="C.gif" alt="C"></p>
```

THE STYLES

```
#A {
  z-index: 100;
  position: absolute;
  top: 175px;
  left: 200px;
}

#B {
  z-index: 5;
  position: absolute;
  top: 275px;
  left: 100px;
}

#C {
  z-index: 1;
  position: absolute;
  top: 325px;
  left: 250px;
}
```

By default, elements later in the document source order stack on top of preceding elements.

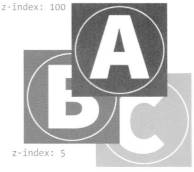

You can change the stacking order with the z-index property. Higher values stack on top of lower values.

FIGURE 15-26. Changing the stacking order with the **z-index** property.

To be honest, the **z-index** property is not often required for most page layouts, but you should know it's there if you need it. If you want to guarantee that a positioned element always ends up on top, assign it a very high **z-index** value, such as 100 or 1000. If you want to make sure it's at the bottom, give it a negative value. The number itself doesn't actually matter.

FIXED POSITIONING

We've covered relative and absolute positioning, so now it's time to take on fixed positioning.

For the most part, fixed positioning works just like absolute positioning. The significant difference is that the offset values for fixed elements are *always* relative to the viewport, which means the positioned element stays put even when the rest of the page scrolls. By contrast, you may remember that when you scrolled the Black Goose Bakery page in EXERCISE 15-3, the award graphic scrolled along with the document—even though it was positioned relative to the initial containing block (equivalent to the viewport). Not so with fixed positioning, where the position is, well, *fixed*.

Fixed elements are often used for menus that stay in the same place at the top, bottom, or side of a screen so they are always available, even when the content scrolls (see **Warning**). Bear in mind that if you fix an element to the bottom of the viewport, you'll need to leave enough space at the end of the document so the content doesn't get hidden behind the fixed element. Fixed elements are also problematic when the document is printed because they will print on every page without reserving any space for themselves. It's best to turn off fixed elements when printing the document. (Targeting print with **@media** is addressed in **Chapter 17, Responsive Web Design**.)

Let's switch the award graphic on the Black Goose Bakery page to a fixed position in EXERCISE 15-4 to see the difference.

EXERCISE 15-4. Fixed positioning

This should be simple. Open the bakery style sheet as you left it in EXERCISE 15-3 and edit the style rule for the **#award div** to make it **fixed** rather than **absolute**:

```
#award {
  position: fixed;
  top: 30px;
  left: 50px;
}
```

Save the styles and open the page in a browser. When you scroll the page, you will see that the award now stays put where we positioned it in the browser window (FIGURE 15-27). You can see that fixed positioned elements have the potential to hide content as the page scrolls. Test well to see the potential pitfalls and weigh them against the benefits.

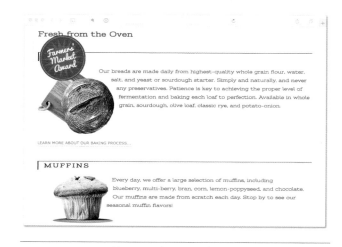

FIGURE 15-27. The award stays in the same place in the top-left corner of the browser when the document scrolls.

That does it for floating and positioning. In the next chapter, you'll learn about flexible boxes and grid layout, which are powerful tools for designing the overall structure of a page and specific page features. But first, try your hand at a few questions about floating and positioning.

TEST YOURSELF

Before we move on, take a moment to see how well you absorbed the principles in this chapter. You'll find the answers in **Appendix A**.

1. Which of the following is *not* true of floated elements?

    a. All floated elements behave as block elements.

    b. Floats are positioned against the padding edge of the containing element.

    c. The contents of inline elements flow around a float, but the element box is unchanged.

    d. You must provide a **width** property for floated block elements.

2. Which of these style rules is incorrect? Why?

    a. `img { float: left; margin: 20px;}`

    b. `img { float: right; width: 120px; height: 80px; }`

    c. `img { float: right; right: 30px; }`

    d. `img { float: left; margin-bottom: 2em; }`

3. How do you make sure a **footer** element always starts below any floated sidebars on the page?

4. Write the name of the positioning method or methods (static, relative, absolute, or fixed) that best matches each of the following descriptions.

    a. Positions the element relative to a containing block.

    b. Removes the element from the normal flow.

    c. Always positions the element relative to the viewport.

    d. The positioned element may overlap other content.

Continued...

e. Positions the element in the normal flow.

f. The space the element would have occupied in the normal flow is preserved.

g. The space the element would have occupied in the normal flow is closed up.

h. You can change the stacking order with **z-index**.

i. Positions the element relative to its original position in the normal flow.

CSS REVIEW: FLOATING AND POSITIONING PROPERTIES

Here is a summary of the properties covered in this chapter.

Property	Description
clear	Prevents an element from being laid out next to a float
float	Moves the element to the right or left and allows the following text to flow around it
position	Specifies the positioning method to be applied
top, bottom, right, left	Specifies the offset amount from each respective edge
shape-outside	Causes content to wrap around a shape instead of the float's bounding box.
shape-margin	Adds a margin to **shape-outside**
shape-image-threshold	Defines the alpha channel threshold used to create the wrap shape
z-index	Specifies the order of appearance within a stack of overlapping positioned elements

CSS LAYOUT WITH FLEXBOX AND GRID

Get ready...this is a *whopper* of a chapter! In it, you will learn about two important CSS page layout tools:

- Flexbox for greater control over arranging items along one axis

- Grid for honest-to-goodness grid-based layouts, like those print designers have used for decades

Each tool has its special purpose, but you can use them together to achieve layouts we've only dreamed of until now. For example, you could create the overall page structure with a grid and use a flexbox to tame the header and navigation elements. Use each technique for what it's best suited for—you don't have to choose just one.

Now that browsers have begun to support these techniques, designers and developers have true options for achieving sophisticated layouts with baked-in flexibility needed for dealing with a wide array of screen sizes. Once old browsers fade from use, we can kiss our old float layout hacks goodbye (in the meantime, they make decent fallbacks).

You may notice that this chapter is big. *Really* big. That's because the specs are overflowing with options and new concepts that require explanation and examples. It's a lot to pack in your mind all at once, so I recommend treating it as two mini-chapters and spend some time getting up to speed with each technique individually.

FLEXIBLE BOXES WITH CSS FLEXBOX

The CSS Flexible Box Layout Module (also known as simply Flexbox) gives designers and developers a handy tool for laying out components of web pages such as menu bars, product listings, galleries, and much more.

According to the spec,

> *The defining aspect of flex layout is the ability to make the flex items "flex," altering their width/height to fill the available space in the main dimension.*

That means it allows items to stretch or shrink inside their containers, preventing wasted space and overflow—a real plus for making layouts fit a variety of viewport sizes. Other advantages include the following:

- The ability to make all neighboring items the same height

- Easy horizontal and vertical centering (curiously elusive with old CSS methods)

- The ability to change the order in which items display, independent of the source

The Flexbox layout model is incredibly robust, but because it was designed for maximum flexibility, it takes a little time to wrap your head around it (at least it did for me). Here's how it helped me to think about it: when you tell an element to become a flexbox, all of its child elements line up on one axis, like beads on a string. The string may be horizontal, it may hang vertically, or it may even wrap onto multiple lines, but the beads are always on one string (or to use the proper term, one axis). If you want to line things up both horizontally *and* vertically, that is the job of CSS Grid, which I'll introduce in the next section of this chapter.

Before we dig in, I have a quick heads-up about browser support. All current browser versions support the latest W3C Flexible Box Layout Module spec; however, older browsers require prefixes and even different, outdated properties and values altogether. I'll be sticking with the current standard properties to keep everything simple while you learn this for the first time, but know

Multicolumn Layout

A third CSS3 layout tool you may want to try is multicolumn layout. The Multi-column Layout Module (*w3.org/TR/css-multicol-1*) provides tools for pouring text content into a number of columns, as you might see in a newspaper (FIGURE 16-1). It is designed to be flexible, allowing the widths and number of columns to automatically fit the available space.

This chapter is already big enough, so I've put this lesson in an article, **"Multicolumn Layout"** (PDF), available at *learningwebdesign.com/articles/*.

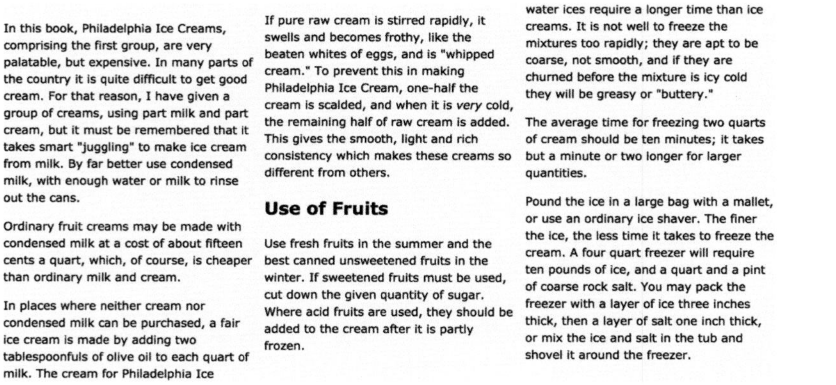

In this book, Philadelphia Ice Creams, comprising the first group, are very palatable, but expensive. In many parts of the country it is quite difficult to get good cream. For that reason, I have given a group of creams, using part milk and part cream, but it must be remembered that it takes smart "juggling" to make ice cream from milk. By far better use condensed milk, with enough water or milk to rinse out the cans.

Ordinary fruit creams may be made with condensed milk at a cost of about fifteen cents a quart, which, of course, is cheaper than ordinary milk and cream.

In places where neither cream nor condensed milk can be purchased, a fair ice cream is made by adding two tablespoonfuls of olive oil to each quart of milk. The cream for Philadelphia Ice

If pure raw cream is stirred rapidly, it swells and becomes frothy, like the beaten whites of eggs, and is "whipped cream." To prevent this in making Philadelphia Ice Cream, one-half the cream is scalded, and when it is *very* cold, the remaining half of raw cream is added. This gives the smooth, light and rich consistency which makes these creams so different from others.

Use of Fruits

Use fresh fruits in the summer and the best canned unsweetened fruits in the winter. If sweetened fruits must be used, cut down the given quantity of sugar. Where acid fruits are used, they should be added to the cream after it is partly frozen.

water ices require a longer time than ice creams. It is not well to freeze the mixtures too rapidly; they are apt to be coarse, not smooth, and if they are churned before the mixture is icy cold they will be greasy or "buttery."

The average time for freezing two quarts of cream should be ten minutes; it takes but a minute or two longer for larger quantities.

Pound the ice in a large bag with a mallet, or use an ordinary ice shaver. The finer the ice, the less time it takes to freeze the cream. A four quart freezer will require ten pounds of ice, and a quart and a pint of coarse rock salt. You may pack the freezer with a layer of ice three inches thick, then a layer of salt one inch thick, or mix the ice and salt in the tub and shovel it around the freezer.

FIGURE 16-1. An example of text formatted with the multicolumn properties.

that production-ready style sheets may require more code. I'll give you the nitty-gritty on browser support at the end of this section.

Setting Up a Flexbox Container

You've already learned about the block layout mode for stacking elements in the normal flow and the inline mode for displaying content within it horizontally. Flexbox is another layout mode with its own behaviors. To turn on flexbox mode for an element, set its **display** property to **flex** or **inline-flex** (see **Note**). It is now a flex container, and all of its direct child elements (whether they are **div**s, list items, paragraphs, etc.) *automatically* become flex items in that container. The flex items (the beads) are laid out and aligned along flex lines (the string).

FIGURE 16-2 shows the effect of simply adding **display: flex** to a **div**, thus turning on the Flexbox switch. I've added a blue border to the container to make its boundaries clear. To save space, I am not showing purely cosmetic styles such as colors and fonts.

THE MARKUP

```
<div id="container">
  <div class="box box1">1</div>
  <div class="box box2">2</div>
  <div class="box box3">3</div>
  <div class="box box4">4</div>
  <div class="box box5">5</div>
</div>
```

THE STYLES

```
#container {
  display: flex;
}
```

Flexbox Resources

You'll learn all the ins and outs of Flexbox in this chapter, but it is always good to get a few perspectives and hands-on tutorials online. If you do a web search, be sure to limit your findings to 2015 posts and later, or you may come across outdated advice based on earlier spec versions. Following are some of the sites that I've found most useful or most entertaining:

A Complete Guide to Flexbox
(css-tricks.com/snippets/css/a-guide-to-flexbox/)

> This summary of Flexbox features by Chris Coyier is one of the most popular Flexbox references out there. Many developers just keep it open in a browser when they do Flexbox work.

Flexbox Froggy (flexboxfroggy.com/)

> Don't miss this online game for learning Flexbox by helping colorful frogs make it back to their lily pads.

What the Flexbox?! (flexbox.io/)

> Wes Bos does a great job walking you through Flexbox properties as well as a few code projects in this free, 20-part video series.

Flexbox Playground (codepen.io/enxaneta/full/adLPwv/)

> As the name says, this page by Gabi lets you play around with all of the Flexbox properties and values and see the results instantly. It's a nice way to get familiar with what Flexbox can do.

Flexy Boxes (the-echoplex.net/flexyboxes/)

> This is another Flexbox playground and code generator.

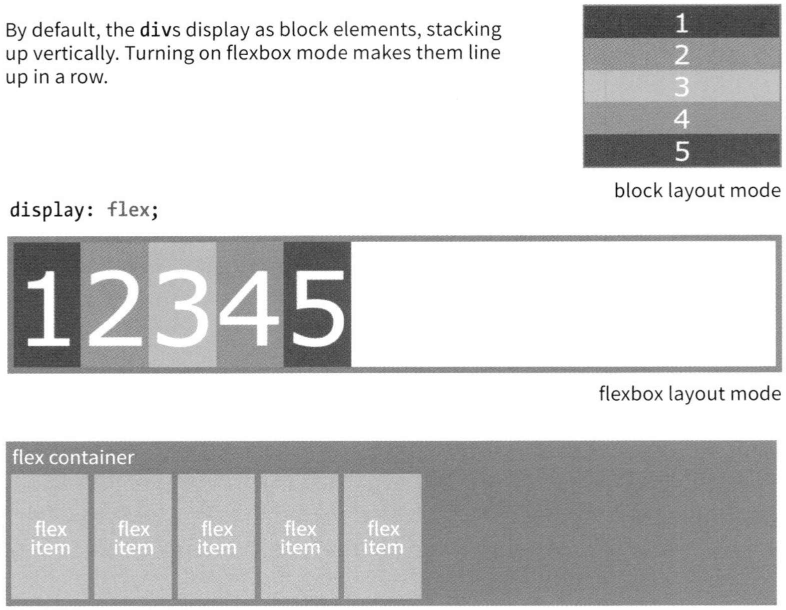

By default, the **divs** display as block elements, stacking up vertically. Turning on flexbox mode makes them line up in a row.

block layout mode

`display: flex;`

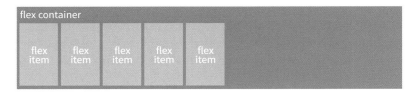

flexbox layout mode

FIGURE 16-2. Applying the flex display mode turns the child elements into flex items that line up along one axis. You don't need to do anything to the child elements themselves.

You can see that the items have lined up in a row from left to right, which is the default Flexbox behavior if your page is in English or another language written in rows from left to right. That is because the default flexbox direction matches the direction of the language the page is written in. It would go from right to left by default in Hebrew or Arabic or in columns if the page is set with a vertical writing direction. Because it is not tied to one default direction, the terminology for specifying directions tends to be a little abstract. You'll see what I mean when we talk about "flow" in the following section.

It is worth noting that you can turn any flex item into a flex container by setting its **display** to **flex**, resulting in a nested flexbox. In fact, you'll get to try that yourself in an upcoming exercise. Some Flexbox solutions use flexboxes nested several layers deep.

Controlling the "Flow" Within the Container

Once you turn an element into a flex container, there are a few properties you can set on that container to control how items flow within it. The flow refers to the direction in which flex items are laid out as well as whether they are permitted to wrap onto additional lines.

Specifying flow direction

You may be happy with items lining up in a row as shown in FIGURE 16-2, but there are a few other options that are controllled with the **flex-direction** property.

flex-direction

Values: row | column | row-reverse | column-reverse

Default: row

Applies to: flex containers

Inherits: no

The default value is **row**, as we saw in the previous example (see the "**Row and Column Direction**" sidebar). You can also specify that items get aligned vertically in a **column**. The other options, **row-reverse** and **column-reverse**, arrange items in the direction you would expect, but they start at the end and get filled in the opposite direction. FIGURE 16-3 shows the effects of each keyword as applied to our simple example.

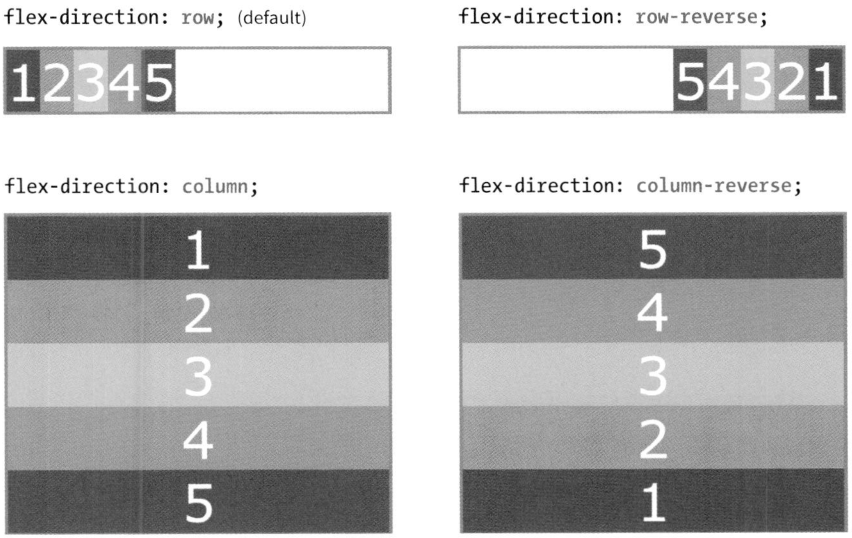

FIGURE 16-3. Examples of **flex-direction** values **row**, **row-reverse**, **column**, and **column-reverse**.

Now that you've seen Flexbox in action, it's a good time to familiarize yourself with the formal Flexbox terminology. Because the system is direction-agnostic, there are no references to "left," "right," "top," or "bottom" in the property values. Instead, we talk about the main axis and the cross axis. The main axis is the flow direction you've specified for the flex container. For primarily horizontal languages, when set to **row**, the main axis is horizontal; for **column**, the main axis is vertical (again, rows and columns are language-dependent, as explained earlier in the **"Row and Column Direction"** sidebar).

Row and Column Direction

In writing systems with horizontal lines of text, the **row** keyword lays items out horizontally, as we Westerners typically think of a "row." Bear in mind that in vertically oriented languages, **row** aligns items vertically, in keeping with the default direction of the writing system. Similarly, **column** results in horizontally aligned items in vertical languages.

This is a behavior worth knowing; however, because we are creating English language sites in this book, I'll be sticking with the assumptions that row = horizontal and column = vertical throughout this chapter for simplicity's sake.

The cross axis is whatever direction is perpendicular to the main axis (vertical for **row**, horizontal for **column**). The parts of a flex container are illustrated in FIGURE 16-4.

In addition to the axes, understanding the other parts of the Flexbox system makes the properties easier to learn. Both the main and cross axes have a start and an end, based on the direction in which the items flow. The main size is the width (or height if it's a column) of the container along the main axis, and the cross size is height (or width if it's a column) along the cross axis.

Wrapping onto multiple lines

If you have a large or unknown number of flex items in a container and don't want them to get all squished into the available space, you can allow them to break onto additional lines with the **flex-wrap** property.

> The main axis is the flow direction you've specified for the flex container.
> The cross axis is perpendicular to the main axis.

> ### ■ DON'T WORRY
>
> Keeping the main and cross axes straight as you switch between rows and columns can feel like mental gymnastics and is one of the trickier things about using Flexbox. With practice, you'll get used to it.

FOR LANGUAGES THAT READ HORIZONTALLY FROM LEFT TO RIGHT:

When **flex-direction** is set to **row**, the main axis is horizontal and the cross axis is vertical.

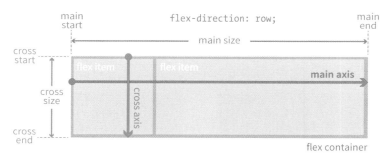

When **flex-direction** is set to **column**, the main axis is vertical and the cross axis is horizontal.

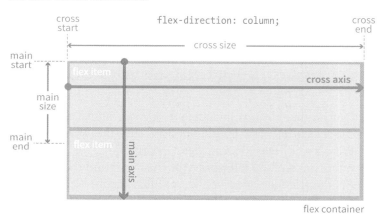

FIGURE 16-4. The parts of a flex container.

`flex-wrap`

Values:	nowrap | wrap | wrap-reverse
Default:	nowrap
Applies to:	flex containers
Inherits:	no

By default, items do the squish thing and do not wrap onto additional lines (**nowrap**). The **wrap** keyword turns on the ability to wrap onto multiple lines in the direction from cross start to cross end. For example, if the direction is row, then lines are positioned from the top down.

wrap-reverse breaks the elements onto multiple lines, but flows them in the opposite direction, from cross end to cross start (from the bottom up, in this case). It feels a little esoteric to me, but you never know when an occasion might arise to put it to use.

I've added more **div**s to our numbered flexbox example and I've given the flex items a width of 25% so that only four will fit across the width of the container. FIGURE 16-5 shows a comparison of the various wrap options when the **flex-direction** is the default **row**.

THE MARKUP

```
<div id="container">
  <div class="box box1">1</div>
  <!-- more boxes here -->
  <div class="box box10">10</div>
</div>
```

THE STYLES

```
#container {
  display: flex;
  flex-direction: row;
  flex-wrap: wrap;
}
.box {
  width: 25%;
}
```

flex-wrap: `wrap`;

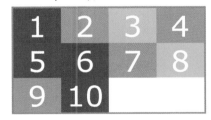

flex-wrap: `wrap-reverse`;

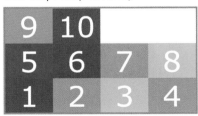

flex-wrap: `nowrap`; (default)

When wrapping is disabled, flex items squish if there is not enough room, and if they can't squish any further, may get cut off if there is not enough room in the viewport.

FIGURE 16-5. Comparing the effects of **nowrap**, **wrap**, and **wrap-reverse** keywords for **flex-wrap**.

By default, when the **flex-direction** is set to **column**, the container expands to contain the height of the items. In order to see wrapping kick in, you need to set a height on the container, as I've done here. FIGURE 16-6 shows how wrapping works for each of the **flex-wrap** keywords. Notice that the items are still 25% the width of their parent container, so there is space left over between the columns.

```
#container {
  display: flex;
  height: 350px;
  flex-direction: column;
  flex-wrap: wrap;
}
.box {
  width: 25%;
}
```

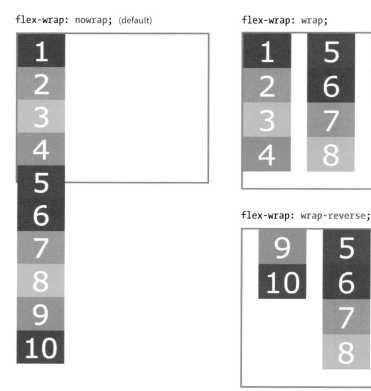

FIGURE 16-6. Comparing **nowrap**, **wrap**, and **wrap-reverse** when the items are in a column.

Putting it together with flex-flow

The shorthand property **flex-flow** makes specifying **flex-direction** and **flex-wrap** short and sweet. Omitting one value results in the default value for its respective property, which means you can use **flex-flow** for either or both direction and wrap.

`flex-flow`

Values:	*flex-direction flex-wrap*
Default:	`row nowrap`
Applies to:	flex containers
Inherits:	no

Using **flex-flow**, I could shorten the previous example (FIGURE 16-6) like so:

```
#container {
   display: flex;
   height: 350px;
   flex-flow: column wrap;
}
```

You've only scratched the surface of Flexbox, but you've got what it takes to whip that ugly **nav** menu on the bakery page into shape in EXERCISE 16-1.

EXERCISE 16-1. Making a navigation bar with Flexbox

Open the most recent version of the style sheet for the bakery home page in a text editor. If you need a fresh start, you will find an updated copy of *bakery-styles.css* in the materials for **Chapter 16**.

Note: Be sure to use one of the Flexbox-supporting browsers listed at the end of this section.

1. Open *bakery-styles.css* in a text editor and start by making the **ul** element in the **nav** element as neutral as possible:

```
nav ul {
   margin: 0;
   padding: 0;
   list-style-type: none;
}
```

Turn that **ul** element into a flexbox by setting its **display** to **flex**. As a result, all of the **li** elements become flex items. Because we want rows and no wrapping, the default values for **flex-direction** and **flex-wrap** are fine, so the properties can be omitted:

```
nav ul {
   …
   display: flex;
}
```

Save the document and look at it in a browser. You should see that the links are lined up tightly in a row, which is an improvement, but we have more work to do.

2. Now we can work on the appearance of the links. Start by making the **a** elements in the **nav** list items display as block elements instead of inline. Give them 1px rounded borders, padding within the borders (.5em top and bottom, 1em left and right), and .5em margins to give them space and to open up the brown navigation bar.

```
nav ul li a {
   display: block;
   border: 1px solid;
   border-radius: .5em;
   padding: .5em 1em;
   margin: .5em;
}
```

3. We want the navigation menu to be centered in the width of the **nav** section. I'm getting a little ahead here because we haven't seen alignment properties yet, but this one is fairly intuitive. Consider it a preview of what's coming up in the next section. Add the following declaration for the **nav ul** element:

```
nav ul {
   …
   display: flex;
   justify-content: center;
}
```

FIGURE 16-7 shows the way your navigation menu should look when you are finished.

IMPORTANT: We'll be using this version of the bakery site as the starting point for EXERCISE 16-6, so save it and keep it for later.

FIGURE 16-7. The list of links is now styled as a horizontal menu bar.

Controlling the Alignment of Flex Items in the Container

So far we've seen how to turn flexbox mode on, turning an element into a flex container and its children into flex items. We've also learned how to change the direction in which items flow, and allow them to wrap onto multiple lines. The remaining set of container properties affects the alignment of items along the main axis (`justify-content`) and cross axis (`align-items` and `align-content`).

Aligning on the main axis

By default, flex items are just as wide as they need to be to contain the element's content, which means the container may potentially have space to spare on the flex line. We saw this back in FIGURE 16-2. Also by default, the items flow in right next to each other from the "main start" (based on language direction and the direction of the flex line).

The `justify-content` property defines how extra space should be distributed around or between items that are inflexible or have reached their maximum size (see **Note**).

`justify-content`

Values: `flex-start | flex-end | center | space-between | space-around`

Default: `flex-start`

Applies to: flex containers

Inherits: no

Apply `justify-content` to the flex container element because it controls spacing within the container itself:

```
#container {
  display: flex;
  justify-content: flex-start;
}
```

FIGURE 16-8 shows how items align using each of the keyword values for `justify-content`. As you would expect, `flex-start` and `flex-end` position the line of items toward the start and end of the main axis, respectively, and `center` centers them.

`space-between` and `space-around` warrant a little more explanation. When `justify-content` is set to `space-between`, the first item is positioned at the start point, the last item goes at the end point, and the remaining space is distributed evenly between the remaining items. The `space-around` property adds an equal amount of space on the left and right side of each item, resulting in a doubling up of space between neighboring items.

justify-content: flex-start; (default)

1234567

justify-content: flex-end;

1234567

justify-content: center;

1234567

justify-content: space-between;

1 2 3 4 5 6 7

justify-content: space-around;

1 2 3 4 5 6 7

FIGURE 16-8. Options for aligning items along the main axis with **justify-content**.

When the direction is set to a column with a vertical main axis, the keywords work the same way; however, there needs to be an explicit container height with space left over in order for you to see the effect. I've changed the size of the text and set a height on the container element in FIGURE 16-9 to demonstrate the same keywords as applied to a vertical main axis.

justify-content: flex-start; (default)

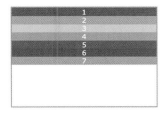

justify-content: flex-end;

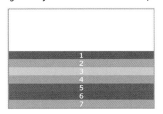

justify-content: center;

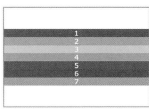

justify-content: space-between;

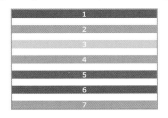

justify-content: space-around;

FIGURE 16-9. Options for aligning items along a vertical main axis (**flex-direction** set to **column**) with **justify-content**.

Aligning on the cross axis

That takes care of arranging things on the main axis, but you may also want to play around with alignment on the cross axis (up and down when the direction is **row**, left and right if the direction is **column**). Cross-axis alignment and stretching is the job of the **align-items** property.

align-items

Values:	flex-start | flex-end | center | baseline | stretch
Default:	stretch
Applies to:	flex containers
Inherits:	no

I've demonstrated the various keyword values for **align-items** as it applies to rows in FIGURE 16-10. In order to see the effect, you must specify the container height; otherwise, it expands just enough to contain the content with no extra space. I've given the container a height to show how items are positioned on the cross axis.

Like **justify-content**, the **align-items** property applies to the flex container (that can be a little confusing because "items" is in the name).

```
#container {
    display: flex;
    flex-direction: row;
    height: 200px;
    align-items: flex-start;
}
```

The **flex-start**, **flex-end**, and **center** values should be familiar, only this time they refer to the start, end, and center of the cross axis. The **baseline** value aligns the baselines of the first lines of text, regardless of their size. It may be a good option for lining up elements with different text sizes, such as headlines and paragraphs across multiple items. Finally, **stretch**, which is the default, causes items to stretch until they fill the cross axis.

align-items: flex-start;

align-items: flex-end;

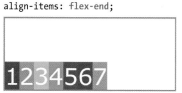

align-items: center;

align-items: stretch; (default)

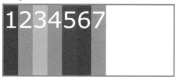

Items are aligned so that the baselines of the first text lines align.

align-items: baseline;

FIGURE 16-10. Aligning along the cross axis with **align-items**.

When the flex container's direction is set to **column**, **align-items** aligns items left and right. Look back at FIGURES 16-2 and 16-9 and you will see that when we set the items in a column and did not provide any alignment information, each item stretched to the full width of the cross axis because **stretch** is the default value.

If you'd like one or more items to override the cross-axis setting, use the **align-self** property on the individual item element(s). This is the first property we've seen that applies to an *item*, not the container itself. **align-self** uses the same values as **align-items**; it just works on one item at a time.

align-self

Values:	flex-start	flex-end	center	baseline	stretch
Default:	stretch
Applies to:	flex items
Inherits:	no

In the following code and FIGURE 16-11, the fourth box is set to align at the end of the cross axis, while the others have the default stretch behavior.

```
.box4 {
  align-self: flex-end;
}
```

FIGURE 16-11. Use **align-self** to make one item override the cross-axis alignment of its container.

Aligning multiple lines

The final alignment option, **align-content**, affects how multiple flex lines are spread out across the cross axis. This property applies only when **flex-wrap** is set to **wrap** or **wrap-reverse** and there are multiple lines to align. If the items are on a single line, it does nothing.

align-content

Values:	flex-start	flex-end	center	space-around	space-between	stretch
Default:	stretch
Applies to:	multi-line flex containers
Inherits:	no

align-content applies only when there are multiple wrapped flex lines.

All of the values you see in the property listing should look familiar, and they work the way you would expect. This time, however, they apply to how extra space is distributed around multiple lines on the cross axis, as shown in FIGURE 16-12.

Again, the **align-content** property applies to the flex container element. A height is required for the container as well, because without it the container would be just tall enough to accommodate the content and there would be no space left over.

```
#container {
  display: flex;
  flex-direction: row;
  flex-wrap: wrap;
  height: 350px;
  align-items: flex-start;
}

box {
  width: 25%;
}
```

align-content: flex-start;

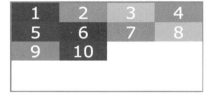

align-content: flex-end;

align-content: center;

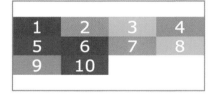

align-content: space-between;

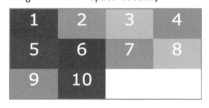

align-content: space-around;

align-content: stretch; (default)

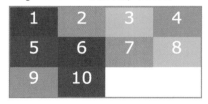

FIGURE 16-12. The **align-content** property distributes space around multiple flex lines. It has no effect when flex items are in a single line.

Aligning items with margins

As long as we're talking about alignment, there is one good trick I'd like to show you that will be useful when you start laying out components with Flexbox.

Menu bars are ubiquitous on the web, and it is common for one element of the bar, such as a logo or a search field, to be set off visually from the others. You can use a margin to put the extra container space on a specified side or sides of a flex item, thus setting one item apart. This should be more clear with an example.

The menu in FIGURE 16-13 has a logo and four menu options. I'd like the logo to stay in the left corner but the options to stay over to the right, regardless of the width of the viewport.

THE MARKUP

```
<ul>
  <li class="logo"><img src="logo.png" alt="LoGoCo"></li>
  <li>About</li>
  <li>Blog</li>
  <li>Shop</li>
  <li>Contact</li>
</ul>
```

Use margins to add space on the sides of particular flex items.

THE STYLES

```
ul {
  display: flex;
  align-items: center;
  background-color: #00af8f;
  list-style: none; /* removes bullets */
  padding: .5em;
  margin: 0;
}
li {
  margin: 0 1em;
}
li.logo {
  margin-right: auto;
}
```

FIGURE 16-13. Using a margin to adjust the space around flex items. In this example, the right margin of the logo item pushes the remaining items to the right.

I've turned the unordered list (**ul**) into a flex container, so its list items (**li**) are now flex items. By default, the items would stay together at the start of the main axis (on the left) with extra space on the right. Setting the right margin on the logo item to **auto** moves the extra space to the right of the logo, pushing the remaining items all the way to the right (the "main end").

This technique applies to a number of scenarios. If you want just the last item to appear on the right, set its left margin to **auto**. Want equal space around the center item in a list? Set both its left and right margins to **auto**. Want to push a button to the bottom of a column? Set the top margin of the last item to **auto**. The extra space in the container goes into the margin and pushes the neighboring items away.

We've covered a lot of territory, so it's a good time to try out Flexbox in EXERCISE 16-2.

HEADS-UP

When you use **margin: auto** *on a flex item, the* **justify-content** *property no longer has a visual effect because you've manually assigned a location for the extra space on the main axis.*

EXERCISE 16-2. A flexible online menu

Now it's time for you to play around with Flexbox properties by using content a bit more complex than links in a menu bar. In this exercise, you'll format a simple online menu with a number of menu items. As always, the materials are available at *learningwebdesign.com/5e/materials*.

Open *flex-menu.html* in a text editor, and you'll see that it has all of the content ready to go as well as an internal style sheet with styles for the cosmetic aspects of the menu (colors, fonts, borders, spacing, etc.). Open the file in a browser, and the menu items should appear in a column because they are block elements. I put a border on the **#menu** wrapper **div** so you can visualize its boundaries.

1. First, we'll go for maximum impact with minimal effort by making the **#menu** wrapper **div** a flex container. There is already a rule for **#menu**, so add this declaration to it:

   ```
   #menu {
       border: 3px solid #783F27;
       display: flex;
   }
   ```

   Save and reload the page in the browser, and BAM!…they're in a row now! And because we haven't added any other flex

properties, they are demonstrating default flexbox behavior (FIGURE 16-14):

- Each item (defined by a **section** element) is the full height of the **#menu** container, regardless of its content.
- The sections have their widths set to 240 pixels, and that measurement is preserved by default. Depending on how wide your browser window is set, you may see content extending beyond the container and getting clipped off, as shown in the figure.

2. By default, flex items appear in the writing direction (a row, left to right, in English). Add the **flex-direction** property to the existing **#menu** rule to try out some of the other values (**row-reverse**, **column**, **column-reverse**). The items are numbered to make their order more apparent.

   ```
   flex-direction: row-reverse;
   ```

3. Set the **flex-direction** back to **row**, and let's play around with the cross-axis alignment by using the **align-items** property. Begin by setting it to **flex-start** (FIGURE 16-15). Save and reload, and see that the items all line up at the start of the cross axis (the top, in this case). Try some of the other values

FIGURE 16-14. The bistro menu in default flexbox mode. By default, the items stay in one row even though there is not enough room for them and content gets clipped.

FIGURE 16-15. Using the **align-items** property to align the items at the start of the cross axis (**flex-start**).

for **align-items** (**flex-end**, **center**, **baseline**, and **stretch**) to get a feel for how each behaves.

```
align-items: flex-start;
```

4. When you are done experimenting, set **align-items** back to **stretch**. Instead of having all the items on one line and getting cropped by the edge of the browser, let's have them wrap onto multiple lines by using the **flex-wrap** property on the **#menu** container:

```
flex-wrap: wrap;
```

Save the file and look at it in the browser (FIGURE 16-16). Resize the browser window and watch the lines rewrap. Notice that each flex line is as tall as the tallest item in that row, but rows may have different heights based on item content.

FIGURE 16-16. The menu with wrapping turned on.

5. If you'd like, you can replace the **flex-direction** and **flex-wrap** declarations with a single **flex-flow** declaration like so:

```
flex-flow: row wrap;
```

6. By default, the items on each flex line are stacked toward the start of the main axis (the left). Try changing the main-axis alignment of items with the **justify-content** property (again, applied to the **#menu** flex container rule). I like how they look centered in the container, but check out the effect of the other values (**flex-start**, **flex-end**, **space-between**, **space-around**) as well.

```
justify-content: center;
```

7. As a final tweak, let's make the price buttons line up at the bottom of each menu item, which is possible if each item is also a flex container. Here, I'm making each item a nested flex container by setting its **display** to **flex** and specifying the direction as **column** so they continue to stack up vertically. Now the **h2** and **p** elements become flex items within the **section** flex container.

```
section {
  …
  display: flex;
  flex-direction: column;
}
```

When you reload the page in the browser, it looks about the same as when the sections were made up of block elements. The subtle difference is that now the neighboring margins between elements stack up and do not collapse.

Now push the paragraphs containing the prices to the bottom using the **margin: auto** trick. Add this declaration to the existing style rule for elements with the class name "price."

```
.price {
  …
  margin-top: auto;
}
```

FIGURE 16-17 shows the final state of the "Bistro Items to Go" menu with nested flexboxes. We'll continue working on this file after we've learned the item-specific properties, so save it for later.

FIGURE 16-17. The menu so far with wrapping flex items and aligned prices.

Determining How Items "Flex" in the Container

One of the great marvels of the flexbox model is that items resize, or flex to use the formal term, to fit the available space. It's this flexibility that makes Flexbox such a powerful tool for designing for the wide array of screen and browser window sizes we encounter as web designers. The beauty is that the browser figures out the sizes on the fly, and that means less math for us! In this section, we'll get to know the flex properties.

Earlier, you learned about the **justify-content** property, which distributes extra space in the container between and around items along the main axis. The concept of flex is concerned with how space is distributed *within* items, growing or shrinking items as required to make them fit.

Flex is controlled with the **flex** property, which specifies how much an item can grow and shrink, and identifies its starting size. The full story is that **flex** is a shorthand property for **flex-grow**, **flex-shrink**, and **flex-basis**, but the spec strongly recommends that authors use the **flex** shorthand instead of individual properties in order to avoid conflicting default values and to ensure that authors consider all three aspects of **flex** for every instance.

flex

Values:	none | *'flex-grow flex-shrink flex-basis'*
Default:	0 1 auto
Applies to:	flex items
Inherits:	no

The value for the **flex** property is typically three flex properties listed in this order:

```
flex: flex-grow flex-shrink flex-basis;
```

For the **flex-grow** and **flex-shrink** properties, the values 1 and 0 work like on/off switches, where 1 "turns on" or allows an item to grow or shrink, and 0 prevents it. The **flex-basis** property sets the starting dimensions, either to a specific size or a size based on the contents.

In this quick example, a list item starts at 200 pixels wide, is allowed to expand to fill extra space (1), but is not allowed to shrink (0) narrower than the original 200 pixels.

```
li {
   flex: 1 0 200px;
}
```

That should give you the general idea. In this section, we'll take a much closer look at growing, shrinking, and base size, in that order.

But first, it is important to note that **flex** and its component properties apply to flex *items*, not the container. Keeping track of which properties go on the container and which go on items is one of the tricks of using Flexbox. See the **"Flex Properties"** sidebar for a handy list of how the properties are divided.

The flex properties apply to flex items, not the container.

Expanding items (flex-grow)

The first value in the **flex** property specifies whether (and in what proportion) an item may stretch larger—in other words, its **flex-grow** value (see **Note**). By default it is set to 0, which means an item is not permitted to grow wider than the size of its content or its specified width. Because items do not expand by default, the alignment properties have the opportunity to go into effect. If the extra space was taken up inside items, alignment wouldn't work.

`flex-grow`

Values: *number*

Default: 0

Applies to: flex items

Inherits: no

If you set the **flex-grow** value for all the items in a container to 1, the browser takes whatever extra space is available along the main axis and applies it equally to each item, allowing them all to stretch the same amount.

Let's take the simple box example from earlier in the chapter and see how it behaves with various flex settings applied. FIGURE 16-18 shows what happens when **flex-grow** is set to 1 for all box items (**flex-shrink** and **flex-basis** are left at their default values). Compare this to the same example with **flex-grow** set to the default 0 (this is the same behavior we observed in FIGURE 16-2).

THE MARKUP

```
<div id="container">
  <div class="box box1">1</div>
  <div class="box box2">2</div>
  <div class="box box3">3</div>
  <div class="box box4">4</div>
  <div class="box box5">5</div>
</div>
```

THE STYLES

```
.box {
  …
  flex: 1 1 auto;
}
```

`flex:` **0 1 auto;** (prevents expansion)

`flex:` **1 1 auto;**   (allows expansion)

FIGURE 16-18. When **flex-grow** is set to 1, the extra space in the line is distributed into the items in equal portions, and they expand to fill the space at the same rate.

NOTE

flex-grow *is the individual property that specifies how an item may expand. Authors are encouraged to use the shorthand* **flex** *property instead.*

■ **AT A GLANCE**

Flex Properties

Now that you've been introduced to all the properties in the Flexible Box Module, it might be helpful to see at a glance which properties apply to containers and which are set on flex items.

Container Properties

Apply these properties to the flex container:

```
display
flex-flow
  flex-direction
  flex-wrap
justify-content
align-items
align-content
```

Flex Item Properties

Apply these properties to flex items:

```
align-self
flex
  flex-grow
  flex-shrink
  flex-basis
order
```

If you specify a higher **flex-grow** integer to an item, it acts as a ratio that applies more space within that item. For example, giving "box4" the value **flex-grow: 3** means that it receives three times the amount of space than the remaining items set to **flex-grow: 1**. FIGURE 16-19 shows the result.

```
.box4 {
    flex: 3 1 auto;
}
```

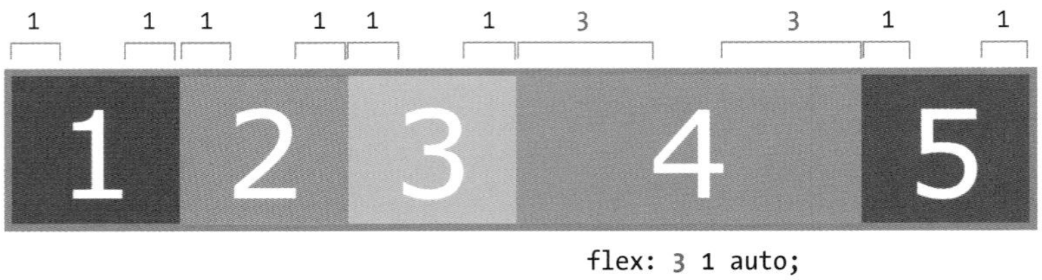

flex: 3 1 auto;

FIGURE 16-19. Assigning a different amount **flex-grow** to an individual item. Here "box4" was set to expand at three times the rate of the other items.

Notice that the resulting item is not three times as wide as the others; it just got three times the amount of space added to it.

If there's not much space left over on the line, there's a chance that each portion of space could be small enough that it would not add up to much difference. You may just need to play around with the **flex-grow** values and adjust the width of the browser until you get the effect you want.

Now that you have that concept down, shrinking should be straightforward because it is based on the same principle.

Squishing items (flex-shrink)

The second **flex** property value, **flex-shrink**, kicks in when the container is not wide enough to contain the items, resulting in a space deficit. It essentially takes away some space from within the items, shrinking them to fit, according to a specified ratio.

flex-shrink

Values:	*number*
Default:	1
Applies to:	flex items
Inherits:	no

By default, the **flex-shrink** value is set to 1, which means if you do nothing, items shrink to fit at the same rate. When **flex-shrink** is 0, items are not permitted to shrink, and they may hang out of their container and out of view of the viewport. Finally, as in **flex-grow**, a higher integer works as a ratio. An item with a **flex-shrink** of 2 will shrink twice as fast as if it were set to 1. You

NOTE

flex-shrink *is the individual property that specifies how an item may contract. Authors are encouraged to use the shorthand* **flex** *property instead.*

will not generally need to specify a shrink ratio value. Just turning shrinking on (1) or off (0) should suffice.

Flex items stop shrinking when they reach their minimum size (defined by **min-width**/**min-height**). By default (when **min-width**/**min-height** is **auto**), this minimum is based on its **min-content** size. But it can easily be set to zero, or 12em, or any other length that seems useful. Watch for this effect when deeply nested items force a flex item to be wider than expected.

You will see the **flex-shrink** property in action in FIGURE 16-20 in the next section.

By default, items may shrink when the container is not wide enough (flex-shrink: 1).

Providing an initial size (flex-basis)

The third **flex** value defines the starting size of the item before any wrapping, growing, or shrinking occurs (**flex-basis**). It may be used instead of the **width** property (or **height** property for columns) for flex items.

flex-basis

Values:	*length* | *percentage* | content | auto
Default:	auto
Applies to:	flex items
Inherits:	no

NOTE

*flex-basis is the individual property that sets the initial size of the item. Authors are encouraged to use the shorthand **flex** property instead.*

In this example, the **flex-basis** of the boxes is set to 100 pixels (FIGURE 16-20). The items are allowed to shrink smaller to fit in the available space (**flex-shrink: 1**), but they are not allowed to grow any wider (**flex-grow: 0**) than 100 pixels, leaving extra space in the container.

```
box {
    flex: 0 1 100px;
}
```

flex: 0 1 100px;

When the container is wide, the items will not grow wider than their **flex-basis** of 100 pixels because **flex-grow** is set to 0.

When the container is narrow, the items are allowed to shrink to fit (**flex-shrink: 1**).

FIGURE 16-20. Using **flex-basis** to set the starting width for items.

Flex settings override specified widths/heights for flex items.

By default, **flex-basis** is set to **auto**, which uses the specified **width/height** property values for the item size. If the item's main size property (**width** or **height**) is not set or is **auto** (its default), **flex-basis** uses the content width. You can also explicitly set **flex-basis** to be the width of the content with the **content** keyword; however, that value is poorly supported as of this writing.

In this example, the flex basis for the boxes is set to 100 pixels because the **auto** value uses the value set by **width**. Items are allowed to grow, taking up any extra space in the container, but they are not allowed to shrink.

```
box {
    width: 100px;
    flex: 1 0 auto;
}
```

When the browser goes about sizing a flex item, it consults the **flex-basis** value, compares it to the available space along the axis, and then adds or removes space from items according to their grow and shrink settings. It's important to note that if you allow an item to grow or shrink, it could end up being narrower or wider than the length provided by **flex-basis** or **width**.

Handy shortcut flex values

The advantage to using the **flex** property is that there are some handy shortcut values that cover typical Flexbox scenarios. Curiously, some of the shortcut values override the defaults of the individual properties, which was confusing to me at first, but in the end it results in more predictable behaviors. When creating a flexbox component, see if one of these easy settings will do the trick:

flex: initial;

> This is the same as **flex: 0 1 auto**. It prevents the flex item from growing even when there is extra space, but allows it to shrink to fit in the container. The size is based on the specified **width/height** properties, defaulting to the size of the content. With the **initial** value, you can use **justify-content** for horizontal alignment.

flex: auto;

> This is the same as **flex: 1 1 auto**. It allows items to be fully flexible, growing or shrinking as needed. The size is based on the specified **width/ height** properties.

flex: none;

> This is equivalent to **flex: 0 0 auto**. It creates a completely inflexible flex item while sizing it to the **width** and **height** properties. You can also use **justify-content** for alignment when flex is set to **none**.

When creating a flexbox component, see if you can take advantage of one of the handy flex shortcuts.

```
flex: integer;
```

> This is the same as **flex:** *integer* **1 0px**. The result is a flexible item with a flex basis of 0, which means it has absolute flex (see the sidebar "**Absolute Versus Relative Flex**") and free space is allocated according to the flex number applied to items.

How are you doing? Are you hanging in there with all this Flexbox stuff? I know it's a lot to take in at once. We have just one more Flexbox item property to cover before you get another chance to try it out yourself.

NOTE

I use Flexbox to format a responsive form in the "Styling Forms" section of **Chapter 19, More CSS Techniques**. *Flex properties allow form fields to adapt to the available width, while labels are set to always stay the same size. Wrapping allows form fields to move below their labels on smaller screens. You've probably got Flexbox in your head right now, so it might be worth taking a look ahead.*

Absolute Versus Relative Flex

In FIGURE 16-19, we saw how extra space is assigned to items based on their flex ratios. This is called relative flex, and it is how extra space is handled whenever the **flex-basis** is set to any size other than zero (0), such as a particular **width**/**height** value or **auto**.

However, if you reduce the value of **flex-basis** to 0, something interesting happens. With a basis of 0, the items get sized proportionally according to the flex ratios, which is known as absolute flex. So with **flex-basis: 0**, an item with a **flex-grow** value of 2 *would* be twice as wide as the items set to 1. Again, this kicks in only when the **flex-basis** is 0.

In practice it is recommended that you always include a unit after the 0, such as **0px** or the preferred **0%**.

In this example of absolute flex, the first box is given a **flex-grow** value of 2, and the fourth box has a **flex-grow** value of 3 via the aforementioned shortcut **flex:** *integer*. In FIGURE 16-21, you can see that the resulting overall size of the boxes is in proportion to the **flex-grow** values because the **flex-basis** is set to 0.

```
.box {
  /* applied to all boxes */
  flex: 1 0 0%;
}
.box1 {
  flex: 2; /* shortcut value for flex: 2 1 0px */
}
.box4 {
  flex: 3; /* shortcut value for flex: 3 1 0px */
}
```

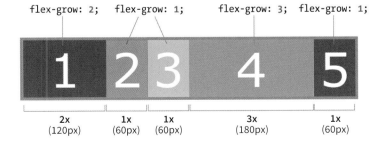

FIGURE 16-21. In absolute flex, boxes are sized according to the flex value ratios.

Changing the Order of Flex Items

One of the killer features of Flexbox is the ability to display items in an order that differs from their order in the source (see the **"When to Reorder (and When Not To)"** sidebar). That means you can change the layout order of elements by using CSS alone. This is a powerful tool for responsive design, allowing content from later in a document to be moved up on smaller screens.

To change the order of items, apply the **order** property to the particular item(s) you wish to move.

order

Values:	*integer*
Default:	0
Applies to:	flex items and absolutely positioned children of flex containers
Inherits:	no

The value of the **order** property is a positive or negative number that affects the item's placement along the flex line. It is similar to the **z-index** property in that the specific number value doesn't matter, only how it relates to other values.

By default, all items have an **order** value of zero (0). When items have the same **order** value, they are laid out in the order in which they appear in the HTML source. If they have *different* **order** values, they are arranged from the lowest **order** value to the highest.

Going back to our colorful numbered box example, I've given **box3** an **order** value of 1. With a higher order value, it appears after all the items set to 0 (the default), as shown in FIGURE 16-22.

```
.box3 {
  order: 1;
}
```

FIGURE 16-22. Changing the order of items with the **order** property. Setting **box3** to **order: 1** makes it display after the rest.

When multiple items share the same **order** value, that group of value-sharing items (called an ordinal group) sticks together and displays in source order. What happens if I give **box2** an **order** value of 1 as well? Now both **box2** and **box3** have an **order** value of 1 (making them an ordinal group), and they get displayed in source order after all the items with the lower **order** value of 0 (FIGURE 16-23).

```
.box2, .box3 {
  order: 1
}
```

FIGURE 16-23. Setting **box2** to **order: 1** as well makes it display after the items with the default order of 0.

You can also use negative values for **order**. To continue with our example, I've given **box5** an order value of −1. Notice in FIGURE 16-24 that it doesn't just move back one space; it moves before all of the items that still have **order** set to 0, which is a higher value than −1.

```
.box5 {
  order: -1
}
```

FIGURE 16-24. Negative values display before items with the default order of 0.

I've used simple values of 1 and −1 in my examples, but I could have used 10008 or −649, and the result would be the same; the order goes from least value to greatest value. Number values don't need to be in sequential order.

Now let's take a look at how we can use **order** for something more useful than moving little boxes around in a line. Here is a simple document with a header, a main section consisting of an article and two aside elements, and a footer:

```
<header>…</header>
<main>
  <article><h2>Where It's At</h2></article>
  <aside id="news"><h2>News></h2></aside>
  <aside id="contact"><h2>Contact</h2><aside>
</main>
<footer>…<footer>
```

NOTE

Although you can create a full-page layout with Flexbox, the task is more appropriately handled with Grid Layout, which we'll cover next. However, because Flexbox has better browser support than Grid Layout, it may be a suitable fallback. Flexbox is better suited for individual components on the page such as navigation, series of product "cards," or anything that you want to put in a line.

In the following CSS, I've made the **main** element a flexbox container so the **article** and **aside** elements line up in a row, creating three columns (FIGURE 16-25). I set the **flex** factor for each item, allowing them to grow and shrink, and set their widths with **flex-basis**. Finally, I used the **order** property to specify the order in which I'd like them to appear. Notice that the Contact section is now first in the row, although it appears last in the source order. And, as an added bonus, all of the columns fill the height of the main container despite the amount of content in them.

```
main {
    display: flex;
}
article {
    flex: 1 1 50%;
    order: 2;
}
#news {
    flex: 1 1 25%;
    order: 3;
}
#contact {
    flex: 1 1 25%;
    order: 1;
}
```

FIGURE 16-25. A columned layout using Flexbox.

That concludes our tour of Flexbox properties! In EXERCISE 16-3, you can put some of the item-level properties to use in the bistro menu. When you are finished, come back for some tips on dealing with varying browser support in the next section.

Browser Support for Flexbox

The current Flexible Box Layout Module became a stable Candidate Recommendation in 2012 (*www.w3.org/TR/css-flexbox-1/*). The good news is that all major desktop and mobile browsers have supported the standard

EXERCISE 16-3. Adjusting flex and order

The online menu is looking pretty good, but let's put a few finishing touches on it. Open the *flex-menu.html* file as you left it at the end of EXERCISE 16-2.

1. Instead of having lots of empty space inside the menu container, we'll make the items fill the available space. Because we want the items to be fully flexible, we can use the **auto** value for **flex** (the same as **flex: 1 1 auto;**). Add this declaration to the **section** rule to turn on the stretching behavior:

```
section {
    …
    flex: auto;
}
```

2. OK, one last tweak: let's make the photos appear at the top of each menu item. Because each section is a flex container, we can use the **order** property to move its items around. In this case, select the paragraphs with the "photo" class name and give it a value less than the default 0. This will make the photo display first in the line (FIGURE 16-26):

```
.photo {
    order: -1;
}
```

If you want to get fancy, you can set the width of the **img** elements to 100% so they always fill the width of the container. The little image I've provided gets quite blurry when it expands larger, so you can see how the responsive image techniques we covered in

Chapter 7, **Adding Images**, might be useful here. It's not the best-looking web page in the world, but you got a chance to try out a lot of the Flexbox properties along the way.

FIGURE 16-26. The final bistro menu with items flexing to fill the extra space and the photos moved to the top of each listing.

since 2015 and a few since as far back as 2013. That covers roughly 80–90% of users as of this writing according to *CanIUse.com*.

The Flexbox specification went through a lot of big changes in its path to stabilization, and along the way, some older browsers implemented those old specs. The three main releases are as follows:

Current version (2012)

Syntax example: `display: flex;`

Supported by: IE11+, Edge 12+, Chrome 21-28 (`-webkit-`), Chrome 29+, Firefox 22–27 (`-moz-`, no wrapping), Firefox 28+, Safari 6–8 (`-webkit-`), Safari 9+, Opera 17+, Android 4.4+, iOS 7–8.4 (`-webkit-`), iOS 9.2+

"Tweener" version (2011)

Syntax example: `display: flexbox;`

Supported by: IE10

Old version (2009)

Syntax example: `display: box;`

Supported by: Chrome <21, Safari 3.1–6, Firefox 2–21, iOS 3.2–6.1, Android 2.1–4.3

What you won't find in these listings is Internet Explorer 9 and earlier, which lack Flexbox support altogether.

Ensuring Flexbox works on the maximum number of browsers requires a gnarly stack of prefixes and alternative properties, the details of which are too complicated to dive into here. It's also not something you'd want to write out by hand anyway, but fortunately there are options.

You can use Autoprefixer to magically generate that gnarly stack for you automatically. As you're learning and practicing your CSS skills, you can convert your styles online at *autoprefixer.github.io*. Just paste in your styles, and it spits out the code (FIGURE 16-27) that you can add to your style sheet.

WARNING

Be aware that although Autoprefixer makes adding prefixes easier, it does not guarantee that your flexboxes will work seamlessly in all browsers. There are behavior differences that can be unpredictable, so be sure to test on all of your target browsers.

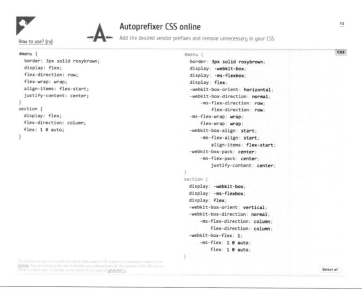

FIGURE 16-27. The Autoprefixer site converts standard Flexbox styles into all the styles needed for full browser support.

When you are ready to bring your workflow to a professional level, you can include Autoprefixer as part of a "build step" that automates a lot of the development gruntwork. If you are using a CSS preprocessor such as SASS, you can also use "mixins" to manage tedious prefixes. We'll look at build tools and preprocessors in **Chapter 20, Modern Web Development Tools**.

You may still want to provide fallback styles for non-supporting browsers (floats, inline blocks, and table display values are all options). If that is the case, you can use a feature detection technique to determine whether the browser supports Flexbox. If the browser fails the test, it gets a fallback set of styles, while supporting browsers get the full Flexbox treatment. We'll take a look at feature detection in **Chapter 19**.

One big layout technique down, one big layout technique to go! Are you still with me? We've covered a lot of nitty-gritty details, and if you're like me, your head may be swimming. That's why I've included FIGURE 16-28. It has nothing to do with CSS layout, but I figured we could use a breather. In fact, why don't you put down this book and take a little walk before taking on grids?

FIGURE 16-28. This adorable red panda has nothing to do with CSS layout, but I figured we could use a breather before moving on to Grid Layout (photo by Teri Finn).

CSS GRID LAYOUT

At long last, we web designers and developers have a CSS module for using an underlying grid to achieve true page layout—and we only had to wait 25 years to get it! The CSS Grid Layout Module provides a system for laying out elements in rows *and* columns (remember that Flexbox lays out elements on one axis only) in a way that can remain completely flexible to fit a variety of screen sizes or mimic a print page layout. You can use grids to create the sort of web page layouts that are familiar today, or get more sophisticated

Re-creation of print jazz
poster using grid

Re-creation of Die Neue
Typography lecture invitation
(1927) using grid

Overlap experiment with
photos by Dorthea Lange

FIGURE 16-29. Examples of grid-based designs from Jen Simmons's "Experimental Layout Lab" page (*labs.jensimmons.com*).

with typography and whitespace as Jen Simmons has done in her Lab demos (FIGURE 16-29). You can also use a grid to format just a portion of a page, such as a gallery of images or products.

In this section, I will give you a good head start on using Grid Layout; however, I should note that there will be a few stones left unturned that you can explore on your own.

The Grid Layout Module is one of the more complex specs in CSS, the finer points of which could fill a book. In fact, Eric Meyer has written that book: *Grid Layout in CSS* (O'Reilly)(see **Note**). I found that Eric helped me make practical sense of the dense language of the spec itself (which you will also want to reference at *www.w3.org/TR/css-grid-1/*). I also highly recommend Grid expert Rachel Andrew's book, *The New CSS Layout* (A Book Apart) for a complete view of how we got to grid layouts and how to use them.

You will also find many great Grid resources online, which I will round up at the end of this section.

The Obligatory Talk About Browser Support

There's great and not-so-great news about browser support for Grid Layout. The great news is that Chrome 57+, Opera, Firefox 52+, Safari 10+, and iOS Safari 10+ all started supporting the Grid standard free and clear of browser prefixes in March 2017. Microsoft Edge added support in version 16 in 2017.

The not-so-great news is that in addition to lingering older versions of those browsers, no version of Internet Explorer supports the current Grid standard (see the **Browser Support Note**).

NOTE

CSS: The Definitive Guide, 4th edition (O'Reilly), by Eric A. Meyer and Estelle Weyl, is a megavolume of everything you could ever want to know about CSS. It contains the entire **Grid Layout in CSS** book as a chapter.

BROWSER SUPPORT NOTE

Internet Explorer versions 10 and 11 and MS Edge through 15 implemented an early draft of the Grid Layout Module, much of which has since been made obsolete. They should be treated as non-supporting browsers when it comes to the standard grid styles outlined in this chapter. However, if those Microsoft browsers are used by a significant share of your target audience, it is probably worth targeting them with an alternative version of your layout written in the older grid syntax they understand.

So, for the time being, you need to provide an alternative layout for non-supporting browsers by using Flexbox or old-fashioned floats (or the older Grid specification for IE and Edge <15), depending on the browsers you need to target. A good way to get your Grid-based layouts to the browsers that can handle them is to use a CSS Feature Query that checks for Grid support and provides the appropriate set of styles. Feature queries are discussed in detail in **Chapter 19**.

Be sure to check *CanIUse.com* for updated browser support information. Another good resource is the Browser Support page at the "Grid by Example" site, created by Rachel Andrew (*gridbyexample.com/browsers*), where she posts browser support news as well as known bugs.

How Grid Layout Works

The process for using the CSS Grid Layout Module is fundamentally simple:

1. **Use the `display` property to turn an element into a grid container.** The element's children automatically become grid items.

2. **Set up the columns and rows for the grid.** You can set them up explicitly and/or provide directions for how rows and columns should get created on the fly.

3. **Assign each grid item to an area on the grid.** If you don't assign them explicitly, they flow into the cells sequentially.

What makes Grid Layout complicated is that the spec provides *so* many options for specifying every little thing. All those options are terrific for customizing production work, but they can feel cumbersome when you are learning Grids for the first time. In this chapter, I'll set you up with a solid Grid toolbox to get started, which you can expand on your own as needed.

Grid Terminology

Before we dive into specific properties, you'll need to be familiar with the basic parts and vocabulary of the Grid system.

Starting with the markup, the element that has the **`display: grid`** property applied to it becomes the grid container and defines the context for grid for-matting. All of its direct child elements automatically become grid items that end up positioned in the grid. If you've just read the Flexbox section of this chapter, this children-become-items scheme should sound familiar.

The key words in that previous paragraph are "direct child," as only those elements become grid items. Elements contained in those elements do not, so you cannot place them on the grid. You can, however, nest a grid inside another grid if you need to apply a grid to a deeper level.

The grid itself has a number of components, as pointed out in FIGURE 16-30.

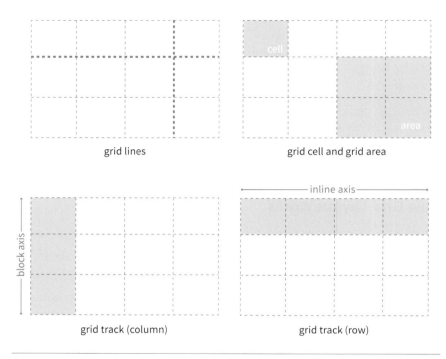

FIGURE 16-30. The parts of a CSS grid.

Grid line

The horizontal and vertical dividing lines of the grid are called grid lines.

Grid cell

The smallest unit of a grid is a grid cell, which is bordered by four adjacent grid lines with no grid lines running through it.

Grid area

A grid area is a rectangular area made up of one or more adjacent grid cells.

Grid track

The space between two adjacent grid lines is a grid track, which is a generic name for a grid column or a grid row. Grid columns are said to go along the block axis, which is vertical (as block elements are stacked) for languages written horizontally. Grid rows follow the inline (horizontal) axis.

It is worth pointing out that the structure established for the grid is independent from the number of grid items in the container. You could place 4 grid items in a grid with 12 cells, leaving 8 of the cells as "whitespace." That's the beauty of grids. You can also set up a grid with fewer cells than grid items, and the browser adds cells to the grid to accommodate them. It's a wonderfully flexible system.

Without further ado, it's time to get into some code.

Declaring Grid Display

To turn an element into a grid container, set its **display** property to **grid** or **inline-grid** (see **Note**).

In this simple example, the **#layout div** becomes a grid container, and each of its children (**#one**, **#two**, **#three**, **#four**, and **#five**), therefore, is a grid item.

THE MARKUP

```
<div id="layout">
  <div id="one">One</div>
  <div id="two">Two</div>
  <div id="three">Three</div>
  <div id="four">Four</div>
  <div id="five">Five</div>
</div>
```

THE STYLES

```
#layout {
  display: grid;
}
```

That sets the stage (or to use the more accurate term, the context) for the grid. Now we can specify how many rows and columns we want and how wide they should be.

Setting Up the Grid

Because I don't want to have to figure out cells and spans in my head, I've made a quick sketch of how I'd like my final grid to look (FIGURE 16-31). A sketch is a good first step for working with grids. From the sketch, I can see that my layout requires three row tracks and three column tracks even though some of the content areas span over more than one cell. This is a pretty standard arrangement for a web page, and although I'm sticking with one-word content so we can focus on structure, you can imagine longer text content filling each area.

NOTE

You probably noticed that this page layout with its header, footer, and three columns looks like the one we made using Flexbox in FIGURE 16-25. And you're right! It just goes to show that there may be several solutions for getting to an intended result. Once Grid Layout becomes solidly supported, it will be the clear winner for creating flexible, whole-page layouts like this one.

NOTE

Inline grids function the same as block-level grids, but they can be used in the flow of content. In this section, I focus only on block-level grids.

As of this writing, work has begun on a Working Draft of CSS Grid Layout Module Level 2, which includes a "subgrid" mode that allows a nested grid to inherit its grid structure from its parent.

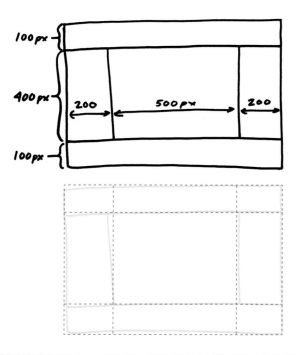

FIGURE 16-31. A rough sketch for my grid-based page layout. The dotted lines in the bottom image show how many rows and columns the grid requires to create the layout structure.

Defining grid tracks

To set up a grid in CSS, specify the height of each row and the width of each column (see **Note**) with the template properties, `grid-template-rows` and `grid-template-columns`, which get applied to the container element.

`grid-template-rows`
`grid-template-columns`

Values:	none | *list of track sizes and optional line names*
Default:	none
Applies to:	grid containers
Inherits:	no

The value of the **grid-template-rows** property is a list of the *heights* for each row track in the grid. The value of the **grid-template-columns** is a list of the *widths* for each column track. The number of track sizes determines the number of rows or columns. For example, if you provide four lengths for **grid-template-columns**, you get a grid that is initially divided into four columns.

You can also include names for the grid lines between tracks, which we'll get to in a moment, but for now, let's start off as simply as possible.

NOTE

Like the Flexbox Module, the Grid Layout Module is dependent on the direction of the language in which the page is written. In this book, I will base grid terminology on the left-to-right, top-to-bottom writing direction.

Grid track sizes

In the following example, I've added template properties to divide the `#layout` container into three columns and three rows with the sizes I designated in my original sketch (FIGURE 16-31):

```
#layout {
  display: grid;
  grid-template-rows: 100px 400px 100px;
  grid-template-columns: 200px 500px 200px;
}
```

Let's see what happens if I do a quick check of the grid so far in the browser. FIGURE 16-32 shows that by default, the grid items flow in order into the available grid cells. I've added background colors to the items so their boundaries are clear, and I used Firefox CSS Grid Inspector (right) to reveal the entire grid structure.

Because there are only five child elements in the `#layout div`, only the first five cells are filled. This automatic flowing behavior isn't what I'm after for this grid, but it is useful for instances in which it is OK for content to pour into a grid sequentially, such as a gallery of images. Soon, we will place each of our items on this grid deliberately, but first, let's look at the template property values in greater depth.

Browser view

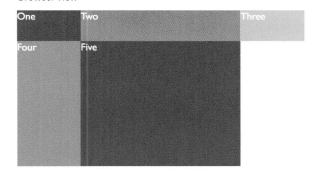

Grid structure revealed with Firefox Grid Inspector

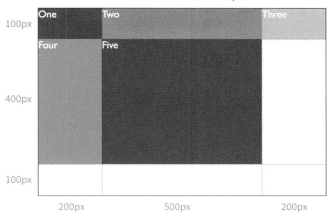

FIGURE 16-32. By default, grid items flow into the grid cells by rows.

Grid line numbers and names

When the browser creates a grid, it also automatically assigns each grid line a number that you can reference when positioning items. The grid line at the start of the grid track is 1, and lines are numbered sequentially from there. FIGURE 16-33 shows how the grid lines are numbered for our sample grid.

Firefox CSS Grid Inspector and Layout Panel

Firefox 52+ includes a great developer tool called the CSS Grid Inspector that overlays a representation of the grid structure for elements with their **display** set to **grid**. It's what I used for the right screenshot in FIGURE 16-32. To get to it, open the Inspector (**Tools → Web Developer → Inspector**). Find an element that is a grid and click the # icon, and you'll see the grid overlaid on the page.

You can also click the Layout tab to access the Layout Panel, which lists all the grid containers on the page and provides tools for analyzing grid lines and areas. It also has a box-model properties component so you can easily see the dimensions, padding, border, and margins for every grid-related element, and more. These visual tools make it easier to tweak your designs.

As this book goes to press, the news is that similar grid layout development tools are coming to Chrome and Safari. The future looks bright for grid designers!

FIGURE 16-33. Grid lines are assigned numbers automatically.

The lines are numbered from the end of tracks as well, starting with −1, and numbers count back from there (−2, −3, etc.), as shown by the gray numbers in FIGURE 16-33. Being able to target the end of a row or column without counting lines (or even knowing how many rows or columns there are) is a handy feature. You'll come to love that −1.

But if you don't like to keep track of numbers, you can also assign names to lines that may be more intuitive. In the following example, I've assigned names that correspond to how I will be using the grid in the final page. Line names are added within square brackets in the position they appear relative to the tracks.

```
#layout {
  display: grid;
  grid-template-rows: [header-start] 100px [content-start] 400px
[footer-start] 100px;
  grid-template-columns: [ads] 200px [main] 500px [links] 200px;
}
```

Based on this example, the grid line at the top of the grid can now be referred to as "header-start," "1," or "−4." I could also name the line that comes after the first row track "header-end" even though I've already named it "content-start." To give a line more than one name, just include all the names in the brackets, separated by spaces:

```
grid-template-rows: [header-start] 100px [header-end content-start]
400px [footer-start] 100px;
```

It is common for each grid line to end up with multiple names and numbers, and you can choose whichever is the easiest to use. We'll be using these numbers and names to place items on the grid in a moment.

Specifying track size values

I provided all of the track sizes in my example in specific pixel lengths to make them easy to visualize, but fixed sizes are one of many options. They also don't offer the kind of flexibility required in our multi-device world. The Grid Layout Module provides a *whole bunch* of ways to specify track sizes, including old standbys like lengths (e.g., pixels or ems) and percentage values, but also some newer and Grid-specific values. I'm going to give you quick introductions to some useful Grid-specific values: the **fr** unit, the **minmax()** function, **auto**, and the content-based values **min-content**/**max-content**. We'll also look at functions that allow you to set up a repeating pattern of track widths: the **repeat()** function with optional **auto-fill** and **auto-fit** values.

Fractional units (flex factor)

The Grid-specific fractional unit (**fr**) allows developers to create track widths that expand and contract depending on available space. To go back to the example, if I change the middle column from **500px** to **1fr**, the browser assigns all leftover space (after the 200-pixel column tracks are accommodated) to that column track (FIGURE 16-34).

```
#layout {
  display: grid;
  grid-template-rows: 100px 400px 100px;
  grid-template-columns: 200px 1fr 200px;
}
```

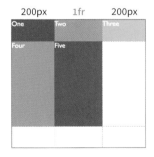

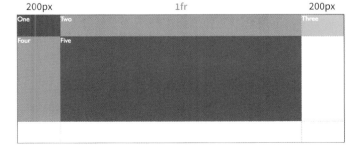

FIGURE 16-34. When the middle column has a track size of 1fr, it takes up the remaining space in the browser window and flexes to adapt to the browser width.

> ■ **AT A GLANCE**
>
> ## Track Size Values
>
> The Grid specification provides the following values for the **grid-template-*** properties:
>
> - Lengths (such as **px** or **em**)
> - Percentage values (%)
> - Fractional units (**fr**)
> - **auto**
> - **min-content**, **max-content**
> - **minmax()**
> - **fit-content()**

NOTE

*Technically, the browser adds up the **fr** units (4 in our example), divides the left-over space into that many portions, and then assigns the portions based on the number of units specified.*

WARNING

***fr** units are not permitted as the minimum value in a **minmax( )** statement.*

The **fr** unit is great for combining fixed and flexible track widths, but I could also use all **fr** units to give all the columns proportional widths. In this example, all of the column widths flex according to the available browser width, but the middle column will always be twice the width of the side columns (see **Note**).

```
grid-template-columns: 1fr 2fr 1fr;
```

Minimum and maximum size range

You can constrict the size range of a track by setting its minimum and maximum widths using the **minmax( )** function in place of a specific track size.

```
grid-template-columns: 200px minmax(15em, 45em) 200px;
```

This rule sets the middle column to a width that is at least 15em but never wider than 45em. This method allows for flexibility but allows the author to set limits.

Content-based sizing

The **min-content**, **max-content**, and **auto** values size the track based on the size of the content within it (FIGURE 16-35).

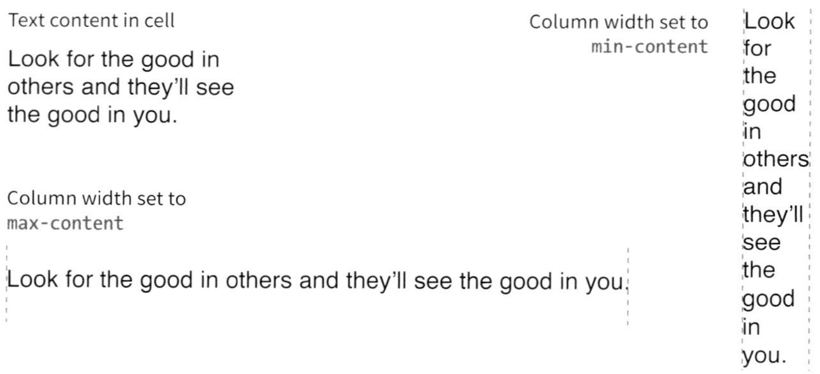

Text content in cell

Look for the good in others and they'll see the good in you.

Column width set to max-content

Look for the good in others and they'll see the good in you.

Column width set to min-content

Look for the good in others and they'll see the good in you.

FIGURE 16-35. The **min-content** and **max-content** track sizing values.

The **min-content** value is the *smallest* that track can get without overflowing (by default, unless overridden by an explicit **min-width**). It is equivalent to the "largest unbreakable bit of content"—in other words, the width of the longest word or widest image. It may not be useful for items that contain normal paragraphs, but it may be useful in some cases when you don't want the track larger than it needs to be. This example establishes three columns, with the right column sized just wide enough to hold the longest word or image:

```
grid-template-columns: 50px 1fr min-content;
```

The **max-content** property allots the maximum amount of space needed for the content, even if that means extending the track beyond the boundaries of the grid container. When used as a column width, the column track will be as wide as the widest content in that track *without* line wrapping. That means if you have a paragraph, the track will be wide enough to contain the text set on one line. This makes `max-content` more appropriate for short phrases or navigation items when you don't want their text to wrap (`auto` may work better because it allows wrapping if there's not enough room).

Using the `auto` keyword for a track size is basically like handing the keys over to the browser. In general, it causes the track to be sized large enough to accommodate its content, while taking into consideration what other restrictions are in place.

In the `minmax()` function, the `auto` keyword behaves very similarly to either `min-content` or `max-content`, depending on whether you put it in the minimum or maximum slot. As a keyword on its own, it functions similarly to `minmax(min-content, max-content)`, allowing the track to squeeze as narrow as it can without anything overflowing, but grow to fit its content without wrapping if there's enough space.

Unlike `max-content`, an `auto` maximum allows `align-content` and `justify-content` to stretch the track beyond the size of the content. As a minimum, it has a few more smarts than `min-content`—for example, using a specified `min-width` or `min-height` on an item (if any) instead of its `min-content` size, and ignoring the contents of any grid items with scrollbars.

If you want to size a track based on its content, but you're not sure which keyword to use, start with `auto`.

> If you want to size a track based on its content, but you're not sure which keyword to use, start with auto.

Repeating track sizes

Say you have a grid that has 10 columns with alternating column widths, like so:

```
grid-template-columns: 20px 1fr 20px 1fr 20px 1fr 20px 1fr 20px 1fr
20px 1fr;
```

That's kind of a bummer to have to type out (I know, I just did it), so the fine folks at the W3C have provided a nice shortcut in the form of the `repeat()` function. In the previous example, the pattern "20px 1fr" repeats five times, which can be written as follows:

```
grid-template-columns: repeat(5, 20px 1fr);
```

Much better, isn't it? The first number indicates the number of repetitions, and the track sizes after the comma provide the pattern. You can use the `repeat()` notation in a longer sequence of track sizes—for example, if those 10 columns are sandwiched between two 200-pixel-wide columns at the start and end:

```
grid-template-columns: 200px repeat(5, 20px 1fr) 200px;
```

You can also provide grid line names before and/or after each track size, and those names will be repeated in the pattern:

```
grid-template-rows: repeat(4, [date] 5em [event] 1fr);
```

auto-fill and auto-fit

In the previous `repeat()` examples, we told the browser how many times to repeat the provided pattern. You can also let the browser figure it out itself based on the available space by using the `auto-fill` and `auto-fit` values instead of an integer in `repeat()`.

For example, if I specify

```
grid-template-rows: repeat(auto-fill, 10em);
```

and the grid container is 35em tall, then the browser creates a row every 10 ems until it runs out of room, resulting in three rows. Even if there is only enough content to fill the first row, all three rows are created and the space is held in the layout.

The `auto-fit` value works similarly, except any tracks that do not have content get dropped from the layout. If there is leftover space, it is distributed according to the vertical (`align-content`) and horizontal (`justify-content`) alignment values provided (we'll discuss alignment later in this section).

Defining grid areas

So far we've been exploring how to divide a grid container into row and column tracks by using the `grid-template-columns` and `grid-template-rows` properties, and we've looked at many of the possible values for track dimensions. We've learned that you can assign names to individual grid lines to make them easy to refer to when placing items on the grid.

You can also assign names to *areas* of the grid, which for some developers is an even more intuitive method than calling out specific lines. Remember that a grid area is made up of one or more cells in a rectangle (no L-shapes or other non-rectangular collections of cells). Naming grid areas is a little funky to implement, but provides nice shortcuts when you need them.

To assign names to grid areas, use the `grid-template-areas` property.

`grid-template-areas`

Values:	none | *series of area names*
Default:	none
Applies to:	grid containers
Inherits:	no

The value of the property is a list of names provided for every cell in the grid, listed row by row, with each row in quotation marks. When neighboring cells share a name, they form a grid area with that name (see **Bonus Grid Line Names** sidebar).

In the following example, I've given names to areas in the example grid we've been working on so far (FIGURE 16-36). Notice that there is a cell name for each of the nine cells as they appear in each row. The row cell lists don't need

---

WARNING

You can only use one auto-repeat for a given declaration, and you cannot use it with `fr` units. You also cannot put content-based size keywords inside an `auto-fill` or `auto-repeat` notation. Note that you can use `minmax()` notation inside an `auto-repeat`, and you can use it with `fr`s or content-based keywords (`auto`, `min-content`, `max-content`) if they're in the max position with a min length.

Bonus Grid Line Names

When you give an area a name with `grid-template-areas`, as an added bonus, you get a set of automatically generated grid line names to go with it. For example, when you name an area "main", the left and top grid lines of that area are automatically named "main-start," and the right and bottom grid lines are named "main-end." You can use those line names when positioning items.

The inverse is true as well. If you explicitly assign line names "portal-start" and "portal-end" around an area, you can use the area name "portal" to assign content to that area later, even if you haven't defined it with `grid-template-areas`. You can keep this shortcut in mind when naming grid lines, but it is not required.

This is a prime example of the flexibility and complexity of the Grid Layout Module.

to be stacked as I've done here, but many developers find it helpful to line up the cell by names using character spaces to better visualize the grid structure.

```
#layout {
   display: grid;
   grid-template-rows: [header-start] 100px [content-start] 400px
[footer-start] 100px;
   grid-template-columns: [ads] 200px [main] 1fr [links] 200px;
   grid-template-areas:
      "header  header  header"
      "ads     main    links"
      "footer  footer  footer";
}
```

"header	header	header"
"ads	main	links"
"footer	footer	footer"

header

ads · main · links

footer

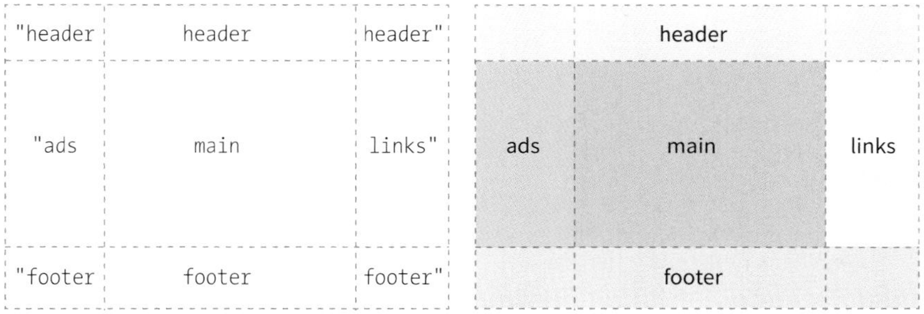

FIGURE 16-36. When neighboring cells have the same name, they form a named area that can be referenced later.

If there are three columns in the grid, there must be three names provided for each row. If you want to leave a cell unnamed, type one or more periods (.) in its place as a space holder so that every cell is still accounted for. Again, a sketch of your grid with the areas identified will make it easier to plan out the **grid-template-areas** value.

Be aware that the track sizes are still coming from the **grid-template-columns** and **grid-template-rows** properties. The **grid-template-areas** property simply assigns names to the areas, making it easier to plop items in them later.

The grid shorthand property

Use the **grid** shorthand property to set values for **grid-template-rows**, **grid-template-columns**, and **grid-template-areas** with one style rule. Bear in mind that any properties you do not use will be reset to their defaults, as is the case for all shorthands.

grid

Values:	none | *row info / column info*
Default:	none
Applies to:	grid containers
Inherits:	no

In **grid**, the row values and column values are separated by a slash, with the row values appearing first:

```
grid: rows / columns
```

It's easier to grasp without the clutter of line and area names, so here is the shorthand declaration for our example grid with just the row and column track information:

```
#layout {
  display: grid;
  grid: 100px 400px 100px / 200px 1fr 200px;
}
```

To include custom line names, add the names in brackets around their respective tracks, as we saw in the earlier named line example.

Including area names looks a little convoluted at first, but if you remember that you list cell names row by row, it makes sense that they appear with the other row information, before the slash. The complete order goes as follows:

```
[start line name] "area names" <track size> [end line name]
```

The line names and area names are optional. Repeat this for each row in the grid, simply listing them one after another with no special character separating rows. You may find it helpful to stack them as I've done in the following example to help keep each row distinct. When the rows are done, add a slash, and list the column track information after it. Here's a complete example of our grid written with the **grid** shorthand:

```
#layout {
  display: grid;
  grid:
    [header-start]  "header   header   header" 100px
    [content-start] "ads      main     links"  400px
    [footer-start]  "footer   footer   footer" 100px
    /[ads] 200px [main] 1fr [links] 200px; }
```

This expands to the following:

```
#layout {
  display: grid;
  grid-template-rows: [header-start] 100px [content-start] 400px
[footer-start] 100px;
  grid-template-columns: [ads] 200px [main] 1fr [links] 200px;
  grid-template-areas:
    "header   header   header"
    "ads      main     links"
    "footer   footer   footer" }
```

NOTE

*The Grid experts I've talked to don't tend to use **grid** or **grid-template** except for the simplest of grid structures. The code becomes overly complex, and one small slip can make the whole grid fall apart. For complicated grid structures, stick to separate properties for defining rows, columns, and areas.*

There is also a **grid-template** property that works exactly like **grid**, but it may be used only with explicitly defined grids (as opposed to implicit grids, which I cover later). The Grid Layout spec strongly recommends that you use the **grid** shorthand instead of **grid-template** (see **Note**) unless you specifically want the cascading behavior of **grid-template**.

I'm thinking that it's a good time for you to put all of these grid setup styles to use in EXERCISE 16-4.

EXERCISE 16-4. Setting up a grid

In this exercise, we'll set up the grid template for the page shown in FIGURE 16-37. We'll place the grid items into the grid in EXERCISE 16-5, so for now just pay attention to setting up the rows and columns.

This page is similar to the bakery page we've been working on, but it has a few more elements and whitespace to make things interesting. The starter document, *grid.html*, is provided with the exercise materials at *learningwebdesign.com/5e/materials*. Open it in a text editor, and you'll see that all of the styles affecting the appearance of each element are provided.

NOTE

You will need to use a browser that supports grids for this exercise. I am using Firefox in order to take advantage of the Grid Inspector tool. Supporting browsers are listed earlier in this section. See the **"Firefox Grid Inspector and Layout Panel"** *sidebar for instructions on how to open the tool.*

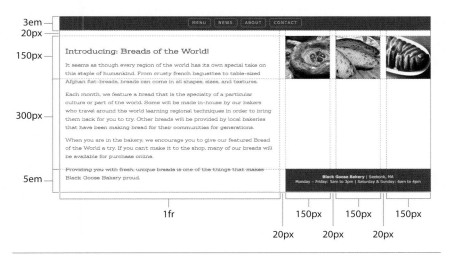

FIGURE 16-37. The Breads of the World page that we will create using Grid Layout.

1. Start by turning the containing element, the **#layout div**, into a grid container by setting its display mode to "grid":

```
#layout {
   ...
   display: grid;
}
```

2. FIGURE 16-37 shows the row and column tracks required to accommodate the content in the desired layout. Start by defining the rows as specified in the sketch, using the **grid-template-rows** property. There should be six values, representing each of the six rows. (Spoiler alert: we'll be tweaking these values when we get to the next exercise. This is just a starting point.)

```
#layout {
   ...
   display: grid;
   grid-template-rows: 3em 20px 150px 300px 5em;
}
```

3. Do the same for the seven columns. Because I want the text column to grow and shrink with the available space, I've specified its width in fractional units (**1fr**). The remaining columns create 150px-wide cells for three images and 20px of space before them.

EXERCISE 16-4. Continued

You can write them all out like this:

```
grid-template-columns: 1fr 20px 150px 20px 150px 20px 150px;
```

However, because the last six columns are a repeating pattern, it would be easier to use the **repeat()** function to repeat the spaces and figure columns three times:

```
grid-template-columns:  1fr repeat(3, 20px 150px);
```

4. Finally, let's assign names to the grid lines that border the grid area where the **main** content element should appear. The names give us some intuitive options for placing that item later. The main area starts at the third row track, so assign the name "main-start" to the grid line between the second and third row track measurements:

```
grid-template-rows: 3em 20px [main-start] 150px 300px 5em;
```

The main area extends into the last row track, so assign the name "main-end" to the last grid line in the grid (after the last row track):

```
grid-template-rows: 3em 20px [main-start] 150px 300px 5em [main-end];
```

5. Now do the same for the grid lines that mark the boundaries of the column track where the main content goes:

```
grid-template-columns:  [main-start] 1fr [main-end] repeat(3, 20px 150px);
```

I've saved my work and looked at it in Firefox with the Grid Inspector turned on (FIGURE 16-38). Because I haven't specified where the grid items go, they flowed into the cells sequentially, making the mess you see in the figure. However, the grid overlay reveals that the structure of the grid looks solid. Save the file and hold on to it until the next exercise.

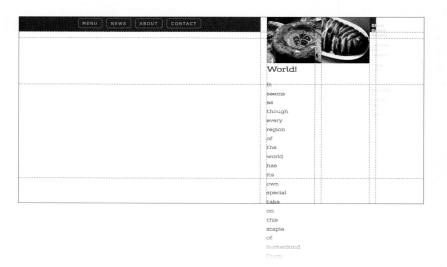

FIGURE 16-38. The grid items are not placed correctly yet, but the Firefox Grid Inspector shows that the grid is set up correctly.

Placing Grid Items

Now that we've covered all the ins and outs of setting up a grid, including giving ourselves handy line and area names, we can move on to assigning items to areas on the grid.

As we saw in FIGURES 16-32 and 16-38, without any explicit placement instruction, grid items flow into the available grid cells sequentially. That's fine for some use cases, but let's tell our grid items where to go!

Positioning using lines

One method for describing a grid item's location on the grid is to specify the four lines bordering the target grid area with four properties that specify the start and end row lines and the start and end column lines. Apply these properties to the individual grid item element you are positioning.

```
grid-row-start
grid-row-end
grid-column-start
grid-column-end
```

Values: auto | *grid line* | span *number* | span *'line name'* | *number 'line name'*

Default: auto

Applies to: grid items

Inherits: no

This set of properties provides a straightforward way to describe an element's position on the grid by identifying either the name or number of the grid line on each border. As an alternative, you can provide just one line identifier and tell the item to "span" a certain number of cells. By default, an item occupies one track width, which is what you get with the **auto** keyword.

Getting back to our five-item example, I would like the first item to go in the top row and span across all three columns (FIGURE 16-39).

One way to do this is to use the four line start/end properties and identify lines by their numbers like so:

```
#one {
  grid-row-start: 1;
  grid-row-end: 2;
  grid-column-start: 1;
  grid-column-end: 4;
}
```

Take a moment to compare this to the position of the **#one div** back in FIGURE 16-36. For **grid-row-start**, the 1 value refers to the first (top) line of the grid container. For **grid-column-start**, 1 refers to the first line on the left edge of the container, and the value 4 for **grid-column-end** identifies the fourth and last line on the right edge of the container.

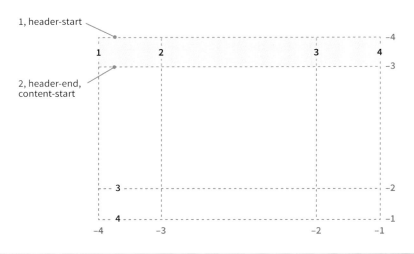

FIGURE 16-39. Positioning a grid item across the top row track in our sample grid.

Here's one more for good measure. This style declaration positions the **#four** item element in the right side column as shown in FIGURE 16-36:

```
#four {
    grid-row-start: 2;
    grid-row-end: 3;
    grid-column-start: 3;
    grid-column-end: 4;
}
```

Remember how grid lines are also numbered in the opposite direction starting at −1? We can use that here. I could specify the **grid-column-end** for **#one** as −1, and it would be the same as 4. In fact, this method has the advantage of guaranteeing to span to the end of the track and avoids miscounting.

I could also use the named lines I set up here. These row values are interchangeable with the previous example:

```
#one {
    grid-row-start: header-start;
    grid-row-end: header-end;
    ...
}
```

If I omit the end line declaration, the row would be one track high (the default). That's what I want here, so omitting the end declaration altogether is one more way to achieve the effect I want.

Ready for yet another option? I can tell the item what line to start on, but instead of providing an end line, I can use the **span** keyword to specify how many tracks to span over. In this example, the item starts at the left edge of the track (line 1) and spans over three columns, effectively ending at line 4.

NOTE

*If you omit a start or end line, the area will be one track wide (the default, **auto**).*

■ **HOT TIP**

If you need to span to the last grid line in a row or column, use the value −1 and save yourself some counting. Also, even if the number of rows or columns changes down the line, −1 will always select the last line, so you won't need to renumber.

```
#one {
    …
    grid-column-start: 1;
    grid-column-end: span 3;
}
```

Spans can work in reverse as well. If you provide only an end line, the span searches toward the start of the track. The following styles have the same effect as our previous examples because they define the target area by its end line at the far right of the grid and span back three columns to the beginning:

```
#one {
    …
    grid-column-start: span 3;
    grid-column-end: -1;
}
```

If four declarations feels like too many, use the shorthand **grid-row** and **grid-column** properties instead.

`grid-row`
`grid-column`

Values:　　　 *start line* / *end line*

Default:　　　 see individual properties

Applies to:　 grid items

Inherits:　　　 no

These properties combine the ***-start** and ***-end** properties into a single declaration. The start and end line values are separated by a slash (/). With the shorthand, I can shorten my example to the following two declarations. Any of the methods for referring to lines work in the shorthand values.

```
#one {
    grid-row: 1 / 2;
    grid-column: 1 / span 3;
}
```

Positioning by area

The other way to position an item on a grid is to tell it go into one of the named areas by using the **grid-area** property.

`grid-area`

Values:　　　 *area name* | *1 to 4 line identifiers*

Default:　　　 see individual properties

Applies to:　 grid items

Inherits:　　　 no

The **grid-area** property points to one of the areas named with **grid-template-areas**. It can also point to an area name that is implicitly created when you name lines delimiting an area with the suffixes "-start" and "-end". With this method, I can drop all of the grid items into the areas I set up with my template earlier (FIGURE 16-40):

```
#one { grid-area: header; }
#two { grid-area: ads; }
#three { grid-area: main }
#four { grid-area: links; }
#five { grid-area: footer; }
```

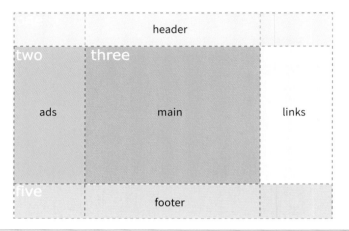

FIGURE 16-40. Assigning grid items by area names.

How easy was *that*?! One benefit of using areas is that you can change the grid, and as long as you provide consistently named grid areas, the items will end up in the right place. There's no need to renumber lines in the style sheet.

You can also use **grid-area** to provide a list of four grid lines that define an area, separated by slashes. The order in which they appear is "row-start," "column-start," "row-end," "column-end" (counterclockwise from the top). There are a lot of rules for what happens when you omit values, but I'm not going to get into all those finer points here. The **grid-area** declaration for the first grid item could be written like this to achieve the same result as previous examples:

```
#one {
  grid-area: 1 / 1 / 2 / span 3;
  /* row-start / column-start / row-end / column-end */
}
```

As you can see, the Grid Layout Module gives you a variety of ways to set up a grid and a variety of ways to place items on it. In fact, the spec includes a few more uses of **span** that you can explore. Choose the methods that work best for the grid you are designing or that work best for your brain.

Now let's finish up the grid we've been working on in EXERCISE 16-5.

EXERCISE 16-5. Placing items on a grid

Now that we have the grid set up for the Breads of the World page, we can place items into the correct grid areas by using line numbers and names.

I'm going to go through them quickly, but feel free to save the file and look at the page in a grid-supporting browser at any step along the way. Refer to the finished layout in FIGURE 16-41 for the final item positions and line number hints.

1. Open *grid.html* in your text editor if it isn't open already. We'll start by placing the **nav** element into the first row of the grid, using the four grid line properties:

    ```
    nav {
      grid-row-start: 1;
      grid-row-end: 2;
      grid-column-start: 1;
      grid-column-end: 8; /* you could also use -1 */
    }
    ```

2. Now place the figures in their positions on the grid. Start by putting the third figure (**#figC**) in its place in the far-right column by using the shorthand **grid-row** and **grid-column** properties. It goes between the 3rd and 4th row grid lines and extends from the 7th to 8th column lines. For columns, instead of 7 and 8, use the negative value for the last line and span it one space to the left to get to the starting point:

    ```
    #figC {
      grid-row: 3 / 4;
      grid-column: span 1 / -1;
    }
    ```

    Now position the **#figA** and **#figB** elements by using the **grid-area** property with line values. Remember that the values go in the order top, left, bottom, right (counterclockwise around the area).

    ```
    #figA {
      grid-area: 3 / 3 / 4 / 4;
    }
    #figB {
      grid-area: 3 / 5 / 4 / 6;
    }
    ```

3. We gave the grid lines around the main area names, so let's use them to place the **main** grid item:

    ```
    main {
      grid-row: main-start / main-end;
      grid-column: main-start / main-end;
    }
    ```

    Do you remember that when you name lines around an area ***-start** and ***-end**, it creates an implicitly named area *****? Because we named the lines according to this syntax, we could also place the **main** element with **grid-area** like this:

    ```
    main {
      grid-area: main;
    }
    ```

4. Finally, we can put the footer into its place. It starts at the last row grid line and spans back one track. For columns, it starts at the third line and goes to the last. Here is one way to write those instructions. Can you come up with others that achieve the same result?

    ```
    footer {
      grid-row: 5 / 6;
      grid-column: 3 / -1;
    }
    ```

Save your file and look at it in the browser. You may spot a problem, depending on the width of your browser window. When

FIGURE 16-41. The final Breads of the World grid layout.

the browser is wide, the layout works fine, but when it is made narrower, the text in the **main** element overflows its cell. That's because the 300-pixel height we gave that row is not sufficient to hold the text when it breaks onto additional lines or is resized larger.

5. We can fix that by changing the measurement of the fifth row track to **auto**. In that way, the height of that row will always be at least big enough to hold the content. The **min-content** value would work as well, but **auto** is always the first value to try:

```
#layout {
  display: grid;
  grid-template-rows: 3em 20px
[main-start] 150px auto 5em
[main-end];
  …
}
```

If you reload the page in the browser, the text is always contained in its grid area, regardless of the width of the window. Everything should fall into place nicely, as shown in FIGURE 16-41.

You now have your first grid layout under your belt. This exercise gives you only a taste of what Grid Layout can do, but we've covered the fundamentals of setting up a grid and placing items in it. You're off to a great start!

Now you know the basics of creating an explicit grid and placing items on it. There are a few more grid-related topics that are important to be familiar with: implicit grids, gutter spaces, and grid alignment. I have space for only a basic introduction to each topic, but when you start implementing grid layouts on your own, you can do the deep dive required to meet your needs.

Implicit Grid Behavior

So far, we've been focusing on ways to define an explicit grid and place items on it deliberately. But along the way, we've encountered a few of the Grid system's automatic, or implicit, behaviors. For example, without explicit placement instructions, grid items flow into the grid sequentially, as we saw in FIGURE 16-32. I also pointed out how creating a named area implicitly generates grid lines with the "-start" and "-end" suffixes, and vice versa.

Another implicit Grid behavior is the creation of row and column tracks on the fly to accommodate items that don't fit in the defined grid. For example, if you place an item outside a defined grid, the browser automatically generates tracks in the grid to accommodate it. Similarly, if you simply have more items than there are cells or areas, the browser generates more tracks until all the items are placed.

By default, any row or column automatically added to a grid will have the size **auto**, sized just large enough to accommodate the height or width of the contents. If you want to give implicit rows and columns specific dimensions, such as to match a rhythm established elsewhere in the grid, use the **grid-auto-*** properties.

```
grid-auto-rows
grid-auto-columns
```

Values:	*list of track sizes*
Default:	auto
Applies to:	grid containers
Inherits:	no

The **grid-auto-row** and **grid-auto-columns** properties provide one or more track sizes for automatically generated tracks and apply to the grid container. If you provide more than one value, it acts as a repeating pattern. As just mentioned, the default value is **auto**, which sizes the row or column to accommodate the content.

In this example, I've explicitly created a grid that is two columns wide and two columns high. I've placed one of the grid items in a position equivalent to the fifth column and third row. My explicit grid isn't big enough to accommodate it, so tracks get added according to the sizes I provided in the **grid-auto-*** properties (FIGURE 16-42).

THE MARKUP

```
<div id="littlegrid">
  <div id="A">A</div>
  <div id="B">B</div>
</div>
```

THE STYLES

```
#littlegrid {
  display: grid;
  grid-template-columns: 200px 200px;
  grid-template-rows: 200px 200px;
  grid-auto-columns: 100px;
  grid-auto-rows: 100px;
}
#A {
  grid-row: 1 / 2;
  grid-column: 2 / 3;
}
#B {
  grid-row: 3 / 4;
  grid-column: 5 / 6;
}
```

The grid has two explicitly defined rows and columns at 200 pixels wide each.

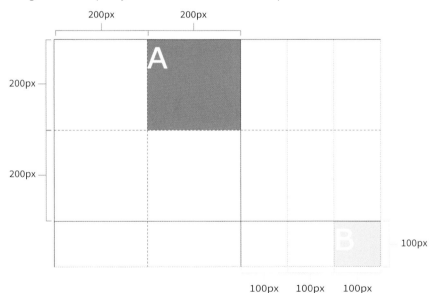

Rows and column tracks are added automatically as needed. They are sized as specified by grid-auto-rows and grid-auto-columns (100 pixels).

FIGURE 16-42. Browsers generate rows and columns automatically to place grid items that don't fit the defined grid.

Hopefully, that example helped you form a mental model for automatically generated rows and columns. A more common use of auto-generated tracks is to tile images, product listings, and the like into columns, letting rows be

The Grid Item Shuffle

So far, you've seen grid items flowing into a grid sequentially and get placed into their own little areas on a grid explicitly. There are a few properties that may be useful for tweaking the position of grid items.

Changing the Order

As in Flexbox, you can apply the **order** property to a grid item element to change the order in which it appears when it is rendered. Keep in mind that the **order** property does not change the order in which it is read by an assistive device. See the section **"Changing the Order of Flex Items"** earlier in this chapter for more information on how to use **order**.

Stacking Order

It is possible to position items in a grid in a way that causes them to overlap. When more than one item is assigned to a grid area, items that appear later in the source are rendered on top of items earlier in the source, but you can change the stacking order by using the **z-index** property. Assigning a higher **z-index** value to earlier item elements makes them render above items that appear later. See the section **"Stacking Order"** in **Chapter 15, Floating and Positioning**, for details on using **z-index**.

created as needed. These styles set up a grid with explicit columns (as many as will fit the width of the viewport, no narrower than 200px) and as many 200px-high rows as needed:

```
grid-template-columns: repeat(auto-fill, minmax(200px, 1fr));
grid-auto-rows: 200px;
```

You can also control the manner in which items automatically flow into the grid with the **grid-auto-flow** property.

Flow direction and density

grid-auto-flow

Values:	row or column | dense *(optional)*
Default:	row
Applies to:	grid containers
Inherits:	no

Use **grid-auto-flow** to specify whether you'd like items to flow in by row or column. The default flow follows the writing direction of the document (left-to-right and top-to-bottom for English and other left-to-right languages).

In this example, I've specified that I'd like grid items to flow in by columns instead of the default rows:

```
#listings {
  display: grid;
  grid-auto-flow: column;
}
```

By default, items are placed in the first area in which they fit. Cells that are too small to accommodate the content will be skipped over until a cell large enough is found for placement. If you include the optional **dense** keyword for the **grid-auto-flow** property, it instructs the browser to fill the grid as densely as possible, allowing the items to appear out of sequence in order to fill the available space:

```
#listings {
  display: grid;
  grid-auto-flow: dense rows;
}
```

The example on the left of FIGURE 16-43 shows the default flow method. Look closely and you'll see that the grid items are in order. When there isn't enough room for the whole item, it moves down and to the left until it fits (similar to floats). This method may leave empty cells as shown in the figure. By comparison, the dense flow example on the right is all filled in, and if you look at the numbering, you can see that putting items wherever they fit makes them end up out of order. Note that dense flow doesn't always result in a completely filled-in grid like the figure, but it is likely to have fewer holes and be more compact than the default mode.

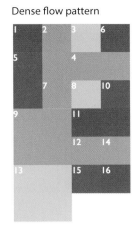

Default flow pattern   Dense flow pattern

FIGURE 16-43. Comparison of default and dense auto-flow modes.

The grid shorthand property revisited

Earlier we saw the **grid** shorthand property used to provide track sizes as well as area names. In that section, we were dealing with explicit grids, but **grid** can be used with implicit grid properties as well.

Adding the **auto-flow** keyword to either the row or track information indicates that the tracks on that axis should be automatically generated at the provided dimension.

Say we want to establish columns explicitly, but let rows generate automatically as needed. The **grid** shorthand for this common scenario is shown here:

```
grid: auto-flow 12em / repeat(5, 1fr);
```

Remember that the **grid** shorthand syntax lists row information first, then a slash, then the column information. Here, the rule says to create rows automatically that are 12 ems high and create 5 columns at 1fr each. When **auto-flow** is applied to rows, the **grid-auto-flow** is set to **row**.

In this example, the resulting grid will have two 300px rows, but 100px-wide columns will be generated on the fly as grid items are added:

```
grid: 300px 300px / auto-flow 100px;
```

With **auto-flow** applied to columns, the **grid-auto-flow** is set to **column**.

It is important to keep in mind that because **grid** is a shorthand property, any omitted value will be reset to its default. Therefore, if you've also used **grid** to set up explicit rows and columns, those will be essentially lost if a **grid** shorthand with implicit grid instructions appears later in the style sheet.

Spacing and Alignment

The remaining properties defined in the Grid Layout Module relate to spacing and alignment. You can add space between tracks and adjust alignment of the grid and its items by using many of the same methods you learned for Flexbox.

Spacing between tracks (gutters)

grid-row-gap
grid-column-gap

Values:	*length (must not be negative)*
Default:	0
Applies to:	grid containers
Inherits:	no

grid-gap

Values:	*grid-row-gap grid-column-gap*
Default:	0 0
Applies to:	grid containers
Inherits:	no

NOTE

These property names will be changing to **row-gap**, **column-gap**, *and* **gap**. *Until browsers start supporting the new syntax, you can still use the* **grid-*** *prefixed versions, which will continue to be supported for backward compatibility.*

Setting a length value for **grid-row-gap** adds space between the row tracks of the grid, and **grid-column-gap** adds space between (you guessed it) column tracks. The effect is as if the grid lines have a width; however, the gap width is applied only to lines between tracks, not outside the first and last lines in the grid. (Spacing on the outside edges can be controlled with padding.) You can use the **grid-gap** shorthand to specify gap widths for rows and columns in one go, with rows first, as usual.

In this example, I've added 20px space between rows and 50px space between columns by using the **grid-gap** shorthand (FIGURE 16-44).

```
div#container {
  border: 2px solid gray;
  display: grid;
  grid: repeat(4, 150px) / repeat(4, 1fr);
  grid-gap: 20px 50px;
}
```

Grid and item alignment

You can align grid items in their cells with the same alignment vocabulary used for Flexbox items (see the **"Box Alignment"** sidebar). I'm going to touch on these quickly, but you can play around with them on your own.

Box Alignment

It's no coincidence that Flexbox and Grid share alignment properties and values. They are all standardized in their own spec called the CSS Box Alignment Module, Level 3, which serves as a reference to a number of CSS modules. You can check it out at *www.w3.org/TR/css-align/*.

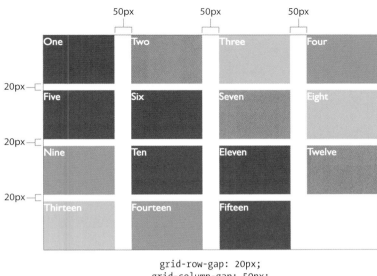

grid-row-gap: 20px;
grid-column-gap: 50px;

FIGURE 16-44. Grid gaps add gutter spaces between tracks.

Aligning individual items

justify-self

Values:	start | end | center | left | right | self-start | self-end | stretch | normal | auto
Default:	auto (looks at the value for justify-items, which defaults to normal)
Applies to:	grid items
Inherits:	no

align-self

Values:	start | end | center | left | right | self-start | self-end | stretch | normal | auto
Default:	auto (looks at the value for align-items)
Applies to:	grid items
Inherits:	no

NOTE

*The **self-start** and **self-end** values look at the writing direction of the content of the item and use its start or end edge for alignment. For example, if an item is in Arabic, its **self-start** edge is on the right, and it would be aligned to the right. The **start** and **end** values consider the writing direction of the grid container. The **left** and **right** keywords are absolute and would not change with the writing system, but they correspond to **start** and **end** in left-to-right languages.*

When a grid item doesn't fill its entire grid area, you can specify how you'd like it to be aligned in that space. Specify the horizontal (inline) alignment with the **justify-self** property. **align-self** specifies alignment on the vertical (block) axis. These properties apply to the grid item element, which makes sense because you want the item to align itself.

FIGURE 16-45 shows the effects of each keyword value. For items with their size set to **auto** (or in other words, not explicitly set with **width** and **height** properties), the default is **stretch**. This is what we've seen in all the previous

■ TIP

If you want a grid item to stay centered in its grid area, set both **align-self** and **justify-self** to center.

FIGURE 16-45. Values for **justify-self** and **align-self** for aligning a grid item within its respective grid area. These values have the same use in the **justify-items** and **align-items** properties that are used to align all the items in the grid.

Speaking of Spacing, What About Margins?

You can add margins to a grid item as you can for any other element. It is useful to know that the item's margin box will be anchored to the cell or grid area, and the margin space is preserved.

You can use margins to move the item around in the grid area. For example, setting the left margin to "auto" pushes the item to the right, as we saw in earlier Flexbox examples. Setting the left and right margins to "auto" (as long as item has a specified width) centers it horizontally. In Grid, you can also set the top and bottom margins to "auto" and, as long as there's a specified height, it centers vertically. Of course, you have the grid item alignment properties to achieve these effects as well.

grid examples. If the grid item has a width and height specified, those dimensions are preserved and the default is **start**.

After reading about Flexbox, you should find these familiar—for example, the use of "start" and "end" to keep the system language direction-agnostic.

Aligning all the items in a grid

justify-items

Values:	start	end	center	left	right	self-start	self-end	stretch	normal
Default:	normal (stretch for non-replaced elements; start for replaced elements)
Applies to:	grid containers
Inherits:	no

align-items

Values:	start	end	center	left	right	self-start	self-end	stretch	normal
Default:	normal (stretch for non-replaced elements; start for replaced elements)
Applies to:	grid containers
Inherits:	no

To align all of the items in a grid in one fell swoop, use the **justify-items** property for horizontal/inline axis alignment and **align-items** for vertical/block axis. Apply these properties to the grid container element so it affects all of the items in the grid. The keywords do the same things shown in

FIGURE 16-43; just picture it happening consistently across the entire grid. Keep in mind that these settings will be overridden by the ***-self** properties.

Aligning tracks in the grid container

There may be instances in which the tracks of your grid do not fill the entire area of their grid container—for example, if you've specified track widths and heights in specific pixel measurements. You can decide how the browser should handle leftover space within the container by using the **justify-content** (horizontal/inline axis) and **align-content** (vertical/block axis) properties.

justify-content

Values:	start | end | left | right | center | stretch | space-around | space-between | space-evenly
Default:	start
Applies to:	grid containers
Inherits:	no

align-content

Values:	start | end | left | right | center | stretch | space-around | space-between | space-evenly
Default:	start
Applies to:	grid containers
Inherits:	no

In FIGURE 16-46, the grid container is indicated with a gray outline. The rows and columns of the drawn grid do not fill the whole container, so something has to happen to that extra space. The **start**, **end**, and **center** keywords move the whole grid around within the container by putting the extra space after, before, or equally on either side, respectively. The **space-around** and **space-between** keywords distribute space around tracks as discussed in the Flexbox section. The **space-evenly** keyword adds an equal amount of space at the start and end of each track and between items.

justify-content:

start	end	center	space-around	space-between	space-evenly
				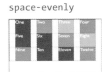	

align-content:

start	end	center	space-around	space-between	space-evenly

FIGURE 16-46. The **justify-content** and **align-content** properties distribute extra space in the container.

Before we close out this discussion of Grid Layout, let's give the Black Goose Bakery page a nice two-column layout in EXERCISE 16-6.

EXERCISE 16-6. A grid layout for the bakery page

The Black Goose Bakery page has come a long way. You've added padding, borders, and margins. You've floated images, positioned an award graphic, and created a navigation bar by using Flexbox. Now you can use your new grid skills to give it a two-column layout that would be appropriate for tablets and larger screens (FIGURE 16-47).

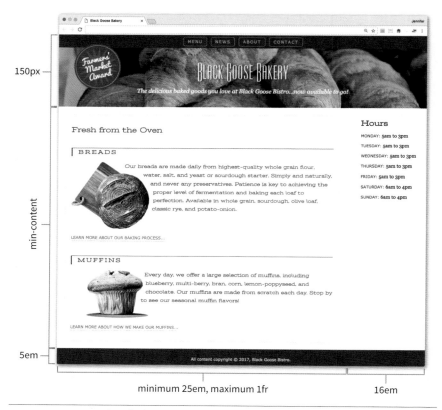

FIGURE 16-47. The Black Goose Bakery page with a two-column grid layout.

Start by opening the bakery file as you left it in EXERCISE 16-1.

1. We need to add a bit of markup that encloses everything in the body of the document in an element that will serve as the grid container. Open the HTML document *bakery.html*, add a **div** around all of the content elements (from **header** to **footer**), and give it the **id** "container". Save the HTML file.

```
<body>
    <div id="container">
        <header>…</header>
        <main>…</main>
        <aside>…</aside>
        <footer>…</footer>
    </div>
</body>
```

In the style sheet (*bakery-styles.css*), add a new style to make the new **div** display as a grid:

```
#container {
    display: grid;
}
```

2. First we'll work on the rows. FIGURE 16-47 shows that we need three rows to create the layout. Set the height of the first row track to **auto** so it will observe the height settings on the elements within it and automatically accommodate the content. The second row has a lot of text, so use the **auto** track value again to guarantee the track will expand at least as much as necessary to fit the text. For the third row, a height of 5em should be sufficient to fit the few lines of text with a comfortable amount of space:

```
#container {
    display: grid;
    grid-template-rows: auto auto 5em;
}
```

3. Now we can set up the column tracks. It looks like we'll need only two: one for the main content and one for the Hours sidebar. I've used the **minmax()** value so I can ensure the text column never gets narrower than 25em, but it can expand to fill the available space in the browser (**1fr**). The Hours column feels right to me at 16em. Feel free to try other values.

```
#container {
    display: grid;
    grid-template-rows: auto auto 5em;
    grid-template-columns: minmax(25em, 1fr) 16em;
}
```

4. Next, name the areas in the grid so we can place the items in it easily and efficiently. Use the **grid-template-areas** property to name the cells in the grid:

```
#container {
    display: grid;
    grid-template-rows: auto auto 5em;
    grid-template-columns: minmax(25em, 1fr) 16em;
    grid-template-areas:
        "banner banner"
        "main   hours"
        "footer footer";
}
```

5. With everything set up, it'll be a breeze to put the content items into their proper places. Create a style rule for each grid item and tell it where to go with **grid-area**:

```
header {
    grid-area: banner;
}
main {
    grid-area: main;
}
aside {
    grid-area: hours;
}
footer {
    grid-area: footer;
}
```

Pretty easy, right? Now would be a good time to save the file and take a look at it in the browser (if you haven't already). The 2.5% margins that we had set on the **main** element earlier give it some nice breathing room in its area, so let's leave that alone. However, I'd like to remove the right margin and border radius we had set on the **aside** so it fills the right column. I'm going to just comment them out so that information is still around if I need to use it later:

```
aside {
    …
    /* border-top-right-radius: 25px; */
    /* margin: 1em 2.5% 0 10%; */
}
```

That does it! Open the *bakery.html* page in a browser that supports CSS grids, and it should look like the screenshot in FIGURE 16-47.

Now the bakery page has a nice two-column layout using a simple grid. In the real world, this would be just one layout in a set that would address different screen sizes as part of a responsive design strategy. We'll be talking about responsive design in the next chapter. And because grids are not supported by Internet Explorer, Edge, and older browsers, you would also create fallback layouts using Flexbox or floats depending on how universally you need the layout to work. I don't mean to kill your buzz, but I do want you to be aware that although this exercise let you sharpen your skills, it's part of a much broader production picture.

Note: For float- and position-based layout techniques that could be used as fallbacks, get the article **"Page Layout with Floats and Positioning"** (PDF) at learningwebdesign.*com/articles/*.

Grid Property Roundup

Here's a nice, handy list of the Grid properties, organized by whether they apply to the container or to individual grid items.

Grid Container Properties
    display: grid | inline-grid
    grid
        grid-template
            grid-template-rows
            grid-template-columns
            grid-template-areas
        grid-auto-rows
        grid-auto-columns
        grid-auto-flow
    grid-gap
        grid-row-gap
        grid-column-gap
    justify-items
    align-items
    justify-content
    align-content

Grid Item Properties
    grid-column
        grid-column-start
        grid-column-end
    grid-row
        grid-row-start
        grid-row-end
    grid-area
    justify-self
    align-self
    order *(not part of Grid Module)*
    z-index *(not part of Grid Module)*

Online Grid Resources

As you continue your Grid Layout adventure, I'm sure you'll find plenty of excellent resources online, as more are popping up all the time. I'd like to point you to a few of the most complete and authoritative resources that I found helpful as I learned about grids myself.

Rachel Andrew's "Grid By Example" site *(gridbyexample.com)*

Rachel Andrew, one of the first champions of Grid Layout, has assembled an incredible collection of articles, free video tutorials, browser support information, and more. You can also try searching the web for her excellent conference talks on the topic.

Jen Simmons' "Experimental Layout Lab" *(labs.jensimmons.com)*

Jen Simmons, who works for Mozilla Foundation, shows off what Grid Layout can do in her Experimental Layout Lab. It's definitely worth a visit for the cool examples of Grid and other emerging CSS technologies as well as exercises that let you code along.

You can find Jen's many articles on CSS Grid at *jensimmons.com/writing*. I also recommend her roundup of resources for learning Grid Layout at *jensimmons.com/post/feb-27-2017/learn-css-grid*. See also Jen's YouTube video series called "Layout Land" *(youtube.com*, search for "Layout Land Jen Simmons").

Grid Garden by Thomas Park *(cssgridgarden.com)*

If you enjoyed the Flexbox Froggy game created by Thomas Park, you will have fun playing his Grid Garden game for getting familiar with CSS Grid Layout.

TEST YOURSELF

We covered lots of ground in this chapter. See how you do on this quiz of some of the highlights. As always, **Appendix A** has the answers.

Flexbox

1. How do you turn an element into a flex item?

2. Match the properties with their functions.

   a. justify-content   1. Distribute space around and between flex lines on the cross axis.

   b. align-self   2. Distribute space around and between items on the main axis.

c. align-content   3. Position items on the cross axis.

d. align-items   4. Position a particular item on the cross axis.

3. How is **align-items** different from **align-content**?
   What do they have in common?

4. Match the properties and values to the resulting effects.

   a. flex: 0 1 auto;   1. Items are completely inflexible, neither shrinking nor growing.

   b. flex: none;   2. Item will be twice as wide as others with flex: 1 and may also shrink.

   c. flex: 1 1 auto;   3. Items are fully flexible.

   d. flex: 2 1 0px;   4. Items can shrink but not grow bigger.

5. Match the following **flex-flow** declarations with the resulting flexboxes (FIGURE 16-48).

   a. flex-flow: row wrap;

   b. flex-flow: column nowrap;

   c. flex-flow: row wrap-reverse;

   d. flex-flow: column wrap-reverse;

   e. flex-flow: row nowrap;

❶  ❷ 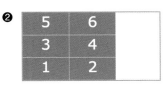 ❸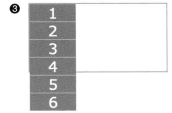

❹ 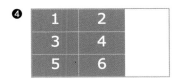 ❺

FIGURE 16-48. Various **flex-flow** settings.

6. Write style rules for displaying the flexbox items in the order shown in FIGURE 16-49.

Source HTML

```
<div id="container">
 <div class="box box1">1</div>
 <div class="box box2">2</div>
 <div class="box box3">3</div>
 <div class="box box4">4</div>
 <div class="box box5">5</div>
 <div class="box box6">6</div>
 <div class="box box7">7</div>
</div>
```

After reordering

6 4 5 7 1 2 3

FIGURE 16-49. Write styles to put items in the shown order.

Grid Layout

7. What is the key difference between Grid Layout and Flexbox? Name at least one similarity (there are multiple answers).

8. Create the grid template for the layout shown in FIGURE 16-50 by using **grid-template-rows** and **grid-template-columns**.

Write it again, this time using the **grid** shorthand property.

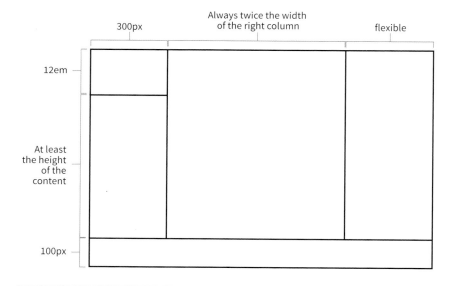

FIGURE 16-50. Create the grid template for this grid structure.

9. Match the following style declarations with the lettered grid items in FIGURE 16-51. In addition to automatic numbering, some of the grid lines have been named, as labeled.

a. _____

```
grid-row-start: 1;
grid-row-end: 3;
grid-column-start: 3;
grid-column-end: 7;
```

b. _____

```
grid-area: 2 / 2 / span 4 / 3;
```

c. _____

```
grid-area: bowie;
```

d. _____

```
grid-row: -2 / -1;
grid-column: -2 / -1;
```

e. _____

```
grid-row-start: george;
grid-row-end: ringo;
grid-column-start: paul;
grid-column-end: john;
```

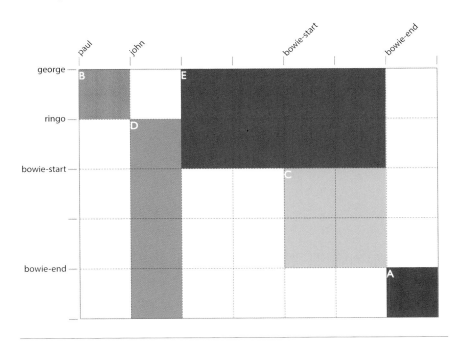

FIGURE 16-51. Match the style examples to the items in this grid.

10. Write a style rule that adds 1em space between columns in a grid container named **#gallery**.

11. Match the tasks with the declarations.

   a. `justify-self: end;`

   b. `align-items: end;`

   c. `align-content: center;`

   d. `align-self: stretch;`

   e. `justify-items: center;`

   _____ Make a particular item stretch to fill its container.

   _____ Position an image on the right edge of its grid area (in a left-to-right reading language).

   _____ Center the whole grid vertically in its container.

   _____ Push all of the images in a grid to the bottom of their respective cells.

   _____ Center all items in their areas horizontally.

CSS REVIEW: LAYOUT PROPERTIES

Here are the properties covered in this chapter, sorted into Flexbox and Grid sections and whether they apply to the container or item.

Flexbox Properties

Flex container properties

`display: flex`	Turns on flexbox mode and makes the element a flex container
`flex-direction`	Indicates the direction in which items are placed in the flex container
`flex-wrap`	Specifies whether the flex items are forced onto a single line or wrapped onto multiple lines
`flex-flow`	Shorthand property for **flex-direction** and **flex-wrap**
`justify-content`	Specifies how space is distributed between and around items on the main axis
`align-content`	Aligns flex lines within the flex container when there is extra space on the cross axis
`align-items`	Specifies how the space is distributed around items on the cross axis

Flex item properties

`align-self`	Specifies how one item is aligned on the cross axis (overrides **align-items**)
`flex`	Shorthand property for **flex-grow**, **flex-shrink**, and **flex-basis**; specifies how items alter their dimensions to fit available space
`flex-basis`	Indicates the initial main size of a flex item
`flex-grow`	Specifies how much a flex item is permitted to grow when there is extra space in the container
`flex-shrink`	Specifies how much a flex item is permitted to shrink when there is not enough room in the container
`order`	Indicates the order used to lay out items in their container

Grid Properties

Grid container properties

`display: grid | inline-grid`	Sets the display mode of an element to a grid context
`grid-template`	Shorthand property for specifying **grid-template-areas**, **grid-template-rows**, and **grid-template-columns**
`grid-template-areas`	Assigns names to areas in the grid
`grid-template-columns`	Specifies track sizes for the columns in explicit grids
`grid-template-rows`	Specifies track sizes for the rows in explicit grids
`grid-auto-columns`	Specifies track sizes for automatically generated columns
`grid-auto-flow`	Indicates the direction and density in which items flow automatically into a grid
`grid-auto-rows`	Specifies track sizes for automatically generated rows
`grid`	Shorthand property for specifying **grid-template-rows**, **grid-template-columns**, and **grid-template-areas**; or **grid-auto-flow**, **grid-auto-rows**, and **grid-auto-columns**
`grid-gap`	Shorthand property for **grid-row-gap** and **grid-column-gap**
`grid-column-gap`	Specifies the width of the gutter between columns
`grid-row-gap`	Specifies the width of the gutter between rows
`justify-items`	Indicates alignment of all the grid items along the inline axis within their respective areas
`justify-content`	Indicates alignment of the grid tracks along the inline axis in its container

`align-items`	Indicates alignment of all the items in a grid along the block axis within their respective grid areas
`align-content`	Indicates alignment of the grid tracks along the block axis in the container

Grid item properties

`grid-column`	Shorthand property for specifying **grid-column-start** and **grid-column-end**
`grid-column-end`	Denotes the end line of the column in which an item is to be placed
`grid-column-start`	Denotes the start line of the column in which an item is to be placed
`grid-row`	Shorthand property for specifying **grid-row-start** and **grid-row-end**
`grid-row-end`	Denotes the end line of the row in which an item is to be placed
`grid-row-start`	Denotes the start line of the row in which an item is to be placed
`grid-area`	Assigns a grid item to a named area or an area described by its four boundary grid lines
`align-self`	Indicates alignment of a single item along the block axis within its grid area
`justify-self`	Indicates alignment of a single grid item along the inline axis within its area
`order`	Specifies the order in which to display the item relative to other items in the source
`z-index`	Specifies the stacking order of an item relative to other items when there is overlap

RESPONSIVE WEB DESIGN

I first introduced you to the concept of Responsive Web Design way back in **Chapter 3, Some Big Concepts You Need to Know**, and we've been addressing ways to keep all screen sizes in mind throughout this book. In this chapter, we get to do a deeper dive into responsive strategies and techniques.

Just to recap, Responsive Web Design (or RWD) is a design and production approach that allows a website to be comfortably viewed and used on all manner of devices. The core principle is that all devices get the same HTML source, located at the same URL, but different styles are applied based on the viewport size to rearrange components and optimize usability. FIGURE 17-1 shows examples of responsive sites as they might appear on a smartphone, tablet, and desktop, but it is important to keep in mind that these sites are designed to work well on the continuum of every screen width in between.

WHY RWD?

Since the iPhone shook things up in 2007, folks now view the web on phones of all sizes, tablets, "phablets," touch-enabled laptops, wearables, televisions, video game consoles, refrigerators, and who knows what else that may be coming down the line.

In 2016, mobile internet usage surpassed desktop usage—an important milestone. The percentage of web traffic that comes from devices other than desktop browsers is steadily increasing. For roughly 10% of Americans, a smartphone or tablet is their *only* access to the internet because of lack of access to a computer or high-speed WiFi at work or home.[*] Younger users may be mobile-only by choice. Furthermore, the vast majority of us access the

---

[*] Pew Research Center, "Smartphone Use in 2015," *www.pewinternet.org/2015/04/01/us-smart-phone-use-in-2015/*.

An Event Apart
aneventapart.com

The Boston Globe
bostonglobe.com

Warwick Public Library
warwicklibrary.org

FIGURE 17-1. Examples of responsive sites that adapt to fit small, medium, and large screens and all sizes in between.

Responsive design is becoming the default way to build a website that meets the demands of our current multidevice environment.

web from a number of platforms (phone, tablet, computer) over the course of the day. And guess what—we expect to have a similar experience using your content or service regardless of how we access your site.

That's where RWD fits in. With one source, you ensure that mobile visitors receive the same content as other visitors (although it might be organized differently). Users are not penalized with stripped-down content or features just because they are using a smartphone. And for visitors who might start using your site on one device and finish it on another, you can ensure a consistent experience.

In fact, for many web designers, "responsive design" is now just "web design." Instead of a niche approach, it is becoming the default way to build a website that meets the demands of our current multidevice environment.

THE RESPONSIVE RECIPE

The deluge of web-enabled mobile devices initially sent shockwaves through the web design community. Accustomed to designing exclusively for large desktop screens, we were unclear about how we could accommodate screens that fit in the palm of your hand.

One solution was to rely on the phone's built-in web display functionality. By default, mobile devices display an entire web page shrunken down to fit on whatever screen real estate is available. Users can pinch to zoom into the details and scroll around to various parts of the page. While that technically works, it is far from an optimal experience. Another approach was to create a separate mobile site just for small screens and people "on the go." There are still many companies and services that use dedicated mobile ("m-dot") sites—Twitter and Facebook come to mind—but in general, m-dot sites are going away in favor of RWD. Google is helping the process along by favoring responsive sites with single URLs over *m.* or *mobile.* versions.

In 2010, Ethan Marcotte gave name to another, more flexible solution in his article "Responsive Web Design" (*alistapart.com/article/responsive-web-design*), which has since become a cornerstone of modern web design. In this chapter, I will follow the "ingredients" for RWD that Ethan outlines in his book *Responsive Web Design* (A Book Apart).

The technique has three core components:

A flexible grid

Rather than remaining at a static width, responsive sites use methods that allow them to squeeze and flow into the available browser space.

Flexible images

Images and other embedded media need to be able to scale to fit their containing elements.

CSS media queries

Media queries give us a way to deliver sets of rules only to devices that meet certain criteria, such as width and orientation.

To this list of ingredients, I would add the viewport **meta** element, which makes the width of the web page match the width of the screen. That's where we'll begin our tour of the mechanics of RWD.

Setting the Viewport

To fit standard websites onto small screens, mobile browsers render the page on a canvas called the viewport and then shrink that viewport down to fit the width of the screen (device width). For example, on iPhones, mobile Safari sets the viewport width to 980 points (see **Note**), so a web page is rendered as though it were on a desktop browser window set to 980 pixels wide. That rendering gets shrunk down to the width of the screen (ranging from 320 to 414 points, depending on the iPhone model), cramming a lot of information into a tiny space.

Mobile Safari introduced the viewport **meta** element, which allows us to define the size of that initial viewport. Soon, the other mobile browsers followed suit. The following **meta** element, which goes in the **head** of the HTML

NOTE

Mobile sites were discussed in the sidebar **"M-dot Sites"** *in* **Chapter 3**.

NOTE

iOS layouts are measured in points, a unit of measurement that is independent from the number of pixels that make up the physical screen. Points and device pixels are discussed in more detail in **Chapter 23, Web Image Basics**.

WARNING

The viewport **meta** *element also allows the* **maximum-scale** *attribute. Setting it to 1 (*maximum-scale=1*) prevents users from zooming the page, but it is strongly recommended that you avoid doing so because resizing is important for accessibility and usability.*

document, tells the browser to set the width of the viewport equal to the width of the device screen (**width=device-width**), whatever that happens to be (FIGURE 17-2). The **initial-scale** value sets the zoom level to 1 (100%).

```
<meta name="viewport" content="width=device-width, initial-scale=1">
```

With the viewport **meta** element in place, if the device's screen is 320 pixels wide, the rendering viewport on that device will also be 320 pixels across (not 980) and will appear on the screen at full size. That is the width we test for with media queries, so setting the viewport is a crucial first step.

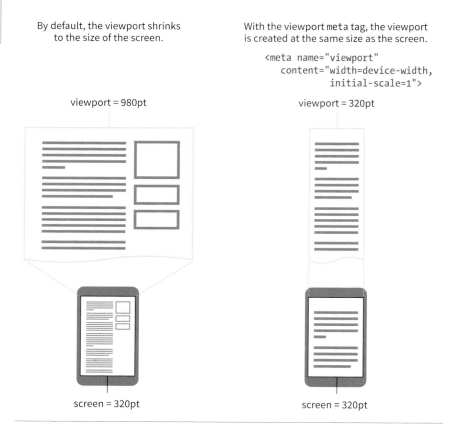

By default, the viewport shrinks to the size of the screen.

With the viewport meta tag, the viewport is created at the same size as the screen.

```
<meta name="viewport"
    content="width=device-width,
        initial-scale=1">
```

viewport = 980pt

viewport = 320pt

screen = 320pt

screen = 320pt

FIGURE 17-2. The viewport **meta** element matches the resolution of the device's browser viewport to the resolution of its screen.

Flexible Grids (Fluid Layouts)

In the Flexbox and Grid discussions in the previous chapter, we saw examples of items expanding and contracting to fill the available space of their containers. That fluidity is exactly the sort of behavior you need to make content neatly fit a wide range of viewport sizes. Fluid layouts (or "flexible grids," as Ethan Marcotte calls them in his article and book) are the foundation of responsive design.

In a fluid layout, the page area and its grid resize proportionally to fill the available width of the screen or window (FIGURE 17-3, top). That is easily accomplished with `fr` and `minmax()` units in CSS Grid layouts and with `flex` property settings in Flexbox. If you need to also target older browsers that don't support CSS layout standards, you can use percentage values for horizontal measurements so elements remain proportional at varying sizes (see the sidebar **"Converting Pixels to Percentages"**).

In the past, when we knew that everyone was looking at our sites on desktop monitors, fixed-width layouts were the norm. (Ahh, those simple pre-mobile days when we only needed to deal with radically incompatible browser support!) As the name implies, fixed-width layouts are created at a specific pixel width (FIGURE 17-3, bottom), with 960 pixels being quite fashionable (see **Note**). Specifying all measurements in pixel values gave designers control over the layout as they might have in print, and ensured that users across all platforms and browsers got similar, if not the same, rendering of the page.

Fluid layouts fill the viewport proportionally.

w3c.org

Fixed layouts stay the same size and may get cut off or leave extra space.

kexp.org

FIGURE 17-3. Fluid and fixed layout examples.

NOTE

Designers landed on 960 pixels wide as a standard page width because it filled the standard desktop width at the time (1,028 pixels) and it was easily divided into an equal columns. Page layout systems based on 12-column grids within the 960-pixel page were also popular.

It didn't take long to realize, however, that it would be impossible to create separate fixed-width designs tailored to every device size. Clearly, fluidity has the advantage. It is based on the intrinsic nature of the normal flow, so we're working *with* the medium here rather than against it. When the layout reflows to fill the available width, you don't need to worry about horizontal scrollbars or awkward empty space in the browser.

On the downside, fluid layouts may allow text line lengths to become uncomfortably long, so that is something to watch out for. We'll go into more detail on layouts later in this chapter.

■ PERSONAL ANECDOTE

When I got started in web design in 1993, the most common PC monitor size was a measly 640 × 480 pixels, unless you were a fancy-pants designer type with a 800 × 600 screen. My earliest designs had a fixed width of an adorable 515 pixels.

Making Images Flexible

Every now and then a solution is simple. Take, for example, the style rule required to make images scale down to fit the size of their container:

```css
img {
    max-width: 100%;
}
```

That's it! When the layout gets smaller, the images in it scale down to fit the width of their respective containers. If the container is larger than the image—for example, in the tablet or desktop layouts—the image does not scale larger; it stops at 100% of its original size (FIGURE 17-4). When you apply the **max-width** property, you can omit the **width** and **height** attributes in the **img** elements in the HTML document. If you do set the **width** attribute, be sure the **height** attribute is set to **auto**; otherwise, the image won't scale proportionately.

```css
img { max-width: 100%, }
```

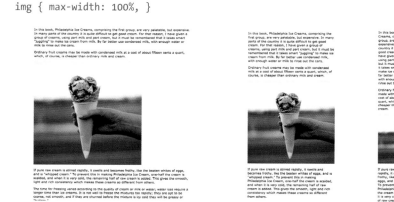

FIGURE 17-4. Setting the **max-width** of inline images allows them to shrink to fit available space but not grow larger than actual size.

Responsive images

But wait—things are never that simple, right? If you think back to our discussion of responsive images in **Chapter 7, Adding Images**, you'll remember that there is some elbow grease required to avoid serving unnecessarily large images to small devices as well as making sure large, high-density monitors get high-resolution images that shine. Choosing the best image size for performance is part of the responsive design process, but we won't be concentrating on that in this chapter. We've got bigger fish to fry!

Other embedded media

Videos and other embedded media (using **object** or **embed** elements) also need to scale down in a responsive environment. Unfortunately, videos do not retain their intrinsic ratios when the width is scaled down, so there are a few more hoops to jump through to get good results. Thierry Koblentz documents one strategy nicely in his article "Creating Intrinsic Ratios for Video" at *www.alistapart.com/articles/creating-intrinsic-ratios-for-video*. There is also a JavaScript plug-in called FitVids.js (created by Chris Coyier and the folks at Paravel) that automates Koblentz's technique for fluid-width videos. It is available at *fitvidsjs.com*.

Media Query Magic

Now we get to the real meat of responsive design—media queries! Media queries apply different styles based on characteristics of the browser: its width, whether it is vertically or horizontally oriented, its resolution, and more. They are what make it possible to send a one-column layout to small screens and a multicolumn layout to larger screens on the fly.

The query itself includes a media type followed by a particular feature and a value for which to test. The criteria are followed by a set of curly brackets that contain styles to apply if the test is passed. The structure of a media query as used within a style sheet goes like this:

```
@media type and (feature: value) {
  /* styles for browsers that meet this criteria */
}
```

Let's clarify that with an example. The following media queries look at whether the viewport is on a screen and in **landscape** (horizontal) or **portrait** (vertical) orientation. When the query detects that the viewport is in landscape mode, the background color of the page is "skyblue"; when it is in portrait orientation, the background is "coral" (FIGURE 17-5). If this were displayed on a smartphone that tips from vertical to horizontal and back again, the colors would change as it tilts. This isn't a very practical design choice, but it does provide a very simple illustration of media queries at work.

```
@media screen and (orientation: landscape) {
  body {
    background: skyblue;
    }
}
@media screen and (orientation: portrait) {
  body {
    background: coral;
    }
}
```

HEADS UP

Having style declaration curly brackets nested inside media query curly brackets can get a little confusing. Be sure that you have the right number of curly brackets and nest them properly. Careful indenting is helpful. Many code-editing programs also use color coding to help you keep them straight.

When the viewport is in portrait mode, the background color is "coral."

When the viewport is in landscape mode, the background color is "skyblue."

FIGURE 17-5. Changing the background color based on the orientation of the viewport with media queries.

Media types

Media types, as included in the first part of a query, were introduced in CSS2 as a way to target styles to particular media. For example, this **@media** rule delivers a set of styles only when the document is printed (it does not test for any specific features or values):

```
@media print {
  /* print-specific styles here */
}
```

The most current defined media types are **all**, **print**, **screen**, and **speech** (see **Note**). If you are designing for screen, the media type is optional, so you can omit it as shown in the syntax example shown here, but including it doesn't hurt. I'll be including the screen **media** type for the sake of clarity in my examples.

```
@media (feature: value) {
   }
```

NOTE

CSS2 also defined **aural**, **handheld**, **braille**, **embossed**, **projection**, **tty**, *and* **tv**, *but they have been deprecated in the latest Media Queries Level 4 spec (currently a Working Draft) and are discouraged from use.*

Media feature queries

CSS3 media queries take targeting one step further by letting us test for a particular *feature* of a viewport or device. We saw an example of testing the orientation of a device in FIGURE 17-5. The most common feature to test for is the viewport width. You can also test for a minimum width (**min-width**) and maximum width (**max-width**).

Here is a simple example that displays headline fonts in a fancy cursive font only when the viewport is 40em or wider—that is, when there is enough space for the font to be legible. Viewports that do not match the query (because they are narrower than 40em) use a simple serif face.

```
h1 {
   font-family: Georgia, serif;
   }

@media screen and (min-width: 40em) {
   h1 {
      font-family: 'Lobster', cursive;
      }
}
```

The complete list of device features you can detect with media queries appears in TABLE 17-1.

> ■ AUTHORING TIP
>
> Minimum-width queries are your go-to for creating mobile-first responsive design.

TABLE 17-1. Media features you can evaluate with media queries

Feature	Description
width	The width of the display area (viewport). Also **min-width** and **max-width**.
height	The height of the display area (viewport). Also **min-height** and **max-height**.
orientation	Whether the device is in **portrait** or **landscape** orientation.
aspect-ratio	Ratio of the viewport's width divided by height (width/height). Example: **aspect-ratio: 16/9**.
color	The bit depth of the display; for example, **color: 8** tests for whether the device has at least 8-bit color.
color-index	The number of colors in the color lookup table.
monochrome	The number of bits per pixel in a monochrome device.
resolution	The density of pixels in the device. This is increasingly relevant for detecting high-resolution displays.
scan	Whether a **tv** media type uses progressive or interlace scanning. (Does not accept **min-**/**max-** prefixes.)
grid	Whether the device uses a grid-based display, such as a terminal window. (Does not accept **min-**/**max-** prefixes.)

Deprecated features

The following features have been deprecated in Media Queries Level 4 Working Draft and are discouraged from use.

device-width	The width of the device's rendering surface (the whole screen). (Deprecated in favor of **width**.)
device-height	The height of the device's rendering surface (the whole screen). (Deprecated in favor of **height**.)
device-aspect-ratio	Ratio of the whole screen's (rendering surface) width to height. (Deprecated in favor of **aspect-ratio**.)

New in Media Queries Level 4

These features have been added in the Working Draft of MQ4. Some may gain browser support, and some may be dropped from future drafts. I include them here to show you where the W3C sees media queries going. For details, see *drafts.csswg.org/mediaqueries-4*.

update-frequency	How quickly (if at all) the output device modifies the appearance of the content.
overflow-block	How the device handles content that overflows the viewport along the block axis.
overflow-inline	Whether the content that overflows the viewport along the inline axis can be scrolled.
color-gamut	The approximate range of colors that are supported by the user agent and output device.
pointer	Whether the primary input mechanism is a pointing device and how accurate it is.
hover	Whether the input mechanism allows the user to hover over elements.
any-pointer	Whether any available input mechanism is a pointing device, and how accurate it is.
any-hover	Whether any available input mechanism allows hovering.

How to use media queries

You can use media queries within a style sheet or to conditionally load external style sheets. Media queries may not be used with inline styles.

Within a style sheet

The most common way to utilize media queries is to use an `@media` ("at-media") rule right in the style sheet. The examples in this chapter so far are all `@media` rules.

When you use media queries within a style sheet, the order of rules is very important. Because rules later in the style sheet override the rules that come before them, your media query needs to come *after* any rules with the same declaration.

The strategy is to specify the baseline styles that serve as a default, and then override specific rules as needed to optimize for alternate viewing environments. In RWD, the best practice is to set up styles for small screens and browsers that don't support media queries, and then introduce styles for increasingly larger screens later in the style sheet.

That's exactly what I did in the headline font-switching example earlier. The `h1` sets a baseline experience with a local serif font, and then gets enhanced for larger screens with a media query.

With external style sheets

For large or complicated sites, developers may choose to put styles for different devices into separate style sheets and call in the whole *.css* file when certain conditions are met. One method is to use the `media` attribute in the `link` element to conditionally load separate *.css* files. In this example, the basic styles for a site are requested first, followed by a style sheet that will be used only if the device is more than 1,024 pixels wide (and if the browser supports media queries):

```
<head>
  <link rel="stylesheet" href="styles.css">
  <link rel="stylesheet" href="2column-styles.css" media="screen and
(min-width:1024px)">
</head>
```

Some developers find this method helpful for managing modular style sheets, but it comes with the disadvantage of requiring extra HTTP requests for each additional *.css* file. Be sure to provide only as many links as necessary (perhaps one for each major breakpoint), and rely on `@media` rules within style sheets to make minor adjustments for sizes in between.

Similarly, you can carry out media queries with `@import` rules that pull in external style sheets from within a style sheet. Notice that the word "media" does not appear in this syntax, only the type and query.

```
<style>
  @import url("/default-styles.css");
  @import url("/wide-styles.css") screen and (min-width: 1024px);
  /* other styles */
</style>
```

Browser support

We can't close out a discussion of media queries without a nod to browser support. The good news is that media queries are supported by virtually all desktop and mobile browsers in use today. The big exceptions are Internet Explorer versions 8 and earlier, which have no support. Because of the staying power of the Windows XP operating system, IE8 continues to show up in browser use statistics (at 1–2% as I write, ahead of IE 9 and 10). If your site has hundreds of thousands of users, that 1% ends up being a significant number of broken experiences.

If you expect to have visitors using old versions of IE, you have a couple of options. First, you could use the Respond.js polyfill, which adds support for `min-width` and `max-width` to non-supporting browsers. It was created by Scott Jehl and is available at *github.com/scottjehl/Respond*.

The other option is to create a separate style sheet with a no-frills desktop layout and deliver it only to users with IE8 or earlier by using a conditional comment. Other browsers ignore the content of this IE-specific comment:

```
<!-- [if lte IE 8]>
    <link rel="stylesheet" href="/path/IE_fallback.css">
<![endif]-->
```

Depending on your site statistics and when you are reading this, you may not need to worry about media query support at all. Lucky you!

CHOOSING BREAKPOINTS

A breakpoint is the point at which we use a media query to introduce a style change. When you specify `min-width: 800px` in a media query, you are saying that 800 pixels is the "breakpoint" at which those particular styles should be used. FIGURE 17-6 shows some of the breakpoints at which Etsy.com makes both major layout changes and subtle design tweaks on its home page.

Choosing breakpoints can be challenging, but there are a few best practices to keep in mind.

When RWD was first introduced, there were only a handful of devices to worry about, so we tended to base our breakpoints on the common device sizes (320 pixels for smartphones, 768 pixels for iPads, and so on), and we created a separate design for each breakpoint. It didn't take long until we had to deal with device widths at nearly every point from 240 to 3,000+ pixels. That device-based approach definitely didn't scale.

A breakpoint is a width at which you introduce a style change.

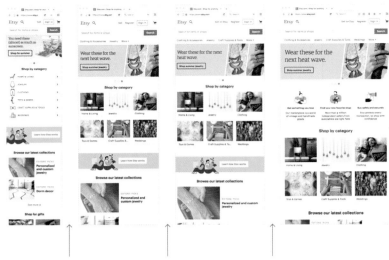

At the **480-pixel breakpoint**, the category navigation changes from a list to photos. "Register" is added to the top navigation bar.

At **501 pixels**, "Sell" becomes "Sell on Etsy" (a very subtle adjustment). You can also see more links in the navigation bar under the search field.

At **640 pixels**, the "How Etsy Works" images and messages move above the categories. In smaller views, they were accessible via the "Learn how Etsy works" link in a yellow bar.

At **901 pixels**, the search input form moves into the top header.

At **981 pixels**, the word "Cart" appears under the shopping cart icon. We now see the full list of navigation options in the header (no "More" link). At this point, the layout expands to fill larger windows until it reaches its maximum width of 1400 pixels. Then margins add space equally on the left and right to keep the layout centered.

FIGURE 17-6. A series of breakpoints used by Etsy's responsive site (2017).

Module-Based Breakpoints

A better approach is to create breakpoints for the individual parts of a page rather than switching out the entire page at once (although for some pages that may work just fine). A common practice is to create the design for narrow screens first, and then resize the browser wider and pay attention to the point at which each part of the page starts to become unacceptable. The navigation might become too awkward and need a breakpoint at 400 pixels wide, but the one-column layout might be OK until it reaches 800 pixels, at which point a two-column design could be introduced.

In his book *Responsive Design: Patterns & Principles* (A Book Apart), Ethan Marcotte calls this "content out" design and puts it like this:

> For me, that "content out" process begins by looking at the smallest version of a piece of content, then expanding that element until its seams begin to show and it starts to lose its shape. Once that happens, that's an opportunity to make a change—to introduce a breakpoint that reshapes the element and preserves its integrity.

If you find that you have a lot of breakpoints within a few pixels or ems of one another, grouping them together may streamline your style sheet and process. And it doesn't hurt to keep the screen sizes of the most popular devices in mind in case nudging your breakpoint down a little helps improve the experience for a whole class of users. The site Screen Sizes (*screensiz.es*) lists the dimensions of a wide range of popular devices. A web search will turn up similar resources.

> It is common to create breakpoints for each component of the page rather than changing the entire page at once.

Em-Based Breakpoints

The examples in this section have been based on breakpoints with pixel measurements. An alternative, and many would say better, method is to use ems instead of pixels in the media query. Remember that an em is equal to the current font size of an element. When used in a media query, an em is based on the base font size for the document (16 pixels by default, although that can be changed by the user or the page author).

Pixel-based media queries don't adapt if the user changes their font size settings, which people do in order to be able to read the page more easily. But em-based media queries respond to the size of the text, keeping the layout of the page in proportion.

For example, say you have a layout that switches to two columns when the page reaches 800 pixels. You've designed it so the main column has an optimum text line length when the base font size is the default 16 pixels. If the user changes their base font size to 32 pixels, that double-sized text will pour into a space intended for text half its size. Line lengths would be awkward.

Using em-based queries, if the query targets browsers wider than 50em, when the base font size is 16 pixels, the switch happens at 800 pixels (as designed).

> Em-based media queries keep the layout proportional to the font size.

However, should the base font size change to 32 pixels, the two-column layout would kick in at 1,600 pixels (50em × 32px = 1,600px), when there is plenty of room for the text to fill the main column with the same line lengths as the original design.

This example used a whole-page layout switch, but media queries on individual components (as discussed earlier) can use ems as well. In the next section, I'll introduce some of the aspects of web pages that require attention when you're choosing breakpoints.

How Wide Is the Viewport?

I've suggested making your browser wider until you see that a breakpoint is needed, but how do you know how wide the window is? There are a number of tools that provide window measurements.

Firefox, Chrome, and Safari all have tools that can show you how a page looks at specific viewport dimensions. In Responsive Mode (or View), you get a resizable window-in-a-window that can be set to standard device sizes or resized manually. The pixel dimensions are displayed as the viewport resizes.

In Firefox, access Responsive Design Mode (FIGURE 17-7) via the Web Developer Tools (**Tools → Web Developer → Responsive Design Mode**). Safari's Responsive Design Mode is accessible via **Develop → Enter Responsive Design Mode**. Chrome offers a Device Toolbar (**View → Developer → Developer Tools**, and then look for the Toggle Device Toolbar icon on the left of the menu bar). They all work about the same, but you may find you prefer one browser's user interface over another.

To find out how your browser window or device responds to media queries, go to MQTest.io (*mqtest.io*) by Viljami Salminen. In addition to viewport width and height, it reports on other device features such as device-pixel-ratio, aspect ratio, and more.

Responsive Design Mode in Firefox shows you the exact pixel dimensions of its viewport. It has shortcuts to resize it to common device dimensions. Chrome and Safari have similar responsive views.

MQTest.io is a web page that reports on how your browser responds to media queries, including width.

FIGURE 17-7. Checking viewport size in Firefox's Responsive Design Mode and MQTest.io.

DESIGNING RESPONSIVELY

We've covered the RWD nuts and bolts—now let's talk about some of the decisions designers make when creating responsive sites. I am only going to be able to scratch the surface here, but you'll find much deeper explorations on these themes in the books and articles listed along the way. For now, I just want to raise your awareness of responsive strategies. At the end of the section, you will use some of these strategies to make the Black Goose Bakery page responsive.

We've seen a few examples in our exercises of content looking wonky when the browser gets very narrow or very wide. A three-column layout just doesn't fit, and text in an image may become unreadable when it is scaled down to fit a 320-pixel-wide screen. At the other end of the spectrum, the line length in single-column layouts becomes too long to read comfortably when the viewport fills a high-resolution desktop monitor. For many aspects of a web page, one size does not fit all. As designers, we need to pay attention to where things fall apart and set breakpoints to "preserve the integrity" of the elements (as Ethan Marcotte so nicely puts it).

In the broadest of strokes, the tricky bits to keep optimized over a wide range of viewport sizes include the following:

- Content hierarchy
- Layout
- Typography
- Navigation
- Images
- Special content such as tables, forms, and interactive features

Content Hierarchy

Content is king on the web, so it is critical that content is carefully considered and organized before any code gets written. These are tasks for Information Architects and Content Strategists who address the challenges of organizing, labeling, planning, and managing web content.

Organization and hierarchy across various views of the site are a primary concern, with a particular focus on the small-screen experience. It is best to start with an inventory of potential content and pare it down to what is most useful and important for all browsing experiences. Once you know what the content modules are, you can begin deciding in what order they appear on various screen sizes.

Keep in mind that you should strive for content parity—that is, the notion that the same content is accessible regardless of the device used to access the site. It might be that visitors need to follow a slightly different navigational path to that information, but dropping portions of your site on small screens because you think mobile users won't need it is false thinking. People do bop between devices mid-task, and you want to be sure they have everything they need.

This is a woefully brief introduction to what is perhaps the most important first step of creating a site, but it is just outside the focus of this book. To get up to speed properly with content strategy, particularly as it applies to RWD, I recommend the following books:

- *Content Strategy for the Web, 2nd Edition,* by Kristina Halvorson and Melissa Rich (New Riders)
- *Content Strategy for Mobile* by Karen McGrane (A Book Apart)

Layout

Rearranging content into different layouts may be the first thing you think of when you picture responsive design, and with good reason. The layout helps form our first impression of a site's content and usability.

As mentioned earlier, responsive design is based on fluid layouts that expand and contract to fill the available space in the viewport. One fluid layout is usually not enough, however, to serve all screen sizes. More often, two or three layouts are produced to meet requirements across devices, with small adjustments between layout shifts.

Designers typically start with a one-column layout that fits well on small handheld devices and rearrange elements into columns as more space is available. They may also have the design for the widest screens worked out early on so there is an end-point in mind. The design process may involve a certain amount of switching between views and making decisions about what happens along the way.

Layout and line length

A good trigger for deciding when to adjust the layout is to look at text line lengths. Lines of text that are too stubby or too long are difficult to read, so you should aim for optimal line lengths of 45 to 75 characters, including spaces. If your text lines are significantly longer, it's time to make changes to the layout such as increasing the margins or introducing an additional column. You might also increase the font size of the text to keep the character count in the desired range.

Clarissa Peterson introduces a neat trick for testing line lengths in her book *Learning Responsive Web Design* (O'Reilly). Put a **span** around the 45th to 75th characters in the text and give it a background color (FIGURE 17-8). That way, you can easily check whether the line breaks are happening in the safe zone

---

Conditional Loading

Content parity doesn't mean that all of the content that fits on a large screen should be stuffed onto the small-screen layout. All that scrolling and extra data to download isn't doing mobile users any favors.

A better approach is to use conditional loading, in which small-screen users get the most important content with links to access supplemental content (comments, product details, ads, lists of links, etc.) when they want it. The information is available to them, just not all at once. Meanwhile, on larger screens, those supplemental pieces of content get displayed in sidebars automatically.

Conditional loading requires JavaScript to implement, so I won't be giving you the specific how-tos here, but it is good to know that there are alternatives to cramming every little thing onto every device.

---

at a glance. Of course, this line length hint would be removed before the site is made public.

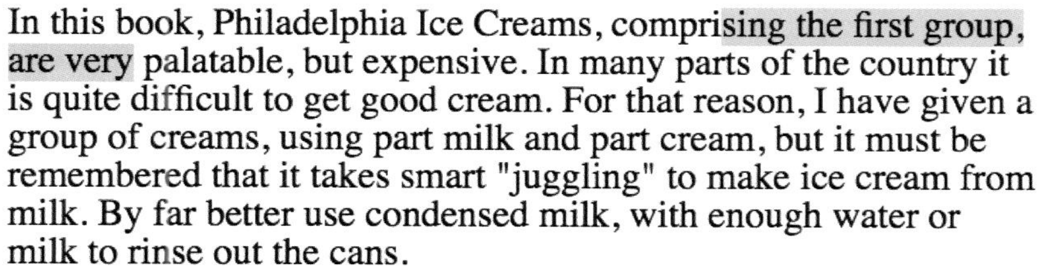

In this book, Philadelphia Ice Creams, comprising the first group, are very palatable, but expensive. In many parts of the country it is quite difficult to get good cream. For that reason, I have given a group of creams, using part milk and part cream, but it must be remembered that it takes smart "juggling" to make ice cream from milk. By far better use condensed milk, with enough water or milk to rinse out the cans.

FIGURE 17-8. Highlight the 45th to 75th characters to test for optimal line lengths at a glance.

Responsive layout patterns

The manner in which a site transitions from a small-screen layout to a wide-screen layout must make sense for that particular site, but there are a few patterns (common and repeated approaches) that have emerged over the years. We can thank Luke Wroblewski (known for his "Mobile First" approach to web design, which has become the standard) for doing a survey of how responsive sites handle layout. The article detailing his findings, "Multi-Device Layout Patterns" (*www.lukew.com/ff/entry.asp?1514*), is getting on in years, but the patterns persist today. Following are the top patterns Luke named in his article (FIGURE 17-9):

Mostly fluid

> This pattern uses a single-column layout for small screens, and another fluid layout that covers medium and large screens, with a maximum width set to prevent it from becoming too wide. It generally requires less work than other solutions.

Column drop

> This solution shifts between one-, two-, and three-column layouts based on available space. When there isn't room for extra columns, the sidebar columns drop below the other columns until everything is stacked vertically in the one-column view.

Layout shifter

> If you want to get really fancy, you can completely reinvent the layout for a variety of screen sizes. Although expressive and potentially cool, it is not necessary. In general, you can solve the problem of fitting your content to multiple environments without going overboard.

Tiny tweaks

> Some sites use a single-column layout and make tweaks to type, spacing, and images to make it work across a range of device sizes.

Mostly fluid

Column drop

Layout shifter

Tiny tweaks

Off canvas

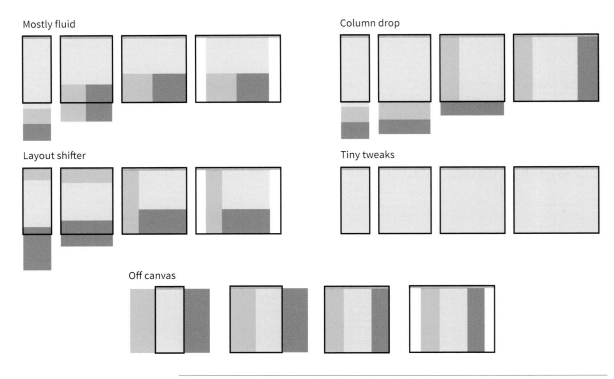

FIGURE 17-9. Examples of the responsive layout patterns identified by Luke Wroblewski.

Off canvas

As an alternative to stacking content vertically on small screens, you may choose to use an "off-canvas" solution. In this pattern, a page component is located just out of sight on the left or right of the screen and flies into view when requested. A bit of the main content screen remains visible on the edge to orient users as to the relationship of moving parts. This was made popular by Facebook, wherein Favorites and Settings were placed on a panel that slid in from the left when users clicked a menu icon.

You can see working examples of these and additional layout patterns on the "Responsive Patterns" page assembled by Brad Frost (*bradfrost.github.io/this-is-responsive/patterns.html*).

Typography

Typography requires fine-tuning along the spectrum from small-screen to wide-screen views in order to keep it legible and pleasant to read. Here are a few typography-related pointers (FIGURE 17-10):

Font face

Be careful about using fancy fonts on small screens and be sure to test for legibility. At small sizes, some fonts become difficult to read because

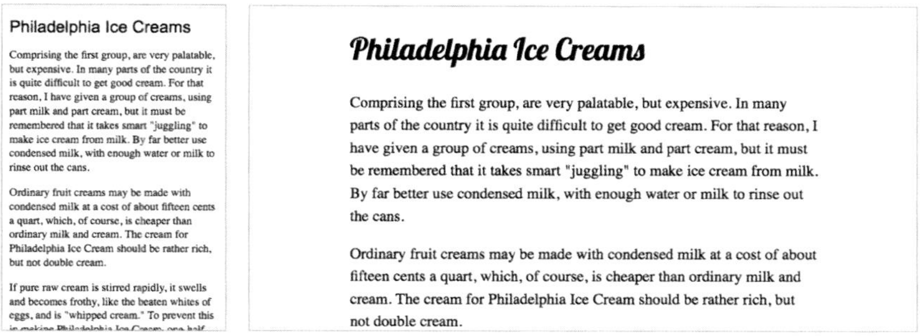

Narrow screens:
- Legible fonts
- Smaller type size
- Tighter line height
- Narrow margins

Wide screens:
- Stylized fonts OK
- Larger type size
- Open line height
- Wider margins

FIGURE 17-10. General typography guidelines for small and large screens.

line strokes become too light or extra flourishes become little blobs. Consider also that small screens may be connecting over cellular, so taking advantage of locally available fonts may be better for performance than requiring a web font to download. If a strict brand identity requires font consistency on all devices, be sure to choose a font face that works well at all sizes. If that is not a concern, consider using a web font only on larger screens. We strive to serve the same design to all devices, but as with everything else in web design, flexibility is important.

Font size

Varying viewport widths can wreak havoc on line lengths. You may find that you need to increase the font size of text elements for wider viewports to maintain a line length of between 45 and 75 characters. It also makes it easier to read from the distance users typically sit from their large screens. Conversely, you could use em-based media queries so that the layout stays proportional to the font size. With em-based queries, line lengths stay consistent.

Line height

Line height is another measurement that you may want to tweak as screens get larger. On average, line height should be about 1.5 (using a number value for the **line-height** property); however, slightly tighter line spacing (1.2 to 1.5) is easier to read with the shorter line lengths on small screens. Large screens, where the type is also likely to be larger, can handle more open line heights (1.4 to 1.6).

Margins

On small screens, make the most of the available space by keeping left and right margins on the main column to a minimum (2–4%). As screens get larger, you will likely need to increase side margins to keep the line

---

Variable Fonts

In late 2016, OpenType released a new font technology called OpenType Font Variations, known less formally as "variable fonts." You can change the weight, width, style (italic), slant, and optical size of a variable font by using **font-*** style properties. The marvel of this technology is that you can deliver one font file (that's just one call to the server) and stretch and manipulate it to suit many purposes, such as to make it narrower to preserve height and line length on small screens. Browser support for variable fonts is due to start kicking in in 2018. For more information, see the article "Get Started with Variable Fonts" by Richard Rutter at *medium.com/@clagnut/get-started-with-variable-fonts-c055fd73ecd7*.

The *axis-praxis.org* site allows you to play around with variable fonts using sliders to adjust the weight and other qualities. Note that you need a browser that supports variable fonts for it to work.

lengths under control and just to add some welcome whitespace to the layout. Remember to specify margins above and below text elements in em units so they stay proportional to the type.

Navigation

Navigation feels a little like the Holy Grail of Responsive Web Design. It is critical to get it right. Because navigation at desktop widths has pretty much been conquered, the real challenges come in re-creating our navigation options on small screens. A number of successful patterns have emerged for small screens, which I will briefly summarize here (FIGURE 17-11):

Top navigation

> If your site has just a few navigation links, they may fit just fine in one or two rows at the top of the screen.

Priority +

> In this pattern, the most important navigation links appear in a line across the top of the screen alongside a More link that exposes additional options. The pros are that the primary links are in plain view, and the number of links shown can increase as the device width increases. The cons include the difficulty of determining which links are worthy of the prime small-screen real estate.

Select menu

> For a medium list of links, some sites use a `select` input form element. Tapping the menu opens the list of options using the select menu UI of the operating system, such as a scrolling list of links at the bottom of the screen or on an overlay. The advantage is that it is compact, but on the downside, forms aren't typically used for navigation, and the menu may be overlooked.

Link to footer menu

> One straightforward approach places a Menu link at the top of the page that links to the full navigation located at the bottom of the page. The risk with this pattern is that it may be disorienting to users who suddenly find themselves at the bottom of the scroll.

Accordion sub-navigation

> When there are a lot of navigation choices with sub-navigation menus, the small-screen solution becomes more challenging, particularly when you can't hover to get more options as you can with a mouse. Accordions that expand when you tap a small arrow icon are commonly used to reveal and hide sub-navigation. They may even be nested several levels deep. To avoid nesting navigation in accordion submenus, some sites simply link to separate landing pages that contain a list of the sub-navigation for that section.

Top navigation

Priority +

KEY

Select menu

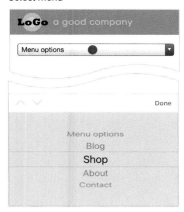

Link to footer menu

Accordion sub-navigation

Overlay toggle (covers top of screen)

Off-canvas/fly-in

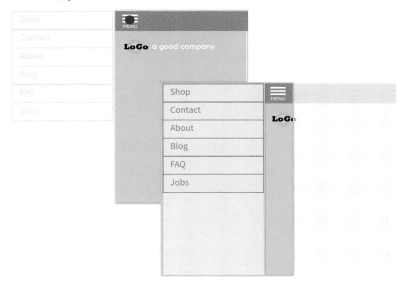

Push toggle (pushes content down)

FIGURE 17-11. Responsive navigation patterns.

> ### Designing for Fingers
>
> Keep in mind that people use their fingers to get around on touch devices, which these days include smartphones, tablets, and even desktop-sized screens like Microsoft Surface and iPad Pro.
>
> Links in navigation should be big enough to easily target with thumbs and fingertips. Apple requires 44 pixels for its apps, and that's a good ballpark to keep in mind for links on web pages as well.
>
> Another consideration for touch devices is that there is no hover state. Hovering has become the convention for opening sub-navigation on web pages on the desktop, but with no mouse, that experience is very different with touch. Most devices open the submenu with a second click. If you use hover in your navigation and elsewhere on your site, you'll need to do thorough device testing. Someday, we may be able to write a media query to test for hover, but in the meantime, either avoid it or test the alternatives.
>
> A really great book about all of this stuff is Josh Clark's *Designing for Touch* (A Book Apart).

Push and overlay toggles

In toggle navigation, the navigation is hidden but expands downward when the menu link is tapped. It may push the main content down below it (push toggle) or slide down in front of the content (overlay toggle).

Off-canvas/fly-in

This popular pattern puts the navigation in an off-screen panel to the left or right of the main content that slides into view when you tap the menu icon.

For a deeper dive into the pros and cons of navigation patterns, read Brad Frost's article "Responsive Navigation Patterns" (*bradfrost.com/blog/web/responsive-nav-patterns*). Brad also includes examples of these patterns and more on his Responsive Patterns page (*bradfrost.github.io/this-is-responsive/patterns.html*).

For working examples of these patterns with the code used to create them, see the "Adventures in Responsive Navigation" page assembled by Eric Arbé at *responsivenavigation.net*.

Images

Images require special attention in responsive designs. Here is a quick rundown of some of the key issues, most of which should sound familiar:

- Use responsive image markup techniques (covered in **Chapter 7**) to provide multiple versions of key images for various sizes and resolutions.

- Serve the smallest version as the default to prevent unnecessary data downloads.

- Be sure that important image detail is not lost at smaller sizes. Consider substituting a cropped version of the image for small screens.

- Avoid putting text in graphics, but if it is necessary, provide alternate versions with larger text for small screens.

Special Content

Without the luxury of wide-open, desktop viewports, some of our common page elements pose challenges when it comes to fitting on smaller screens:

Forms

Forms often take a little finagling to fit the available space appropriately. Flexbox is a great tool for adding flexibility and conditional wrapping to form fields and their labels. A web search will turn up some fine tutorials. Also make sure that your form is as efficient as possible, with no unnecessary fields, which is good advice for any screen size. Finally, consider that form inputs will be used with fingertips, not mouse pointers, so increase the target size by adding ample padding or margins and by making labels tappable to select an input.

Tables

One of the greatest challenges in small-screen design is how to deal with large data tables. Not surprisingly, because there are many types of tables, there are also many solutions. See the **"The Trouble with Tables"** sidebar for more information and resources.

Interactive elements

A big embedded map may be great on a desktop view of a site, but it is less useful when it is the size of a postage stamp. Consider whether some interactive features should be substituted for other methods for performing the same task. In the case of the map, adding a link to a map can trigger the device's native mapping app to open, which is designed to provide a better small-screen experience. Other interactive components, such as carousels, can be adapted for smaller viewports.

The Trouble with Tables

Large tables, such as those shown back in FIGURE 8-1, can be difficult to use on small-screen devices. By default, they are shrunk to fit the screen width, rendering the text in the cells too small to be read. Users can zoom in to read the cells, but then only a few cells may be visible at a time, and it is difficult to parse the organization of headings and columns.

Designers and developers have created a number of approaches for making tables responsive. To be honest, using tables on small devices is still relatively new, so right now what we're seeing is a lot of experimentation and throwing solutions against the wall to see what sticks. Most solutions involve some advanced web development mojo (more than we can take on with only a few chapters under your belt), but I do want you to be familiar with responsive tables. There are three general approaches: scrolling, stacking, and hiding.

For scrolling solutions, the table stays as wide as it needs to be, and users can scroll to the right to see the columns that won't fit. This can be accomplished with JavaScript or CSS alone. You can even anchor the left column to the window so that it stays put when the rest of the table scrolls.

Another approach is to stack up the entries in a long, narrow scroll. Each entry repeats the headers, so the data is always presented with the proper context. Again, you could do this with JavaScript or CSS alone. The downside is that the list can end up very long, and it makes it difficult to compare entries, but at least all of the information is visible without horizontal scrolling.

You may also choose to hide certain columns of information when the page first loads on small devices and give the user the option to click to see the whole table or to toggle on and off specific columns. That is a little more risky from an interaction design perspective. Those columns just might not be seen at all.

CSS Tables and Flexbox are other options for making tabular material responsive. The best approach entirely depends on the type of data you're publishing and how the table is expected to be used. If you are interested in learning more, I recommend the following resources:

- "Accessible, Simple, Responsive Tables" by Davide Rizzo on CSS-Tricks (*css-tricks.com/accessible-simple-responsive-tables/*): A roundup of solutions using CSS tables.

- "CSS-only Responsive Tables" by David Bushell (*dbushell.com/2016/03/04/css-only-responsive-tables/*): A CSS-only scrolling approach using CSS shadows for improved usability.

- "Picking a Responsive Tables Solution" by Jason Grigsby at Cloud Four (*cloudfour.com/thinks/picking-responsive-tables-solution/*).

- Responsive Tables by ZURB Studios (*zurb.com/playground/responsive-tables*): A fixed-left-column scrolling solution using JavaScript and CSS.

- Tablesaw by Filament Group (*github.com/filamentgroup/tablesaw*): A group of JQuery (JavaScript) plug-ins for creating a variety of responsive table effects.

That should give you a feel for some of the aspects of a site that need special attention in a responsive design. We covered content hierarchy, various layout patterns, typography tweaks, responsive navigation patterns, and image strategies, and addressed tables, forms, and interactive features. I'd say that's enough lecturing. Now you'll get some hands-on time in EXERCISE 17-1.

EXERCISE 17-1. Making the bakery home page responsive

We've done a lot of work on the Black Goose Bakery site over the last few chapters, but the resulting site works best on large screens. In this exercise, we're going to back up a few steps and build it again using a small-screen-first strategy, making changes to layout, navigation, typography, and more at strategic breakpoints.

I've done the heavy lifting of writing the necessary styles for each breakpoint, but I will talk you through each step and share the reasoning for the changes. The starting style sheet (*bakery-rwd.css*) as well as the finished style sheet (*bakery-rwd-finished.css*) and the other files for the site are provided with the materials for this chapter. The HTML file, *bakery.html*, hasn't changed since we added the container element to it in **Chapter 16, CSS Layout with Flexbox and Grid**, and we will not need to edit it again.

Getting Started

Open the HTML file (*bakery.html*) in a browser with a Responsive View (see the previous sidebar, **"How Wide Is the Viewport?"**) so you can expand the viewport window and watch the changing pixel dimensions. FIGURE 17-12 shows the page at 320 pixels wide with the default, narrow-screen styles that will be the starting point for this design.

The content of the page is the same as in previous chapters, but if you worked on the exercises in **Chapter 16**, you'll notice that I've changed a few styles to make the initial layout suitable for small screens. Allow me to point out the characteristics of this baseline design:

- **Layout**: The page has a one-column layout for small screens. There are no borders around the main text area, and the Hours section has a scalloped edge on the top instead of the side. That maintains the look and feel, but is more appropriate when the sections are stacked.
- **Navigation:** The navigation menu, which was created with Flexbox, couldn't flex small enough to fit across a small screen. To make it fit, I turned on wrapping (**flex-wrap: wrap;**) and set the width of each **li** to 50% so there would be two on each row. I also made it so they can both grow and shrink as needed (**flex: 1 1 50%**).
- **Conditional header text:** The tagline was taking up a lot of vertical space, and I decided it wasn't critical. I hid the paragraph (**display: none;**) and I will make it visible again when there is more room.

- **Typography:** On small screens, I decided to use a legible sans-serif font for the text and not to employ my web font because it is likely to be difficult to read at small sizes.
- **Images:** I set the **img** elements for the bread and muffin images to **display: block** so they have the full width of the viewport to themselves with no text sneaking in next to them. Setting the side margins to **auto** keeps them centered horizontally.
- **Miscellaneous:**

  — The award appears at the bottom of the page because there is not enough space for it to be positioned at the top.

  — I highlighted a **span** from the 45th to 75th characters to reveal when the line lengths get too long.

FIGURE 17-12. The small-screen design is our starting point.

Fixing the Navigation

Now we can start tailoring the design for other screen sizes. Using a Responsive View tool, I can resize the viewport and get an instant readout of the dimensions of the window. Give it a try on your browser. Keep making it wider, and you'll see that some things look OK, and some things start looking awkward pretty quickly.

One thing that looks awkward to me right away is the stacked navigation at the top. I'd like it to switch to one centered line as soon as there is room, which to my eye happens when the viewport is 400 pixels wide (FIGURE 17-13).

Are you ready to write your first media query? Open the style sheet (*bakery-rwd.css*) in a text editor. Remember that media queries need to come after other rules for the same declaration, so to keep this exercise simple, we'll add them at the end of the style sheet, before **</style>**. Add this query as you see it here. Remember to make sure you have the right number of nesting curly brackets:

```
@media screen and (min-width: 400px) {
  nav ul li {
    flex: none;
  }
  nav ul {
    justify-content: center;
  }
}
```

This tells the browser that when the page is on a screen and the viewport is 400 pixels or wider, set the "flex" of menu list items to "none." The **none** keyword is equivalent to **flex: 0 0 auto;**, so the items are not allowed to grow or shrink and will be sized based on their content. I've centered the flexbox container by setting **justify-content: center**.

Save the style sheet and reload the page in the browser. Try resizing the viewport to see how it works at wider sizes. I think this centered arrangement will work for even the widest of screens, so navigation is all set. If you had navigation with additional elements such as an inline logo and a search box, you might find it best to create a few different arrangements over a number of breakpoints.

Floating Images

As I continue to make the viewport gradually wider, I notice that the main images start looking very lonely on a line alone, and that there is room to start wrapping text around them again at about 480 pixels wide. Let's take care of that awkward whitespace by floating the images to the left once the screen reaches 480 pixels (FIGURE 17-14):

```
@media screen and (min-width: 480px) {
  main img {
    float: left;
    margin: 0 1em 1em 0;
  }
}
```

NOTE: If you like, you can include the CSS shapes from **Chapter 15, Floating and Positioning,** for a more interesting text wrap. I've omitted them here for brevity and because of limited browser support.

Text and Typography

Once the screen gets to be about 600 pixels wide, I feel like there is enough room to introduce some embellishments. There is room for the tagline in the header, so I'll set that to display again.

Now some attention to typography. I like the Stint Ultra Expanded web font, but it isn't key to the company's brand, so I omitted it on the narrow layout because of line length issues. At this breakpoint, I can begin using it because I know it will be more legible and result in comfortable line lengths. I've also loosened up the line height a little. I'll take advantage of the extra space to add a

Before breakpoint change

After

A breakpoint is needed to fill in the awkward space around the image.

At 480 pixels wide, the image is floated to the left.

FIGURE 17-13. The navigation started to look awkward, so I add a breakpoint at 400 pixels to switch it to one line.

FIGURE 17-14. The images float left once there is enough width to accommodate wrapping text.

EXERCISE 17-1. Continued

FIGURE 17-15. This medium size layout is well suited for tablet-sized devices.

rounded border around the main text area to bring it closer to the original brand identity for the site. The result is an enhanced one-column layout that is well suited for tablet-sized devices (FIGURE 17-15).

Here is the media query for the 600-pixel breakpoint. Add this to the bottom of the style sheet after the other two queries:

```
@media screen and (min-width: 600px) {
  header p {
    display: block;
    margin-top: -1.5em;
    font-family: Georgia, serif;
    font-style: italic;
    font-size: 1.2em;
  }
  main, h2, h3 {
    font-family: 'Stint Ultra Expanded', Georgia, serif;
  }
  h2, h3 {
    font-weight: bold;
  }
  main {
    line-height: 1.8em;
    padding: 1em;
    border: double 4px #EADDC4;
    border-radius: 25px;
    margin: 2.5%;
  }
}
```

Multicolumn Layout

As I continue to make the viewport wider and pay attention to the yellow highlighted span of characters, I see that the text line is growing longer than 75 characters. I could increase the font size or the margins, but I think this is a good point to introduce a second column to the layout. If you aren't targeting a specific device, the exact breakpoint is subjective. I've chosen 940 pixels as the point above which the page gets a columned layout.

I've simply taken the grid layout styles from the previous chapter and reapplied them here. On the **aside** element, I moved the scalloped background graphic to the left edge. In addition, I set a maximum width of 1200px on the container and set its side margins to **auto**, so if the browser window is wider than 1,200 pixels, the layout will stay a fixed width and get centered in the viewport. Finally, I absolutely positioned the award graphic at the top of the page now that there's enough room (FIGURE 17-16).

Add this final media query at the end of the style sheet. You can copy and paste them from the final exercise in **Chapter 16** (that's what I did) and make a few tweaks to the **#container** and **#aside** rules as shown:

```
@media screen and (min-width: 940px) {
  #container {
    display: grid;
    grid-template-rows: auto min-height 5em;
    grid-template-columns: minmax(25em, 1fr) 16em;
    grid-template-areas:
      "banner banner"
      "main hours"
      "footer footer";
    max-width: 1200px;
```

```
    margin: 0 auto;
    position: relative;
}
header {
    grid-area: banner;
}
main {
    grid-area: main;
}
aside {
    grid-area: hours;
    background: url(images/scallop.png) repeat-y left top;
    background-color: #F6F3ED;
    padding: 1em;
    padding-left: 45px;
}
footer {
    grid-area: footer;
}
#award {
    position: absolute;
    top: 30px;
    left: 50px;
}
}
```

And we're done! Is this the most sophisticated responsive site ever? Nope. Is there even more we could do to improve the design at various screen sizes? Certainly! But now you should have a feel for what it's like to start with a small-screen design and make changes that optimize for increasingly larger sizes. Consider it a modest first step to future adventures in RWD.

FIGURE 17-16. The two-column grid layout is appropriate for viewports over 940 pixels. On very wide screens, as shown here, the container stops expanding at 1,200 pixels wide and is centered horizontally.

NOTE

The highlighted background on the length span should be turned off before you publish, but I've left it visible in the figures so you can see how our line length is faring across layouts.

A FEW WORDS ABOUT TESTING

In the previous exercise, we relied on the Responsive View in a modern browser to make decisions about style changes at various sizes, but although it's a handy tool for creating an initial design, much more testing is required before the design can be considered ready for final launch. That is even more critical for sites that include features that rely on JavaScript or server-side functionality.

There are three general options for testing sites: real devices, emulators, and third-party services. We'll look at each in this section.

Real Devices

There is really no substitute for testing a site on a variety of real devices and operating systems. Beyond just seeing how the site looks, testing on real devices shows you how your site *performs*. How fast does it load? Are the links easy to tap? Do all the interactive features work smoothly? Do they work at all?

Web development companies may have a device lab comprising iPhones and iPads of various sizes, Android smartphones and tablets of various sizes, and Macs and PCs with recent operating systems (Windows and Linux) that can be used by designers and developers for testing sites (FIGURE 17-17). The size of the device lab depends on the size of the budget, of course (electronic devices aren't cheap!).

<aside>
Building a Device Lab

If you want to set up your own device lab, I recommend reading the primer *Building a Device Lab* by Destiny Montague and Lara Hogan (Five Simple Steps Publishing). The book is a summary of everything the authors learned while creating a killer device lab for Etsy. It is available for free at *buildingadevicelab.com*.
</aside>

FIGURE 17-17. The device lab at Filament Group in Boston, Massachusetts.

If you don't have the luxury of working at a big company with a big lab, there are alternatives:

- If you live in a big city, you may be near a device lab that is open for public use. Check the *opendevicelab.com* site to see if there is one near you.

- You can build your own lab with a collection of used devices. At minimum, you should have access to an iPhone, Android phone, iPad, 7" tablet (like iPad Mini), and computers running macOS and Microsoft Windows. The good news is that you generally don't need a data plan for every device because you can test over WiFi.

- If buying devices is not feasible, you can ask friends and coworkers to borrow their phones and tablets briefly. Asking permission at a mobile retail store to load web pages on their devices is not unheard of.

If you do have multiple real devices for testing, using a synchronization tool makes the process a whole lot smoother. Software like BrowserSync (*browser-sync.io*) and Ghostlab (*www.vanamco.com/ghostlab/*) runs on your computer and beams whatever is on your screen to all your devices simultaneously so you don't need to load the page on each one individually. It's like magic!

Emulators

If a particular device is out of your reach, you could use an emulator, a desktop application that emulates mobile device hardware and operating systems. The emulator presents a window that shows exactly how your site would behave on that particular device (FIGURE 17-18). Emulators require a lot of space on your computer and they can be buggy, but it is certainly better than not testing on that device at all.

A good starting point for exploring emulators is Maximiliano Firtman's "Mobile Emulators & Simulators: The Ultimate Guide" (*www.mobilexweb.com/emulators*).

The Android Emulator lets you set up a wide variety of phones, televisions, wearables, and tablets for testing. I chose a Nexus 5X.

The Nexus 5X emulator displays an image of the device at actual size. All of the buttons work as they would on the phone.

The Bakery page viewed on the Nexus 5X emulator.

FIGURE 17-18. Examples of the Android Emulator (download at *developer.android.com/studio/index.html*).

Third-Party Services

Another option for testing your site on over 1,000 devices is to subscribe to a service like BrowserStack (*browserstack.com*) or CrossBrowserTesting (*crossbrowsertesting.com*). For a monthly fee, you get access to a huge variety of device simulators (FIGURE 17-19). There are many such services available, some of which are free or offer free trials. They don't give you the same insights as testing on actual devices, but it is another better-than-nothing alternative.

BrowserStack.com

CrossBrowserTesting.com

FIGURE 17-19. Screenshots generated by BrowserStack and CrossBrowserTesting (using free trial tools). Notice the variation in how the bakery page displays. This is why we test!

MORE RWD RESOURCES

We've covered the mechanics of using fluid layouts, flexible images, and media queries to make a page that is usable across a wide range of screen sizes. We've looked at the design concerns and some common responsive patterns for layout, navigation, typography, and images. You even got a chance to try out creating a responsive page on your own. But this is really only the tip of the iceberg, and I encourage you to continue learning about RWD, particularly if you are considering web design or development as a career. Following is a list of RWD resources that I've found helpful and should point you in the right direction.

Books

Responsive Web Design, 2e, by Ethan Marcotte (A Book Apart)

This book is required reading. Ethan goes into much greater detail than I was able to here on how to calculate flexible grids and how to use media queries. Plus, it's just plain fun to read.

Learning Responsive Web Design: A Beginner's Guide by Clarissa Peterson (O'Reilly)

> Clarissa provides a comprehensive overview of all aspects of responsive design, from detailed code examples to broad strategies on workflow and mobile-first design.

Smashing Book #5: Real-Life Responsive Web Design, various authors (Smashing Magazine)

> A collection of practical techniques and strategies from prominent web designers.

Atomic Design by Brad Frost (self-published)

> Brad describes his modular approach to RWD, which has become quite popular for large site development.

Responsive Design Workflow by Stephen Hay (New Riders)

> Stephen Hay introduces his "design in the browser" method to creating responsive sites. This book is jam-packed with suggestions on how to approach web design and development.

Implementing Responsive Design by Tim Kadlec (New Riders)

> Tim Kadlec is a leader in the mobile web design community, and his book is a comprehensive guide to designing and building a responsive site.

NOTE

Most of these titles were written before CSS Grid Layout became a viable option. Keep in mind that you have advanced tools for flexible layouts not mentioned in these books.

Online Resources

Responsive Web Design Is… (*responsivedesign.is*)

> A collection of articles and podcasts about web design. You can also sign up for the "RWD Weekly" newsletter and keep your finger on the pulse of RWD. The site is a side project of Justin Avery and Simple Things.

Responsive Resources (*bradfrost.github.io/this-is-responsive/resources.html*)

> For one-stop shopping for everything you could possibly want to know about RWD, look no further than Brad Frost's Responsive Resources. He has gathered hundreds of links to resources related to strategy, design tools, layout, media queries, typography, images, components, development, testing, content management systems, email, tutorials, and more. Seriously, there is enough here to keep you busy for months.

Media Queries (*mediaqueri.es*)

> A gallery of exceptional examples of responsive websites curated by Eivind Uggedal.

TEST YOURSELF

Here we are at the end of another chapter, so you know what that means... *quiz time*! Get the answers in **Appendix A** if you're stumped.

1. What makes a responsive site different from a mobile (m-dot) site?

2. What does this do?

    ```
    <meta name="viewport" content="width=device-width, initial-scale=1">
    ```

3. How do you make sure an image gets smaller when its container gets smaller in the layout?

4. What does this do?

    ```
    @media screen and (min-width: 60em) {
      body {
        margin: 0 10%;
      }
    }
    ```

5. What are some strategies for creating a layout that adjusts to the available width of the viewport?

6. What is the advantage of using ems as a measurement in media queries?

7. List three ways in which a media query may be used.

8. Name three tweaks you may make to typography to make it work well on small screens.

9. How might you handle navigation with a lot of submenus on a small screen?

10. List three options for testing websites on multiple devices.

TRANSITIONS, TRANSFORMS, AND ANIMATION

We've seen CSS used for visual effects like rounded corners, color gradients, and drop shadows that previously had to be created with graphics. In this chapter, we'll look at some CSS3 properties for producing animated interactive effects that were previously possible only with JavaScript or Flash.

We'll start with CSS Transitions, a nifty way to make style changes fade smoothly from one to another. Then we'll discuss CSS Transforms for repositioning, scaling, rotating, and skewing elements and look at how you can animate them with transitions. I'm going to close out the chapter with brief introductions to 3-D Transforms and CSS Animation, which are important to know about but are too vast a topic to cover here, so I'll give you just a taste.

The problem with this chapter is that animation and time-based effects don't work on paper, so I can't show them off right here. I did the next best thing, though, and made the source code for the figures available in the materials for this chapter (*learningwebdesign.com/5e/materials*) in a folder called *figures*. Just open the file in your browser.

EASE-Y DOES IT (CSS TRANSITIONS)

Picture, if you will, a link in a navigation menu that changes from blue to red when the mouse hovers over it. The background is blue...mouse passes over it...BAM! Red! It goes from state to state instantly, with no states in between. Now imagine putting your mouse over the link and having the background gradually change from blue to red, passing through several shades of purple on the way. It's smoooooth. And when you remove the mouse, it fades back down to blue again.

IN THIS CHAPTER

Creating smooth transitions

Moving, rotating, and scaling elements

Combining transitions and transforms

A few words about 3-D transforms

Keyframe animations

CSS Transition Support

The good news is that all modern browsers released since 2013 support CSS transition properties without the need for prefixes. There are a few holes in support you should know about:

- Most notably, Internet Explorer versions 9 and earlier do not support transitions and ignore transition properties entirely.

- Chrome and Safari versions released between 2010 and 2013 support transitions with the **-webkit-** prefix. Later versions do not require a prefix.

- On mobile, iOS versions 3.1–6.0 (2010–2013) and Android versions 2.1–4.3 (2009–2013) require the **-webkit-** prefix. Later versions do not require prefixes.

- Firefox versions released between 2011 and 2012 require the **-moz-** prefix, but they are nearly extinct as I write this.

As always, check your own server's statistics (be sure to pay attention to mobile use) to see which browsers you need to support, and check *CanIUse.com* for support and bug details.

In the examples throughout this chapter, I use only the standard (non-prefixed) properties. If you need to support browsers that require prefixes, I suggest using Autoprefixer, which is discussed in **Chapter 19, More CSS Techniques**. And remember, when using prefixed properties, always include the non-prefixed version last for forward compatibility with supporting browsers.

That's what CSS Transitions do. They smooth out otherwise abrupt changes to property values between two states over time by filling in the frames in between. Animators call that tweening. When used with reserve, CSS Transitions can add sophistication and polish to your interfaces and even improve usability.

CSS Transitions were originally developed by the WebKit team for the Safari browser, and they are a Working Draft at the W3C (see **Note**). Browser support for Transitions is excellent (see the **"CSS Transition Support"** sidebar), so there is no reason not to use them in your designs, particularly if you treat them as an enhancement. For example, on the rare non-supporting browser (I'm looking at you, old IE), our link snapping directly from blue to red is not a big deal.

NOTE

You can read CSS Transitions Module for yourself at www.w3.org/TR/css-transitions-1/.

Transition Basics

Transitions are a lot of fun, so let's give them a whirl. When applying a transition, you have a few decisions to make, each of which is set with a CSS property:

- Which CSS property to change (**transition-property**) (*Required*)

- How long it should take (**transition-duration**) (*Required*)

- The manner in which the transition accelerates (**transition-timing-function**)

- Whether there should be a pause before it starts (**transition-delay**)

Transitions require a beginning state and an end state. The element as it appears when it first loads is the beginning state. The end state needs to be triggered by a state change such as **:hover**, **:focus**, or **:active**, which is what we'll be using for the examples in this chapter. You could use JavaScript to change the element (such as adding a **class** attribute) and use that as a transition trigger as well.

Let's put that all together with a simple example. Here is that blue-to-red link you imagined earlier (FIGURE 18-1). There's nothing special about the markup. I added a **class** so I could be specific about which links receive transitions.

The transition properties are applied to the object that will be transitioned—in this case, the **a** element in its normal state. You'll see them in the set of other declarations for **.smooth**, like **padding** and **background-color**. I've changed the background color of the link to red by declaring the **background-color** for the **:hover** state (and **:focus** too, in case someone is tabbing through links with a keyboard).

THE MARKUP

```
<a href="…" class="smooth">awesomesauce</a>
```

THE STYLES

```
.smooth {
  display: block;
  text-decoration:none;
  text-align: center;
  padding: 1em 2em;
  width: 10em;
  border-radius: 1.5em;
  color: #fff;
  background-color: mediumblue;
  transition-property: background-color;
  transition-duration: 0.3s;
}
.smooth:hover, .smooth:focus {
  background-color: red;
}
```

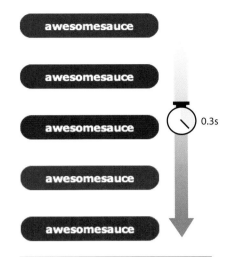

FIGURE 18-1. The background color of this link gradually fades from blue to red over .3 seconds when ~~awesome-sauce~~ a transition is applied.

Specifying the property

transition-property

Values:	*property-name* | all | none
Default:	all
Applies to:	all elements, :before and :after pseudo-elements
Inherits:	no

transition-property identifies the CSS property that is changing and that you want to transition smoothly. In our example, it's the **background-color**. You can also change the foreground color, borders, dimensions, font- and text-related attributes, and many more. TABLE 18-1 lists the animatable CSS properties as of this writing. The general rule is that if its value is a color, length, or number, that property can be a transition property.

Add the transition properties to the object that will be transitioned.

How long should it take?

transition-duration

Values:	*time*
Default:	0s
Applies to:	all elements, :before and :after pseudo-elements
Inherits:	no

transition-duration sets the amount of time it takes for the animation to complete in seconds (**s**) or milliseconds (**ms**). I've chosen .3 seconds, which is just enough to notice something happened but not so long that the transition feels sluggish or slows the user down. There is no correct duration, of course, but I've found that .2s seems to be a popular transition time for UI elements. Experiment to find the duration that makes sense for your application.

Timing Functions

`transition-timing-function`

Values:	ease | linear | ease-in | ease-out | ease-in-out | step-start | step-end | steps | cubic-bezier(#,#,#,#)
Default:	ease
Applies to:	all elements, `:before` and `:after` pseudo-elements
Inherits:	no

The property and the duration are required and form the foundation of a transition, but you can refine it further. There are a number of ways a transition can roll out over time. For example, it could start out fast and then slow down, start out slow and speed up, or stay the same speed all the way through, just to name a few possibilities. I think of it as the transition "style," but in the spec, it is known as the timing function or easing function.

The timing function you choose can have a big impact on the feel and believability of the animation, so if you plan on using transitions and CSS animations, it is a good idea to get familiar with the options.

If I set the **transition-timing-function** to **ease-in-out**, the transition will start out slow, then speed up, then slow down again as it comes to the end state.

```
.smooth {
  ...
  transition-property: background-color;
  transition-duration: 0.3s;
  transition-timing-function: ease-in-out;
}
```

The **transition-timing-function** property takes one of the following keyword values:

ease

Starts slowly, accelerates quickly, and then slows down at the end. This is the default value and works just fine for most short transitions.

linear

Stays consistent from the transition's beginning to end. Because it is so consistent, some say it has a mechanical feeling.

ease-in

Starts slowly, then speeds up.

ease-out

Starts out fast, then slows down.

ease-in-out

Starts slowly, speeds up, and then slows down again at the very end. It is similar to **ease**, but with less pronounced acceleration in the middle.

cubic-bezier(*x1,y1,x2,y2*)

The acceleration of a transition can be plotted with a curve called a Bezier curve. The steep parts of the curve indicate a fast rate of change, and the flat parts indicate a slow rate of change. FIGURE 18-2 shows the Bezier curves that represent the function keywords as well as a custom curve I created. You can see that the **ease** curve is a tiny bit flat in the beginning, gets very steep (fast), then ends flat (slow). The **linear** keyword, on the other hand, moves at a consistent rate for the whole transition.

You can get the feel of your animation *just right* by creating a custom curve. The site *Cubic-Bezier.com* is a great tool for playing around with transition timing and generating the resulting code. The four numbers in the value represent the x and y positions of the start and end Bezier curve handles (the pink and blue dots in FIGURE 18-2).

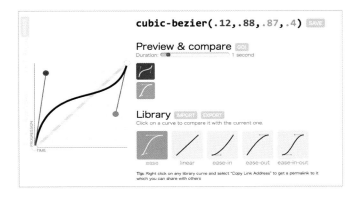

FIGURE 18-2. Examples of Bezier curves from Cubic-Bezier.com. On the left is my custom curve that starts fast, slows down, and ends fast.

steps(#, start|end)

Divides the transitions into a number of steps as defined by a stepping function. The first value is the number of steps, and the **start** and **end** keywords define whether the change in state happens at the beginning (**start**) or end of each step. Step animation is especially useful for keyframe animation with sprite images. For a better explanation and examples, I recommend the article "Using Multi-Step Animations and Transitions," by Geoff Graham on CSS-Tricks (*css-tricks.com/using-multi-step-animations-transitions/*).

step-start

Changes states in one step, at the beginning of the duration time (the same as **steps(1,start)**). The result is a sudden state change, the same as if no transition had been applied at all.

step-end

Changes states in one step, at the end of the duration time (the same as **steps(1,end)**).

TABLE 18-1. *Continued.*

margin-left

margin-top

padding-bottom

padding-left

padding-right

padding-top

Position

top

right

bottom

left

z-index

clip-path

Transforms
(not in the spec as of this writing, but supported)

transform

transform-origin

NOTE

The W3C has broken out the timing functions into their own spec so they are easier to share among modules. It is available at www.w3.org/TR/css-timing-1/.

It's difficult to show the various options on a still page, but I have put together a little demo, which is illustrated in FIGURE 18-3 and available in the *figures* folder with the materials for this chapter. The width of each labeled element (white with a blue border) transitions over the course of 4 seconds when you hover over the green box. They all arrive at their full width at exactly the same time, but they get there in different manners. The image shown in FIGURE 18-3 was taken at the 2-second mark, halfway through the duration of the transition.

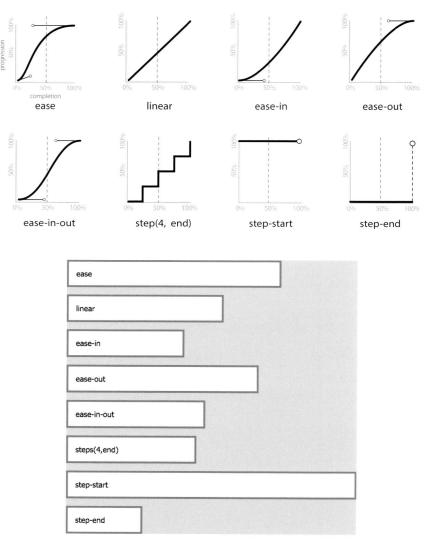

The width of the white boxes is set to transition from 0 to 100% width over 4 seconds. This screenshot shows the progress after 2 seconds (50%) for each timing function.

FIGURE 18-3. In this **transition-timing-function** demo, the elements reach full width at the same time but vary in the manner in which they get there. If you'd like to see it in action, the *ch18_figures.html* file is available with the materials for this chapter.

Setting a Delay

`transition-delay`

Values: *time*

Default: 0s

Applies to: all elements, `:before` and `:after` pseudo-elements

Inherits: no

The **transition-delay** property, as you might guess, delays the start of the animation by a specified amount of time. In the following example, the background color transition starts .2 seconds after the pointer moves over the link.

```
.smooth {
...
  transition-property: background-color;
  transition-duration: 0.3s;
  transition-timing-function: ease-in-out;
  transition-delay: 0.2s;
}
```

The Shorthand transition Property

Thankfully, the authors of the CSS3 spec had the good sense to give us the shorthand **transition** property to combine all of these properties into one declaration. You've seen this sort of thing with the shorthand **border** property. Here is the syntax:

```
transition: property duration timing-function delay;
```

The values for each of the **transition-*** properties are listed out, separated by character spaces. The order isn't important as long as the duration (which is required) appears before delay (which is optional). If you provide only one time value, it will be assumed to be the duration.

Using the blue-to-red link example, we could combine the four transition properties we've applied so far into this one line:

```
.smooth {
...
  transition: background-color 0.3s ease-in-out 0.2s;
}
```

Definitely an improvement.

Applying Multiple Transitions

So far, we've changed only one property at a time, but it is possible to transition several properties at once. Let's go back to the "awesomesauce" link example. This time, in addition to changing from blue to red, I'd like the **letter-spacing** to increase a bit. I also want the text color to change to black, but more slowly than the other animations. FIGURE 18-4 attempts to show these transitions on this static page.

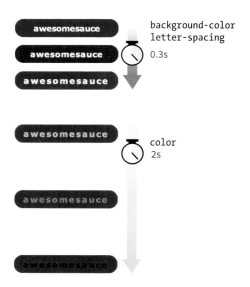

FIGURE 18-4. The **color**, **background-color**, and **letter-spacing** change at different paces.

One way to do this is to list all of the values for each property separated by commas, as shown in this example:

```
.smooth {
    …
    transition-property: background-color, color, letter-spacing;
    transition-duration: 0.3s, 2s, 0.3s;
    transition-timing-function: ease-out, ease-in, ease-out;

}
.smooth:hover, .smooth:focus {
    background-color: red;
    letter-spacing: 3px;
    color: black;
}
```

The values are matched up according to their positions in the list. For example, the transition on the **color** property (second in the list) has a duration of 2s and uses the **ease-in** timing function. If one list has fewer values than the others, the browser repeats the values in the list, starting over at the beginning. In the previous example, if I had omitted the third value (.3s) for **transition-duration**, the browser would loop back to the beginning of the list and use the first value (.3s) for **letter-spacing**. In this case, the effect would be the same.

You can line up values for the shorthand **transition** property as well. The same set of styles we just saw could also be written as follows:

```
.smooth {
  ...
  transition: background-color 0.3s ease-out,
              color 2s ease-in,
              letter-spacing 0.3s ease-out;
}
```

A Transition for All Occasions

But what if you just want to add a little bit of smoothness to all your state changes, regardless of which property might change? For cases when you want the same duration, timing function, and delay to apply to all transitions that might occur on an element, use the **all** value for **transition-property**. In the following example, I've specified that any property that might change for the **.smooth** element should last .2 seconds and animate via the **ease-in-out** function.

```
.smooth {
  ...
  transition: all 0.2s ease-in-out;
}
```

For user interface changes, a short, subtle transition is often all you need for all your transitions, so the **all** value will come in handy. Well, that wraps up our lesson on CSS3 Transitions. Now you give it a try in EXERCISE 18-1.

EXERCISE 18-1. **Trying out transitions**

In this exercise, we're going to create the rollover and active states for a menu link (FIGURE 18-5) with animated transitions. I've put together a starter document (*exercise_18-1.html*) for you in the *materials* folder for this chapter at *learningwebdesign. com/5e/materials*. Be sure you are using an up-to-date desktop browser to view your work (see **Note**).

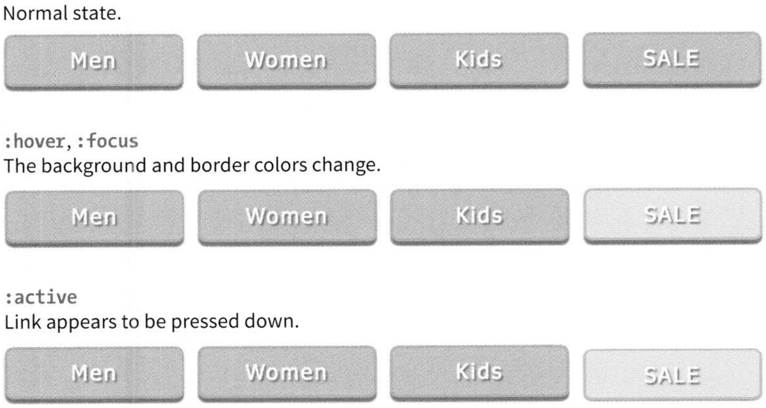

Normal state.

:hover, :focus
The background and border colors change.

:active
Link appears to be pressed down.

FIGURE 18-5. In this exercise, we'll create transitions between these link states.

EXERCISE 18-1. Continued

First, take a look at the styles that are already applied. The list has been converted to a horizontal menu with Flexbox. The **a** element has been set to display as a block element, underlines are turned off, dimensions and padding are applied, and the color, background color, and border are established. I used the **box-shadow** property to make it look as though the links are floating off the page.

1. Now we'll define the styles for the hover and focus states. When the user puts the pointer over or tabs to the link, make the background color change to green (**#c6de89**) and the border color change to a darker shade of green (**#a3c058**).

```
a:hover, a:focus {
    background-color: #c6de89;
    border-color: #a3c058;
}
```

2. While the user clicks the link (**:active**), make it move down by 3 pixels as though it is being pressed. Do this by setting the **a** element's **position** to relative and its **top** position to 0px , and then change the value of the **top** property for the active state. This moves the link 3 pixels away from the top edge (in other words, down).

NOTE: Setting the top to 0px in the initial state is for working around a bug that arises when transitioning the **top**, **bottom**, **left**, and **right** properties.

```
a {
    …
    position: relative;
    top: 0px;
}
a:active {
    top: 3px;
}
```

3. Logically, if the button were pressed down, there would be less room for the shadow, so we'll reduce the **box-shadow** distance as well.

```
a:active {
    top: 3px;
    box-shadow: 0 1px 2px rgba(0,0,0,.5);
}
```

4. Save the file and give it a try in the browser. The links should turn green and move down when you click or tap them. I'd say it's pretty good just like that. Now we can enhance the experience by adding some smooth transitions.

5. Make the background and border color transition ease in over 0.2 seconds, and see how that changes the experience of using the menu. I'm using the shorthand **transition** property to keep the code simple. I'm also using the default **ease** timing function at first so we can omit that value.

I'm not using any vendor prefixes here because modern

browsers don't need them. If you wanted to support mobile browsers released in 2013 and earlier, you could include the **-webkit-** prefixed version as well, but since this isn't production code, we're fine without it.

```
a {
    transition: background-color 0.2s,
                border-color 0.2s;
}
```

6. Save your document, open it in the browser, and try moving your mouse over the links. Do you agree it feels nicer? Now I'd like you to try some other duration values. See if you can still see the difference with a 0.1s duration. Now try a full second (1s). I think you'll find that 1 second is surprisingly slow. Try setting it to several seconds and trying out various **timing-function** values (just add them after the duration times). Can you tell the difference? Do you have a preference? When you are done experimenting, set the duration back to 0.2 seconds.

7. Now let's see what happens when we add a transition to the downward motion of the link when it is clicked or tapped. Transition both the **top** and **box-shadow** properties because they should move in tandem. Let's start with a 0.2s duration like the others.

```
a {
    transition:
        background-color 0.2s,
        border-color 0.2s,
        top 0.2s,
        box-shadow 0.2s;
}
```

Save the file, open it in the browser, and try clicking the links. That transition really changes the experience of using the menu, doesn't it? The buttons feel more difficult to "press." Try increasing the duration. Do they feel even more difficult? I find it interesting to see the effect that timing has on the experience of a user interface. It is important to get it right and not make things feel sluggish. I'd say that a very short transition such as 0.1 second—or even no transition at all—would keep these buttons feeling snappy.

8. If you thought increasing the duration made the menu uncomfortable to use, try adding a short 0.5-second delay to the **top** and **box-shadow** properties.

```
a {
    transition:
        background-color 0.2s,
        border-color 0.2s,
        top 0.1s 0.5s,
        box-shadow 0.1s 0.5s;
}
```

I think you'll find that little bit of extra time makes the whole thing feel broken. Timing is everything!

CSS TRANSFORMS

transform

Values:	rotate() | rotateX() | rotateY() | rotateZ() | rotate3d() | translate() | translateX() | translateY() | scale() | scaleX() | scaleY() | skew() | skewX() | skewY() | none
Default:	none
Applies to:	transformable elements (see sidebar)
Inherits:	no

The CSS3 Transforms Module (*www.w3.org/TR/css-transforms-1*) gives authors a way to rotate, relocate, resize, and skew HTML elements in both two- and three-dimensional space. It is worth noting up front that transforms change how an element displays, but it is not motion- or time-based. However, you can animate from one transform state to another using transitions or keyframe animations, so they are useful to learn about in the context of animation.

This chapter focuses on the more straightforward two-dimensional transforms because they have more practical uses. Transforms are supported on virtually all current browser versions without vendor prefixes (see the sidebar **"CSS Transforms Support"** for exceptions).

You can apply a transform to the normal state of an element, and it appears in its transformed state when the page loads. Just be sure that the page is still usable on browsers that don't support transforms. It is common to introduce a transform only when users interact with the element via **:hover** or a JavaScript event. Either way, transforms are a good candidate for progressive enhancement—if an IE8 user sees an element straight instead of at a jaunty angle, it's probably no biggie.

FIGURE 18-6 shows a representation of four two-dimensional transform functions: **rotate()**, **translate()**, **scale()**, and **skew()** (see **Note**). The dashed outline shows the element's original position.

Transformable Elements

You can apply the **transform** property to most element types:

- HTML elements with replaced content, such as **img**, **canvas**, form inputs, and embedded media

- Elements with their display set to **block**, **inline-block**, **inline-table** (or any of the **table-*** display types), **grid**, and **flex**

It may be easier to note the element types you *cannot* transform, which include:

- Non-replaced inline elements, like **em** or **span**

- Table columns and column groups (but who'd want to?)

NOTE

*There are actually five 2-D transform functions in the CSS spec. The fifth, **matrix()**, allows you to craft your own combined transformation using six values and some badass trigonometry. There are tools that can take a number of transforms and combine them into a matrix function, but the result isn't very user-friendly. Fascinating in theory, but more than I want to take on personally.*

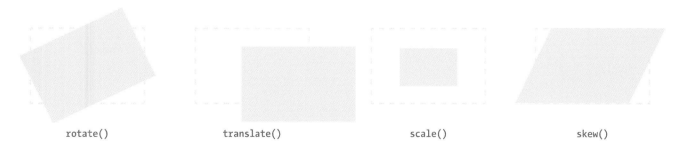

| rotate() | translate() | scale() | skew() |

FIGURE 18-6. Four types of transforms: **rotate()**, **translate()**, **scale()**, and **skew()**.

CSS Transforms Support

As of this writing, CSS Transforms are supported by every major browser without vendor prefixes; however, that support has happened more recently than Transitions, and there are a few more holes. Here are a few browser-related pointers:

- Internet Explorer 8 and earlier have no support for transforms. Version 9 supports Transforms with the **-ms-** prefix.

- IE 10 and 11 and all versions of Edge support transforms without prefixes, but they do not support transforms on elements in SVGs.

- Use the **-webkit-** prefix if you need to support the following browsers:

  — Android v2.1 to 4.4.4 (prefixes dropped in 2017)

  — OS Safari v3.2 to 8.4 (prefixes dropped in 2015)

  — Safari 8 and earlier (prefixes dropped in 2015)

  — Opera versions up to v.22 (prefixes dropped in 2014)

As of this writing, it is still recommended that you include **-ms-** and **-webkit-** prefixes for **transform**, but that may no longer be the case by the time you are reading this. Check *CanIUse.com* for updated browser information, and *ShouldIPrefix.com* for recommendations.

When an element transforms, its element box keeps its original position and influences the layout around it, in the same way that space is left behind by a relatively positioned element. It is as though the transformation magically picks up the pixels of the rendered element, messes around with them, and lays them back down on top of the page. So, if you move an element with **transform**, you're moving only a picture of it. That picture has no effect on the surrounding layout. Let's go through the transform functions one by one, starting with **rotate()**.

Transforming the Angle (rotate)

If you'd like an element to appear on a bit of an angle, use the **rotate()** transform function. The value of the **rotate()** function is an angle specified in positive (clockwise) or negative (counterclockwise) degrees. The image in FIGURE 18-7 has been rotated −10 degrees (350 degrees) with the following style rule. The tinted image shows the element's original position for reference.

```
img {
    width: 400px;
    height: 300px;
    transform: rotate(-10deg);
}
```

Notice that the image rotates around its center point, which is the default point around which all transformations happen. But you can change that easily with the **transform-origin** property.

transform: rotate(-10deg);

FIGURE 18-7. Rotating an **img** element by using **transform: rotate()**.

transform-origin

Values: *percentage* | *length* | left | center | right | top | bottom

Default: 50% 50%

Applies to: transformable elements

Inherits: no

The value for **transform-origin** is either two keywords, length measurements, or percentage values. The first value is the horizontal offset, and the second is the vertical offset. If only one value is provided, it will be used for both. The syntax is the same as you learned for **background-position** back in **Chapter 13, Colors and Backgrounds**. If we wanted to rotate our image around a point at the center of its top edge, we could write it in any of the following ways:

```
transform-origin: center top;
transform-origin: 50%, 0%;
transform-origin: 200px, 0;
```

The images in FIGURE 18-8 have all been rotated 25 degrees, but from different origin points. It is easy to demonstrate the origin point with the **rotate()** function, but keep in mind that you can set an origin point for any of the transform functions.

transform-origin: center top;

transform-origin: 100% 100%;

transform-origin: 400px 0;

Transforming the Position (translate)

Another thing you can do with the **transform** property is give the element's rendering a new location on the page by using one of three **translate()** functions, as shown in the examples in FIGURE 18-9. The **translateX()** function allows you to move an element on a horizontal axis; **translateY()** is for moving along the vertical axis; and **translate()** combines both x and y values.

```
transform: translateX(50px);
transform: translateY(25px);
transform: translate(50px, 25px); /* (translateX, translateY) */
```

FIGURE 18-8. Changing the point around which the image rotates by using **transform-origin**.

transform: translate(90px, 60px);

transform: translate(-5%, -25%);

FIGURE 18-9. Moving an element around with the **translate()** function.

Provide length values in any of the CSS units or as a percentage value. Percentages are calculated on the width of the bounding box—that is, from border edge to border edge (which, incidentally, is how percentages are calculated in SVG, from which transforms were adapted). You can provide positive or negative values, as shown in FIGURE 18-9.

If you provide only one value for the shorthand **translate()** function, it will be presumed to be the **translateX** value, and **translateY** will be set to zero. So **translate(20px)** would be equivalent to applying both **translateX(20px)** and **translateY(0)**.

How do you like the **transform** property so far? We have two more functions to go.

Transforming the Size (scale)

Make an element appear larger or smaller by using one of three scale functions: **scaleX()** (horizontal), **scaleY()** (vertical), and the shorthand **scale()**. The value is a unitless number that specifies a size ratio. This example makes an image 150% its original width:

```
a img {
   transform: scaleX(1.5);
}
```

The **scale()** shorthand lists a value for **scaleX** and a value for **scaleY**. This example makes an element twice as wide but half as tall as the original:

```
a img {
   transform: scale(2, .5);
}
```

Unlike **translate()**, however, if you provide only one value for **scale()**, it will be used as the scaling factor in both directions. So specifying **scale(2)** is the same as applying **scaleX(2)** and **scaleY(2)**, which is intuitively the way you'd want it to be.

FIGURE 18-10 shows the results of all our scaling endeavors.

transform: scale(1.25);

transform: scale(.75);

transform: scale(1.5, .5);

FIGURE 18-10. Changing the size of an element with the **scale()** function.

Making It Slanty (skew)

The quirky collection of skew properties—**skewX()**, **skewY()**, and the short-hand **skew()**—changes the angle of either the horizontal or vertical axis (or both axes) by a specified number of degrees. As for **translate()**, if you provide only one value, it is used for **skewX()**, and **skewY()** will be set to zero.

The best way to get an idea of how skewing works is to take a look at some examples (FIGURE 18-11):

```
a img {
    transform: skewX(15deg);
}

a img {
    transform: skewY(30deg);
}

a img {
    transform: skew(15deg, 30deg);
}
```

transform: skewX(15deg);

transform: skewY(30deg);

Applying Multiple Transforms

It is possible to apply more than one transform to a single element by listing out the functions and their values, separated by spaces, like this:

```
transform: function(value) function(value);
```

In the example in FIGURE 18-12, I've made the forest image get larger, tilt a little, and move down and to the right when the mouse is over it or when it is in focus:

```
img:hover, img:focus {
    transform: scale(1.5) rotate(-5deg) translate(50px,30px);
}
```

transform: skew(15deg, 30deg);

FIGURE 18-11. Slanting an element by using the **skew()** function.

Normal state

:hover, :focus
rotate(), translate(), and scale() applied

FIGURE 18-12. Applying **scale()**, **rotate()**, and **translate()** to a single element.

It is important to note that transforms are applied in the order in which they are listed. For example, if you apply a **translate()** and then **rotate()**, you get a different result than with a **rotate()** and then a **translate()**. Order matters.

Another thing to watch out for is that if you want to apply an additional transform on a different state (such as **:hover**, **:focus**, or **:active**), you need to repeat all of the transforms already applied to the element. For example, this **a** element is rotated 45 degrees in its normal state. If I apply a **scale()** transform on the **hover** state, I would lose the rotation unless I explicitly declare it again:

```
a {
  transform: rotate(45deg);
}
a:hover {
  transform: scale(1.25);  /* rotate on a element would be lost */
}
```

To achieve both the rotation and the scale, provide both transform values:

```
a:hover {
  transform: rotate(45deg) scale(1.25);  /* rotates and scales */
}
```

Smooooooth Transforms

The multiple transforms applied to the redwood forest image look interesting, but it might *feel* better if we got there with a smooth animation instead of just BAM! Now that you know about transitions and transforms, let's put them together and make some magic happen. And by "magic," of course I mean some basic animation effects between two states. We'll do that together, step-by-step, in EXERCISE 18-2.

EXERCISE 18-2. Transitioning transforms

In this exercise, we'll make the travel photos in the gallery shown in FIGURE 18-13 grow and spin out to an angle when the user mouses over them—and we'll make it smoooooth with a transition. A starter document (*exercise_18-2.html*) and all of the images are available in the *materials* folder for this chapter.

1. Open *exercise_18-2.html* in a text editor, and you will see that there are already styles that arrange the list items horizontally and apply a slight drop shadow. The first thing we'll do is add the **transform** property for each image.
2. We want the transforms to take effect only when the mouse is over the image or when the image has focus, so the **transform** property should be applied to the **:hover** and **:focus** states. Because I want each image to tilt a little differently, we'll need to write a rule for each one, using its unique ID as the selector. You can save and check your work when you're done.

FIGURE 18-13. Photos get larger and tilt on **:hover** and **:focus** . A transition is used to help smooth out the change between states. You can see how it works when you are finished with this exercise (or check it out in the *ch18_figures.html* page).

```
a:hover #img1, a:focus #img1 {
   transform: rotate(-3deg);
}
a:hover #img2, a:focus #img2 {
   transform: rotate(5deg);
}
a:hover #img3, a:focus #img3 {
   transform: rotate(-7deg);
}
a:hover #img4, a:focus #img4 {
   transform: rotate(2deg);
}
```

NOTE

As of this writing, prefixes are still recommended for the **transform** *property, so for production-quality code, the complete rule would look like this:*

```
a:hover #img1, a:focus #img1 {
   -webkit-transform: rotate(-3deg);
   -ms-transform: rotate(-3deg); /* for IE9 */
   transform: rotate(-3deg);
}
```

Because we are checking our work on a modern browser, we can omit the prefixes for this exercise.

3. Now let's make the images a little larger as well, to give visitors a better view. Add **scale(1.5)** to each of the **transform** values. Here is the first one; you do the rest:

```
a:hover #img1 {
   transform: rotate(-3deg) scale(1.5);
}
```

Note that my image files are created at the larger size and then scaled down for the thumbnail view. If we started with small images and scaled them larger, they would look crummy.

4. As long as we are giving the appearance of lifting the photos off the screen, let's make the drop shadow appear to be a little farther away by increasing the offset and blur, and lightening the shade of gray. All images should have the same effect, so add one rule using **a:hover img** as the selector.

```
a:hover img {
   box-shadow: 6px 6px 6px rgba(0,0,0,.3);
}
```

Save your file and check it out in a browser. The images should tilt and look larger when you mouse over them. But the action is kind of jarring. Let's fix that with a transition.

5. Add the **transition** shorthand property to the normal **img** state (i.e., not on **:hover** or **:focus**). The property we want to transition in this case is **transform**. Set the duration to 0.3 seconds and use the **linear** timing function.

```
img {
   …
   transition: transform 0.3s linear;
}
```

NOTE

The prefixed **transform** *property should be included in the context of a transition as well, as shown in this fully prefixed declaration:*

```
-webkit-transition: -webkit-transform .3s linear;
```

The **-ms-** *prefix is not needed because transitions are not supported by IE9. Those users will see an immediate change to the transformed image without the smooth transition, which is fine.*

And that's all there is to it! You can try playing around with different durations and timing functions, or try altering the transforms or their origin points to see what other effects you can come up with.

3-D Transforms

In addition to the two-dimensional transform functions we've just seen, the CSS Transforms spec also describes a system for creating a sense of three-dimensional space and perspective. Combined with transitions, you can use 3-D transforms to create rich interactive interfaces, such as image carousels, flippable cards, or spinning cubes! FIGURE 18-14 shows a few examples of interfaces created with 3-D transforms.

It's worth noting that this method does not create 3-D objects with a sense of volume; it merely tilts the otherwise flat element box around on three axes (animation expert Val Head calls them "postcards in space"). The rotating cube example in the figure merely stitches together six element boxes at different angles. That said, 3-D transforms still add some interesting depth to an otherwise flat web page.

Animated book covers by Marco Barria
tympanus.net/Development/AnimatedBooks/

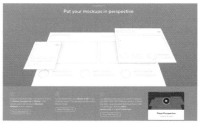

Webflow transform tools example
3d-transforms.webflow.com

Movie poster animation by Marco Kuiper
demo.marcofolio.net/3d_animation_css3/

3D CSS Rotating Cube by Paul Hayes
paulrhayes.com/experiments/cube-3d/

FIGURE 18-14. Some examples of 3-D transforms. The book covers, movie posters, and 3-D cube also have cool animation effects, so it's worth going to the links and checking them out. Webflow is a visual web design tool that includes the ability to create 3-D transformed elements.

3-D transforms are not a need-to-know skill for folks just starting out in web design, so I'm not going to go into full detail here, but I will give you a taste of what it takes to add a third dimension to a design. If you'd like to learn more, the following tutorials are good places to start (although the browser support information they contain may be out-of-date):

- "Adventures in the Third Dimension: CSS 3D Transforms" by Peter Gasston (*coding.smashingmagazine.com/2012/01/06/adventures-in-the-third-dimension-css-3-d-transforms/*)

- "Intro to CSS 3D Transforms" by David DeSandro (*desandro.github.com/3dtransforms/*)

To give you a very basic example, I'm going to use the images from EXERCISE 18-2 and arrange them as though they are in a 3-D carousel-style gallery (FIGURE 18-15).

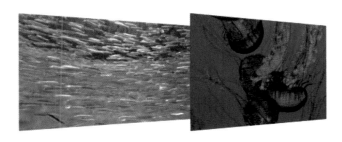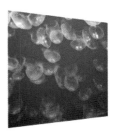

FIGURE 18-15. Our aquarium images arranged in space…*space*…*space*…

The markup is the same unordered list used in the previous exercise:

```
<ul>
   <li><a href=""><img src="anchovies.jpg" id="img1" alt=""></a></li>
   <li><a href=""><img src="jellyfish1.jpg" id="img2" alt=""></a></li>
   <li><a href=""><img src="bluejellyfish.jpg" id="img3" alt=""></a>
   </li>
   <li><a href=""><img src="seadragon.jpg" id="img4" alt=""></a></li>
</ul>
```

The first step is to add some amount of "perspective" to the containing element by using the **perspective** property. This tells the browser that the child elements should behave as though they are in 3-D space. The value of the **perspective** property is some integer larger than zero that specifies a distance from the element's origin on the z-axis. The lower the value, the more extreme the perspective. I have found that values between 300 and 1,500 are reasonable, but this is something you need to fuss around with until you get the desired effect.

```
ul {
   width: 1000px;
   height: 100px;
   list-style-type: none;
   padding: 0;
   margin: 0;
   perspective: 600;
}
```

NOTE

When using the **-webkit-** *prefix for* **transform**, *include the prefixed version of* **perspective** *as well (*-webkit-perspective*).*

The **perspective-origin** property (not shown) describes the position of your eyes relative to the transformed items. The values are a horizontal position (**left**, **center**, **right**, or a length or percentage) and a vertical position (**top**, **bottom**, **center**, or a length or percentage value). The default (FIGURE 18-15) is centered vertically and horizontally (**perspective-origin: 50% 50%**). The final transform-related property is **backface-visibility**, which controls whether the reverse side of the element is visible when it spins around.

With the 3-D space established, apply one of the 3-D transform functions to each child element—in this case, the **li** within the **ul**. The 3-D functions include **translate3d**, **translateZ**, **scale3d**, **scaleZ**, **rotate3d**, **rotateX**, **rotateY**, **rotateZ**, and **matrix3d**. You should recognize some terms in there. The ***Z** functions define the object's orientation relative to the z-axis (picture it running from your nose to this page, whereas the x- and y-axes lie flat on the page).

In our example in FIGURE 18-15, each **li** is rotated 45 degrees around its y-axis (vertical axis) by using the **rotateY** function, which works as though the element boxes are rotating around a pole.

Compare the result to FIGURE 18-16, in which each **li** is rotated on its x-axis (horizontal axis) by using **rotateX**. It's as though the element boxes are rotating around a horizontal bar.

```
li {
    float: left;
    margin-right: 10px;
    transform: rotateX(45deg);
}
```

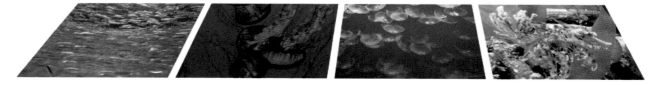

FIGURE 18-16. The same list of images rotated on their horizontal axes with **rotateX()**.

Obviously, I'm barely scratching the surface of what can be done with 3-D transforms, but this should give you a mental model for how it works. Next up, I'll introduce you to a more sophisticated way to set your web pages in motion.

KEYFRAME ANIMATION

The CSS Animations Module allows authors to create real, honest-to-goodness keyframe animation. FIGURE 18-17 shows just a few examples that you can see in action online. Unlike transitions that go from a beginning state to

WATCH **MADMANIMATION**

MADMANIMATION
by Anthony Calzadilla and Andy Clarke
stuffandnonsense.co.uk/content/demo/
madmanimation/—hint: click WATCH

How I Learned to Walk
by Andrew Wang-Hoyer
andrew.wang-hoyer.com/experiments/
walking/

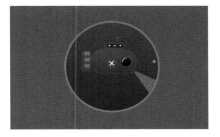

Adorable animated submarine
by Alberto Jerez
codepen.io/ajerez/pen/EaEEOW

Animated Web Banner
by Caleb Jacob
tympanus.net/codrops/2012/01/10/
animated-web-banners-with-css3/

FIGURE 18-17. Examples of animations using only CSS.

CSS transitions are animations with two keyframes: a start state and an end state. More complex animations require many keyframes to control property changes in the sequence.

an end state, keyframe animation allows you to explicitly specify other states at points along the way, allowing for more granular control of the action. Those "points along the way" are established by keyframes that define the beginning or end of a segment of animation.

Creating keyframe animations is complex, and more than I can cover here. But I would like for you to have some idea of how it works, so I'll sketch out the minimal details. The following resources are good starting points for learning more:

- *CSS Animations Level 1 (a Working Draft at the time of this writing) at www.
  w3.org/TR/css-animations-1/.*

- *Transitions and Animations in CSS* by Estelle Weyl (O'Reilly).

- "Animation & UX Resources" by Val Head (*valhead.com/ui-animation/*). Val has compiled a mega-list of resources regarding web animation, including links to tutorials, articles, tools, galleries, and more. It is not limited to CSS keyframe animation, but as long as you're delving into animation, you can trust Val to point you to good stuff.

NOTE

Keyframe animation is known as explicit animation *because you program its behavior. By contrast, transitions are an example of* implicit animation *because they are triggered only when a property changes.*

Animation Tools

If you want to add a simple animation effect to an element—a quick flip here or a little shimmy there—you may be able to find a premade effect you can apply to your design. Here are a few sites that provide ready-made CSS for common animation effects (some also use JQuery plug-ins, but they explain how to use them):

- **Animate.css** by Daniel Eden (*daneden.github.io/animate.css/*)

- **CSS Animation Cheat Sheet** by Justin Aguilar (*www.justinaguilar. com/animations/index.html*)

- **AngryTools CSS Animation Kit** (*angrytools.com/css/animation/*)

- "CSS: Animation" course by Val Head on Lynda.com (*www.lynda.com/ CSS-tutorials/CSS-Animation/439683-2.html*). You'll need a subscription to Lynda.com, but if you are in web-design-learning mode, it may be a good investment.

- "CSS Animation for Beginners" by Rachel Cope (*robots.thoughtbot.com/ css-animation-for-beginners*). This is a clearly written tutorial with lots of examples.

- "The Guide to CSS Animation: Principles and Examples" by Tom Waterhouse (*www.smashingmagazine.com/2011/09/the-guide-to-css-animation-principles-and-examples/*). This tutorial goes beyond CSS code to include tips for creating natural animation effects.

Establishing the Keyframes

The animation process has two parts:

1. Establish the keyframes with a **@keyframes** rule.

2. Add the animation properties to the elements that will be animated.

Here is a very simple set of keyframes that changes the background color of an element over time. It's not a very action-packed animation, but it should give you a basic understanding of what a **@keyframes** rule does.

```
@keyframes colors {
  0% { background-color: red; }
  20% { background-color: orange; }
  40% { background-color: yellow; }
  60% { background-color: green; }
  80% { background-color: blue; }
  100% { background-color: purple; }
}
```

The keyframes at-rule identifies the name of the animation, the stages of the animation represented by percentage (%) values, and the CSS properties that are affected for each stage. Here's what a **@keyframes** rule looks like abstracted down to its syntax:

```
@keyframes animation-name {
  keyframe { property: value; }
  /* additional keyframes */
}
```

The sample **@keyframes** rule says: create an animation sequence called "colors." At the beginning of the animation, the **background-color** of the element should be red; at 20% through the animation runtime, the background color should be orange; and so on, until it reaches the end of the animation. The browser fills in all the shades of color in between each keyframe (or *tweens* it, to use the lingo). This is represented the best I could in FIGURE 18-18.

Each percentage value and the property/value declaration defines a keyframe in the animation sequence.

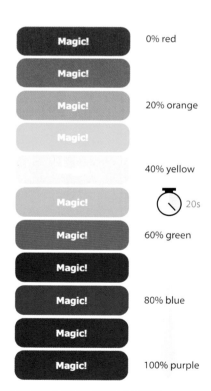

0% red

20% orange

40% yellow

20s

60% green

80% blue

100% purple

FIGURE 18-18. Animating through the colors of the rainbow by using keyframes.

As an alternative to percentages, you can use the keyword **from** for the start of an animation sequence (equivalent to 0%) and the keyword **to** for denoting the end (100%). The following example makes an element slide in from right to left as the left margin reduces to 0:

```
@keyframe slide {
    from { margin-left: 100% }
    to { margin-left: 0%; }
}
```

Adding Animation Properties

Now we can apply this animation sequence to an element or multiple elements in the document by using a collection of animation properties that are very similar to the set of transition properties that you already know.

I am going to apply the rainbow animation to the **#magic div** in my document:

```
<div id="magic">Magic!</div>
```

In the CSS rule for **#magic**, I make decisions about the animation I want to apply:

- Which animation to use (**animation-name**) (*Required*).

- How long it should take (**animation-duration**) (*Required*).

- The manner in which it should accelerate (**animation-timing-function**). This property uses the same timing function keywords that we covered for CSS Transitions.

- Whether to pause before it starts (**animation-delay**).

Looks familiar, right? There are a few other animation-specific properties to know about as well:

animation-iteration-count

How many times the animation should repeat. This can be set to a whole number or **infinite**.

animation-direction

Whether the animation plays forward (**normal**), in reverse (**reverse**), or alternates back and forth starting at the beginning (**alternate**), or alternates starting from the end (**alternate-reverse**).

animation-fill-mode

The animation fill mode determines what happens with the animation before it begins and after it ends. By default (**none**), the animation shows whatever property values were not specified via **@keyframes**. If you want the last keyframe to stay visible after the animation plays, use the **forwards** keyword. If there is a delay set on the animation and you want the first keyframe to show during that delay, use **backwards**. To retain the beginning and end states, use **both**.

■ **SUPPORT TIP**

CSS Keyframe Browser Support

All current versions of major desktop and mobile browsers support CSS keyframe animation without vendor prefixes. Here are the exceptions:

- Internet Explorer 9 and earlier do not support keyframe animation at all. The animation will appear in its start state, so be sure that first frame is an acceptable fallback.

- You need to use the **-webkit-** prefix to support the following browsers: Safari and iOS Safari 8 and earlier (2014), Chrome 41 and earlier (2015), Opera 29 and earlier (2015), and Android 4.4.4 and earlier (2014). As I am writing this, these browsers represent enough traffic that it is still recommended that you include the **-webkit-** prefix, but that may change based on when you are doing development and who your target audience is.

  Note that you need the prefixed keyframe at-rule as well as prefixed **animation-*** properties. As always, the standard, unprefixed rules go after prefixed versions.

  `@-webkit-keyframes`

  `-webkit-animation-*`

---

animation-play-state

Whether the animation should be **running** or **paused** when it loads. The play-state can be toggled on and off based on user input with JavaScript or on hover.

The **animation-name** property tells the browser which keyframe sequence to apply to the **#magic div**. I've also set the duration and timing function, and used **animation-iteration-count** to make it repeat infinitely. I could have provided a specific number value, like 2 to play it twice, but how fun are only two rainbows? And for fun, I've set the **animation-direction** to **alternate**, which makes the animation play in reverse after it has played forward. Here is the resulting rule for the animated **div**:

```
#magic {
    …
    animation-name: colors;
    animation-duration: 5s;
    animation-timing-function: linear;
    animation-iteration-count: infinite;
    animation-direction: alternate;
}
```

That gets a bit verbose, especially when you consider that each property may also follow a prefixed version. You can also use the **animation** shorthand property to combine the values, just as we did for **transition**:

```
#magic {
    animation: colors 5s linear infinite alternate;
}
```

Those are the bare bones of creating keyframes and applying animations to an element on the page. To make elements move around (what we typically think of as "animation"), use keyframes to change the position of an element on the screen with **translate** (the best option for performance) or with the **top**, **right**, **bottom**, and **left** properties. When the keyframes are tweened, the object will move smoothly from position to position. You can also animate the other transform functions such as **scale** and **skew**.

When to Use Keyframe Animation

To keep my example simple, I chose to change only the background color of a button element, but of course, keyframe animations can be used to create real animations, especially when combined with the CSS transform functions for spinning and moving elements around on the page. If you only need to change an element from one state to another, a transition is the way to go. But if you have a linear animation such as moving a character, an object, or its parts around, keyframe animation is the most appropriate choice.

For more complex keyframe animations, particularly those that change with user interaction or require complex physics, using JavaScript for animation may be a better choice than CSS animation. JavaScript animation also has

Animation Inspectors

Both Chrome and Firefox offer tools to inspect and modify web animations (FIGURE 18-19). When you inspect an animated element in the Developer Tools, click the Animations tab to see a timeline of all the animations applied to that object. You can slow down the animation to reveal what is happening on a detailed level. You can also modify the animation by making changes to the timing, delay, duration, and keyframes. For more information, see the following:

- Firefox Animation Inspector (*developer.mozilla.org/en-US/docs/Tools/Page_Inspector/How_to/Work_with_animations*)
- Chrome Animation Inspector (*developers.google.com/web/tools/chrome-devtools/inspect-styles/animations*)

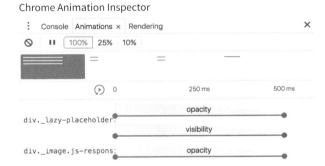

FIGURE 18-19. Animation inspectors are part of the developer tools offered by Firefox and Chrome browsers.

better support in older browsers, making it preferable if animation is critical to the mission of the page. CSS keyframe animation is a good solution for simple animations used as an enhancement to a baseline experience.

I should note that as I write this, there is a lot of excitement in the web community for animating SVG graphics. When you place the source code for an SVG directly in the HTML document, the elements in it are available to be animated. As of this writing, there are still limitations and browser support issues around using CSS to animate SVGs, but as browser support grows, this approach looks very promising. In the meantime, JavaScript has better access to SVG properties, has better browser support, and is the more common solution for SVG animation.

WRAPPING UP

I hope I've helped you to wrap your head around how CSS can be used to add a little motion and smoothness to your pages. For adding motion to a web page, we have CSS Transitions to smooth out changes from one state to another and CSS Keyframe Animation for animating a series of states. We also looked at CSS Transforms for repositioning, spinning, resizing, or skewing an element when it is rendered on the screen.

Used thoughtfully, animation can make your interfaces more intuitive and enhance your brand personality. It's powerful stuff, but with great power comes great responsibility. To learn how to use web animation to enhance the user experience in a meaningful way, I recommend the book *Designing Interface Animation: Meaningful Motion for User Experience* by Val Head (Rosenfeld Media).

Now let's see if you were paying attention with a 12-question quiz!

TEST YOURSELF

Think you know your way around transitions, transforms, and keyframe animations? Here are a few questions to find out (answers in **Appendix A**):

1.   What is tweening?

2.   If a transition had keyframes, how many would it have?

3.   Write out the transition declaration (property and value) you would use to accomplish the following:

     a.   Wait .5 seconds before the transition starts.

     b.   Make the transition happen at a constant speed.

     c.   Make the transition last .5 seconds.

     d.   Make the lines of text slowly grow farther apart.

4. Which of the following can you *not* animate?

   a. `width`

   b. `padding`

   c. `text-transform`

   d. `word-spacing`

5. Which timing function will be used if you omit the **transition-timing-function** property? Describe its action.

6. In the following transition, what does .2s describe?
   ```
   transition: color .2s linear;
   ```

7. Which transition will finish first?

   a. `transition: width 300ms ease-in;`

   b. `transition: width 300ms ease-out;`

8. Write the **transform** declaration to accomplish the following:

   a. Tilt the element 7 degrees clockwise.

   b. Reposition the element 25 pixels up and 50 pixels to the left.

   c. Rotate the element from its bottom-right corner.

   d. Make a 400-pixel-wide image display at 500 pixels wide.

9. In the following transform declaration, what does the 3 value describe?
   ```
   transform: scale(2, 3)
   ```

10. Which 3-D transform would look more angled and dramatic?

    a. `perspective: 250;`

    b. `perspective: 1250;`

11. What happens halfway through this animation?

    ```
    @keyframes border-bulge {
      from { border-width: 1px; }
      25% { border-width: 10px; }
      50% { border-width: 3px; }
      to { border-width: 5px; }
    }
    ```

12. Write the animation declaration you would use to accomplish the following:

    a. Make the animation play in reverse.

    b. Make the entire animation last 5 seconds.

    c. Wait 2 seconds before running the animation.

    d. Repeat the animation three times and then stop.

    e. The end state of the animation stays visible after the animation is done playing.

CSS REVIEW: TRANSITIONS, TRANSFORMS, AND ANIMATION

Here is a summary of the properties covered in this chapter.

Property	Description
animation	A shorthand property that combines animation properties
animation-name	Specifies the named animation sequence to apply
animation-duration	Specifies the amount of time the animation lasts
animation-timing-function	Describes the acceleration of the animation
animation-iteration-count	Indicates the number of times the animation repeats
animation-direction	Specifies whether the animation plays forward, in reverse, or alternates back and forth
animation-play-state	Specifies whether the animation is running or paused
animation-delay	Indicates the amount of time before the animation starts running
animation-fill-mode	Overrides limits to when animation properties can be applied
backface-visibility	Determines whether the reverse side of an element may be visible in 3-D transforms
perspective	Establishes an element as a 3-D space and specifies the perceived depth
perspective-origin	Specifies the position of your viewpoint in a 3-D space
transform	Specifies that the rendering of an element should be altered via one of the 2-D or 3-D transform functions
transform-origin	Denotes the point around which an element is transformed
transform-style	Preserves a 3-D context when transformed elements are nested
transition	A shorthand property that combines transition properties
transition-property	Defines which CSS property will be transitioned
transition-duration	Specifies the amount of time the transition animation lasts
transition-timing-function	Describes the manner in which the transition happens (changes in acceleration rates)
transition-delay	Specifies the amount of time before the transition starts

MORE CSS TECHNIQUES

By now you have a solid foundation in writing style sheets. You can style text and element boxes, float and position objects, create responsive page layouts using Flexbox and Grid, and even add subtle animation effects to your designs. But there are a few more common techniques that you should know about.

If you look over at the **"In This Chapter"** list, you'll see that this chapter is a grab bag of sorts. It starts with general approaches to styling forms and the special properties for table formatting. We'll cover other tricks of the trade including clearing out browser styles with a CSS reset, using images in place of text (only when necessary!), reducing the number of server requests with CSS sprites, and checking whether a browser supports a particular CSS feature. Let's dig in!

STYLING FORMS

Web forms can look a bit hodgepodge right out of the box with no styles applied (FIGURE 19-1), so you'll certainly want to give them a more professional appearance using CSS. Not only do they look better, but studies show that forms are much easier and faster to use when the labels and inputs are lined up nicely. In this section, we'll look at how various form elements can be styled.

Now, I'm not going to lie: styling forms is somewhat of a dark art because of the variety of ways in which browsers handle form elements. And for really slick, custom forms, you will generally need to turn to JavaScript. But the efforts are well worth it to improve usability.

There aren't any special CSS properties for styling forms; just use the standard color, background, font, border, margin, and padding properties that

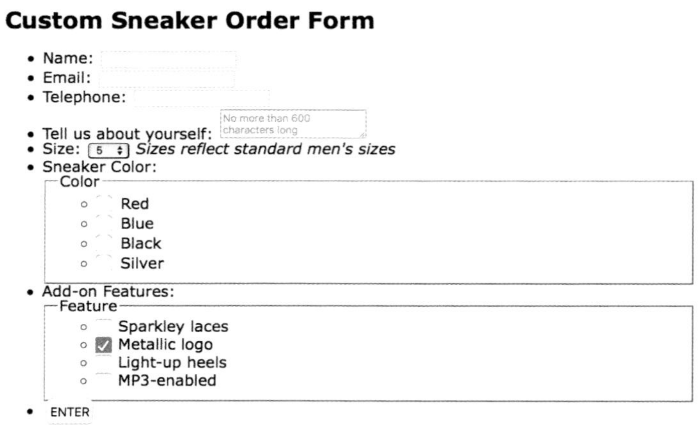

Custom Sneaker Order Form

- Name:
- Email:
- Telephone:

- Tell us about yourself: [No more than 600 characters long]
- Size: [5 ⬍] *Sizes reflect standard men's sizes*
- Sneaker Color:

    Color
    - ○ Red
    - ○ Blue
    - ○ Black
    - ○ Silver

- Add-on Features:

    Feature
    - ○ Sparkley laces
    - ☑ Metallic logo
    - ○ Light-up heels
    - ○ MP3-enabled

- ENTER

FIGURE 19-1. Forms tend to be ugly and difficult to use with HTML alone. Don't worry—this one gets spiffed up in FIGURE 19-2.

---

you've learned in the previous chapters. The following is a quick rundown of the types of things you can do for each form control type.

Text inputs (text, password, email, search, tel, url)

Change the appearance of the box itself with **width**, **height**, **background-color**, **background-image**, **border**, **border-radius**, **margin**, **padding**, and **box-shadow**. You can also style the text inside the entry field with the **color** property and the various font properties.

The textarea element

This can be styled in the same way as text-entry fields. **textarea** elements use a monospace font by default, so you may want to change that to match your other text-entry fields. Because there are multiple lines, you may also specify the line height. Note that some browsers display a handle on the lower-right corner of the **textarea** box that makes it resizable, but you can turn it off by adding the style **resize: none**. Text areas display as **inline-block** by default, but you can change them to **block** with the **display** property.

Button inputs (submit, reset, button)

Apply any of the box properties to submit and reset buttons (**width**, **height**, **border**, **background**, **margin**, **padding**, and **box-shadow**). It is worth noting that buttons are set to the border-box sizing model by default. Most browsers also add a bit of padding by default, which can be overridden by your own padding value. You can also style the text that appears on the buttons.

Radio and checkbox buttons

The best practice for radio and checkbox buttons is to leave them alone. If you are tenacious, you can use JavaScript to change the buttons altogether.

Drop-down and select menus (`select`)

You can specify the width and height for a `select` element, but note that it uses the border-box box-sizing model by default. Some browsers allow you to apply `color`, `background-color`, and font properties to `option` elements, but it's probably best to leave them alone to be rendered by the browser and operating system.

Fieldsets and legends

You can treat a `fieldset` as any other element box, adjusting the border, background, margin, and padding. Turning the border off entirely is one way to keep your form looking tidy while preserving semantics and accessibility. By default, `legend` elements are above the top border of the `fieldset`, and, unfortunately, browsers make them very difficult to change. Some developers use a `span` or `b` element within the `legend` and apply styles to the contained element for more predictable results. Some choose to hide it in a way that it will still be read by screen readers (`legend {width: 1px; height: 1px; overflow: hidden;}`).

Now we know what we can do to style individual controls, but the grander goal is to make the form more organized and easier to use. FIGURE 19-2 shows the "after" shots of the unstyled form from FIGURE 19-1. There color, font, border, and spacing changes, and the labels and input elements are nicely aligned as well. And not only that, the form is responsive! I've used Flexbox to

HEADS UP

The following form elements cannot be changed with CSS alone: inputs for range, color, date pickers, file picker, `option`, `optgroup`, `datalist`, `progress`, and `meter`. It is possible to customize them by using JavaScript, which is beyond the scope of this book.

Wide viewport   Narrow viewport

FIGURE 19-2. This responsive form uses Flexbox to allow text inputs to resize and to shift the position of the labels on small screens.

make the labels stack on top of their respective inputs and fieldsets on narrow screens so there is no wasted space.

If you'd like to take a look at the actual markup and styles, the document *sneakerform.html* is available with the materials for this chapter (*learningweb-design.com/5e/materials*). I've left careful and thorough comments throughout that explain exactly what each style is for. My approach to styling the Custom Sneaker Order Form can be summarized as follows:

- Set the **box-sizing** to **border-box** for the whole document. This makes sizing form elements more predictable.

- Give the **form** a **max-width** (so it can shrink to fit smaller viewports) and optional decorative styling like the green background and rounded border in the example.

- Get rid of the bullets and spacing around the unordered lists that were used to mark up the form semantically.

- Turn list items (each containing a label and some sort of input or fieldset) into flex containers by setting their **display** to **flex** (see **Note**). Turn on wrapping, which is what allows the input to shift below the labels on small screens.

- Give the labels fixed widths (**flex: 0 0 8em;**) so they are sized the same regardless of screen size. Because labels on checkboxes and radio buttons work differently, set them to override the 8em width (**flex: 1 1 auto;**).

- Allow the **input**, **textarea**, and **fieldset**s to grow to fill the remaining space (**flex: 1 1 20em;**). When the screen is too narrow for them to fit next to the labels, they wrap below.

- Set the text input fields' **font-family** to **inherit** so they use the same font as the rest of the document instead of whatever font the browser uses for forms. Text inputs also get heights, borders, and a little padding.

- Fieldsets and legends are tricky to style. Turn off the border and padding on the **fieldset**, and then hide the **legend** in a way that it will still be read aloud before each checkbox or radio button option. Because there is both a label and a legend for each fieldset, I made sure they are not exactly the same so they won't be redundant when read aloud by a screen reader. The legend should be shorter because it is repeated for each option.

- The submit button has a rounded border, background color, and font styling. Set the side margins to **auto** so it will always be centered in the width of the form.

This is a very simple example, but it should give you a general idea of how forms can be styled. You may also want to add highlight styles for interactivity, such as **:hover** styles on the buttons and **:focus** styles for text inputs when they are selected.

NOTE

If you don't want to use Flexbox, you can line up labels by using floats. Set labels to **display: block***, give them a width and height, and float them to the left. You need to clear the* **li** *elements (***clear: both***) so they start below the previous floated pair.*

STYLING TABLES

Like any other text content on a web page, content within table cells can be formatted with various font, text, and background properties.

You will probably want to adjust the spacing in and around tables. To adjust the amount of space within a cell (cell padding), apply the **padding** property to the **td** or **th** element. Spacing between cells (cell spacing) is a little more complicated and is related to how CSS handles cell borders. CSS provides two methods for displaying borders between table cells: separated or collapsed. These options are specified with the table-specific **border-collapse** property with **separate** and **collapse** values, respectively.

border-collapse

Values:	separate | collapse
Default:	separate
Applies to:	table and inline-table elements
Inherits:	yes

Separated Borders

By default, borders are separated, and a border is drawn on all four sides of each cell. The **border-spacing** property lets you specify the space between cell borders.

border-spacing

Values:	*horizontal-length vertical-length*
Default:	0
Applies to:	table and inline-table elements
Inherits:	yes

The values for **border-spacing** are two length measurements. The horizontal value comes first and applies between columns. The second measurement is applied between rows. If you provide one value, it will be used both horizontally and vertically. The default setting is 0, causing the borders to double up on the inside grid of the table (see **Note**).

The table in FIGURE 19-3 is set to **separate** with 15 pixels of space between columns and 5 pixels of space between rows. A purple border has been applied to the cells to make their boundaries clear.

NOTE

*Although the **border-spacing** default is 0, browsers generally add 2 pixels of space for the obsolete **cellspacing** attribute by default. If you want to see the borders double up, you need to set the **cellspacing** attribute to 0 in the **table** element.*

NOTE

*In the past, cell padding and spacing were handled by the **cellpadding** and **cellspacing** attributes in the **table** element, respectively, but they have been made obsolete in HTML5 because of their presentational nature.*

```
td {
    border: 3px solid purple;
}
table {
    border-collapse: separate;
    border-spacing: 15px 5px;
    border: none;
}
```

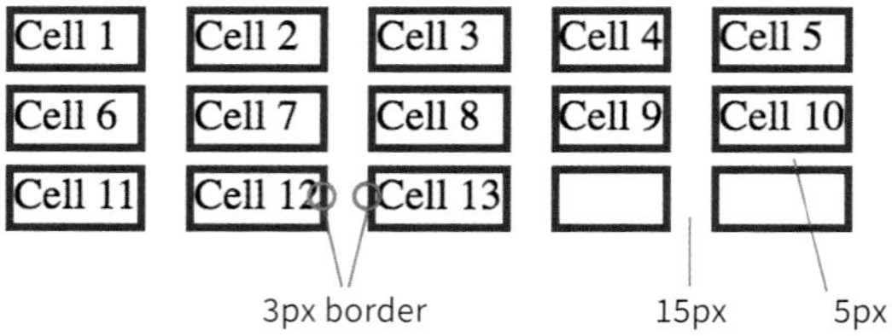

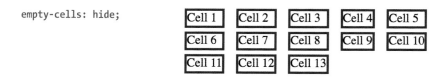

FIGURE 19-3. The separated table border model.

For tables with separated borders, you can indicate whether you want empty cells to display their backgrounds and borders by using the **empty-cells** property. For a cell to be "empty," it may not contain any text, images, or non-breaking spaces. It may contain carriage returns and space characters.

empty-cells

Values:	show | hide
Default:	show
Applies to:	table cell elements
Inherits:	yes

FIGURE 19-4 shows the previous separated table-border example with its empty cells (what would be Cell 14 and Cell 15) set to **hide**.

empty-cells: hide;

FIGURE 19-4. Hiding empty cells with the **empty-cells** property.

Collapsed Borders

In the collapsed border model, the borders of adjacent borders "collapse" so that only one of the borders is visible and the space is removed (FIGURE 19-5). In the example, although each table cell has a 3-pixel border, the borders between cells measure a total of 3 pixels, not 6. In instances where neighboring cells have different border styles, a complicated pecking order is called in to determine which border will display, which you can read in the spec.

The advantage to using the collapsed table-border model is that you can style the borders for **tr**, **col**, **rowgroup**, and **colgroup** elements. With the separated model, you can't. Strategic use of horizontal and vertical borders improves the readability of complicated tables, making the collapsed model an attractive choice.

```
td {
   border: 3px solid purple;
}
table {
   border-collapse: collapse;
   border: none;
}
```

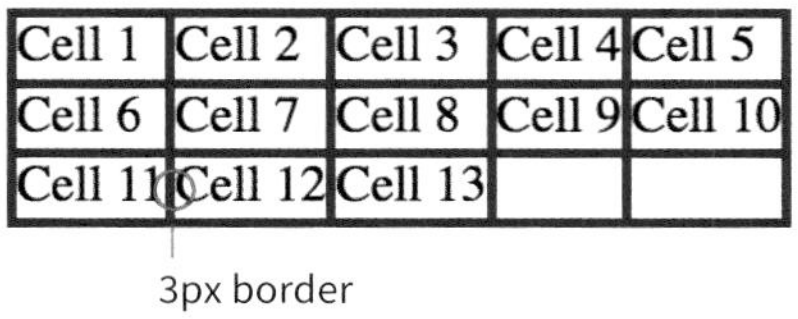

Cell 1	Cell 2	Cell 3	Cell 4	Cell 5
Cell 6	Cell 7	Cell 8	Cell 9	Cell 10
Cell 11	Cell 12	Cell 13		

3px border

FIGURE 19-5. The collapsed border model.

Table Layout

table-layout

Values: auto | fixed

Default: auto

Applies to: table or inline-table elements

Inherits: yes

The **table-layout** property allows authors to specify one of two methods of calculating the width of a table. The **fixed** value bases the table width on **width** values provided for the table, columns, or cells. The **auto** value bases the width of the table on the minimum width of the contents of the table. Auto layout may display nominally more slowly because the browser must calculate the default width of every cell before arriving at the width of the table.

That covers basic form and table formatting. I know this is a beginner's book, but in the next section, I'm going to introduce you to a few intermediate CSS techniques that may make your work easier and your pages faster.

Pick a Side

When you use the **caption** element in a table, it will appear above the table by default. If you'd prefer it to be below the table, you can use the **caption-side** property to position it there.

caption-side

Values: top | bottom

Default: top

Applies to: table caption element

Inherits: yes

Table Display Properties

CSS 2.1 includes a number of values for the **display** property that allow authors to attach table display behaviors to elements. The table-related **display** values are **table**, **inline-table**, **table-row-group**, **table-header-group**, **table-footer-group**, **table-row**, **table-column-group**, **table-column**, **table-cell**, and **table-caption**.

The original intent for these values was to provide a mechanism for applying table display behaviors to XML languages that may not have elements like **table**, **tr**, or **td** in their vocabularies.

In recent years, table display values have become another method for achieving page layout effects such as vertical centering and flexible column widths. CSS table layout may be useful as a fallback design for older browsers that do not support CSS Grid or Flexbox. Note that this is not the same as using table-based layout with HTML markup. With CSS table layout, the semantics of the source document stay intact. If you'd like to learn more, I recommend the article "Layout Secret #1: The CSS Table Property" by Massimo Cassandro (*www.sitepoint.com/solving-layout-problems-css-table-property/*).

Now that Flexbox and Grid are gaining momentum, I suspect the table layout methods will eventually go by the wayside.

A CLEAN SLATE
(RESET AND NORMALIZE.CSS)

As you know, browsers have their own built-in style sheets (called user agent style sheets) for rendering HTML elements. If you don't supply styles for an **h1**, you can be certain that it will display as large, bold text with space above and below. But just how much larger and how much space may vary from browser to browser, giving inconsistent results. Furthermore, even if you do provide your own style sheet, elements in your document may be secretly inheriting certain styles from the user agent style sheets, causing unexpected results.

There are two methods for getting a consistent starting point for applying your own styles: a CSS reset or normalize.css. They take different approaches, so one or the other may be the best solution for what you need to achieve.

CSS Reset

The older approach is a CSS reset, a collection of style rules that overrides *all* user agent styles and creates a starting point that is as neutral as possible. With this method, you need to specify all the font and spacing properties for every element you use. It's a truly from-scratch starting point.

The most popular reset was written by Eric Meyer (the author of too many CSS books to list). It is presented here, and I've also included a copy of it in the *materials* folder for this chapter for your copy-and-paste pleasure (see **Note**). If you look through the code, you'll see that the margins, border, and padding have been set to 0 for a long list of block elements. There are also styles that get typography to a neutral starting point, clear out styles on lists, and prevent browsers from adding quotation marks to quotes and block-quotes.

NOTE

You can get the CSS reset on the web at meyerweb.com/eric/tools/css/reset/.

```
/* http://meyerweb.com/eric/tools/css/reset/
 v2.0 | 20110126 License: none (public domain)*/
html, body, div, span, applet, object, iframe,
h1, h2, h3, h4, h5, h6, p, blockquote, pre,
a, abbr, acronym, address, big, cite, code,
del, dfn, em, img, ins, kbd, q, s, samp,
small, strike, strong, sub, sup, tt, var,
b, u, i, center, dl, dt, dd, ol, ul, li,
fieldset, form, label, legend,
table, caption, tbody, tfoot, thead, tr, th, td,
article, aside, canvas, details, embed,figure, figcaption, footer,
header, hgroup,menu, nav, output, ruby, section, summary,
time, mark, audio, video {
    margin: 0;
    padding: 0;
    border: 0;
    font-size: 100%;
    font: inherit;
    vertical-align: baseline;
}
```

```
/* HTML5 display-role reset for older browsers */
article, aside, details, figcaption, figure,footer, header, hgroup,
menu, nav, section {
    display: block;
}
body {
    line-height: 1;
}
ol, ul {
    list-style: none;
}
blockquote, q {
    quotes: none;
}
blockquote:before, blockquote:after,
 q:before, q:after {
    content: '';
    content: none;
}
table {
    border-collapse: collapse;
    border-spacing: 0;
}
```

To use the reset, place these styles at the top of your own style sheet so your own styles override them. You can use them exactly as you see them here or customize them as your project requires. I also recommend reading Eric's posts about the thinking that went into his settings at *meyerweb.com/eric/tools/css/reset/* and *meyerweb.com/eric/thoughts/2007/04/18/reset-reasoning/*. A web search will reveal other, potentially smaller, CSS reset options.

Normalize.css

A more nuanced approach is to use Normalize.css, created by Nicolas Gallagher and Jonathan Neal. They painstakingly combed through the user agent styles of every modern browser (desktop and mobile) and created a style sheet that tweaks their styles for consistency, rather than just turning them all off. Normalize.css gives you a reasonable starting point: paragraphs still have some space above and below, headings are bold in descending sizes, lists have markers and indents as you would expect. It also includes styles that make form widgets consistent, which is a nice service. FIGURE 19-6 shows the difference between CSS reset and Normalize.css starting points.

You can download Normalize.css at *necolas.github.io/normalize.css/* and include it before your own styles. It is too long to print here, but you will find that it is well organized and includes comments with clear explanations for each section. For Nicolas's thoughts on the project, see *nicolasgallagher.com/about-normalize-css/*.

Normalize.css is considered a superior successor to the cruder CSS reset, but I think it is important to be aware of both options. Or, if slight differences from browser to browser are just fine with you (as they are for a lot of professional developers), you don't need to use either.

CSS reset   Normalize.css

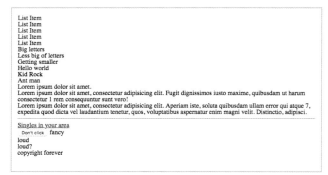

FIGURE 19-6. The difference between CSS reset (left) and Normalize.css (right). (Credit: screenshot of a Codepen created by Zach Wolf.)

IMAGE REPLACEMENT TECHNIQUES

Before web fonts were a viable option, we needed to use an image anytime we wanted text in a font fancier than Times or Helvetica. Fortunately, that is no longer the case, but every now and then, it may still be necessary to replace a text element with an image in a way that is still accessible to screen readers. One common scenario is using a stylized logo in place of a company name in a heading (see **Note**).

Removing the text altogether and replacing it with an **img** element is a bad idea because the text content is gone forever. The solution is to use a CSS-based image replacement technique that uses the image as a background in the element, then shifts the text out of the way so that it is not rendered on the page. Visual browsers see the background image, while the text content stays in the file for the benefit of search engines, screen readers, and other assistive devices. Everybody wins!

Many image replacement techniques have been developed over the years (see **Note**), but the most popular is the Phark technique created by Mike Rundle. It uses a large negative indent to move the text off to the left of the visible page.

In the example in FIGURE 19-7, I use the Phark technique to display the Jenware logo in place of the **h1** "Jenware" text in the HTML source. The markup is simple:

```
<h1 id="logo">Jenware</h1>
```

NOTE

Before going through the effort of an image replacement technique, consider whether the **alt** *text in an* **img** *element is all you need. In the case of a logo, the* **alt** *text could represent the company name should the image of the logo not be seen. Frankly, the logo example in this section could probably be handled that way. That said, there may be instances in which you need to replace an actual string of text with an image, in which case an image replacement technique might be a good thing to have in your CSS toolbox.*

The style rule is as follows:

```
#logo {
    width: 450px;
    height: 80px;
    background: url(jenware.png) no-repeat;
    text-indent: -9999px;
}
```

NOTE

You can view a gallery of old techniques at "The Image Replacement Museum," assembled by Marie Mosley (css-tricks. com/the-image-replacement-museum/).

What users see:

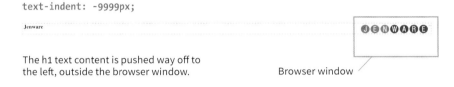

What is actually happening:

text-indent: -9999px;

The h1 text content is pushed way off to the left, outside the browser window.

Browser window

FIGURE 19-7. The Phark image replacement technique hides the HTML text by pushing it out of the visible element box with a large negative text indent so only the background image displays.

There are a few things of note here. First, the **h1** element displays as a block by default, so we can just specify its **width** and **height** to match the dimensions of the image used as a background. The **text-indent** property pushes the word *Jenware* over to the left by 9,999 pixels. This requires the browser to render a very wide element box, but the performance hit is minimal.

The downside to any image replacement approach is that it means an extra request to the server for every image used. It can also be more work creating graphics every time a heading changes. Again, before you reach for an image replacement, consider whether a web font or inline image with **alt** text may do the trick. In the next section, we'll look at a way to curb unnecessary server requests.

CSS SPRITES

When I talked about performance back in **Chapter 3, Some Big Concepts You Need to Know**, I noted that you can improve site performance by reducing the number of requests your page makes to the server (a.k.a. HTTP requests). One strategy for reducing the number of image requests is to combine all your little images into one big image file so that only one image gets requested. The large image that contains multiple images is known as a sprite, a term coined by the early computer graphic and video game industry. That image gets positioned in the element via the **background-position** property in such a way that only the relevant portion of it is visible. An example should make this clear.

If I want to show a collection of six social media icons on my page, I can turn those six graphics into one sprite and reduce the number of HTTP requests accordingly (FIGURE 19-8). You can see in the figure that the icons have been stacked into one tall graphic (*social.png*). This example also uses an image replacement technique so the text for each link is still available to screen readers.

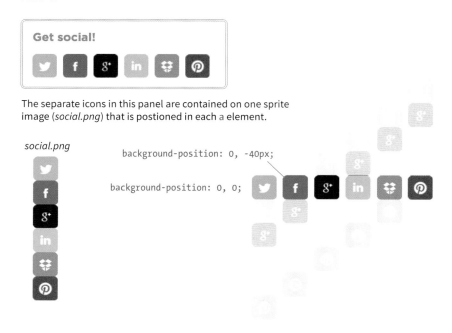

FIGURE 19-8. Replacing separate graphic files with one sprite image cuts down on the number of HTTP requests to the server and improves site performance.

THE MARKUP

```
<ul>
  <li><a href="" class="hide twitter">Twitter</a></li>
  <li><a href="" class="hide fb">Facebook</a></li>
  <li><a href="" class="hide gplus">Google+</a></li>
  <li><a href="" class="hide linkedin">LinkedIn</a></li>
  <li><a href="" class="hide dropbox">Dropbox</a></li>
  <li><a href="" class="hide pinterest">Pinterest</a></li>
</ul>
```

THE STYLES

```
.hide {
  text-indent: 100%;
  white-space: nowrap;
  overflow: hidden;
}
```

```
li a {
  display: block;
  width: 40px;
  height: 40px;
  background-image: url(social.png);
}
li a.twitter { background-position: 0 0; }
li a.fb { background-position: 0 -40px; }
li a.gplus { background-position: 0 -80px; }
li a.linkedin { background-position: 0 -120px; }
li a.dropbox { background-position: 0 -160px; }
li a.pinterest { background-position: 0 -200px; }
```

In the markup, each item has two **class** values. The **hide** class is used as a selector to apply an image replacement technique. This one was developed by Scott Kellum and uses a left indent of 100% to move the text out of sight. The other **class** name is particular to each social network link. The unique **class** values allow us to position the sprite appropriately for each link.

At the top of the style sheet you'll see the image replacement styles. Notice in the next rule that all link (**a**) elements use *social.png* as their background image.

Finally, we get to the styles that do the heavy lifting. The **background-position** is set differently for each link in the list, and the visible element box works like a little window revealing a portion of the background image. The first item has the value **0,0**; this positions the top-left corner of the image in the top-left corner of the element box. To make the Facebook icon visible, we need to move the image *up* by 40 pixels, so its vertical position is set to −40px (its horizontal position of 0 is fine). The image is moved up by 40-pixel increments for each link, revealing image areas farther and farther down the sprite stack.

In this example, all of the icons have the same dimensions and stack up nicely, but that is not a requirement. You can combine images with a variety of dimensions on one sprite. The process of setting a size for the element and then lining the sprite up perfectly with the **background-position** property is the same.

> ## Sprite Generators
>
> There are many online tools that create sprite image files and their respective styles automatically. Just upload or drag-and-drop your individual graphics to the page, and the tool does the rest. One that I find easy to use is CSSsprites (*css. spritegen.com*). If you need your sprites to be responsive, use their responsive version at *responsive-css. spritegen.com*.

CSS FEATURE DETECTION

One of the dominant challenges facing web designers and developers is dealing with uneven browser support. Useful new CSS properties emerge regularly, but it takes a while for them find their way into browsers, and it takes much longer for the old non-supporting browsers to fade into extinction.

Fortunately, we have a few methods for checking to see if a browser supports a particular feature so we can take advantage of cutting-edge CSS while also providing thoughtful fallbacks for non-supporting browsers. Using feature detection with fallbacks sure beats the alternatives of a) not using a property until it is universally supported, or b) using it and letting users with non-supporting browsers have a broken experience.

We'll look at two ways to detect whether a feature is supported: feature queries with a new CSS at-rule (**@supports**) and a JavaScript-based tool called Modernizr.

CSS Feature Queries (@supports)

The CSS3 Conditional Rules Module Level 3 (*www.w3.org/TR/css3-conditional/*) introduces the **@supports** rule for checking browser support of a particular property and value declaration. Commonly referred to as a feature query, it works like a media query in that it runs a test, and if the browser passes that test, it applies the styles contained in the brackets of the at-rule. The syntax for **@supports** is as follows:

```
@supports (property: value) {
   /* Style rules for supporting browsers here */
}
```

Note that the query is for an entire declaration, both the property and a value. It was designed this way because sometimes you may test for a new property (such as **initial-letter**), and sometimes you may need to test for a new value for an existing property. For example, the **display** property is universally supported, but the newer **grid** keyword value is not. Note also that there is no semicolon at the end.

Let's look at a more specific example. I think it would be cool to use the new **mix-blend-mode** property to make a photo of watermelons blend in with the background (similar to a Layer Blending Mode in Photoshop). As of this writing, it is supported only in Firefox, Chrome, and Safari. As a fallback for non-supporting browsers, I create a somewhat less interesting blended effect using the **opacity** property (FIGURE 19-9).

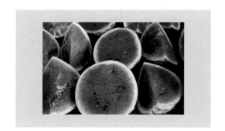

Original image (no effect)

As seen on browsers that support
mix-blend-mode: multiply;

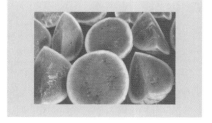

Fallback for non-supporting browsers
(opacity: .5)

FIGURE 19-9. The original image (left), the result using the **mix-blend-mode** property with **multiply** keyword (center), and the fallback style using **opacity** (right).

As of this writing, the best practice is to specify the fallback styles first, and then override them with a set of styles targeted at browsers that support the feature. Note that I also need to set the **opacity** back to 1 so it overrides my fallback style.

THE MARKUP

```
<div id="container">
  <figure class="blend">
    <img src="watermelon.jpg" alt="">
  </figure>
</div>
```

THE STYLES

```
#container {
  background-color: #96D4E7;
  padding: 5em;
}
.blend img {
  opacity: .5;
}
@supports (mix-blend-mode: multiply) {
  .blend img {
    mix-blend-mode: multiply;
    opacity: 1;
  }
}
```

WARNING

The browser has to report for itself whether it has implemented the feature. If the feature is implemented in a buggy way, you may still encounter problems even when using feature queries.

Operators

The **@supports** rule can be used with three operators to refine the feature test: **not**, **and**, and **or**:

not

The **not** operator lets us test for when a specific property/value pair is *not* supported.

```
@supports not (mix-blend-mode: hue) {
  /* styles for non-supporting browsers */
}
```

Someday, this will be useful for supplying fallback styles, but with the current browser support, you risk non-supporting browsers skipping everything in the **@supports** rules, including the fallbacks. That's why I used the override method in the previous example.

and

Applies styles only when all of the conditions in a series of two or more are met.

```
@supports (border-radius: 10em) and (shape-outside: circle()) {
  /* styles that apply only when the browser supports
     shape-outside AND border-radius */
}
```

or

Use the **or** operator to apply styles when any of a series of conditions are met. This one is particularly useful for vendor-prefixed properties.

```
@supports (-webkit-transform: rotate(10deg)) or
          (-ms-transform: rotate(10deg)) or
          (transform: rotate(10deg))
  /* transform styles */
}
```

Browser support

Feature queries began working in Chrome, Firefox, and Opera back in 2013, and they are supported by every version of Microsoft Edge. Safari added support in version 9 in 2015. Unfortunately, no version of Internet Explorer supports feature queries, which leaves a big hole in the support picture until those old browsers go away.

Non-supporting browsers use your fallback design, so make sure that it is usable at the very least. Beware, however, of browsers that do not support **@supports** but may support newer CSS features that you might be inclined to test. Flexbox is a great example. Safari 8 recognizes the Flexbox properties, but does not recognize **@supports**, so if all of your Flexbox layout rules are tucked away inside a feature query, Safari 8 won't see them. That's why feature queries aren't the best tool for detecting Flexbox or any property that has better support than **@supports** itself. Grid Layout, on the other hand, is a great place to put feature queries to work because every browser that supports **display: grid** also supports **@supports**. Again, *CanIUse.com* is a good resource for comparing support.

Pros and cons

Feature queries are an exciting new tool for web development. They allow us to take advantage of new CSS properties sooner in a way that doesn't rely on JavaScript (we'll look at Modernizr, a JavaScript solution, next). Downloading and running a script (even a small one) is slower than using CSS alone.

On the downside, limited browser support (for now) means **@supports** is not as far-reaching as Modernizr. However, if it accomplishes your goals, it should be your first choice. Fortunately, the browser environment will only continue to improve, giving CSS feature queries the advantage over a script-based solution in the long run.

So what is this "Modernizr" you're hearing so much about?

Modernizr

Modernizr is a lightweight JavaScript library that runs behind the scenes and tests for a long list of HTML5 and CSS3 features when the page is loaded in

---

■ **AUTHORING TIP**

Not every new feature needs a feature query. Some features, such as **border-radius**, simply don't render on non-supporting browsers, and that is just fine.

---

the browser. For each feature it tests, it stores the result (supports/doesn't support) in a JavaScript object that can be accessed with scripts and optionally as a class name in the `html` root element that can be used in CSS selectors. I'm going to focus on the latter CSS method.

How it works

When Modernizr runs, it appends the `html` element with a class name for each feature it detects. For example, if it is configured to test for Flexbox, when it runs on a browser that *does* support Flexbox, it adds the `.flexbox` class name to the `html` element:

```
<html class="js flexbox">
```

If the feature is not supported, it adds the feature name with a `.no-` prefix. On a non-supporting browser, the Flexbox test would be reported like this:

```
<html class="js no-flexbox">
```

With the class name in place on the root element, everything on the page becomes part of that class. We can use the class name as part of a selector to provide different sets of styles depending on feature support:

```
.flexbox nav {
  /* flexbox styles for the nav element here */
}

.no-flexbox nav {
  /* fallback styles for the nav element here */
}
```

This example is short and sweet for demonstration purposes. Typically, you'll use Modernizr to test for many features, and the `html` tag gets filled with a long list of class names.

How to use it

First, you need to download the *Modernizr.js* script. Go to *Modernizr.com* and find the Download link. From there you can customize the script to contain just the HTML and CSS features you want to test, a nice way to keep the file size of the script down. Click the Build button, and you will be given several options for how it can be saved. A simple click on Download saves the script in a *.js* file on your computer.

Once you have your script, put it in the directory with the rest of the files for your project. Add it to the `head` of your HTML document, before any linked style sheets or other scripts that need to use it:

```
<head>
  <script src="modernizr-custom.js"></script>
  <!--other scripts and style sheets -->
</head>
```

> Modernizr is a lightweight JavaScript library that tests for a variety of HTML and CSS features.

Finally, open your HTML document and assign the **no-js** class name to the **html** element.

```
<html class="no-js">
```

Modernizr will change it to **js** once it detects that the browser supports JavaScript. If JavaScript (and therefore Modernizr) fails to run, you will not know whether or not features are supported.

Pros and cons

Modernizr is one of the most popular tools in web developers' arsenals because it allows us to design for particular features rather than whole browsers. It is easy to use, and the Modernizr site has thorough and clear documentation to help you along. Because it's JavaScript, it works on the vast majority of browsers. The flip side to that, however, is that because it relies on JavaScript, you can't be 100% certain that it will run, which is its main disadvantage. It will also be slightly slower than using CSS alone for feature detection.

WRAPPING UP STYLE SHEETS

That concludes our whirlwind tour of Cascading Style Sheets. You've come a long way since styling an **h1** and a **p** back in **Chapter 11, Introducing Cascading Style Sheets**. By now, you should be comfortable formatting text and even doing basic page layout. While CSS is easy to learn, it takes a lot of time and practice to master. If you get stuck, you will find that there are many resources online to help you find the answers you need. The nice thing about CSS is that you can start with just the basics and then build on that knowledge as you gain proficiency in your web development skills.

In the next chapter, I'll introduce you to tools that web developers use to improve their workflow, including tools for writing CSS more efficiently and optimizing the results. But if you're feeling overwhelmed with CSS properties, you can breathe a sigh of relief. We're *done*!

TEST YOURSELF

See how well you picked up the CSS techniques in this chapter with these questions. As you may have guessed, the answers are available in **Appendix A**.

1. What is the purpose of a CSS reset?

    a. To override browser defaults

    b. To make presentation more predictable across browsers

    c. To prevent elements from inheriting unexpected styles

    d. All of the above

2. What is the purpose of a CSS sprite?

    a. To improve site performance

    b. To use small images in place of large ones, reducing file size

    c. To reduce the number of HTTP requests

    d. a and c

    e. All of the above

3. What is the purpose of an image replacement technique?

    a. To achieve really big text indents

    b. To use a decorative graphic in place of text

    c. To remove the text from the document and replace it with a decorative image

    d. To maintain the semantic content of the document

    e. b and d

    f. All of the above

4. Name two approaches to aligning form controls and their respective labels without tables. A general description will do here.

5. Match the style rules with their respective tables in FIGURE 19-10.

    a. ```
table { border-collapse: collapse;}
td { border: 2px black solid; }
```

    b. ```
table { border-collapse: separate; }
td { border: 2px black solid; }
```

    c. ```
table {
   border-collapse: separate;
   border-spacing: 2px 12px; }
td { border: 2px black solid; }
```

    d. ```
table {
   border-collapse: separate;
   border-spacing: 5px;
   border: 2px black solid; }
td { background-color: #99f; }
```

    e. ```
table {
   border-collapse: separate;
   border-spacing: 5px; }
td { background-color: #99f;
   border: 2px black solid; }
```

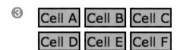

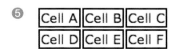

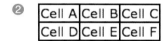

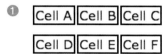

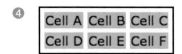

FIGURE 19-10. Match these tables with the code examples in Question 5.
```

6. Using Modernizr to test for **border-radius**, say whether the **div** will display with rounded corners based on the following generated class results:

```
.border-radius div {
  border: 1px solid green;
  border-radius: .5em;
}
```

a. `<html class="js .no-border-radius">`

b. `<html class="js .border-radius">`

c. `<html class="no-js">`

7. As of this writing, what advantage does Modernizr have over CSS feature detection? What long-term advantage will CSS feature detection have over Modernizr?

CSS REVIEW: TABLE PROPERTIES

The following is a summary of the properties covered in this chapter.

Property	Description
border-collapse	Specifies whether borders between cells are separate or collapsed
border-spacing	Denotes the space between cells set to render as separate
caption-side	Specifies the position of a table caption relative to the table (top or bottom)
empty-cells	Specifies whether borders and backgrounds should render for empty cells
table-layout	Specifies how table widths are calculated

MODERN WEB DEVELOPMENT TOOLS

In the exercises in this book, you've been writing static HTML pages with embedded style sheets, saving them, and opening them in your browser. Although that is a perfectly valid approach, it is likely not the way you would work if you were doing web development for a living. I figure if you are learning web design and development, you should be familiar with how things are done in a professional environment.

This chapter introduces you to some of the tools used by web developers to make their work easier and their code more robust:

- CSS processors for writing CSS more efficiently and optimizing the resulting code so it works across all browsers

- Build tools that automate the sorts of repetitive tasks you encounter when producing code

- Git, a version control program that keeps track of your previous versions and makes it easy for teams to work together on the same code

What these advanced tools have in common is that they are generally used with a command-line interface (CLI). So, before we look at specific tools, let's first get up to speed with the command line.

GETTING COZY WITH THE COMMAND LINE

You probably use a computer with a graphical user Interface (GUI), with icons that stand for files and folders, pull-down menus full of options, and intuitive actions like dragging files from folder to folder or into the trash.

Computer users in the '60s and '70s didn't have that luxury. The only way to get a computer to perform a task was to type in a command. Despite our fancy GUIs, typing commands into a command-line terminal is far from obsolete. In fact, the more experienced you become at web development, the more likely it is you'll dip into the command line for certain tasks. If you are already a programmer, the command line will be nothing new.

The command line is still popular for a number of reasons. First, it is useful for accessing remote computers, and developers often need to access and manage files on remote web servers. In addition, it is easier to write a program for the command line than a standalone application with a GUI, so many of the best tools for optimizing our workflow exist as command-line programs only. A lot of those tools can be used together in a pipeline for accomplishing complex tasks.

The time- and sanity-saving benefits are powerful incentives to take on the command line. Trust me: if you can learn all those elements and style properties, you can get used to typing a few commands.

The Command-Line Terminal

The program that interprets the commands you type is called a shell (visual interfaces are also technically a shell; they're just fancier). Every Mac and Linux machine comes installed with Terminal, which uses a shell program called bash. On macOS, you will find the Terminal program in **Applications →** **Utilities** (FIGURE 20-1).

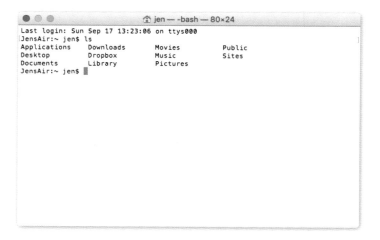

FIGURE 20-1. The Terminal window in macOS.

Windows users have a few more hoops to jump through to get set up. The default command-line tool on Windows is Command Prompt (most easily accessed with Search), which can perform many of the functions you may want to do as a developer; however, it does not use bash. Because so many tools use bash, it is better to install a bash-based shell emulator like

Cygwin (*cygwin.com*) or cmder (*cmder.net*). If you use Windows 10, it is recommended that you install a Linux environment on your machine by using Windows Subsystem (*msdn.microsoft.com/en-us/commandline/wsl/about*) or Ubuntu, available in the Windows store (*www.microsoft.com/en-us/store/p/ ubuntu/9nblggh4msv6*).

Getting Started with Commands

When you launch a Terminal window, the first thing you see is a command-line prompt, which is a string of characters that indicates the computer is ready to receive your command:

```
$: _
```

The dollar sign is common, but you may see another symbol in your terminal program (see **Terminal Tip**). The underscore in this example stands for the cursor position, which may appear as a little rectangle or a flashing line.

The complete prompt that I see in Terminal begins with my computer's name ("JensAir") and an indication of the working directory—that is, the directory the shell is currently looking at. In GUI terms, the working directory is the folder you are "in." In this example, the tilde (~) indicates that I am looking at my root User directory. The "jen" before the prompt character is my username. In future examples, I will abbreviate the prompt to simply **$:**.

```
JensAir:~ jen$: _
```

When you see the prompt, type in a command, and hit Enter. The computer executes the command and gives you a new prompt when it is finished. It is very no-nonsense about it. For some commands, there may be feedback or information displayed before the next prompt appears. Sometimes everything happens behind the scenes, and all you see is a fresh prompt.

When you're learning about the command line, it is common to start with the built-in commands for navigating the file system, tasks typically handled by the Finder on the Mac and My Computer on Windows. Because they are fairly intuitive, that's where I'm going to start my simple command-line lesson as well.

A nice little utility to try as a beginner is **pwd** (for "print working directory"), which displays the complete path of the working (current) directory. To use it, simply type **pwd** after the prompt. It's a good one to try first because you can't break anything with it, but for seasoned users, it is useful for figuring out exactly where you've landed if you're disoriented. The forward slash indicates that this path starts at the root directory for the entire computer.

```
$: pwd
/Users/jen
```

Here's another easy (and low-risk!) example. Typing the **ls** command at the prompt returns a list of the files and directories in the working directory

NOTE

Your user directory is the default root directory in Terminal and is represented by a tilde (~) in the prompt, as we saw in the previous example.

(*/Users/jen*). You can compare it to the Finder view of the same folder in FIGURE 20-2. They are two ways of looking at the same thing, just as *directory* and *folder* are two terms for the same thing depending on your view.

```
JensAir:~ jen$ ls
Applications    Downloads    Movies      Public
Desktop         Dropbox      Music       Sites
Documents       Library      Pictures
JensAir:~ jen$
```

FIGURE 20-2. Finder view of the *jen* home folder.

Some utilities, like **pwd**, require only their name at the prompt to run, but it is more common that you'll need to provide additional information in the form of flags and arguments. A flag changes how the utility operates, like an option or a preference. It follows the command name and is indicated by a single or double dash (-). In many cases, flags can be abbreviated to just their first letter because they are used in context with a particular utility. For example, I can modify the **ls** utility with the **-l** flag, which instructs the computer to display my directory contents in "long" format, including permission settings and creation dates:

```
JensAir:~ jen$ ls -l
total 0
drwxr-xr-x     5 jen   staff    170 Jul  8  2016 Applications
drwx------    57 jen   staff   1938 Sep 11 09:47 Desktop
drwx------    26 jen   staff    884 May 18 11:34 Documents
drwx------+  151 jen   staff   5134 Sep  3 15:47 Downloads
drwx------@   48 jen   staff   1632 Aug 16 16:34 Dropbox
drwx------@   72 jen   staff   2448 Jul 15 11:21 Library
drwx------    22 jen   staff    748 Oct  6  2016 Movies
drwx------    12 jen   staff    408 Sep 29  2016 Music
drwx------    14 jen   staff    476 Oct 13  2016 Pictures
drwxr-xr-x     6 jen   staff    204 May  6  2015 Public
drwxr-xr-x    11 jen   staff    374 Jul 10  2016 Sites
JensAir:~ jen$
```

An argument provides the specific information required for a particular function. For example, if I want to change to another directory, I type **cd** (for "change directory") as well as the name of the directory I want to go to (see **Mac Terminal Tip**). To make my Dropbox directory the new working directory, I type this:

```
JensAir:~ jen$: cd Dropbox
```

After I hit Enter, my prompt changes to **JensAir:Dropbox jen$**, indicating that I am now in the Dropbox directory. If I entered **ls** now, I'd get a list of the files and folders contained in the Dropbox folder (definitely way too long to show here).

To go up a level, and get back to my home user directory (~), I can use the Unix shorthand for "go up a level": **..** (remember that from your URL path lesson?). The returned prompt shows I'm back at my root directory (~).

```
JensAir:Dropbox jen$ cd ..
JensAir:~ jen$
```

Some other useful file-manipulation commands include **mv** (moves files and folders), **cp** (copies files), and **mkdir** (creates a new empty directory). The **rm** command removes a file or folder in the working directory. Be careful with this command, however, because it doesn't just move files to the Trash; it removes them from your computer entirely (see the **"A Word of Caution"** note).

Another handy command is **man** (short for *manual*), which displays documentation for any command you pass to it. For example, **man ls** shows a description of the **ls** (list) command and all of its available flags. Some man pages are long. To move down in the scroll, hitting the Return key moves you down one line at a time. To move down a page at a time, hit fn+down arrow on a Mac or Shift+Page Down on Linux. To go back up a page, it's fn+up arrow or Shift+Page Up, respectively. Finally, to quit out of the man page, type **q** to return to the prompt.

Learning More

Not surprisingly, these commands are just the tip of the tip of the iceberg when it comes to command-line utilities. For a complete list of commands that can be used with bash, see "An A–Z Index of the Bash Command Line for Linux" at *ss64.com/bash/*. You'll pick these up on an as-needed basis, so don't get overwhelmed. In addition, as you start installing and using new tools like the ones listed in this chapter, you'll gradually learn the commands, flags, and arguments for those too. All part of a day's work!

Clearly, I don't have the space (and if I'm being honest, the experience) to write a comprehensive tutorial on the command line in this chapter, but you will find books and plenty of tutorials online that can teach you. I found Michael Hartl's tutorial "Learn Enough Command Line to Be Dangerous"

■ MAC TERMINAL TIP

On the Mac, Terminal is well connected to Finder. If you need to enter a pathname to a directory or a file, you can drag the icon for that file or folder from Finder to Terminal, and it will fill in the pathname for you.

■ COMMAND-LINE TIP

Typing **cd** followed by a space always takes you back to your home directory.

A WORD OF CAUTION

The command line allows you to muck around in critical parts of your computer that your GUI graciously protects from you. It's best not to type in a command if you don't know exactly what it does and how it works. Make a complete backup of your computer before you start playing around with command line so you have the peace of mind that your files are still available if something goes horribly wrong.

Here's the Thing About Development Tools

Be aware that the development tool landscape is ever-shifting. Tools come and go in rapid-fire fashion, with the whole development community jumping on one framework bandwagon, then moving on to the next new thing. It's difficult to write about specific tools in a book that has to last a couple of years. I have made an effort to present the most established and stable tools as of early 2018, but you should know that there are many more niche tools out there, and by the time you read this, some new tool may be all the rage. As you read this chapter, focus on the functions the tools perform, start with the ones mentioned here when you're ready, and keep your ear to the ground for newer options.

NOTE

Hat tips to Stefan Baumgartner, whose article "Deconfusing Pre- and Post-Processing" (medium.com/@ddprrt/ deconfusing-pre-and-post-processing-d68e3bd078a3) helped me sort out all this CSS processing stuff, and David Clark for his clarifying article "It's Time for Everyone to Learn About PostCSS" (davidtheclark.com/its-time-for-every-one-to-learn-about-postcss/).

to be thorough and accessible if you are starting from square one (*www.learnenough.com/command-line-tutorial#sec-basics*). I also recommend the series of tutorials from Envato Tuts+, "The Command Line for Web Design" (*webdesign.tutsplus.com/series/the-command-line-for-web-design--cms-777*). If you enjoy video tutorials, try the "Command Line for Non-Techies" course by Remy Sharp (*terminal.training*).

Now that you have a basic familiarity with the command line, let's look at tools you might use it for, beginning with tools for writing and optimizing CSS.

CSS POWER TOOLS (PROCESSORS)

I know that you are just getting used to writing CSS, but I would be negligent if I didn't introduce you to some advanced CSS power tools that have become central to the professional web developer workflow. They fall into two general categories:

- Languages built on top of CSS that employ time-saving syntax characteristics of traditional programming languages. These are traditionally known as preprocessors. The most popular preprocessors as of this writing are Sass, LESS, and Stylus. When you write your styles in one of these languages, you have to use a program or script to convert the resulting file into a standard CSS document that browsers can understand.

- CSS optimization tools take your clean, standard CSS and make it even better by improving cross-browser consistency, reducing file size for better performance, and enhancing many other tasks. Tools that optimize browser-ready CSS are commonly known as postprocessors.

Before you get too comfortable with the terms *preprocessor* and *postprocessor*, you should know that the distinction is not exactly clear-cut. Preprocessors have always been able to do some of the optimization tasks that postprocessors are good for, and postprocessors are starting to allow some functions typically found in preprocessors. The lines are blurring, so some folks refer to all of these tools simply as CSS processors, including souped-up special syntaxes for authoring as well as CSS optimizers. Many CSS processor functions are also built in to third-party tools such as CodeKit (*codekitapp.com*, *Mac only*) for one-stop shopping. I think it is beneficial for you to be familiar with the traditional terms as they are still in widespread use, and I'm going to use them here for the sake of simplicity.

Introduction to Preprocessors (Especially Sass)

Preprocessors consist of an authoring syntax and a program that translates (or compiles, to use the proper term) files written in that syntax to plain old CSS files that browsers can use (FIGURE 20-3). For example, in Sass, you write in the Sass syntax language and save your files with the *.scss* suffix, indicating it is in that language and not a CSS file. The Sass program, originally written in the Ruby language (see **Technical Note**), converts the SCSS syntax to standard CSS syntax and saves the resulting file with the *.css* suffix. LESS and Stylus work the same way, but they use JavaScript for conversion. All of these tools are installed and run via the command line.

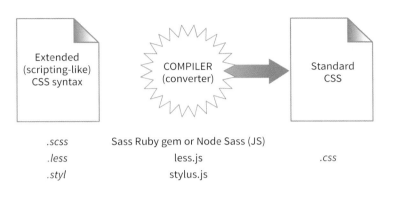

.scss   Sass Ruby gem or Node Sass (JS)
.less   less.js   .css
.styl   stylus.js

FIGURE 20-3. A simplified view of the role of a preprocessor.

By far, the most popular preprocessor is Sass ("Syntactically awesome style sheets"), created by Hampton Catlin and Nathan Weizenbaum, who were tired of the repetitiveness of normal CSS. Their new syntax allowed CSS authors to use the type of shortcuts typical in scripting. Originally, it used an indented, bracket-free syntax (which is still an option), but a later release known as SCSS (for "Sassy CSS") is based on the bracketed ({ }) CSS format we know and love. In fact, a valid CSS document would also be a valid SCSS document. This makes it much easier to get started with Sass, because it is familiar, and you can use just a little bit of Sass in style sheets written the way you've learned in this book.

I'm going to show you a few examples of Sass syntax to give you the general idea. When you are ready to take on learning Sass, a great first step is Dan Cederholm's book *Sass for Web Designers* (A Book Apart). I've listed additional resources at the end of the section. In the meantime, let's look at three of the most popular Sass features: nesting, variables, and mixins.

Nesting

Let's say you have an HTML document with a **nav** element that contains an unordered list for several menu options. Sass lets you nest the style rules for the **nav**, **ul**, and **li** elements to reflect the structure of the HTML markup. That alleviates the need to type out the selectors multiple times—the Sass compiler does that for you. The following example shows nested styles as they can be written in Sass syntax:

■ TECHNICAL NOTE

The Sass project wrote a newer version in C++ that can be used with other languages. Most developers now compile *.scss* files with Node Sass because it integrates more smoothly into a workflow with other Node.js tools.

Sass lets you nest styles to match the structure of the markup.

```
nav {
  margin: 1em 2em;

  ul {
    list-style: none;
    padding: 0;
    margin: 0;

    li {
      display: block;
      width: 6em;
      height: 2em;
    }
  }
}
```

When Sass converts the SCSS file to standard CSS, it compiles to this:

```
nav {
  margin: 1em 2em;
}

nav ul {
  list-style: none;
  padding: 0;
  margin: 0;
}

nav ul li {
  display: block;
  width: 6em;
  height: 2em;
}
```

Variables

A variable is a value you can define once, and then use multiple times throughout the style sheet. For example, O'Reilly uses the same shade of red repeatedly on its site, so their developers could create a variable named "oreilly-red" and use the variable name for color values. That way, if they needed to tweak the shade later, they need to change the variable value (the actual RGB color) only in one place. Here's what setting up and using a variable looks like in Sass:

```
$oreilly-red: #900;

a {
  border-color: $oreilly-red;
}
```

When it compiles to standard CSS, the variable value is plugged into the place where it is called:

```
a {
  border-color: #900;
}
```

The advantage of using a variable is that you can change the value in one place instead of searching and replacing through the whole document. When teams use variable names, it also helps keep styles consistent across the site.

> A variable is a value that you define once and reuse throughout the style sheet.

Mixins

Sass allows you to reuse whole sets of styles by using a convention called mixins. The following example saves a combination of background, color, and border styles as a mixin named "special." To apply that combination of styles, **@include** it in the declaration and call it by name:

```
@mixin special {
  color: #fff;
  background-color: #befc6d;
  border: 1px dotted #59950c;
}
a.nav {
  @include special;
}
a.nav: hover {
  @include special;
  border: 1px yellow solid;
}
```

When compiled, the final CSS looks like this:

```
a.nav {
  color: #fff;
  background-color: #befc6d;
  border: 1px dotted #59950c;
}
a.nav: hover {
  color: #fff;
  background-color: #befc6d;
  border: 1px dotted #59950c;
  border: 1px yellow solid;
}
```

Notice that the hover state has a second border declaration that overrides the values in the mixin, and that's just fine. Mixins are a popular solution for dealing with vendor prefixes. Here is a mixin for **border-radius** that includes an argument (a placeholder for a value you provide indicated with a **$**):

```
@mixin rounded($radius) {
  -webkit-border-radius: $radius;
    -moz-border-radius: $radius;
        border-radius: $radius;
}
```

When including the mixin in a style rule, provide the value for **$radius**, and it gets plugged into each instance in the declarations:

```
aside {
  @include rounded(.5em);
  background: #f2f5d5;
}
```

This compiles to the following:

```
aside {
  -webkit-border-radius: .5em;
    -moz-border-radius: .5em;
        border-radius: .5em;
  background: #f2f5d5;
}
```

Mixins are sets of rules
that can be reused.

LESS and Stylus

Sass is the most widely used preprocessor, but it's not the only game in town for nesting, variables, mixins, and more.

LESS (*lesscss.org*) is another CSS extension with scripting-like abilities. It is very similar to Sass, but it lacks advanced programming logic features (such as **if**/**else** statements) and has minor differences in syntax. For example, variables in LESS are indicated by the **@** symbol instead of **$**. The other major difference is that a LESS file is processed into regular CSS with JavaScript (*less.js*) instead of Ruby. Note that compiling a LESS file into CSS is processor-intensive and would bog down a browser. For that reason, it is best to do the conversion to CSS before sending it to the server. LESS offers a very active developer community and the "LESShat" mixin library.

Stylus (*stylus-lang.com*) is the relative new kid on the preprocessor block. It combines the logic features of Sass with the convenience of a JavaScript-based compiler (*stylus.js*). It also offers the most flexible syntax: you can include as much CSS "punctuation" (brackets, colons, and semicolons) as you like, prepend variables with a **$** or not, and treat mixin names like regular properties. Developers who use Stylus like how easy it is to write and compile. Nib and Axis are two mixin libraries available for Stylus.

When you are ready to take your CSS authoring to the next level, you can give each of these a try. The one you choose is a matter of personal preference; however, if you are working on a professional development team, one may be chosen for you.

Building a mixin around fill-in-the-blank arguments makes them reusable and even shareable. Many developers create their own mixin libraries to use on multiple projects. You can also take advantage of existing mixin libraries in tools like Compass (an open source CSS authoring framework at *compass-style.org*) or Bourbon (*bourbon.io*). By the time you read this, there may be others, so search around to see what's available.

Sass resources

Nesting, variables, and mixins are only a tiny fraction of what Sass can do. It can handle math operations, "darken" and "lighten" colors mathematically on the fly, and process **if**/**else** statements, just to name a few features.

Once you get some practice under your belt and feel that you are ready to take your style sheets to the next level, explore some of these Sass and LESS articles and resources:

- The Sass site (*sass-lang.com*)

- "Getting Started with Sass," by David Demaree (*alistapart.com/articles/getting-started-with-sass*)

- "An Introduction to LESS, and LESS Vs. Sass," by Jeremy Hixon (*www.smashingmagazine.com/2011/09/an-introduction-to-less-and-comparison-to-sass/*)

Introduction to Postprocessors (Mostly PostCSS)

As I mentioned earlier, postprocessors are scripts that optimize standard CSS code to make it better (FIGURE 20-4). "Better" usually means consistent and bug-free browser support, but there are hundreds of postprocessing scripts that do a wide variety of cool things. We'll look at some examples in a moment.

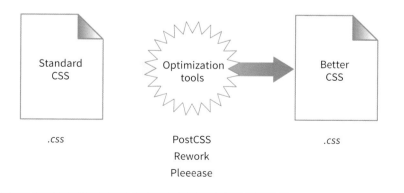

FIGURE 20-4. Postprocessors optimize existing, standard CSS files.

The poster child for postprocessing is Autoprefixer, which takes the CSS styles you write, scans them for properties that require vendor prefixes, and then inserts the prefixed properties automatically. What a time- and headache-saver!

Back in **Chapter 16, CSS Layout with Flexbox and Grid**, we used Autoprefixer via a web page interface (*autoprefixer.github.io*) to generate the required prefixes. Although the web page is handy (especially while you are learning), it is more common for postprocessors to be implemented with a task runner such as Grunt or Gulp. We'll take a quick look at them later in this chapter.

As of this writing, the postprocessing scene is dominated by PostCSS (*postcss.org*). PostCSS is "a tool for transforming CSS with JavaScript" created by Andrey Sitnik, who also created Autoprefixer. PostCSS is both a JavaScript-based program (a Node.js module, to be precise) and an ecosystem of community-created plug-ins that solve all sorts of CSS problems.

PostCSS parses the CSS (or a CSS-like syntax such as Sass or LESS), analyzes its structure, and makes the resulting "tree" available for plug-ins to manipulate the code (see **Note**).

This open API makes it easy for anyone to create a PostCSS plug-in, and as a result, there are literally hundreds of plug-ins created and shared by developers (see them at *www.postcss.parts*). They range from the life-saving to the esoteric, but because it is a modular system, you can pick and choose just the tools that you find useful or even create your own. Here are just a few:

> **NOTE**
>
> *The "tree" is formally known as the Abstract Syntax Tree (AST) and is the API for PostCSS plug-ins.*

- Stylelint (*stylelint.io*) checks your CSS file for syntax errors (a process called linting) and redundancies.

- CSSNext (*cssnext.io*) allows you to use future CSS Level 4 features today by generating fallbacks that work across browsers that haven't implemented those features yet.

- PreCSS (*github.com/jonathantneal/precss*) is a bundle of plug-ins that lets you write Sass-like syntax (loops, conditionals, variables, mixins, and so on) and converts it to standard CSS. This is an example of a postprocessor being used to aid authoring, which is where the line between pre- and postprocessing gets blurred.

- Fixie (*github.com/tivac/fixie*) inserts hacks that are required to make effects work in old versions of Internet Explorer ("Fix-IE," get it?).

- Color format converters translate alternative color formats (such as HWB, HCL, and hex + alpha channel) to standard RGB or hexadecimal.

- The Pixrem plug-in converts rem units to pixels for non-supporting browsers.

- The List-selectors plug-in lists and categorizes the selectors you've used in your style sheet for code review. It is an example of a plug-in that does not alter your file but gives you useful information about it.

NOTE

PostCSS is not the only postprocessor out there. Other frameworks include Rework (github.com/reworkcss/rework) and Pleeease (pleeease.io), but they are not as full featured. By the time you read this, there may be many more. So goes the world of web development tools.

From that short list, you can probably see why postprocessors have become so popular. They free you up to write CSS with the syntax you want, taking advantage of cutting-edge properties and values, but with the peace of mind that everything will work well across browsers. They also eliminate the need to know about every browser idiosyncrasy, past and present, in order to do your job. It's definitely worth knowing about even if you aren't quite ready to take it on right away. Check out these resources for more information:

- Drew Minns' article "PostCSS: A Comprehensive Introduction" for *Smashing Magazine* (*www.smashingmagazine.com/2015/12/introduction-to-postcss/*)

- The Envato Tuts+ tutorial "PostCSS Deep Dive" (*webdesign.tutsplus.com/series/postcss-deep-dive--cms-889*)

BUILD TOOLS (GRUNT AND GULP)

In the world of software, a build process is required to test source code and compile it into a piece of executable software. As websites evolved from a collection of static HTML files to complex JavaScript-reliant applications, often generated from templates, build tools have become integral to the web development workflow as well. Some web build tools like Grunt and Gulp are commonly referred to as task runners. You use them to define and run various tasks (anything you might do manually from the command line) on your working HTML, JavaScript, CSS, and image files to get them ready to publish.

Automation

You can automate your tasks, too, so they happen in the background without your needing to type commands. To do this, you tell the build tool to "watch" your files and folders for changes. When a change is detected, it triggers the relevant tasks to run automatically as you've configured them.

Once you have the task runner configured and set to watch your files, you can go about your business writing CSS, and all that command-line stuff happens for you without ever touching a terminal appplication. Here's how that might look. Imagine making a change to your Sass file and saving it. Grunt instantly sees that the *.scss* file has changed, automatically converts it to *.css* (see **Note**), and then reloads the browser to reflect your change.

NOTE

There is a Grunt plug-in for converting SCSS files, but it is not as full featured as Ruby.

Some Common Tasks

The previous section on CSS processors should have given you an idea of some things that would be nice to automate. Allow me to list several more to give you a solid view of the ways task runners make your job easier.

- Concatenation. It is common for web teams to divide style sheets and scripts into small, specialized chunks of *.css* and *.js*. When it's time to publish, however, you want as few calls to the server as possible for performance purposes, so those little chunks get concatenated (put together) into master files.

- Compression and "minification." Another way to improve performance is to make your files as small as possible by removing unnecessary spaces and line returns. Build tools can compress your CSS and minify JavaScript.

- Checking your HTML, CSS, and JavaScript for errors (linting).

- Optimizing images with tools that squeeze down the file size of all the images in a directory.

- Help committing or pushing changes to a version control repository (Git).

- Refreshing your browser to reflect whatever changes you just made to a file (LiveReload plug-in).

- Building final HTML files from templates and content data (see the sidebar **"Building Sites with Data and Templates"**).

- Running CSS pre- and postprocessors.

Grunt and Gulp

The first and most established web build tool is Grunt (*gruntjs.com*), presumably named for handling all of the "grunt work" for you. It is a JavaScript tool built on the open source Node.js framework, and you operate it using the command line. The compelling thing about Grunt is that the development community has created literally thousands of plug-ins that perform just about any task you can think of. Just download one, configure it, and start using it. You do not have to be a JavaScript master to get started.

Another popular option is Gulp (*gulpjs.com*), which has the advantage of running a little faster but also requires more technical knowledge than Grunt because you configure it with actual JS code. Other contenders as of this writing are Webpack (quite popular!), Brunch, Browserify, and Broccoli. New tools with amusing names pop up on a regular basis. Some developers simply use Node.js-based scripts without using a task-runner program as a go-between. The point is, there are plenty of options.

You will find many online tutorials for learning how to download and configure the build tool of your choice when you are ready to automate your workflow. I hope that I have made you aware of the possibilities, and when a job interviewer mentions Grunt and Gulp, you'll know they aren't just suffering from indigestion.

Building Sites with Data and Templates

Throughout this book, we've been writing the HTML for our pages manually, wrapping tags around content elements in a logical source order. All of the content for the page is contained right there in the *.html* document. Of course, it is completely acceptable to build whole sites out of static web pages such as these, but in the real world—where sites might have thousands of pages with content tailored to individual users—a more robust solution is required.

It is more common these days to use a template system or framework to generate web pages from content stored as data. The templates use regular HTML markup, so everything you've learned so far will serve you well, but instead of specific content between the tags, special data markers are placed to pull in content from a database or data file.

There are a vast number of tool options for site generation, all of which are well beyond the scope of this book. However, as usual, I'd like to give you a taste of what the templating process might look like.

I once worked on a site that used a template tool called Handlebars (*handlebarsjs.com*) to pull content in from data files written in the YAML (*www.yaml.org/start.html*) language. These are just two options for doing this sort of thing. Let's look at a small example of how a template and data were used to assemble the web content shown in FIGURE 20-5.

FIGURE 20-5. A small portion of a speaker web page that was created with Handlebars and YAML.

Here is a small snippet of the data as it appears in the YAML (*.yml*) file:

```
speaker--name: "Jennifer Robbins"
speaker--description: "Designer, Author, ARTIFACT
Co-founder"
speaker--photo: "/img/speakers/jennifer-robbins.
jpg"
#HTML
speaker--biography: |
  <p>Jennifer has been designing for the web since
1993 when she worked on the first commercial web
site, GNN, from O'Reilly Media. Since then she has
```

gone on to write several books on web design for O'Reilly, including `<i>`Web Design in a Nutshell `</i>`, `<i>`Learning Web Design`</i>`, and the `<i>`HTML5 Pocket Reference`</i>`. More recently, Jennifer's days are filled with organizing the ARTIFACT Conference. …`</p>`

```
speaker--links:
  - link--label: "Website"
    link--target: "http://www.jenville.com"
    link--title: "jenville.com"
  - link--label: "Twitter"
    link--target: "http://www.twitter.com/jenville"
    link--title: "@jenville"
```

And here is the markup from the Handlebars template document, *speakers.hbs*. (I've edited it slightly for brevity.) If you look at the highlighted code, you see that instead of actual content, there are the same data labels used in the YAML file between curly brackets. (If you turn a curly bracket on its side, it looks like a handlebar mustache, thus the name!). Notice also that the template has markup for one label/link pair, but it loops through and displays all the **speaker--links** in the data file:

```
<div class="layout--container">
<div class="speaker--photo-container">
  <img src="{{page-data.speaker--photo}}">
</div>
<article class="speaker--content">
  <div class="speaker--biography">
    {{{page-data.speaker--biography}}}
  </div>
  <ul class="speaker--links">
    {{#each page-data.speaker--links}}
    <li class="speaker--link-item">{{link--label}}:
<a href="http://{{link--target}}" class="speaker--
link">{{link--title}}</a></li>
    {{/each}}
  </ul>
</article>
</div
```

This is just one example of how templates cut down on redundancy in markup. The Handlebars site (*handlebarsjs.com*) has a nice description of semantic templates right on the home page if you'd like more information on how it works.

Of course, browsers have no idea what to do with these file formats, so before the site can be published, it needs to be built or assembled, merging all the data into the template modules and all the modules into whole web pages. That is the job of scripts and build tools like the ones introduced in this section. Hopefully, this brief example gives you an inkling of how generated sites work.

VERSION CONTROL WITH GIT AND GITHUB

If you've done any sort of work on a computer, you've probably used some sort of system for keeping track of the versions of your work. You might have come up with a system of naming drafts until you get to the "final" version (and the "final-final" version, and the "final-final-no-really" version, and so on). You might take advantage of macOS's Time Machine to save versions that you can go back to in an emergency. Or you might have used one of the professional version control systems that have been employed by teams for decades.

The king of version control systems (VCS) for web development is a robust program called Git (*git-scm.com*). At this point, knowing your way around Git is a requirement if you are working on a team and is a good skill to have even for your own projects.

In this section, I'll introduce you to the terminology and mental models that will make it easier to get started with Git. Teaching all the ins and outs of how to configure and use Git from the command line is a job for another book and online tutorials (I list a few at the end of the section), but I wish someone had explained the difference between a "branch" and a "fork" to me when I was starting out, so that's what I'll do for you.

We'll begin with a basic distinction: Git is the version control program that you run on your computer; GitHub (*github.com*) is a service that hosts Git projects, either free or for a fee. You interact with GitHub by using Git, either from the command line, with the user interface on the GitHub website, or using a standalone application that offers a GUI interface for Git commands. This was not obvious to me at first, and I want it to be clear to you from the get-go.

GitHub and services like it (see **Note**) are mainly web-based wrappers around Git, offering features like issue tracking, a code review tool, and a web UI for browsing files and history. They are convenient, but keep in mind that you can also set up Git on your own server and share it with your team members with no third-party service like GitHub involved at all.

Why Use Git

There are several advantages to making Git (and GitHub) part of your work-flow. First, you can easily roll back to an earlier version of your project if problems show up down the line. Because every change you make is logged and described, it helps you determine at which point things might have gone wrong.

Git also makes it easy to collaborate on a shared code source. You may tightly collaborate with one or more developers on a private project, merging all of

> ■ **FUN FACT**
>
> Git was created by Linus Torvalds, the creator of the Linux operating system, when he needed a way to allow an enormous community to contribute to the Linux project.

NOTE

Beanstalk (beanstalkapp.com), GitLab (gitlab.com), and Bitbucket (bitbucket.org) are other Git hosting services aimed at enterprise-scale projects. GitLab has a free option for public projects, similar to GitHub, and because it is open source, you can host it yourself.

your changes into a primary copy. As an added benefit, the sharing process is a way to get an extra set of eyes on your work before it is incorporated. You may also encourage loose collaboration on a public project by welcoming contributions of people you don't even know in a way that is safe and managed. Git is a favorite tool for this type of collaboration on all sorts of open source projects.

Getting up to speed with GitHub in particular is important because it's what everyone is using. If your project is public (accessible to anyone), the hosting is free. For private and commercial projects, GitHub charges a fee for hosting. In addition to hosting projects, they provide collaboration tools such as issue tracking. You may have already found that some of the links to tools I mentioned in this book go to GitHub repositories. I want you to know what you can do when you get there.

How Git Works

Git keeps a copy of every revision of your files and folders as you go along, with every change (called a commit) logged in with a unique ID (generated by Git), a message (written by you) describing the change, and other metadata. All of those versions and the commit log are stored in a repository, often referred to as a "repo."

Once you have Git installed on your computer, every time you create a new repository or clone an existing one, Git adds a directory and files representing the repo's metadata alongside other files in the project's folder. Once the Git repository is initialized, you can commit changes and take advantage of the "time machine" feature if you need to get back to an earlier version. In this way, Git is a good tool for a solo workflow.

More likely you'll be working with a team of other folks on a project. In that case, a hub model is used in which there is an official repository on a central server that each team member makes a local copy of to work on. Each team member works on their own machine, committing to their local repo, and at logical intervals, uploads their work back to the central repository.

That's what makes Git a distributed version control system compared to other systems, like SVN, that require you to commit every change directly to the server. With Git, you can work locally and offline.

The first part of mastering Git is mastering its vocabulary. Let's run through some of the terminology that will come in handy when you're learning Git and the GitHub service. FIGURE 20-6 is a simplified diagram that should help you visualize how the parts fit together.

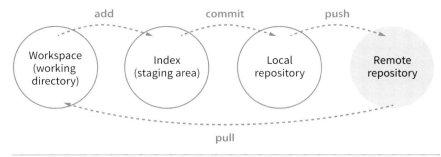

FIGURE 20-6. Visualization of Git structure.

Working directory

The working directory is the directory of files on your computer in which you do your actual work. Your working copy of a file is the one that you can make changes to, or to put it another way, it's the file you can open from the hard drive by using Finder or My Computer.

Repository

Your local Git repository lives alongside the files in your working directory. It contains copies, or snapshots, of all the files in a single project at every step in its development, although these are kept hidden. It also contains the metadata stored with each change. There may also be a central repository for the project that lives on a remote server like GitHub.

Commit

A commit is the smallest unit of Git interaction and the bulk of what you will do with Git. Git uses "commit" as a verb and a noun. You may "save" your working document frequently as you work, but you commit (v.) a change when you want to deliberately add that version to the repository. Usually you commit at a logical pause in the workflow—for example, when you've fixed a bug or finished changing a set of styles.

When you commit, Git records the state of all the project files and assigns metadata to the change, including the username, email, date and time, a unique multidigit ID number (see the **"Hashes"** sidebar), and a message that describes the change. These stored records are referred to as commits (n.). A commit is like a snapshot of your entire repository—every file it contains—at the moment in time you made the commit.

Commits are additive, so even when you delete a file, Git adds a commit to the stack. The list of commits is available for your perusal at any time. On GitHub, use the History button to see the list of commits for a file or folder.

The level of granularity in commits allows you to view the repository (project) at any state it's ever been at, ever. You *never* lose work, even as you proceed

Git Visualization Resources

Need more help picturing how all these pieces and commands work together? Try these visualization resources:

- The Git Cheatsheet from NDP Software provides a thorough interactive mapping of how various Git commands correspond to the workspace and local and remote repositories. It's worth checking out at *ndpsoftware.com/git-cheatsheet.html#loc=workspace;*.

- A Visual Git Reference (*marklodato. github.io/visual-git-guide/index-en.html*) is a collection of diagrams that demonstrate most common Git commands.

- "Understanding the GitHub Flow" (*guides.github.com/introduction/ flow/*) explains a typical workflow in GitHub.

Hashes

The unique ID that Git generates for each commit is technically called a *SHA-1 hash*, more affectionately known as simply a *hash* in the developer world. It is a 40-character string written in hexadecimal (0–9 and A–F are used), so the odds of having a duplicate hash are astronomical. It is common to use short hashes on projects instead of the full 40 characters. For example, on GitHub, short hashes are seven characters long, and you'll see them in places like a project's Commits page. Even with just seven characters, the chances of collision are tiny.

further and further. It's a great safety net. Indirectly this also means that there's nothing you can do with Git that you can't undo—you can't ever get yourself into an impossible situation.

Staging

Before you can commit a change, you first have to make Git aware of the file (or to track it, to use the proper term). This is called staging the file, accomplished by adding it to Git. In the command line, it's **git add** *filename*, but other tools may provide an Add button to stage files. This creates a local index of files that you intend to commit to your local repository but haven't been committed yet. It is worth noting that you need to "add" any file that you've changed, not just new files, before committing them. Staging as a concept may take a little while to get used to at first because it isn't especially intuitive.

Branch

A branch is a sequential series of commits, also sometimes referred to as a stack of commits. The most recent commit on any given branch is the head (see **Note**). You can also think of a branch as a thread of development. Projects usually have a primary or default branch, typically (although not necessarily) called master, which is the official version of the project. To work on a branch, you need to have it checked out.

When working in a branch, at any point you can start a new branch to do a little work without affecting the source branch. You might start a new branch to experiment with a new feature, or to do some debugging, or to play around with presentation. Branches are often used for small, specific tasks like that, but you can create a new branch for any purpose you want.

For example, if you are working on "master," but want to fix a bug, you can create a new branch off master and give the branch a new descriptive name, like "bugfix." You can think of the bugfix branch as a copy of master at the point at which bugfix was created (FIGURE 20-7), although that's not exactly what is happening under the hood.

To work on the bugfix branch, you first need to check it out (**git checkout bugfix**), and then you can go about your business of making changes, saving them, adding them to Git, and committing them. Eventually, the new branch ends up with a commit history that is different from the source branch.

NOTE

There are exceptions, as it is possible to reorder commits; however, it is almost always true that the head commit is also the most recent.

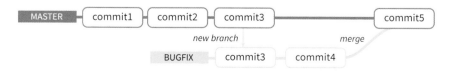

FIGURE 20-7. Creating and merging a new branch.

When you are done working on your new branch, you can merge the changes you made back into the source branch and delete the branch. If you don't like what's happening with the new branch, delete it without merging, and no one's the wiser.

Merging

Merging is Git's killer feature for sharing code. You can merge commits from one branch into another (such as all of the commits on a feature branch into master) or you might merge different versions of the same branch that are on different computers. According to the Git documentation, merging "incorporates changes from the named commits (since the time their histories diverged from the current branch) into the current branch." Put another way, Git sees merging as "joining two histories together," so it useful to think of merging happening at the commit level.

Git attempts to merge each commit, one by one, into the target branch. If only one branch has changed, the other branch can simply fast-forward to catch up with the changes. If both branches have commits that are not in the other branch—that is, if both branches have changes—Git walks through each of those commits and, on a line-by-line basis, attempts to merge the differences. Git actually changes the code inside files for you automatically so you don't have to hunt for what's changed.

However, if Git finds conflicts, such as two different changes made to the same line of code, it gives you a report of the conflicts instead of trying to change the code itself. Conflicts are pointed out in the source files between ======= and <<<<<<< characters (FIGURE 20-8). When conflicts arise, a real person needs to read through the list and manually edit the file by keeping the intended change and deleting the other. Once the conflicts are resolved, the files need to be added and committed again.

```
    docs.css
    docs.css

55    p {
56        margin-top: 0;
57        margin-bottom: 1rem;
58    }
59    .container > p {
60  ┌ <<<<<<< big-load-comin-through-container
61  │     margin: .6rem auto 1rem;
62  │     max-width: 880px;
63  ├ =======
64  │     margin: .5rem auto 1rem;
65  │     max-width: 900px;
66  └ >>>>>>> gh-pages
67    }
68
69    hr {
70        max-width: 100px;
71        margin: 3rem auto;
72        border: 0;
73        border-top: .1rem solid #eee;
74    }
```

FIGURE 20-8. GitHub conflict report.

Remotes

All of the features we've looked at so far (commits, branches, merges) can be done on your local computer, but it is far more common to use Git with one or more remote repositories. The remote repo could be on another computer within your organization, but it is likely to be hosted on a remote server like GitHub. Coordinating with a remote repository opens up a few other key Git features.

Clone

Cloning is making an exact replica of a repository and everything it contains. It's common to clone a repo from a remote server to your own computer, but it is also possible to clone to another directory locally. If you are getting started on an existing project, making a clone of project's repo is a logical first step.

Push/pull

If you are working with a remote repository, you will no doubt need to upload and download your changes to the server. The process of moving data from your local repository to a remote repository is known as pushing. When you push commits to the remote, they are automatically merged with the current version on the server. To update your local version with the version that is on the server, you pull it, which retrieves the metadata about the changes and applies the changes to your working files. You can think of pushing and pulling as the remote version of merging.

It is a best practice to pull the remote master frequently to keep your own copy up-to-date. That helps eliminate conflicts, particularly if there are a lot of other people working on the code. Many GUI Git tools provide a Sync button that pulls and pushes in one go.

> ■ **GIT TIP**
>
> Always *pull* before you *push* to avoid conflicts.

Fork

You may hear talk of "forking" a repo on GitHub. Forking makes a copy of a GitHub repository to your GitHub account so you have your own copy to play around with. Having the repo in your account is not the same as having a working copy on your computer, so once you've forked it, you need to clone (copy) it to your own computer (FIGURE 20-9).

People fork projects for all sorts of reasons (see **Note**). You might just want to have a look under the hood. You may want to iterate and turn it into something new. You may want to contribute to that project in the form of pull requests. In any scenario, forking is a safeguard for repository owners so they can make the project available to the public while also controlling what gets merged back into it.

NOTE

Forking is most often used for contributing to an open source project. For commercial or personal projects, you generally commit directly to the repository shared by your team.

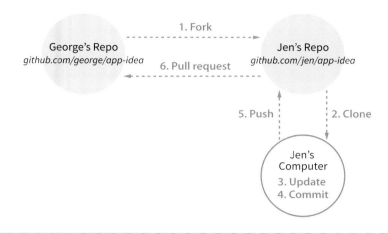

FIGURE 20-9. Once you fork a repository on GitHub, you need to clone it to get a local working copy. (Based on a diagram by Kevin Markham.)

Pull request

It is important to keep in mind that your forked copy is no longer directly connected to the original repository it was forked from. You will not be able to push to the original. If you come up with something you think is valuable to the original project, you can do what is called a pull request—that is, asking the owner to pull your changes into the original master.

You can also do a pull request for a repo that you have access to, not just one that you've forked. For example, if you've made a branch off the main project branch, you can do a pull request to get your team to review what you've done and give you feedback before merging your changes back in. In fact, pull requests may be used earlier in the process to start a discussion about a possible feature.

Git Tools and Resources

Most Git users will tell you that the best way to use Git is with the command line. As David Demaree says in his book *Git for Humans*, "Git's command-line interface is its native tongue." He recommends typing commands and seeing what happens as the best way to learn Git. The downside of the command line, of course, is that you need to learn all the Git commands and perhaps also tackle the command-line interface hurdle itself. The following resources will help get you up to speed:

- *Git for Humans* by David Demaree (A Book Apart) is a great place to start learning Git via the command line (or however you intend to use it!).

- *Pro Git* by Scott Chacon and Ben Straub (Apress) is available free online (*git-scm.com/book/en/v2*).

- "Git Cheat Sheet" from GitHub is a list of the most common commands (*services.github.com/on-demand/downloads/github-git-cheat-sheet.pdf*).

- The Git Reference Manual on the official Git site provides a thorough listing of commands and features (*git-scm.com/docs*).

There are also several graphical Git applications available for those who prefer icons, buttons, and menus for interacting with their repositories, and there's no shame in it. I know many developers who use a graphical app and Terminal side by-side, choosing the tool that most easily allows them to do the task they need to do. If you feel more comfortable getting started with a graphical Git tool, I recommend the following:

- GitHub Desktop (from GitHub) is free and available for Mac and Windows (*desktop.github.com*).

- Git Tower 2 (Mac and Windows) costs money, but it is more powerful and offers a thoughtfully designed interface, including visualizations of branches and merges (*www.git-tower.com*).

Many code editors have built-in Git support or Git/GitHub plug-ins as well.

If you go to the GitHub.com site, they do a good job of walking you through the setup process with easy-to-follow tutorials. You can set up an account and gain some basic GitHub skills in a matter of minutes. Their online documentation is top-notch, and they even have a YouTube channel with video tutorials aimed at beginners (*www.youtube.com/githubguides*).

And speaking of GitHub, for a good introduction to the ins and outs of the GitHub interface, I recommend the book *Introducing GitHub: A Non-Technical Guide* by Brent Beer (O'Reilly).

When you are ready to get started using Git for version control, you'll find all the support you need.

CONCLUSION

This concludes the web developer "power tools" chapter. We began with an introduction to the command line, and looked at some strong incentives for learning to use it. You can write CSS faster and make it more cross-browser compliant. You can take advantage of task runners and build tools that automate a lot of the repetitive grunt work you come across as a developer. Finally, although the command line is not required to use Git, it may make learning Git easier and will give you repo superpowers as you begin to master it.

We've talked a fair amount about JavaScript in this chapter. In **Part IV**, I hand over the keyboard to JavaScript master Mat Marquis, who will introduce you to JavaScript and its syntax (also somehow managing to make it very entertaining). I'll be back in **Part V** to talk about web images.

TEST YOURSELF

It's time to test your knowledge of the topics introduced in this chapter. See **Appendix A** for the answers.

1. In the computer world, what is a *shell*?

2. Why might you want to learn to use the command line?

   a. It is a good way to manipulate files and folders on your own computer.

   b. It is a good way to manipulate files and folders on a remote server.

   c. It is required for many useful web development tools.

   d. All of the above.

3. What is a *prompt*?

4. What would you expect to happen if you type `mkdir newsite` after a command-line prompt?

5. Name the two primary functions of CSS processors.

6. Name one advantage of learning Sass.

7. Name two features you might use a CSS postprocessor for.

8. What is a task (in relation to a build tool/task runner)?

9. What does "Grunt is watching this file" mean?

10. What makes Git a *distributed* version control system?

11. In Git, what does it mean if a file is *staged*?

12. What is the difference between a *branch* and a *fork*?

13. Why should you pull before you push?

14. What is a pull request?

IV

JAVASCRIPT FOR BEHAVIOR

INTRODUCTION TO JAVASCRIPT

by Mat Marquis

In this chapter, I'm going to introduce you to JavaScript. Now, it's possible you've just recoiled a little bit, and I understand. We're into full-blown "programming language" territory now, and that can be a little intimidating. I promise, it's not so bad!

We'll start by going over what JavaScript is—and what it isn't—and discuss some of the ways it is used. The majority of the chapter is made up of an introduction to JavaScript syntax—variables, functions, operators, loops, stuff like that. Will you be coding by the end of the chapter? Probably not. But you will have a good head start toward understanding what's going on in a script when you see one. I'll finish up with a look at some of the ways you can manipulate the browser window and tie scripts to user actions such as clicking or submitting a form.

WHAT IS JAVASCRIPT?

If you've made it this far in the book, you no doubt already know that JavaScript is a programming language that adds interactivity and custom behaviors to our sites. It is a client-side scripting language, which means it runs on the user's machine and not on the server, as other web programming languages such as PHP and Ruby do. That means JavaScript (and the way we use it) is reliant on the browser's capabilities and settings. It may not even be available at all, either because the user has chosen to turn it off or because the device doesn't support it, which good developers keep in mind and plan for. JavaScript is also what is known as a dynamic and loosely typed programming language. Don't sweat this description too much; I'll explain what all that means later.

First, I want to establish that JavaScript is kind of misunderstood.

What It Isn't

Right off the bat, the name is pretty confusing. Despite its name, JavaScript has nothing to do with Java. It was created by Brendan Eich at Netscape in 1995 and originally named "LiveScript." But Java was all the rage around that time, so for the sake of marketing, "LiveScript" became "JavaScript." Or just "JS," if you want to sound as cool as one possibly can while talking about JavaScript.

JS also has something of a bad reputation. For a while it was synonymous with all sorts of unscrupulous internet shenanigans—unwanted redirects, obnoxious pop-up windows, and a host of nebulous "security vulnerabilities," just to name a few. There was a time when JavaScript allowed less reputable developers to do all these things (and worse), but modern browsers have largely caught on to the darker side of JavaScript development and locked it down. We shouldn't fault JavaScript itself for that era, though. As the not-so-old cliché goes, "with great power comes great responsibility." JavaScript has always allowed developers a tremendous amount of control over how pages are rendered and how our browsers behave, and it's up to us to use that control in responsible ways.

What It Is

Now we know what JavaScript isn't: it isn't related to Java, and it isn't a mustachioed villain lurking within your browser, wringing its hands and waiting to alert you to "hot singles in your area." Let's talk more about what JavaScript *is*.

JavaScript is a lightweight but incredibly powerful scripting language. We most frequently encounter it through our browsers, but JavaScript has snuck into everything from native applications to PDFs to ebooks. Even web servers themselves can be powered by JavaScript.

As a dynamic programming language, JavaScript doesn't need to be run through any form of compiler that interprets our human-readable code into something the browser can understand. The browser effectively reads the code the same way we do and interprets it on the fly.

JavaScript is also loosely typed. All this means is that we don't necessarily have to tell JavaScript what a variable is. If we're setting a variable to a value of 5, we don't have to programmatically specify that variable as a number; that is, 5 is a number, and JavaScript recognizes it as such.

Now, you don't necessarily need to memorize these terms to get started writing JS, mind you—to be honest, I didn't. This is just to introduce you to a

NOTE

JavaScript was standardized in 1996 by the European Computer Manufacturers Association (ECMA), which is why you sometimes hear it called ECMAScript.

few of the terms you'll hear often while you're learning JavaScript, and they'll start making more and more sense as you go along. This is also to provide you with conversation material for your next cocktail party! "Oh, me? Well, I've been really into loosely typed dynamic scripting languages lately." People will just nod silently at you, which I think means you're doing well conversationally. I don't go to a lot of cocktail parties.

What JavaScript Can Do

Most commonly we'll encounter JavaScript as a way to add interactivity to a page. Whereas the "structural" layer of a page is our HTML markup, and the "presentational" layer of a page is made up of CSS, the third "behavioral" layer is made up of our JavaScript. All of the elements, attributes, and text on a web page can be accessed by scripts using the DOM (Document Object Model), which we'll be looking at in **Chapter 22, Using JavaScript.** We can also write scripts that react to user input, altering either the contents of the page, the CSS styles, or the browser's behavior on the fly.

You've likely seen this in action if you've ever attempted to register for a website, entered a username, and immediately received feedback that the username you've entered is already taken by someone else (FIGURE 21-1). The red border around the text input and the appearance of the "sorry, this username is already in use" message are examples of JavaScript altering the contents of the page. Blocking the form submission is an example of JavaScript altering the browser's default behavior. Ultimately, verifying this information is a job for the server—but JavaScript allows the website to make that request and offer immediate feedback without the need for a page reload.

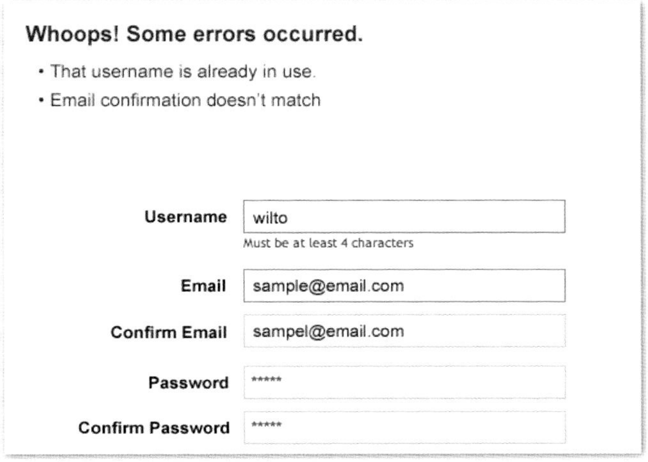

Whoops! Some errors occurred.

• That username is already in use.
• Email confirmation doesn't match

Username	wilto
	Must be at least 4 characters
Email	sample@email.com
Confirm Email	sampel@email.com
Password	*****
Confirm Password	*****

FIGURE 21-1. JavaScript inserts a message, alters styles to make errors apparent, and blocks the form from submitting. It can also detect whether the email entries match, but the username would more likely be detected by a program on the server.

In short, JavaScript allows you to create highly responsive interfaces that improve the user experience and provide dynamic functionality, without waiting for the server to load up a new page. For example, we can use JavaScript to do any of the following:

- Suggest the complete term a user might be entering in a search box as he types. You can see this in action on Google.com (FIGURE 21-2).

FIGURE 21-2. Google.com uses JavaScript to automatically complete a search term as it is typed in.

- Request content and information from the server and inject it into the current document as needed, without reloading the entire page—this is commonly referred to as "Ajax."

- Show and hide content based on a user clicking a link or heading, to create a "collapsible" content area (FIGURE 21-3).

FIGURE 21-3. JavaScript can be used to reveal and hide portions of content.

- Test for browsers' individual features and capabilities. For example, one can test for the presence of "touch events," indicating that the user is interacting with the page through a mobile device's browser, and add more touch-friendly styles and interaction methods.

- Fill in gaps where a browser's built-in functionality falls short, or add some of the features found in newer browsers to older browsers. These kinds of scripts are usually called shims or polyfills.

- Load an image or content in a custom-styled "lightbox"—isolated on the page with CSS—after a user clicks a thumbnail version of the image (FIGURE 21-4).

This list is nowhere near exhaustive!

FIGURE 21-4. JavaScript can be used to load images into a lightbox-style gallery.

ADDING JAVASCRIPT TO A PAGE

As with CSS, you can embed a script right in a document or keep it in an external file and link it to the page. Both methods use the **script** element.

Embedded Script

To embed a script on a page, just add the code as the content of a **script** element:

```
<script>
  … JavaScript code goes here
</script>
```

External Scripts

The other method uses the **src** attribute to point to a script file (with a *.js* suffix) by its URL. In this case, the **script** element has no content:

```
<script src="my_script.js"></script>
```

The advantage to external scripts is that you can apply the same script to multiple pages (the same benefit external style sheets offer). The downside, of course, is that each external script requires an additional HTTP request of the server, which slows down performance.

NOTE

For documents written in the stricter XHTML syntax, you must identify the content of the script element as CDATA by wrapping the code in the following wrapper:

```
<script type="text/javascript">
  // <![CDATA[
  …JavaScript code goes here
  // ]]>
</script>
```

Script Placement

The **script** element can go anywhere in the document, but the most common places for scripts are in the **head** of the document and at the very end of the **body**. It is recommended that you don't sprinkle them throughout the document, because they would be difficult to find and maintain.

For most scripts, the end of the document, just before the **</body>** tag, is the preferred placement because the browser will be done parsing the document and its DOM structure:

```
<!DOCTYPE html>
  <html lang="en">
  <head>
    <meta charset="utf-8">
  </head>
  <body>
    …contents of page…
    <script src="script.js"></script>
  </body>
</html>
```

Consequently, that information will be ready and available by the time it gets to the scripts, and they can execute faster. In addition, the script download and execution blocks the rendering of the page, so moving the script to the bottom improves the perceived performance.

However, in some cases, you might want your script to do something before the body completely loads, so putting it in the **head** will result in better performance. For example, Modernizr (the feature detection tool discussed in **Chapter 19, More CSS Techniques**) recommends its script be placed in the head so the feature detection tests can be run up front.

THE ANATOMY OF A SCRIPT

There's a reason why the book *JavaScript: The Definitive Guide* by David Flanagan (O'Reilly) is 1,100 pages long. There's a *lot* to say about JavaScript! In this section, we have only a few pages to make you familiar with the basic building blocks of JavaScript so you can begin to understand scripts when you encounter them. Many developers have taught themselves to program by finding existing scripts and adapting them for their own needs. After some practice, they are ready to start writing their own from scratch. Recognizing the parts of a script is the first step, so that's where we'll start.

Originally, JavaScript's functionality was mostly limited to crude methods of interaction with the user. We could use a few of JavaScript's built-in functions (FIGURE 21-5) to provide user feedback, such as **alert()** to push a notification to a user, and **confirm()** to ask a user to approve or decline an action. To request the user's input, we were more or less limited to the built-in **prompt()** function. Although these methods still have their time and place today, they're

```
alert("Hi there");
```

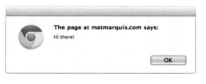

```
confirm("I'm gonna do something, okay?");
```

```
prompt("What should I do?");
```

FIGURE 21-5. Built-in JavaScript functions: **alert()** (top), **confirm()** (middle), and **prompt()** (bottom).

jarring, obtrusive, and—in common opinion, at least—fairly obnoxious ways of interacting with users. As JavaScript has evolved over time, we've been afforded much more graceful ways of adding behavior to our pages, creating a more seamless experience for our users.

In order to take advantage of these interaction methods, we have to first understand the underlying logic that goes into scripting. These are logic patterns common to all manner of programming languages, although the syntax may vary. To draw a parallel between programming languages and spoken languages: although the vocabulary may vary from one language to another, many grammar patterns are shared by the majority of them.

By the end of this section, you're going to know about variables, arrays, comparison operators, `if`/`else` statements, loops, functions, and more. Ready?

The Basics

There are a few common syntactical rules that wind their way though all of JavaScript.

It is important to know that JavaScript is case-sensitive. A variable named `myVariable`, a variable named `myvariable`, and a variable named `MYVariable` will be treated as three different objects.

JavaScript is case-sensitive.

Also, whitespace such as tabs and spaces is ignored, unless it's part of a string of text and enclosed in quotes. All of the character spaces added to scripts such as the ones in this chapter are for the benefit of humans—they make reading through the code easier. JavaScript doesn't see them.

Statements

A script is made up of a series of statements. A statement is a command that tells the browser what to do. Here is a simple statement that makes the browser display an alert with the phrase "Thank you":

```
alert("Thank you.");
```

The semicolon at the end of the statement tells JavaScript that it's the end of the command, just as a period ends a sentence. According to the JavaScript standard, a line break will also trigger the end of a command, but it is a best practice to end each statement with a semicolon.

Comments

JavaScript allows you to leave comments that will be ignored at the time the script is executed, so you can provide reminders and explanations throughout your code. This is especially helpful if this code is likely to be edited by another developer in the future.

There are two methods of using comments. For single-line comments, use two slash characters (**//**) at the beginning of the line. You can put single-line comments on the same line as a statement, as long as the comment comes after the statement. It does not need to be closed, as a line break effectively closes it.

```
// This is a single-line comment.
```

Multiple-line comments use the same syntax that you've seen in CSS. Everything within the **/* */** characters is ignored by the browser. You can use this syntax to "comment out" notes and even chunks of the script when troubleshooting.

```
/* This is a multiline comment.
Anything between these sets of characters will be
completely ignored when the script is executed.
This form of comment needs to be closed. */
```

I'll be using the single-line comment notation to add short explanations to example code, and we'll make use of the **alert()** function we saw earlier (FIGURE 21-5) so we can quickly view the results of our work.

Variables

A variable is like an information container.

If you're anything like me, the very term "variables" triggers nightmarish flashbacks to eighth-grade math class. The premise is pretty much the same, though your teacher doesn't have a bad comb-over this time around.

A variable is like an information container. You give it a name and then assign it a value, which can be a number, text string, an element in the DOM, or a function—anything, really. This gives us a convenient way to reference that value later by name. The value itself can be modified and reassigned in whatever way our scripts' logic dictates.

The following declaration creates a variable with the name **foo** and assigns it the value 5:

```
var foo = 5;
```

We start by declaring the variable by using the **var** keyword. The single equals sign (=) indicates that we are assigning it a value. Because that's the end of our statement, we end the line with a semicolon. Variables can also be declared without the **var** keyword, which impacts what part of your script will have access to the information they contain. We'll discuss that further in the section **"Variable Scope and the var Keyword"** later in this chapter.

You can use anything you like as a variable name, but make sure it's a name that will make sense to you later. You wouldn't want to name a variable something like **data**; it should describe the information it contains. In our earlier very specific example, **productName** might be a more useful name than **foo**. There are a few rules for naming a variable:

- It must start with a letter or an underscore.

- It may contain letters, digits, and underscores in any combination.

- It may not contain character spaces. As an alternative, use underscores in place of spaces, or close up the space and use camel case instead (for example, `my_variable` or `myVariable`).

- It may not contain special characters (e.g., `!` `.` `,` `/` `\` `+` `*` `=`).

You can change the value of a variable at any time by redeclaring it anywhere in your script. Remember: JavaScript is case-sensitive, and so are those variable names.

Data types

The values we assign to variables fall under a few distinct data types:

Undefined

The simplest of these data types is likely **undefined**. If we declare a variable by giving it a name but no value, that variable contains a value of **undefined**.

```
var foo;
alert(foo); // This will open a dialog containing "undefined".
```

Odds are you won't find a lot of use for this right away, but it's worth knowing for the sake of troubleshooting some of the errors you're likely to encounter early on in your JavaScript career. If a variable has a value of **undefined** when it shouldn't, you may want to double-check that it has been declared correctly or that there isn't a typo in the variable name. (We've all been there.)

Null

Similar to **undefined**, assigning a variable of **null** (again, case-sensitive) simply says, "Define this variable, but give it no inherent value."

```
var foo = null;
alert(foo); // This will open a dialog containing "null".
```

Numbers

You can assign variables numeric values.

```
var foo = 5;
alert(foo); // This will open a dialog containing "5".
```

The word **foo** now means the exact same thing as the number 5 as far as JavaScript is concerned. Because JavaScript is loosely typed, we don't have to tell our script to treat the variable **foo** as the *number* 5. The variable behaves the same as the number itself, so you can do things to it that you would do to any other number by using classic mathematical notation: **+**, **-**, *****, and **/** for plus, minus, multiply, and divide, respectively. In this example, we use the plus sign (**+**) to add **foo** to itself (**foo + foo**).

```
var foo = 5;
alert(foo + foo); // This will alert "10".
```

Strings

Another type of data that can be saved to a variable is a string, which is basically a line of text. Enclosing characters in a set of single or double quotes indicates that it's a string, as shown here:

```
var foo = "five";
alert( foo ); // This will alert "five"
```

The variable **foo** is now treated exactly the same as the word *five*. This applies to any combination of characters: letters, numbers, spaces, and so on. If the value is wrapped in quotation marks, it will be treated as a string of text. If we were to wrap the number 5 in quotes and assign it to a variable, that variable wouldn't behave as a number; instead, it would behave as a string of text containing the character "5."

Earlier we saw the plus sign (**+**) used to add numbers. When the plus sign is used with strings, it sticks the strings together (called concatenation) into one long string, as shown in this example.

```
var foo = "bye"
alert(foo + foo);   // This will alert "byebye"
```

Notice what the alert returns in the following example when we define the value 5 in quotation marks, treating it as a string instead of a number:

```
var foo = "5";
alert( foo + foo ); // This will alert "55"
```

If we concatenate a string and a number, JavaScript will assume that the number should be treated as a string as well, since the math would be impossible.

```
var foo = "five";
var bar = 5;
alert( foo + bar ); // This will alert "five5"
```

Booleans

We can also assign a variable a true or false value. This is called a Boolean value, and it is the lynchpin for all manner of advanced logic. Boolean values use the **true** and **false** keywords built into JavaScript, so quotation marks are not necessary.

```
var foo = true; // The variable "foo" is now true
```

Just as with numbers, if we were to wrap the preceding value in quotation marks, we'd be saving the word *true* to our variable instead of the inherent value of **true** (i.e., "not false").

In a sense, everything in JavaScript has either an inherently true or false value. For example, **null**, **undefined**, **0**, and empty strings (**" "**) are all inherently false, while every other value is inherently true. These values, although not identical to the Booleans **true** and **false**, are commonly referred to as being "truthy" and "falsy." I promise I didn't make that up.

Arrays

An array is a group of multiple values (called members) that can be assigned to a single variable. The values in an array are said to be indexed, meaning you can refer to them by number according to the order in which they appear in the list. The first member is given the index number 0, the second is 1, and so on, which is why one almost invariably hears us nerds start counting things at zero—because that's how JavaScript counts things, and many other programming languages do the same. We can avoid a lot of future coding headaches by keeping this in mind.

So, let's say our script needs all of the variables we defined earlier. We could define them three times and name them something like **foo1**, **foo2**, and so on, or we can store them in an array, indicated by square brackets ([ ]).

```
var foo = [5, "five", "5"];
```

Now anytime you need to access any of those values, you can grab them from the single **foo** array by referencing their index number:

```
alert( foo[0] ); // Alerts "5"
alert( foo[1] ); // Alerts "five"
alert( foo[2] ); // Also alerts "5"
```

Comparison Operators

Now that we know how to save values to variables and arrays, the next logical step is knowing how to compare those values. There is a set of special characters called comparison operators that evaluate and compare values in different ways:

==	Is equal to
!=	Is not equal to
===	Is identical to (equal to and of the same data type)
!==	Is not identical to
>	Is greater than
>=	Is greater than or equal to
<	Is less than
<=	Is less than or equal to

There's a reason all of these definitions read as parts of a statement. In comparing values, we're making an assertion, and the goal is to obtain a result that is either inherently true or inherently false. When we compare two values, JavaScript evaluates the statement and gives us back a Boolean value depending on whether the statement is true or false.

```
alert( 5 == 5 ); // This will alert "true"
alert( 5 != 6 ); // This will alert "true"
alert( 5 < 1 ); // This will alert "false"
```

Equal versus identical

The tricky part is understanding the difference between "equal to" (==) and "identical to" (===). We already learned that all of these values fall under a certain data type. For example, a string of "5" and a number 5 are similar, but they're not quite the same thing.

Well, that's exactly what === is meant to check.

```
alert( "5" == 5 ); // This will alert "true". They're both "5".

alert( "5" === 5 );
/* This will alert "false". They're both "5", but they're not the same
data type. */

alert( "5" !== 5 );
/* This will alert "true", since they're not the same data type. */
```

Even if you have to read through this part a couple of times, understanding the difference between "equal" and "identical to" means you've already begun to adopt the special kind of crazy one needs to be a programmer. Welcome! You're in good company.

Mathematical operators

The other type of operator is a mathematical operator, which performs mathematical functions on numeric values (and, of course, variables that contain numeric values). We touched briefly on the straightforward mathematical operators for add (+), subtract (-), multiply (*), and divide (/). There are also some useful shortcuts you should be aware of:

+=	Adds the value to itself
++	Increases the value of a number (or a variable containing a number value) by 1
--	Decreases the value of a number (or a variable containing a number value) by 1

if/else statements

if/else statements are how we get JavaScript to ask itself a true/false question. They are more or less the foundation for all the advanced logic that can be written in JavaScript, and they're about as simple as programming gets. In fact, they're almost written in plain English. The structure of a conditional statement is as follows:

```
if( true ) {
    // Do something.
}
```

It tells the browser "if this condition is met, then execute the commands listed between the curly brackets ({ })." JavaScript doesn't care about whitespace in our code, remember, so the spaces on either side of the (true) are purely for the sake of more readable code.

Here is a simple example using the array we declared earlier:

```
var foo = [5, "five", "5"];

if( foo[1] === "five" ) {
    alert("This is the word five, written in plain English.");
}
```

Since we're making a comparison, JavaScript is going to give us a value of either **true** or **false**. The highlighted line of code says "true or false: the value of the **foo** variable with an index of **1** is identical to the word 'five'?"

In this case, the alert would fire because the **foo** variable with an index of **1** (the second in the list, if you'll remember) is identical to "five". It is indeed true, and the alert fires.

We can also explicitly check if something is false by using the **!=** comparison operator, which reads as "not equal to."

```
if( 1 != 2 ) {
    alert("If you're not seeing this alert, we have bigger problems than
JavaScript.");
    // 1 is never equal to 2, so we should always see this alert.
}
```

I'm not much good at math, but near as I can tell, 1 will never be equal to 2. JavaScript says, "That '1 is not equal to 2' line is a true statement, so I'll run this code."

If the statement doesn't evaluate to **true**, the code inside the curly brackets will be skipped over completely:

```
if( 1 == 2 ) {
    alert("If you're seeing this alert, we have bigger problems than
JavaScript.");
    // 1 is not equal to 2, so this code will never run.
}
```

That covers "if," but what about "else"?

Lastly—and I promise we're almost done here—what if we want to do one thing if something is true and something *else* if that thing is false? We could write two **if** statements, but that's a little clunky. Instead, we can just say, "else, do something...else."

```
var test = "testing";
if( test == "testing" ) {
        alert( "You haven't changed anything." );
} else {
    alert( "You've changed something!" );
}
```

> ### Idiomatic JavaScript
>
> There is an effort in the JavaScript community to create a style guide for writing JavaScript code. The document "Principles of Writing Consistent, Idiomatic JavaScript" states the following: "All code in any code-base should look like a single person typed it, no matter how many people contributed." To achieve that goal, a group of developers has written an Idiomatic Style Manifesto that describes how whitespace, line breaks, quotation marks, functions, variables, and more should be written to achieve "beautiful code." Learn more about it at *github.com/rwldrn/ idiomatic.js/*.

EXERCISE 21-1.
English-to-JavaScript translation

In this quick exercise, you can get a feel for variables, arrays, and **if/else** statements by translating the statements written in English into lines of JavaScript code. You can find the answers in **Appendix A**.

1. Create a variable called **friends** and assign it an array with four of your friends' names.

2. Show the user a dialog that displays the third name in your list of **friends**.

3. Create a variable called **name** and assign it a string value that is your first name.

4. If the value of **name** is identical to **Jennifer**, show the user a dialog box that says, "That's my name too!"

5. Create a variable called **myVariable** and assign it a number value between 1 and 10. If **myVariable** is greater than five, show the user a dialog that says "upper." If not, show the user a dialog that says "lower."

Changing the value of the **test** variable to something else—anything other than the word *testing*—will trigger the alert "You've changed something!"

EXERCISE 21-1 gives you a chance to write a bit of JavaScript yourself.

Loops

There are cases in which we'll want to go through every item in an array and do something with it, but we won't want to write out the entire list of items and repeat ourselves a dozen or more times. You are about to learn a technique of *devastating power*, readers: loops.

I know. Maybe I overstated how exciting loops can be, but they *are* incredibly useful. With what we've covered already, we're getting good at dealing with single variables, but that can get us only so far. Loops allow us to easily deal with huge sets of data.

Say we have a form that requires none of the fields to be left blank. If we use the DOM to fetch every text input on the page, the DOM provides an array of every text input element. (I'll tell you more about how the DOM does this in the next chapter.) We could check every value stored in that array one item at a time, sure, but that's a lot of code and a maintenance nightmare. If we use a loop to check each value, we won't have to modify our script, regardless of how many fields are added to or removed from the page. Loops allow us to act on every item in an array, regardless of that array's size.

There are several ways to write a loop, but the **for** method is one of the most popular. The basic structure of a **for** loop is as follows:

```
for( initialize the variable;  test the condition;  alter the value; ) {
   // do something
}
```

Here's an example of a **for** loop in action:

```
for( var i = 0; i < 2; i++ ) {
  alert( i ); // This loop will trigger three alerts, reading "0",
"1", and "2" respectively.
}
```

That's a little dense, so let's break it down:

for()

First, we're calling the **for()** statement, which is built into JavaScript. It says, "For every time this is true, do this." Next we need to supply that statement with some information.

var i = 0;

This creates a new variable, **i**, with its value set to zero. You can tell it's a variable by the single equals sign. More often than not, you'll see coders using the letter "i" (short for "index") as the variable name, but keep in mind that you could use any variable name in its place. It's a common convention, not a rule.

We set that initial value to 0 because we want to stay in the habit of counting from zero up. That's where JavaScript starts counting, after all.

i <= 2;

With **i <= 2;**, we're saying, "for as long as **i** is less than or equal to 2, keep on looping." Since we're counting from zero, that means the loop will run three times.

i++

Finally, **i++** is shorthand for "every time this loop runs, add one to the value of **i**" (**++** is one of the mathematical shortcut operators we saw earlier). Without this step, **i** would always equal zero, and the loop would run forever! Fortunately, modern browsers are smart enough not to let this happen. If one of these three pieces is missing, the loop simply won't run at all.

{ *script* }

Anything inside those curly brackets is executed once for each time the loop runs, which is three times in this case. That **i** variable is available for use in the code the loop executes as well, as we'll see next.

Let's go back to the "check each item in an array" example. How would we write a loop to do that for us?

```
var items = ["foo", "bar", "baz"]; // First we create an array.
for( var i = 0; i < items.length; i++ ) {
  alert( items[i] ); // This will alert each item in the array.
}
```

This example differs from our first loop in two key ways:

items.length

Instead of using a number to limit the number of times the loop runs, we're using a property built right into JavaScript to determine the "length" of our array, which is the number of items it contains. **.length** is just one of the standard properties and methods of the **Array** object in JavaScript. In our example, there are three items in the array, so it will loop three times.

items[i]

Remember how I mentioned that we can use that **i** variable inside the loop? Well, we can use it to reference each index of the array. Good thing we started counting from zero; if we had set the initial value of **i** to 1, the first item in the array would have been skipped. The result of our **for** loop example is that each item in the array (the text strings **foo**, **bar**, and **baz**) gets returned after each loop and fed to an alert.

Now no matter how large or small that array should become, the loop will execute only as many times as there are items in the array, and will always hold a convenient reference to each item in the array.

There are literally dozens of ways to write a loop in JavaScript, but this is one of the more common patterns you're going to encounter out there in the wild. Developers use loops to perform a number of tasks, such as the following:

- Looping through a list of elements on the page and checking the value of each, applying a style to each, or adding/removing/changing an attribute on each. For example, we could loop through each element in a form and ensure that users have entered a valid value for each before they proceed.

- Creating a new array of items in an original array that have a certain value. We check the value of each item in the original array within the loop, and if the value matches the one we're looking for, we populate a new array with only those items. This turns the loop into a filter of sorts.

Functions

The structure of a function:

```
function() {
}
```

I've introduced you to a few functions already in a sneaky way. Here's an example of a function that you might recognize:

```
alert("I've been a function all along!");
```

A function is a bit of code for performing a task that doesn't run until it is referenced or called. **alert()** is a function built into our browser. It's a block of code that runs only when we explicitly tell it to. In a way, we can think of a function as a variable that contains *logic*, in that referencing that variable will run all the code stored inside it. Functions allow code to be reused any time it is referenced so you don't need to write it over and over.

All functions share a common pattern (FIGURE 21-6). The function name is always immediately followed by a set of parentheses (no space), then a pair of curly brackets that contains their associated code. The parentheses sometimes contain additional information used by the function called arguments. Arguments are data that can influence how the function behaves. For example, the **alert()** function we know so well accepts a string of text as an argument, and uses that information to populate the resulting dialog.

Multiple arguments are separated by commas   Not all functions take arguments

Function name   Arguments

```
addNumbers( a, b ) {
    return a + b;
}
```

Code to execute

```
addNumbers( ) {
    return 2 + 2;
}
```

FIGURE 21-6. The structure of a function.

There are two types of functions: those that come "out of the box" (native JavaScript functions) and those that you make up yourself (custom functions). Let's look at each.

Native functions

Hundreds of predefined functions are built into JavaScript, including these:

`alert()`, `confirm()`, *and* `prompt()`

These functions trigger browser-level dialog boxes.

`Date()`

Returns the current date and time.

`parseInt("123")`

This function will, among other things, take a string data type containing numbers and turn it into a number data type. The string is passed to the function as an argument.

`setTimeout(functionName, 5000)`

Executes a function after a delay. The function is specified in the first argument, and the delay is specified in milliseconds in the second argument (in the example, 5,000 milliseconds, which equals 5 seconds).

There are scores more beyond this as well. Note that names of functions are case-sensitive, so be sure to write **setTimeout** instead of **SetTimeout**.

Custom functions

To create a custom function, we type the **function** keyword followed by a name for the function, followed by opening and closing parentheses, followed by opening and closing curly brackets:

```
function name() {
    // Our function code goes here.
}
```

Just as with variables and arrays, the function's name can be anything you want, but all the same naming syntax rules apply.

If we were to create a function that just alerts some text (which is a little redundant, I know), it would look like this:

```
function foo() {
    alert("Our function just ran!");
    // This code won't run until we call the function 'foo()'
}
```

We can then call that function and execute the code inside it anywhere in our script by writing the following:

```
foo(); // Alerts "Our function just ran!"
```

We can call this function any number of times throughout our code. It saves a lot of time and redundant coding.

Arguments

Having a function that executes the exact same code throughout your script isn't likely to be all that useful. We can "pass arguments" (provide data) to native and custom functions in order to apply a function's logic to different sets of data at different times. To hold a place for the arguments, create a variable name (or a series of comma-separated names) in the parentheses after the name of the function at the time the function is defined.

An argument is a value or data that a function uses when it runs.

For example, let's say we wanted to create a very simple function that alerts the number of items contained in an array. We've already learned that we can use `.length` to get the number of items in an array, so we just need a way to pass the array to be measured into our function. We do that by supplying the array to be measured as an argument. In the code, I've defined a new function named **alertArraySize()** and created the variable **arr** that holds a place for the argument. That variable will then be available inside the function and will contain whatever argument we pass when we call the function.

```
function alertArraySize(arr) {
        alert(arr.length);
}
```

When we call that function, anything we include between the parentheses after the function name (in this case, **test**) will be passed to the argument with the **arr** placeholder as the function executes. Here we've defined the variable **test** as an array of five items. We've passed that variable to the function, and now that array gets plugged in and the length is returned.

```
var test = [1,2,3,4,5];
alertArraySize(test); // Alerts "5"
```

Returning a value

This part is particularly wild and incredibly useful.

It's pretty common to use a function to calculate something and then give you back a value that you can use elsewhere in your script. We could accomplish this using what we know now, through clever application of variables, but there's a much easier way.

The **return** keyword inside a function effectively turns that function into a variable with a dynamic value! This one is a little easier to show than it is to tell, so bear with me while we consider this example:

```
function addNumbers(a,b) {
    return a + b;
}
```

We now have a function that accepts two arguments and adds them together. That wouldn't be much use if the result always lived inside that function, because we wouldn't be able to use the result anywhere else in our script. Here we use the **return** keyword to pass the result out of the function. Now any reference you make to that function gives you the result of the function—just like a variable would:

```
alert( addNumbers(2,5) ); // Alerts "7"
```

In a way, the **addNumbers()** function is now a variable that contains a dynamic value: the value of our calculation. If we didn't return a value inside our function, the preceding script would alert **undefined**, just like a variable that we haven't given a value.

The **return** keyword has one catch. As soon as JavaScript sees that it's time to return a value, the function ends. Consider the following:

```
function bar() {
    return 3;
    alert("We'll never see this alert.");
}
```

When you call this function by using **bar()**, the alert on the second line never runs. The function ends as soon as it sees it's time to return a value.

Variable Scope and the var Keyword

There are times when you'll want a variable that you've defined within a function to be available anywhere throughout your script. Other times, you may want to restrict it and make it available *only* to the function it lives in. This notion of the availability of the variable is known as its scope. A variable that can be used by any of the scripts on your page is globally scoped, and a variable that's available only within its parent function is locally scoped.

JavaScript variables use functions to manage their scope. If a variable is defined outside a function, it will be globally scoped and available to all scripts. When you define a variable within a function and you want it to be used only by that function, you can flag it as locally scoped by preceding the variable name with the **var** keyword:

```
var foo = "value";
```

To expose a variable within a function to the global scope, we omit the **var** keyword and simply define the variable:

```
foo = "value";
```

You need to be careful about how you define variables within functions, or you could end up with unexpected results. Take the following JavaScript snippet, for example:

```
function double( num ){
    total = num + num;
    return total;
}
var total = 10;
var number = double( 20 );
alert( total ); // Alerts 40.
```

You may expect that because you specifically assigned a value of 10 to the variable **total,** the **alert(total)** function at the end of the script would return 10. But because we didn't scope the **total** variable in the function with the **var** keyword, it bleeds into the global scope. Therefore, although the variable **total** is set to 10, the following statement runs the function and grabs the value for **total** defined there. Without the **var**, the variable "leaked out."

As you can see, the trouble with global variables is that they'll be shared throughout all the scripting on a page. The more variables that bleed into the global scope, the better the chances you'll run into a "collision" in which a variable named elsewhere (in another script altogether, even) matches one of yours. This can lead to variables being inadvertently redefined with unexpected values, which can lead to errors in your script.

Remember that we can't always control all the code in play on our page. It's very common for pages to include code written by third parties, for example:

- Scripts to render advertisements
- User-tracking and analytics scripts
- Social media "share" buttons

It's best not to take any chances on variable collisions, so when you start writing scripts on your own, locally scope your variables whenever you can (see the sidebar **"Keeping Variables Out of the Global Scope"**).

This concludes our little (OK, not so little) introductory tour of JavaScript syntax. There's a lot more to it, but this should give you a decent foundation for learning more on your own and being able to interpret scripts when you see them. We have just a few more JavaScript-related features to tackle before we look at a few examples.

THE BROWSER OBJECT

In addition to being able to control elements on a web page, JavaScript also gives you access to and the ability to manipulate the parts of the browser

Keeping Variables Out of the Global Scope

If you want to be sure that all of your variables stay out of the global scope, you can put all of your JavaScript in the following wrapper:

```
<script>
(function() {
  //All your code here!
}());
<script>
```

This little quarantining solution is called an IIFE (Immediately Invoked Functional Expression), and we owe this method and the associated catchy term to Ben Alman (*benalman.com/news/2010/11/ immediately-invoked-function- expression/*).

window itself. For example, you might want to get or replace the URL that is in the browser's address bar, or open or close a browser window.

In JavaScript, the browser is known as the **window** object. The **window** object has a number of properties and methods that we can use to interact with it. In fact, our old friend **alert()** is actually one of the standard browser object methods. TABLE 21-1 lists just a few of the properties and methods that can be used with **window** to give you an idea of what's possible. For a complete list, see the Window API reference at MDN Web Docs (*developer.mozilla.org/en-US/docs/Web/API/Window*).

TABLE 21-1. Browser properties and methods.

Property/method	Description
event	Represents the state of an event
history	Contains the URLs the user has visited within a browser window
location	Gives read/write access to the URI in the address bar
status	Sets or returns the text in the status bar of the window
alert()	Displays an alert box with a specified message and an OK button
close()	Closes the current window
confirm()	Displays a dialog box with a specified message and an OK and a Cancel button
focus()	Sets focus on the current window

EVENTS

JavaScript can access objects in the page and the browser window, but did you know it's also "listening" for certain events to happen? An event is an action that can be detected with JavaScript, such as when the document loads or when the user clicks an element or just moves her mouse over it. HTML 4.0 made it possible for a script to be tied to events on the page, whether initiated by the user, the browser itself, or other scripts. This is known as event binding.

In scripts, an event is identified by an event handler. For example, the **onload** event handler triggers a script when the document loads, and the **onclick** and **onmouseover** handlers trigger a script when the user clicks or mouses over an element, respectively. TABLE 21-2 lists some of the most common event handlers. Keep in mind that these are also case-sensitive.

Event handlers "listen" for certain document, browser, or user actions and bind scripts to those actions.

TABLE 21-2. Common events.

Event handler	Event description
onblur	An element loses focus.
onchange	The content of a form field changes.
onclick	The mouse clicks an object.
onerror	An error occurs when the document or an image loads.
onfocus	An element gets focus.
onkeydown	A key on the keyboard is pressed.
onkeypress	A key on the keyboard is pressed or held down.
onkeyup	A key on the keyboard is released.
onload	A page or an image is finished loading.
onmousedown	A mouse button is pressed.
onmousemove	The mouse is moved.
onmouseout	The mouse is moved off an element.
onmouseover	The mouse is moved over an element.
onmouseup	A mouse button is released.
onsubmit	The submit button is clicked in a form.

There are three common methods for applying event handlers to items within our pages:

- As an HTML attribute

- As a method attached to the element

- Using `addEventListener()`

In the upcoming examples of the latter two approaches, we'll use the `window` object. Any events we attach to `window` apply to the entire document. We'll be using the `onclick` event in all of these as well.

As an HTML Attribute

You can specify the function to be run in an attribute in the markup, as shown in the following example:

```
<body onclick="myFunction();"> /* myFunction will now run when the user
clicks anything within 'body' */
```

Although still functional, this is an antiquated way of attaching events to elements within the page. It should be avoided for the same reason we avoid using **style** attributes in our markup to apply styles to individual elements. In this case, it blurs the line between the semantic layer and behavioral layers of our pages, and can quickly lead to a maintenance nightmare.

As a Method

This is another somewhat dated approach to attaching events, though it does keep things strictly within our scripts. We can attach functions by using helpers already built into JavaScript:

```
window.onclick = myFunction; /* myFunction will run when the user
clicks anything within the browser window */
```

We can also use an anonymous function rather than a predefined one:

```
window.onclick = function() {
    /* Any code placed here will run when the user clicks anything
within the browser window */
};
```

This approach has the benefit of both simplicity and ease of maintenance, but does have a fairly major drawback: we can bind only one event at a time with this method.

```
window.onclick = myFunction;
```

```
window.onclick = myOtherFunction;
```

In the example just shown, the second binding overwrites the first, so when the user clicks inside the browser window, only **myOtherFunction** will run. The reference to **myFunction** is thrown away.

addEventListener

Although a little more complex at first glance, this approach allows us to keep our logic within our scripts and allows us to perform multiple bindings on a single object. The syntax is a bit more verbose. We start by calling the **addEventListener()** method of the target object, and then specify the event in question and the function to be executed as two arguments:

```
window.addEventListener("click", myFunction);
```

Notice that we omit the preceding "on" from the event handler with this syntax.

Like the previous method, **addEventListener()** can be used with an anonymous function as well:

```
window.addEventListener("click", function(e) {

});
```

This was just a brief introduction, so I recommend getting more information on **addEventListener()** at the "eventTarget.addEventListener" page on the MDN Web Docs (*developer.mozilla.org/en/DOM/element.addEventListener*).

PUTTING IT ALL TOGETHER

Now you have been introduced to many of the important building blocks of JavaScript. You've seen variables, data types, and arrays. You've met **if/else** statements, loops, and functions. You know your browser objects from your event handlers. That's a lot of bits and pieces. Let's walk through a couple of simple script examples to see how they get put together.

Example 1: A Tale of Two Arguments

Here's a simple function that accepts two arguments and returns the greater of the two values:

```
greatestOfTwo( first, second ) {
  if( first > second ) {
    return first;
  } else {
    return second;
  }
}
```

We start by naming our function **greatestOfTwo**. We set it up to accept two arguments, which we'll just call "first" and "second" for want of more descriptive words. The function contains an **if/else** statement that returns **first** if the first argument is greater than the second, and returns **second** if it isn't.

Example 2: The Longest Word

Here's a function that accepts an array of strings as a single argument and returns the longest string in the array. It returns the first occurrence of one of the longest strings (in case they are of the same length).

```
longestWord( strings ) {
  var longest = strings[0];

  for( i = 1; i < strings.length; i++ ) {
    if ( strings[i].length > longest.length ) {
      longest = strings[i];
    }
  }
  return longest;
}
```

First, we name the function and allow it to accept a single argument. Then, we set the **longest** variable to an initial value of the first item in the array: **strings[0]**. We start our loop at 1 instead of 0 since we already have the first value in the array captured. Each time we iterate through the loop, we compare the length of the current item in the array to the length of the value saved in the **longest** variable. If the current item in the array contains more characters than the current value of the **longest** variable, we change the value of **longest** to that item. If not, we do nothing. After the loop is complete we return the value of **longest**, which now contains the longest string in the array.

LEARNING MORE ABOUT JAVASCRIPT

Now that you've seen the basic building blocks and a few simple examples, does it whet your appetite for more? Here are a few resources to take you to the next step:

JavaScript Resources at MDN Web Docs
(developer.mozilla.org/en-US/docs/Web/JavaScript)

The folks at MDN Web Docs have assembled excellent tutorials as well as thorough documentation on all the components of JavaScript. It's a great site to visit when you're just starting out, and it is likely to be a go-to reference even after you have years of experience.

JavaScript for Web Designers **by Mat Marquis (A Book Apart)**

I can say a lot more in a book than in a chapter, so if you're looking for a little more depth in a beginner-level manual, I wrote this book for you.

Learning JavaScript **by Ethan Brown (O'Reilly)**

For a deeper dive into JavaScript, this book will take you to the next level.

Why not see how you're doing with JavaScript so far with EXERCISE 21-2 and a quick quiz? In the next chapter, you'll see how we use these tools in the context of web design.

EXERCISE 21-2. You try it

In this exercise, you will write a script that updates the page's title in the browser window with a "new messages" count. You may have encountered this sort of script in the wild from time to time. We're going to assume for the sake of the exercise that this is going to become part of a larger web app someday, and we're tasked only with updating the page title with the current "unread messages" count.

I've created a document for you already (*title.html*), which is available in the *materials* folder for this chapter on *learningwebdesign.com*. The resulting script is in **Appendix A**.

1. Start by opening *title.html* in a browser. You'll see a blank page, with the title element already filled out. If you look up at the top of your browser window, you'll notice it reads "Million Dollar WebApp".

2. Now open the document in a text editor. You'll find a **script** element containing a comment just before the closing **</body>** tag. Feel free to delete the comment.

3. If we're going to be changing the page's title, we should save the original first. Create a variable named **originalTitle**. For its value, we'll have the browser get the title of the document using the DOM method **document.title**. Now we have a saved reference to the page title at the time the page is loaded. This variable should be global, so we'll declare it outside any functions.

```
var originalTitle = document.title;
```

4. Next, we'll define a function so we can reuse the script whenever it's needed. Let's call the function something easy to remember, so we know at a glance what it does when we encounter it in our code later. **showUnreadCount()** works for me, but you can name it whatever you'd like.

```
var originalTitle = document.title;

function showUnreadCount() {
}
```

EXERCISE 21-2. Continued

5. We need to think about what the function needs to make it useful. This function does something with the unread message count, so its argument is a single number referred to as **unread** in this example.

```
var originalTitle = document.title;

function showUnreadCount( unread ) {
}
```

6. Now let's add the code that runs for this function. We want the document title for the page to display the title of the document plus the count of unread messages. Sounds like a job for concatenation (**+**)! Here we set the **document.title** to be (**=**) whatever string was saved for **originalTitle** plus the number in **showUnreadCount**. As we learned earlier, JavaScript combines a string and a number as though they are both strings.

```
var originalTitle = document.title;

function showUnreadCount( unread ) {
  document.title = originalTitle + unread;
}
```

7. Let's try out our script before we go too much further. Below where you defined the function and the **originalTitle** variable, enter **showUnreadCount(3);**. Now save the page and reload it in your browser (FIGURE 21-7).

```
var originalTitle = document.title;

function showUnreadCount( unread ) {
  document.title = originalTitle + unread;
}
showUnreadCount(3);
```

FIGURE 21-7. Our title tag has changed! It's not quite right yet, though.

8. Our script is working, but it's not very easy to read. Fortunately, there's no limit on the number of strings we can combine at once. Here we're adding new strings that wrap the count value and the words "new messages" in parentheses (FIGURE 21-8).

```
var originalTitle = document.title;

function showUnreadCount( unread ) {
  document.title = originalTitle + "(" + unread + " new messages!)";
}
showUnreadCount(3);
```

FIGURE 21-8. Much better!

TEST YOURSELF

We covered a lot of new material in this chapter. Here's a chance to test what sunk in. You will find the answers in **Appendix A**.

1. Name one good thing and one bad thing about linking to external *.js* files.

2. Given the following array

   ```
   var myArray = [1, "two", 3, "4"]
   ```

   write what the alert message will say for each of these examples:

   a. ```
      alert(myArray[0]);
      ```

   b. ```
      alert( myArray[0] + myArray[1] );
      ```

   c. ```
      alert(myArray[2] + myArray[3]);
      ```

   d. ```
      alert( myArray[2] - myArray[0] );
      ```

3. What will each of these alert messages say?

   a. ```
      var foo = 5;
      foo += 5;
      alert(foo);
      ```

   b. ```
      i = 5;
      i++;
      alert( i );
      ```

   c. ```
      var foo = 2;
      alert(foo + " " + "remaining");
      ```

   d. ```
      var foo = "Mat";
      var bar = "Jennifer";
      if( foo.length > bar.length ) {
        alert( foo  + " is longer." );
      } else {
        alert( bar + " is longer." );
      }
      ```

   e. ```
      alert(10 === "10");
      ```

4. Describe what this does:

   ```
   for( var i = 0; i < items.length;  i++ ) {  }
   ```

5. What is the potential problem with globally scoped variables?
   ```

6. Match each event handler with its trigger.

    a. onload   1. The user finishes a form and hits the submit button.

    b. onchange   2. The page finishes loading.

    c. onfocus   3. The pointer hovers over a link.

    d. onmouseover   4. A text-entry field is selected and ready for typing.

    e. onsubmit   5. A user changes her name in a form field.

USING JAVASCRIPT

AND THE DOCUMENT OBJECT MODEL

by Mat Marquis

Now that you have a sense for the language of JavaScript, let's look at some of the ways we can put it to use in modern web design. First, we'll explore DOM scripting, which allows us to manipulate the elements, attributes, and text on a page. I'll introduce you to some ready-made JavaScript and DOM scripting resources, so you don't have to go it alone. You'll learn about polyfills, which provide older browsers with modern features and normalize functionality. I'll also introduce you to JavaScript libraries that make developers' lives easier with collections of polyfills and shortcuts for common tasks.

MEET THE DOM

You've seen references to the Document Object Model (DOM for short) several times throughout this book, but now is the time to give it the attention it deserves. The DOM gives us a way to access and manipulate the contents of a document. We commonly use it for HTML, but the DOM can be used with any XML language as well. And although we're focusing on its relationship with JavaScript, it's worth noting that the DOM can be accessed by other languages too, such as PHP, Ruby, C++, and more. Although DOM Level 1 was released by the W3C in 1998, it was nearly five years later that DOM scripting began to gain steam.

The DOM is a programming interface (an API) for HTML and XML pages. It provides a structured map of the document, as well as a set of methods to interface with the elements contained therein. Effectively, it translates our markup into a format that JavaScript (and other languages) can understand. It sounds pretty dry, I know, but the basic gist is that the DOM serves as a map to all the elements on a page and lets us *do* things with them. We can use it to find elements by their names or attributes, and then add, modify, or delete elements and their content.

The DOM gives us a way to access and manipulate the contents of a document.

Without the DOM, JavaScript wouldn't have any sense of a document's contents—and by that, I mean the *entirety* of the document's contents. Everything from the page's **doctype** to each individual letter in the text can be accessed via the DOM and manipulated with JavaScript.

The Node Tree

A simple way to think of the DOM is in terms of the document tree as diagrammed in FIGURE 22-1. You saw documents diagrammed in this way when you were learning about CSS selectors.

```
<!DOCTYPE html>
<html>
<head>
  <title>Document title</title>
  <meta charset="utf-8">
</head>
<body>
  <div>
    <h1>Heading</h1>
    <p>Paragraph text with a <a href="foo.html">link</a> here.</p>
  </div>
  <div>
    <p>More text here.</p>
  </div>
</body>
</html>
```

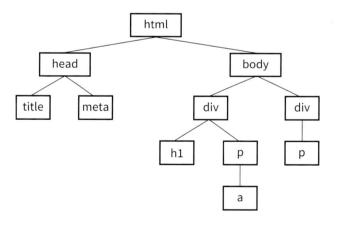

FIGURE 22-1. A simple document.

Each element within the page is referred to as a node. If you think of the DOM as a tree, each node is an individual branch that can contain further branches. But the DOM allows deeper access to the content than CSS because it treats the actual content as a node as well. FIGURE 22-2 shows the structure of the first **p** element. The element, its attributes, and its contents are all nodes in the DOM's node tree.

```
<p>Paragraph text with a <a href="foo.html">link</a> here.</p>
```

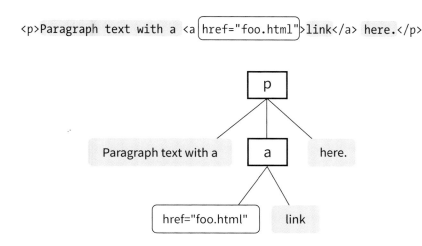

FIGURE 22-2. The nodes within the first **p** element in our sample document.

The DOM also provides a standardized set of methods and functions through which JavaScript can interact with the elements on our page. Most DOM scripting involves reading from and writing to the document.

There are several ways to use the DOM to find what you want in a document. Let's go over some of the specific methods we can use for accessing objects defined by the DOM (we JS folks call this "crawling the DOM" or "traversing the DOM"), as well as some of the methods for manipulating those elements.

Accessing DOM Nodes

The **document** object in the DOM identifies the page itself, and more often than not will serve as the starting point for our DOM crawling. The **document** object comes with a number of standard properties and methods for accessing collections of elements. This is reminiscent of the **length** property we learned about in **Chapter 21, Introduction to JavaScript**. Just as **length** is a standard property of all arrays, the **document** object comes with a number of built-in properties containing information about the document. We then wind our way to the element we're after by chaining those properties and methods together, separated by periods, to form a sort of route through the document.

To give you a general idea of what I mean, the statement in this example says to look on the page (**document**), find the element that has the **id** value "beginner", find the HTML content within that element (**innerHTML**), and save those contents to a variable (**foo**):

```
var foo = document.getElementById("beginner").innerHTML;
```

Because the chains tend to get long, it is also common to see each property or method broken onto its own line to make it easier to read at a glance.

Remember, whitespace in JavaScript is ignored, so this has no effect on how the statement is parsed.

```
var foo = document
  .getElementById("beginner")
    .innerHTML;
```

There are several methods for accessing nodes in the document.

By element name

`getElementsByTagName()`

We can access individual elements by the tags themselves, using **document. getElementsByTagName()**. This method retrieves any element or elements you specify as an argument.

For example, **document.getElementsByTagName("p")** returns every paragraph on the page, wrapped in something called a collection or nodeList, in the order they appear in the document from top to bottom. nodeLists behave much like arrays. To access specific paragraphs in the nodeList, we reference them by their index, just like an array.

```
var paragraphs = document.getElementsByTagName("p");
```

Based on this variable statement, **paragraphs[0]** is a reference to the first paragraph in the document, **paragraphs[1]** refers to the second, and so on. If we had to access each element in the nodeList separately, one at a time...well, it's a good thing we learned about looping through arrays earlier. Loops work the exact same way with a nodeList.

```
var paragraphs = document.getElementsByTagName("p");
for( var i = 0; i < paragraphs.length; i++ ) {
 // do something
}
```

Now we can access each paragraph on the page individually by referencing **paragraphs[i]** inside the loop, just as with an array, but with elements on the page instead of values.

By id attribute value

`getElementById()`

This method returns a single element based on that element's ID (the value of its **id** attribute), which we provide to the method as an argument. For example, to access this particular image

```
<img src="photo.jpg" alt="" id="lead-photo">
```

we include the **id** value as an argument for the **getElementById()** method:

```
var photo = document.getElementById("lead-photo");
```

NOTE

nodeLists are living collections. If you manipulate the document in a nodeList loop—for example, looping through all paragraphs and appending new ones along the way—you can end up in an infinite loop. Good times!

By class attribute value

getElementsByClassName()

Just as it says on the tin, this allows you to access nodes in the document based on the value of a **class** attribute. This statement assigns any element with a **class** value of "column-a" to the variable **firstColumn** so it can be accessed easily from within a script:

```
var firstColumn = document.getElementsByClassName("column-a");
```

Like **getElementsByTagName()**, this returns a nodeList that we can reference by index or loop through one at a time.

WARNING

This is a relatively new method for accessing DOM nodes. Although **getElements-ByClassName()** *is available in the current versions of modern browsers, it will not work in IE8 or below.*

By selector

querySelectorAll()

querySelectorAll() allows you to access nodes of the DOM based on a CSS-style selector. The syntax of the arguments in the following examples should look familiar to you. It can be as simple as accessing the child elements of a specific element:

```
var sidebarPara = document.querySelectorAll(".sidebar p");
```

or as complex as selecting an element based on an attribute:

```
var textInput = document.querySelectorAll("input[type='text']");
```

querySelectorAll() returns a nodeList, like **getElementsByTagName()** and **getElementsByClassName()**, even if the selector matches only a single element.

WARNING

querySelectorAll() *isn't supported in IE7 or below.*

Accessing an attribute value

getAttribute()

As I mentioned earlier, elements aren't the only thing you can access with the DOM. To get the value of an attribute attached to an element node, we call **getAttribute()** with a single argument: the attribute name. Let's assume we have an image, *stratocaster.jpg*, marked up like this:

```
<img src="stratocaster.jpg" alt="electric guitar" id="lead-image">
```

In the following example, we access that specific image (**getElementbyId()**) and save a reference to it in a variable ("bigImage"). At that point, we could access any of the element's attributes (**alt**, **src**, or **id**) by specifying it as an argument in the **getAttribute()** method. In the example, we get the value of the **src** attribute and use it as the content in an alert message. (I'm not sure *why* we would ever do that, but it does demonstrate the method.)

```
var bigImage = document.getElementById("lead-image");
alert( bigImage.getAttribute("src") ); // Alerts "stratocaster.jpg".
```

Manipulating Nodes

Once we've accessed a node by using one of the methods discussed previously, the DOM gives us several built-in methods for manipulating those elements, their attributes, and their contents.

setAttribute()

To continue with the previous example, we saw how we *get* the attribute value, but what if we wanted to *set* the value of that **src** attribute to a new pathname altogether? Use **setAttribute()**! This method requires two arguments: the attribute to be changed and the new value for that attribute.

In this example, we use a bit of JavaScript to swap out the image by changing the value of the **src** attribute:

```
var bigImage = document.getElementById("lead-image");
bigImage.setAttribute("src", "lespaul.jpg");
```

Just think of all the things you could do with a document by changing the values of attributes. Here we swapped out an image, but we could use this same method to make a number of changes throughout our document:

- Update the **checked** attributes of checkboxes and radio buttons based on user interaction elsewhere on the page.

- Find the **link** element for our *.css* file and point the **href** value to a different style sheet, changing all the page's styles.

- Update a **title** attribute with information on an element's state ("this element is currently selected," for example).

innerHTML

innerHTML gives us a simple method for accessing and changing the text and markup inside an element. It behaves differently from the methods we've covered so far. Let's say we need a quick way of adding a paragraph of text to the first element on our page with a class of **intro**:

```
var introDiv = document.getElementsByClassName("intro");
introDiv[0].innerHTML = "<p>This is our intro text</p>";
```

The second statement here adds the content of the string to **introDiv** (an element with the **class** value "intro") as a *real live element* because **innerHTML** tells JavaScript to parse the strings "<p>" and "</p>" as markup.

style

The DOM also allows you to add, modify, or remove a CSS style from an element by using the **style** property. It works similarly to applying a style with the inline **style** attribute. The individual CSS properties are available as properties of the **style** property. I bet you can figure out what these statements are doing by using your new CSS and DOM know-how:

```
document.getElementById("intro").style.color = "#fff";

document.getElementById("intro").style.backgroundColor = "#f58220";
    //orange
```

In JavaScript and the DOM, property names that are hyphenated in CSS (such as **background-color** and **border-top-width**) become camel case (**backgroundColor** and **borderTopWidth**, respectively) so the "-" character isn't mistaken for an operator.

In the examples you've just seen, the **style** property is used to set the styles for the node. It can also be used to get a style value for use elsewhere in the script. This statement gets the background color of the **#intro** element and assigns it to the **brandColor** variable:

```
var brandColor = document.getElementById("intro").style.backgroundColor;
```

Adding and Removing Elements

So far, we've seen examples of getting and setting nodes in the existing document. The DOM also allows developers to change the document structure itself by adding and removing nodes on the fly. We'll start out by creating new nodes, which is fairly straightforward, and then we'll see how we add the nodes we've created to the page. The methods shown here are more surgical and precise than adding content with **innerHTML**. While we're at it, we'll remove nodes, too.

createElement()

To create a new element, use the aptly named **createElement()** method. This function accepts a single argument: the element to be created. Using this method is a little counterintuitive at first because the new element doesn't appear on the page right away. Once we create an element in this way, that new element remains floating in the JavaScript ether until we add it to the document. Think of it as creating a *reference* to a new element that lives purely in memory—something that we can manipulate in JavaScript as we see fit, and then add to the page once we're ready:

```
var newDiv = document.createElement("div");
```

createTextNode()

If we want to enter text into either an element we've created or an existing element on the page, we can call the **createTextNode()** method. To use it, provide a string of text as an argument, and the method creates a DOM-friendly version of that text, ready for inclusion on the page. Like **createElement()**, this creates a reference to the new text node that we can store in a variable and add to the page when the time comes:

```
var ourText = document.createTextNode("This is our text.");
```

appendChild()

So we've created a new element and a new string of text, but how do we make them part of the document? Enter the **appendChild()** method. This method takes a single argument: the node you want to add to the DOM. You call it on the existing element that will be its *parent* in the document structure. Time for an example.

Here we have a simple **div** on the page with the **id** "our-div":

```
<div id="our-div"></div>
```

Let's say we want to add a paragraph to **#our-div** that contains the text "Hello, world!" We start by creating the **p** element (**document.createElement()**) as well as a text node for the content that will go inside it (**createTextNode()**):

```
var ourDiv = document.getElementById("our-div");
var newParagraph = document.createElement("p");
var copy = document.createTextNode("Hello, world!");
```

Now we have our element and some text, and we can use **appendChild()** to put the pieces together:

```
newParagraph.appendChild( copy );
ourDiv.appendChild( newParagraph );
```

The first statement appends **copy** (that's our "Hello, world!" text node) to the new paragraph we created (**newParagraph**), so now that element has some content. The second line appends the **newParagraph** to the original **div** (**ourDiv**). Now **ourDiv** isn't sitting there all empty in the DOM, and it will display on the page with the content "Hello, world!"

You should be getting the idea of how it works. How about a couple more?

insertBefore()

The **insertBefore()** method, as you might guess, inserts an element before another element. It takes two arguments: the first is the node that gets inserted, and the second is the element it gets inserted in front of. You also need to know the parent to which the element will be added.

So, for example, to insert a new heading before the paragraph in this markup

```
<div id="our-div">
  <p id="our-paragraph">Our paragraph text</p>
</div>
```

we start by assigning variable names to the **div** and the **p** it contains, and then create the **h1** element and its text node and put them together, just as we saw in the last example:

```
var ourDiv = document.getElementById("our-div");
var para = document.getElementById("our-paragraph");

var newHeading = document.createElement("h1");
var headingText = document.createTextNode("A new heading");
newHeading.appendChild( headingText );
// Add our new text node to the new heading
```

Finally, in the last statement shown here, the **insertBefore()** method places the **newHeading h1** element before the **para** element inside **ourDiv**.

```
ourDiv.insertBefore( newHeading, para );
```

replaceChild()

The **replaceChild()** method replaces one node with another and takes two arguments. The first argument is the new child (i.e., the node you want to end up with). The second is the node that gets replaced by the first. As with **insertBefore()**, you also need to identify the parent element in which the swap happens. For the sake of simplicity, let's say we start with the following markup:

```
<div id="our-div">
  <div id="swap-me"></div>
</div>
```

And we want to replace the **div** with the **id** "swap-me" with an image. We start by creating a new **img** element and setting the **src** attribute to the pathname to the image file. In the final statement, we use **replaceChild()** to put **newImg** in place of **swapMe**.

```
var ourDiv = document.getElementById("our-div");
var swapMe = document.getElementById("swap-me");
var newImg = document.createElement("img");
// Create a new image element

newImg.setAttribute( "src", "path/to/image.jpg" );
// Give the new image a "src" attribute
ourDiv.replaceChild( newImg, swapMe );
```

removeChild()

To paraphrase my mother, "We brought these elements into this world, and we can take them out again." You remove a node or an entire branch from the document tree with the **removeChild()** method. The method takes one argument, which is the node you want to remove. Remember that the DOM thinks in terms of *nodes*, not just elements, so the child of an element may be the text (node) it contains, not just other elements.

Like **appendChild()**, the **removeChild()** method is always called on the parent element of the element to be removed (hence, "remove *child*"). That means we'll need a reference to both the parent node and the node we're looking to remove. Let's assume the following markup pattern:

```
<div id="parent">
  <div id="remove-me">
    <p>Pssh, I never liked it here anyway.</p>
  </div>
</div>
```

Our script would look something like this:

```
var parentDiv = document.getElementById("parent");
var removeMe = document.getElementById("remove-me");
```

```
parentDiv.removeChild( removeMe );
// Removes the div with the id "remove-me" from the page.
```

For Further Reading

That should give you a good idea of what DOM scripting is all about. Of course, I've just barely scratched the surface of what can be done with the DOM, but if you'd like to learn more, definitely check out the book *DOM Scripting: Web Design with JavaScript and the Document Object Model, Second Edition*, by Jeremy Keith and Jeffrey Sambells (Friends of Ed).

POLYFILLS

You've gotten familiar with a lot of new technologies in this book so far: new HTML5 elements, new ways of doing things with CSS3, using JavaScript to manipulate the DOM, and more. In a perfect world, all browsers would be in lockstep, keeping up with the cutting-edge technologies and getting the established ones right along the way (see the sidebar **"The Browser Wars"**). In that perfect world, browsers that couldn't keep up (I'm looking at you, IE8) would just vanish completely. Sadly, that is not the world we live in, and browser inadequacies remain the thorn in every developer's side.

I'll be the first to admit that I enjoy a good wheel reinvention. It's a great way to learn, for one thing. For another, it's the reason our cars aren't rolling around on roundish rocks and sections of tree trunk. But when it comes to dealing with every strange browser quirk out there, we don't have to start from scratch. Tons of people smarter than I am have run into these issues before, and have already found clever ways to work around them and fix the parts of JavaScript and the DOM where some browsers may fall short. We can use JavaScript to fix JavaScript.

Polyfill is a term coined by Remy Sharp to describe a JavaScript "shim" that normalizes differing behavior from browser to browser (*remysharp. com/2010/10/08/what-is-a-polyfill*). Or, as Paul Irish put it, a polyfill is

> *A shim that mimics a future API providing fallback functionality to older browsers.*

There's a lot of time travel going on in that quote, but basically what he's saying is that we're making something new work in browsers that don't natively support it—whether that's brand-new technology like detecting a user's physical location or fixing something that one of the browsers just plain got wrong.

There are tons of polyfills out there targeted to specific tasks, such as making old browsers recognize new HTML5 elements or CSS3 selectors, and new ones are popping up all the time as new problems arise. I'm going to fill you in on the most commonly used polyfills in the modern developer's toolbox as

---

The Browser Wars

JavaScript came about during a dark and lawless time, before the web standards movement, when all the major players in the browser world were—for want of a better term—winging it. It likely won't come as a major surprise to anyone that Netscape and Microsoft implemented radically different versions of the DOM, with the prevailing sentiment being "may the best browser win."

I'll spare you the gory details of the Battle for JavaScript Hill, but the two competing implementations were so different that they were both largely useless, unless you wanted to either maintain two separate code bases or add a "best viewed in Internet Explorer/Netscape" warning label to your sites.

Enter the web standards movement! During this cutthroat time, the W3C was putting together the foundations for the modern-day standardized DOM that we've all come to know and love. Fortunately for us, Netscape and Microsoft got on board with the standards movement. The standardized DOM is supported all the way back to Internet Explorer 5 and Netscape Navigator 6. Unfortunately, Internet Explorer's advancements in this area stagnated for quite some time following IE6. As a result, older versions of IE have a few significant differences from the modern-day DOM. Fortunately with Internet Explorer 9 and later, they're catching right back up.

The trouble is, your project likely still needs to support those users with older versions of IE. It's a pain, but we're up for it. We have an amazing set of tools at our disposal, such as polyfills and JavaScript libraries full of helper functions, that normalize the strange little quirks we're apt to encounter from browser to browser.

---

of the release of this book. You may find that new ones are necessary by the time you hit the web design trenches. You may also find that some of these techniques aren't needed for the browsers you need to support.

HTML5 shim (or shiv)

You may remember seeing this one back in **Chapter 5, Marking Up Text,** but let's give it a little more attention now that you have some JavaScript under your belt.

An HTML5 shim/shiv is used to enable Internet Explorer 8 and earlier to recognize and style newer HTML5 elements such as **article**, **section**, and **nav**.

There are several variations on the HTML5 shim/shiv, but they all work in much the same way: crawl the DOM looking for elements that IE doesn't recognize, and then immediately replace them with the same element so they are visible to IE in the DOM. Now any styles we write against those elements work as expected. Sjoerd Visscher originally discovered this technique, and many, many variations of these scripts exist now. Remy Sharp's version is the one in widest use today.

The shim must be referenced in the **head** of the document, in order to "tell" Internet Explorer about these new elements before it finishes rendering the page. The script is referenced inside an IE-specific conditional comment and runs only if the browser is less than (**lt**) IE9—in other words, versions 8 and earlier:

```
<!--[if lt IE 9]>
    <script src="html5shim.js"></script>
<![endif]-->
```

The major caveat here is that older versions of Internet Explorer that have JavaScript disabled or unavailable will receive unstyled elements. To learn more about HTML5 shim/shiv, try these resources:

- The Wikipedia entry for HTML Shiv (*en.wikipedia.org/wiki/HTML5_Shiv*)

- Remy Sharp's original post
  (*remysharp.com/2009/01/07/html5-enabling-script*)

Selectivizr

Selectivizr (created by Keith Clark) allows Internet Explorer 6–8 to understand complex CSS3 selectors such as **:nth-child** and **::first-letter**. It uses JavaScript to fetch and parse the contents of your style sheet and patch holes where the browser's native CSS parser falls short.

Selectivizr must be used with a JavaScript library (I talk about them in the next section). The link to the script goes in an IE conditional comment after the link to the library *.js* file, like so:

NOTE

If you don't need to support IE8 and earlier, you don't need an HTML5 shim.

NOTE

If you don't need to support IE8 and earlier, you don't need Selectivizr.

```
<script type="text/javascript" src="[JS library]"></script>
<!--[if (gte IE 6)&(lte IE 8)]>
  <script type="text/javascript" src="selectivizr.js"></script>
  <noscript><link rel="stylesheet" href="[fallback css]" /></noscript>
<![endif]-->
```

Because we're forgoing the native CSS parser here, we may see a slight performance hit in applicable browsers. See the Selectivizr site (*selectivizr.com*) for more information.

Picturefill (A Responsive Image Polyfill)

Picturefill enables support for the **picture** element, **srcset** and **sizes** attributes, and features related to delivering images based on viewport size and resolution (also known as responsive images, as discussed in **Chapter 7, Adding Images**). It was created by Scott Jehl of Filament Group and is maintained by the Picturefill group.

To use Picturefill, download the script and add it to the **head** of the document. The first script creates a **picture** element for browsers that don't recognize it. The second script calls the Picturefill script itself and the **async** attribute tells the browser it can load Picturefill asynchronously—that is, without waiting for the script to finish before loading the rest of the document.

```
<head>
  <script>
    // Picture element HTML5 shiv
    document.createElement( "picture" );
  </script>
  <script src="picturefill.js" async></script>
</head>
```

On the downside, browsers without JavaScript that also do not support the **picture** element will see only alt-text for the image. Download Picturefill and get information about its use at *scottjehl.github.io/picturefill/*.

JAVASCRIPT LIBRARIES

Continuing on the "you don't have to write everything from scratch yourself" theme, it's time to take on JavaScript libraries. A JavaScript library is a collection of prewritten functions and methods that you can use in your scripts to accomplish common tasks or simplify complex ones.

There are many JS libraries out there. Some are large frameworks that include all of the most common polyfills, shortcuts, and widgets you'd ever need to build full-blown Ajax web applications (see the sidebar **"What Is Ajax?"**). Some are targeted at specific tasks, such as handling forms, animation, charts, or math functions. For seasoned JavaScript-writing pros, starting with a library is an awesome time-saver. And for folks like you who are just getting started, a library can handle tasks that might be beyond the reach of your own skills.

What Is Ajax?

Ajax (sometimes written AJAX) stands for Asynchronous JavaScript And XML. The "XML" part isn't that important—you don't have to use XML to use Ajax (more on that in a moment). The "asynchronous" part is what matters.

Traditionally, when a user interacted with a web page in a way that required data to be delivered from the server, everything had to stop and wait for the data, and the whole page needed to reload when it was available. This made for a not especially smooth user experience.

But with Ajax, because the page can get data from the server in the background, you can make updates to the page based on user interaction smoothly and in real time without the page needing to be reloaded. This makes web applications feel more like "real" applications.

You see this on a number of modern websites, although sometimes it's subtle. On Twitter, for example, scrolling to the bottom of a page loads in a set of new tweets. Those aren't hardcoded in the page's markup; they're loaded dynamically as needed. Google's image search uses a similar approach. When you reach the bottom of the current page, you're presented with a button that allows you to load more, but you never navigate away from the current page.

The term "Ajax" was first coined by Jesse James Garrett in an article "Ajax: A New Approach to Web Applications." Ajax is not a single technology, but rather a combination of HTML, CSS, the DOM, and JavaScript, including the `XMLHttpRequest` object, which allows data to be transferred asynchronously. Ajax may use XML for data, but it has become more common to use JSON (JavaScript Object Notation), a JavaScript-based and human-readable format, for data exchange.

Writing web applications with Ajax isn't the type of thing you would do right out of the gate, but many of the JavaScript libraries discussed in this chapter have built-in Ajax helpers and methods that let you get started with significantly less effort.

The disadvantage of libraries is that because they generally contain all of their functionality in one big *.js* file, you may end up forcing your users to download a lot of code that never gets used. But the library authors are aware of this and have made many of their libraries modular, and they continue to make efforts to optimize their code. In some cases, it's also possible to customize the script and use just the parts you need.

jQuery and Other Libraries

As of this writing, the overwhelmingly dominant JavaScript library is jQuery (*jquery.com*). Chances are, if you use a library, it will be that one (or at least that one first). Written in 2005 by John Resig, jQuery has found its way into over two-thirds of all websites. Furthermore, if a site uses a library at all, there is a 97% chance that it's jQuery.

It is free, it's open source, and it employs a syntax that makes it easy to use if you are already handy with CSS, JavaScript, and the DOM. You can supplement jQuery with the jQuery UI library, which adds cool interface elements such as calendar widgets, drag-and-drop functionality, expanding accordion lists, and simple animation effects. jQuery Mobile is another jQuery-based library that provides UI elements and polyfills designed to account for the variety of mobile browsers and their notorious quirks.

Of course, jQuery isn't the only library in town. Others include MooTools (*mootools.net*), Dojo (*dojotoolkit.org*), and Prototype (*prototypejs.org*). As for smaller JS libraries that handle specialized functions, because they are being created and made obsolete all the time, I recommend doing a web search for

"JavaScript libraries for _____" and see what is available. Some library categories include the following:

- Forms

- Animation

- Image carousels

- Games

- Information graphics

- Image and 3-D effects for the **canvas** element

- String and math functions

- Database handling

- Touch gestures

How to Use jQuery

It's easy to implement any of the libraries I just listed. All you do is download the JavaScript (*.js*) file, put it on your server, point to it in your **script** tag, and you're good to go. It's the *.js* file that does all the heavy lifting, providing prewritten functions and syntax shortcuts. Once you've included it, you can write your own scripts that leverage the features built into the framework. Of course, what you actually do with it is the interesting part (and largely beyond the scope of this chapter, unfortunately).

As a member of the jQuery Mobile team, I have a pretty obvious bias here, so we're going to stick with jQuery in the upcoming examples. Not only is it the most popular library anyway, but they said they'd give me a dollar every time I say "jQuery."

Download the jQuery .js file

To get started with jQuery (*cha-ching*), go to *jQuery.com* and hit the big Download button to get your own copy of *jquery.js*. You have a choice between a production version that has all the extra whitespace removed for a smaller file size, or a development version that is easier to read but nearly eight times larger in file size. The production version should be just fine if you are not going to edit it yourself.

Copy the code, paste it into a new plain-text document, and save it with the same filename that you see in the address bar in the browser window. As of this writing, the latest version of jQuery is 3.2.1, and the filename of the production version is *jquery-3.2.1.min.js* (the *min* stands for "minimized"). Put the file in the directory with the other files for your site. Some developers keep their scripts in a *js* directory for the sake of organization, or they may simply keep them in the root directory for the site. Wherever you decide put it, be sure to note the pathname to the file because you'll need it in the markup.

Add it to your document

Include the jQuery script the same way you'd include any other script in the document, with a **script** element:

```
<script src="pathtoyourjs/jquery-3.2.1.min.js"></script>
```

And that's pretty much it. There is an alternative worth mentioning, however. If you don't want to host the file yourself, you can point to one of the publicly hosted versions and use it that way. One advantage to this method is that it gets cached by the browser, so there's a chance some of your users' browsers already have a copy of it. The jQuery Download page lists a few options, including the following link to the code on Google's server. Simply copy this code exactly as you see it here, paste it into the **head** of the document or before the **</body>** tag, and you've got yourself some jQuery!

```
<script src="https://ajax.googleapis.com/ajax/libs/jquery/3.2.1/ →
jquery.min.js"></script>
```

Get "ready"

You don't want to go firing scripts before the document and the DOM are ready for them, do you? Well, jQuery has a statement known as the ready event that checks the document and waits until it's ready to be manipulated. Not all scripts require this (for example, if you were only firing a browser alert), but if you are doing anything with the DOM, it is a good idea to start by setting the stage for your scripts by including this function in your custom **script** or *.js* file:

```
<script src="pathtoyourjs/jquery-3.2.1.min.js"></script>

<script>
$(document).ready(function(){

    // Your code here

});
</script>
```

Scripting with jQuery

Once you're set up, you can begin writing your own scripts using jQuery. The shortcuts jQuery offers break down into two general categories:

- A giant set of built-in feature detection scripts and polyfills

- A shorter, more intuitive syntax for targeting elements (jQuery's selector engine)

You should have a decent sense of what the polyfills do after making your way through that last section, so let's take a look at what the selector engine does for you.

One of the things that jQuery simplifies is moving around through the DOM because you can use the selector syntax that you learned for CSS. Here is an example of getting an element by its **id** value *without* a library:

```
var paragraph = document.getElementById( "status" );
```

The statement finds the element with the ID "status" and saves a reference to the element in a variable (**paragraph**). That's a lot of characters for a simple task. You can probably imagine how things get a little verbose when you're accessing lots of elements on the page. Now that we have jQuery in play, however, we can use this shorthand:

```
var paragraph = $("#status");
```

That's right—that's the **id** selector you know and love from writing CSS. And it doesn't just stop there. *Any* selector you'd use in CSS will work within that special helper function.

You want to find everything with a class of **header**? Use **$(".header");**.

By the element's name? Sure: **$("div");**.

Every subhead in your sidebar? Easy-peasy: **$("#sidebar .sub");**.

You can even target elements based on the value of attributes: **$("[href='http://google.com']");**.

But it doesn't stop with selectors. We can use a huge number of helper functions built into jQuery and libraries like it to crawl the DOM like so many, uh, Spider-men. Spider-persons. Web-slingers.

jQuery also allows us to chain objects together in a way that can target things even CSS can't (an element's parent element, for example). Let's say we have a paragraph and we want to add a **class** to that paragraph's parent element. We don't necessarily know what that parent element will be, so we're unable to target the parent element directly. In jQuery we can use the **parent()** object to get to it:

```
$("p.error").parent().addClass("error-dialog");
```

Another major benefit is that this is highly readable at a glance: "find any paragraph(s) with the class 'error' and add the class 'error-dialog' to their parent(s)."

But What If I Don't Know How to Write Scripts?

It takes time to learn JavaScript, and it may be a while before you can write scripts on your own. But not to worry. If you do a web search for what you need (for example, "jQuery image carousel" or "jQuery accordion list"), there's a very good chance you will find lots of scripts that people have created and shared, complete with documentation on how to use them. Because jQuery uses a selector syntax very similar to CSS, it makes it easier to customize jQuery scripts for use with your own markup.

BIG FINISH

In all of two chapters, we've gone from learning the very basics of variables to manipulating the DOM to leveraging a JavaScript library. Even with all we've covered here, we've just barely begun to cover all the things JavaScript can do.

The next time you're looking at a website and it does something cool, view the source in your browser and have a look around for the JavaScript. You can learn a lot from reading and even taking apart someone else's code. And remember, there's nothing you can break with JavaScript that can't be undone with a few strokes of the Delete key.

Better still, JavaScript comes with an entire community of passionate developers who are eager to learn and just as eager to teach. Seek out like-minded developers and share the things you've learned along the way. If you're stuck on a tricky problem, don't hesitate to seek out help and ask questions. It's rare that you'll encounter a problem that nobody else has, and the open source developer community is always excited to share the things they've learned. That's why you've had to put up with me for two chapters, as a matter of fact.

TEST YOURSELF

Just a few questions for those of you playing along at home. If you need some help, peek in **Appendix A** for the answers.

1. Ajax is a combination of what technologies?

2. What does this do?

    ```
    document.getElementById("main")
    ```


3. What does this do?

    ```
    document.getElementById("main").getElementsByTagName("section");
    ```

4. What does this do?

```
document.body.style.backgroundColor = "papayawhip"
```

5. What does this do? (This one is a little tricky because it nests functions, but you should be able to piece it together.)

```
document
  .getElementById("main")
    .appendChild(
      document.createElement("p")
        .appendChild(
          documentCreateTextNode("Hey, I'm walking here!")
        )
    );
```

6. What is the benefit of using a JavaScript library such as jQuery?

    a. Access to a packaged collection of polyfills

    b. Possibly shorter syntax

    c. Simplified Ajax support

    d. All of the above

V
WEB IMAGES

WEB IMAGE BASICS

Unless you plan to publish text-only sites, chances are you'll need images. For many of you, that might mean getting your hands on an image-editing program for the first time and acquiring some basic graphics production skills. If you are a seasoned designer, you may need to adapt your style and process to make graphics that are appropriate for web delivery.

In **Chapter 7, Adding Images**, we covered the basics of embedding images in the HTML document, including the difference between bitmapped graphic formats and the vector-based SVG. This chapter covers the fundamentals of the images themselves. We'll start by reviewing sources for imagery. From there, we'll get to know the file formats available for web graphics to help you decide which one to use. We'll look at image resolution and how it relates to the resolution of the screens on which they appear, including high-density displays. I'll also walk you through a series of questions that will help you form a strategy for creating images for your site. Finally, the chapter wraps up with a quick Favicon how-to.

IMAGE SOURCES

You need to *have* an image to save an image, so before we jump into the nitty-gritty of file formats, let's look at some ways to get images in the first place. There are many options: from scanning, shooting, or illustrating them yourself, to using available stock photos and clip art, to just hiring someone to create images for you.

Create Your Own Images

In most cases, the most cost-effective way to generate images for your site is to make your own from scratch. The added bonus is that you know you have

■ SCANNING TIPS

When you're scanning sources for use on the web, these tips will help you create images with better quality:

- Because it is easier to maintain image quality when resizing smaller than resizing larger, **scan the image larger than you actually need**. This gives you more flexibility for creating other sizes later. Issues of image size are discussed in more detail in the **"Image Size and Resolution"** section later in this chapter.

- **Scan black-and-white images in grayscale (8-bit) mode**, not in black-and-white (1-bit, or bitmap) mode. This enables you to make adjustments in the midtone gray areas once you have sized the image to its final dimensions and resolution. If you really want only black-and-white pixels, convert the image as the last step.

- If you are scanning an image that has been printed, you need to **eliminate the dot pattern that results from the printing process.** The best way to do this is to apply a slight blur to the image (in Photoshop, use the Gaussian Blur filter), resize the image slightly smaller, and then apply a sharpening filter. This will eliminate those pesky dots. Make sure you have the rights to use the printed image, too, of course.

full rights to use the images (we'll address copyright in a moment). Designers may generate imagery with scanners, cameras, or a drawing program:

Photographs

You can capture the world around you and pipe it right into an image-editing program. Depending on the type of imagery you're after, you may get sufficient quality with the camera in your phone. Keep in mind that it's always a good idea to create high-resolution versions of your images and save smaller copies as needed.

Electronic illustration

If you have illustration skills, you can make your own image in a drawing or photo-editing application. Every designer has her own favorite tools and techniques. For logos and line drawings, I recommend starting with a vector drawing program like Adobe Illustrator, Corel Draw, or Sketch, and then saving to a web-appropriate copy as needed.

Scanning

Scanning is a great way to collect source material. You can scan almost anything, from flat art to small 3-D objects. Beware, however, the temptation to scan and use found images. Keep in mind that most images you find are probably copyright-protected and may not be used without permission, even if you modify them considerably. See the **"Scanning Tips"** sidebar for some how-to information.

Stock Photography and Illustrations

If you aren't confident in your design skills, or you just want a head start with some fresh imagery, there are plenty of collections of ready-made photos, illustrations, buttons, animations, and textures available for sale or for free. Stock photos and illustrations generally fall into two broad categories: rights-managed and royalty-free.

Rights-managed

Rights-managed means that the copyright holder (or a company representing them) controls who may reproduce the image. In order to use a rights-managed image, you must obtain a license to reproduce it for a particular use and for a particular period of time. One of the advantages to licensing images is that you can arrange to have exclusive rights to an image within a particular medium (such as the web) or a particular business sector (such as the health-care industry or banking). You also know that the source of the image is verified (i.e., it is not stolen).

On the downside, rights-managed images get quite pricey. Depending on the breadth and length of the license, the price tag may be many thousands of dollars for a single image. If you don't want exclusive rights and you want to use the image only on the web, the cost is more likely to be a few hundred dollars, depending on the source.

Getty Images (*gettyimages.com*) is the largest stock image house for rights-managed images, having acquired most of its competitors over recent years. It also offers royalty-free images, which we'll look at next.

Royalty-free

If you don't have a four-digit or even three-digit budget for images, consider using royalty-free artwork for which you don't need to pay a licensing fee. Royalty-free artwork is available for a one-time fee that gives you unlimited use of the image, but you have no control over who else is using it. Royalty-free images are available from the top-notch professional stock houses such as Getty Images for as little as 50 bucks for a small image appropriate for the web (like the blissed-out kangaroo in FIGURE 23-1), and from other sites for less (or even for free).

One of my favorite sources is iStockPhoto (*istockphoto.com*). They have a huge collection of images starting around US$10 a pop. You can buy one image at a time or get a subscription plan.

Creative Commons

Another way to get free images is to find photos and drawings released by the artists under a Creative Commons license. There are a few types of Creative Commons licenses, so be sure to check the terms. Some artists make their work free to use however you want; some artists ask only that you give them credit ("attribution-only"); and some limit the image use to non-commercial purposes.

There are a number of resources for images released on a Creative Commons license, but these are three good first stops:

Flickr Creative Commons (*www.flickr.com/creativecommons*)

The photo-sharing service Flickr is my first stop for finding photos released on a Creative Commons license. The quality varies, but I can usually find what I need (such as the red panda in FIGURE 16-28) for the cost of a photo credit.

Unsplash (*unsplash.com*)

Unsplash provides free images of top-notch quality, "gifted by the world's most generous community of photographers." It is the source of many of the food images I use in this book.

Wikimedia Commons (*commons.wikimedia.org/wiki/Main_Page*)

A sister site to Wikipedia, Wikimedia Commons is a vast resource of millions of Creative Commons and public domain images and other media files. They are contributed by the community and free to use.

FIGURE 23-1. One blissed-out kangaroo, an example of a royalty-free image I got on Gettyimages.com for your amusement.

> ■ **FURTHER READING**
>
> For more information about Creative Commons licenses, go to *creativecommons.org/licenses/*.

Clip Art and Icons

Clip art refers to collections of royalty-free illustrations, animations, buttons, and other doodads that you can copy and paste for a wide range of uses. There are a number of resources online, and the good news is that some of these sites give graphics away for free, although you may have to suffer through a barrage of pop-up ads. Others charge a membership fee, anywhere from $10 to $200 a year. The drawback is that a lot of them are poor quality or kind of hokey (but then, "hokey" is in the eye of the beholder). The following are two sites to get you started:

Clipart.com (*www.clipart.com*)

This service charges a membership fee, but is well organized and tends to provide higher-quality artwork than the free sites.

#1 Free Clip Art (*www.1clipart.com*)

Another no-frills free clip-art site.

It is also easy to find icons for web pages and applications for free or for a low price (a simple search for "free icons" will do the trick). Here are two resources to start you off:

The Noun Project (*thenounproject.com*)

The Noun Project collects and organizes classic, one-color icons from around the world. Dozens of collections are available for free, and a yearly subscription fee gives you access to everything.

Icon Finder (*www.iconfinder.com*)

This is a good resource for full-color icons of all styles. Some are free, but most are available via a monthly subscription plan. Be sure to check the terms of the Creative Commons license, which varies by icon set.

Hire a Designer

Finding and creating custom images takes time and particular talents. If you have more money than either of those things, consider hiring a graphic designer, photographer, or illustrator to generate the imagery for your site for you. The advantage to hiring a professional is that you get custom images tailored to your message or brand, not just generic stock images. If you start with high-quality original images, you can use the skills you learn in this book to produce web versions as you need them.

MEET THE FORMATS

Once you have your hands on some images, you need to get them into a format that will work on a web page. There are dozens of graphics file formats out there in the world. For example, if you use Windows, you may be familiar with BMP graphics, or if you are a print designer, you may commonly use images in TIFF and EPS format. On the web, bitmapped (pixel-based) images can be saved in the following formats (see **Note**): JPEG ("jay-peg"), PNG ("ping" or "Pee-en-gee"), GIF (pronounced "giff" or "jiff"), and WebP (I've seen it referred to as "weppy," but "web-p" sounds fine to me).

There is also the vector format SVG (Scalable Vector Graphics) that we looked at it in terms of markup back in **Chapter 7**. SVG is a bit of an oddball in that it is generated by an XML text file. It is so unique, in fact, that I've given it its own chapter: **Chapter 25, SVG**. This chapter and the next focus primarily on the bitmap formats.

When you're saving an image asset for a web page, it is important that it has the best image quality at the smallest file size. The first step to achieving those goals is making sure you save the image in the most appropriate format based on the image type. This section tackles terminology and digs deep into the features and functions of GIF, JPEG, PNG, and WebP. Knowing how they work will help you make the best format decision.

The Photogenic JPEG

One of the most popular graphic formats on the web is JPEG, which stands for Joint Photographic Experts Group, the standards body that created it.

JPEG is the best format to use if your image is a photograph or contains soft, smooth color transitions (FIGURE 23-2). The JPEG compression scheme *loves* gradient and blended colors, but doesn't work especially well on flat colors or hard edges.

NOTE

The WebP format is so new as of this writing that few browsers and image software programs support it. Still, I include it here because it is a promising option once support improves.

Name Files Properly

Be sure to use the proper file extensions for your image files:

- GIF files end with the *.gif* suffix.
- JPEG files use the *.jpg* (or the less common *.jpeg*) suffix.
- PNG files end in *.png*.
- WebP files end in *.webp*.
- SVG files end in *.svg*.

> JPEG is the best format to use if your image is a photograph or contains soft, smooth color transitions.

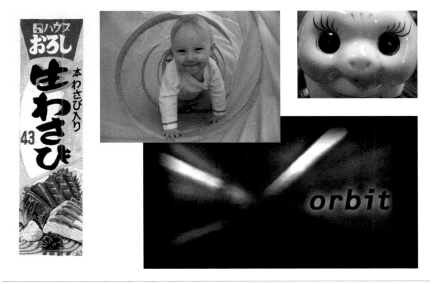

FIGURE 23-2. The JPEG format is ideal for photographs (color or grayscale) or any image with subtle color gradations.

24-bit Truecolor images

JPEGs are capable of displaying millions of colors in the RGB color space (also referred to as the Truecolor space; see **Note**). This is also known as 24-bit color because each of the three color channels (Red, Green, and Blue) is defined with 8 bits of information.

Displaying 24-bit color is one aspect that makes JPEGs ideal for photographs—they have all the colors you'll ever need. By comparison, other formats such as PNG-8 and GIF use a palette that limits the number of colors in the image to 256 *total* (we'll talk about why in a moment).

Lossy compression

The JPEG compression scheme is lossy, which means that some of the image information is thrown out in the compression process (see **Warning**). Fortunately, this loss is not discernible for most images at most compression levels. When an image is compressed with high levels of JPEG compression, you begin to see color blotches and squares (referred to as artifacts) that result from the way the compression scheme samples the image (FIGURE 23-3).

Original   Maximum compression

FIGURE 23-3. JPEG compression discards image detail to achieve smaller file sizes. At high compression rates, image quality suffers, as shown in the image on the right.

In most programs, you can control how aggressively you want the image to be compressed with a Quality setting when saving or exporting. This involves a trade-off between file size and image quality. The more you compress the image (for a smaller file size), the more the image quality suffers. Conversely, when you maximize quality, you also end up with larger files. The best compression level is based on the particular image and your objectives for the site.

Progressive JPEGs

Progressive JPEGs display in a series of passes, starting with a low-resolution version that gets clearer with each pass, as shown in FIGURE 23-4. In some image editing programs, you can specify the number of passes it takes to fill in the final image (3, 4, or 5).

NOTE

RGB color is explained in **Chapter 13, Colors and Backgrounds.**

WARNING

Cumulative Image Quality Loss

Be aware that once image quality is lost in JPEG compression, you can never get it back again. For this reason, you should avoid resaving a JPEG as a JPEG. The image loss is cumulative—in other words, you lose image quality **every time***.*

It is better to hang on to the original image and export JPEG copies as needed. That way, if you need to make a change, you can go back to the original and do a fresh save or export.

FIGURE 23-4. Progressive JPEGs render in a series of passes.

The advantage to using progressive JPEGs is that viewers can get an idea of the image before it downloads completely. Also, making a JPEG progressive usually reduces its file size slightly. The disadvantage is that progressive JPEGs take more processing power, which can make them problematic for low-end mobile devices. Despite that minor hitch, the best practice is to make all JPEGs progressive, not only for the smaller file size, but because they appear on the page faster, improving perceived performance.

The Powerful PNG

The PNG (Portable Network Graphics) format was designed to replace GIF for online purposes and TIFF for image storage and printing. A PNG can be used to save many image types: 8-bit indexed color, 24- and 48-bit RGB color, and 16-bit grayscale, but for the purposes of web production, you need to choose only between 8-bit (PNG-8) and 24-bit (PNG-24).

Despite getting off to a slow start in terms of browser support, PNGs have become developers' first choice in web graphics formats, and for good reason. PNGs offer an impressive lineup of features:

- Lossless compression
- Multiple-level (alpha) or simple on/off (binary) transparency
- Progressive display in multiple passes
- Embedded gamma (brightness) adjustment information
- Embedded text for attaching information about the image

PNG-8

PNG-8 is good for images that have flat colors, such as logos, line art, and icons (FIGURE 23-5). You can save photographs or textured images too, but they won't be saved as efficiently, resulting in larger file sizes. However, PNG-8 does work nicely for images with a combination of small amounts of photographic imagery and large, flat areas of color. The two key characteristics of PNG-8s are that they use an indexed color model and they support transparency. These concepts are worth exploring a bit deeper.

The Wide World of JPEG

The Joint Photographic Experts Group has been busy since releasing the original JPEG format we know and love. They have released several newer JPEG standards (JPEG 2000, JPEG XR, JPEG-LS, JPEG XS, and others) that aim to keep pace with changing image requirements in all arenas, from digital cameras to medical imaging. Newer formats include features such as lossless compression, the ability to store 16-bit information in the RGB color channels, the CMYK color model, and lightweight implementations that are easier to encode and decode. Read more about them at *JPEG.org*.

Grayscale PNGs

PNG supports 16-bit grayscale images—that's as many as 65,536 shades of gray (2^{16}), enabling black-and-white photographs and illustrations to be stored with enormous subtlety of detail, although they are not appropriate for the web. In addition to the large file sizes required to store that much image information, that level of subtlety in grays would be lost on most computer monitors.

NOTE

Because they are simple illustrations, the images in FIGURE 23-5 could also have been drawn with vectors and saved in SVG format.

FIGURE 23-5. The PNG-8 format is efficient at compressing graphical images comprising mainly flat colors and hard edges.

8-bit indexed color

I mentioned earlier that PNG-8 files contain a maximum of 256 colors. Let's talk about why.

NOTE

GIFs are also 8-bit indexed color images, so this discussion of bit depth and palettes applies to GIFs as well.

PNG-8 files are indexed color images that contain 8-bit color information (they can also be saved at lower bit depths). Let's decipher that statement one term at a time. First, 8-bit means PNG-8s can contain up to 256 colors—the maximum number that 8 bits of information can define ($2^8 = 256$). Lower bit depths result in fewer colors and also reduce file size. For example, 4-bit images contain only 16 colors ($2^4 = 16$).

Indexed color means that the set of colors in the image, its palette, is stored in a color table (also called a color map). Each pixel in the image contains a numeric reference (or index) to a position in the color table. Let's make this clear with a simple demonstration. FIGURE 23-6 shows how a 2-bit (4-color) indexed color image references its color table for display. For 8-bit images, there are 256 slots in the color table.

Image-editing programs generally allow you to view the color table for an image. In Photoshop, you can view (and even edit) the color table by selecting Image → Mode → Color Table (FIGURE 23-7). In GIMP, go to Windows → Dockable Dialogs → Color Map (the image must be converted to indexed color mode first).

Most source images (scans, illustrations, photos, etc.) start out in RGB format, so they need to be converted to indexed color in order to be saved as a PNG-8 or GIF. When an image goes from RGB to indexed mode, the colors in the image are reduced to a palette of 256 colors or fewer, a process known as quantization. For most programs, including Photoshop, the conversion takes place when you save or export the image. Some image-editing programs, like

1	1	1	1	1	1	1	1	1
1	1	3	3	3	3	3	1	1
1	3	3	2	3	2	3	3	1
1	3	3	3	4	3	3	3	1
1	3	2	3	3	3	2	3	1
1	3	3	2	2	2	3	3	1
1	1	3	3	3	3	3	1	1
1	1	1	1	1	1	1	1	1

Color table

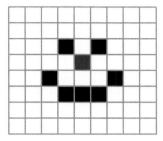

The pixels in an indexed color image contain numerical references to the color table for the image.

The color table matches numbers to RGB color values. This is the map for a 2-bit image with 4 colors.

The image displays with the colors in place.

FIGURE 23-6. A 2-bit image and its color table.

Image reduced to 64 indexed colors

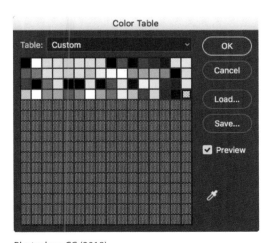

Photoshop CC (2018)

GIMP

FIGURE 23-7. The color tables in Photoshop and GIMP display the 64-pixel colors used in the image.

GIMP, may require you to convert the image to indexed color manually first, and then export the PNG-8 as a second step.

In either case, you might be asked to select a palette for the indexed color image. The sidebar **"Common Color Palettes"** outlines the various palette options available in the most popular image tools. It is recommended that you use Selective or Perceptual in Photoshop and Optimized Median Cut in PaintShop Pro for the best results for most image types. In GIMP, "Generate optimum palette" should do the trick, although it also provides a long list of crazy custom palettes you *could* use (Coldfire, Plasma, Paintjet, and Bears, to name just a few).

Transparency

You can make parts of a PNG-8 image fully transparent so that the background image or color shows through. Although all bitmapped graphics are rectangular by nature, transparency creates the illusion that the image has a more interesting shape (FIGURE 23-8). In the most commonly supported type of PNG-8 transparency, pixels are either fully transparent or fully opaque, also known as binary transparency.

PNG-8 files are also capable of storing multiple levels of transparency in their indexed color maps, allowing soft edges and shadows to blend in with the background. In the past, although browsers supported PNG-8 with variable levels, it was a challenge to find an image-editing tool that could create them. Today, you can create transparent PNG-8s right from Photoshop CC, and there are a number of tools for converting a PNG-24 to PNG-8 while maintaining its transparency levels.

FIGURE 23-8. Transparency allows the striped background to show through the bottom image.

Common Color Palettes

All 8-bit indexed color images, like PNG-8 and GIF, use palettes to define the colors in the image, and there are several standard palettes to choose from. Some are methods for producing a custom palette based on the colors in the image. Others apply a preexisting palette to the image.

Exact. Creates a custom palette out of the actual colors in the image if the image already contains fewer than 256 colors.

Adaptive. Creates a custom palette using the most frequently used pixel colors in the image. It allows for color-depth reduction while preserving the original character of the image.

Perceptual (Photoshop only). Creates a custom color table by giving priority to colors for which the human eye has greater sensitivity. Unlike Adaptive, it is based on algorithms, not just a pixel count. It generally results in images with better color integrity than Adaptive palette images.

Selective (Photoshop only). Similar to Perceptual, but it gives preference to areas of broad color.

Web Adaptive, Restrictive, or Web216. Creates a palette of colors exclusively from a palette of 216 colors that do not dither on 8-bit monitors. Because 8-bit monitors are a thing of the past, this palette (known as the "web palette") is no longer relevant or recommended.

Custom. Allows you to load a palette that was previously saved and apply it to the current image. Otherwise, it preserves the current colors in the palette.

System (Windows or Macintosh). Uses the colors in the specified system's default palette.

Optimized Median Cut (Paint Shop Pro Photo only). Reduces the image to a few colors using something similar to an Adaptive palette.

Optimized Octree (Paint Shop Pro Photo only). Is recommended if the original image has just a few colors and you want to keep those exact colors.

We'll look at both binary and variable transparency as it applies to PNG-8 files in the **"Working with Transparency"** section in **Chapter 24, Image Asset Production**.

PNG-24

A PNG can also be saved as a Truecolor image, with each channel (red, green, and blue) defined by 8- or 16-bit information, resulting in 24- or 48-bit RGB images, respectively. In many graphics programs, 24-bit RGB PNGs are identified as PNG-24. It should be noted that 48-bit images, while great for storage of high-quality originals, are useless for the web becuse of file size, and even 24-bit images may not be the best choice. Like JPEG, PNG-24 is good for photographic images where you want the maximum color range.

The two key characteristics of PNG-24s are that they are "lossless" and they can contain multiple levels of transparency. Let's dig into that a bit deeper.

Lossless compression

We learned that in JPEG's lossy compression algorithm, image data is tossed out in order to reduce the size of the file. PNG-24 files are lossless, meaning nothing is sacrificed. Because it is a lossless format, a 24-bit PNG is nearly always significantly larger than a lossy JPEG of the same image. For that reason, JPEGs are the best choice for photos on the web.

However, PNG-24 was the first format to include a killer feature that has made it one of the web's most popular formats, and that is…

Alpha transparency

PNG-24 files can contain multiple levels of transparency, commonly referred to as alpha transparency. They do this by storing 8-bit transparency information (256 levels) in a fourth channel, called the alpha channel.

NOTE

You sometimes see PNG-24 with alpha transparency referred to as a 32-bit PNG because there are 8 bits for each of four channels: red, green, blue, and alpha.

FIGURE 23-9 shows the same PNG against two different background images. The orange circle is entirely opaque, but the drop shadow contains multiple levels of transparency, ranging from nearly opaque to entirely transparent. The multiple transparency levels stored in the PNG allow the drop shadow to blend seamlessly with any background. The ins and outs of alpha transparency will be addressed in the section **"Working with Transparency"** in **Chapter 24**.

The two key characteristics of PNG-24s are that they are "lossless" and they can contain multiple levels of transparency.

FIGURE 23-9. Alpha-channel transparency allows multiple levels of transparency, as shown in the drop shadow around the orange circle PNG.

Additional features

There are a few other features that make PNG a Pretty Nifty Graphic format (see what I did there?).

Gamma correction

Gamma refers to the brightness setting of a monitor. PNGs can be tagged with information regarding the gamma setting of the environment in which they were created. When implemented in the image and the browser, the PNG retains its intended brightness and color intensity. Unfortunately, this feature is not consistently supported. In fact, image-optimizing tools typically remove the chunk of code that controls gamma. With poor browser support for gamma anyway, nothing is lost but unnecessary bytes.

Embedded color profile information

The PNG format can also store the ICC color profile information of the system it was created on. In fact, if you are finding that it is difficult to match an RGB value in a PNG to the same RGB value in a background color, the embedded color profile is to blame. The block of code for storing ICC profiles also generally gets tossed by image optimizers.

Embedded text

PNGs also have the ability to store strings of text. This is useful for permanently attaching text to an image, such as copyright information or a description of what is in the image. Ideally, the meta-information in the PNG would be accessible via right-clicking the graphic in a browser, but this feature has never been implemented.

Progressive display (interlacing)

PNGs can also be coded for interlaced display, revealing the image in a series of seven passes, filling in the image both horizontally and vertically. Interlacing adds to the file size and is usually not necessary, so to keep files as small as possible, turn interlacing display off. I'm finding that most tools these days don't give you the option to turn it on anyway.

In conclusion…

Before we move on, here's the skinny on what you should know about PNGs:

- If you have a bitmapped image with areas of flat color, with or without transparent areas, PNG-8 is the most appropriate format as it will likely result in the smallest file size.

- If you need variable levels of transparency, regardless of the image type, PNG-24 may be the only option based on the tools you are working with; however, the file will be smaller as a PNG-8.

- If you have a photographic image with no transparency, you *could* use PNG-24, but JPEG will almost always result in a smaller file.

NOTE

Safari now supports ICC color profiles. This article on CSS Tricks by Chris Coyier provides a good overview: css-tricks.com/color-rendering-difference-firefox-vs-safari/.

Animated PNGs

The APNG (Animated PNG) format is an extension to PNG that adds the ability to animate frames. In addition to 8-bit animations, it includes support for animated 24-bit images with alpha transparency. APNG is supported by current versions of Chrome and both desktop and mobile versions of Firefox, Safari, and Opera. No versions of Internet Explorer or MS Edge support APNG. Once they add support and old versions fall out of use, the APNG will certainly give animated GIFs a run for their money.

Ol' Grandpa GIF

The GIF (Graphic Interchange Format) file was the first image format supported by web browsers and for a while, it was the *only* file format that would display in a browser window. (I know. I was there.) Although not designed specifically for the web, it was adopted for its versatility, small file size, and cross-platform compatibility.

These days, GIF is synonymous with "animated viral meme," and, as the only well-supported web image format capable of animation, the GIF format still has a place at the table (at least until APNG and animated WebP have more thorough support). For still images, however, GIF has lost ground to the PNG format, which can do everything GIF can do and usually better. Furthermore, newer graphics tools are simply omitting the option to save files in GIF format. Our old friend GIF may be heading for retirement. That's OK...we just fight about how to pronounce it anyway.

That said, let's quickly look at what makes GIF tick.

8-bit indexed color

Like PNG-8, GIF is an 8-bit indexed color format. You can save a GIF at even lower bit depths, resulting in fewer colors and smaller file sizes.

GIF compression

GIF compression is lossless, although some image information is lost when the RGB image is converted to indexed color. It uses a compression scheme (called "LZW" for "Lempel-Ziv-Welch") that takes advantage of repetition in data. When it encounters a string of pixels of identical color, it compresses them into one data description (FIGURE 23-10). This is why images with large areas of flat color condense better than images with textures. PNG uses a similar like-color compression scheme.

Transparency

GIF images use binary transparency, in which pixels are either entirely opaque or transparent.

Interlacing

Interlacing makes a GIF display in a series of passes, like progressive JPEGs. Each pass is clearer than the pass before, until the image is fully rendered in the browser window (FIGURE 23-11). Over a fast connection, these effects (interlacing or image delays) may not be perceptible. However, over slow connections, interlacing large images may be a way to provide a hint of the image to come.

GIF compression stores repetitive pixel colors as a single description.

"14 blue"

In an image with gradations of color, information must be saved for every pixel in the row. The longer description means a larger file size.

"1 blue, 1 aqua, 2 light aqua..." (and so on)

FIGURE 23-10. A simplified demonstration of the LZW compression scheme. What actually happens in technical terms is more complicated, of course, but this example provides a good mental model.

FIGURE 23-11. Interlaced GIFs display in a series of passes, each clearer than the pass before.

Animation

Another feature built into the GIF file format is the ability to display simple animations (FIGURE 23-12). Many of the spinning, blinking, fading, or otherwise moving ad banners you see are animated GIFs, and they certainly show up in your social media feeds.

FIGURE 23-12. All the frames of this simple animation are contained in one GIF file.

Animated GIFs contain a number of animation frames, which are separate images that, when viewed together quickly, give the illusion of motion or change over time, kind of like a flipbook. All of the frames are stored within a single GIF file along with settings that describe how they should be played. Settings include whether and how many times the sequence repeats, how long each frame stays visible (frame delay), the manner in which one frame replaces another (disposal method), whether the image is transparent, and whether it is interlaced.

There are many tools for creating animated GIFs (just do a quick search). Many are web apps that you can use right in the browser or mobile device, and many are free. You can also make an animated GIF in Photoshop by using the Timeline window and clicking Create Frame Animation.

The Performant WebP

There's a new image format in town, and it's here to beat up all the other formats. Google calls its open source WebP format "the Swiss Army knife of image formats." It has virtually all the features we've looked at in JPEG, PNG, and GIF at sizes that are typically 25–35% smaller:

Lossless or lossy compression

> WebP can be saved in a lossy format (like JPEG) or lossless (like PNG). Its lossy compression scheme uses the same encoding used in the VP8 video codec.

Alpha transparency

> WebP has an alpha channel for multiple levels of transparency, like PNG-24. Alpha transparency can be used with either the lossless (PNG-like) image compression or—and this is special—lossy (JPEG-like) compression. It is the only format that can combine a *lossy* RGB channel with a

lossless alpha channel, resulting in a file that is 60–70% smaller than a PNG-24 of the same image.

Animation

It is also possible to animate WebP images. Sorry GIF, there goes your advantage.

Metadata

Like PNG, the WebP container can store metadata right in its code.

Color profile

The WebP container can also embed color profile (ICC) information.

Support

Here's where we get to the "sad trombone" portion of the story. Because WebP is new, it has sparse browser support. As of this writing, it is supported in only newer Chrome, Android, Opera, Vivaldi, and Samsung browsers. But that doesn't mean you can't use it! The modern web developer knows it's a good approach to supply the best (in this case, fastest) experience to browsers that can handle it and the next best thing to the rest.

You can use Modernizr (covered in **Chapter 19, More CSS Techniques**) to detect WebP in its lossy, lossless, alpha-channel, and animated varieties. You can also use the **picture** element to deliver a *.webp* image to browsers that can use it and a JPEG as a fallback, as we saw back in **Chapter 7**:

```
<picture>
  <source type="image/webp" srcset="pizza.webp">
  <img src="pizza.jpg" alt="pizza">
</picture>
```

It is also common to have the server make the call and deliver WebP images when it detects that the browser supports them (based on the "accept encoding header"). Backend solutions are beyond the scope of this discussion, but it's an option you should be aware of.

Creating WebP files

As with browsers, it will take a while for WebP to find its way into image creation tools. You can already make WebP files in Sketch, Pixelmator, and a few other graphics programs. You will find a current list of supporting programs on the WebP Wikipedia page (*en.wikipedia.org/wiki/WebP*). There is word that full WebP support will be added to GIMP in version 2.10, which has not yet been released as of this writing.

If you use Adobe Photoshop, there are two plug-ins that let you save to WebP format. The first, by Toby Thain, is at *telegraphics.com.au/sw/product/ WebPFormat*, and a newer one by Brendan Bolles is available at *github.com/ fnordware/AdobeWebM*). Once you install the plug-in, you'll see WebP in the list of formats you can save to.

Finally, you may also use the **cwebp** command-line tool (see, they're not just for coders!) to convert PNG and JPEG images to WebP format. The corresponding **dwebp** command converts WebP to PNG.

Where to learn more

WebP has an official site at *developers.google.com/speed/webp*, where you will find detailed documentation, an explanation of its compression schemes, updated lists of supporting tools and browsers (including links to download the aforementioned plug-ins and command-line tools), and a gallery of samples. It's definitely worth reading if you enjoy geeking out on image formats. WebP is certainly worth keeping an eye on.

Choosing the Best Bitmapped Format

The first step to making quality web graphics that maintain quality and download quickly is choosing the right format. TABLE 23-1 provides a good starting point. Because of poor support for WebP as of this writing, I will stick with the supported bitmap formats PNG, JPEG, and GIF here.

Note that SVG should be your first choice for illustrations and icons with flat colors. SVG may also result in smaller files for images with a combination of flat colors and a small areas of bitmapped image, gradients, or effects like drop shadows. You'll learn all about them in **Chapter 25**, but for now, TABLE 23-1 should help you sort out the bitmapped file options.

That concludes our exploration of image formats. I think we just took the very long way around to say, "if it's a photo, use JPEG, and if it's mostly flat colors, use PNG-8," but I think it's important to understand *why*.

TABLE 23-1. Choosing the best bitmapped (raster) file format

If your image...	use...	because...
Is graphical, with flat colors	8-bit PNG or GIF	PNG and GIF excel at compressing flat color.
Is a photograph or contains graduated color	JPEG	JPEG compression works best on images with blended colors. Because it is lossy, it generally results in smaller file sizes than 24-bit PNG.
Is a combination of flat and photographic imagery	8-bit PNG or GIF	Indexed color formats are best at preserving and compressing flat color areas. The pixelation (dithering) that appears in the photographic areas as a result of reducing to a palette is usually not problematic.
Requires transparency	GIF or PNG-8	Both GIF and PNG allow on/off transparency in images.
Requires multiple levels of transparency	PNG-24 or PNG-8	Only PNG supports multiple levels of transparency. PNG-24s with alpha transparency have a much larger file size, but it is easier to find tools to create them. WebP also supports alpha transparency, and may be a better option once it is better supported.
Requires animation	GIF	GIF is the only supported format that can contain animation frames. APNG and WebP may be better options in the future.

IMAGE SIZE AND RESOLUTION

There is a new term floating around to describe folks who design web pages and apps: screen designer. I like it. As the web and smartphones evolve, it is clear that the requirements and concerns of designing for screens are distinct from designing for print. As a web designer, you will need to be well versed in how images display on screens, so let's zoom in.

One thing that GIF, JPEG, PNG, and WebP images have in common is that they are all bitmapped (also called raster) images. When you zoom in on a bitmapped image, you can see that it is like a mosaic made up of many pixels (tiny, single-colored squares). These are different from vector graphics that are made up of smooth lines and filled areas, all based on mathematical formulas. FIGURE 23-13 illustrates the difference between bitmapped and vector graphics.

Bitmapped images are made up of a grid of variously colored pixels, like a mosaic.

Vector images use mathematical equations to define shapes.

FIGURE 23-13. Bitmapped and vector graphics.

Image Resolution

Image-editing programs keep track of how many pixels an image has per inch. This pixel per inch (ppi) measurement is the resolution of the digital image. When an image is printed on paper, higher ppi means sharper, higher quality because there is more information packed into each square inch (see the **"DPI Versus PPI"** sidebar). In the print world, image resolutions of 300ppi and 600ppi are common.

On the web, however, the notion of "inches" is irrelevant because the final display size of the image is dependent on the resolution of the screen on which it is displayed (FIGURE 23-14).

If we're throwing out "inches," we have to toss out "pixels per inch" as well. The only thing we know for sure is that the graphic in FIGURE 23-14 is 72 pixels across, and it will be twice as wide as a graphic that is 36 pixels across. Here's the bottom line: *web images are measured in number of pixels, and the ppi at which they are created is irrelevant.*

DPI Versus PPI

The resolution of digital images is measured in pixels per inch (ppi). When it comes to print, however, printers and printed pages are measured in dots per inch (dpi), which describes the number of printed dots in each inch of the image. The more ink dots per inch, the sharper the image. The dpi of the printed image may or may not be the same as the ppi for the digital image.

In your travels, you may hear the terms "dpi" and "ppi" used interchangeably (albeit incorrectly), but now you know the difference.

Web images are measured in number of pixels. The resolution (ppi) at which they are created is not important.

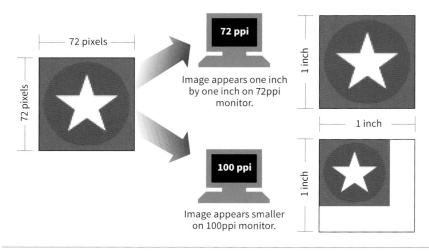

FIGURE 23-14. Inches, and therefore "pixels per inch," are not relevant for digital media, where the size of an image is dependent on the resolution of the screen.

That said, it is the recommended practice to create images at 72ppi if you are designing in a bitmap image editor like Photoshop or GIMP. This is the default and keeps images at roughly the size they'll appear on a desktop monitor. You are welcome to create your images at a different ppi, but just be sure to be consistent so images don't get resized when you're copying and pasting from one file to another.

Screen Resolution

Screen displays are made up of pixels, so you can measure their resolution in pixels per inch (ppi) as well. This is often referred to as the pixel density of the screen (see **Note**).

The first Macintosh computers had 72ppi screens, which is pretty crude by today's standards. Early PCs used 96ppi. These days, standard desktop and laptop monitors have resolutions of about 109 to 160ppi. Over the years, manufacturers have been pushing resolution of displays higher and higher, which leads us to...

High-density displays

From the 1980s to 2010, we could pretty much count on the pixels in our images mapping one-to-one with the hardware pixels in the desktop monitor, as shown in FIGURE 23-14. Of course, there were exceptions—browsers could zoom images larger or smaller on command, and images were scaled down to fit on smartphone screens—but that was the general rule.

There was a seismic shift in 2010, however, when Apple introduced the iPhone 4 with its Retina display. The Retina display packed literally twice the number of pixels into the same physical screen space, resulting in images that were much sharper (remember, the more pixels per inch, the better the image quality). The flip side of that, of course, was that the bitmapped images we were already using got rendered by twice as many pixels, and ended up looking a bit blurry (FIGURE 23-15).

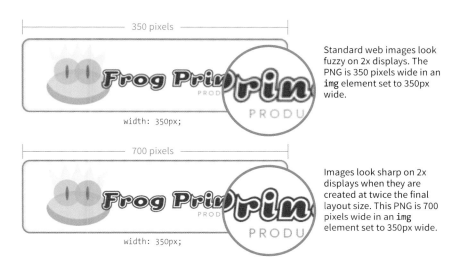

350 pixels

width: 350px;

Standard web images look fuzzy on 2x displays. The PNG is 350 pixels wide in an **img** element set to 350px wide.

700 pixels

width: 350px;

Images look sharp on 2x displays when they are created at twice the final layout size. This PNG is 700 pixels wide in an **img** element set to 350px wide.

FIGURE 23-15. Typical web graphics look slightly pixel-y on a 2x display.

The Retina screen was just the beginning. There are now both 2x and 3x Apple devices (including tablets and laptops), and Android devices come in with 1.5x, 2x, 3x, and even 4x standard pixel densities. As a result, an actual device pixel is so small that images and text would be illegibly tiny if they were mapped one to one. What to do?!

Reference pixels: PT and DP

If you think back to our responsive images discussion in **Chapter 7**, you'll remember that we've got a solution. High-resolution devices use a measurement called a reference pixel that can be used for the purposes of layout. Reference pixels go by different names and get calculated slightly differently depending on the operating system, but they enable us to specify pixel sizes without getting caught up in pixel densities.

Apple calls its reference pixels points (PT). One point on a standard 1x screen equals one device pixel. On a 2x screen, a point is 2×2 device pixels, and on 3x screens, a point is 3×3 device pixels. They all look about the same size because the high-resolution pixels are so incredibly small. Android calls its reference pixels device-independent pixels, or DiP, or simply DP. They are always equal to one pixel at 160ppi, but they work the same way.

You would probably use the terms PT and DP more when designing graphics to be used in native smartphone apps. For the web, it is sufficient to do the layout design in pixels and relevant CSS units. For example, you would say that the image in FIGURE 23-15 has a width of 350 (reference) pixels in the layout, even though the image file itself is 700 pixels wide for 2x displays.

The Upshot

At the end of the day, you can go about your business creating images at the pixel dimensions you intend for the layout. For important images, however, you may decide that you want them to look as crisp as possible on high-density displays. In that case, you'll need to create several versions and deliver them with responsive image markup or let the server handle it. If you have a product shot that appears at 150×150 pixels at 1x, you'll need at least a 2x version (300×300) and perhaps a 3x version (450×450) as well, knowing that they will all occupy 150 reference pixels in the layout.

In **Chapter 24**, we'll look at tools and techniques for creating multiple image sizes aimed at high-density displays. The markup for delivering the right image size to the right device is covered in **Chapter 7**.

IMAGE ASSET STRATEGY

Now you know where to get images, are acquainted with the various web format options, and have a feel for screen resolution. Throughout this book, you've also gotten to know the important principles of performance and Responsive Web Design. Let's put all of this know-how together in a strategy for approaching image production.

As a conscientious web designer concerned with providing the best experience across a wide range of devices, you should have these priorities in mind when creating graphics for a site:

- Keeping the file sizes of images as small as possible
- Minimizing the number of HTTP requests to the server
- Not downloading more image data than is needed for devices with smaller screens
- Delivering high-quality images to high-density displays

It may be helpful to approach your image requirements systematically, ruling out classes of images and unnecessary tasks, so you are left with a clear set of production options. FIGURE 23-16 diagrams a series of questions you can use to cull your image production options. In this section, we'll address each step of the process at a conceptual level. In **Chapter 24**, you'll get to try out specific image production techniques that address these goals.

First off, let's determine whether you need an image at all.

■ **FURTHER READING**

For much more in-depth explanations of image and screen resolution, I recommend theses articles:

- "Pixel Density, Demystified" by Peter Nowell (*medium.com/@pnowelldesign/pixel-density-demystified-a4db63ba2922*)
- "Designer's guide to DPI," by Sebastien Gabriel (*sebastien-gabriel.com/designers-guide-to-dpi/*)

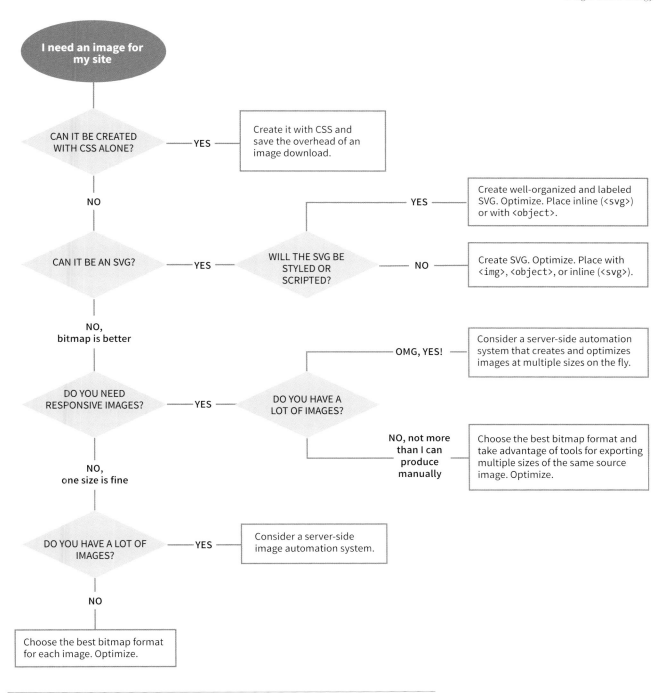

FIGURE 23-16. This flowchart may look a little crazy, but it is intended to help you narrow down the options for image asset production. It is the foundation of the discussion in this section.

Can It Be Done with CSS?

Before you break out Photoshop, consider whether you can achieve what you're after with CSS alone. Not only will the effect be a fraction of the file size, but you'll also avoid another call to the server.

Effects like rounded corners and gradients that once required images are now achievable with CSS properties (**border-radius** and **radial-gradient**/**linear-gradient**, respectively).

It is also possible to make little drawings with CSS, which may be useful in place of icons (FIGURE 23-17). Basic shapes such as circles, rectangles, triangles, and more can be created with empty **div** elements and some trickery with borders and transforms. Some people have created amazingly complex illustrations using HTML and CSS, but the technique, which had its heyday around 2010–11, is largely for demonstration purposes rather than for serious production.

I don't want to stray too far from image production in this chapter, so I will leave you with these articles, where you can learn more about CSS shapes and illustrations:

- "The Shapes of CSS," a gallery of one-element CSS shapes with the code used to create them, compiled by Chris Coyier: *css-tricks.com/examples/ShapesOfCSS/*

- "Beginners Guide to Pure CSS Images," a step-by-step tutorial by Michael Mangialardi for creating the koala bear in FIGURE 23-17: *medium.com/coding-artist/a-beginners-guide-to-pure-css-images-ef9a5d069dd2*

- A collection of "not-so-semantic drawings made with CSS," on Codepen, collected by Hugo Giraudel: *codepen.io/collection/kFeDz/3/*

If you need something more complex than a CSS effect, it's time to think about image formats.

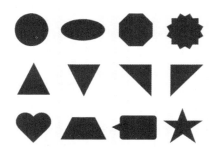

Shapes by Chris Coyier
css-tricks.com/examples/ShapesOfCSS/

Koala by Michael Mangialardi
codepen.io/mikemang/pen/oYMePj

Cheesecake by Sasha Tran
codepen.io/sashatran/pen/ggGeZr

FIGURE 23-17. These little drawings are created with HTML markup and CSS alone.

Can It Be an SVG?

If your image is a logo, icon, or other illustration, creating it in a vector drawing tool and saving it as an SVG offers the benefits of small file size and resolution independence. Now that browser support is reliable, it is a good solution to dealing with the variety of devices and displays we need to design for.

If you place the SVG code inline, with the **svg** element, you save another HTTP request and gain the ability to style and script the elements. Or, if a static illustration is all you need, embedding the SVG in the document with the `img` element is a perfectly fine option.

In **Chapter 25**, you'll take a long journey through the SVG format, so I won't say much more here other than the fact that SVG should be your first choice if you can create the image or illustration in vector format.

If SVG is not appropriate for your image type or if your target audience is known to use non-supporting browsers in significant numbers, then you may need to go with a bitmapped format. There are still a few things to consider.

What Is the Best Bitmapped Format?

Image format has a large impact on file size, so choosing the most appropriate format for your image is an important step to optimizing images. As we learned, PNG-8 is the best option for images with areas of flat color, and JPEG is the best format for photographic images. In **Chapter 24**, I'll show you how to save images in various formats, and you'll get to see how format affects file size firsthand.

Consider also saving the image in the much smaller WebP format and using the **picture** element to deliver it to the browsers that can render it (see the **"Responsive Image Markup"** section in **Chapter 7**, for details). It helps speed things up on supporting browsers and provides a reliable JPEG or PNG fallback for the others.

With the format decided, it's time to start thinking about how many versions of each image you need to create.

Does Your Layout Require Responsive Images?

The next thing to consider is whether your layout requires responsive images.

No, one size is fine

Some pages, such as text-heavy pages with small illustrations, might get by fine with just one version of each image that serves all screen sizes. If that is the case, save or export your image in the most appropriate file format and you're nearly done. The final step is to optimize the image to make it as small as it can be. Optimization techniques are discussed in detail in **Chapter 24**.

Yes, I need each image saved at multiple sizes

Your responsive layout may require that you take advantage of the responsive image techniques we outlined in **Chapter 7**. To recap, "responsive images" refers to the process of providing images that are tailored to the user's viewing environment. This includes preventing browsers on small screens from downloading more image data than they need as well as providing images large enough to look crisp on high-density displays. You can also provide alternative versions of the image based on content (called the "art direction" scenario) or to take advantage of newer formats, such as WebP.

If you're going the responsive images route, things start getting interesting.

Does Your Site Have a Lot of Images?

Yes, my site has a ton of images (Hint: Automate it!)

Although it is terrific to have an HTML solution for getting the right images to the right browsers, the current system is a bit cumbersome with stacks of code and the need to produce multiple images. If you work on a large, image-heavy site, it could prove to be unmanageable. Image processing is a task that begs to be automated. The solution: let the *server* do it!

Fortunately, there are many tools and services, both open source and for pay, that let the server do the work of creating appropriate image versions on the fly. You upload the image at the highest quality and largest size required and let the server handle the rest—no need to create and store multiple versions of every image. Some services go beyond simple resizing, including the ability to crop images intelligently, add special effects such as sepia tones, or otherwise transform images on the fly.

Some content management systems have image-resizing features built in. Another option is to install software or an open source script (like Glide, *glide.thephpleague.com*) on your own server. Bear in mind, however, that requiring JavaScript to be running is less than ideal. There are also third-party solutions that provide image-resizing services (like *Cloudinary.com*, *Akamai.com*, or *Kraken.io*), for a fee. For large, image-heavy sites, they are worth looking into.

For more information, read "Image Resizing Services" by Jason Grigsby of Cloud Four (*cloudfour.com/thinks/image-resizing-services/*). He maintains a list of current image services, which you can find linked from the article.

No, I can handle images manually

If your site has a reasonable number of images that are updated on a reasonable schedule, you should be able to produce them by hand on your computer and upload them to the server. The good news is that there's a whole slew of new tools designed especially to support the web image asset production process, including ways to create several versions at once and to optimize them in batches. Even our old standby, Adobe Photoshop, is evolving to better support the needs of web image producers. We'll look at these tools in the following chapter.

FAVICONS

As long as we're talking about images, there is one last site-related image to cover: the favicon. A favicon is the little icon that shows up to the left of the page title in the browser tab and in bookmark lists (FIGURE 23-18). First introduced as an Internet Explorer 5 feature in 1999, favicons were quickly adopted by other browsers. Favicons aren't required, but they do help users identify and find your site in a long lineup of tabs or bookmarks. They're a little attention to detail that can strengthen your brand.

FIGURE 23-18. Favicons for Adobe.com, W3C.org, and Firefox.com in browser tabs (shown in Firefox).

Other web-enabled devices use site-associated icons that are similar to favicons. For example, Apple iPhone and iPad represent sites or web apps with an icon (called a touch icon) when you save them to the home screen. Site icons are also used by Microsoft Metro tiles, GoogleTV, and other systems.

This section introduces what it takes to create a basic desktop favicon as well as a full icon set that covers all the bases. We'll also look at one tool that does all the repetitive work for you.

Old-Fashioned Browser Favicons

For desktop browsers, the standard favicon process is easy:

1. Save your icon in ICO format and name it *favicon.ico*.

2. Put that file in the root directory of the site, where browsers know to look for it.

3. There is no third step. That's it!

This is the method that is supported by the most browsers, and the *only* favicon method supported by Internet Explorer 10 and earlier.

There are a few important things to know about the *favicon.ico* file itself. Favicons should be created at 16 × 16 pixels with an additional 32 × 32 pixel version for crisp display on Retina display devices. The good news is that you need only one *favicon.ico* file because the ICO format is capable of storing multiple images in a single file. The bad news is that most graphics tools, including Adobe Photoshop, can't save images in ICO format, so you need to use a conversion tool that takes in PNG or JPEG and spits out ICO. There are several free drag-and-drop ICO converters online, such as *icoconverter.com* and *convertico.com*. If you are on a Mac and want a more full-featured conversion tool, check out Icon Slate by Kodlian (*www.kodlian.com/apps/icon-slate*) available in the App Store for US$5.

As mentioned previously, once you have your *favicon.ico* file, just place it in the root directory for the site alongside *index.html*, and the browser will find it automatically. There is no need to add any markup in the files.

Full Favicon Set

You may decide to go the extra mile and create a complete favicon set to represent your site on other devices. You can save these icons in good old PNG format and even include transparent areas, so it's a more familiar process.

When your icons are in PNG format, you must link them to your files with the `link` element in the markup, as in this example that adds a touch icon for the iPhone with a Retina screen (see the sidebar **"iOS Icon Effects"**):

```
<link rel="apple-touch-icon-precomposed" sizes="120x120"
href="apple-touch-icon-120x120.png">
```

TABLE 23-2 lists most of the standard icon sizes as of this writing.

TABLE 23-2. Most popular standard favicon sizes

Size (in pixels)	Purpose
32 × 32	Standard for most desktop browsers
57 × 57	Standard iOS screen (iPod Touch, iPhone first generation)
76 × 76	iPad home screen icon
96 × 96	GoogleTV icon
120 × 120	iPhone Retina
128 × 128	Chrome web store
144 × 144	IE10 Metro tile for pinned site
152 × 152	iPad touch icon; Android icon (auto-downscaled as needed)
167 × 167	iPad Retina touch icon
180 × 180	iPhone 6 plus
196 × 196	Chrome for Android home screen
228 × 228	Opera Coast icon

---

iOS Icon Effects

By default, iOS adds visual effects to your icon file so it matches the style of other icons on the home screen:

- Rounded corners
- Drop shadow
- A "shiny" reflection effect

If you like your icon just as it is and want to turn the special effects off, tell iOS that the icon is "precomposed" by setting the value of **rel** to **apple-touch-icon-precomposed** as shown in the example. If you'd like to take advantage of those effects, set **rel** to simply **apple-touch-icon**.

Icon Creation

For ultimate control over icon quality, it's best to create your icons by hand. Everyone has their own process, but it is generally recommended to start with a vector-based original and export to the required sizes. If you start with a bit-mapped image, scale down in increments and check the quality at each step.

For very small icons (32- and especially 16-pixel square), you'll likely need to do some pixel-by-pixel fine-tuning to get the best result. If your logo is complicated, consider using just a distinctive detail as O'Reilly Media does (FIGURE 23-19).

■ **COOL TOOL**

If you want to use just the initial letter of your site's name as a favicon, *Favicon.io* is a neat online tool that generates icons based on your character, font, and color selections.

FIGURE 23-19. O'Reilly Media uses a detail from their logo in their favicon.

For excellent how-to advice on creating icons in general, I heartily recommend *The Icon Handbook* (Five Simple Steps), by icon expert John Hicks. John shares his tricks for effective icon design and how to maintain the best quality at small sizes.

If manually creating all your icons feels like a burden, an easier option is to use a favicon generator that creates all the icons from one original and generates all of the required code as well. There are a few of them out there, but one I like is Favic-o-matic (*www.favicomatic.com*) shown in FIGURE 23-20. Just upload one PNG larger than 300px square, and the tool does the rest.

■ **FURTHER READING**

With a PNG-to-ICO converter and favicon generator tool, you now have a basic toolkit for creating complete favicon sets. However, you may want to read up on the finer details that I was not able to include here. The following are a few resources that I found to be helpful:

- "The 2017 Guide to FavIcons for Nearly Everyone and Everyone and Every Browser," from Emerge Interactive (*www.emergeinteractive.com/ insights/detail/The-Essentials-of-FavIcons-in-2017*)

- "How to Make a Favicon" by Nick Pettit at Treehouse (*blog.teamtreehouse.com/how-to-make-a-favicon*)

- The Favicon entry on Wikipedia (*en.wikipedia.org/wiki/Favicon*)

FIGURE 23-20. The Favic-o-matic favicon and code generator.

SUMMING UP IMAGES

We've covered a lot of ground in this chapter. If I've done my job, you should now have a good foundation in web graphics, including where to find an image and what file format to save it in. You know about image resolution and screen resolution, including working with high-density displays. You also have a strategy for identifying your image requirements in order to whittle down the wide array of options. And of course, you know what it takes to add a favicon to your site.

In the next chapter, you'll get hands-on experience creating and optimizing web images as we explore the particulars of the production process. But first, a little quiz.

TEST YOURSELF

Answer the following questions to see if you got the big picture on web graphics. The answers appear in **Appendix A**.

1. What is the primary advantage to using rights-managed images?

2. What does "ppi" stand for?

3. What is "indexed color"? What file formats use it?

4. How many colors are in the color table for an 8-bit image? If you are up for a bit of math, figure out the maximum number of colors in a 5-bit image.

5. Name two things you can do with a GIF that you can't do with a JPEG.

6. Name one thing you can do with a GIF that you can't do with a PNG.

7. Name one thing you can do with a PNG that you can't do with a GIF.

8. JPEG's lossy compression is cumulative. What does that mean? Why is it important to know?

9. What is the difference between binary and alpha transparency?

10. Pick the best bitmap file format for each of the images in FIGURE 23-21. You should be able to make the decision just by looking at the images as they're printed here and explain your choice. Some images may have more than one option.

FIGURE 23-21. Choose the best file format for each image.

IMAGE ASSET PRODUCTION

IN THIS CHAPTER

Selecting web file formats
when exporting

Binary and alpha transparency

Producing responsive images

Image optimization tools
and techniques

In the previous chapter, you learned a lot about images, but now we're going to focus on *making* them. Because images typically make up 60–70% of the data on the web, it is critical to approach image creation thoughtfully, with a mind toward responsive design requirements and performance. Once again, we'll be working with bitmapped formats: JPEG, PNG, and GIF. SVG has a different set of considerations and has been given the next chapter all to itself. This chapter is all about pixel-pushing!

You'll get a chance to save or export images in a variety of bitmap formats and create an image with transparent areas. You'll learn some shortcuts for creating multiple versions of an image at once for responsive layouts and high-density displays. Finally, you'll pick up some optimization tools and techniques so you can make your image files as small as they can be.

Let's start out with the most basic of image production tasks, saving an image in a web-appropriate format.

SAVING IMAGES IN WEB FORMATS

Let's dig right in with saving web images in Photoshop CC and GIMP. You may be thinking, "Why just those two?" I wrote you a little sidebar, **"Why Just Photoshop and GIMP?"** to explain. If you use one of the dozens of other image editors, the process and terminology is likely similar to those described here.

In most programs, you can count on seeing JPEG and PNG options (if there's only one PNG option, it's PNG-24) when you Save or Export the final graphic. GIF is available in more established programs like Photoshop, GIMP, and PaintShop Pro; and WebP is beginning to make an appearance.

This section goes over the process of saving or exporting images step-by-step for those who may not be familiar with using graphics tools. If you are already pretty handy with image editors, this could be a review, or you might skip right to EXERCISE 24-1.

Adobe Photoshop CC

There are a number of ways to save graphics in web-appropriate formats in Photoshop:

Export As

The recommended and most streamlined method is to use the Export As function, either from the File → Export → Export As menu, or by right-clicking (Control-clicking on a Mac) a layer to export its contents (FIGURE 24-1, **A**). From there, you get a dialog box with an image preview and a File Settings pop-up menu for selecting JPEG, PNG, GIF, or SVG format **B**. When you use Export As, Photoshop uses aggressive compression options to give you the smallest file size.

The Export As dialog box includes format-specific options with a preview of the image as it appears with the settings applied.

— For JPEG **C**, you can set the Quality level (higher quality equals larger files).

— For PNG **D**, you can choose to preserve transparent areas in the image so soft edges and shadows blend in with the background. By default, Photoshop exports PNG-24 files, but you can select "Smaller File (8-bit)" to export as a PNG-8 while still preserving multiple transparency levels.

— For GIF **E**, you get no options. I think that's Adobe's way of saying you're much better off with PNG.

The Export As dialog box **B** also gives you the option to resize the image. This is useful for maintaining a full-size original while exporting copies sized for different layouts.

Save As

You can also use File → Save As to save the file you're working on in a new format (you'll see the web-friendly formats in the long list of options). You'll generally get a few more options with Save As, such as the ability to turn on interlacing and select a palette for GIFs and to make a JPEG progressive, but you miss out on the extra compression. And it's a lot of compression. Depending on the image and the file type, a Saved As image could be 10× larger than its exported counterpart.

Why Just Photoshop and GIMP?

There are dozens of programs out there for creating images. In this chapter, I will be sticking with Adobe Photoshop CC and GIMP in the examples because I feel like they represent the far ends of the commitment spectrum. Most importantly, both are available for macOS and Windows, and you can get copies to work with for free.

On one end of the spectrum, Photoshop is the most popular image-editing program for design professionals, but it is costly, available via a monthly subscription fee as part of the Adobe Creative Cloud suite of products. You can download a free trial version at *www.adobe.com/creativecloud/catalog/desktop.html* if you'd like to work along with the exercises.

On the other end, GIMP (GNU Image Manipulation Program) is an open source image editor with many of the same features as Photoshop and it is absolutely *free*! Like, forever—not just a limited trial. Download it at *gimp.org*.

Convert to sRGB? YES!

In Photoshop's Export As dialog box, toward the bottom under Color Space, you will find the option Convert to sRGB. You definitely want to select that option because that is the color encoding that the web uses. Adobe has its own expanded RGB color space, so you will get unpredictable results if you do not convert to sRGB first.

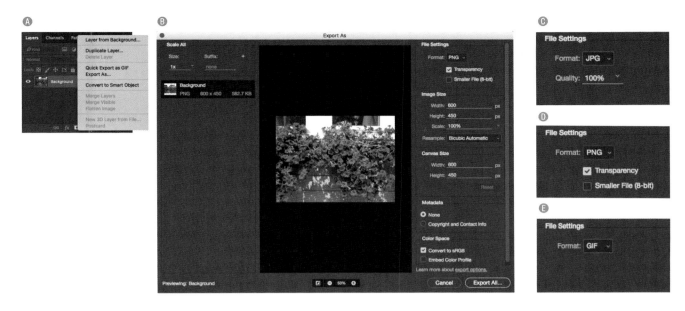

FIGURE 24-1. Selecting a file type in Photoshop's Export As dialog box.

Save for Web (legacy)

Photoshop's Save for Web function provides settings for manually optimizing the size of a file while keeping an eye on the resulting image in a preview window, and even comparing up to four settings at a time. For GIF and PNG-8 you can reduce the number of colors (the bit depth), reduce dithering, and turn on interlacing, among other settings. For JPEG, you can choose the quality, make it progressive or optimized, or apply a slight amount of blur to the image to reduce its file size.

Adobe has tagged the Save for Web function as "legacy" starting around 2014, and it will be going away entirely in future versions with no substitutes for many of the settings. But the fact is that there are tools available now that achieve the same amount of compression without all the manual work. If you have access to an older version of Photoshop, you can give it a try, but don't get too attached (as I am!).

GIMP

In GIMP, working files are always in GIMP's native XCF format. From there, you need to choose File → Export As to select your file format. The quickest way to get the format you want is to type *.jpg*, *.png*, or *.gif* at the end of the filename in the Name field. For example, typing "name.png" triggers GIMP to export that file in PNG format. Alternatively, you can select a file type from the list of options in the Select File Type menu (shown in FIGURE 24-2, Ⓐ).

After you hit the Export button, you get a dialog box with settings appropriate for the format you've chosen.

- For PNG **B**, deselect all of the options, as many of them store unnecessary metadata in the file and others are of limited use when you are exporting a layered file. You may choose to make the image interlaced.

- For GIF **C**, you can make the image interlaced and embed a comment. You can also save it as an animation if your layers are set up in that way.

- For JPEG **D**, you can play with the Quality setting, with the option to view the resulting quality as well as its file size in an image window (recommended). Under Advanced Options, you can Optimize the JPEG, make it Progressive, and apply a slight blur (Smoothing) to reduce the file size. Under Subsampling, the 4:4:4 (best quality) is a good choice, especially if your image has areas of flat color, although 4:2:2 produces smaller files. You can see the results of these settings in the image window.

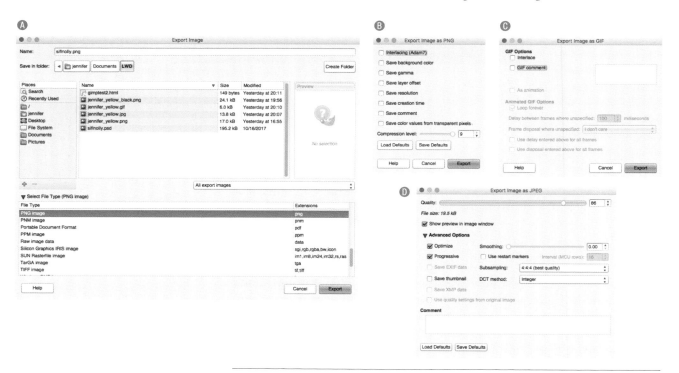

FIGURE 24-2. Selecting your file format in GIMP.

Why don't you give this web-image-making a try in EXERCISE 24-1? You'll find that the format you choose greatly impacts the size of the file. If you have Photoshop or GIMP, you can follow the instructions just listed, but if you don't, there's a good chance that whatever image creation tool you do have will have similar save or export options. Remember that you can download a free trial of Photoshop, and GIMP is always free.

That takes care of basic web image output. After the exercise, we'll turn our attention to one of the core features of web images that you will certainly want to become handy with: transparency.

EXERCISE 24-1. Formats and file size

In this exercise, we're going to see the effect the image format has on file size by exporting two images in a variety of formats and comparing file sizes. I have provided two image files with the materials for this chapter (FIGURE 24-3), but you could also experiment with your own.

boats.png

asian.png

FIGURE 24-3. Export these images in various formats to see how each affects their file size.

1. First, open *boats.png* in the program of your choice and export it in JPEG format. If your image editor does not have an export function, you may need to do a Save As. Be sure that you always start with the original image throughout this exercise.

   If you are using Photoshop or GIMP, slide the Quality slider from 100% all the way down to 0%, and pay attention to how the image quality changes in the preview or image window. Make a note of the file sizes at 100%, 60%, and 10% quality. Save the final JPEG at 60% quality.

   Alternatively, if you do not have a preview in your tool, you can export three separate JPEGs with the quality set to 100%, 60%, and 10%. Open the images in your image tool or a browser window to check the quality and use the Finder or File Explorer to check the resulting file size.

2. Now export the full-color image again as a PNG-24 (in Photoshop, do *not* select the 8-bit option).

3. Finally, convert the image to Indexed color (**Image → Mode → Indexed**) and select 256 colors. Export the image as a PNG-8 (in Photoshop, select "Smaller File (8-bit)"; GIMP saves indexed color images as PNG-8 automatically. While the original is still in indexed color mode, export again in GIF format. When you are done, you can revert the image to RGB color or close it without saving.

4. Let's see what we've got! Here are the resulting file sizes for the *boats* images that I got in Photoshop and GIMP. Note that file sizes differ depending on the tool because of the compression algorithms they use. Yours will likely be different from these, but in the general ballpark.

Tool	JPEG (100)	JPEG (60)	JPEG (10)	PNG-24	PNG-8	GIF
PhotoshopCC	130.3 KB	**33.1 KB**	9.2 KB	221 KB	67.6 KB	74.1 KB
GIMP	179 KB	**20.9 KB**	7.4 KB	225 KB	73.7 KB	80.3 KB

Work in RGB Mode

Regardless of the final format of your file, you should always do your image-editing work in RGB mode (grayscale is fine for non-color images). To check the color mode of the image in Photoshop or GIMP, select **Image → Mode** and make sure there is a checkmark next to RGB Color.

JPEG and PNG-24 files compress the RGB color image directly. If you are saving the file as a GIF or PNG-8, the RGB image must be converted to indexed color mode, either manually or as part of the export process.

Indexed Color

If you need to edit an existing GIF or PNG-8, convert the image to RGB as the first step before editing. This enables the editing tool to use colors from the full RGB spectrum when adjusting the image. If you resize the original indexed color image, you'll get lousy results because the new image is limited to the colors from the existing color table.

CMYK

If you have experience creating graphics for print, you may be accustomed to working in CMYK mode (printed colors are made up of Cyan, Magenta, Yellow, and blacK ink). CMYK mode is irrelevant and inappropriate for web graphics, so convert to RGB mode at the beginning of the image-editing process.

EXERCISE 24-1. Continued

Conclusion: The best format for the *boats* image is JPEG, and a quality of around 60 gives the best balance of image quality and small file size. The PNG-8 and GIF versions are twice as large and they look pretty bad. Of course, "quality" is subjective. You might decide that an image is so important that pristine 100% quality is worth the extra download time, but generally, you can shave a lot of bytes off an image while keeping quality acceptable.

5. OK, now we're going to repeat all the previous steps, this time using the *asian.png* image. Export the original image as a JPEG at various settings (or just make notes on the file size based on the preview) and as a PNG-24. When you convert the image to indexed color, play around with the numbers of colors to see how few you can get away with. Does the image still read well with 128 colors? 64? 32?

I really went for it and reduced the palette to 32 colors, and then exported as PNG-8 and GIF. Here are my results:

Tool	JPEG (100)	JPEG (60)	JPEG (10)	PNG-24	PNG-8 (32 colors)	GIF (32 colors)
PhotoshopCC	22.7 KB	8.7 KB	3.3 KB	14.8 KB	**4.2 KB**	4.3 KB
GIMP	27.3 KB	6.8 KB	3.3 KB	14.5 KB	**3.3 KB**	3.8 KB

Conclusion: For the *asian* image, the PNG-8 with a reduced color palette is the winner. Sure, the 10% JPEG file size is smaller, but the quality is disastrous! The PNG-8 offers the smallest file size while keeping the flat colors artifact-free.

WORKING WITH TRANSPARENCY

Both GIF and PNG formats allow parts of an image to be transparent, so that the background color or image shows through. In this section, we'll take a closer look at transparent graphics, including tips on how to make them.

Remember that there are two types of transparency. In binary transparency, pixels are either entirely transparent or entirely opaque, like an on/off switch. Both GIF and PNG-8 files support binary transparency.

In alpha (or alpha-channel) transparency, a pixel may be totally transparent, totally opaque, or up to 254 levels of opacity in between (a total of 256 opacity levels). Only PNG, WebP, and JPEG 2000 support true alpha-layer transparency (see **Note**). The advantage of PNGs with alpha transparency is that they blend seamlessly with any background color or pattern, as shown back in FIGURE 23-9. PNG-8 also allows multiple levels of transparency, but it handles it a little differently, as you'll learn in a moment.

In this section, you'll become familiar with how each type of transparency works, and learn how to make transparent images using GIMP and Photoshop.

NOTE

Because of poor tool and browser support for WebP and JPEG 2000, we'll be focusing on alpha transparency in PNGs in this section.

How Binary Transparency Works

Remember that the pixel colors for PNG-8s and GIFs are stored in an indexed color table. Transparency is simply treated as a separate color, occupying one position in the color table. FIGURE 24-4 shows the color table in Photoshop for a simple transparent GIF. The slot in the color table that is set to transparent is indicated by a checker pattern. Pixels that correspond to that position in the color map are completely transparent when the image displays in the browser. Note that only one slot is transparent—all the other pixel colors are opaque.

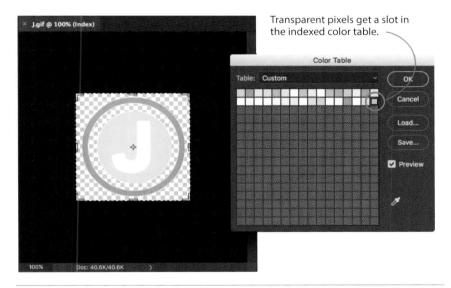

Transparent pixels get a slot in the indexed color table.

FIGURE 24-4. Transparency is treated as a color in the indexed color table.

Avoiding halos

When an image has multiple transparency levels, it blends seamlessly with the web page background. With binary transparency, however, there is a risk that the soft edges around the image will have a fringe of pixels that don't match the color behind it (FIGURE 24-5). This fringe is commonly known as a halo and it is a potential hazard of binary transparency.

Prevention is the name of the game when it comes to dealing with binary transparency and halos. The trick is to blend the semitransparent pixels in the original image (such as the anti-aliased edges around text or a shape with feathered edges) with a color that is as close as possible to the background color of the page. Many image-editing tools that support web graphic formats provide a way to pick the blend color (also known as the matte color) when saving or exporting.

Some programs use whatever color is selected as the background color to fill in soft edges. Others may allow you to pick your blend color manually. For

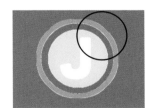

FIGURE 24-5. This GIF with binary transparency has a halo because the semitransparent edges of the original image were blended with a light color that doesn't match the teal background of the page.

example, in Photoshop's legacy Save for Web feature, you can select a matte color whenever transparency is turned on for the image (see **Note**). The matte color is also used to fill in any transparent image areas when you're converting an image to JPEG. GIMP, on the other hand, prevents halos by avoiding any sort of blend at all. You get the choice of hard, stair-stepped edges or a dithering pattern made of color and transparent pixels meant to simulate the blurred edge. Neither option looks good, but hey, no halos.

Of course, avoiding halos with these methods requires that you know the RGB values of the page's background color in advance so you can match the matte color to it. If the page color changes, you need to go back and export the graphics again with the new color. That's where alpha transparency has a real advantage—you can change the background, and everything will still blend in perfectly.

How Alpha Transparency Works

RGB images, such as JPEGs and PNG-24s, store color in separate channels: one for red, one for green, and one for blue. PNG-24 files add another channel, called the alpha channel, to store transparency information. In that channel, each pixel may display one of 256 values, which correspond to 256 levels of transparency when the image is displayed. The black areas of the alpha channel mask are transparent, the white areas are opaque, and the grays are on a scale in between. I think of it as a blanket laid over the image that tells each pixel below it how transparent it is (FIGURE 24-6).

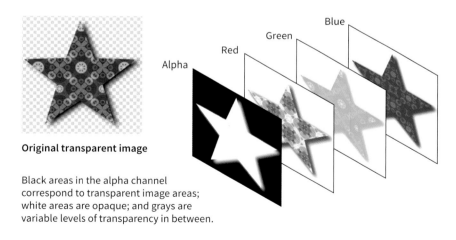

Original transparent image

Black areas in the alpha channel correspond to transparent image areas; white areas are opaque; and grays are variable levels of transparency in between.

FIGURE 24-6. Transparency information is stored as a separate (alpha) channel in 24-bit PNGs.

PNG-8 Alpha Transparency

Variable levels of transparency are not limited to 24-bit PNGs—PNG-8 files can do it too! Although they are referred to as PNG8+alpha or alpha-palette PNGs, they do *not* store transparency information in a separate alpha channel overlay as we saw in FIGURE 24-6.

PNG expert Greg Roelofs explains PNG-8 "alpha" transparency well in this excerpt from his 1999 book *PNG: The Definitive Guide* (O'Reilly):

> *A PNG alpha-palette image is just that: an image whose palette also has alpha information associated with it, not a palette image with a full alpha mask. In other words, each pixel corresponds to an entry in the palette with red, green, blue, and alpha components. So if you want to have bright red pixels with four different levels of transparency, you must use four separate palette entries to accommodate them—all four entries will have identical RGB components, but the alpha values will differ. If you want all of your colors to have four levels of transparency, you've effectively reduced your total number of available colors from 256 to 64.*

No image program (that I know of) displays PNG-8 color tables with multiple transparency levels, so I've simulated one for you in FIGURE 24-7. I based it on the orange circle with the soft drop shadow from FIGURE 23-9, with the palette reduced to just 16 colors. The resulting image has a bit of dithering in the drop shadow, but it's not that noticeable when it appears over a background pattern. With file size savings of 75%, it's worth it.

Original PNG-24 with alpha transparency (8.4 KB).

Saved as PNG-8 with 16 colors and multiple levels of transparency (1.6 KB).

When used over a pattern, you can't see the dithering.

Simulation of the color table for the PNG-8 with multiple transparency levels for the drop shadow.

FIGURE 24-7. A simulation of a PNG-8 color table with multiple levels of transparency. The PNG-8 is over 80% smaller than the similar PNG-24 with very similar quality.

Making Transparent PNGs and GIFs

The easiest way to make parts of an image transparent is to design them that way from the start and preserve the transparent areas when you export. Although it is possible to doctor up an existing flattened opaque image and make areas transparent, it is usually difficult to get a seamless blend with the background while avoiding jagged edges.

Instead of just telling you, I'll let you create a layered image and preserve the transparent areas in EXERCISE 24-2. When you create your layered Photoshop or GIMP file, be sure that the background layer appears as a gray checkerboard pattern and is not filled with a color. If you end up with a color in the background anyway, you can select it all and delete it.

When you've finished playing with transparency, you can come back for some tips on responsive images.

RESPONSIVE IMAGE PRODUCTION TIPS

If your site is responsive, chances are you'll need responsive images to go with it. When it comes to bitmapped images, "responsive" actually means "multiple versions" (see **Note**).

In the **"Responsive Image Markup"** section in **Chapter 7, Adding Images**, you learned about four responsive image scenarios, but it's worth a refresher here (that was *hundreds* of pages ago, after all). Whereas in the past one image did the trick, in our current environment we may choose to do the following:

- Provide a set of images of various dimensions for use in responsive layouts on different **viewport sizes**.

- Provide versions of the image with varying amounts of detail based on the device size and orientation (also known as the **art direction** use case).

- Provide large-scale images that look crisp on **high-density screens**.

- Provide **alternative image formats** that store the same image at much smaller file sizes.

This section introduces tools, tips, and general strategies for producing (or automating!) the images you need for the first three scenarios. Alternative image formats were addressed in **Chapter 23, Web Image Basics**.

Images for Responsive Layouts

The first scenario addresses providing a range of image sizes that the browser selects from based on the viewport size. In HTML, you would specify these using `srcset` with a w-selector that provides the exact pixel width of the image, and the `sizes` attribute that tells the browser how large the image will appear in the layout.

NOTE

Responsive SVGs are covered in **Chapter 25, SVG**.

■ FURTHER READING

If you are an Adobe Photoshop user (or intend to become one), you will find expert advice on working Photoshop into your Responsive Web Design workflow in Dan Rose's book *Responsive Web Design with Adobe Photoshop* (Adobe).

EXERCISE 24-2. Creating transparent images

In this exercise, we're going to start from scratch, so you'll get the experience of creating a layered image with transparent areas. I'm going to keep it simple, but you can apply these techniques to fancier designs, of course.

Because Photoshop and GIMP have different approaches, I'm going to step through the processes for them separately. You can use another tool as long as it uses layers in its interface.

Photoshop CC (2018)

1. Start a new file and make it 250×250 pixels with a resolution of 72 (FIGURE 24-8). On the New Document dialog **Ⓐ**, look for Background Contents and select Transparent from the pop-up menu. Click Create. You should see a square filled with a gray checkerboard pattern indicating the background is transparent.

2. Select the ellipse Marquee tool and set the Feather setting to 10. Draw a circle in the center of the document and fill it with a color. You should have a shape with blurry edges where the checkerboard shows through. That's all we need for the purposes of this exercise, but you can feel free to add more elements.

3. Now you can select **File → Export As**, select PNG from File Settings, and be sure the Transparency box is checked **Ⓑ**. Also be sure "Convert to sRGB" is checked. Click Export All, name the file *circle24.png*, and click Export.

4. Let's save it as a PNG-8 as well: Export As, PNG, Transparency, but this time select "Smaller File (8-bit)." Name the file *circle8.png*, and click Export.

5. Just for comparison, Export As again, but this time select GIF from the File Settings menu. In the preview, you will see that the areas that are not 100% opaque are blended with white **Ⓒ**, which is not ideal, but save the file anyway as *circle.gif*. The Export As function does not offer a way to change the fill (matte) color for GIFs and JPEGs.

Now that you have your transparent files *circle24.png*, *circle8.png*, and *circle.gif*, you can skip ahead to the section **"How do they look?"**

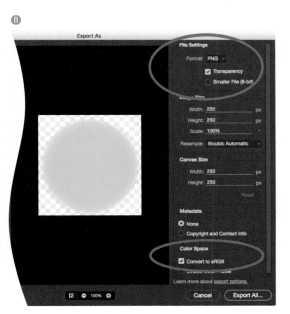

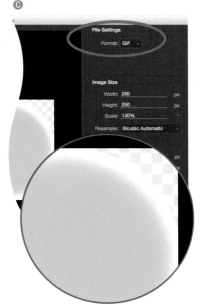

Start with a transparent layered image document.

When you select PNG, either 24-bit (default) or 8-bit (Smaller), multiple levels of transparency are preserved.

GIF can store only binary transparency, so the semitransparent pixels are blended with solid white.

FIGURE 24-8. Exporting an image with soft transparent edges in Photoshop CC.

GIMP

1. Create a new file (**File → New**), set the dimensions to 250 pixels wide and high, set X and Y resolution to 72.000 pixels/in. Select Transparency from the "Fill with:" pop-up menu. You can remove the "Created with GIMP" comment. Click OK. You should have a new image window filled with a gray, checkered background. Save the working copy with the name *circle.xcf*.

2. Time to draw a shape. Select the Ellipse Select Tool from the Toolbox and under Tool Options, turn on Feather Edges, and set the radius to 10. Now draw a circle in the image window. Set the foreground color to something you like and drag the color into your circle to fill it (FIGURE 24-9, **Ⓐ**). That's all we need to do for the purposes of this exercise, but you can add more embellishments if you like.

3. Now let's export it. Select **File → Export As** and name the file *circle24.png* **Ⓑ**. The suffix tells GIMP to save the file in PNG format, and because the original image is RGB with transparent areas, GIMP creates a 24-bit PNG with alpha transparency. In

GIMP, this is the best transparency option. In the Export Image as PNG dialog box **Ⓒ**, uncheck all of the boxes.

4. For comparison, let's see how GIMP handles binary transparency. To export an 8-bit image in GIMP, you need to convert it to indexed color first (**Image → Color Mode → Indexed Color**). Use the optimum palette with 256 colors. Leave the "Enable dithering of transparency" box unchecked for now, and click Convert. All those soft edges are gone, and the pixels are either opaque or transparent. I recommend zooming in to 200% (the zoom setting is at the bottom of the window) to see the stair-stepped edges **Ⓓ**.

5. OK, revert the file to RGB (**File → Revert**) and convert it to indexed color again, only this time, click the box next to Enable Dithering. If you're zoomed in, you can see that GIMP creates a pattern out of solid and transparent pixels that *kinda* simulates the blurred edges of the circle **Ⓓ**. Export this file in PNG format as *circle8.png*. You could also save it in GIF format.

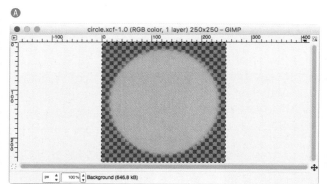

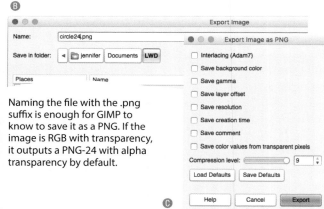

Naming the file with the .png suffix is enough for GIMP to know to save it as a PNG. If the image is RGB with transparency, it outputs a PNG-24 with alpha transparency by default.

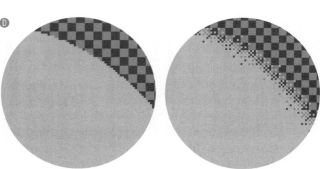

Converted to indexed color, the soft edges get converted to on/off transparency with hard edges (left) or dithered edges (right). I find both of these options unacceptable, so in GIMP, go for the PNG-24 option.

FIGURE 24-9. Creating a transparent image in GIMP.

How do they look?

Now that I have some transparent graphics, I'm going to try them out on a minimal web page with a white background. The images and *transparency.html* file are provided with the materials for this chapter if you'd like to work along. You could also use the graphics you created.

```html
<!DOCTYPE html>
<html>
<head>
  <title>Transparency test</title>
  <style>
    body {background-color: white;}
    p {text-align: center;}
    img {margin: 2em;}
  </style>
</head>
<body>
  <p>
  <img src="circle.gif" alt="">    <!-- left -->
  <img src="circle24.png" alt=""> <!-- center -->
  <img src="circle8.png" alt="">  <!-- right -->
  </p>
</body>
</html>
```

When I open the file in a browser, the graphics look more or less the same against the white background (FIGURE 24-10, top). But if I change the background color of the web page to teal (**background-color: teal;**), the difference between the alpha and binary transparency becomes very obvious (bottom). You can clearly see the halo on the GIF on the left. Both the PNG-8 and the PNG-24 versions as exported in Photoshop have smooth alpha transparency.

Wrapping up

In summary, if you work in Photoshop CC, export transparent images as 8-bit PNGs. In other tools, use PNG-24 with alpha transparency, but keep an eye on the file size. If the file is unacceptably large, you can convert it to a PNG-8 + alpha by using one of the tools listed in the **"Image Optimization"** section. Your other option is to try it with binary transparency and a matte color that matches the background of the page. If your tool doesn't have a Matte feature, see the **"Matte Alternative"** sidebar.

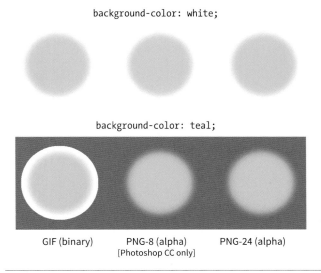

background-color: white;

background-color: teal;

GIF (binary)   PNG-8 (alpha)   PNG-24 (alpha)
[Photoshop CC only]

FIGURE 24-10. The difference between binary and alpha transparency becomes very clear when the background color of the page changes.

Matte Alternative

If your graphics tool doesn't have the Matte feature (GIMP and Photoshop CC 2018 come to mind), create a new layer at the bottom of the layer "stack" and fill it with the background color of your page. When the image is flattened as a result of being changed to indexed color, the anti-aliased edges blend with the proper background color. Just select that background color to be transparent when exporting to GIF or PNG, and your image should be halo-free.

If selecting a transparent color is not an option in the tool you use, you can copy the important parts of the image including the blended edges, copy and paste it into a new transparent image file, and then export it as a GIF or PNG-8.

That's a lot of work for each image, which is why using alpha transparency is a superior choice.

This example should look familiar:

```
<img src="strawberries-640.jpg" alt="baskets of ripe strawberries"
    srcset="strawberries-240.jpg 240w,
            strawberries-480.jpg 480w,
            strawberries-672.jpg 672w"
    sizes="(max-width: 480px) 100vw,
           (max-width: 960px) 70vw,
           240px">
```

For this particular **img** element, we've provided JPEGs of the strawberry image at 240, 480, and 672 pixels wide. Other layouts may require fewer or more breakpoints for each image. The first question you may ask when producing images for responsive layouts is, "How many images do I need to create?" That is a good question that doesn't have an easy answer.

Start by determining the smallest and largest dimensions at which you know the image is likely to appear. Then, decide how many interim sizes would be useful to meet the goal of reducing unnecessary downloads. If the range isn't that large, you might find that providing small, medium, and large versions is fine and better than nothing. If there is a large difference between the extremes, more breakpoints may be required. If there is very little difference, one image size may suffice.

Resize them manually

If you find you need only a few versions, resizing images on export is a fine option. FIGURE 24-11 shows resizing options in Photoshop CC's Export As dialog box, but you will find similar settings in other programs. Alternatively, you could use the Image Size tool to resize the image manually before saving or exporting. That gives you an opportunity to make adjustments to the image (such as sharpening it up) before committing to the export.

Remember that you always want to start with the image at its largest size in your image editor, and resize it *smaller* to your target image sizes. Resizing larger (upscaling) results in blurry images.

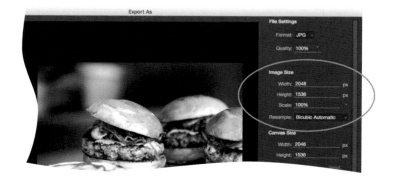

FIGURE 24-11. Resizing images manually (as shown here in Photoshop CC) is an option if you have a manageable number of images to produce.

Generate images based on file size

If your image is used at a wide range of sizes, more breakpoints than "small, medium, and large" may be required. In that case, providing a range of selections based on *file size*, not pixel dimensions, is a more appropriate approach (see **Further Reading**). Keep in mind that the primary goal for viewport-based responsive images is limiting wasted data downloads. Remember also that the browser makes the final image file selection based on the user's viewing environment—we only provide options with our responsive image markup. We can trust the browser to make the right selection, scaling up or down slightly as required.

In the file-size approach to breakpoints, you create a set of images with file sizes that step up in fixed increments, such as 20 KB, 40 KB, or 80 KB, to cover all the possibilities and fine-tune the amount of data that gets downloaded. Granted, that takes a lot of extra work and may not be feasible to do manually for a site with a lot of images.

Fortunately, there is a tool that generates the images for you. The Responsive Image Breakpoints Generator by Cloudinary (*responsivebreakpoints.com*) lets you upload a large image and set the maximum/minimum dimensions, the size step, and the maximum number of images, and it generates all the images automatically. FIGURE 24-12 shows how I used the tool to create strawberry images at 20 KB increments. By the time you are reading this, there may be more tools like this, so it's worth a quick web search to see what's available.

> **■ FURTHER READING**
>
> I recommend two articles that discuss the file-size approach to responsive breakpoints that go into more detail than I am able to here:
>
> - "Responsive Image Breakpoints Generator, A New Open Source Tool," by Nadav Soferman at *Smashing Magazine* (*www.smashingmagazine.com/2016/01/responsive-image-breakpoints-generation/*). This article introduces the image generator mentioned in this section and provides a lot of background information about the approach.
>
> - "Responsive Images 101, Part 9: Image Breakpoints," by Jason Grigsby on the Cloud Four blog (*cloudfour.com/thinks/responsive-images-101-part-9-image-breakpoints/*), introduces the idea of basing breakpoints on a "performance budget," among other solutions.

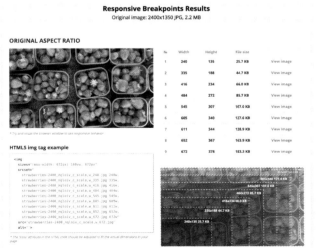

FIGURE 24-12. Responsive Image Breakpoints Generator by Cloudinary (*responsivebreakpoints.com*) generates image files for you.

Art-Directed Images

For some images, simply resizing to fit a layout isn't sufficient. It may be necessary to crop or alter the image so that it works successfully at smartphone size as well as desktop monitor size. This is what is known as the "art direction" case for responsive images. **Chapter 7** has a full explanation and examples of art direction–based selections, but as a quick reminder, this is a scenario for the **picture** element:

```
<picture>
   <source media="(min-width: 1024px)" srcset="icecream-large.jpg">
   <source media="(min-width: 760px)" srcset="icecream-medium.jpg">
   <img src="icecream-small.jpg" alt="Savor the Summer">
</picture>
```

If you want total control over what appears in an image at each size, you need to design and export each image manually in your favorite image editor. Each art-directed version may also need to be generated at several sizes, depending on your breakpoints. That may be just fine if you don't have too many images to deal with.

But hold onto your hat! Cloudinary figured out a way to automate art direction too. You can use the tools in the bottom-right corner of the Responsive Image Breakpoints Generator to specify image proportions for desktops, laptops, tablets, and smartphones. Cloudinary's tool does some sophisticated image analysis, including edge detection, face detection, and visual uniqueness to determine the most important parts of the image. The final image is cropped to include the visually "hot" spots. For more information on how it's done, read the article "Automating Art Direction with the Responsive Image Breakpoints Generator" by Eric Portis at *www.smashingmagazine. com/2016/09/automating-art-direction-with-the-responsive-image-breakpoints-generator/*.

Other image hosting and automation services also offer face detection and features that improve the quality of the images they generate. If you are shopping for such a service, check to see if smart cropping is available.

Images for High-Density Displays

If you want an image to look its sharpest on high-density screens (@1.5x, @2x and @3x), it needs to be created large enough to cover the device pixels at the highest densities. For example, if you want an image to be 300 pixels wide in your layout, you'll need a 300-pixel-wide version for standard displays, a 600-pixel-wide version for 2x displays, and a 900-pixel-wide version targeted to 3x displays.

To review, this high-resolution scenario uses the **srcset** attribute in the **img** element with an x-descriptor that specifies the target screen density for each image:

NOTE

To brush up on the special requirements of high-density displays, see **Chapter 7**, *where I first introduced device-pixel-ratios as well as the markup for targeting images to specific densities. See also the discussion of image and screen resolutions in* **Chapter 23**.

```
<img
  src="/images/apple-300px.jpg" alt="apple"
  srcset="/images/apple-600px.jpg 2x,
          /images/apple-900px.jpg 3x" >
```

Thankfully, the people who make our image creation programs get it, and they've begun building features into their tools that make it easier to output multiple high-density versions at once.

Export multiple high-density versions

Photoshop CC 2018, Sketch, Illustrator, and Affinity Designer are four tools aimed at screen designers that make it easy to set up simultaneous exports at multiple scales. It's a nice little time (and math!) saver. If you use another design tool, check to see if it is an option (it is generally located wherever your tool handles exporting). Later in this section, I'll give you some strategies for making sure the image quality stays crisp even at larger scales.

Adobe Photoshop CC 2018

Photoshop lets you add scales on the top-left corner of the Export As dialog box (FIGURE 24-13). To export a whole artboard, choose Export As (File → Export → Export As). You can also export a specific element by right-clicking (Control-clicking on a Mac) its layer name and selecting Export As from the pop-up menu. In the Scale All section, click the + button to add more scales for export. The little down arrows open a menu of standard scales (1x, .5x, 3x, etc.). Click the garbage can to remove a scale. When you click Export All, all of the images are created at once, named with the -@*nx* suffix (see **Note**).

Adobe Illustrator CC

In Illustrator, to export the entire artboard, choose File → Export → Export for Screens. You'll find the option to Add Scale in the right column (FIGURE 24-13). You can also export individual assets (such as icons and other elements) via the Assets Export panel (Window → Assets Export), which has its own export settings. Just drag elements into the panel, and they are ready to go. The Export As dialog box also provides access to individual assets via the Assets tab, but they need to be added to the Assets Export panel first. One click on Export, and voilà! All your scaled assets exported at once!

Sketch

Sketch (Mac only) is a tool for designing website and app interfaces that has rapidly grown in popularity. In Sketch, select an artboard or a page element and click the + icon next to Make Exportable in the bottom-right corner of the Sketch window. In the revealed Export panel (FIGURE 24-13), select a file format and click the + icon to add more scales to be created on export.

NOTE

The "@nx" (@1x, @2x, etc.) convention was established in the Apple iOS Developer Library. It seems to have crossed over to the web world as well.

Photoshop CC 2018
Right-click a layer to export one layer element at a time.

Select the file format under File Settings (right). Add scales in the Scale All section (left).

Illustrator CC
Choose Export for Screens from the File menu to export the entire artboard. Choose the file format and add scales under Formats.

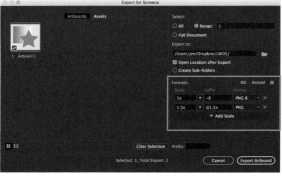

Export one element at a time from the Asset Export dialog box. Add assets by dragging them into the panel.

Sketch
Select the item to export and click Make Exportable in the bottom-right corner of the application. In the Export settings, select file formats and add scales.

Affinity Designer
Enter the Export Persona by clicking its icon. Click the arrow icon next to the slice you want to export to reveal format and scale settings.

 Export Persona icon

FIGURE 24-13. Newer design tools allow you to export multiple high-density sizes at once.

Affinity Designer

Affinity Designer has an export mode (which it calls a "Persona") in which you access all of its export settings. Create slices for the elements you want to export. Enter the Export Persona (using the menu **Affinity Designer → Export Persona** or clicking the icon that looks like a molecule). Select the slice or slices you want to export in the Slices panel (FIGURE 24-13); then click the small arrow to the left of the slice name to expose export settings, including file format and the ability to add scales with the + icon. When you are ready, click Export Slices.

The problem to watch out for with all of these tools is that if you design at standard (@1x) resolution, the exported @2x and @3x versions will be much *bigger* than they are in your working document. That should raise a red flag in your mind, because doubling or tripling the dimensions of images typically makes them blurry. There are ways around that, however, which I'll discuss next.

Work at @1x scale

Even if you are creating high-definition versions of your images, it is still recommended that you do your design work at @1x scale (see **Note**). In other words, the pixel dimensions in your working document (whether it's in Photoshop, Sketch, or some other tool) should match the layout pixels of your design. In Photoshop and other image-editing tools, @1x scale is equivalent to 72ppi. The advantages to working at @1x scale include the following:

- It's easier to specify font size and other length measurements as they appear in your working documents without the need to divide everything by two. If you work at @2x and you want 16pt type, you need to make it 32pt in your image document. If you want 10 pixels of padding in the layout, you need to create it at 20 pixels, and so on.

- Pixel-snap features work more reliably at @1x. Snapping to even pixels is a way to keep edges crisp in detailed elements such as icons.

- File sizes are much smaller for a design created at @1x, so it is better for performance on your computer. Complex files with lots of artboards and layers at @2x can get sluggish and slow down your work.

- It creates a more realistic sense of how much space you have to work with. A @2x design space might give the impression that you have more room to fit in elements, but they will end up too small and cramped when reduced 50% for @1x displays.

Start with vectors when possible

One way to maintain quality when your design is upscaled is to use vector source images whenever possible. As you've learned, vectors can scale up with no loss of quality, so they make a great starting point for web and app design.

NOTE

On the other hand, some designers strongly prefer to work at 2x and reduce everything by half for standard displays, particularly if they do their design work on Retina displays. Dan Rodney is one such designer, and you can read his argument for @2x design at www.dan-rodney.com/blog/designing-retina-web-graphics-in-photoshop-should-you-work-at-1x-or-2x/.

Many new UI design tools for screen and web interfaces, such as Sketch, Affinity Designer, and Adobe XD, are vector-based by default, so you'll have no problem outputting larger versions of elements you create there (the same goes for vector-based Adobe Illustrator). If you prefer to design in Photoshop, make sure to use its vector tools such as shapes, paths, and imported vector smart objects for common web page elements like buttons, icons, and illustrations whenever possible.

Embed large-scale bitmaps

To preserve the image quality of photographs and other necessarily bitmapped page elements at large scales, start with an image source that is at least as large as your largest scale. For example, if you know that your @3x version is 2,880 pixels wide, your source image should be that wide or wider.

In Illustrator, Sketch, and Affinity Designer, "placing" the high-resolution source image on the @1x artboard and resizing it to fit the needs of the layout gives the program all the pixel information it needs to export high-quality, large-scale assets.

In Photoshop CC, to take advantage of the full image resolution, the trick is to add the image to your design as a linked Smart Object. The Smart Object is like a placeholder for the image in your @1x design, with the high-resolution original remaining separate. When it comes time to export at various scales, Photoshop references the high-res version, and you end up with full-resolution exports (see **Important Warning**). To place an image as a Smart Object, choose File → Place Linked and resize the image to fit into your design.

Viva la Automation!

I mentioned this in the section **"Image Asset Strategy"** in the previous chapter, but it bears repeating—if your site is image-heavy, consider using server software that automates the process of responsive image generation. As Jason Grigsby says in his article, "Humans shouldn't be doing this." I couldn't agree more (unless you have a penchant for repetitive tasks).

You may choose to install software on your own server, or as a convenience, use a third-party vendor that provides hosted image management services. Again, some popular services currently are Cloudinary (*cloudinary.com*), Akamai (*akamai.com*), and Kraken.io (*kraken.io*).

I hope that you've come away with some strategies to improve the workflow for creating multiple versions of images for responsive layouts. Or perhaps you've just decided to let the server handle it! Let's move on to the final topic in our image asset production deep-dive: optimization.

IMPORTANT WARNING

As of this writing, there is a bug in Photoshop CC 2018 that prevents this technique from working with JPEG images. When you link a large-scale JPEG, Photoshop ignores it and scales up a screenshot of the image in the current file. The workaround is to convert the high-resolution JPEG image to a PSD file before adding it as a Smart Object. Adobe knows about this bug, so hopefully they will fix it in an upcoming release.

■ **RESOURCE**

Jason Grigsby maintains a spreadsheet of image-resizing services, available at *tinyurl.com/ pmpbyzj*. See also his associated article "Image Resizing Services" (*cloudfour.com/thinks/image-resizing-services/*).

IMAGE OPTIMIZATION

Because a web page is published over a network, it needs to zip through the lines as little packets of data in order to reach the end user. It is fairly intuitive, then, that larger amounts of data will require a longer time to arrive. And guess which part of a standard web page packs a whole lotta bytes—that's right, the images.

Thus is born the conflicted relationship with images on the web. On the one hand, images make a web page more interesting than text alone, and the ability to display images is one of the factors contributing to the web's success. On the other hand, images also try the patience of users with slow internet connections and gobble the data plans of mobile devices.

If you study the flowchart back in FIGURE 23-16, you will see that all paths end with "Optimize." Making your image files as small as they can be is critical for fast-loading sites, so all web designers and developers should have multiple image optimization tricks up their sleeves.

As you saw firsthand in EXERCISE 24-1, choosing the appropriate file format is your first line of defense against bloated file sizes, but it doesn't stop there. It's possible to squeeze a lot more data out of the images that your image editor exports.

Optimization approaches fall into two broad categories:

- Efforts you make manually and deliberately during the design and export process

- Post-export compression tools that root through the code and crunch them down even further, generally by throwing out unused data

This section starts with general guidelines for limiting file size. Next, because each image format is slightly different under the hood, we'll examine optimization strategies for JPEG, PNG-24, PNG-8, and GIF files (see **Note**). Finally, we'll round up some optimization tools that work on multiple formats and are a good last step in any image production process.

General Optimization Guidelines

Regardless of the image or file type, there are a few basic strategies to keep in mind for limiting file size. In the broadest of terms, they are as follows:

Start with a high-quality original

> Start with the best-quality source image you can get your hands on. From there, you can make copies at various sizes and compression settings, but you'll want to keep that original safe.

All web designers should have multiple image optimization tricks up their sleeves.

NOTE

*Of course it is important to optimize SVGs as well, but I've saved that discussion for the SVG chapter (***Chapter 25***).*

Limit dimensions

Although fairly obvious, the easiest way to keep file size down is to limit the dimensions of the image itself. There aren't any magic numbers; just don't make images any larger than they need to be. By simply eliminating extra space in the graphic in FIGURE 24-14, I was able to reduce the file size by 3 KB (23%).

600 x 200 pixels (**13 KB**)

500 x 136 pixels (**10 KB**)

FIGURE 24-14. You can reduce the size of your files by cropping out extra space.

Reuse and recycle

If you use the same image repeatedly in a site, it is best to create only one image file and point to it repeatedly wherever it is needed. This allows the browser to take advantage of the cached image and avoid additional downloads.

Use appropriate tools

If you know you will be doing a lot of web image production work, it is worth investing in professional image-editing software with web-specific features. Whether you choose Photoshop, Sketch, PaintShop Pro, or some other program mentioned in this book is up to your personal preference and budget limitations.

Run the image through an optimizer

You should have a number of image optimization tools at your disposal. I'll list several throughout this section, many of which are free to use.

Optimizing JPEGs

Here are the general strategies for reducing the file size of JPEGs:

- Be aggressive with compression.

- Choose Optimized if available.

- Soften the image (Blur/Smoothing).

- Avoid hard edges and sharp details.

Be aggressive with compression

Your number one tool for optimizing JPEGs is the Quality setting that you'll find in just about every graphics tool. The Quality setting allows you to set the rate of compression; lower quality means higher compression and smaller files. If your image editor has a preview, you can keep an eye on the image quality while changing the compression level. Different images can withstand different amounts of compression, but in general, images hold up reasonably well at moderate (50–70) and even low (30–40) quality settings. The quality at particular settings varies from program to program, so use whatever setting results in the best balance of quality and file size for your particular image.

Choose Optimized if available

Optimized JPEGs have slightly smaller file sizes and better color fidelity than standard JPEGs (although I've never been able to see the difference). For this reason, you should select the Optimized option if your image software offers it.

Blur the image

Because soft images compress smaller than sharp ones, you can try applying a slight Gaussian blur to the image to give the JPEG compression something to chew on. Even an imperceptible blur over the whole image can reduce file size. In GIMP's Export as JPEG dialog box, there is a Smoothing setting that does just that. Photoshop's legacy Save for Web feature also includes an option to apply varying amounts of blur across the whole image.

You might also choose to apply a more aggressive blur to less important areas of the image while preserving areas of interest. In FIGURE 24-15, I applied a blur to all areas of the image except the face, which remains at the original quality, and reduced the file size by 6 KB, or 23%. For this image, I'd say the savings are worth the loss of detail around the edges, but of course, you should decide whether blurring is appropriate based on the content and purpose of your images.

Avoid hard edges and details

JPEGs compress areas of smooth, blended colors more efficiently than areas with high contrast, hard edges, and sharp detail. To demonstrate the difference,

26 KB
Quality: 60%, no blur

20 KB
Quality: 60%, Gaussian blur applied to areas except the face

FIGURE 24-15. Applying blur to less important parts of an image can help reduce the size of the exported JPEG.

gradient.jpg (**12 KB**)

detail.jpg (**49 KB**)

FIGURE 24-16. JPEG compression works better on smooth, blended colors than hard edges and detail.

Alternatives to PNG-24

PNG-24 images have large file sizes, so developers look for ways to avoid them entirely. Here are some options for achieving multiple levels of transparency without using PNG-24:

- Convert them to PNG-8, as discussed in this section.

- Place a JPEG version of the image inside an SVG; then use the SVG clipping or masking features (covered in **Chapter 25**) to create transparent areas.

- Apply transparent areas by using CSS Masks (*www.w3.org/TR/ css-masking-1/*), which are not covered in this book but are worth looking into.

- Use a new image format, such as WebP and JPEG 2000, that supports alpha transparency. These will be good alternatives to PNG-24 once support improves in image-creation tools and browsers.

FIGURE 24-16 shows two similar graphics with blended colors. The image with more contrast and detail is more than four times larger at the same quality setting. You can keep this principle in mind when creating your images. If a photograph has a lot of hard edges, consider whether they can be softened or edited out. Also see whether a PNG-8 might offer similar image quality at a smaller size.

"Optimizing" PNG-24

Because PNG-24 is a lossless format, there isn't much you can do to these images in terms of optimization. Your best bets are to do the following:

- Avoid them for photographs in favor of JPEGs.

- Run them through an optimization utility.

- Convert them to PNG-8 with multiple levels of transparency.

PNG's lossless compression makes PNG-24 a wonderful format for preserving quality in images, but the same image will always be smaller saved as a lossy JPEG. Therefore, your first "lean and mean" strategy for photographs is to avoid PNG-24 and go with JPEG instead.

You may be using PNG-24 because you need multiple levels of transparency (a valid reason). If that is the case, you have two options. Running the image through one of the image optimizers listed later in this section is a good way to strip out useless metadata but preserve the image. The other option is to convert it to a PNG-8 while maintaining alpha transparency.

Converting to PNG-8

Until recently, we didn't have tools for making PNG-8 with alpha transparency (see **Note**). Now Photoshop CC gives you the option to make PNG-8 with alpha transparency and a smaller file size right in the Export As dialog box.

NOTE

Adobe Fireworks had the little-known ability to create PNG-8 + alpha, but it was discontinued in 2013.

You can also use a standalone utility for converting a PNG-24 to PNG-8 with alpha transparency. Some options are as follows:

- **ImageAlpha** (*pngmini.com*) is a Mac-only program created by Kornel Lesiński for converting PNG-24 to PNG-8 (**FIGURE 24-17**). For the image of the orange circle, I was able to reduce the size from 8.4 KB to 2.6 KB, a savings of 69%. Because the circle had flat colors, I was able to reduce the color palette to 64 colors without any significant change in appearance.

- **TinyPNG** (*tinypng.com*) allows you to drag PNGs right onto their web page for conversion. They also offer a paid Pro version and developer APIs that let you use the "tinify" tool with most backend platforms.

- **PunyPNG Pro** (*punypng.com*) is another compressor with a web interface that offers "lossy" conversion from PNG-24 to PNG-8, although you get that feature only with the paid Pro account.

> **■ FUN FACT**
>
> All of these tools use the **pngquant** compression library, created by Kornel Lesiński (*pngquant.org*), which reduces the number of colors from 24-bit to 8-bit while assigning transparency levels to slots in the indexed color map.

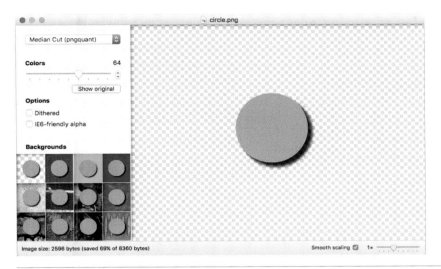

FIGURE 24-17. The ImageAlpha compression tool (Mac only) turns PNG-24s with alpha transparency into PNG-8s while retaining multiple transparency levels.

Optimizing PNG-8 and GIF

Follow these optimization strategies in the PNG-8 and GIF creation and export process:

- Reduce the number of colors (bit depth).

- Avoid or reduce dithering.

- Design with flat colors.

Reduce the number of colors (bit depth)

The most effective way to reduce the size of an indexed color image, and therefore the first stop in your optimization journey, is to reduce the number of colors in the image.

Although PNG-8s and GIFs can contain up to 256 colors, there's no rule that says they have to. In fact, by reducing the number of colors (bit depth), you significantly reduce the file size of the image. One reason for this is that files with lower bit depths contain less data. Another byproduct of the color

Bit Depth

Bit depth is a way to refer to the maximum number of colors a graphic can contain. This chart shows the number of colors each bit depth represents:

1-bit	2 colors
2-bit	4 colors
3-bit	8 colors
4-bit	16 colors
5-bit	32 colors
6-bit	64 colors
7-bit	128 colors
8-bit	256 colors

You'd be surprised how many images look perfectly fine with only 32 pixel colors.

reduction is that you create more areas of flat color by combining similar, abutting pixel colors. More flat color areas mean more-efficient compression.

Photoshop and GIMP give you the opportunity to reduce the number of colors when you convert the image from RGB to indexed color. In Photoshop, select Image → Mode → Indexed Color, and enter the number of colors to use in the color map in the Colors box. If you have access to Photoshop's legacy Save for Web feature, there is a bit-depth setting you can play around with while observing the resulting image in the preview before saving the image. In GIMP, go to Image → Mode → Indexed and enter the "Maximum number of colors" you'd like to use.

If you reduce the number of colors too far, of course, the image begins to fall apart or may cease to communicate effectively. For example, in FIGURE 24-18, once I reduced the number of colors in the PNG to eight, I lost the rainbow, which was the whole point of the image. This "meltdown" point is different from image to image. (Granted, this barn and sky image should be a JPEG, but it demonstrates the effects of optimization dramatically, so thank you for bearing with me.)

You'll be surprised to find how many images look perfectly fine with only 32 pixel colors (5-bit), such as the Asian Cuisine image in EXERCISE 24-1. That is usually my starting point for color reduction, and I go higher only if necessary. Some image types fare better than others with reduced color palettes, but as a general rule, the fewer the colors, the smaller the file.

The real size savings kick in when there are large areas of flat color. Keep in mind that even if your image has 8 pixel colors, if it has a lot of blends, gradients, and detail, you won't see the kind of file size savings you might expect with such a severe color reduction.

256 colors (**21 KB**)

64 colors (**13 KB**)

8 colors (**6 KB**)

FIGURE 24-18. Reducing the number of colors in an image reduces the file size.

Reduce dithering

When the colors in an RGB image are reduced to a specific palette, the colors that are *not* in that palette get approximated by dithering. Dithering is a speckle pattern that results when palette colors are mixed to simulate an unavailable color. When converting to indexed color, Photoshop and GIMP (and most other image editors) allow you to specify whether and how the image dithers.

In photographic images, dithering is not a problem and can even be beneficial; however, dithering in flat color areas is usually distracting and undesirable. In terms of optimization, dithering is undesirable because the speckles disrupt otherwise smooth areas of color. Those stray speckles stand in the way of the compression and result in larger files.

One way to shave bytes off a PNG or GIF is to turn off dithering entirely. For some images, that may result in a banding effect as shown in FIGURE 24-19. If that is unacceptable, you can turn the dithering back on or try a higher number of colors if the bit depth was set to less than 8-bit.

NOTE

Not all image-editing tools give you control over the amount of dithering.

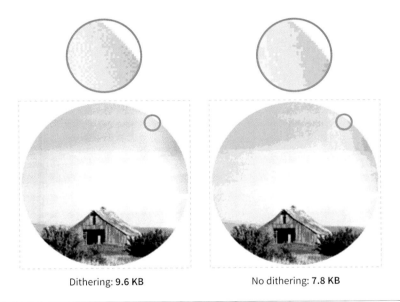

Dithering: **9.6 KB**   No dithering: **7.8 KB**

FIGURE 24-19. Turning off or reducing the amount of dithering reduces the file size. Both images have 32 pixel colors and use an adaptive palette.

Design with flat colors

When designing your images keep in mind the fact that PNGs and GIFs are good at compressing areas of flat color.

Choosing flat colors over gradients and patterns makes a big difference in file size, as shown in FIGURE 24-20. Reducing the colors from 256 to 8 goes a long way in reducing the file size, but the colors in the blend are approximated with a dither pattern, which we just learned is counterproductive to GIF and PNG compression. However, if you create the image with flat colors in the first place, the file size is half that of the dithered version, even though both images have been reduced to 8 colors.

I feel obliged to say that images like this one should be drawn with vectors and saved in SVG format, which will be smaller and more versatile than bit-mapped versions. However, if you have a reason for saving PNGs, design them in a way that complements the compression. Similarly, if you are starting with a bitmapped source image, you may be able to edit it in a way that eliminates unnecessary color blends and patterns.

13.5 KB
PNG with gradient blends and 256 colors.

6.8 KB
PNG with dithering pattern and only 8 colors.

3.7 KB
PNG designed with flat colors (8-color palette).

FIGURE 24-20. For PNG-8 and GIF, you can keep file sizes small by replacing gradients and patterns with flat colors.

Optimization Tools

Even if you design images to take advantage of their end compression scheme and take full advantage of all the optimizations in your image-editing tool, there's a good chance that you can squeeze down the file size of your images even further using an optimization tool. These tools are generally lossless, meaning they do not alter the appearance of your image. They find the file savings by tossing out chunks of code dedicated to metadata, color profiles, and other redundant code.

It is recommended that you always run your images through an optimization tool as the last step in the image production process. The good news is, there are many ways to do it, so you will surely find one that fits into your work-flow. Let's look at some options.

Online image optimizers

One easy solution is to use one of the freely available online optimizers. Just drag your images onto the web page interface and download the resulting compressed files. They are a good option if you don't have too many images to process, and they have the advantage of being cross-platform. In addition to free web-based tools, most of these companies also offer Pro packages that allow you to upload more data and provide additional compression options. Some also offer server-side solutions:

Always run your images through an optimization tool as the last step in the image production process.

- **Optimizilla** (*optimizilla.com*) can optimize both JPEGs and PNGs and allows you to compress up to 20 images at once. It is free to use.

- **Kraken.io** (*kraken.io/web-interface*) offers a free web interface in addition to their commercial server-side services. They give you the option of lossy, lossless, manual "expert" settings, and the ability to resize the image as well.

- **TinyPNG** (*tinypng.com*) was mentioned earlier as a way to convert transparent PNG-24 to PNG-8, but you can use it to compress any PNG or JPEG.

- **PunyPng** (*punypng.com*) boasts that they produce the smallest file sizes for JPEGs, PNGs and GIFs. They also offer a Pro package that gives you more compression options, such as the PNG-24 to PNG-8 conversion mentioned earlier.

Standalone optimization apps

You might prefer to have an optimization program running on your own computer. If that is the case, look into these popular downloadable tools:

- **ImageOptim** (*imageoptim.com*) is a Mac-only tool with an easy drag-and-drop interface for optimizing PNGs, JPEGs, GIF (including animated GIF), and even SVG. It was created by Kornel Lesiński, who also brought you ImageAlpha.

- **PNGGauntlet** (*pnggauntlet.com*) is a Windows-only tool for PNG optimization. It can also convert JPEG, GIF, TIFF, and BMP files to PNG format.

- **JPEGmini** (*www.jpegmini.com*) is a program for Mac and Windows that compresses JPEGs. The free trial is good for 200 images; after that, you need to pay for the Pro version. They offer a free web interface as well as a server-side option.

- **Trimage** (*trimage.org*) is an optimization tool similar to ImageOptim that works on the Linux platform.

Grunt and Gulp plug-ins

If your workflow is based around a task runner such as Grunt or Gulp, you can make optimization of PNGs and JPEGs an automated task with the "imagemin" plug-in. imagemin is maintained at *github.com/gruntjs/grunt-contrib-imagemin*, where you can get instructions and links to download.

Now you should have some strategies for making your images as lean and mean as possible, including techniques for each file format during the creation process as well as tools for squooshing them down even further after they are made. Let's put them to the test in EXERCISE 24-3.

EXERCISE 24-3. Optimize some images

In this exercise, we'll take the best images we exported in EXERCISE 24-1 and see if we can make them even smaller using an online optimization tool. I've included starter images *boats-60.jpg* and *asian-32.png* in the *materials* folder if you'd like to use the same images shown here.

I'm going to use Kraken.io because it gives me a few more options, such as the choice between lossy and lossless compression. Click the Try Free Web Interface button on their home page to get to the online tool (FIGURE 24-21).

1. Let's start with the *asian-32.png* file, which if you'll remember, was reduced to 32 pixel colors and saved as a PNG-8. Using Photoshop's best compression tool (the Export As function), we get a file size for this image of 3.35 KB, which isn't bad, but let's see if we can make it even smaller. Drag it into the Kraken.io optimizer, selecting the "lossless" mode, which means it won't touch the image data but will find other data in the image that can be removed.

   The "Kraked" (optimized) file size is 2.96 KB, a file savings of 11.8% without the image being altered at all. For what it's worth, I tried compressing this same image at TinyPNG.com and got a file reduction of 15%, so keep in mind that tools offer varying results based on their compression algorithms.

2. Now let's see what we can do with the *boats-60.jpg* image. First, try it using the "lossless" optimization mode, keeping the image exactly as it is. The file size went from 34.74 KB to 31.56 KB, which is just over 9% smaller. Next drag it into Kraken.io again using "lossy" mode, allowing the tool to throw out a little image data to compress it even smaller.

   The resulting file size is just 24.9 KB, a savings of 28%! I downloaded both the lossy and lossless versions and compared them in an image editor, and to my eye, there was no discernable difference. I'd go with the much smaller lossy version for this one. By comparison, TinyPNG was only able to reduce *boats-60.jpg* by 3%.

You can see that running exported images through an optimizer is well worth the effort. You can probably also see that doing each one individually could get a little cumbersome, so if you have a lot of images to produce, consider using a tool that allows batch processing, or automate the process with a task runner or a server-side image management tool or service.

FIGURE 24-21. Optimizing images with the Kraken.io online image tool.

And with that, we end our tour of image asset production techniques. You should feel comfortable opening an image in an image-editing application and saving or exporting to the various web image formats. You've gotten to know the various ways image formats store transparency information and how to pick the most appropriate format for transparent images. You've picked up some tricks for generating sets of images for responsive sites, and finally, you have some options for optimizing your images as a final step.

As usual, this chapter ends with a quiz so you can put your new knowledge to work.

TEST YOURSELF

Are you an image asset master? Answer these questions to find out. Answers are in **Appendix A**.

1. What are your file format options if you want multiple levels of transparency in a bitmapped image?

2. What is your number one tool for optimizing a JPEG?

3. What is your number one tool for optimizing an indexed-color image like PNG-8 or GIF?

4. How does dithering affect the file size of an indexed color PNG or GIF?

5. How does adding a blur affect the file size of a JPEG?

6. sRGB: Yes or no? Why?

7. Why might you need to create @2x and @3x scales of an image?

8. Why might you hire a company like Cloudinary or Akamai?

SVG

(SCALABLE VECTOR GRAPHICS)

SVGs (Scalable Vector Graphics) have made several guest appearances in this book, but in this chapter they finally get to be the star.

When rendered in a browser window, an SVG graphic may look like an image in any other format, but it's what's under the hood that makes it truly unique and versatile. First, as the name says, it is a vector format, meaning shapes within SVGs are defined by coordinates and lines, not grids of pixels. That's what makes them scalable—they can resize infinitely without loss of quality.

FIGURE 25-1 shows the same tiger image saved as an SVG and a PNG. The SVG can scale very large without any change in quality. Lines and text stay sharp, regardless of whether the image is viewed at 100 pixels or 10,000 pixels—try doing that with a bitmapped image! Now that our web pages and interfaces must work on all devices of all scales, from smartphones to high-density monitors and large-screen televisions, the ability to create a single image that looks great in all contexts is an epic win.

The vector nature of SVG makes it a good choice for icons, logos, charts, and other line drawings (FIGURE 25-2). And because these drawings are made up of shapes and paths, the file size is often significantly smaller than the same image made up of a grid of pixels.

SVGs may contain raster image content as well—in fact, you can do some pretty cool effects with them, but you miss out on the file size savings. SVGs are also an attractive choice for adding animation and interactivity to an interface. We'll review all of these capabilities throughout this chapter.

Scalability and reduced file sizes make SVG a great format for icons and simple illustrations.

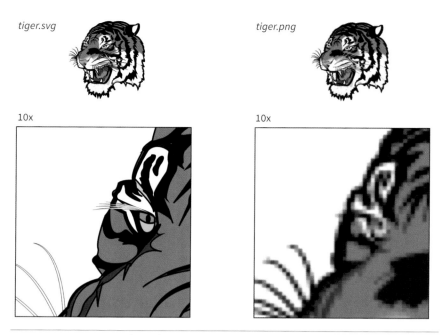

tiger.svg

tiger.png

10x

10x

FIGURE 25-1. Vector-based SVG images scale without loss of quality.

The Noun Project

"ben" , Open Clip Art

Ozer Kavak, Open Clip Art

Ghostscript tiger

FIGURE 25-2. SVG format is appropriate for line-style illustrations.

SVG History and Browser Support

SVG has had a long ramp-up over 20 years. It was first introduced by the W3C SVG Working Group in 1998, and SVG 1.0 finally achieved Recommendation status in 2001. SVG 1.1 (a more modularized version) was released in 2003, then cleaned up and republished again in 2011 (*www.w3.org/TR/SVG11/*).

Browser support for SVG 1.1 is excellent, but not quite ubiquitous. Browsers began supporting SVG natively (without plug-ins) between 2004 and 2006. The good news is that all modern browsers now support SVG placed as a standalone image and as inline code. The notable holes in support are Internet Explorer 8 and earlier and Android 2.x, which thankfully are on the verge of being obsolete (but check your own stats). There are other inconsistencies in browser support when you get down to the property level and other syntax minutiae. These are the growing pains all promising web standards go through. For an overview of feature support, see the Comparison of Layout Engines (SVG) page on Wikipedia at *en.wikipedia.org/wiki/Comparison_of_layout_engines_(Scalable_Vector_Graphics)*.

The W3C also released SVG Tiny 1.2 (*www.w3.org/TR/SVGTiny12*), a subset of SVG 1.1 aimed at pre-smartphone mobile devices. It is not supported on regular desktop or smartphone browsers.

SVG 2 (*www.w3.org/TR/SVG2/*) is under development with the aim to be more integrated with HTML5, CSS, and WOFF (Web Open Font Format). Browsers are already beginning to roll out support for individual modules from the SVG 2 spec, which you can begin using with testing and fallbacks.

DRAWING WITH XML

That takes care of the "scalable" and "vector" aspects of SVG. What really sets SVG apart from other formats, though, is that it is an XML language (see the sidebar **"A Quick Introduction to XML"**) for describing two-dimensional graphics, including shapes, paths, text, and even special filter effects. Bitmapped graphics are stored as largely unintelligible code (should you care to peek inside), but SVG images are generated by text files that are fairly human-readable. In fact, it is possible to create SVG graphics by typing out the code directly in a code editor instead of using a graphics program.

SVG Elements

SVG is a markup language, just like HTML, only it includes elements for two-dimensional graphics, such as the following:

- Elements for drawing lines and shapes: `circle`, `rect`, `ellipse`, `path`, `line`, `polyline`, and `polygon`

- A `text` element for adding text content

- Elements for organization, such as **g** for grouping shapes together, and **use** and **symbol** for reusing drawings

- Elements for clipping (`clipPath`) and masking (`mask`) image areas into interesting shapes

- Elements for raster effects such as `linearGradient` and `filter` for Photoshop-like filter effects

A Quick Introduction to XML

XML (which stands for eXtensible Markup Language) is not a specific language in itself, but rather a robust set of rules for creating other markup languages. It is a meta-language.

To use a simplified example, if you were publishing recipes, you might use XML to create a custom Recipe Markup Language (RML) that includes the elements **<ingredient>**, **<instructions>**, and **<servings>** to accurately describe the types of information in your recipe documents. Once labeled correctly, that information can be treated as data. In fact, XML has proven to be a powerful tool for sharing data between applications. Despite the fact that XML was developed with the web in mind, it has had a larger impact outside the web environment because of its data-handling capabilities. There are XML files working behind the scenes in an increasing number of software applications, such as Microsoft Office and Apple iTunes.

A few of the XML languages that are used on the web are as follows:

- **XHTML**: HTML rewritten according to the stricter rules of XML

- **RSS** (Really Simple Syndication, or RDF Site Summary): allows your content to be shared as data and read with RSS feed readers

- **MathML**: Used to describe mathematical notation

- **SVG**: The image description language that you'll learn all about in this chapter

XML Syntax Requirements

Because it is possible for multiple XML languages to appear in the same document, it is important that the syntax be very strict to keep things straight. Shortcuts that are fine in HTML (such as omitting end tags) won't fly in XML languages.

SVG follows the stricter XML syntax, so it is important to follow these code requirements when you're writing SVG:

- Element and attribute names must be lowercase.

- All elements must be closed (terminated), which means they must have a closing tag. To close elements without content (a.k.a. empty elements), you add a slash before the closing bracket (for example, **<rect/>**).

- Attribute values must be in quotation marks. Single or double quotation marks are acceptable as long as they are used consistently. Furthermore, there should be no extra whitespace (character spaces or line returns) before or after the attribute value inside the quotation marks.

- All attributes must have explicit attribute values. XML does not support attribute minimization, the practice in which certain attributes can be reduced to just the attribute value. This is best explained with an example from XHTML, a stricter version of HTML rewritten in XML. In HTML, you can write **checked** to indicate that a form button should be checked when the form loads, but in XHTML you need to explicitly write out **checked="checked"**.

- Proper nesting of elements is strictly enforced.

- Special characters must always be represented by character entities (e.g., **&amp;** for the & symbol). Note that most HTML named entities do not work in XML. Use the numeric Unicode code point reference instead.

- Scripts must be contained in a CDATA section so they will be treated as simple text characters and not parsed as XML markup. There is an example in the **"Interactivity with JavaScript"** section later in this chapter.

Of course, this is by no means an exhaustive list (see **Note**), but it should give you the general idea of what SVG is about. A simple example should make it even clearer. FIGURE 25-3 shows an SVG image, *simple.svg*, that contains a sampling of simple SVG elements. It's not a masterpiece, I know, but it will introduce you to some common SVG elements.

Here are the contents of the *simple.svg* file that generates the image in FIGURE 25-3. If you read through it closely, I think you'll find it's fairly intuitive, but my annotations follow.

```
<?xml version="1.0" encoding="utf-8"?>  Ⓐ
<svg version="1.1"  Ⓑ
  xmlns="http://www.w3.org/2000/svg"
  xmlns:xlink="http://www.w3.org/1999/xlink"
  width="150" height="200" viewBox="0 0 150 200">  Ⓒ

<defs>  Ⓓ
  <radialGradient id="fade">  Ⓔ
    <stop offset="0" stop-color="white"/>
    <stop offset="1" stop-color="orange"/>
  </radialGradient>
</defs>

<g id="greenbox">  Ⓕ
  <rect x="25" y="25" width="100" height="100" fill="#c6de89"
    stroke-width="2" stroke="green"/>  Ⓖ
  <circle cx="75" cy="75" r="40" fill="url(#fade)"/>
  <path d="M 13 100 L 60 50 L 90 90 L 140 30" stroke="black"
stroke-width="2" fill="none"/>  Ⓗ
</g>

<text x="25" y="150" fill="#000000" font-family="Helvetica"
font-size="16">A Simple SVG</text>  Ⓘ

</svg>
```

Let's take a closer look at the various parts of *simple.svg*:

Ⓐ Because this is an XML file, it starts off with some XML business. The first line is an XML declaration that identifies the file as XML. For web SVGs, this declaration is not necessary unless you are using a character encoding other than the default UTF-8, but you are likely to see it in code exported by graphics programs.

Ⓑ The entire document is contained in the **svg** root element. Drawing programs generally include the version number (1.1), although it is not necessary. The two **xmlns** attributes declare the XML namespace, which tells the browser to interpret this document by using the vocabulary defined in SVG (see **Note**). The **xmlns:xlink** attribute allows you to put links and references to external files in the SVG document. Namespaces help keep element names straight, especially when there is more than one XML language used in a document.

Ⓒ The **width** and **height** attributes in the root **svg** element establish a drawing area (viewport) that is 150 pixels wide by 200 pixels tall. The viewport

NOTE

Lists of all the SVG elements and attributes can be found at www.w3.org/TR/SVG11/.

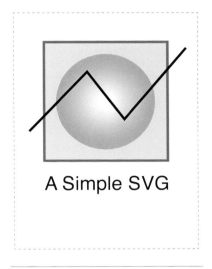

FIGURE 25-3. A basic SVG image, *simple.svg*. The dotted line has been added to indicate the edges of the viewport but is not part of the SVG code.

NOTE

The **xmlns** *and* **xmlns:xlink** *attributes are not required when the SVG is placed inline in an HTML5 document.*

NOTE

The viewport and viewbox are discussed in more detail in the section "**Responsive SVGs**" later in this chapter.

SVG Coordinates

The coordinates in SVGs start at the top-left corner and increase down and to the right (FIGURE 25-4). The square created with the **rect** element in the example has the coordinates **x="25" y="25"**, which means its top-left corner is positioned 25 pixels from the left edge of the viewport/viewbox and 25 pixels down from the top edge. Some elements, like circles and ellipses, may be positioned based by their center points (**cx** and **cy**).

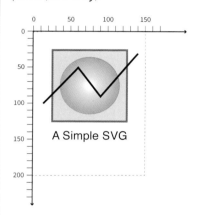

FIGURE 25-4. In SVG, x coordinates start on the left and increase to the right, and y coordinates start at the top and increase downward. The 0,0 origin point is in the top-left corner of the viewport.

is indicated in FIGURE 25-3 by a dotted line, but this is for illustration purposes only and wouldn't appear in the browser. Pixels are the default measurement unit in SVG, so you don't need the "px." The **viewBox** attribute controls the size of the drawing itself and enables the graphic to scale neatly if you change the width and height later. (See **Note**.)

Ⓓ Next we get to the **defs** element, which defines elements and effects that will be referenced later in the document by their **id** values. Elements in the **defs** section are created but not immediately rendered. Here we are using **defs** to store a radial gradient pattern, but it could also be used for shapes (like **circle**) or symbols that get rendered in the document via the **use** element. Defining a shape, drawing, or effect once, then reusing it, is a good way to eliminate redundancy in your SVG code.

Ⓔ This **radialGradient** element is made up of two color **stop** elements, one for white, and one for orange. It is given an **id** of **"fade"**.

Ⓕ Finally, we get to the elements that describe the drawing itself. The rectangle (**rect**), circle (**circle**), and path (**path**) that make up the drawing are grouped together with the **g** element and given the name **"greenbox"**. This makes it easy to access in CSS or a script later.

Ⓖ The square is created using the **rect** (for "rectangle") element with its width and height set to 100 pixels. Notice that this and other empty element are closed (terminated) with a slash (**/**) before the closing bracket, as is required in XML languages.

The **x** and **y** attributes position it on the pixel grid within the viewport (see FIGURE 25-4 in the **"SVG Coordinates"** sidebar). You can see that attributes are used to provide the dimensions, fill color, stroke width, and stroke color (see **Note**). The center of the **circle** element is positioned with the **cx** and **cy** attributes, and its radius is set with **r**. This **circle** is filled with the radial gradient we defined earlier, which is called by its **id** "fade" in the **url()** notation.

NOTE

"Stroke" is what SVG calls the line or border around a shape.

Ⓗ The crooked line is defined by a **path** element. The **d** (data) attribute provides a series of x, y coordinates that make up the points along the path. All paths start with **M** ("moveto"), which sets the starting position. Each **L** draws a "lineto" the next set of coordinates. Coordinates can be separated by a character space (as shown) or a comma.

Ⓘ Finally, we have a bit of text defined with the **text** element. You can see that it is styled with attributes like **font-size** and **font-family**, which should look familiar now that you've learned about CSS. There are many similarities between SVG attributes and CSS styles.

Beyond Simple Shapes

SVGs have some cool image features in addition to drawing lines and shapes.

Embedded bitmap images

SVGs aren't limited to vector drawings; you can embed bitmap images in them too. You might do this in order to apply special effects or add some sort of behavior or interactivity that a PNG or JPEG can't do on its own. Images are embedded with the **image** element.

```
<image xlink:href="kangaroo.jpg" x="45" y="0" width="100"
height="150"/>
```

Note that because SVG is an XML format, it requires the **xlink:href** attribute to point to the external image file.

Clipping and masking

SVG lets you selectively show parts of an image and hide others by clipping and masking.

In clipping, a vector path is used to "cut out" a section of an image. The parts of the image that fall outside the clipping path are hidden completely. FIGURE 25-5 uses a path in the shape of a star to clip the starry sky image. Clipping paths are defined with the **clipPath** element.

```
<defs>
  <clipPath id="star">
  <polygon points="390,12 440,154 590,157 470,250 513,393 390,307
266,393 310,248 189,157 340,154 390,12" style="fill: none"/>
  </clipPath>
</defs>

<image xlink:href="starrysky_600.jpg" width="600" height="400"
style="clip-path: url(#star)"/>
```

The star-shaped path positioned over the image.

The image is clipped to the path (dotted border indicates the SVG viewport but is not part of the SVG).

FIGURE 25-5. The star-shaped path is used as a clipping path that reveals part of the underlying image.

NOTE

If the mask is a color image, it is converted to grayscale based on its luminance (brightness) using a formula that interprets yellows and greens as lighter than reds and blues.

WARNING

Masking is not supported in Android versions 4.3 and earlier.

■ COOL TRICK

It is possible to simulate transparency in a JPEG by embedding it in an SVG and using a clipping path or mask to make certain areas within the image transparent. That lets you take advantage of the small file size of JPEGs for full-color images while gaining the transparency effects available only with PNG-24. On the downside, there are browser support issues that you don't run into with PNG-24.

Masking works similarly but is a pixel-based effect. Varying levels of darkness in the mask result in varying amounts of transparency at each point, similar to an alpha channel. In SVG masks, pure white areas correspond to 100% opacity, and pure black corresponds to 0% opacity (fully transparent). Levels of gray in between result in levels of semitransparency.

You can play with the fill color of the mask to reveal more or less of the object it is masking. The effect is more interesting when the mask contains gradients rather than solid fill colors. You can even use an image as a mask (see **Note**).

FIGURE 25-6 shows the same star shape filled with a gradient and used as a mask over the starry sky photograph. Note that the areas of the image that fall outside the mask object are completely transparent, just like the clipping path.

```
<defs>
  <linearGradient id="blend">
    <stop offset="0%" stop-color="#ffffff"/>
    <stop offset="100%" stop-color="#000000"/>
  </linearGradient>

  <mask id="star" x="0" y="0" width="400" height="381">
    <polygon points="390,12 440,154 590,157 470,250 513,393 390,307
266,393 310,248 189,157 340,154 390,12" style="fill: url(#blend)"/>
  </mask>
</defs>

<image xlink:href="starrysky_600.jpg" width="600" height="400"
style="mask: url(#star);"/>
```

The star-shaped path is filled with a gradient.

The gradient works as a mask in which the light areas allow more of the image to show through. The darker the mask, the lighter the masked image.

FIGURE 25-6. The star shape has a gradient fill that affects the transparency of the masked image.

Filter effects

You might be surprised to learn that a vector-based graphic format includes Photoshop-like filters for manipulating images. SVG features more than a dozen filter effects that can be used alone or layered and combined for all sorts of effects, such as simple Gaussian blurs, color shifting, mosaic-like patterns, and good ol' drop shadows.

The nice thing about filters is that the original image is untouched; all the messing around happens when the browser renders the image with the filters applied. FIGURE 25-7 shows just a few SVG filters to give you an idea of what can be done.

Original image

Gaussian blur

Color matrix: saturate

Morphology

Turbulence + Displacement map

FIGURE 25-7. Examples of SVG filters.

To give you a brief taste of how filters work, here is an example that puts a blur effect on an ellipse element. The filter is defined with a **filter** element, which contains one or more filter primitives (a very specific effect that can be combined with other effects). The filter is given an **id** and then is called in as a style on the element that uses it. FIGURE 25-8 shows the ellipse without and with the blur filter.

NOTE

This example and the next use the **style** *attribute (the same one we use in HTML) to add inline styles to elements. We'll talk about options for styling SVGs in the next section.*

```
<defs>
  <filter id="blurry">
    <feGaussianBlur in="SourceGraphic" stdDeviation="4"/>
  </filter>
</defs>

<ellipse cx="200" cy="50" rx="150" ry="100" style="fill: orange;"/>

<ellipse cx="200" cy="300" rx="150" ry="100" style="fill: orange;
filter: url(#blurry);"/>
```

FIGURE 25-8. A Gaussian blur filter applied to an **ellipse** element.

FIGURE 25-9. A drop shadow created with SVG filters.

■ **FUN FACT**

The masking, filter, and transform features in CSS are extensions of SVG. The standards bodies are aiming to make them work together as seamlessly as possible and to bring some of the best aspects of SVG into CSS and standard browser behavior.

NOTE

Because symbols won't render, you don't need to put them in a **defs** *section, but it's a good practice because it is a logical container for elements you're defining for later use.*

To make a drop shadow, the blur filter is defined and then merged with an offset that moves it down and to the right. FIGURE 25-9 shows the result.

```
<defs>
<filter id="shadow">
  <feGaussianBlur in="SourceAlpha" stdDeviation="4" result="blur"/>
  <feOffset in="blur" dx="7" dy="5" result="offsetBlur" />
  <feMerge>
    <feMergeNode in="offsetBlur"/>
    <feMergeNode in="SourceGraphic"/>
  </feMerge>
</filter>
</defs>
<polygon points="390,12 440,154 590,157 470,250 513,393 390,307
266,393 310,248 189,157 340,154 390,12" style="fill: pink; filter:
url(#shadow)"/>
```

Of course, there is a *lot* more to SVG filters than I can cover here, but I hope that I've provided a good introduction.

Reuse and recycle

A powerful feature in SVG is the ability to define a shape or effect once and then reuse it wherever you need it, as many times as you need it. This keeps the file small by removing redundant code and is a good example of DRY (Don't Repeat Yourself) coding.

The trick is defining the element you want to repeat, such as an icon, in a **symbol**. The **symbol** element does not get rendered; it just sets up a drawing for future use (see **Note**).

```
<symbol id="iconA" viewBox="0 0 44 44">
  <!-- all the paths and shapes that make up the icon -->
</symbol>
```

When you want to use the symbol on the page, call it up with the **use** element, which triggers the symbol to render. The following is a minimal **use** element example. The reused symbol scales to whatever dimensions are set on **svg.icon** in the web page's style sheet.

```
<svg class="icon">
  <use xlink:href="#iconA" />
</svg>
```

You could include other attributes with instructions such as x,y coordinates for positioning, width and height dimensions, and styles that override styles inherited by the copy of the symbol.

The **use** element doesn't work only with **symbol**. You can use it to reuse any basic SVG shape, image, or group in a similar manner. The advantage to making the initial SVG a symbol is you can include the **viewBox** attribute to enable proportional scaling.

The **symbol** and **use** elements are the tools behind SVG sprites. Sprites are a technique in which multiple SVG drawings (such as an icon set, to use the most popular example) are defined in one SVG, either in the HTML document or as an external *.svg* file. In the HTML document, the **use** element (inside an inline **svg**) pulls a particular icon symbol onto the page. It is a powerful tool for managing SVG icons. You will find plenty of tutorials for SVG sprites online, and Chris Coyier includes a nice how-to in his book *Practical SVG* (A Book Apart).

So far you've seen SVG used to draw basic shapes, embed images, clip and mask selected areas, and add some pretty groovy special effects. The SVG drawing features are core to the SVG format; however, if we focus only on what gets drawn in the browser window, we would be missing out on some of the best features of SVG. Let's look at them now.

FEATURES OF SVG AS XML

Now you know that behind every SVG that renders on a screen is a structured text document. In that respect, it's pretty much the same as HTML. Furthermore, SVG, as a structured document language, has a DOM that includes objects, properties, and methods related to manipulating graphic elements. This opens up some really exciting possibilities that make SVG more flexible and useful than its static-image counterparts.

Styling

You can target elements in an SVG (or the **svg** element itself if it's inline) to change their presentation with CSS—for example, applying the same color or border style to HTML elements on the page as well as shapes within the SVG.

Styles are added to SVG in four ways:

Presentation attributes

The earlier "Simple SVG" example in FIGURE 25-3 uses presentational attributes defined in the SVG language, such as **fill** and **stroke-width**, to control how shapes should appear. Presentation attributes are always overridden by styles applied with CSS rules.

```
<rect x="25" y="25" width="100" height="100" fill="#c6de89"
  stroke-width="2" stroke="green"/>
```

Inline styles

SVG elements may use the inline **style** attribute, which works the same as it does in HTML elements. Many developers prefer this approach. The same **rect** element could also be written as follows:

```
<rect x="25" y="25" width="100" height="100" style="fill:#c6de89;
  stroke-width:2; stroke:green;" />
```

Internal style sheet

As in HTML, you can include a **style** element at the top of the **svg** (or in the **defs** section if there is one) that contains all the styles used in the SVG document:

```
<svg> <!-- XML business omitted for brevity -->
  <style>
    /* styles here */
  </style>
  <!--drawing here -->
</svg>
```

External style sheet

If your SVG is inline or placed on the page with the **object** or **iframe** elements, you can import an external style sheet with the **@import** rule in the **style** element. Remember that external files won't work for standalone SVGs embedded with the **img** element. That includes the style sheet itself as well as references to external resources using the **url()** notation within style rules.

```
<svg>
  <style type="text/css">
    @import "svg-style.css";
    /* more styles */
  </style>
  <!-- drawing here -->
</svg>
```

For inline SVGs, you can also style elements with a style sheet linked to the HTML document with the **link** element:

```
<head>
  <!-- additional head elements -->
  <link href="svg-style.css" rel="stylesheet" type="text/css">
</head>
<body>
  <svg>
  <!-- drawing here -->
  </svg>
</body>
```

Adding SVG to a Page: A Refresher

Chapter 7, Adding Images, went into detail about the ways to add an SVG to a page, but I thought it would be good to have a little refresher now in the context of our SVG deep-dive. See the original discussion in **Chapter 7** for more markup details. SVGs can be added to an HTML document in the following ways:

As an image

You can add a self-contained *.svg* file to a page with the **img** element as you would any other graphic:

```
<img src="star.svg" alt="star icon">
```

An SVG can also be used in any CSS property that accepts images, such as **background-image**.

When standalone SVGs are added to pages like simple graphics, they behave as simple graphics. You can no longer style or script the elements in the SVG, it won't be interactive (i.e., won't register user events like clicks or hover), and it won't load any external files like embedded images, style sheets, or scripts. if a static image is all you need, this is a reliable option.

As an embedded object

You can use the **object** element to embed an SVG on a page. This method's advantage is that it allows scripts to run and external files to load. You can also provide a fallback image for non-supporting browsers (although there aren't many):

```
<object data="star.svg" type="image/svg+xml">
  <img src="fallback.png" alt="">
</object>
```

As inline SVG code

The entire SVG file can be pasted right into the HTML source as an **svg** element. This option gives you total access to the SVG's DOM for styling and scripting, which is a big advantage. On the downside, the code for an SVG can get very long.

Interactivity with JavaScript

SVGs aren't just pretty pictures—SVGs are images you can *program*! You can add interactivity to the elements in an SVG with JavaScript because all of its element and attribute nodes are accessible in the DOM. It is worth noting that SVGs may also include simple **a** links, are a basic kind of interactivity.

For example, because an SVG can listen for mouseovers, you can create fun hover effects that add personality to UI elements. You can also trigger changes in the SVG on a click or a tap. JavaScript can do everything from adding a little motion to an icon to creating whole Flash-like game interfaces and multimedia presentations, as shown in FIGURE 25-10.

FIGURE 25-10. An example of an SVG game interface created with the Snap.svg JavaScript library. When you put the pointer over each dot, a funny little worm pops up. See more interactive SVG demos at *snapsvg.io/demos*.

If your SVG is inline, scripts in the HTML document can access elements within the SVG. For standalone SVGs, you can use SVG's **script** element. Because it is an XML document, the code needs to be wrapped in an XML Character Data Block (`<![CDATA[    ]]>`) so <, >, and & symbols are parsed correctly, as shown in this example:

```
<script><![CDATA[

  //script here

]]></script>
```

> ### SVG Versus Canvas
>
> In **Chapter 10, Embedded Media**, we looked at the HTML5 **canvas** element and API that creates a space for a two-dimensional, dynamic drawing on a web page. The difference is that an SVG image is drawn with a structural markup language and a canvas is drawn with JavaScript commands. Both can contain images, videos, animation, and dynamic updates in real time.
>
> **canvas** is better for quick redraws on the fly (it's only pixels, after all), making it better suited for designing games, editing images, and saving images to bitmapped formats. SVG offers advantages in the ease of scripting, animation, and accessibility; however, complicated SVG documents require more processing power than **canvas** elements.

Animation

SVG is a popular choice for adding animated elements to a web page. FIGURE 25-11 is my attempt to capture some charming animation in a still image. For more inspiration, I recommend going to *codepen.io* and searching for "SVG animation."

FIGURE 25-11. An example of an animated SVG by Chris Gannon. You can see it in action at *codepen.io/chrisgannon/pen/emVgMg*.

There are a number of ways to animate an SVG: animation elements in SVG, CSS animation, and JavaScript:

SVG/SMIL

The SVG specification includes animation effects based on SMIL (Synchronized Multimedia Integration Language), an XML language for creating synchronized audio, video, and animated elements. Each animation effect is defined by an element, with attributes for fine-tuning. Although the built-in SVG/SMIL animation elements provide good tools for all sorts of animation tasks, lack of browser support means that it's not a great option if animation is critical to your message.

CSS animation

SVG elements can also be animated with CSS transitions and keyframes. It should be noted that CSS can animate only CSS properties, not attribute values, which may be limiting for SVG, which uses attributes for most of the geometry and layout. This technique is also hampered by limited browser support (see **Note**), although that continues to improve. CSS animation is good for simple, non-critical animation effects.

JavaScript

With JavaScript, you can create complex, interactive animations that compete with the functionality Flash once offered. There is much better browser support, although there is always the possibility that some users don't have JavaScript enabled and will miss out. If you don't want to reinvent the wheel, you can take advantage of the many SVG Animation JavaScript libraries (see the **"SVG Animation JS Libaries"** sidebar).

If you'd like to learn more about SVG animation, I recommend *SVG Animations* by Sarah Drasner (O'Reilly) and *Creating Web Animations* by Kirupa Chinnathambi (O'Reilly).

BROWSER SUPPORT NOTE

No Microsoft browser (Internet Explorer or Edge) supports SVG/SMIL animation. Chrome temporarily deprecated it, which sent a message to other browser vendors to stop active development of SVG/SMIL support. With CSS and JavaScript offering better animation options, this part of the SVG spec may wither on the vine.

BROWSER SUPPORT NOTE

*CSS animation is not supported in Internet Explorer 9 and earlier (at all, not just for SVGs), and there is no SVG support (at all) in IE8 and earlier. IE 10 and 11 support animation of CSS properties, but not SVG-specific properties (*fill*, *stroke*, etc.). In MSEdge and Firefox browsers released prior to 2017, CSS animation won't work if the SVG is added with the *img* element. Older Chrome and Safari browsers require the *-webkit-* prefix.*

Data Visualization

SVGs have become a go-to tool of the data visualization ("dataviz") world because they can be generated dynamically with real data. For example, you could make the temperature level on an SVG thermometer illustration rise and fall with real weather data gathered in the user's location, or you could change progress bars or pie charts as data updates in real time. FIGURE 25-12 shows examples of SVG used for dataviz from the D3.js Gallery. D3.js is a JavaScript library created specifically for "data-driven documents." Find out more at *d3js.org*.

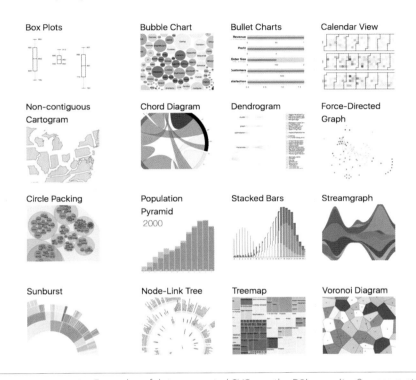

FIGURE 25-12. Examples of data-generated SVGs on the D3js.org site. See more at *github.com/d3/d3/wiki/Gallery*.

The methods for generating SVGs with data are dependent on the type of data and the programming language used. One option is to translate the XML document that contains the data into the SVG by using XSLT. XSLT (eXtensible Stylesheet Language Transformations) is an XML language that provides structured instructions for translating one XML language into another. Clearly, that is some advanced XML mojo that we will not be delving into here, but I thought you ought to know. Other options include JavaScript and server-side template languages (also more than we'll take on here).

If you are eager to know more about data-generated SVGs, the book *Interactive Data Visualization for the Web* by Scott Murray (O'Reilly) is a good place to start.

SVG Animation JS Libraries

These are just a few of the JavaScript libraries available to help you add animation effects to your SVGs more efficiently:

Snap.svg (snapsvg.io)

This is a multipurpose SVG building and animating library created by Dmitry Baranovskiy. It is open source and freely available.

SVG.js (svgjs.com)

SVG.js is an extremely lightweight library (just 11 KB!) for basic SVG animation. It is modular, too, so you can use just what you need.

Velocity (velocityjs.org)

As the name says, Velocity makes animations render very quickly, and it has a jQuery-like syntax that makes it easy to use.

Bonsai (bonsaijs.org)

Bonsai is a robust SVG animation library that includes support for fonts, audio, video, and images.

Path animators

Have you ever seen a graphic on a web page that appears to get drawn before your eyes? It was likely an SVG animated with a path animator. There are a number of one-trick-pony JS libraries that can animate the lines in your SVG: Walkway (*connoratherton. com/walkway*), LazyLinePainter (*lazylinepainter.info*), and Vivus (*maxwellito.github.io/vivus*).

Accessibility

Unlike text in bitmapped image formats, the text in SVGs can be accessed by search engines and read by screen readers when labeled properly. There are a few things you can do to make your SVGs more accessible to screen readers:

- Use the SVG `title` element to provide a short name for the **svg** element itself or any container (such as **g**) or element it contains. The `title` element should be the first child element of its parent.

- Use the SVG `desc` element to provide long text descriptions for elements.

- Add ARIA roles to the **svg** element and its components to ensure that screen readers interpret them correctly and efficiently. Recommendations include the following:

  — Add `role="img"` to the **svg** element, but only if you want it to be treated as a single, non-interactive image. The child elements will not be accessible separately.

  — Add `aria-labelledby="title desc"` to the **svg** element to improve support for `title` and `desc`.

  — If parts of the SVG should be accessible (text, links, interactive elements, etc.), do not set a role on **svg**, but add `role="presentation"` to shapes (such as `circle`) and paths to prevent screen readers from announcing the occurrence of every shape in the graphic.

SVG TOOLS

Technically, all you need to create SVG graphics is a text editor (and genius visualization skills plus heroic patience!), but you'll be much happier having a graphics program do the heavy lifting for you. It is also common for designers to create the complex illustrations in a graphics program, and then bring them into a text editor to clean up the code and add scripts and styles manually. It's a matter of preference based on your skills and interests.

Vector Illustration Tools

The most appropriate tool for creating SVGs is a vector drawing tool such as Adobe Illustrator, although even image editors like Photoshop and GIMP use shapes that can be exported as SVG. These days, there are many vector software options, ranging from pricey to free, and full-featured to bare-bones.

Adobe Illustrator

Illustrator is the granddaddy of vector illustration tools and is available today as part of Adobe's Creative Suite for a monthly fee. Illustrator is a vector tool, but it uses PostScript natively and needs to translate those vectors to SVG. Although it is possible to "Save" a drawing in SVG format, the better option is to "Export As" because the resulting SVG will be web-optimized. If you use Illustrator, it is worth doing a search for how to create optimized SVGs in Illustrator because people have published all sorts of tips that will help your design and production process.

Inkscape

Inkscape (*inkscape.org*) is an open source image editor made specifically for SVG (SVG is its native format). It is available for Windows, Mac (see **Note**), and Linux. Inkscape's interface has evolved quite a bit over the last few years (FIGURE 25-13), but if you are accustomed to Adobe tools, it may take a little getting used to. You definitely can't beat the price (free)!

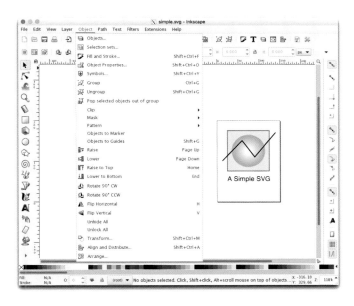

FIGURE 25-13. Inkscape was created for SVGs, so its interface features are SVG-centric, including menu items for Fill and Stroke, Symbols, Clip, and Mask.

SVG-specific tools

There are a number of nifty little SVG-specific drawing tools available for little or no investment. Because they are designed just for SVG, they have a manageable number of tools and settings that map to SVG capabilities (no wading through hundreds of tools you don't need). Some of them allow you to view and edit the underlying SVG code as well. Here are a couple of SVG editors of note:

Boxy (*boxy-svg.com*)

Boxy is a full-featured graphics program available for Mac, Windows, and Linux for a modest US$10 (as of this writing). It has an easy-to-use interface as well as a code inspector (FIGURE 25-14).

SVG-Edit (*github.com/SVG-Edit/svgedit*)

SVG-Edit works right in the browser (*svg-edit.github.io/svgedit/releases/svg-edit-2.8.1/svg-editor.html*) or as a downloaded program. It provides all the basic drawing tools, layers, and the ability to view and edit the SVG source (FIGURE 25-14). You can also export to PNG, JPEG, BMP, and WebP. And it's free, so there's no reason not to give it a try.

Boxy   SVG-Edit

FIGURE 25-14. SVG-creation tools Boxy and SVG-Edit.

Interface design tools

A whole slew of tools have recently emerged for designing web page and app interfaces, such as Sketch, AdobeXD, and Affinity Designer. All of them are vector-based and make it easy to export components in SVG format. As with many visual design tools that export code, the results are not always as well constructed as you might like, particularly if you intend to use the SVG programmatically with JavaScript, CSS, and animation.

Code Editors

If writing SVG by hand is your thing, or if you need to tinker with preexisting SVGs, you should look to see if your code editor of choice has an SVG preview extension that renders your code as you write. SVG previews are available for these editors:

• Atom Editor (free from GitHub): Get the SVG Preview package at *atom.io/packages/svg-preview*.

• Brackets (free from Adobe): Get the SVG extension by Peter Flynn at *github.com/peterflynn/svg-preview*.

SVG PRODUCTION TIPS

When you create an SVG drawing in a graphical tool, keep in mind that the end result is a text file. As with any file that is being delivered on a web page, you want that file to be as small as possible. If you have plans to style the SVG with CSS or manipulate it with JavaScript, you want the markup to be structured as well as possible.

The downside to using graphical tools is that you don't have much control over the code they output. Most of them export SVG code that is inefficient, redundant, and full of proprietary cruft. There are measures you can take while designing and after you export the SVG to ensure it is as lean and mean as possible. Many a blog post has been written about SVG optimization, but the following tips, although not comprehensive, should point you in the right direction. In the end, you will need to get familiar with your chosen tool's quirks to anticipate and correct its shortcomings.

Pre-Export Best Practices

Decisions you make in the design space can improve your SVG output in terms of organization and file size. Again, keeping in mind that the final product is a text file is useful for optimization. Here are some production tips that will help you create SVGs with the best quality at smallest file sizes:

Define the artboard or drawing size in pixels

> The artboard dimensions correspond to the viewport (**width** and **height** attributes) of the **svg** element.

Use layers to group elements logically

> If you plan on animating or scripting your SVG, keeping your design document well organized as you work will help with accessing the pieces you need later. In Illustrator and most other tools, layers are converted to group (**g**) elements, and nested layers are stored as nested groups.

Give elements and layers meaningful names

> The names you give elements and layers are used as **class** and **id** values in the SVG code, so make sure they are descriptive. Names should be all lowercase and with no character spaces so they are appropriate as attribute values.

Simplify paths

> The more points and handles used to define a path, the more coordinates appear in the SVG source. More coordinates means more characters and a larger file size. Take advantage of any "simplify path" function your tool offers. Also consider using methods that reduce the number of elements in the file, such as merging objects that always appear as one unit and using one wide stroke instead of two strokes and a fill. If possible, ensure your tool uses shape elements like **circle** and **rect** instead of multipoint

paths for simple shapes. If your tool does not provide a way to do this, it is possible to replace the path code with the simple shape element manually.

Be aware of decimal places

Keeping in mind that more characters results in a larger file size, you can shave bytes off your file by limiting the number of characters after the decimal points in your designs. For example, an x, y coordinate "100.3004598, 248.9998765" requires more data than simply "100.3, 249". Many tools allow you to limit the number of decimal places on export. You may also choose to "snap to pixels" when you set up the document so that points always fall on even integers. The general rule of thumb is that the smaller the image, the more decimal places are required to accurately define the points in objects. Large images can tolerate lower accuracy without compromising quality. You may need to experiment to find the right balance of decimal places and quality for the type of image.

Avoid raster effects inside the SVG

SVG's efficiency lies in the fact that it is vector-based. When you introduce raster (bitmapped) image material to the SVG, that file size advantage is lost. In some cases, you may be adding a raster image deliberately for manipulation in the SVG, which is fine. But be aware that certain effects in drawing programs—such as blurs, drop shadows, glows, and so on— often generate a raster image area when you may not be expecting it, adding greatly to the file size. Some filter effects, such as drop shadows, can be done in code after export more efficiently. If you find that your *.svg* file is unusually large, unexpected raster image material is a likely suspect.

Pay attention to fonts

Like any font style suggestion on the web, there is no guarantee that your chosen font will be available on the user's machine, so the font you use in your SVG may not display. Be sure to test and provide fallbacks. If there is a small amount of text, and it doesn't need to be searchable or read aloud by an assistive device, consider whether converting the text to paths is a better option.

Use centered strokes

Although not related to file size, you will achieve better results if you design with strokes set to be centered over the path because that is how SVG handles strokes natively. Some tools, like Sketch, make adjustments to compensate for an outside or inside stroke, but just centering your strokes is a better starting point.

Of course, there are many tool-specific tips that I am not able to cover here. Adobe offers tips for optimizing SVGs in Illustrator on its "About SVG" page (*helpx.adobe.com/illustrator/using/svg.html*). If you use Sketch, you may want to invest in Peter Nowell's "SVG Workflows in Sketch" video course at *Sketchmaster.com*.

Post-Export Optimization

Even with careful planning up front, exported SVGs have a lot of redundant code, unnecessary metadata, hidden elements, and other fluff that can be safely removed without affecting the way the SVG renders. It is a good idea to run your SVGs through an optimizer to strip all that out and slim down the file size.

SVGO

The best SVG optimizer in town as of this writing is SVGO (*github.com/svg/svgo*). It uses plug-ins that affect individual tweaks—such as removing empty attributes, removing the **xmlns** attribute (just fine if the SVG is used inline), removing comments, and dozens more—so you can pick and choose how you want to squeeze down the file depending on its end use.

The best thing about SVGO is that there are so many ways to use it! It is Node.js-based, so you can use it as a Node.js module or incorporate it in a Grunt or Gulp task. There are SVGO plug-ins for Illustrator (SVGNow), Inkscape (SVGO-Inkscape), and Sketch (SVGO Compressor). It's also available as a macOS folder action, whereby optimization is performed when you drag files into it. The full list of options is listed on the SVGO site.

The easiest way to see SVGO in action is to use the web-based SVGOMG tool, created by Jake Archibald, which provides a graphical user interface (GUI) for SVGO (*jakearchibald.github.io/svgomg/*). SVGOMG lets you toggle the various optimization plug-ins individually and view the results in the live preview (FIGURE 25-15), which is a handy feature during development.

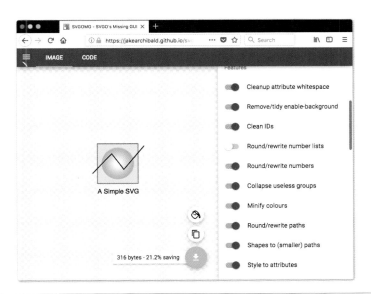

FIGURE 25-15. SVGOMG provides a GUI for the SVGO optimizing tool (*jakearchibald.github.io/svgomg*). You can toggle optimization methods to see the resulting image quality and file size.

File compression

Because they are text files, SVGs can be compressed with tools such as Gzip or Brotli.

Gzip is a utility on the server that compresses text files with fancy algorithms. Gzipped SVGs may result in files that are a mere 16–25% of their original size. A gzipped SVG file uses the suffix *.svgz*. In order to use Gzip for SVG, you must configure it on the server, which is beyond the scope of this chapter, but you can find plenty of tutorials online. The file savings are well worth the effort.

Brotli is an open source compression algorithm released by Google in 2015 that is giving Gzip a run for its money in terms of compression and performance. Like Gzip, Brotli must be configured on the server. Browsers began supporting Brotli content encoding in 2017. There is a nice explanation of Brotli on the MaxCDN site at *www.maxcdn.com/one/visual-glossary/brotli/*. The official Brotli GitHub page is at *github.com/google/brotli*.

RESPONSIVE SVGS

I've talked a lot about how the scalable nature of SVGs makes them great for use in responsive layouts, where they can scale to fit changing element widths with no loss of quality. Although that is absolutely true, the reality is that there are a few hoops to jump through to ensure SVGs scale predictably across all browsers.

In Responsive Web Design, we often want graphics to stretch or shrink to fit the width of a text container. With bitmap images, this is easy. Just set the width of the **img** to **100%**, and its height is set to **auto** by default. The browser automatically calculates the auto height based on the width you specify and determines the aspect ratio (the ratio of its width to height) of the image based on its dimensions in pixels. That allows the image to scale proportionally, without being stretched or distorted.

With SVG, it's a little more complicated. First, you have to give your graphic an explicit aspect ratio. SVGs can be drawn at any size, and do not have intrinsic aspect ratios by default. Second (in some cases), you have to work around browser bugs involving automatic height calculations.

The Viewport and Viewbox

NOTE

When the SVG is embedded with **img**, **object**, *or* **iframe**, *the* **width** *and* **height** *attributes on those elements set up the viewport size.*

To understand how SVGs scale, you need to have a good grasp of the SVG viewport and its viewbox. The viewport, defined by the **width** and **height** attributes on the **svg** element (see **Note**), is like a window through which you can see the drawing area. You can think of the viewport as a little browser window (which we've also been referring to as the "viewport" throughout this book) or an **iframe** element displaying an HTML document. Just as there is no guarantee that the *entire* HTML document will fit inside the browser window or iframe, there is no guarantee that the entire SVG drawing will fit perfectly within its viewport. It might be smaller; it might be bigger and get cropped off. The dimensions of the drawing space (also called user space) and the viewport dimensions are independent of one another.

Earlier in this chapter, we saw that the viewport uses a set of coordinates (the viewport coordinate system) that start at 0 in the top-left corner and increase to the right and downward. The drawing space has its own set of coordinates, the user coordinate system, which is established with the **viewBox** attribute in the **svg** element and works the same way. This **viewBox** attribute is the key to making responsive scaling possible while preserving the aspect ratio of the drawing.

The syntax for the **viewBox** attribute is as follows:

```
viewBox="x y width height"
```

The x and y values determine the position of the top-left corner of the view-box within the viewport. The **width** and **height** attributes give it dimensions and establish its aspect ratio. Values may be separated by space characters, as shown, or by commas. The x and y coordinates may have negative values, but width and height must always be positive integers.

The SVG in this example has both its viewport (**width** and **height**) and its viewbox (**viewBox**) set to 400×500 pixels:

```
<svg width="400" height="500" viewBox="0 0 400 500">
  <!-- drawing content here -->
</svg>
```

The viewbox matches the viewport in this example (this is the default behavior if **viewBox** is omitted), but let's see what happens when we change the viewbox dimensions. Keeping the viewport the same size, we can reduce the size of the viewbox by half (**viewBox="0 0 200 250"**). The result is the drawing scales up in the viewport by twice its size (FIGURE 25-16). The two coordinate systems (user and viewport), which are the same by default, now have different scales: one user unit is now equal to two viewport units. The point of this example is merely to demonstrate that the dimensions and coordinate systems of the viewport and the viewbox work independently of one another and can be used to adjust scale.

I could fill half a chapter describing the full capabilities and effects of the **viewBox** attribute. I want you to know everything about it, but for the sake of space, I will refer you to this wonderful tutorial by Sara Soueidan: "Understanding SVG Coordinate Systems and Transformations (Part 1)— The viewport, viewBox, and preserveAspectRatio" (*www.sarasoueidan.com/ blog/svg-coordinate-systems/*). You will also find thorough explanations in the SVG books recommended at the end of the chapter.

> The viewBox attribute is the key to making responsive scaling possible while preserving the aspect ratio of the drawing.

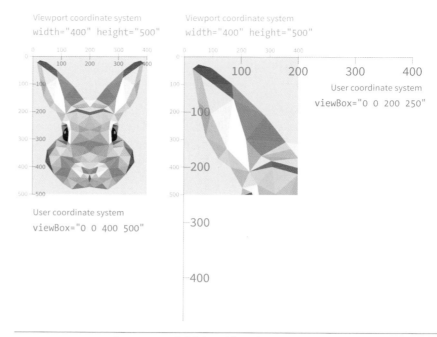

FIGURE 25-16. The viewport (**width** and **height**) and the viewbox (**viewBox**).

For the purposes of this responsive SVG discussion, however, just keep in mind that the **viewBox** attribute is the key to establishing the width and height and the resulting user coordinate system of the SVG drawing itself, independent of the viewport "window" it will be displayed in.

The preserveAspectRatio Attribute

The **preserveAspectRatio** attribute in the **svg** element is responsible for making sure the drawing maintains its aspect ratio, so it is important to our goal of creating a proportional responsive SVG. Conveniently, it is turned on by default, which means you don't need to include it if that is your desired effect. Setting it to **none** means you can stretch and squish the drawing however you like, just as you can a bitmapped image.

The **preserveAspectRatio** attribute also takes keyword values for how the viewbox should be aligned in its viewport. They work a lot like percentage values for the **background-image-position** CSS property.

```
<svg viewBox="0 0 300 200"  preserveAspectRatio="xMaxYMax meet">
```

In this example, **xMaxYMax** places the viewbox all the way to the right and against the bottom axis of the viewport ("Max" is equivalent to 100%). The **meet** keyword says to size it until it meets either the height or the width of the viewport (similar to **contain** for background images). The alternative is **slice**, which sizes the drawing so that it covers the entire viewport, even if some of the drawing is cut off (like **cover** for background images).

Again, I recommend you get to know the capabilities of `preserveAspectRatio` on your own, but for now, know that it is the attribute that does the work of keeping the aspect ratio intact, even if we take advantage of the default setting and don't include it explicitly.

Now that you have some familiarity with the SVG scaling mechanisms at work behind the scenes, let's look at the techniques for making SVGs in web pages scale proportionally within a changing container size.

Responsive SVGs Embedded with img and object

If you embed your SVG in the source document with the `img` or `object` elements, the process for making it scale automatically is pretty straightforward.

First, in the SVG file itself, make sure the `svg` element includes the `viewBox` attribute to establish the dimensions of the drawing. By default, the aspect ratio will be preserved even if you don't include the `preserveAspectRatio` attribute. If you want the graphic to completely fill the width of its container, omit the `width` and `height` attributes for the `svg` element because they default to 100%, which is the behavior we are after (see **Note**).

Now let's look at the `img` or `object` element that embeds it. The width and height applied to the embedding element determines the size at which the SVG appears in the layout. Because `width` and `height` properties are `auto` by default, if you omit them, the dimensions of the SVG (100%) will be used. If you specify just `width` or just `height`, the browser uses the aspect ratio of the viewbox to calculate the unspecified dimension.

Relying on the default sizing of the `img` or `object` elements works in current browsers, but you'll get better results in older browsers (particularly Internet Explorer; see **Warning**) if you explicitly set the `width` and `height` of the embedding element. For example:

```
img {
  width: 100%;
  height: auto;
}
```

This approach leaves nothing to chance. The result is an SVG file with its default width and height of 100% filling an `img` element set to fill the width of its container proportionally.

In the following example, I embedded an SVG with an `img` element in a `div` that is always set to 50% of the browser window width, as might occur in a responsive layout (FIGURE 25-17). Note that there are no `width` and `height` attributes in the SVG source, and the `viewBox` defines the aspect ratio. As the window gets larger and smaller, the SVG scales with it, maintaining that crisp, vector quality at all scales. An outline on the `div` reveals its boundaries, and I've set its side margins to `auto` to keep it centered in the browser window:

THE SVG MARKUP *(flowers.svg)*

```
<?xml version="1.0" encoding="utf-8"?>
<svg version="1.1" viewBox="0 0 160 120">
  <!-- flower drawing -->
</svg>
```

THE HTML MARKUP

```
<div class="container">
  <img src="flowers.svg" alt="flowers">
</div>
```

THE STYLES

```
.container {
  width: 50%;
  outline: 1px solid gray;
  margin: 2em auto;
}

/* IE fix */
img {
  width: 100%;
  height: auto;
}
```

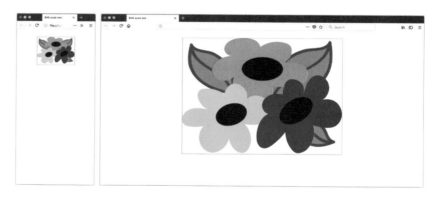

FIGURE 25-17. The SVG scales automatically and proportionally with the size of its container.

Responsive Inline SVGs

I'll just let you know up front that preserving the aspect ratio of inline SVGs placed in the source with the **svg** element is not as simple as the previous example. You need to employ an interesting hack to get many browsers to comply. I will explain the technique here as efficiently as possible.

First, as with embedded media, include the **viewBox** attribute and omit the **width** and **height** attributes on the **svg** element if you want the width to be 100% of the container (taking advantage of their default values).

In the absence of a style rule specifically overriding the **svg** defaults, the width will be 100%, and its aspect ratio will be preserved. Current browser versions support this as expected—scaling the SVG in its container proportionally. However, older browsers (including all versions of Internet Explorer) do not, so we need to employ the "padding hack" to maintain the proportions of the inline SVG.

The padding hack is a little tricky, but the steps are as follows (FIGURE 24-18):

1. Put the **svg** in a container **div**.

2. Set the **height** of that **div** to 0 or 1 pixel.

3. Apply an amount of padding to the top of the **div** that gives it the same aspect ratio as the SVG (there is a bit of math involved here).

4. Once the **div** is expanded to the proper proportions with padding, absolutely position the **svg** element in the top-left corner of the container **div**.

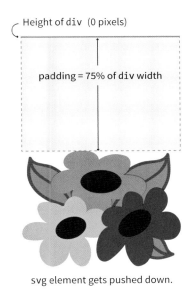

Height of div (0 pixels)

padding = 75% of div width

svg element gets pushed down.

svg is absolutely positioned in top-left corner of div.

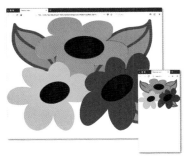

The container is set to 100% width, and the svg scales with it.

FIGURE 25-18. How the padding hack works to make inline SVGs maintain their aspect ratio on all browsers that support SVG.

It's a little convoluted (they don't call it a "hack" for nothing!), but it works. The foundation of this hack is the defined behavior of padding. Padding, when specified in percentage values, is always based on the *width* of the element (even top and bottom values). That means that as the width of the container **div** changes, so too does the amount of padding, always maintaining the same relationship. That sets up a constant aspect ratio for the SVG to fill.

Here's an example that shows how the padding hack works:

THE MARKUP

```
<div class="container">
  <svg version="1.1" viewBox="0 0 160 120">
    /* drawing contents */
  </svg>
</div>
```

THE STYLES

```
.container {
  width: 100%;
  height: 0;
  padding-top: 75%; /* (120/160)*100% */
  position: relative;
}
svg {
  position: absolute;
  top: 0;
  left: 0;
  width: 100%;
  height: 100%;
}
```

In the markup, you see the **svg** element in its **#container div** and its viewbox dimensions set to 160 × 120 pixels. The width of the container is set to 100% (it could also be set to a different percentage) with a 0 height. The **padding-top** declaration expands the **div** to the proper aspect ratio, which is calculated by dividing the height of the SVG by its width, and multiplying the result by the percentage width of the **div**:

*(svg-height / svg-width) * div-width%*

In our example, the padding is set to 75% [(120 / 160) × 100% = 75%], which matches the 4:3 aspect ratio of the SVG. Notice also that the container is relatively positioned to create the positioning context for the **svg** child element (do you remember turning elements into positioning contexts with **position: relative** from **Chapter 15, Floating and Positioning**?)

Additional Resources

This section cut to the chase and provided just what you need to know to make SVGs scale in responsive layouts. Of course, there is a lot more to the story, so I recommend these articles for additional background information and techniques:

- "How to Scale SVG" by Amelia Bellamy-Royds for CSS-Tricks (*css-tricks.com/scale-svg/*)

- "Making SVGs Responsive with CSS" by Sara Soueidan for Codrops (*tympanus.net/codrops/2014/08/19/making-svgs-responsive-with-css/*)

To provide an even more customized SVG experience in your user interface, go beyond simple scaling and change the design of the icon with an adaptive SVG (see the sidebar **"Adaptive Icons"**).

Adaptive Icons

The problem with simply scaling SVGs (or any image, really) smaller is that details may get lost at small sizes. One approach to solving that problem is to provide simplified versions of icons or logos when the image is very small. Adaptive (or responsive) icons use media queries to test the viewport size and some clever styling in the SVG to deliver the appropriate amount of detail at various sizes. FIGURE 25-19 shows a set of icons created by Joe Harrison, with an explanation at *responsiveicons.co.uk*.

There are several methods for achieving the effect. Joe's house icon was done with an SVG sprite. You could also reveal and hide groups of drawing elements in the SVG based on viewport size. These articles provide some how-tos:

- "Making SVGs Responsive with CSS" by Sara Soueidan includes a section at the end on making adaptive SVGs with media queries (*tympanus.net/codrops/2014/08/19/making-svgs-responsive-with-css/*).

- "Rethinking Responsive SVG" by Ilya Pukhalski outlines several adaptive SVG approaches (*www.smashingmagazine.com/2014/03/rethinking-responsive-svg/*).

FIGURE 25-19. An example of adaptive icons by Joe Harrison.

FURTHER SVG EXPLORATION

Obviously, I could only scratch the surface of Scalable Vector Graphics in this chapter. When you are ready to use SVG on your site, you'll have more brushing up to do. There are many volumes and online tutorials written about SVG, but these are the resources that helped me the most in my own exploration. I recommend them heartily.

- *SVG Essentials, 2nd Edition* by J. David Eisenberg and Amelia Bellamy-Royds (O'Reilly)

- *Using SVG with CSS3 and HTML5* by Amelia Bellamy-Royds, Kurt Cagle, and Dudley Storey (O'Reilly)

- *Practical SVG* by Chris Coyier (A Book Apart)

- Developer and SVG expert Sara Soueidan has written many useful SVG articles on her blog at *www.sarasoueidan.com*.

TEST YOURSELF

I just threw a lot of SVG info at you. Try taking this quiz to see what stuck. The answers appear in **Appendix A**.

The first four questions refer to this SVG element:

```
<rect x="0" y="0" width="600" height="400" />
```

1. What is **rect**?

2. What do **x** and **y** do?

3. What do `width` and `height` do?

4. Explain the **/** character.

Now back to our regularly scheduled questions:

5. What is the primary difference between SVG clipping and masking?

6. Name three ways to reduce the file size of an SVG.

7. What is the most widely supported version of SVG?

    a. SVGTiny

    b. SVG 1.1

    c. SVG 2

    d. SVG, Electric Boogaloo

8. Name three of the five ways you can style elements in an SVG.

9. Which of the following can be used to animate elements in an SVG?

    a. Special SVG elements for animation

    b. JavaScript

    c. CSS transitions and keyframe animation

    d. All of the above

AND...WE'RE DONE!

Hey! Here we are at the end of the book! I hope that you've enjoyed this detailed tour through HTML, CSS, JavaScript, and image production. I know the content here is pretty dense, but remember that you don't have to learn it all at once, and you don't need to keep it all in your head. Heck, I *wrote* this book, and I still go back to it to look up attributes, properties, and values. With practice, however, a lot of it will become second-nature to you.

I hope that you will find plenty of opportunities to put your new knowledge to use. Best of luck in your web endeavors!

VI
APPENDICES

ANSWERS

Chapter 1: Getting Started in Web Design

1. b, d, a, c

2. The W3C guides the development of web-related technologies.

3. c, d, a, b

4. Frontend development is concerned with aspects of the site that appear in or are related to the browser. Backend development involves the applications and databases required on the server for site functionality.

5. An FTP tool is used to transfer files between computers over the internet, such as between your local machine and the server. You may use an FTP tool provided by your hosting company, built into a code editor, or as a standalone application.

Chapter 2: How the Web Works

1. c; 2. j; 3. h; 4. g; 5. f; 6. i; 7. b; 8. a; 9. d; 10. e

Chapter 3: Some Big Concepts You Need to Know

1. There are a number of unknown factors when you're developing a site. Some that were addressed in this chapter include:

    — The size of the screen or browser window

    — The user's internet connection speed

    — Whether JavaScript is enabled

    — Whether the browser supports specific features

    — Whether the user is at a desk or on the go (context and attention span)

2. 1. c; 2. d; 3. e; 4. a; 5. b

3. The four general disability categories include:

   — Sight impairment: make sure the content is semantic and in logical order for when it is read by a screen reader.

   — Hearing impairment: provide transcripts for audio and video content.

   — Mobility impairment: use measures that help users without a mouse or keyboard.

   — Cognitive impairment: content should be simple and clearly organized.

4. You would use a waterfall chart to evaluate your site's performance in the optimization process.

Chapter 4: Creating a Simple Page

1. A tag is part of the markup (brackets and element name) used to delimit an element. An element consists of the content and its tags.

2. The recommended markup for a minimal HTML5 document is as follows:

```
<!DOCTYPE html>
<html>
  <head>
    <meta charset="utf8">
    <title>Title</title>
  </head>
  <body>
  </body>
</html>
```

3. a. *Sunflower.html*—Yes.

   b. *index.doc*—No, it must end in *.html* or *.htm*.

   c. *cooking home page.html*—No, there may be no character spaces.

   d. *Song_Lyrics.html*—Yes.

   e. *games/rubix.html*—No, there may be no slashes in the name.

   f. *%whatever.html*—No, there may be no percent symbols.

4. a. It is missing the **src** attribute: `<img src="birthday.jpg">`

   b. The slash in the end tag is missing: `<em>Congratulations!</em>`

   c. There should be no attribute in the end tag:
      `<a href="file.html">linked text</a>`

   d. The slash should be a forward slash:
      `<p>This is a new paragraph</p>`

5. Make it a comment:
   `<!-- product list begins here -->`

Chapter 5: Marking Up Text

1. Here is the markup for a thematic break between these paragraphs:

```
<p>People who know me know that I love to cook.</p>
<hr>
<p>I've created this site to share some of my favorite recipes.</p>
```

2. A **blockquote** is a block-level element used for long quotations or quoted material that may consist of other block elements. The **q** (quote) element is for short quotations that go in the flow of text and do not cause line breaks.

3. The **pre** element.

4. The **ul** element is an unordered list element. It is used for lists that don't need to appear in a particular sequence. They display with bullets by default. The **ol** element is an ordered list in which sequence matters. The browser automatically inserts numbers for ordered lists.

5. Use a style sheet to remove bullets from an unordered list.

6. `<abbr title="World Wide Web Consortium">W3C</abbr>`

7. **dl** is the element used to identify an entire description list. The **dt** element is used to identify just one term within that list.

8. The **id** attribute is used to identify a unique element in a document, and the name in its value may appear only once in a document. **class** is used to classify multiple elements into conceptual groups.

9. An **article** element is intended for a self-contained body of content that would be appropriate for syndication or might appear in a different context. A **section** element divides content into thematically related chunks.

Chapter 6: Adding Links

Exercise 6-7

1. `<p><a href="tapenade.html">Go to the tapenade recipe</a></p>`

2. `<p><a href="../salmon.html">Try this with Garlic Salmon.</a></p>`

3. `<p><a href="pasta/linguine.html">Try the Linguine with Clam Sauce</a></p>`

4. `<p><a href="../../about.html">About Jen's Kitchen</a></p>`

5. `<p><a href="http://www.allrecipes.com">Go to Allrecipes.com</a></p>`

Test Yourself

1. `<a href="tutorial.html">...</a>`

2. `<a href="examples/instructions.html">...</a>`

3. `<a href="examples/people/family.html">...</a>`

4. `<a href="/examples/things/boot.html">...</a>`

5. `<a href="../index.html">...</a>`

6. `<a href="http://www.learningwebdesign.com">...</a>`

7. `<a href="../instructions.html">...</a>`

8. `<a href="../../index.html">...</a>`

9. `<img src="images/arrow.gif" alt="" />`

10. `<img src="../images/arrow.gif" alt="" />`

11. `<img src="../../images/bullet.gif" alt="" />`

Chapter 7: Adding Images

1. The **src** and **alt** attributes are required for the document to be valid. If the **src** attribute is omitted, the browser won't know which image to use. You may leave the value of the **alt** attribute empty if alternative text would be meaningless or clumsy when read in context.

2. `<img src="furry.jpg" alt="">`

3. a) Because HTML documents are not valid if the **alt** attribute is omitted, and b) **alt** improves accessibility by providing a description of the image if it is not available or not viewable.

4. The three likely causes for a missing image are a) the URL is incorrect, so the browser is looking in the wrong place or for the wrong filename (names are case-sensitive); b) the image file is not in an acceptable format; and c) the image file is not named with the proper suffix (*.gif*, *.jpg*, or *.png*, as appropriate).

5. x-descriptors specify the screen resolution used for targeting high-resolution monitors. The w-descriptor provides the actual size of the image file that the browser uses to make the best selection based on viewport width.

6. A device pixel is the square of colored light that makes up the screen display. CSS pixels (also called "reference pixels") make up the grid that devices use to lay out what appears on the screen. The CSS pixel may be made up of multiple device pixels.

7. b, c, d, a, d, b

8. The **picture** element provides a set of images for the browser to choose from. When the viewport is 480 pixels or wider, the image will appear at

80% of the viewport width. For smaller viewport sizes, it fills 100% of the viewport. There is a set of images in WebP format for browsers that support them; otherwise, the browser will choose from the set of JPEGs.

9. Disk cache is where browsers temporarily store files downloaded over the network so they can be reused. Taking advantage of cached resources eliminates the need for repeated server requests for the same file and can increase performance.

10. Advantages include simple and familiar markup, excellent browser support, image caching, and available fallbacks. Disadvantages include the inability to manipulate the parts of the SVG with style sheets or JavaScript.

11. Advantages of inline SVGs include the ability to take advantage of all of SVG's features (animation, scripting, and applying CSS style rules), good browser support, and fewer server requests. Disadvantages include potentially unwieldy amounts of code in the HTML document, more complicated image maintenance, and lack of caching.

12. When it is purely presentational and not part of the editorial content of the page.

13. `image/svg+xml` is the MIME type of an SVG file. You may need to include it as the value of the `type` attribute in the `picture` element or use it to configure your server to recognize SVG files as images.

14. `http://www.w3.org/2000/svg` is the pointer to the SVG namespace as standardized by the W3C. It appears as the value of the `xmlns` (XML namespace) attribute in **svg** elements.

Chapter 8: Table Markup

1. The table itself (**table**), rows (**tr**), header cells (**th**), data cells (**td**), and an optional caption (**caption**).

2. The **table** element can directly contain **tr**, **caption**, **colgroup**, **thead**, **tbody**, and **tfoot** elements.

3. The **tr** element can contain only some number of **th** and **td** elements.

4. Use the **col** element if you want to include additional information about the structure of a table, to specify widths to speed up display, or to add certain style properties to a column of cells.

5. a) The **caption** should be the first element inside the **table** element;

   b) There may not be text directly in the **table** element; it must go in a **th** or **td**;

   c) The **th** elements must go inside the **tr** element;

   d) The second **tr** element is missing a closing tag;

   e) There is no **colspan** element; it should be a **td** with a **colspan** attribute.

Chapter 9: Forms

1. a. POST (because of security issues)

    b. POST (because it uses the file selection input type)

    c. GET (because you may want to bookmark search results)

    d. POST (because it is likely to have a lengthy text entry)

2. a. Drop-down menu: `<select>`

    b. Radio buttons: `<input type="radio">`

    c. `<textarea>`

    d. Eight checkboxes: `<input type="checkbox">`

    e. Scrolling menu: `<select multiple="multiple">`

3. a. The **type** attribute is missing.

    b. **checkbox** is not an element name; it is a value of the **type** attribute in the **input** element.

    c. The **option** element is not empty. It should contain the value for each option (for example, `<option>Orange</option>`).

    d. The required **name** attribute is missing.

    e. The width and height of a text area are specified with the **cols** and **rows** attributes, respectively.

Chapter 10: Embedded Media

1. A nested browsing context works like a browser window inside another browser window. You can create one with an **iframe** element or an **object** element (bonus points if you got both).

2. The **sandbox** attribute allows developers to set limitations on what nested content can do, and is important for security reasons.

3. To specify it with the required type attribute in a **source** element and to configure the server to recognize the media type.

4. a. container, b. video codec, c. video codec, d. audio codec, e. container, f. video codec, g. audio codec, h. container

5. The **poster** attribute specifies an image that appears in the video player until the video is played.

6. A *.vtt* file is a text file in the WebVTT format that contains subtitles, captions, descriptions, chapter titles, or metadata that are synchronized to a video or audio file.

7. SVG is a vector format, and canvas is pixel-based (raster). SVGs can scale without loss of quality, but canvas is resolution-dependent and does not scale well. You can style the elements in an SVG with CSS and affect them with JavaScript, but canvas can be manipulated with JavaScript only.

8. `strokeRect()` and `fill()`

Chapter 11: Introducing Cascading Style Sheets

1. selector: `blockquote`; property: `line-height`; value: `1.5`; declaration: `line-height: 1.5;`

2. The paragraph text will be gray because when there are conflicting rules of identical weight, the last one listed in the style sheet will be used.

3. a. Use one rule with multiple declarations applied to the **p** element.

   ```
   p {
     font-family: sans-serif;
     font-size: 1em;
     line-height: 1.2em;
   }
   ```

   b. The semicolons are missing.

   ```
   blockquote {
     font-size: 1em;
     line-height: 150%;
     color: gray;
   }
   ```

   c. There should not be curly brackets around every declaration, only around the entire declaration block.

   ```
   body {background-color: black;
     color: #666;
     margin-left: 12em;
     margin-right: 12em;
   }
   ```

   d. This could be handled with a single rule with a grouped element type selector.

   ```
   p, blockquote, li {
     color: white;
   }
   ```

   e. This inline style is missing the property name.

   ```
   <strong style="color: red">Act now!</strong>
   ```

4.

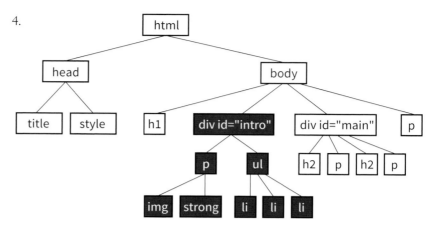

NOTE: color styles applied to the img element are displayed on the border only (if there is one).

FIGURE A-1. Answer to Chapter 11, question 4.

Chapter 12: Formatting Text

1. a. 4; b. 1; c. 7; d. 3; e. 2; f. 9; g. 8; h. 5; i. 6

2. a. `body {color: red;}`

   b. `h2 {color: red;}`

   c. `h1, p {color: red;}`

   d. `.special {color: red; }`

   e. `#intro {color: red;}`

   f. `#main strong {color: red;}`

   g. `h2 + p {color: red;}`

Chapter 13: Colors and Backgrounds

1. g. a, b, and c

2. d. rgb(FF, FF, FF)

3. a. 5; b. 1; c. 4; d. 6; e. 2; f. 3

4. a. 1; b. 3; c. 2; d. 6; e. 5; f. 4

Chapter 14: Thinking Inside the Box

Ⓐ `border: double black medium;`

Ⓑ `padding: 2em;`

Ⓒ `padding: 2em; border: 4px solid red;`

Ⓓ `border: 4px solid red; margin: 2em;`

Ⓔ `padding: 1em 1em 1em 6em; border: 4px dashed black; margin: 1em 6em;`

or

`padding: 1em; padding-left: 6em; border: 4px dashed; margin: 1em 6em;`

Ⓕ `padding: 1em 50px; border: 2px solid black; margin: 0 auto;`

Chapter 15: Floating and Positioning

1. b is not true. Floats are positioned against the content edge, not the padding edge.

2. c is incorrect. Floats do not use offset properties, so there is no reason to include **right**.

3. Clear the **footer** to make it start below a floated sidebar on either side: `footer {clear: both;}`

4. a) absolute; b) absolute, fixed; c) fixed; d) relative, absolute, fixed; e) static; f) relative; g) absolute, fixed h) relative, absolute, fixed; i) relative

Chapter 16: CSS Layout with Flexbox and Grid

1. Turn its parent element into a flex container by setting **display** to **flex**. The child element becomes a flex item automatically with no extra code.

2. a. 2; b. 4; c. 1; d. 3

3. The **align-items** property positions items relative to their flex line, while **align-content** distributes space around and within multiple lines. Both properties are applied to the container, and both are concerned with positioning along the cross axis.

4. a. 4; b. 1; c. 3; d. 2

5. a. 4; b. 3; c. 2; d. 5; e. 1

6. Style rules for displaying the items in the order shown in FIGURE 16-49.
   ```
   .box6 {order: -1;}
   .box1, .box2, .box3 {order: 1;}
   ```

7. The key difference between Grid Layout and Flexbox is that Grid creates layouts in two dimensions—rows and columns—but Flexbox arranges elements on one axis. (*Continued...*)

Similarities between Grid and Flexbox include:

— For both Grid and Flexbox, making an element a container automatically turns its direct children into items.

— They are both based on the language direction of the document.

— Both can create whole-page layouts (although Grid is better suited to the task).

— You can change the order of the items with the **order** property.

— They both use the Box Alignment Module for item and content alignment.

8. Grid template for the layout shown in FIGURE 16-50:

```
grid-template-rows: 12em min-content 100px;
grid-template-columns: 300px 2fr 1fr;
```

Using the **grid** shorthand property:

```
grid: 12em min-content 100px / 300px 2fr 1fr;
```

(Note: **auto** could be used instead of **min-content** in both examples.)

9. a. E; b. D; c. C; d. A; e. B

10. #gallery:
```
    column-gap: 1em;
}
```

11. d, a, c, b, e

Chapter 17: Responsive Web Design

1. A responsive site delivers the same HTML source at the same URL regardless of the device used. An m-dot site sends a document at a separate URL when it receives a request from a mobile device. Mobile-specific sites also tend to reduce the number of options and content on the first screen.

2. It sets the size of the viewport the mobile browser uses to render the page to the same size as the screen.

3. img { max-width: 100%; }

4. It sets the margin on the left and right side of the page to 10% if the viewport is 60em or wider.

5. If the layout is created with CSS Grid Layout, use **fr** and **minmax()** units to make columns and rows flexible while setting limits. If you have page elements in Flexbox, use the flex properties to let them grow and shrink as needed. Otherwise, use percentage values for page elements so they resize proportionally. Avoid fixed pixel measurements.

6. When you use ems for media queries, the page elements stay proportional to the size of the type. This can help keep line lengths consistent.

7. In an **@media** rule in a style sheet, in **@import** rules that call in external style sheets, and in the **link** element to an external style sheet.

8. Use a legible font, make the size slightly smaller, use a tighter line height, and use smaller margins.

9. You could use an accordion to hide and reveal the submenu options, or put the submenu on a separate landing page and link to it from the main navigation.

10. Test it on real devices, use an emulator, or use a third-party testing service.

Chapter 18: Transitions, Transforms, and Animation

1. Tweening is the process in animation in which frames are generated between two end point states.

2. A transition would have two keyframes, one for the beginning state and one for the end.

3. a. `transition-delay: 0.5s;`

   b. `transition-timing-function: linear;`

   c. `transition-duration: 0.5s;`

   d. `transition-property: line-height;`

4. c. **text-transform** is not an animatable property.

5. **ease** is the default timing function. It starts out slowly, speeds up quickly, and then slows down again at the very end.

6. .2s is the **transition-duration** value (how long the animation lasts).

7. Trick question! They will arrive at the same time, 300ms after the transition begins. The timing function has no effect on the total amount of time it takes.

8. a. `transform: rotate(7deg);`

   b. `transform: translate(-50px, -25px);`

   c. `transform-origin: right bottom;`

   d. `transform: scale(1.25);`

9. The 3 value indicates that the element should be resized three times larger than its original *height*.

10. **perspective: 250;** because lower number values indicate closer distance and are more dramatic.

11. The border is 3 pixels wide at 50% through the animation.

12. a. `animation-direction: reverse;`

    b. `animation-duration: 5s;`

    c. `animation-delay: 2s;`

    d. `animation-iteration-count: 3;`

    e. `animation-fill-mode: forwards;`

Chapter 19: More CSS Techniques

1. d. All of the above.

2. d. a and c

3. e. b and d

4. Use Flexbox or floats.

5. a. 2; b. 5; c. 1; d .4; e. 3

6. a. no; b. yes; c. no (if the `.border` class is required for styles to appear)

7. As of this writing, Modernizr has better browser support than CSS feature detection. Once all browsers support CSS feature detection, CSS will be faster and more reliable than a solution that requires JavaScript.

Chapter 20: Modern Web Development Tools

1. It is the program that interprets commands you type into a command-line tool.

2. d. All of the above.

3. A string of characters that indicates the computer is ready to receive a command.

4. You'd create a new directory (folder) in the current directory with the name "newsite".

5. Providing a more efficient syntax for *authoring* (traditionally known as "preprocessing") and *optimizing* (known as "postprocessing") standard CSS files.

6. Once you learn the syntax, Sass (or LESS and Stylus) can make writing styles less redundant and easier to edit. You may also be required to know Sass for some web development jobs.

7. Common CSS postprocessor tasks include error checking, adding vendor prefixes, inserting hacks that fix bugs in old versions of IE, including fallbacks for newer CSS features, converting rems to pixels, converting color formats to RGB, and analyzing the structure of your CSS code. This is by no means an exhaustive list, so you may come up with other features.

8. It is anything you might do manually from the command line.

9. It means that the task runner, Grunt, has been configured to "watch" the file so that when it detects any changes to that file, it automatically performs a series of tasks.

10. Each user has a local copy of the shared repository that they can work on even offline.

11. When a file is staged, it means that it has been added to the Git index, and Git is tracking it, but it has not yet been committed.

12. A *branch* is a sequential series of commits and reflects a thread of development. A *fork* is a copy of somebody else's repository that you can work on and that is not linked to the original.

13. Pulling refers to merging the recent copy of the remote master repo into your local version. You should pull in a fresh copy to be sure you have the most up-to-date version before you push your changes to the master. This helps prevent conflicts if other users have been making changes to the same files.

14. A pull request is when you ask the owner of a repo you forked to merge in your changes.

Chapter 21: Introduction to JavaScript

Exercise 21-1

1. `var friends = ["name", "othername", "thirdname", "lastname"];`

2. `alert( friends[2] );`

3. `var name = "yourName";`

4. `if( name === Jennifer ) { alert("That's my name too! ");}`

5.
```
var myVariable = #;|
if(myVariable > 5) {
  alert ("upper");
} else {
 alert ("lower");
}
```

Exercise 21-2

```
<script>
var originalTitle = document.title;
function showUnreadCount( unread ) {
  document.title = originalTitle + " (" + unread + "new
message!");
}
showUnreadCount(3);
</script>
```

Test Yourself

1. When you link to an external *.js* file, you can reuse the same scripts for multiple documents. The downside is that it requires an additional HTTP request.

2. a. 1; b. 1two; c. 34; d. 2

3. a. 10; b. 6; c. "2 remaining"; d. "Jennifer is longer."; e. false

4. It loops through a number of items by starting at the first one in the array and ending when there are no more left.

5. Globally scoped variables may "collide" with variables with the same names in other scripts. It is best to use the **var** keyword in functions to keep your variables scoped locally.

6. a. 2; b. 5; c. 4; d. 3; e. 1

Chapter 22: Using JavaScript

1. Ajax is a combination of HTML, CSS, and JavaScript (with the **XMLHttpRequest** JavaScript method used to get data in the background).

2. It accesses the element that has the **id** value "main".

3. It creates a nodeList of all the **section** elements in the element with the **id** of "main".

4. It sets the background color of the page (**body** element) to "papayawhip".

5. It creates a new text node that says, "Hey, I'm walking here!", inserts it in a newly created **p** element, and puts the new **p** element in the element with the **id** "main".

6. d. All of the above.

Chapter 23: Web Image Basics

1. You can get a license to have exclusive rights to an image so that your competitor doesn't use the same photo on their site. You also know the source of the image is verified (i.e., it's not stolen).

2. ppi stands for "pixels per inch" and is a measure of resolution.

3. Indexed color is a mode for storing pixel color information. GIF and PNG-8 formats are indexed color images.

4. There are 256 colors in an 8-bit graphic, and 32 colors in a 5-bit graphic.

5. GIF can contain animation and transparency. JPEG cannot.

6. GIF can contain animation. Regular PNGs cannot (although APNG format can).

7. PNGs can have multiple levels of transparency. GIF has only binary (on/off) transparency.

8. Cumulative lossy compression means you lose image data every time you save an image as a JPEG. If you open a JPEG and save it as a JPEG again, even more image information is thrown out than the first time you saved it. Be sure to keep your full-quality original and save JPEG copies as needed.

9. In binary transparency, a pixel is either entirely transparent or entirely opaque. Alpha transparency allows up to 256 levels of transparency.

10. **A** GIF or PNG-8 because it is text, flat colors, and hard edges. **B** JPEG because it is a photograph. **C** GIF or PNG-8 because although it has some photographic areas, most of the image is flat colors with hard edges. **D** GIF or PNG-8 because it is a flat graphical image. **E** JPEG because it is a photograph.

Chapter 24: Image Asset Production

1. PNG-24 or PNG-8+alpha are the best supported. The WebP and JPEG 2000 formats also include alpha transparency, but lack tool and browser support.

2. Adjusting the Quality setting is the most effective tool for optimizing a JPEG.

3. Reducing the number of colors in the color palette has the greatest effect on the size of indexed color images.

4. The pattern in the dithering breaks up solid areas of color and results in larger files. Dithering should be turned off or limited.

5. Because JPEG compression works well on smooth transitions of color and less well on hard edges, blurring the image slightly improves compression and results in a smaller file.

6. sRGB: Yes, because it is the RGB encoding used by the web.

7. If the image needs to look crisp on high-density screens.

8. If your site has a lot of images, companies like Cloudinary and Akamai generate and host multiple, optimized versions of every image automatically. They keep you from doing all the image creation manually.

Chapter 25: SVG

1. **rect** is the SVG element that creates a rectangle.

2. The **x** and **y** coordinates position the rectangle element in the top-left corner of the SVG viewport.

3. The **width** and **height** attributes establish the dimensions of the SVG viewport, the area on which the drawing will be rendered.

4. In XML, all elements must be closed. When the element is a standalone element (without an opening and closing tag), it is closed with a forward slash (/) character before the closing bracket.

5. Clipping uses a vector shape to reveal or hide portions of an image. Masking is pixel-based, using the lightness and darkness of a raster image to hide and reveal the masked image.

6. Ways to reduce the size of an SVG include:

   — Simplifing paths.

   — Reducing the number of decimal places.

   — Using shapes instead of complex paths when possible.

   — Avoiding raster images and effects in the SVG.

   — Running it through an optimizer like SVGO.

   — Enabling Gzip compression on the server.

7. b. SVG 1.1 (and for the record, SVG Electric Boogaloo isn't a thing).

8. You can style SVGs in the following ways:

   — SVG presentation attributes

   — The inline **style** attribute

   — A style sheet in the SVG itself (**style** element)

   — An external style sheet called into the SVG (for SVGs placed with the **img** element)

   — If the SVG is inline, the style sheet in the HTML document in which it appears

9. d. All of the above.

HTML5 GLOBAL ATTRIBUTES

The following attributes may be used with any HTML element.

Attribute	Values	Description
accesskey	*single text character*	Assigns an access key (shortcut key command) to the link. Access keys are also used for form fields. Users may access the element by pressing Alt-<key> (PC) or Ctrl-<key> (Mac). Example: **accesskey="B"**
class	*text string*	Assigns one or more classification names to the element. Multiple values are separated by spaces.
contenteditable	**true** | **false**	Indicates the user can edit the element. If the value is an empty string, it is the same as "true." By default, the element inherits the edit setting from its parent.
dir	**ltr** | **rtl** | **auto**	Specifies the inline text direction of the element ("left to right" or "right to left") and scopes bidirectional reordering, isolating the text from influencing surrounding content. When set to **auto**, it uses the first letter to determine direction.
draggable	**true** | **false**	A **true** value indicates the element is draggable in the UI (an event configured with JavaScript), meaning the user can move it by clicking and holding it, and then moving it to a new position in the window.
hidden	In HTML, list value only: **hidden** In XHTML, include attribute name: **hidden="hidden"**	Prevents the element and its descendants from being rendered in the user agent (browser). Any scripts or form controls in hidden sections will still execute but will not be presented to the user.
id	*text string* (may not contain spaces)	Assigns a unique identifying name to the element.
lang	*ISO language code* (see *www.loc.gov/standards/ iso639-2/php/code_list.php*)	Specifies the primary language for the content of an element and its attribute values. When **lang** is omitted, the language of the element is the same as the language of the parent element.

753

Attribute	Values	Description
spellcheck	**true** | **false**	Indicates whether the element is to have its spelling and grammar checked. When **spellcheck** is omitted, the element follows the default behavior for that element, possibly inheriting the parent's spellcheck state.
style	Semicolon-separated list of style rules (**property: value** pairs)	Associates style information with an element. For example: `<h1 style="color: red; border: 1px solid">Heading</h1>`
tabindex	*number*	Indicates that the element is focusable, and specifies its position in the tabbing order for the current document. The value must be between 0 and 32,767. It is used for tabbing through links on a page or fields in a form and is useful for assistive browsing devices. A value of −1 is allowable to remove elements from the tabbing flow and make them focusable only by JavaScript.
title	*text string*	Provides a title or advisory information about the element, typically displayed as a tooltip. If a title is not specified, an element inherits the title from its nearest ancestor element with a title.
translate	**yes** | **no**	Specifies whether an element's attribute values and the values of its **Text** node children are to be translated when the page is localized, or whether to leave them unchanged. If it is not specified, the element inherits the translate state from its parent.

CSS SELECTORS, LEVELS 3 AND 4

The following table lists the selectors in the Selectors Level 4 Editor's Draft (*drafts.csswg.org/selectors-4/*, December 2017).

Note that selectors marked "(Level 4)" are new and may not yet be implemented by browsers. Check *CanIUse.com* and be sure to test well if you use them. All other selectors are part of CSS3 and are generally well supported.

Selector	Type of selector	Description
Simple selectors and combinators		
*	Universal selector	Matches any element.
A	Type selector	Matches the name of an element.
A, B	Compound selector	Matches elements A and B.
A B	Descendant combinator	Matches element B only if it is a descendant of element A.
A>B	Child combinator	Matches any element B that is a child of element A.
A+B	Next-sibling combinator	Matches any element B that immediately follows any element A, where A and B share the same parent.
A~B	Subsequent-sibling combinator	Matches any element B that is preceded by A, where A and B share the same parent.
Class and ID selectors		
.classname A.classname	Class selector	Matches the value of the **class** attribute in all elements or in a specified element.
#idname A#idname	ID selector	Matches the value of the **id** attribute in an element.

Selector	Type of selector	Description
Attribute selectors		
`A[att]`	Simple attribute selector	Matches any element A that has the given attribute defined, whatever its value.
`A[att="val"]`	Exact attribute value selector	Matches any element A that has the specified attribute set to the specified value.
`A[att="val" i]` *(Level 4)*	Case-insensitive attribute value selector	Matches any element A that has the specified attribute set to the specified value, even if it does not match its capitalization (even in XML languages that may be case-sensitive). This example matches images named *Icon.png*, *ICON.png*, *icon.png*, and so on. `img[src="Icon.png" i] {border: 1px solid yellow;}`
`A[att~="val"]`	Partial attribute value selector	Matches any element A that has the specified value as one of the values in a list given to the specified attribute. `table[class~="example"] {background: yellow;}`
`A[att|="val"]`	Hyphenated prefix attribute selector	Matches any element A that has the specified attribute with a value that is equal to or begins with the provided value. It is most often used to select languages, as shown here. `a[lang|="en"] {background-image: url(en_icon.png);}`
`A[att^="val"]`	Beginning substring attribute selector	Matches any element A that has the specified attribute and its value begins with the provided string. `img[src^="/images/icons"] {border: 3px solid;}`
`A[att$="val"]`	Ending substring attribute selector	Matches any element A that has the specified attribute and its value ends with the provided string. `img[src$=".svg"] {border: 3px solid;}`
`A[att*="val"]`	Arbitrary substring attribute selector	Matches any element A that has the specified attribute and its value contains the provided string. `img[title*="July"] {border: 3px solid;}`
Pseudo-class selectors		
`:any-link` *(Level 4)*	Link pseudo-class selector	Specifies a style for a link regardless of whether it has been visited.
`:link`	Link pseudo-class selector	Specifies a style for links that have not yet been visited.
`:target`	Target pseudo-class selector	Selects an element that is used as a fragment identifier.
`:target-within` *(Level 4)*	Generalized target pseudo-class selector	Selects an element that is used as a fragment identifier or contains an element that does.
`:visited`	Link pseudo-class selector	Specifies a style for links that have already been visited.
`:active`	User action pseudo-class selector	Selects any element that has been activated by the user, such as a link as it is being clicked.
`:hover`	User-action pseudo-class selector	Specifies a style for elements (typically links) that appear when the mouse is placed over them.
`:focus`	User action pseudo-class selector	Selects any element that currently has the input focus, such as a selected form input.
`:focus-within` *(Level 4)*	Generalized input pseudo-class selector	Selects any element that has user-input focus or contains an element that has input focus.

Selector	Type of selector	Description
`:focus-visible` (*Level 4*)	User action pseudo-class selector	Selects any element that has user-input focus and the user agent has determined that a focus ring or other indicator should be drawn for that element.
`:drop(active)` (*Level 4*)	Drag-and-drop pseudo-class selector	Selects an element that is the current drop target for the item being dragged.
`:drop(valid)` (*Level 4*)	Drag-and-drop pseudo-class selector	Selects an element that could receive the item currently being dragged.
`:drop(invalid)` (*Level 4*)	Drag-and-drop pseudo-class selector	Selects an element that cannot receive the item currently being dragged but could receive some other item.
`:dir(ltr)` (*Level 4*)	Directionality pseudo-class	Selects an element with a particular writing direction. In this example, the direction is left to right. The document language determines how directionality is determined.
`:lang(xx)`	Language pseudo-class selector	Selects an element that matches the two-character language code. `a:lang(de) {color: green;}`
`:nth-child()`	Structural pseudo-class selector	Selects an element that is the nth child of its parent. The notation can include a number, a notation, or the keywords odd or even.
`:nth-last-child()`	Structural pseudo-class selector	Selects an element that is the nth child of its parent, counting from the last one.
`:nth-of-type()`	Structural pseudo-class selector	Selects the nth element of its type.
`:nth-last-of-type()`	Structural pseudo-class selector	Selects the nth element of its type, counting from the last one.
`:first-child`	Structural pseudo-class selector	Selects an element that is the first child of its parent element.
`:last-child`	Structural pseudo-class selector	Selects an element that is the last child of its parent element.
`:only-child`	Structural pseudo-class selector	Selects an element that is the only child of its parent.
`:first-of-type`	Structural pseudo-class selector	Selects an element that is the first sibling of its type.
`:last-of-type`	Structural pseudo-class selector	Selects an element that is the last sibling of its type.
`:only-of-type`	Structural pseudo-class selector	Selects an element that is the only sibling of its type.
`:root`	Tree-structural pseudo-class selector	Selects an element that is the root of the document. In HTML, it is the `html` element.
`:empty`	Tree-structural pseudo-class selector	Selects an element that has no text and no child elements.
`:blank`	Tree-structural pseudo-class selector	Selects an element that has no content except maybe whitespace.
`:enabled`	UI pseudo-class selector	Selects a UI element if it is enabled.
`:disabled`	UI pseudo-class selector	Selects a UI element if it is disabled.
`:checked`	UI pseudo-class selector	Selects a UI element (radio button or checkbox) that is checked.
`:read-write` (*Level 4*)	Mutability pseudo-class selector	Selects a UI element if it is user alterable.
`:read-only` (*Level 4*)	Mutability pseudo-class selector	Selects a UI element if it is not user alterable.
`:placeholder-shown` (*Level 4*)	Mutability pseudo-class selector	Selects an input control currently showing placeholder text.

Selector	Type of selector	Description
:default *(Level 4)*	Default-option pseudo-class selector	Selects a UI element that is the default item in a group of related choices.
:indeterminate *(Level 4)*	Indeterminate-value pseudo-class selector	Selects a UI element that is an indeterminate state (neither checked nor unchecked).
:valid *(Level 4)*	Validity pseudo-class selector	Selects a UI element that meets its data validity semantics.
:invalid *(Level 4)*	Validity pseudo-class selector	Selects a UI element that does not meet its data validity semantics.
:in-range *(Level 4)*	Range pseudo-class selector	Selects a UI element whose value is in a specified range.
:out-of-range *(Level 4)*	Range pseudo-class selector	Selects a UI element whose value is not in a specified range.
:required *(Level 4)*	Optionality pseudo-class selector	Selects a UI element that requires input.
:optional *(Level 4)*	Optionality pseudo-class selector	Selects a UI element that does not require input.
:not(A)	Negation pseudo-class selector	Selects an element that does not match the simple selector A. Can also be used with compound selectors, in which case it selects an element that does not match either A or B. `:not(A, B) { color: #ccc; }`
:matches(A, B) *(Level 4)*	Matches-any pseudo-class selector	Selects an element that matches A and/or B. `:matches(h2, h3) { color: #ccc;}`
E:has(rA, rB) *(Level 4)*	Relational pseudo-class selector	Selects an element E if either of the relative selectors rA or rB, when evaluated with the element as the **:scope** elements, matches an element. The following example matches only **a** elements that contain an **img**: `a:has(> img) { margin: .5em 0; }`

Pseudo-element selectors

::first-letter	Pseudo-element selector	Selects the first letter of the specified element.
::first-line	Pseudo-element selector	Selects the first letter of the specified element.
::before	Pseudo-element selector	Inserts generated text at the beginning of the specified element and applies a style to it.
::after	Pseudo-element selector	Inserts generated content at the end of the specified element and applies a style to it.

Grid-structural selectors

A || B *(Level 4)*	Grid-structural selector	Selects an element B that represents a cell in a grid/table belonging to a column represented by an element A.

FROM HTML+ TO HTML5

I'm not sure any HTML specification has had such fanfare as HTML5. It offers so many promising possibilities, in fact, that it has become something of a buzzword with connotations far beyond the spec itself. When marketers and journalists use the term "HTML5," they are sometimes referring to any new web technology that replaces Flash. Throughout this book, you have gotten familiar with the elements of HTML5, and in this appendix, I'll tell you a bit more about the spec itself, so you can join those of us who are irked when we hear "HTML5" used incorrectly. The important thing, however, is that mainstream awareness of web standards is certainly a win and makes our job easier when we're communicating with clients.

But first, I think it's important to know how we got here and what makes HTML5 a breakthrough. I'll start with a brief history of HTML, and then point out some unique qualities of HTML5, including its APIs.

AN ABBREVIATED HISTORY OF HTML

Understanding where we've been provides useful context for where we are going. Our journey to HTML5 passes through the frontier of the early web, the dangerous battlegrounds of the Browser Wars, and a flirtatious fling with XML.

The Wild Frontier

The story of HTML, from Tim Berners-Lee's initial draft in 1991 to the HTML5 standard in development today, is both fascinating and tumultuous. Early versions of HTML (HTML+ in 1994 and HTML 2.0 in 1995) built on Tim's early work with the intent of making it a viable publishing option.

■ **FURTHER READING**

For a detailed history of HTML from 1989 to 1998, read David Raggett's account from his book *Raggett on HTML4* (Addison-Wesley), available on the W3C site (*www.w3.org/People/ Raggett/book4/ch02.html*).

759

But when the World Wide Web (as it was adorably called back in the day) took the world by storm, browser creators, most notably Mosaic Netscape and later Microsoft Internet Explorer, each said, "We ain't waitin' for no stinkin' standards!" They gave the people what they wanted by creating a slew of browser-specific elements for improving the look of pages on their respective browsers. This divisive one-upping is what has come to be known as the Browser Wars. As a result, it became common in the late 1990s to create two entirely separate versions of a site that targeted each of the Big Two browsers. Signs on sites reading "Best viewed in Netscape" were the norm. I shudder just thinking about it.

A Call for Reason

In 1996, the newly formed W3C put a stake in the ground and released its first Recommendation: HTML 3.2. It is a snapshot of all the HTML elements in common use at the time, and includes many presentational extensions to HTML (such as the **font** and **center** elements) that were the result of the Netscape/IE feud and the lack of a style sheet alternative. HTML 4.0 (1998) and HTML 4.01 (the slight revision that superseded it in 1999) aimed to get HTML back on track by emphasizing the separation of structure and presentation and improving accessibility. All matters of presentation were handed over to the newly minted Cascading Style Sheets standard that was gaining support.

HTML 4.01—along with XHTML 1.0, its stricter XML-based sibling (discussed next)—became the cornerstone of the web standards movement (see the sidebar **"The Web Standards Project"**).

Enter XML and XHTML

Around the same time that HTML 4.01 was in development, folks at the W3C became aware that one limited markup language wasn't going to cut it for describing all the sorts of information (chemical notation, mathematical equations, multimedia presentations, financial information, and so on) that might be shared over the web. Their solution: XML (eXtensible Markup Language), a metalanguage for creating markup languages. XML was a simplification of SGML (Standardized Generalized Markup Language), the big kahuna of metalanguages that Tim Berners-Lee used to create his original HTML application. But SGML itself proved to be more complex than the web required.

The W3C had a vision of an XML-based web with many specialized markup languages working together—even within a single document. Of course, to pull that off, everyone would have to mark up documents very carefully, strictly abiding by XML syntax, to rule out potential confusion.

The Web Standards Project

In 1998, at the height of the Browser Wars, a grassroots coalition called the Web Standards Project (WaSP for short) began to put pressure on browser creators (primarily Netscape and Microsoft at the time) to start sticking to the open standards as documented by the W3C. Not stopping there, it educated the web developer community on the many benefits of developing with standards. Its efforts revolutionized the way sites are created and supported. Now browsers (even Microsoft) brag of standards support while continuing to innovate.

In 2013, WaSP declared, "Our work here is done," and disbanded. You can still read its mission statement, history, and reference materials on the WaSP site (*webstandards.org*).

Their first step was to rewrite HTML according to the rules of XML so that it could play well with others. The result is XHTML (eXtensible HTML). The first version, XHTML 1.0, is nearly identical to HTML 4.01, sharing the same elements and attributes, but with stricter syntax requirements (see the **"XHTML Markup Requirements"** sidebar).

But the W3C didn't stop there. With a vision of an XML-based web in mind, they began work on XHTML 2.0, an even bolder attempt to make things work "right" than HTML 4.01 had been. The problem was that it was not backward-compatible with old standards and browser behavior. The writing and approval process dragged on for years with no browser implementation. Without browser implementation, XHTML 2.0 was stuck.

XHTML Markup Requirements

XHTML syntax follows the strict markup requirements of XML, as follows:

- Element and attribute names must be lowercase. In HTML, element and attribute names are not case-sensitive.

- All elements must be closed (terminated). You close empty elements by adding a slash before the closing bracket (for example, **
**).

- Attribute values must be in quotation marks. Single or double quotation marks are acceptable as long as they are used consistently. Furthermore, there must be no extra whitespace (character spaces or line returns) before or after the attribute value inside the quotation marks.

- All attributes must have explicit attribute values. XML (and therefore XHTML) does not support attribute minimization, the SGML practice in which certain attributes can be reduced to just the attribute value. So, while in HTML you can write **checked** to indicate that a form button should be checked when the form loads, in XHTML you need to explicitly write out **checked="checked"**.

- Proper nesting of elements is strictly enforced. Some exisiting elements got new nesting restrictions.

- Start tags and end tags are required.

- Special characters must always be represented by character entities (e.g., **&** for the & symbol).

- Scripts must be contained in a CDATA section so they will be treated as simple text characters and not parsed as XML markup. Here is an example of the syntax:

```
<script type="type/javascript">
  // <![CDATA[
  ... JavaScript goes here...
  // ]]>
</script>
```

While HTML parsers are forgiving of incorrect markup, errors in XHTML syntax stop the parser in its tracks. Running your XHTML code through a validator is a good idea to catch syntax errors before pages get launched.

Hello HTML5!

Meanwhile…

In 2004, members of Apple, Mozilla, and Opera formed the Web Hypertext Application Technology Working Group (WHATWG, *whatwg.org*), separate from the W3C. The goal of the WHATWG was to further the development of HTML to meet new demands in a way that was consistent with real-world authoring practices and browser behavior (in contrast to the start-from-scratch ideal that XHTML 2.0 described). Their initial documents, Web Applications 1.0 and Web Forms 1.0, were rolled together into HTML5. Today, the WHATWG maintains an unnumbered, "living" HTML standard.

The W3C eventually established its own HTML5 Working Group based on the work done by the WHATWG. HTML5 reached formal Recommendation status in October 2014. As of early 2018, the latest version is HTML 5.2, which is a "Proposed Recommendation."

Work on the HTML5 specification is happening in both organizations in tandem, sometimes with slight inconsistencies. For the most part, browser vendors use the WHATWG copy as their implementation reference.

And XHTML 2.0? At the end of 2009, the W3C officially put it out of its misery, pulling the plug on the Working Group and putting its resources and efforts into HTML5.

So that's how we got here. Now let's get to know HTML5 a little better.

HTML5: MORE THAN MARKUP

■ **FURTHER READING**

The following books will help fill out your knowledge of HTML5:

- *HTML5 for Web Designers, 2e* by Rachel Andrew and Jeremy Keith (A Book Apart)
- *HTML5: Up and Running* by Mark Pilgrim (O'Reilly and Google Press)
- *Introducing HTML5, 2e* by Bruce Lawson and Remy Sharp (New Riders)

Prior HTML versions concerned themselves mainly with elements for marking up content to be viewed on web pages. HTML5 is a bundle of new methods for accomplishing tasks that previously required special programming or proprietary plug-in technology such as Flash or Silverlight. Solutions include both markup and scripting components, including APIs for things like putting audio and video on the page, storing data locally, working offline, taking advantage of location information, and more. With HTML5 for common tasks, developers can rely on built-in browser capabilities and not reinvent the wheel for every application.

Much of what's new in HTML5 requires advanced web development skills, so it's unlikely you'll use those features right away (if ever), but as always, I think it is beneficial to everyone to have a basic familiarity with what can be done. And "basic familiarity" is what I'm aiming at here. For more in-depth discussions of HTML5 features, see the **"Further Reading"** sidebar.

HTML5 Markup Component

You've been learning the elements and attributes of HTML5 throughout this book.

HTML5 is based on HTML 4.01 Strict, the version of HTML that did not include any presentation-based or other deprecated elements and attributes. That means the vast majority of HTML5 is made up of the same elements that were used for years, and browsers know what to do with them.

HTML5 introduced a number of new elements, form input types, and global attributes. It also made many deprecated elements and attributes in HTML 4.01 officially obsolete.

One departure from previous HTML versions is that HTML5 is the first specification that includes detailed instructions for how browsers should handle malformed and legacy markup. It bases the instructions on legacy browser behavior, but for once, there is a standard protocol for browser makers to follow when browsers encounter incorrect or non-standard markup.

HTML5 in XML

HTML5 can also be written according to the stricter syntax of XML (called the XML serialization of HTML5). Some developers have come to prefer the tidiness of well-formed XHTML (lowercase element names, quoted attribute values, closing all elements, and so on), so that way of writing is still an option, although not required. In edge cases, an HTML5 document may be required to be served as XML in order to work with other XML applications, in which case it can use the XML syntax and be ready to go.

A DTD-Free DOCTYPE

As we saw in **Chapter 4, Creating a Simple Page**, HTML documents should begin with a Document Type (DOCTYPE) declaration that identifies which version of HTML the document follows. The HTML5 declaration is short and sweet:

```
<!DOCTYPE html>
```

Compare that to a declaration for a Strict HTML 4.01 document:

```
<!DOCTYPE HTML PUBLIC "-//W3C//DTD HTML 4.01//EN"
   "http://www.w3.org/TR/HTML4.01/strict.dtd">
```

Why so complicated? For documents written in HTML 4.01 and XHTML 1.0 and 1.1, the declaration must point to the public DTD (Document Type Definition), a document that defines all of the elements in a markup language as well as the rules for using them. DTDs are a remnant of SGML and proved to be less helpful on the web than originally thought, so the authors of HTML5 simply didn't use one. As a result, the DOCTYPE declaration is much simpler.

Validators—software that checks that all the markup in a document is correct (see **Note**)—use the DOCTYPE declaration to make sure the document abides by the rules of the specification it claims to follow.

Both HTML 4.01 and XHTML 1.0 had three separate DTDs (for Traditional, Strict, and Frameset versions of each spec), so there were a lot of little details to keep track of. For a full list of DOCTYPE declarations (including DTD references) for HTML 4.01, XHTML, SVG, and other document types, go to *www.w3.org/QA/2002/04/valid-dtd-list.html*.

NOTE

To check whether your HTML document is valid, use the online validator at the W3C (validator.w3.org). An HTML5-specific validator is also available at html5.validator.nu.

Meet the APIs

HTML specifications prior to HTML5 included only documentation of the elements, attributes, and values permitted in the language. That's fine for simple text documents, but the creators of HTML5 had their minds set on making it easier to create web-based applications that require scripting and programming. For that reason, HTML5 also defines a number of new APIs for making it easier to communicate with an application.

An API (application programming interface) is a documented set of commands, data names, and so on, that lets one software application communicate with another. For example, the developers of Twitter documented the names of each data type (users, tweets, timestamps, etc.) and the methods for accessing them in an API document (*dev.twitter.com/docs*) that lets other developers include Twitter feeds and elements in their programs. That is why there are so many Twitter programs and widgets available. Amazon.com also opens up its product data via an API. In fact, publishers of every ilk are recognizing the power of having their content available via an API.

But let's bring it back to HTML5, which includes APIs for tasks that traditionally required proprietary plug-ins (like Flash) or custom programming. The idea is that if browsers offer those features natively—with standardized sets of hooks for accessing them—developers can do all sorts of nifty things and count on them working in all browsers, just as we count on the ability to embed an image on a page today. Of course, we have a way to go before there is ubiquitous support of these cutting-edge features, but we're getting there steadily. Some APIs have a markup component, such as embedding multimedia with the new HTML5 **video** and **audio** elements. Others happen entirely behind the scenes with JavaScript or server-side components, such as creating web applications that work even when there is no internet connection (Offline Web Application API).

The W3C and WHATWG are working on *lots and lots* of APIs for use with web applications, all in varying stages of completion and implementation. Most have their own specifications, separate from the HTML5 spec itself, but they are generally included under the wide HTML5 umbrella that covers web-based applications. HTML5 includes specifications for these APIs:

NOTE

For a list of all the APIs, see the "HTML5 Overview" by Erik Wilde (html5-overview. net). The W3C lists all the documents they maintain, many of which are APIs, at www.w3.org/TR/tr-title-all.

Media Player API

For controlling audio and video players embedded on a web page, used with the new **video** and **audio** elements.

Editing API

Provides a set of commands that could be used to create in-browser text editors, allowing users to insert and delete text; format text as bold, italic, or hypertext; and more. In addition, there is a new **contenteditable** attribute that allows any content element to be editable right on the page.

Session History API

Exposes the browser history for better control over the Back button.

Drag and Drop API

Adds the ability to drag a text selection or file to a target area on the page or another web page. The **draggable** attribute indicates the element can be selected and dragged.

The following are just a handful of the APIs in development at the W3C with specifications of their own:

Canvas API

The **canvas** element adds a dynamic, two-dimensional drawing space to a page. The **canvas** element is discussed in **Chapter 10, Embedded Media**.

Service Workers API

This specification describes a method that enables web applications to work while offline.

Web Storage API

Allows data to be stored in the browser's cache so that an application can use it later. Traditionally, that has been done with "cookies," but the Web Storage API allows more data to be stored. It also controls whether the data is limited to one session (**sessionStorage**: when the window is closed, the data is cleared) or based on domain (**localStorage**: all open windows pointed to that domain have access to the data).

Geolocation API

Lets users share their geographical location (longitude and latitude) so that it is accessible to scripts in a web application. This allows the app to provide location-aware features such as suggesting a nearby restaurant or finding other users in your area.

Web Sockets API

Creates a socket, which is an open connection between the browser client and the server. This allows information to flow between the client and the server in real time, with no lags for the traditional HTTP requests. You can think of a web socket as an ongoing telephone call between the browser and server compared to the walkie-talkie, one-at-a-time style of traditional browser/server communication. (A hat tip to Jen Simmons for this analogy.) It is useful for multiplayer games, chat, or data streams that update constantly, such as sports or stock tickers or social media streams.

WHERE WE GO FROM HERE

With a system in place that seems to be working, all indications are that the HTML specification will continue to undergo minor revisions in order to keep up with the changing demands of how we use the web and the devices we use it on. Minor revisions generally include adding attributes, elements, and APIs and putting to rest features that were never implemented. In other words, I have not heard talk of another seismic shift such as the switch from XHTML to HTML5.

At the W3C, HTML 5.2 (the 5th major version and second minor revision of HTML) became a Recommendation on December 14, 2017. As this book goes to press, there is already a Working Draft of HTML 5.3. Meanwhile, the WHATWG maintains its "living" (unnumbered) version of HTML that is continually updated and forms the basis for most browser vendors' implementation.

So know that HTML is always changing, and as a web designer or developer, you will need to keep your ear to the ground. There is always something new to learn.

INDEX

Symbols

$ (dollar sign) 323, 569
£ (pound) 108
¥ (yen) 108
€ (euro) 108
& (ampersand) 105–106
<> (angle brackets) 27, 30, 56
' (apostrophe) 106
* (asterisk) 187, 285, 601
\ (backslash) 56, 116
: (colon) 316, 320
, (comma) 263
/* */ (comments) 245
© (copyright) 108
{} (curly brackets) 243, 491, 573, 604,
    608–609
:: (double colons) 320
... (ellipsis) 108
— (em dash) 108
– (en dash) 108
= (equals sign) 64
== (equal to) operator 603–604
>= (greater than or equal to) operator
    603
> (greater than sign) 106, 603
=== (identical to) operator 603–604
<= (less than or equal to) operator 603
< (less than sign) 106, 603
- (minus sign) 601
!= (not equal to) operator 603
!== (not identical to) operator 603
(octothorpe symbol) 124, 282–283, 325
() (parentheses) 608–610

% (percent sign) 413
+ (plus sign) 601–602, 604
" (quotation marks). *See* quotation
    marks
® (registered trademark) 108
; (semicolon) 105–106, 243, 245, 599
/ (slash). *See* slash (/)
~ (tilde) 569
™ (trademark) 108
_ (underscore) 54, 569, 601

A

AAC audio codec 220–221
a (anchor) element
    about 89, 113, 130
    applying styles to 318–319
    href attribute 84, 114–128, 132
    target attribute 127
abbr (abbreviation) element 89, 92, 112
abbr attribute, th element 176
absolute flex 441
absolute pathnames 24–25, 114–115, 135
absolute positioning
    about 393, 405, 408–409
    columned layouts 408
    containing blocks 409–411
    specifying position 411–414
    stacking order 414–415
absolute URLs 24–25, 114–115, 135, 351
absolute values 253–254
Abstract Syntax Tree (AST) 577
accept attribute, input element types
    198, 212–213

accept-charset attribute, form element
    209
accessibility
    about 42
    alternate text 136–137
    assistive technology for 23
    color-blind-friendly pages 314
    form considerations 181, 184, 187, 192,
        203–205
    government requirements 43
    improving with ARIA 102–105
    SVG and 718
    tables 169–171
    web design considerations 42–45
Accessible Rich Internet Applications
    (ARIA) 102–105, 205, 718
accesskey global attribute 101, 753
acronym element 89, 92
action attribute, form element 180–181,
    209
:active selector 317–319, 518, 756
Active Server Pages (ASP) 180
adaptive icons 731
addEventListener() method 615
address element 82, 87, 112
Adobe
    Animate software 228
    code editors 16, 50
    Creative Cloud tool suite 17–18, 672
    Dreamweaver 16, 307
    Flash Player 218
    Illustrator 17, 142, 642, 687, 718
    Photoshop. *See* Photoshop
    RGB color space 672, 675
    Typekit service 265, 280